Taxation

Theory and Practice
2002/2003 Edition

Kath Nightingale

 Prentice Hall
FINANCIAL TIMES

An imprint of **Pearson Education**
Harlow, England • London • New York • Boston • San Francisco • Toronto • Sydney • Singapore • Hong Kong
Tokyo • Seoul • Taipei • New Delhi • Cape Town • Madrid • Mexico City • Amsterdam • Munich • Paris • Milan

To Barry

Pearson Education Limited
Edinburgh Gate
Harlow
Essex CM20 2JE
England

and Associated Companies throughout the world

Visit us on the World Wide Web at
www.pearsoneduc.com

First published by Pitman Publishing in 1997
Second edition published 1999
Third edition published 2000
Fourth edition published 2002

© Pearson Professional Limited 1997
© Pearson Education Limited 1999, 2000, 2002

ISBN 0273-65573-6

British Library Cataloguing in Publication Data
A CIP catalogue record for this book can be obtained from the British Library.

Typeset in 10pt Palatino by 30.

Transferred to digital print on demand, 2009

Printed and bound in Great Britain by CPI Antony Rowe, Chippenham and Eastbourne

Taxation

Theory and Practice

CONTENTS

PREFACE TO FIFTH EDITION

The 2002/03 edition of this book has been updated to reflect the tax changes announced in the Budget 2002. The structure of the book for 2002/03 remains unchanged; answers to self-assessment questions are provided in Appendix 3, the answers to the Practice questions being available to lecturers on request.

Kath Nightingale
April 2002

PREFACE TO FOURTH EDITION

The 2001/02 edition of this book has been updated to include the tax changes announced in the Budget 2001.

The structure of this book remains unchanged; answers to the self assessment questions continue to be provided in Appendix 3, and answers to the Practice questions are available to lectures on request.

Kath Nightingale
April 2001

PREFACE TO THIRD EDITION

The third edition of this book has been updated to include the tax changes announced in the Budget 2000.

The structure of the book remains unchanged; answers to the self assessment questions are contained in Appendix 3, and answers to the Practice questions are available in the Instructor's Manual.

Kath Nightingale
April 2000

PREFACE TO SECOND EDITION

The second edition of this book has been updated to include the tax changes announced in the Budget 1999.

To enable students to practise their computational skills, self assessment questions have been included where appropriate, with suggested solutions provided for the students' use. Apart from this addition, the structure of the book remains unchanged; answers to the Practice questions at the end of each Part continue to be provided in the Instructor's Manual.

Kath Nightingale
July 1999

PREFACE TO FIRST EDITION

The book is intended to provide a comprehensive core text for undergraduates studying taxation as part of their degree course. Although there are some excellent publications covering the economic theory of taxation, my experience of teaching taxation to undergraduates over the past 13 years has been that they need a sound understanding of the basic concepts at an elementary level in order to progress satisfactorily to the more involved articles and texts. Therefore, in Part 1 of this book I have attempted to introduce taxation theory in a simple and uncomplicated manner in the hope that, having grasped the essentials, students will feel inspired to extend their knowledge by undertaking the more advanced readings given at the end of each chapter in that Part.

Despite the fact that the book was written primarily for undergraduates, the technical detail in Parts 2–5 is such that the book should also be useful to professional students preparing for the taxation examinations of the following bodies:

- Chartered Association of Certified Accountants (ACCA)
  Paper 7 Tax Framework
- Chartered Institute of Management Accountants (CIMA)
  Paper 12 Business Taxation
- Association of Taxation Technicians (ATT)
  Personal and Business taxation
- Institute of Chartered Accountants in England and Wales (ICAEW)
  Intermediate Level.

Parts 2–5 of the book cover the practical applications of income tax, capital gains tax, corporation tax and value added tax respectively. The aim of these parts is that students should not only be able to calculate complex tax liabilities, they should also know 'why' as well as 'how'. This is achieved by illustrative worked examples throughout the chapters, together with sound explanations and reference to relevant sources of tax law. For ease of computation, most figures appearing in these worked examples have been rounded up or down to the nearest pound sterling. Tax-planning opportunities are also included where relevant.

Part 6 examines the Pay As You Earn system (PAYE) and the administrative organisation of the Inland Revenue incorporating the new self-assessment regime for income tax and capital gains tax which was introduced from 1996/7. The system of pay and file and the transition to self-assessment for companies is also included in this part of the book. At the end of Part 6 the student should understand the procedures involved in dealing with the Inland Revenue with regard to income tax, capital gains tax and corporation tax.

Practice questions without answers are provided at the end of each Part. The answers to these questions are available to lecturers adopting this book in a companion Instructor's Manual. At the end of the book there is a more detailed coverage of the case law referred to in the main body of the text.

Note that changes to the taxation system introduced by the Chancellor's Budget speech on 2 July 1997 have been incorporated where possible. This information has been based on Inland Revenue press releases.

Kath Nightingale
July 1997

ACKNOWLEDGEMENTS

I am very grateful to my friends and students for their valued support during the long process of preparing this book. I would especially like to thank Helen Tague and Penny Heaney for their administrative support in preparing the manuscript for publication, any errors or omissions being entirely my responsibility.

I would also like to express my thanks to my long-suffering family, especially my husband, without whose help and encouragement this book would never have been completed.

Finally, I would like to thank the Chartered Institute of Management Accountants, the Chartered Association of Certified Accountants and the Institute of Taxation, for their permission to incorporate past examination questions in the book. The answers to these questions are in no way the liability of the bodies concerned; they are entirely my own work.

LIST OF ABBREVIATIONS

AC	Appeal Cases
ACCA	The Chartered Association of Certified Accountants
A&M	Accumulation and Maintenance Trust
ATII	Associate Member of the Chartered Institute of Taxation
BA	Balancing Allowance
BC	Balancing Charge
BSI	Building Society Interest
BTC	British Tax Cases
CAA 2001	Capital Allowance Act 2001
CCE	Commissioners of Customs and Excise
CEN	Capital Export Neutrality
CGT	Capital Gains Tax
CIMA	Chartered Institute of Management Accountants
CIN	Capital Import Neutrality
CIR	Commissioners of the Inland Revenue
CT	Corporation Tax
CTSA	Corporation Tax Self Assessment
CYB	Current Year Basis
DIY	Do-It-Yourself
DPTC	Disabled Person's Tax Credit
DTR	Double Tax Relief
EC	European Community
EIS	Enterprise Investment Scheme
EU	European Union
ESC	Extra Statutory Concession
FA	Finance Act
FII	Franked Investment Income
FP	Franked Payment
FY	Financial Year
GCT	Gross Corporation Tax
ICTA 1988	Income and Corporation Taxes Act 1988
IR	Inland Revenue
ISA	Individual Savings Account

IT	Income Tax
MV	Market Value
NIC	National Insurance Contribution
PA	Personal Allowance
PAYE	Pay As You Earn
PCTCT	Profit Chargeable to Corporation Tax
PPS	Personal Pension Scheme
PR	Personal Representative
PYB	Prior Year Basis
R&D	Research and Development
RPI	Retail Price Index
S	Section
SEM	Single European Market
SERPS	State Earnings Related Pension Scheme
SP	Statement of Practice
STC	Simons Tax Cases
TC	Tax Cases
TCGA 1992	Taxation of Chargeable Gains Act 1992
TESSA	Tax Exempt Special Savings Account
TMA 1970	Taxes Management Act 1970
UII	Unfranked Investment Income
VAT	Value Added Tax
VATA 1994	Value Added Tax Act 1994
VATTR	Value Added Tax Tribunal
VCT	Venture Capital Trust
WDA	Writing Down Allowance
WFTC	Working Families Tax Credit

Where other abbreviations and statutes are used they are defined where they appear in the text.

PART 1

The theory of taxation

Taxation has existed since the birth of early civilisations, and it could be said that it is part of the price to be paid for living in an organised society.

However, taxation is not just a means of transferring money to the government, to spend as it thinks fit, it also has a tendency to reflect prevailing social values and priorities. In this respect it could be argued that a system of taxation is a socioeconomic model, representing society's social, political and economic needs at any one time; changes in these needs often being reflected by changes to the system of taxation. This characteristic explains why no two countries' tax systems will be identical in every respect and indeed why the UK tax system is continually changing.

This Part aims to introduce the basic theory of taxation in a plain and easily understood manner. This is by no means underestimating the complexity of the theoretical issues involved, but in this respect Part 1 is an introductory text, and further recommended reading is provided at the end of each chapter.

Chapter 1 introduces most of the basic terminology, setting out the objectives of taxation and the various ways in which taxes can be classified. No tax system is perfect but an 'ideal' tax should conform to certain principles if it is to achieve its objectives without producing negative effects, and so this chapter concludes by examining the criteria for evaluating a modern tax system.

After giving a brief historical background of the major UK taxes, the next four chapters analyse and evaluate the current UK tax system. Chapter 6 discusses avoidance and evasion in the UK, examining tax morality and the current legal status regarding tax avoidance. Chapter 7 examines the choice of tax base and considers the alternatives available.

The final chapter in this Part examines the rationale for harmonising direct taxes within Europe, the difficulties involved, and the progress in this area to date.

Introduction to the theory of taxation

The objectives of taxation

The rationale for imposing taxes in a market economy such as the UK stems from the government responsibilities listed below.

1. To provide public goods

A pure public good is one that displays the following characteristics:

(a) displays zero marginal cost, i.e. no extra cost is incurred in supplying the good to more than one person;

(b) individuals cannot be excluded from consuming the good, even if they have no desire for it;

(c) all members of society must consume the same amount, it cannot be rejected, e.g. law and order.

A good example of a pure public good is defence. The provision of national defence protects all members of society from hostilities at zero marginal cost, no individual can be excluded and it cannot be rejected by those who disagree in principle, e.g. pacifists.

If left to the market, individuals with no desire for the good would be unwilling to pay the price, yet at the same time they could not be excluded from benefiting; as a consequence a free market would be inefficient in the provision of public goods, and as a result they become the responsibility of the state.

2. Redistribution of income and wealth

The mechanism for the redistribution of income and wealth by the use of transfer payments and benefits to those members of society who are less well off promotes social equality.

3. To promote social and economic welfare

Government often takes on a paternalistic role by providing 'merit' goods, e.g. health and education. Merit goods, unlike public goods, can be provided privately, but if left completely to market forces merit goods would be under consumed, and so there is some merit in the state providing such goods as everyone benefits from living in a healthy and educated society, i.e. there are external benefits in the provision of merit goods.

In the same respect, demerit goods, e.g. alcohol and cigarettes are discouraged by government in order to reduce the external costs to society, e.g. health risks and pollution.

4. Economic stability

The government is responsible for avoiding high levels of inflation and unemployment in order to promote economic stability and sustainable growth.

5. The single European market

With the introduction of the single market in January 1993, there is more pressure on the government to be in harmony with other member states.

6. Regulation

Legislation and regulatory controls made on producers in order to protect consumers, employees and the general public is the responsibility of any socially aware government.

Given these general responsibilities, taxation can be a powerful tool in the hands of any government as a means of ensuring that the social, political and economic policies of the government in power are brought to fruition.

From this we can deduce that there are *four* main objectives of a modern tax system:

1. Revenue raising

Historically taxes were raised in order to fund the monarchy and to pay for defence in times of strife. Revenue raising is still a primary objective of a modern tax system to help finance public sector expenditure.

2. Redistribution of income and wealth

The tax system is a means of ensuring the redistribution of income and wealth in order to reduce poverty and promote social welfare.

3. Economic regulator

The tax system is a means of promoting economic welfare and creating a sound infrastructure for businesses.

4. Harmonisation

The philosophy of the single market in Europe is to provide for the free movement of goods/services, capital and people between member states, suggesting harmonisation to be a modern objective of European tax systems.

How well the current UK tax system fulfils these objectives will be discussed in later chapters.

The classification of taxes

A tax is a compulsory contribution, imposed by government, and while taxpayers may receive nothing identifiable in return for their contribution, they nevertheless have the benefit of living in a relatively educated, healthy and safe society. Taxes can be classified in the following ways:

1. By tax base

Taxes have to be levied on some basis or other, and a convenient way of classifying a tax is to do so according to what is being taxed. Three main tax bases are used in the present UK tax system, *see* Fig 1.1.

Using the tax base is a convenient classification for economic analysis, for example, in examining who exactly bears the burden of a tax, known as the incidence of taxation; but the tax base can cause problems in terms of definition – how, for example, should income be defined? These issues will be considered later in this section.

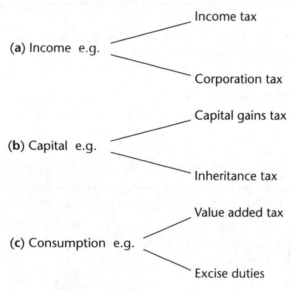

(a) Income e.g.
— Income tax
— Corporation tax

(b) Capital e.g.
— Capital gains tax
— Inheritance tax

(c) Consumption e.g.
— Value added tax
— Excise duties

Fig 1.1 Main UK tax bases

2. Direct/indirect

A direct tax is one levied directly on the person who is intended to pay the tax, whereas an indirect tax is borne by a person other than the one from whom the tax is collected. This classification can prove to be misleading at times as the incidence of some direct taxes, for example, corporation tax, can easily be shifted.

Classification under this heading of the main UK taxes examined in this Part is as indicated in Fig 1.2.

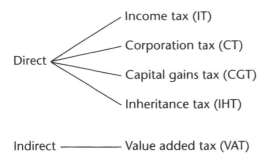

Fig 1.2 Classification of UK direct/indirect taxes

3. Unit/*ad valorem*

A unit or specific tax is levied on the volume of what is being taxed; many excise duties are specific taxes, for example, tobacco tax is charged by weight of tobacco.

An *ad valorem* tax is levied on the value of the tax base, for example income tax is charged at 10 per cent to 40 per cent, depending on the level and type of income.

4. Distribution of the tax burden

The way in which the burden of tax is distributed among the taxpaying community is another way in which taxes may be classified. The rates of tax can be set in such a way so that they are:

(a) *Progressive*. Progressive taxes take an increasing portion as the value of the tax base rises and depends on the marginal rate of tax* being greater than the average rate of tax.**

(b) *Proportional*. Proportional taxes take a constant portion of the value of the tax base and depends on the marginal and average rates of tax being equal.

(c) *Regressive*. Regressive taxes take a declining portion as the value of the tax base rises and depends on the average rate of tax being greater than the marginal rate of tax.

$$* \text{ The Marginal Rate of Tax} = \frac{\Delta \text{ change in tax paid}}{\Delta \text{ change in income}}$$

$$** \text{ The Average Rate of Tax} = \frac{\text{total tax paid}}{\text{total income}}$$

The principles of an 'ideal' tax

No one really likes paying taxes, yet they are inevitable for the provision of social welfare. Would anyone really like to put the clock back to the days when healthcare and education were not freely available, and the fate of old people without any private means of support was the workhouse? Despite the need for taxes in a modern society, the tax system adopted must be acceptable to the general public if dissension is to be avoided, an example is the unrest caused by the introduction of the community charge in the UK in 1990. Indeed, it was the introduction of a poll tax that caused the Peasants Revolt in the fourteenth century, and throughout history, unfair or seemingly unfair systems of taxation have been at the heart of many such conflicts.

In his book, *The Wealth of Nations* (1776), Adam Smith proposed that a 'good' tax should display the following characteristics:

- it should reflect a person's ability to pay;
- it should be certain;
- it should be convenient; and
- it should be administratively efficient and not cause economic distortion.

These principles still hold good today, and in a modern tax system an 'ideal' tax should conform as far as possible to the following criteria:

1. Simple, certain and convenient

The tax should be relatively simple for taxpayers to understand their liability, and it should be administered in such a way that they are aware of the amount they should pay, and the due date for payment. Finally, the method of payment should not be inconvenient.

2. Flexible

The structure and rate of a tax should be capable of being altered without too much difficulty to cope with changes in circumstances if the system of taxation is to be used as a means of regulating the economy, which is one of the stated aims of taxation.

3. Administratively efficient

The costs of administering the tax should not be too high in proportion to the revenue raised, e.g. one of the reasons for abolishing the dog licence, a form of taxation, was that administration costs were higher than the revenue raised. The efficiency of a tax includes not only the costs incurred by the tax authorities, i.e. administration costs, but also the costs incurred by the taxpayer in complying with the tax legislation, known as compliance costs, e.g. professional tax advice.

Both administration and compliance costs should not be overlooked when evaluating the tax system as they no doubt impinge on the welfare effects of the various taxes.

Compliance costs are, in practice, much more difficult to ascertain than administration costs; Sandford[1] refers to these costs as 'hidden costs' and suggested that compliance costs should be kept reasonably low in preference to administration costs for the following reasons:

(a) administration costs are met from public revenue, whereas compliance costs are regressive in nature, falling more heavily on smaller businesses, pensioners, etc., i.e. on those persons least able to afford them; and

(b) increased administration costs would not create the same taxpayer resentment as increased compliance costs.

4. Neutral

A tax is said to be neutral if it does not distort economic choices; this distortion of economic choice is known as the excess burden of taxation, causing substitution effects resulting in economic inefficiency.

All economic activities have costs and benefits associated with them, e.g. the cost of working could be said to be the loss of leisure time, and the benefit is the income received in wages; when taxation enters the equation distortions are introduced by creating what is known as a tax wedge. This wedge is the difference between the marginal cost of the activity and the marginal benefits received, the degree of distortion depending on the size of the tax wedge.

Any tax that impinges on economic activity cannot be completely neutral in its effect, and indeed governments would not wish them to be, if they are to use fiscal policy as a means of manipulating the economy. In this respect it is the degree of neutrality that is important when evaluating a tax system.

5. Equitable

Taxes must not only be fair they must also be seen to be fair if the taxpaying public is to find them acceptable. There is also a greater tendency for tax evasion when the tax system is perceived to be inequitable; it is often said that if there is widespread tax evasion, then it is the system of taxation that is at fault, and not the taxpayer.

There are two types of equity to be considered:

(a) *Horizontal equity* – requires that people in similar situations are treated in a similar way.

(b) *Vertical equity* – requires that people in unequal situations are treated with the necessary degree of inequality. Vertical equity would require the rich to pay more than the poor, which advocates a progressive system of taxation.

Horizontal equity is easier to achieve through the tax system than vertical equity as there are different attitudes as to what is a necessary degree of inequality. Equity is concerned with the distribution of the tax burden.

There are two traditional approaches as to how the tax burden should be distributed among the taxpaying community:

1. Benefit theory

This theory is based on the idea that taxes should be levied in proportion to the benefit received. On the face of it, this approach would seem to be fair. However, in practice the benefit is difficult to measure, for example, childless couples may not always feel they should contribute to the provision of state education, and yet indirectly they will derive a benefit from living in an educated community.

In a market economy there will always be poor people who must be supported by the state by means of transfer payments paid for out of taxation, and here the benefit theory is of little use as the benefits received by the poor by redistribution cannot then be subjected to taxation.

By and large the general public do not always see public spending on social goods and taxation as synonymous; there is always a large percentage of the population who feel that more money should be spent on health and education while at the same time perceive that taxes are too high.

The benefit approach, which advocates that taxes should be paid by those who benefit the most from the expenditure, suggests a case for earmarking taxes for specific goods and services, for example, government expenditure on roads should be financed from taxes on car ownership such as the vehicle excise licence and taxes on fuel, etc. In the absence of earmarked taxes, the road user would always wish to see money spent on roads and lower taxes on vehicle ownership. In fact, the vehicle excise licence was originally to be an earmarked tax, but currently finds its way into the general pool of tax revenue.

According to Musgrave,[2] earmarked taxes, or hypothecation, could increase efficiency and equity and lead to better expenditure decisions. The arguments in favour of earmarked taxes put forward by Deran[3] are that earmarking:

- applies the benefit theory of taxation;
- assures the minimum level of expenditure for government functions;
- can reduce the costs of specific projects by assuring continuity; and
- can overcome resistance to new taxes or increased rates of tax.

2. Ability to pay

Unlike the benefit approach, which would seek to match government expenditure with taxation in proportion to the benefit received, this approach is based on the idea that the burden of taxation should be spread in such a way as to give rise to an equality of sacrifice among the taxpaying community, e.g. £1 is less of a sacrifice to a person earning £25 000 than to one earning £15 000 all other things being equal. In principle, the ability-to-pay approach would tend to satisfy vertical equity in that people in different situations should be treated differently and it would require a progressive system of taxation. If the tax system is to provide for both types of equity, items such as gifts and inheritances should logically be included in the tax base, e.g. horizontal equity would require that a person who invests £10 000 in shares and another who invests £10 000 in non-income producing assets should be treated equally.

The main problem with this approach is deciding on the best indication of a person's ability to pay; in reality it is no more helpful than the benefit theory in formulating tax policy.

As equity is concerned with the fair distribution of the tax burden, it is also important to consider the incidence of a tax, as the formal incidence, i.e. the person on whom the tax is levied, is not always the same as the effective incidence, i.e. the person who actually bears the burden of the tax.

It is impossible for any one tax to conform to all these principles, e.g. in the pursuit of simplicity equity is often reduced, provisions for taxpayers in different situations can only be achieved by increased legislation, thereby making the system more complex. By the same token, equity may only be achieved at the expense of efficiency.

Which of these principles are considered to be most important is a matter of judgement and, of course, politics, and so we must be careful not to evaluate a tax on these criteria in absolute terms, but in the degree to which they are achieved and how important the tax is in the tax system as whole.

REFERENCES

1 Sandford, C.T., Goodwin, M. and Hardwick, P. (1989) *Administration and Compliance Costs of Taxation*, Fiscal Publications, Bath.
2 Musgrave, R. and Musgrave, P. (1980) *Public Finance in Theory and Practice* (5th edn), McGraw Hill.
3 Deran, E. (1965) 'Earmarking and expenditures: a survey and a new test', *National Tax Journal* (December).

FURTHER READING

Bracewell-Milnes, B. (1991) *The Case for Earmarked Taxes*, Institute of Economic Affairs, February.

Bracewell-Milnes, B., *et al.* (1990) *Which Road to Fiscal Neutrality*, Institute of Economic Affairs, September.

Brown, C.V. and Jackson, P.M. (1990) *Public Sector Economics*, Blackwell.

Collard, D. and Godwin, M. (1999) 'Compliance costs for employers: UK PAYE and National Insurance, 1995–96', *Fiscal Studies*, Vol. 20, No. 4, pp 423–49.

James, S. and Nobes, C. (2000/01) *The Economics of Taxation*, Prentice Hall.

Kay, J.A. and King, M.A. (1990) *The British Tax System*, Oxford University Press.

Meade, J.E. (1978) *The Structure and Reform of Direct Taxation*, Chapter 2, Institute of Fiscal Studies.

Musgrave, R. (1959) *The Theory of Public Finance*, McGraw-Hill.

Newbery, D.M. and Santos, G. (1999) 'Road taxes, road user charges and earmarking', *Fiscal Studies*, Vol. 20, No. 2, pp 103–102.

CHAPTER 2

Income taxation

Brief history of UK income tax

Income tax is a relatively modern tax compared to other forms of taxation employed in the UK. Throughout the eighteenth century the main sources of public revenue came from assessed taxes on property and indirect taxes. All manner of commodities were taxed, direct taxation being used mainly as an emergency measure.

Towards the end of the eighteenth century, the national debt was escalating due to increased borrowing to finance the war with France. In his Budget speech in 1798, William Pitt revealed his proposals to introduce a tax on incomes to help fund the Napoleonic war to be effective from January 1799. Pitt's income tax of 1799, requiring a general return of income and a measure of self assessment was very unpopular and evasion was widespread. Pitt had estimated a revenue of £10 million in its first year but it actually raised only £6 million. Pitt resigned in 1801 and was succeeded by Addington, who repealed the income tax in 1802 following the Treaty of Amiens.

However, hostilities with France erupted again in 1803 and income tax was re-introduced. Addington's income tax of 1803, levied at graduated rates on incomes over £60, was markedly different from Pitt's income tax of 1799, and was the true forerunner of the modern income tax. Addington introduced two aspects that are still present in today's income tax:

- the schedules of income tax; and
- tax deduction at source.

When the war with France ended, income tax was again repealed. Between 1816 and 1842 revenue was raised from the traditional customs duties, excise duties and land tax. When Peel re-introduced Addington's income tax in 1842 as a temporary measure to compensate for the revenue lost as a result of repealing the Corn Laws, he added two important features that shaped the administration of income tax in the UK:

- the right of appeal to the special commission that had been created in 1805; and
- a system of penalties.

Although when Gladstone came to power he was proposing to abolish the income tax by 1860, it remained as a temporary tax. Even today income tax is a temporary tax and has to be re-introduced each year via the Finance Act.

Towards the end of the Second World War the number of people paying income tax had trebled and in 1944 the pay as you earn (PAYE) system of tax collection was introduced, which greatly improved the Revenue's cash flow. The twentieth century witnessed the birth of the welfare state, no longer was income tax seen as an emergency measure in times of strife but as a means of achieving the social, political and economic aims of government. Rates of income tax steadily increased and by the late 1970s the top rate of income tax had risen to 98 per cent (83 per cent top rate income tax plus an additional 15 per cent investment income surcharge). Such confiscatory rates of tax caused economic inefficiency and the exodus of high income earners to pastures new.

When the Conservatives came to power in 1979 they set out to reduce the disincentive effects caused by high levels of taxation aiming for a more neutral system of taxation that would not distort economic choices. However, even in the 1980s the tax treatment of married women reflected Victorian social values. It was not until 1990 that the inequality with which the tax system treated married women was redressed with the introduction of independent taxation from April 1990.

The administration of UK income tax remained largely unchanged for over a century, however, the introduction of self assessment from 1996/7 has given taxpayers more control over their tax affairs by shifting responsibilities from the Revenue to the taxpayer.

Income tax and the incentive to work

Any tax that significantly distorts economic choices creates an excess burden resulting in economic inefficiency. The degree of this distortion depends on the size of the tax wedge, i.e. the difference between the marginal cost of the activity and the marginal benefits received. Taxes on income have two opposing effects on the incentive to work:

1. The income effect

The income effect has a tendency to increase effort as individuals work harder in order to maintain their pre-tax position. This depends on the average rate of tax.

2. The substitution effect

The substitution effect has a tendency to decrease effort as individuals substitute leisure for work when they perceive that the cost of the extra work in lost leisure time is greater than the extra income received. This depends on the marginal rate of tax.

If the average rate of tax is equal to the marginal rate of tax, i.e. where the tax is proportional, the net effect will be neutral, and only when the marginal rate exceeds the average rate, i.e. when the tax is progressive, are there likely to be substitution effects, creating a disincentive to work.

In reality, the decision of whether to work or not, or how little or how much work to undertake, is not simply related to the tax system, as working may be 'more than a means of economic support'.[1] Even where monetary rewards are the prime reasons for working, individuals may not be in a position to vary the hours they work.

Research carried out in 1969[2] concluded that for the majority of workers, higher taxation did not affect the incentive to work, while for 5–15 per cent of the population, mainly those who could vary the hours they worked, e.g. middle-aged people, those without dependants and wealthy individuals, higher taxation created disincentive effects. At the other end of the spectrum, for individuals with large families and those who are less well off, higher taxes were more likely to increase the incentive to work.

Research carried out in 1988[3] on the effect of the cuts in the top rates of income tax between 1978 (98 per cent) and 1988 (40 per cent) concluded that there was a small incentive in cutting the top rates of income tax. There is, however, a strong argument that taxes on income create disincentive effects for the lower paid and unemployed individuals receiving state benefits. This situation arises mainly because the income tax system and the social security system have been developed separately. As many benefits are means tested, i.e. related to income, low paid workers can find themselves in a situation where they earn above the threshold for income tax and National Insurance contributions purposes but are entitled to state benefits. If the individual earns more money, the situation can arise where not only does this result in extra income tax and National Insurance contributions, but the increased income takes them above the threshold for means tested benefits, with the result that the individual is worse off in real terms for the increase in income. This is known as *the poverty trap*, and arises because the tax imposed and the benefits lost give the taxpayer a higher marginal rate of tax resulting in increased substitution effects.

A similar situation occurs with the *unemployment trap*, i.e. when individuals are no better off in work than they are on benefits. If benefits are in the region of 90 per cent of the expected bring home pay, the individual will probably be better off unemployed, especially when the costs of working are taken into account, e.g. travel expenses and loss of leisure time. Individuals caught in the poverty and unemployment traps are unlikely to better themselves through their own effort, creating a disincentive to work.

Alleviating the *poverty trap* and achieving a greater degree of redistribution of income has been the main aim of recent income tax and benefit changes introduced by the Labour government.

In July 1997, the new Labour government announced its intentions to reform the tax and benefit system under its Welfare-to-Work programme, in order to make working more worthwhile than claiming benefit. This requires tackling the disincentive effects caused by the poverty trap, the unemployment trap and the lack of inexpensive childcare facilities for working families. However, this is not as straightforward as it may first appear.

In 1998 the Chancellor announced the introduction of the Working Families Tax Credit (WFTC), which was introduced in October 1999, and from April 2000 is to be paid through the employee's wages. The notion of a tax credit system is not a new idea; Green Papers on the subject were produced in 1972 and 1985. The main problem appears to be how the WFTC will be administered. If it were based on individual assessments it would be simpler to administer, but it would mean that the credit could find its way into second wages of relatively well-off families, thereby defeating its main objective. To avoid this the WFTC would have to be based on a joint assessment if it is to be fully integrated with the tax system, which would necessitate a return to the joint assessment of husband and wife and the abandonment of independent taxation. If on the other hand the WFTC was to run alongside the tax system, without integration, it would amount to little more than a renamed Family Credit.

Increasing support for individuals in work will no doubt reduce the unemployment trap, but with more people in work and claiming WFTC, there is a likelihood that the number of families caught in the poverty trap may increase as more people in work face losing benefit as income rises. This may affect families where both husband and wife go out to work, by creating a disincentive for the second earner to continue working. The new 10 per cent starting rate for income tax is also unlikely to benefit the poorest families, as the benefit system is a major consideration when calculating marginal rates of tax for the lower paid.

Help with the costs of childcare was introduced in the 1999 Budget; parents applying for WFTC after 5 October 1999 can claim up to 70 per cent of the cost, subject to a restriction of £100 per week for one child, increasing to £150 per week where two or more children receive eligible childcare.

Research published in 1999[4] on the combined effect of the initial Welfare-to-Work reforms, i.e. WFTC, National Insurance contribution reforms, and the new 10 per cent starting rate for income tax, concluded that the measures were effective in reducing unemployment, with the WFTC having the greatest effect at the lowest cost; the report estimates that in the long run the reforms could reduce unemployment by almost 4 per cent.

Further measures to reform the UK tax and benefit system were announced in the 2000 Budget. The government introduced a Children's Tax Credit (CTC) in April 2001, as a substitute for withdrawing the Married Couples' Allowance from 6 April 2000.

The present WFTC is a combination of a payment for child support and a payment for work, which is means tested from details of family income. The government intends to extend the principle of the work related credit in the WFTC by introducing the Employment Tax Credit (ETC), which would then be available to childless individuals and couples on low incomes. Proposals were also made to integrate child support measures under the Integrated Child Credit (ICC), 'to bring together the different strands of support for children in the Working Families Tax Credit, in Income Support and in the Children's Tax Credit, to create an integrated and seamless system of financial support for children paid to the main carer, building upon the foundation of universal Child Benefit'.[5]

The Budget 2002 outlined these new credits, to be introduced from April 2003 as:

(i) The Child Tax Credit (CTC), which brings together the child element of support in current benefits, and

(ii) The Working Tax Credit (WTC), which represents the adult support in the current WFTC and DPTC, but will be available to adults without children over the age of 25.

The case for a progressive income tax

'The purpose of progressive income taxation is to allocate the burden of tax fairly between different members of the community.'[6]

Whether a progressive income tax is desirable depends on the extent to which it is believed that the tax system should be used to achieve social equality. Social justice in the distribution of the tax burden advocates that the tax system should provide for vertical equity among taxpayers, i.e. the rich should pay more than the poor.

A *proportional* income tax would tax each £1 of taxable income at the same rate regardless of the total level of income, e.g. a taxpayer with £50 000 of taxable income would pay five times the income tax of an individual with £10 000 of taxable income.

Under a progressive income tax, the rate of tax would increase as the level of income increased, e.g. a taxpayer with £50 000 of taxable income would pay greater than five times the income tax of the individual with £10 000 of taxable income.

In either case, individuals with more income pay more income tax but under progressive rates the difference is disproportionate, which may in itself be considered to be inequitable. Progressive taxation implies that the system should be used to correct income inequalities. The arguments in favour of a progressive income tax are as follows:

1. Vertical equity

Tax rates should be progressive in order to promote vertical equity in the tax system. Vertical equity is concerned with the equality of sacrifice, i.e. the loss of £1 to a rich person is less of a burden than the loss of £1 to a poor person.

2. Redistribution of income

Socially aware governments seeking to reduce poverty and promote social welfare can use progressive taxation to achieve a greater degree of redistribution.

3. Benefit theory

Progressive taxation may be justified on the grounds that wealthier individuals receive more benefit from public services such as defence and law and order as they have more to lose than poorer individuals with few possessions.

4. To achieve equity in the tax system as a whole

A progressive income tax can compensate for regressive taxes in the tax system, e.g. excise duties, so that the total burden of taxation from all taxes is proportional.

In contrast, the arguments against a progressive income tax are as follows:

1. Simplicity

Simplicity is one of the principles of a good tax and it is argued that steeply progressive rates of income tax make it more complicated increasing the incentive to avoid and evade the tax.

2. Political objection

The fact that a government is voted in by the majority of the electorate but the highest progressive rates of tax would only apply to a minority may be politically unacceptable, as in effect the majority would be allowed to determine rates of tax that would fall exclusively on the minority.

3. Economic efficiency

Progressive income taxation may result in economic inefficiency affecting both the incentive to work, by increasing the marginal rate of tax, and the incentive for risk taking, e.g. saving and investment, by lowering the after tax rate of return.

'Progression changes the odds on the risk involved in all investments and the change is always in the direction of making them less attractive.'[7]

Although these economic effects are largely indeterminable, the more progressive the tax the more likely it is that revenue collected at the highest rates, from the wealthiest individuals, would be collected from money that would have been saved or invested rather than being spent. In this way highly progressive rates of income tax are likely to reduce savings and the creation of capital, making society as a whole worse off. As with all taxes, there is often a trade off between equity and efficiency and a reasonable balance between the two may be preferable to achieving one at the expense of the other.

Income tax and the move to self assessment

One of the principles of taxation is that a tax should be administratively efficient, i.e. the costs of collecting the tax should be low in relation to the revenue collected. Up until 1996/7 the administration of income tax had changed little since it was re-introduced by Peel in 1842. The system depended on the Revenue raising assessments and formal demands for tax, based on the information contained in the tax return, with each particular source of income having its own due date for payment. In the absence of a tax return, estimated assessments were issued with the taxpayer having the right of appeal, and the system was often used in order to delay the payment of income tax.

The self assessment regime will have the effect of improving cash flow and administrative efficiency for the following reasons:

(a) tax is automatically payable without demand on set payment dates;

(b) the number of appeals will be substantially reduced so that less revenue will be held up in the system; and

(c) the shift in responsibility from the Revenue to the taxpayer will have the effect of reducing administrative costs at the expense of taxpayer compliance costs.

Self assessment requires a tax system that is certain and relatively simple for the taxpayer to understand in order to encourage compliance. In theory, increased certainty should lead to more cost effective administration and also has implications for the enforcement of the tax laws. The Keith Committee Report set out the following principles with regard to enforcement:[8]

(a) enforcement powers should be precise;

(b) administrative discretion should be reduced to a minimum and particular consequences should follow particular acts or omissions;

(c) automatic civil surcharges and penalties are more appropriate than criminal sanctions;

(d) opportunities for tax evasion should be reduced; and

(e) effective criminal sanctions should be available in the case of serious fraud.

Prior to the introduction of self assessment, the administration of income tax was laborious and time consuming, which had the effect of reducing the efficiency of the tax. The process of change is always expensive to manage, but once the change is complete, the move to self assessment will make the income tax system more cost effective for the Revenue although taxpayer compliance costs are likely to rise as responsibility is shifted from the Revenue to the taxpayer.

Compliance costs create an excess burden reducing the overall efficiency of the tax, and tend to be regressive in nature, i.e. they fall more heavily on those members of society who are least able to afford them, e.g. pensioners.

Compliance costs are more difficult to ascertain than administration costs and include non-financial as well as financial costs to the taxpayer such as the:

- cost of obtaining professional advice;
- time spent completing tax returns, etc.;
- stress and anxiety caused by having to comply with complicated legislation.

Costs of complying with the tax legislation may also be incurred indirectly by third parties, for example:

1. Employers

The operation of the PAYE system imposes additional costs on employers which can be particularly burdensome for the small employer.

2. Statutory requirement to provide information

The statutory obligation to provide information imposes additional costs on the bodies concerned; for example, banks are under a statutory obligation to supply information to the Revenue, however, the introduction of tax deduction at source had the effect of reducing the compliance costs for banks in respect of the supply of information relating to payments of interest.

The move to self assessment will no doubt have the effect of increasing compliance costs, despite the arguments that they should be kept reasonably low in preference to administration costs.[9]

The reduction of compliance costs would demand a tax system that is simple for taxpayers to understand and comply with. In reality, however, even the most capable and intelligent individuals appear to suffer some sort of mental block when faced with a tax return.

REFERENCES

1 Morse, N.C. and Weiss, R. (1955) 'The function and meaning of work and the job', *American Sociological Review*, Vol. 20.

2 Brown, C.V. and Dawson, D.A. (1969) 'Personal taxation, incentives and tax reforms', *Political and Economic Planning*.

3 Dilnot, A. and Kell, M. (1988) 'Top rate tax cuts and incentives: some empirical evidence', *Fiscal Studies*, Vol. 9, No. 4, pp. 70–92.

4 Gregg, P., Johnson, P. and Reed, H. (1999) *Entering Work and the British Tax and Benefit System*, Institute of Fiscal Studies, March.

5 HM Treasury, *The Modernisation of Britain's Tax and Benefit System, Number 5: Supporting Children through the Tax and Benefit System 1999*, p. 39.

6 *The Report of the Royal Commission on the Taxation of Profits and Incomes* (1955) CMND 9474, HMSO.

7 Blum, W.J. and Kalven, H. (1953) *The Uneasy Case for Progressive Taxation*, University of Chicago Press.

8 *The Keith Committee Report on Enforcement Powers of the Revenue Departments* (1983), Vols 1 and 2, CMND 8822, HMSO.

9 Sandford, C.T., Goodwin, M. and Hardwick, P. (1989) *Administration and Compliance Costs of Taxation*, Fiscal Publications, Bath.

FURTHER READING

Blum, W.J. and Kalven, H. (1953) *The Uneasy Case for Progressive Taxation*, University of Chicago Press.

Blundell, R. (1992) 'Labour supply and taxation: a survey', *Fiscal Studies*, Vol. 13, No. 3, pp. 15–40.

Blundell, R., Duncan, A., McCrae, J and Meghir, C. (2000) 'The labour market impact of the Working Families Tax Credit', *Fiscal Studies*, Vol. 21, No. 1, pp. 75–104.

Fry, V. and Stark G., (1993) *The Take Up of Means Tested Benefits 1984–90*, London Institute of Fiscal Studies, January.

Gregg, P., Johnson, P. and Reed H. (1999) *Entering Work and the British Tax and Benefit System*, Institute of Fiscal Studies, March.

Houghton, R.W. (1973) *Public Finance: Selected Readings* (2nd edn), Penguin Books.

James, S. and Nobes, C. (2001/02) *The Economics of Taxation*, Prentice Hall.

Kay, J.A. and King, M.A. (1990), *The British Tax System* (5th edn), Oxford University Press.

Robson, M.H. (1995) 'Taxation and household saving: reflections on the OECD report', *Fiscal Studies*, Vol. 16, No. 1, pp. 38–57.

Walker, R. and Wiseman, M. (1997) 'The possibility of a British earned income tax credit', *Fiscal Studies*, Vol. 18, No. 4, pp. 401–25.

CHAPTER 3

The taxation of wealth

The rationale for including capital in the tax base

Although the main objective of any tax should be to raise revenue for public expenditure, the inclusion of capital in the tax base is justified on the grounds of equity and the redistribution of wealth. The Labour Chancellor, James Callaghan, made this point when introducing capital gains tax in 1965: 'Yield is not my main purpose . . . The failure to tax capital gains is . . . the greatest blot on our system of direct taxation . . . This new tax will provide a background to equity and fair play'.[1]

The equity argument for capital taxation

Equity in the tax system demands that people in similar situations should be treated in a similar way (horizontal equity), e.g. an individual earning £20 000 should not be treated differently from an individual with realised capital gains of £20 000 but no earned income. The equity argument is also based on the ability to pay, or equality of sacrifice, i.e. individuals in unequal situations should be treated differently (vertical equity). The ownership of wealth increases living standards and security, bringing with it status and economic power and as such it could be argued that wealthy individuals have a greater ability to pay taxes. In the absence of capital taxes, the wealthiest individuals would be in a position to avoid paying income tax merely by converting their income into capital. The equity argument for capital taxation was supported by the Meade Committee Report: 'capital produces an income which unlike earning capacity does not decline with age and is not gained at the expense of leisure'.[2]

The redistribution of wealth argument for capital taxation

The second argument for imposing taxes on capital is that it is presumed that extreme inequalities in the distribution of wealth can be corrected. However, capital taxes have been in existence for many years, with little effect on the distribution of wealth. The extent to which social equality is an objective of the tax system is highly sensitive to the political persuasion of the government concerned. Historically, Labour governments have seen taxing the wealthy as a means of achieving social equality, albeit without much success. The income tax system was often used as a means of correcting the imbalance by:

(a) taxing the income derived from wealth at a higher rate than earned income; and

(b) leaving higher rate taxpayers with less net income with which to accumulate wealth.

During the 1970s the top rate of income tax was 83 per cent with an additional 15 per cent charged on investment incomes over a certain amount. However, despite these oppressive rates of tax, the concentration of wealth has changed little in the past 50 years, any distribution that has taken place has tended to be from the very rich to the rich. This is not surprising when it is considered that the highest concentrations are a result of inherited wealth and often held in forms that yield little taxable income. This would indicate that if social equality is an objective of government policy, an effective inheritance tax and/or the introduction of a wealth tax may go some way in achieving this goal. It was the seemingly unfair distribution of wealth and the intent to achieve social equality that led the government in 1974 to produce a Green Paper on the introduction of a wealth tax in the UK, its opening paragraphs stated: 'The government is committed to using the taxation system to promote greater social and economic equality. This requires a redistribution of wealth as well as income'.[3]

The taxation of wealth

Basically, there are three ways in which wealthy individuals may be taxed on their stock of capital assets:

(a) on the income derived from the assets, e.g. dividends received from the ownership of shares;

(b) on the capital value of the assets. This may be achieved either:
 – on a recurrent basis, e.g. annually; or
 – on the transfer of capital, e.g. on death; and

(c) on the increase in the value of assets, e.g. on the disposal of an asset.

The main types of taxes on capital are as follows:

1. Investment income surcharge

Investment income surcharge taxes the income derived from investment in capital assets at a higher rate than earned income. Such a system existed in the UK until 1984 when it was abolished. This type of tax can have a distortionary effect on the economy as wealthy individuals switch their investments to non-income producing assets, e.g. antiques, in order to avoid the tax.

Another criticism of this tax was that the idea that investment income was being subjected to higher taxation was somewhat illusionary when consideration is given to the fact that earned income, unlike investment income, is liable to National Insurance contributions.

2. Wealth tax

An annual wealth tax may be imposed on the capital value of the wealth. Many European countries operate an annual wealth tax levied at fairly low rates, most of these being introduced at about the same time as the UK introduced the investment income surcharge. The UK tax system does not have a wealth tax, although this was given consideration by the government in 1974. The implications of a wealth tax are considered more fully in Chapter 7.

3. Taxes on the transfer of capital

Tax may be charged on the capital value of wealth transferred either on death or during the individuals lifetime via:

(a) Capital transfer tax

The capital transfer tax (CTT) that was introduced in the UK in 1974 taxed the capital value of transfers on death and during the individual's lifetime on a cumulative basis. The fact that lifetime gifts were included in CTT ought to have meant that the objective of redistribution was easier to achieve, however, this was not the case, probably as a result of the relatively low rates of tax and the many exemptions and reliefs that were available. In the UK, CTT was replaced by the present inheritance tax in 1986.

(b) Estate duty

Estate duties tax the transfer of capital on death based on the value of the estate. In the UK estate duty was replaced in 1974 by CTT only to be reintroduced in 1986 under the inappropriate name of inheritance tax. Estate duty takes account of the donor's circumstances at death, a true inheritance tax would be a donee-based tax.

(c) Inheritance tax

An inheritance tax would take account of the circumstances of the beneficiary rather than the size of the estate, and would arguably promote the redistribution of wealth.

(d) Accessions tax

An accessions tax, like an inheritance tax, would be based on the circumstances of the donee, taking into account the individual's lifetime gifts and legacies so that the tax is administered on a cumulative basis. This type of tax however, would undoubtedly lead to higher administrative costs.

4. Stamp duties

Stamp duties may also be considered to be a tax on the transfer of capital. Stamp duties are levied on documents connected with certain capital transactions, e.g. conveyancing. However, Sandford considered that in many ways stamp duties 'are more akin to taxes on outlay than on capital. They are not an essential part of the fabric of the system of capital taxation'.[4] For these reasons, stamp duty will not be considered further in this chapter.

5. Capital gains tax

Capital gains tax is imposed on the increase in the value of capital assets on their disposal. Some countries only tax short-term gains, and in other countries long-term gains are treated less harshly than short-term gains. In the UK the distinction between short-term and long-term gains was arbitrary until 1971, after which all capital gains were subject to the same tax treatment.

However, radical changes to capital gains tax following the Finance Act 1998 once again make the distinction between long-term and short-term gains by the use of a taper, lowering the effective rate of tax on long-term gains, the taper being more generous in respect of business assets. Business assets are defined as:

- assets used for trading purposes; or
- shareholdings in unquoted trading companies; or
- shareholdings held by employees in quoted trading companies; or
- shareholdings in quoted trading companies of at least 5 per cent of the voting shares, where the individual is not an employee.

The rest of this chapter will consider in more detail the two major UK taxes on capital.

UK taxes on capital

The present UK tax system includes capital gains tax (CGT), a tax on the chargeable gains arising from the disposal of assets, and inheritance tax (IHT), a tax on the value of capital transferred on death and into certain types of trust.

Capital gains tax

Historical background

Prior to 1962, gains arising on the disposal of capital assets escaped tax altogether. However, from 10 April 1962, Schedule D of income tax was extended and Case VII taxed the gains arising on the disposal of assets held for less than six months, this period was extended to three years for land and buildings. Because there was no provision for charging long-term gains, the tax system provided the incentive for wealthy individuals to convert income gains, into capital gains and so avoid tax.

This situation changed in 1965 with the introduction of CGT for long-term gains and the simultaneous modification of Schedule D Case VII in respect of the short-term gains liable to income tax, such that:

(a) CGT was charged at a flat rate of 30 per cent on the chargeable gains arising on the disposal of assets held for more than 12 months; and

(b) Schedule D Case VII continued to treat short-term gains as income but the holding period was increased from six to 12 months.

This situation continued until 1971, from which time all capital gains were subject to CGT at the flat rate of 30 per cent. During the 1970s, with escalating rates of inflation, concern was expressed that CGT was being levied on inflationary rather than real gains and eroding the underlying capital. After several years of debate an indexation allowance was introduced with effect from April 1982. However, besides implying that no inflation existed before 1982, the allowance was limiting in two other ways:

(a) the first 12 months of ownership were excluded for assets acquired after April 1982; and

(b) the indexation could not be used to create or increase a loss.

The system of indexation was modified in 1985 by removing these restrictions, but in 1993 the legislation was changed yet again and indexation can no longer be used to increase or create a loss.

The Finance Act 1988 brought two major changes to the system of CGT.

(a) Assets were rebased to their value at 31 March 1982, so that effectively gains accruing before this date were no longer chargeable on disposals made after April 1988. This was probably logical to a government whose previous legislation had presumed no inflation before 1982.

(b) The rate of CGT was changed from a flat rate of 30 per cent to the individual's marginal rate of income tax, on the basis that 'there is little economic difference between income and capital gains'.[5]

Whether this is true or not is an area for debate, as taxing capital gains in the same way as income may well be justified on the grounds of horizontal equity but on efficiency grounds it may be more expedient to charge a lower rate of tax on capital gains in order to encourage investment in more risky projects.

The case for a capital gains tax examined

Capital gains tax is administratively cumbersome and raises very little revenue; the legislation is complicated and full of anomalies, detracting from the principle of simplicity and resulting in high taxpayer compliance costs.

In the light of these poor qualities, the main arguments in favour of a CGT are now examined.

1. Equity

An individual with a capital gain should not be treated more favourably by the tax system than an individual receiving an equal amount of income. Realised gains give rise to spending power in much the same way as income gains and *horizontal equity* would demand that they should be taxed equally.

The existence of a CGT also improves *vertical equity* in the tax system by reducing the incentive for wealthy individuals to avoid income tax by converting income gains into capital gains. During the period when gains were charged at a flat rate of 30 per cent there was an incentive for higher rate income tax payers to receive a capital gain in preference to additional income. Aligning the rate of CGT to income tax rates has substantially reduced this incentive with the result that vertical equity is improved.

2. Equality

Wealthy individuals are more likely to hold a large proportion of their wealth in capital assets that are potentially liable to CGT; the existence of a CGT should therefore, in theory at least, promote the redistribution of wealth.

3. Efficiency

The existence of a CGT reduces distortion in investment choices, making the system more neutral between income producing assets and non-income producing assets;

and charging CGT at income tax rates increases economic efficiency by making the system more neutral between income and capital, which was the Chancellor's main objective when introducing the reform. 'Taxing capital gains at income tax rates makes for greater neutrality in the tax system.'[6]

Given that these are the main arguments in favour of taxing capital gains, it may be surprising to learn that the UK CGT as it stands violates each of these arguments to a certain degree.

1. Equity revisited

The present CGT undermines the principle of equity for the following reasons.

(a) The existence of an annual exemption at a higher level than the personal income tax allowances still provides the incentive for higher rate taxpayers to receive a capital gain rather than additional income.

(b) The CGT legislation provides for a number of reliefs and exemptions, which can act as a tax shelter for wealthier individuals.

(c) Assets that can be fragmented give the taxpayer a distinct advantage. For example, compare a taxpayer holding shares that had increased £20 000 in value over the past five years with a taxpayer holding investment property with an equal increase in value over the same time period. The shareholder could have realised the gain over the period of ownership to take advantage of the annual exemption and pay no CGT. On the other hand, the property holder would be liable to CGT if the gain was realised, as the disposal cannot be fragmented. This clearly violates horizontal equity.

2. Equality revisited

The redistribution of wealth may be undermined for the following reasons.

(a) Since general gift relief was withdrawn in 1989, the present system of CGT inhibits the redistribution of wealth by way of gifts.

(b) As only realised gains are charged to tax, there is an incentive to become 'locked in' to the investment which restricts the mobility of capital; the recent changes to CGT increase this incentive.

3. Efficiency revisited

The present system of CGT may reduce economic efficiency for the following reasons.

(a) Taxing both capital and income gains at the same rates discourages investment in risky projects. There is therefore an argument for taxing gains more lightly than income in order to encourage risk taking and enterprise.

(b) The existence of substantial exemptions and reliefs may discourage investment in chargeable assets.

(c) The system encourages individuals to hold on to their investments in order to defer a liability to CGT which may result in economic inefficiency.

In conclusion, there is no doubt that without some means of taxing gains, the tax system as a whole would be less equitable. The present government is seeking to actively encourage long-term investment and entrepreneurship through its radical tax reform. However, it is likely that the recent changes to CGT will reinforce the incentive to become 'locked in' to the investment, which will not enhance the over-all efficiency of the tax.

Inheritance tax

Historical background

Taxes on death have a longer history in Britain than other taxes. The latter end of the seventeenth century saw the development of a hotchpotch of death duties starting with probate duty in 1694. Probate duty, or probate and administration duty, as it was sometimes known, was essentially a stamp duty, charged on obtaining probate, i.e. proving the validity of a will. When probate duty was first introduced, it was at a flat rate of five shillings on estates over £20, but in 1779 three progressive rates were introduced and in 1780 legacy duty, a second stamp duty, was levied on receipts given to legatees receiving personalty from an estate, i.e. the receipt was stamped and charged to legacy duty. However, as there was no legal requirement to provide the legatee with a receipt, the duty could easily be avoided.

This was remedied by Pitt in 1796 by modifying the duty and transforming it into an inheritance tax charged at graduated rates depending on the relationship of the legatee to the deceased, the more remote the relationship, the higher the rate of tax, demonstrating that redistribution had no place in eighteenth-century Britain.

By 1822, the revenue from legacy duty and probate duty reached almost £2 mil-lion, representing approximately 3 per cent of public revenue. Real property remained untaxed until 1853 when succession duty was introduced, calculated on the value of the inheritance and levied on all property not covered by legacy duty. The use of death duties to promote social equality did not emerge until 1894 when William Harcourt introduced estate duty, a donor-based tax levied at progressive rates on the value of the estate at death. In the same year probate duty was abolished but legacy duty and succession duty, which were true inheritance taxes, i.e. reflecting the circumstances of the donee rather than the value of the estate, remained on the statute books alongside estate duty. The year after estate duty was introduced the revenue from death duties amounted to £14 million rising to £18 million in 1908. In 1949 legacy duty and succession duty were abolished and the top rate of estate duty rose to 80 per cent, ten times higher than when it was introduced by Harcourt.

Despite the high rates of estate duty, the revenue began to decline steadily after the end of the Second World War, and by the time it was replaced with capital trans-fer tax (CTT) in 1974, it contributed only 2.4 per cent of tax revenue. The reason for the poor yield was that the tax could easily be avoided by setting up trusts and making lifetime gifts, and the tax became 'a voluntary tax paid by those who dislike the Revenue less than they dislike their heirs'.[7]

Death bed bequests were frequently used to avoid estate duty. To counter this avoidance, the legislation was amended and the period in which gifts could be made before death without attracting a charge to estate duty was increased from three months to seven years. This meant that only the 'healthy, wealthy and well advised'[8] could organise their affairs so as to avoid the tax.

Probably one of the main reasons why estate duty had little effect on the redistri-bution of wealth was that the tax was donor-based rather than donee-based. Although replacing estate duty with CTT in 1974 was an attempt to close the loophole on lifetime gifts, CTT remained a donor-based tax and, together with exemptions, reliefs and lower rates of tax, raised even less revenue than the old estate duty. Although a Conservative government came to power in 1979, CTT remained until 1986, when it was replaced with the present IHT, which is nothing more than the old estate duty resurrected under the new and inappropriate name of IHT.

When IHT was introduced, the existing CTT legislation of 1984 was amended and renamed the Inheritance Tax Act 1984, which is confusing in itself since the tax was introduced in 1986. Tinkering with the CTT legislation at the edges, instead of starting afresh, has resulted in the legislation being both complicated and full of anomalies. The new IHT suffers from all the problems of the old estate duty but is likely to raise even less revenue because all the exemptions and reliefs introduced with CTT have been retained and even extended in some instances, while the tax base has been narrowed by increasing the threshold to £250 000 (2002/03).

Inheritance tax examined

The present IHT, unlike its name suggests, does not reflect the circumstances of the beneficiary; it is really a donor-based estate tax. Instead of drafting new legislation in 1986, the previous CTT legislation was amended by exempting lifetime gifts made within seven years of death and adding to the copious amount of anti-avoidance legislation. The legislation is full of anomalies and extremely complicated, undermining the principle of simplicity. This has the effect of increasing compliance costs as wealthy individuals contrive to mitigate the effects of the tax, as with careful planning the tax can easily be avoided. Taxes on death do not sit easily with the principle of certainty; death is its own master with little respect for age or timing. The convenience of the tax is also compromised if assets have to be sold to pay the tax at a time when there is no readily available market or the market is depressed. On the basis of this, the justification for including taxes on the transfer of wealth on death is based on achieving a degree of equity and redistribution in the tax system.

Consideration will now be given as to how well the current IHT achieves these objectives.

1. Equity

Wealth gives rise to a taxable capacity that should not be ignored if the tax system is to be fair. However, the present IHT does not take account of the circumstances of the beneficiary. Switching from a donor-based tax to a donee-based tax would achieve a greater degree of equity. Equity is also violated as estates of the same size may be subject to different amounts of tax depending on:

- the frequency of transfer, i.e. the tax system favours the healthy and long-lived; and
- the ease with which the assets can be valued, e.g. if one estate consists of readily saleable assets for which there is a market and another consists of rare works of art that may have been under or over valued, horizontal equity is not maintained.

The more the estate consists of assets that are difficult to value, the more likely it is to be inequitable.

2. Redistribution

Reducing wealth inequalities is seen as the main reason for taxing the transfer of wealth on death, as inherited wealth is the major cause of wealth inequality. The extent to which redistribution is an objective of the tax system depends on value judgements and the extent to which an egalitarian society is desirable. Inheritance tax in its current form does little to encourage the dispersion of wealth. In order to improve the effectiveness with which IHT achieves equity and redistribution, consideration should be given to the following:

(a) Donor / donee-based tax?

Taking into account the circumstances of the beneficiary rather than the size of the estate would provide for greater equity. Is it fair that wealth should be taxed 'in proportion to the amount left by those who can no longer enjoy it'?[9] A donor-based tax can only achieve redistribution if it raises sufficient revenue, i.e. wealth is transferred to the public sector with redistribution being effected by transfer payments, etc. A donee-based tax would also transfer wealth from the private sector to the public sector but may also encourage estates to be split into smaller inheritances.

(b) Lifetime gifts?

The present system of IHT exempts lifetime gifts, provided that the person making the gift survives for at least seven years. This favours the more wealthy members of society as they are more likely to be able to pass on wealth during their lifetime and therefore avoid tax. A system that had some mechanism for taxing lifetime gifts would achieve a greater degree of redistribution, and if this was coupled with a donee-based tax, equity would be improved.

(c) Exemptions and reliefs?

The present system of IHT gives an enormous amount of reliefs and exemptions, which only serve to create inequalities between individuals holding different forms of wealth, creating economic inefficiency by distorting the choice between exempt and chargeable assets.

Concessions and reliefs may have the effect of not actually benefiting the interests of those they were meant to protect. Once a relief is given it tends to become capitalised in the price of the asset, e.g. agricultural property relief has pushed up the price of farmland. The system would therefore provide for more equity and redistribution if exemptions and reliefs were kept minimal.

REFERENCES

[1] James Callaghan in his Budget speech, 1965.
[2] Meade, J.E. (Chairman) (1978) *The Meade Committee Report on the Structure and Reform of Direct Taxation*, Institute of Fiscal Studies, George Allen & Unwin.
[3] Government Green Paper, *The Introduction of a Wealth Tax*, (1974) CMND 5704, HMSO.
[4] Sandford, C.T. (1971) *Taxing Personal Wealth*, George Allen & Unwin.
[5] Nigel Lawson in his Budget speech, 1988.
[6] *Ibid.*
[7] Sandford, C.T. (1971) *Taxing Personal Wealth*, George Allen & Unwin.
[8] Kay, J.A. and King, M.A. (1990) *The British Tax System* (5th edn), Oxford University Press.
[9] *Hansard* Parliamentary Debates, 10 May 1894.

FURTHER READING

Bracewell-Milnes, B.B. (1992) *A Discredited Tax*, Institute of Fiscal Studies.

James, S. and Nobes, C. (2000/01) *The Economics of Taxation*, Prentice Hall.

Kay, J.A. and King, M.A. (1990) *The British Tax System* (5th edn), Oxford University Press.

Meade, J.E. (Chairman) (1978) *The Meade Committee Report on The Structure and Reform of Direct Taxation*, Institute of Fiscal Studies, George Allen & Unwin.

Robinson, B. (1989) 'Reforming the taxation of capital gains, gifts and inheritances', *Fiscal Studies*, Vol. 10, No. 1, pp. 32–40.

Sandford, C. (1987) 'Death duties: taxing estates or inheritances', *Fiscal Studies*, Vol. 8, No. 4, pp. 32–40.

CHAPTER 4

Company taxation

Systems of corporation tax

The economic effect of corporate taxes depends largely on the system of corporation tax (CT) that is adopted. The main systems for taxing company profits being as follows.

1. Classical system

A classical system of CT does not differentiate between a company's distributed and retained earnings, and its shareholders are treated as being completely independent of the company. The taxation consequences of this are that:

(a) the company is liable to CT on all its taxable income and gains whether distributed or retained;

(b) the shareholder is liable to income tax (IT) on dividends received from the company; and

(c) the shareholder is liable to CGT on taxable gains that are realised on the disposal of shares in the company.

Although a classical system of corporation tax is simple to understand and administer, it is often criticised for its distortionary effects on the economy.

(a) Because the company and the shareholders are treated separately for tax purposes, the system gives rise to the double taxation of dividends, which could distort the company's dividend policy.

(b) The system is not neutral between debt and equity capital; the double taxation of dividends encourages the company to be highly geared as interest is deductible from pre-tax profits.

(c) The classical system of CT encourages companies to retain earnings, which could lead to a potential double taxation when shareholders dispose of their shares.

(d) The system encourages investment to be funded from retained earnings, which could distort investment decisions and lead to the inefficient use of resources.

2. Imputation system

Under the imputation system of CT, all or part of the underlying CT on distributions is imputed to the shareholder as a tax credit, therefore avoiding the problem of the double taxation of dividends.

There are two types of imputation system:

(a) Full imputation

Under a full imputation system, all the underlying CT on the distribution is imputed to the shareholder. The economic significance of full imputation is that the system is neutral between debt and equity finance (ignoring retentions).

(b) Partial imputation

Part of the underlying CT on the distribution is imputed to the shareholder. Under partial imputation, the system will become more neutral between debt and equity the nearer the CT rate is to the rate of imputation.

On the whole, imputation systems of CT alleviate many of the problems of a classical system, but in doing so they ignore the possible double taxation with regard to retained earnings and CGT.

3. Split rate systems

Split rate systems of CT make the distinction between distributed and retained profit by charging a lower rate of tax on distributed profits in order to avoid the double taxation of dividends. Using a lower rate for distributed profit can operate either under a classical or imputation system of CT.

The rationale for taxing company profits

The Meade Committee Report[1] considered the following reasons for justifying taxing company profits:

1. Privileges of incorporation

Incorporated businesses enjoy limited liability and it is argued that the company should pay for such a privilege.

2. Equity

As unincorporated businesses have to pay tax even on retained earnings, then on equity grounds, if a company's retained earnings cannot be allocated to shareholders, there should be some method of taxing undistributed company profits.

3. Revenue raising

A CT levied at higher rates than the basic rate of income tax may be a convenient way of raising extra revenue.

4. CT exists

Perhaps the most convincing argument for maintaining a CT is that it already exists and to abolish it would mean substantial windfall gains for a large number of shareholders.

However, there are opposing views on whether there is a genuine case for taxing companies on their income and gains in the first place.[2] The logic behind the arguments for not imposing a separate tax on companies stems from the fact that although in law a company is a separate legal entity, its activities and therefore any tax imposed on these activities can only affect the individuals concerned with that company, for example shareholders, customers, creditors, employees, etc. If companies were not taxed at all, it is quite probable that the loss of CT revenue would be compensated for as follows:

(a) As shareholders pay IT on the dividends they receive, without a CT the company's distributable profits may be increased, with a corresponding increase in IT revenue.

(b) If the company decided to retain the extra profit generated by the absence of CT, then the value of the company would increase, and as the gain arising on the disposal of shares would be liable to CGT, there would be a corresponding increase in CGT revenue.

(c) In the absence of CT, there would be no backward shifting of CT on to the employees of the company and higher wages would result in an increase of IT payable by the employees of the company.

(d) It is possible that a company can shift the burden of CT over to the customers, in the form of higher prices, depending on the elasticity of supply and demand for the product; the absence of CT may mean more stable prices for the consumer.

The most compelling argument against taxing companies is that eventually the burden of the tax must fall on individuals. When considering the burden or incidence of a tax, a distinction must be made between the statutory/formal incidence, i.e. the person on whom the tax is levied, and the economic/effective incidence, i.e. the person who eventually bears the burden of the tax. Equity would be satisfied if the burden of a CT remained with the shareholders, as in this case the tax could be considered to be fairly progressive, on the assumption that shareholders pay income tax above the basic rate. However, shareholders require a certain rate of return from their investment, and, to the extent that a CT would reduce the return on capital employed for investors, the burden of a CT may be shifted either:

- backwards – on to the employees of the company; or
- forwards – on to the customers.

The extent to which the incidence of a CT can be shifted depends on the elasticity of supply and demand for the product and the labour market. These arguments would tend to favour an integrated system of taxing companies. Under an integrated system, the company would not be liable to pay a CT, but its profits, both distributed and retained would be allocated to the shareholders in proportion to their holdings, and taxed accordingly.

The UK corporation tax

1. The system up to 1965

At the outset, the UK tax system did not differentiate between incorporated and unincorporated businesses: they were both liable to pay income tax on their income. However, companies, not being individuals, were not eligible for personal reliefs and allowances, nor were they liable to pay income tax at graduated rates, but paid income tax at the basic rate on all their income.

After the outbreak of the First World War in 1914, an excess profits duty was levied in 1915, and in 1920 a corporation profits tax was levied at 5 per cent, arguably because individuals at that time were liable to surtax. However, excess profits duty was abolished in 1924. Between 1924 and 1937 companies reverted to paying income tax at the basic rate, and no additional taxes were levied.

In 1937 the national defence contribution was introduced at the rate of 5 per cent and when war broke out in 1939 an excess profits tax was imposed on companies to augment the national defence contribution, and continued until after the end of the war.

In the Income Tax Act 1945 initial allowances were introduced for all businesses investing in plant and machinery and industrial buildings, laying the foundations for the modern capital allowance system.

The national defence contribution was only intended to be a temporary measure, but in 1947 it was renamed profits tax and at the same time excess profits tax was abolished.

The 1947 profits tax made the distinction between distributed and retained profit by charging a lower rate on distributed profit, effectively amounting to a split rate system of CT. However, following the recommendations of the Royal Commission on the taxation of profits and income in 1955, profits tax was levied at a single rate on all corporate profits. This state of affairs remained until 1965 when James Callaghan introduced a separate tax on companies, to replace the income tax and profits tax previously levied on incorporated businesses.

2. 1965 to 1973

When a separate tax on companies was first introduced in 1965, it was under a classical system, which does not differentiate between distributed and retained profit, resulting in the double taxation of dividends.

This had the effect of encouraging companies to become highly geared as debt capital became more tax efficient than equity capital, and during this period preference shares practically became extinct.

As it is often difficult for a company to change its capital structure overnight, this period also witnessed an increase in the number of takeovers and mergers as companies attempted to achieve the most tax efficient capital structures.

Because the classical system of CT results in the double taxation of dividends, it encourages retained earnings. In theory this should have encouraged companies to use these retained earnings for worthwhile investments in order to sustain growth. In reality, together with the accelerated depreciation for plant and machinery and industrial buildings available by 1971, many companies were undertaking capital investment programmes merely to gain a tax advantage and many such investments proved to produce poor and often negative returns, leading to a misallocation of resources.

The system of CT during this period fulfilled few of the objectives of taxation; CT revenue was depressed because many companies were tax exhausted, i.e. interest on debt was tax deductible and this, together with accelerated depreciation, meant that many companies had negative tax profits. Although the CT could be used to regulate the economy, the outcome was not always as government intended.

As a result of the economic effects, the CT during this period conformed to few of the principles of a good tax. Increased legislation meant that the system of CT was far from simple and certainty was undermined because the rates of CT were set in arrears, i.e. the rates were set in the spring Budget for the previous financial year.

The tax was not neutral between different forms of capital expenditure or between debt and equity finance, with the consequence that it caused economic inefficiency. Many large companies were able to undertake large capital investment programmes and reduce their taxable capacity, i.e. those companies most able to pay the tax had negative tax profits.

With the increase in first year allowances (FYA) to 100 per cent for capital expenditure on plant and machinery and 75 per cent for industrial buildings, the situation intensified. One outcome of these FYAs was the huge growth in the leasing industry, as the lessor could claim the capital allowances and the lessee could deduct the lease payments as a revenue expense. The classical system of CT was heavily criticised for its distortionary effects on the economy and in 1973 it was replaced by the imputation system, alleviating the double taxation of dividends and aligning the UK corporate tax system with the system most widely adopted by members of the European Community (EC) at that time.

3. 1973 to 1984

In 1973 the UK adopted a partial imputation system of CT, where part of the underlying CT on distributed profits is imputed to the shareholder. While this reduces the double taxation of dividends, it does not take into account the possibility of double taxation with regard to retained earnings and CGT, and unless the rate of imputation is equal to the rate of CT there is still a bias in favour of debt finance.

During the early 1970s many companies were facing liquidity problems as inflation escalated, to alleviate this problem, the government introduced stock relief in 1975. The original stock relief was based on the increase in the value of stocks during the company's accounting period, but it made no distinction between changes in volume and changes in value, which meant that the system could be exploited by increasing the level of stocks at the end of the period of account. As a result of this, the scheme was modified in 1981 by calculating the relief with reference to opening stocks in excess of £2000:

Stock relief = (opening stock − £2000) × percentage increase in stocks

Any unused stock relief could be carried forward as a loss for a maximum of six years. In the early 1980s with increasing inflation and unemployment the CT system again came under close scrutiny as a result of its distortionary effects on the economy, the main considerations being as follows:

- The system of capital allowances was not neutral between different kinds of capital investment; expenditure on plant and machinery and industrial buildings receiving preferential treatment. During this time of such high unemployment, firms were encouraged by the tax system to invest in capital rather than labour.

- With high rates of CT, 52 per cent for large companies and 40 per cent for small companies, the system was not neutral between debt and equity finance.

- More than 50 per cent of companies during the early 1980s were tax exhausted causing a huge build up of tax losses.

- With many companies having negative tax profits, unrelieved ACT was becoming a problem.

Despite the fundamental change to the system of CT in 1973, the CT in 1984 was no better at achieving the objectives and principles of taxation than its predecessor. From the early 1980s, consideration was given to reducing the economic distortions caused by the system of CT and the government produced a Green Paper on the possibilities for reform in 1982. However, many of the criticisms stemmed from the bias in favour of certain types of investment and financing methods rather than the system of CT itself and addressing these issues was seen as the way forward.

4. The 1984 reforms to CT

The main reasoning behind the 1984 reforms to CT was to increase fiscal neutrality and so avoid unnecessary economic distortions within the tax system. The move to a more neutral system of CT was achieved by:

- the withdrawal of stock relief in 1984;
- the systematic reduction in the rates of CT over a two-year period; and
- the phasing out of first year allowances over a two-year period.

The main effects of the 1984 reforms are as follows:

(a) The capital allowance system was more neutral between different types of capital expenditure with allowances more closely representing economic depreciation.

(b) The system was more neutral between debt and equity; there was still a bias towards debt finance but the nearer the CT rate moves to the rate of imputation then the more neutral the system is between debt and equity.

(c) The tax base was widened as more companies were eligible to pay CT, i.e. fewer companies were becoming tax exhausted with the withdrawal of first year allowances and stock relief.

(d) The widening of the tax base also reduced the problem of surplus ACT, although this was somewhat short-lived. The mid 1980s saw the UK economy in recession, and by the early 1990s the surplus ACT problem had returned. The reduction in the rate of ACT from 1993/94 went some way to reducing this problem, but did not go far enough. The problem was more acute with regards multinational companies resident in the UK, as overseas income will form a large portion of their total income. The Finance Act 1994 introduced the Foreign Income Dividend Scheme to provide a measure of relief for such companies, extending the relief further to companies owned at least 80 per cent by non-UK residents, by allowing the foreign income dividend to be paid without accounting for ACT.

On balance, the post 1984 CT achieved the objectives of taxation and caused less economic distortion than previously, although it has been suggested that it actively discourages business investment.[3] Prior to the 1990 Budget, concern by the CBI and industrial unions called for a return to higher FYAs.

The UK CT has been the subject of many changes since its introduction in 1965 and, while the post 1984 system reduced the excess burden of the tax, it has been argued that, as around two-thirds of business investment is funded from retained earnings, a truly neutral CT would require that the cost of capital should be the same for both debt finance and retained earnings, i.e. the CT system would require an allowable deduction for the opportunity cost of such finance in the same way as the allowable deduction for interest on debt finance.[4]

5. Recent reforms to CT

Recent changes to the system of CT indicate that the Labour government continues to see neutrality as the way forward. Since coming to power in 1997 they have undertaken a series of radical reforms to the system of CT in an attempt to improve the overall economic efficiency of the tax.

The abolition of reclaimable tax credits on dividends paid to pension funds and corporate shareholders after 2 July 1997 ought, in theory at least, to encourage companies to retain profits for investment, rather than distribute them as dividends.

Because the existence of ACT affects a company's cash flow position, it can distort dividend policy; the problem of surplus ACT also unfairly penalises UK-based multinationals. Both these distortions should be alleviated when the system of ACT is abolished from 6 April 1999, and will go a long way to improving the neutrality of the tax.

In order to stimulate investment, the FA 1997 (No. 2) introduced a 50 per cent FYA for small and medium-sized businesses investing in plant and machinery between 2 July 1997 and 1 July 1998.

The enhancement of capital allowances has been extended in successive Finance Acts since 1998 with a FYA of 40 per cent being available for small and medium-sized businesses investing in plant and machinery, this feature being made permanent in the FA 2000. In fact, many of the recent reforms to CT made by the present government have largely been targeted at smaller companies, namely:

- enhanced FYAs for plant and machinery;
- 0 per cent starting rate for companies with profits up to £10 000 from April 2002;
- research and development Tax Credits;
- share ownership schemes;
- increase in the threshold for the quarterly PAYE scheme.

The government intends that these measures will help to encourage investment, innovation and growth in these companies by improving their cash flow and reducing their tax bills.

As smaller companies tend to incur higher compliance costs, taxing them less heavily can be justified on equity grounds.

REFERENCES

[1] Meade, J.E. (Chairman) (1978) *The Meade Committee Report on the Structure and Reform of Direct Taxation*, Institute of Fiscal Studies, George Allen & Unwin.

[2] Kay, J.A. and King, M.A. (1990) *The British Tax System* (5th edn), Oxford University Press.

[3] Devereux, M. (1988) 'Corporation tax: The effect of the 1984 reforms on the incentive to invest', *Fiscal Studies*, Vol. 9, No. 1, pp. 62–79.

[4] Bond, S., Denny, K. and Devereux, M. (1993) 'Capital allowances and the impact of corporation tax on investment in the UK', *Fiscal Studies*, Vol. 14, No. 2, pp. 1–14.

FURTHER READING

Bond, S., Denny, K. and Devereux, M. (1993) 'Capital allowances and the impact of corporation tax on investment in the UK', *Fiscal Studies*, Vol. 14, No. 2, pp. 1–14.

Devereux, M. (1987) 'On the growth of corporation tax revenues', *Fiscal Studies*, Vol. 8, No. 2, pp. 77–85.

Devereux, M. (1988) 'Corporation tax: the effect of the 1984 reforms on the incentive to invest', *Fiscal Studies*, Vol. 9, No. 1, pp. 62–79.

Freeman, H. and Griffith, R. (1993) 'Surplus ACT – a solution in sight?', *Fiscal Studies*, Vol. 14, No. 4, pp. 58–73.

Government Green Paper on Corporation Tax, (1982) CMND 8456, HMSO.

Kay, J.A. and King, M.A. (1990) *The British Tax System* (5th edn), Oxford University Press.

Meade, J.E. (1978) *The Structure and Reform of Direct Taxation*, Institute of Fiscal Studies, George Allen & Unwin.

CHAPTER 5

Indirect taxation

Historical background

Throughout history indirect taxes have played a major role in the British tax system, contributing significantly to government revenue. Long before Parliament existed, monarchs had the right to open and close ports and impose duties on imports and exports, making customs duties one of the main sources of revenue for the monarchy.

In 1643, during the civil war in England, an innovative form of taxation, the excise, was introduced. Unlike customs duties, which were levied on imports and exports, excise duties were a form of sales tax applied to domestic goods, and were administered by the Inland Revenue. The excise was a revolutionary method of taxation for a country that had previously escaped onerous levels of taxation, and Samuel Johnson referred to it as 'a hateful tax levied on commodities'. The tax was extremely regressive as it was imposed on many essential items and applied equally to rich and poor.

Until the introduction of income tax, customs and excise duties were the main forms of taxation applying to all manner of goods including carriages, watches, bachelors, hearths, windows, wines, spirits, tobacco and even mousetraps. The re-introduction of income tax in 1842 gave Robert Peel the means of reducing many customs and excise duties that fell heavily on the poorer members of society and interfered with trade. Up until 1909 excise duties continued to be administered by the Inland Revenue but on the grounds of administrative efficiency, responsibility for the collection of excise duties was transferred to Customs from 3 December 1909.

With income tax becoming a more important source of revenue after the First World War, excise duties on a few selective items and customs duties remained the main indirect taxes in Britain. However, during the Second World War a tax on domestic goods which operated like the old excise was introduced under the guise of purchase tax.

In order to help fund the war effort, purchase tax was introduced in 1940 on a wide range of specific goods. Purchase tax, which was levied at the wholesale stage, was administratively simple and efficient, raising large sums of revenue and, in consequence, continued long after the war ended. Although purchase tax was intended to be a tax on luxury goods, the luxuries of the present often become the necessities of the future and purchase tax was criticised as an extremely inequitable tax that distorted consumer choice and production patterns. By 1968, purchase tax, which was then levied at four rates ($12\frac{1}{2}$ per cent, 20 per cent, $33\frac{1}{3}$ per cent and 50 per cent), had become full of anomalies and there seemed to be little logic in the way the tax was levied, for example, pianos and organs were exempt while other musical instruments were taxed at the highest rate. Toothbrushes were exempt from the tax while toothpaste suffered a higher rate of purchase tax than confectionery. Other items taxed at the highest rate included clocks, watches, radios, televisions, wallets and purses. There seemed little sense in a tax that charged a higher rate on soap than it did on ice cream. A second criticism of purchase tax was that because it was levied on wholesalers it could not be used to tax services, making the tax inequitable.

A tax on employment in the service industries, selective employment tax, was introduced in 1966 partly as a means of taxing services and partly to encourage employment in the manufacturing industries. The tax was charged at a fixed sum per worker with rebates and premiums paid in respect of individuals employed in manufacturing. The tax was ill-thought out, and extremely unpopular. Like purchase tax, selective employment tax was plagued with inequities, for example self-employment was exempt.

'Selective taxation gives rise to distortion of trade and personal consumption patterns and can lead to an inefficient allocation of resources'[1] and so in the FA 1972 both these distortionary taxes were replaced by the present system of value added tax.

UK indirect taxes

The present UK tax system includes the following indirect taxes:

1. Customs duties

In the present UK tax system customs duties are no longer the important taxes they once were and are mainly governed by international agreements. The introduction of the single European market in January 1993 has seen the erosion of customs duties on cross frontier activities.

2. Local taxation

The present local taxation includes council tax and uniform business rate.

(a) Council tax

The tax that was introduced in 1993 is based on property values similar to the old rating system but where the rating system was very inequitable, as it did not take into account personal circumstances, the council tax remedies this in two ways:

- a rebate of up to 100 per cent is available to individuals and families on low incomes or state benefit; and
- a rebate of 25 per cent is available to adults living in a property on their own.

(b) Uniform business rate

Although, since April 1990, businesses are dealt with under the old rating system, the rateable poundage is set by central government, so that there is one uniform business rate for the whole country. The local authority collects the business rate but it is paid into a central fund and the proceeds redistributed to local authorities depending on the number of adults in the area.

3. Vehicle excise duty

The road fund licence fee charged on motorists evidenced by the licence disc is an indirect tax on the use of public roads.

4. Betting and gaming tax

Following consultation, the Budget 2001 announced that Gaming Duty bands were to be amended in line with inflation, in order to help casinos, and radical reforms were proposed to Betting Duty, in response to the increase in the amount of off-shore betting. Under the proposed system, the bookmaker would absorb the tax charge, horse-race levy and administration charges.

5. Excise duties

Excise duties still figure in the present UK tax system as specific indirect taxes levied on selective items. Excise duties raise a significant amount of revenue principally from three main categories:

- tobacco;
- alcohol; and
- hydrocarbon oils.

Because they are levied on such a narrow base, these taxes are extremely regressive.

6. Value added tax

Value added tax (VAT) is a multistage *ad valorem* tax charged at each stage of the production and distribution chain, but as VAT registered traders are able to reclaim their input tax through the VAT system the final burden of the tax falls on the consumer, i.e. VAT is a tax on spending. A broad-based tax applying to a wide range of goods and services, it replaced purchase tax and selective employment tax from 1 April 1973.

Although excise duties raise a significant amount of revenue, the main indirect tax in the UK is VAT.

Value added tax

The rationale for VAT

Arguably, when Britain decided to become a formal member of the EC on 1 January 1973, it committed itself to the introduction of VAT at some point, since this was the method of indirect taxation chosen by the EC to become fully harmonised over time to allow for the free movement of goods between member states. However, at the time, no steps had been taken to harmonise the rates or the scope of VAT, these matters being left to those members who had adopted the tax. The only formal requirement of EC membership was that the tax would eventually be used as the main indirect tax throughout the EC, and some countries, such as Italy, had postponed the introduction of a VAT many times.

When the UK introduced VAT in the FA 1972, to be effective from 1 April 1973, it was not out of immediate necessity. Although the introduction of VAT was a first step in preparation for its impending membership and an indication of Britain's intention to co-operate with European tax harmonisation, it was also 'a means of improving our tax system'.[2]

Many of the arguments in favour of adopting VAT at this early stage were based on the numerous shortcomings of its predecessors, purchase tax and selective employment tax, as the 'existing pattern of indirect taxation in this country is open to the objection that it is selective and based on too narrow a range of expenditure'.[3]

VAT examined

VAT is a broad-based tax that is difficult to avoid. It achieves the objectives of taxation while being flexible, certain, convenient and administratively efficient. As with all taxes, there is an ultimate trade-off between equity and efficiency, i.e. a tax that is completely equitable can only be so at the expense of economic efficiency and vice versa. These two aspects with respect to VAT are now examined in more detail.

1. Equity

The tax is levied at the same rate on goods and services regardless of personal circumstances, so that in principle the tax is regressive. However, the existence of zero rating makes VAT less regressive than other indirect taxes. Because many essential items are zero rated, wealthier individuals will tend to pay a larger proportion of their incomes in VAT than individuals who are less well off, making the tax more proportional in its effect.

2. Efficiency

VAT is less selective than its predecessors, purchase tax and selective employment tax, making the tax more economically efficient, i.e. it is less likely to distort consumer choice making the tax more neutral between:

- goods and services; and
- different types of businesses.

Although selectivity may be desirable where society is of the opinion that certain goods should be discouraged, for example, tobacco and alcohol, this can be achieved by the use of specific excise duties. If the existence of the tax distorts taxpayer choice, an excess burden is created, depending on the substitution effects. To the extent that a taxed good can be substituted for an untaxed good, this excess burden disappears; if the good cannot be substituted and the taxpayer rejects the good because of the existence of the tax, then it is assumed that the taxpayer and therefore society as a whole must be worse off, creating an excess burden. In this respect, as VAT is less selective, it is less likely to distort choice. VAT would arguably be more efficient if zero rating was abolished. However, this increase in efficiency would only be gained at the expense of equity because VAT levied on all goods and services at the same rate would make the tax regressive.

As VAT is a self assessed tax, compliance costs are likely to be high creating an excess burden for the taxpayer. For very large businesses, however, these costs may be more than offset by the cash flow advantage gained by holding on to the VAT collected during the VAT period, before it is handed over to HM Customs and Excise, whereas for smaller businesses this cash flow advantage is probably less significant compared with the administration necessary to comply with the legislation.

One spin off from the administrative burden on taxpayers operating VAT is that management information is improved because the VAT system requires records to be maintained to provide an audit trail for Customs and Excise. It has been noted that 'the standard of the nations book-keeping has undoubtedly improved in consequence of the tax'.[4]

Direct *v* indirect taxation

All governments use a mixture of direct and indirect taxes in the tax system, but since the late 1970s there has been a shift in emphasis from direct to indirect taxation. In order to determine whether a bias in favour of indirect taxes has any real merit, the relative advantages and disadvantages of direct and indirect taxes are considered with respect to the following:

1. Equity

'A tax must not only be fair, it must be seen to be fair.'[5]

The income tax system is arguably more equitable taking into account the ability to pay, unlike indirect taxes, which fall equally on rich and poor alike. Any system that relies too heavily on indirect taxes must as a whole be less progressive. Many indirect taxes are regressive, e.g. excise duties, or at best proportional, e.g. VAT, undermining the principle of equity in the tax system. However, as everyone benefits from public expenditure, if it is believed, as a consequence of this, that everyone should contribute to the public housekeeping, then indirect taxation is the only way of raising revenue from those members of society with small incomes.

2. Economic regulator

Indirect taxes are generally more flexible, as the rates of tax can be varied at any time by statutory instruments, unlike income tax which can generally only be changed in the Budget, making them a better tool for regulating the economy.

3. Economic efficiency

It is often argued that indirect taxes are psychologically more acceptable for two reasons. First, the tax is less noticeable, and second, the taxpayer has the satisfaction of consumption. However, there is evidence to suggest that consumers are well aware of the effect of indirect taxes on prices.[6]

(a) Indirect taxation and the incentive to work

The argument that indirect taxes may be preferable to an income tax on the grounds that they are less likely to create a disincentive to work is generally unfounded. Low rates of income tax may leave the individual with more disposable income, but if this is offset with high levels of indirect taxation the individual has less purchasing power, and the net effect is the same.

The extent to which indirect taxes affect the incentive to work depends to some extent on the elasticity of demand for the product. Where the good has an inelastic demand, it is more likely that the tax will be reflected in higher prices, with the net result that there is little difference between the effects of a direct tax as opposed to an indirect tax.

(b) Taxation and the incentive to save

The existence of income taxes may affect the incentive to save because savings made from taxed income are themselves subject to tax. Indirect taxes avoid this double taxation and are less likely to affect the incentive to save. This argument, however, is weakened by the present system of income taxation which favours certain types of saving by removing this double taxation element, e.g. ISAs.

4. Social and economic welfare

(a) Social welfare

Indirect taxation can be used to promote social welfare and reduce externalities, e.g. companies that cause pollution impose social costs, and indirect taxation can be used to reflect these costs. The government can use the system of indirect taxes to discourage those goods that are considered harmful to society, for example cigarettes and alcohol, and encourage the use of those goods considered to be a benefit to society, e.g. unleaded petrol.

However, the government raises large amounts of revenue from excise duties on tobacco and alcohol, and while it is argued that these products impose costs on society with pollution and higher costs of medical care, if more people stopped smoking and drinking in the hope of living longer, healthier lives, government revenue would suffer and savings made in the health service may only be deferred as more elderly people would need care and medical attention.

(b) Economic welfare

Direct taxes reduce disposable income and so it could be argued that indirect taxes give the taxpayer more choice. However, this depends on the system of indirect taxation; an individual may be able to avoid tax by giving up smoking, but generally broad-based taxes like VAT are very difficult to avoid completely.

5. Administrative efficiency

With the introduction of self assessment from 1996/7 administration costs are likely to be much lower (although taxpayer compliance costs will rise), which weakens previous arguments in favour of indirect taxes on the basis of administrative efficiency.

REFERENCES

[1] Government Green Paper, *Value Added Tax* (1971), CMND 4621, HMSO.
[2] *The United Kingdom and European Communities* (1971), CMND 4715, HMSO.
[3] Government Green Paper, *op cit.*
[4] *Report of the VAT Task Force* (1977), Conservative Central Office, March.
[5] Cripps, J.G.A. (1973) 'Stirring the VAT', *Financial Executive*, October.
[6] Stanlake, G.F. (1982) *Public Finance*, Longman Economic Studies.

FURTHER READING

Baker, P. and Brechling, V. (1992) 'The impact of excise duty changes on retail prices in the UK', *Fiscal Studies*, Vol. 13, No. 2, pp. 48–65.

James, S. and Nobes, C. (2000/01) *The Economics of Taxation*, Prentice Hall.

Kay, J.A. and King, M.A. (1990) *The British Tax System* (5th edn), Oxford University Press.

Prest, A.R. (1980) *Value Added Tax: The Experience of the United Kingdom*, American Enterprise Institution.

Sandford, C.T. (1981) *Costs and Benefits of VAT*, Heinemann.

CHAPTER 6

Tax evasion and avoidance

Tax avoidance is the legal arrangement of the taxpayer's affairs in order to minimise the tax liability, whereas tax evasion is illegal. Sometimes, however, the borderline between avoidance and evasion can become blurred, a fact that is evidenced by the huge body of anti-avoidance legislation and the development of case law in this area.

Tax evasion

Tax evasion involves the intentional disregard of the legislation in order to escape the liability to tax. Tax evasion may be achieved by understating income, overstating expenses, making false claims for allowances or failing to disclose a chargeability to tax.

Undeclared income probably counts for the bulk of evaded taxes in the UK, and is referred to as the black economy, where individuals work for cash-in-hand without declaring the income for tax purposes. This sort of tax evasion, or 'moonlighting', may be carried out by individuals who are lower paid or unemployed to escape the poverty trap or unemployment trap (*see* Chapter 2), and it has been suggested that as many as 1.6 million workers receive unrecorded incomes.[1] However, there is a view that, provided evasion is not widespread, its existence could have the effect of reducing the disincentive effects of taxation.[2] Because of its illegal nature, there is little hard evidence as to the true extent of tax evasion in the UK, with estimates varying between 2–14 per cent of national income.

Whatever the actual level of evasion, it is likely to be more prevalent when the tax system is perceived to be unfair or levied at confiscatory rates. Tax evasion is illegal and the offender may be liable to prosecution, however, the authorities will usually only resort to criminal prosecution where the case involves substantial amounts of lost revenue; many minor cases of tax evasion that are discovered by the Revenue are generally settled out of court. The Revenue gleans its information from a variety of sources:

1. Information supplied by the taxpayer

2. Statutory rights to information

The following are obliged to supply the Revenue with information if required:

- banks;
- theatres, clubs, etc. with regard to fees, commissions, etc. paid to entertainers;
- construction businesses with regard to details of any subcontractors;
- other government departments, e.g. HM Customs & Excise.

3. Information from internal sources

Information may be exchanged between Revenue departments.

4. Information from other public bodies

The Revenue is informed when a business registers or obtains a licence from a public body, e.g. licences to sell alcohol.

5. Information from other sources

Local newspapers can be a useful source of information for the Revenue, e.g:

- advertisements;
- reports on robberies;
- reports on social functions (how much was spent?); and
- reports of deceased's estate.

Information is often provided by jealous neighbours or ex-spouses bearing a grudge.

If tax evasion is to be curtailed, the tax laws must be properly enforced: 'If . . . some people are perceived to be escaping their obligations, great dissatisfaction is likely to be aroused among the majority of conscientious taxpayers. Further, more and more of them will be inclined to become less conscientious and join the ranks of the evaders. Thus the tax yield will become progressively eroded. Enforcement powers are therefore necessary not only to coerce the dishonest and neglectful, but to encourage the honest and conscientious'.[3]

Taxpayer compliance can be improved by:

- tax deduction at source;
- matching information; and
- auditing.

Addington had introduced the concept of deduction of tax at source in 1803 and it was an effective means of reducing the widespread evasion witnessed in the income tax of 1799. The introduction of self assessment brings with it the notion of voluntary compliance with the tax legislation. Under self assessment the onus is on the taxpayer to declare a chargeability, file a tax return, maintain records and pay the tax due. Failure to comply with any of these requirements may render the taxpayer liable to automatic interest and penalties. Although a large percentage of the returns may never be audited to verify their completeness and correctness, the possibility of the taxpayer being the subject of a Revenue enquiry may be sufficient to persuade taxpayers to comply with current tax legislation. This may be achieved because:

(a) of the fear of being caught out and becoming liable to interest and penalties; and

(b) taxpayer education promoting a positive attitude towards the tax system may instil a sense of moral obligation.

Increased international trade provides a further source of tax evasion by the use of foreign jurisdictions. To counter this problem some co-operation between the tax authorities in different countries would seem to be the way forward.

Tax avoidance

A tax such as VAT can be avoided simply by not buying the taxed good or service, in this respect, DIY can be seen to be a form of tax avoidance. The arrangement of an individual's affairs so as to mitigate the liability to tax is tax avoidance, and provided that the taxpayer acts within the framework of the law, tax avoidance is legal. However, where the activity is within the letter of the law but outside the spirit of the law, the distinction between avoidance and evasion may become blurred.

Many forms of tax avoidance are merely tax planning opportunities that exist in the legislation for reducing the liability to tax, for example, choosing the most tax efficient savings and investments or making sure that all available reliefs are used to their full advantage.

However, loopholes in the legislation also create opportunities for tax avoidance. For example, a common ploy up to 1987 was for company directors to pay themselves in gilts, so as to avoid paying National Insurance contributions. However, once a loophole has been exploited, the Revenue react by introducing legislation to close that particular loophole.

The increasing body of anti-avoidance legislation merely makes the tax system more complicated, detracting from the cannon of simplicity even though it has been suggested that 'an economy breathes through its loopholes'.[4] The tax avoidance industry grew to enormous proportions during the 1970s as high rates of tax made the costs of elaborate avoidance schemes worthwhile, supporting the view that 'the existence of widespread avoidance is evidence that the system, not the taxpayer, stands in need of radical reform'.[5]

By the 1980s the courts began to look not just at the form of the transaction but at the substance, and the scheme will not be allowed to stand if the whole reason was purely to avoid tax. The present judicial approach to tax avoidance schemes developed during the 1980s through the following cases:

1. *Ramsey (WT) Ltd* v *IRC* [1981] STC 174
The taxpayer had implemented an elaborate tax avoidance scheme with the sole purpose of reducing a liability to capital gains tax by creating allowable losses. The House of Lords held that although every transaction in the scheme was genuine, they were self-cancelling and the court should look at the effect of the transaction, which was to avoid tax. The scheme as a whole produced neither gain nor loss and so should be disregarded for tax purposes.

2. *Furniss* v *Dawson* [1984] STC 153

The *Ramsay* principle was extended in this case beyond the self-cancelling transactions. A scheme will also be rejected where steps in the transaction are inserted that have no commercial purpose other than to avoid tax.

3. *Craven* v *White* [1988] STC 476

In this case the House of Lords followed a more restrictive approach to *Furniss* v *Dawson*, in that the principle will be limited to a pre-ordained series of transactions which at the time of the first transaction was intended and likely to occur.

Since coming to power in 1997, the new Labour government has indicated its intentions to clamp down on tax avoidance schemes. Legislation to close loopholes in the tax laws has been enacted in the Finance Acts since July 1997, in order to prevent tax leakage through avoidance.

In the first Labour Budget in July 1997, the Inland Revenue were set the task of carrying out a wide ranging assessment of direct tax avoidance, and giving consideration to the possibility of a general anti-avoidance rule (GAAR).

In November 1997 the Tax Law Review Committee for the Institute for Fiscal Studies published a report on tax avoidance, giving consideration as to whether anti-avoidance provisions should continue to develop through case law, or whether a GAAR was the way forward to counteract tax avoidance in the UK. They concluded that a GAAR was possibly the way forward, but that it would have to be drafted so that there is no infringement of taxpayer rights, and that normal commercial transactions are not jeopardised in the process.

The Inland Revenue published a Consulative Document for a GAAR with respect to direct taxation in October 1998, which proposed initially to confine a GAAR to corporate activities. This would in itself produce anomalies that would reduce its effectiveness, e.g. such a GAAR may restrict corporate schemes that may be acceptable if undertaken by individuals, unless judicial decisions indicated otherwise, in which case there would be little need of a GAAR, especially when consideration is given to the fact that the majority of case law in this area concerns avoidance by individuals.

The Tax Law Review Committee's response to the consultative document was to oppose the proposed GAAR. The two main reasons for this opposition were that the burden would be on the taxpayer, rather than the Revenue, to show whether the scheme fell within or outside the GAAR; and that clearance procedures were inadequate. In his 1999 Budget speech, the Chancellor announced that there would be no action taken on the GAAR for corporate direct taxes at the present time, but that it would remain a consideration for the future.

General anti-avoidance rules have been tried in Australia, New Zealand and Canada with little success, which would indicate that targeted legislation may be more desirable. However, the policy makers are faced with the dilemma of how wide or narrow anti-avoidance legislation should be; too narrow and it may fail in its objectives, too wide and it may well be applied to situations for which it was not intended.

In the 1999 Budget Gordon Brown announced that the Finance Bill 2000 would include proposals to modernise the Inland Revenue's powers where serious fraud is suspected, allowing them to obtain evidence from third parties.

In the FA 2000, Gordon Brown promised more guidance and support to taxpayers, in particular he announced proposals to:

- provide more payroll help for small employers;
- reduce the number of individuals who have to fill in self assessment forms;
- provide more understandable self assessment statements;
- allow self assessment taxpayers and employers to pay by Debit Card, either on-line or over the telephone, or on account by direct debit;
- revise the formal notice of a self assessment enquiry, making it less threatening;
- provide clearer information for pensioners.

Theoretically these measures should encourage compliance with the tax legislation, and reduce the costs for the taxpayers affected.

Whatever steps are taken to counter tax avoidance, the principle of certainty of taxation would require a definition of legitimate tax planning which may be difficult to frame as 'The boundaries move with public sentiment, with developing financial techniques and with the introduction of new statutory relief. Tax law will always have to address this question and to determine where the line will be drawn'.[6]

REFERENCES

[1] Johnson, C. (1982) 'Light on the black economy', *Lloyds Bank Economic Bulletin*, February.

[2] Kay, J.A. and King, M.A. (1990) *The British Tax System* (5th edn), Oxford University Press.

[3] *The Keith Committee Report on Enforcement Powers of the Revenue Dept* (1983), CMND 8822, HMSO.

[4] Bracewell-Milnes, B.B. (1979) 'Tax Avoidance can be good news for the tax collector', *Daily Telegraph*, 16 July.

[5] Kaldor, N. (1980) *Reports on Taxation*, Duckworth & Co.

[6] Troup, E. (1992) 'Unacceptable discretion: countering tax avoidance and preserving the rights of the individual', *Fiscal Studies*, Vol. 13, No. 4.

FURTHER READING

James, S. and Nobes, C. (2000/01) *The Economics of Taxation*, Prentice Hall.

Kay J.A. (1979) 'The economics of tax avoidance', *The British Tax Review*, pp. 354–65.

Kay, J.A. and King, M.A. (1990) *The British Tax System* (5th edn), Oxford University Press.

Spicer, M. (1975) 'New approaches to the problem of tax evasion', *The British Tax Review*.

Troup, E. (1992) 'Unacceptable discretion: countering tax avoidance and preserving the rights of the individual', *Fiscal Studies*, Vol. 13, No. 4, pp. 128–38.

CHAPTER 7

The UK tax system as a whole

The UK tax base

The UK tax system employs a mixture of income, capital and consumption in its tax base in order to achieve its overall objectives.

Income is probably the best measure of a person's ability to pay with personal and corporate taxes on income accounting for the bulk of the revenue raised from direct taxes. *See* Table 7.1.

Although the present UK taxes on capital are themselves inefficient and ineffective, without some means of taxing capital, the tax system as a whole would be less equitable, as wealthier individuals would aspire to convert their income 'gains' into capital 'gains', undermining the principle of equity in the tax system.

The replacement of purchase tax and selective employment tax with a broad based VAT made the UK system of indirect taxation less distortionary. VAT raises a substantial amount of revenue and although indirect taxes are generally regressive in nature, the existence of zero rating makes VAT on the whole a proportional tax for all but the bottom 20 per cent or so of income earners.

The shift in the balance of taxation from direct to indirect over recent years has had the effect of making the tax system as a whole less progressive, remaining mildly progressive for the bottom one third of households and broadly proportional for the rest. Since the beginning of the twentieth century successive governments have used taxation to help them accomplish a particular set of objectives, and there is no doubt that taxation can be instrumental in achieving the social, political and economic goals of government.

Table 7.1 Revenue raised from direct taxes (£ million)

Year	Income tax	Corporation tax	Capital gains tax	Inheritance tax
1994/95	63 100	19 390	926	1 411
1995/96	68 049	23 570	796	1 518
1996/97	69 071	27 788	1 131	1 558
1997/98	76 838	30 437	1 453	1 684
1998/99	86 507	30 032	2 002	1 805
1999/00	92 986	34 322	2 122	2 047
2000/01	101 155	32 420	3 236	2 221
2001/02	102 500	33 100	2 900	2 400

Source: Inland Revenue Statistics, HMSO

Traditionally simplicity, equity and efficiency have been high on the agenda in judging the relative merits of the tax system. However, it has already been noted in earlier chapters that these principles are often in conflict with each other, and it is a matter of value judgement as to which of these criteria are considered to be the most important.

The high rates of taxation that existed in the UK at the end of the 1970s were justified on the grounds that progressive rates of tax provided a greater degree of equity and redistribution. However, it soon became clear that excessively high rates of tax encourage avoidance and evasion, undermining the very principle on which they were based. These steeply progressive rates of tax indicated an overriding objective to achieve social equality, but during the last decade vertical equity has taken a back seat in favour of economic efficiency and horizontal equity.

We will now examine the principles of equity, efficiency and simplicity in the light of the reforms that have taken place since the mid 1980s.

1. Equity

Tax changes have indicated a switch in emphasis from vertical to horizontal equity. The systematic broadening of the tax base and simultaneous reduction in the rates of tax since 1984 have eroded the extent to which the tax system provides for vertical equity. At the same time, taxing capital gains at the marginal rate of income tax since 1988 and the introduction of independent taxation in 1990 have improved fairness in the tax system but the emphasis has been on providing horizontal equity rather than vertical equity.

2. Efficiency

Many of the tax reforms instituted since the mid 1980s were aimed at making the tax system more neutral, to remove economic distortions and improve efficiency, for example:

- reduction in reliefs, e.g. mortgage interest relief removing the bias in favour of home ownership;
- bringing capital allowances more in line with economic depreciation making the tax system more neutral between different forms of capital investment;
- reduction in the rates of CT makes the corporate tax system more neutral between debt and equity finance;
- taxing capital gains at income tax rates makes the tax system more neutral between capital and income.

Philip Chappel[1] suggested that to achieve fiscal neutrality the tax system should apply the following principles:

(a) *Simplicity* – the system should be simple for the taxpayer to understand reducing compliance costs.

(b) *Plainness* – a single flat rate of tax should be applied.

(c) *Rate* – the rate of tax should be set at a level that makes tax avoidance unprofitable.

(d) *Universality* – the single flat rate should apply universally in the same way as VAT, and perks, privileges and allowances should be phased out.

(e) *Comprehensiveness* – a proportion of tax should be levied on income as well as expenditure as an overall switch to expenditure is undesirable.

(f) *Even handedness* – the system should not distort between different forms of saving and ideally there should be no distortion between spending and saving.

3. Simplicity

Simplifying the tax system has been a major issue during the 1990s. The introduction of self assessment calls for a more simplified tax system in order to gain taxpayer confidence and encourage voluntary compliance, which in turn makes the system more simple for the tax authorities to administer and enforce. However, reforms to simplify the system must be undertaken with care if equity and efficiency are not to be lost.

Alternative tax bases

Towards the end of the 1970s the need for tax reform was becoming evident, giving rise to much discussion on the direction of reform. In the end, reforms were aimed at making the tax system more neutral, simpler for the taxpayer to understand and increasing horizontal equity. However, during this period alternative bases for taxation were given serious consideration:

1. Comprehensive income tax

The idea of a comprehensive income tax (CIT) was discussed at length by the Royal Commission on Taxation[2] and by the Meade Committee.[3] Under a CIT, income from all sources would be treated equally, e.g. there would be no distinction between income and capital, which would achieve both equity and neutrality, and do away with the need for separate taxes on gifts and inheritances.

With a CIT the tax base is the annual increase in value of all assets. However, the Meade Committee concluded that there were several serious problems with adopting a CIT:

(a) the annual increase in value of some assets would be difficult to ascertain, e.g. pensions;

(b) comprehensive income would fluctuate widely from year to year which may call for some sort of averaging procedure;

(c) retained company profits would have to be allocated to individual shareholders, which would require the corporate tax system to be fully integrated with the personal tax system.

Despite the fact that a CIT was rejected, some elements of the idea have been adopted, e.g. capital gains are now taxed at income tax rates.

2. Expenditure tax

An expenditure tax (ET) was considered by Kaldor[4] who was instrumental in setting up an expenditure tax in India and Sri Lanka, despite the fact that they had little success. An ET would be a tax on spending but not in the same way as indirect taxes such as VAT, but rather a direct ET to replace the personal income tax. The idea of a universal expenditure tax (UET) was considered by the Meade Committee in 1978.[5]

Under a UET the tax base would be calculated as follows:

income + dissavings – savings

To achieve this, assets would be classed as registered and unregistered assets and only registered assets would be included in the tax base. Gifts and bequests would be treated as expenditure obviating the need for separate taxes on the transfer of capital.

The main arguments in favour of an ET are that:

- it is more equitable to tax a person on what is taken out of society rather than what is put in;
- an ET removes the disincentives to work and save; and
- under an ET there would be no need for separate taxes on capital.

However, the idea of an ET has not generally found favour with governments, the main problems being that:

- it would encourage emigration;
- relations with other countries which did not operate an ET would be difficult and double taxation agreements would be more complex; and
- capital markets would be distorted as the attractiveness of assets would depend on whether they were registered/unregistered.

With an expenditure tax, the nominal rate of tax would have to be set at a higher rate than an equivalent income tax as it would have to be expressed on the expenditure net of tax. Therefore an income tax of, say, 20 per cent would become an ET of 25 per cent (i.e. 20/80). However, it is unrealistic to compare the theoretical notion of an ET with the income tax, which works reasonably well in practice, while an ET may seem simpler it is likely that in time it would develop its own problems in the same way as a tax on income.

3. Annual wealth tax

The Meade Committee also actively considered the possibility of an annual wealth tax (AWT). An AWT based on the annual valuation of wealth could be used to replace all or part of the income tax and could possibly be levied at lower rates than income tax to achieve the same yield. For example, capital assets valued at £50 000 producing an income of say £6000 per year would yield income tax of £1200 at a 20 per cent tax rate. An annual wealth tax need only be levied at 2.4 per cent to achieve the same yield, i.e. £50 000 × 2.4 per cent = £1200.

The main arguments in favour of an AWT are as follows:

(a) Horizontal equity

The possession of wealth confers advantages over and above the income derived from wealth and it could be argued that an income tax is insufficient to achieve horizontal equity.

(b) Efficiency

It is argued that a wealth tax would not affect the incentive to work as it would tax past rather than present effort. This argument is limited by the extent to which income taxes create a disincentive to work and extent to which individuals work in order to save or spend.

(c) Redistribution of wealth

Only an annual wealth tax would tax wealth as it stands, income taxes can only tax wealth to the extent that the assets generate income.

(d) Administrative control

It is argued that an AWT would generate information that could be used to control tax evasion.

The government considered the introduction of a wealth tax in 1974[6] but in the end abandoned the idea because of the difficulties involved, the main arguments against a wealth tax being:

(a) Practical difficulties

Annual valuations of all personal wealth would be required and for assets such as pension rights, or antiques, this could prove difficult. Discrepancies in valuation undermines horizontal equity in the tax system. The problem of valuation was one of the main reasons why the introduction of a wealth tax was abandoned in the 1970s.

(b) Administrative control

Cross checking is only possible if the assets concerned generate an income, and capital markets may be distorted in favour of non-income producing assets. The system may encourage evasion with non-income producing assets being undeclared.

(c) Economic consequences

Although the largest concentrations of wealth are a result of inherited wealth, it may also be the result of entrepreneurship and accumulated saving which may both be discouraged under an AWT.

The main difficulties with an AWT stem from a satisfactory definition of wealth, for example, should human capital be included? If money is used to increase future skills and earning power, it is just as much an investment as dealing on the Stock Exchange.

All these alternative tax bases use the notion of economic power over resources as the basis for assessing the ability to pay as opposed to an income tax which measures the ability to pay on the current increment of economic power.

Future trends in taxation policy

A system of taxation can be considered to be a socioeconomic model, tending to reflect prevailing social and economic values and priorities, thereby representing society's social, political and economic needs at any one time.

Since 1997, significant reforms to the system of corporation tax and capital gains tax have been implemented. The main thrust behind the reforms has been to encourage worthwhile investment and entrepreneurship, whilst at the same time there has been a determination by the government to clamp down on tax avoidance and evasion.

One of the issues facing governments at the start of the new millennium stems from the growing concern for environmental issues, '... in securing the long term, nothing is more important than the environment'.[7] The idea of using the tax system to address environmental issues is embedded in economic theory. Taxation can be used to solve the problem of externalities, i.e. the external costs incurred as a result of carrying out an activity; imposing taxation on such activities to reflect environmental costs is one way to address the problem. There is no doubt that environmental issues will be a prime concern for the government and businesses in the next century, but are green issues being tackled in a way likely to have any real effect, or is government merely paying lip-service to a very real problem? During the 1990s, in the UK, measures to tackle the level of carbon dioxide emissions, although being justified on the grounds of environmental benefits, were implemented for their revenue raising potential.

Following the Kyoto conference on climatic change in December 1997, the UK government is legally committed to reducing greenhouse gas emissions by 2008–12 to 12.5 per cent below their 1990 levels. On top of this, the government has a self-imposed target to reduce carbon dioxide emissions to 20 per cent below their 1990 levels by 2010. In the late 1990s most of the measures to reduce pollution were aimed at road fuels. However, in order to help the government reach its target reductions, the FA 2000 introduced legislation to implement the climate change levy, to be administered by Customs and Excise, from April 2001 at the following rates:

Energy product	Rate per kWh
Electricity	0.43
Coal	0.15
Natural gas	0.15
LPG	0.07

NB: Electricity generated from renewable energy sources are exempt, and energy intensive sectors formally agreeing to energy efficiency targets benefit from an 80 per cent discount on the levy. It is intended that the climate change levy will be revenue neutral and the revenue raised will be used to fund energy efficiency and reduce employer NIC costs.

The use of eco-taxes on fuel, as opposed to subsidising energy saving materials, would increase efficiency, as the price of fuel would reflect social costs, pollution and environmental damage, rather than artificially making the cost of energy saving materials too low in comparison with other goods. The introduction of specific eco-taxes into the tax system will depend on an increase in political support for environmental issues in the future.

Sophisticated communication networks, increased international trade and the globalisation of capital markets have brought with them a need for greater co-operation between nations, as they become increasingly economically linked. With this in mind, it is not surprising to learn that the tax reforms that have been implemented over the last ten years or so have not been confined to Britain. The international mobility of capital has increased the influence of tax differentials providing more scope for avoidance and evasion, and the increasing number of large multinational enterprises have brought with them their own particular problems, calling for a co-ordination of international taxation policies.

REFERENCES

[1] Chappell, P. (1990) 'The assault on fiscal privilege: A simpler system with lower tax rates', in Bracewell-Milnes, B. (ed.) *Which Road to Fiscal Neutrality?*, Institute of Economic Affairs.

[2] The Report of the Royal Commission on Taxation (Canada), 1966.

[3] Meade, J.E. (Chairman) (1978) *The Meade Committee Report on the Structure and Reform of Direct Taxation*, Institute of Fiscal Studies, George Allen & Unwin.

[4] Kaldor, N. (1955) *An Expenditure Tax*, George Allen & Unwin.

[5] Meade, J.E, *op. cit.*

[6] Government Green Paper, *A Wealth Tax*, (1974) CMND 5704, HMSO.

[7] Gordon Brown in his 1998 pre-Budget speech.

FURTHER READING

Barker, T and Köhler, J. (1998) 'Equity and ecotax reform in the EU: achieving a 10 per cent reduction in CO_2 emissions using excise duties', *Fiscal Studies*, Vol. 19, No. 4, pp. 375–402.

Bracewell-Milnes, B. (ed.) (1990) *Which Road to Fiscal Neutrality*, Institute of Economic Affairs.

James, S. and Nobes, C. (2000/01) *The Economics of Taxation*.

Kaldor, N. (1955) *An Expenditure Tax*, George Allen & Unwin.

Kay, J.A. and King, M.A. (1990) '*The British Tax System*' (5th edn), Oxford University Press.

Meade, J.E. (Chairman) (1978) *The Meade Committee Report on the Structure and Reform of Direct Taxation*, Institute of Fiscal Studies, George Allen & Unwin.

Pechman, J.A. (ed.) (1977) *Comprehensive Income Taxation*, A Report of a Conference sponsored by the Fund for Public Policy Research, The Brookings Institution.

Sandford, C.T., Willis, J.R.M. and Ironside, D.J. (1975) *An Annual Wealth Tax*, Heinemann.

CHAPTER 8

Taxation and international trade

In the modern world, advanced technology and sophisticated communication systems have led to a greater interdependence between nations as firms increasingly operate at an international level. Tax differentials cause problems for governments in respect of multinational enterprises (MNEs) with regard to the following:

1. Tax competition

Increased tax competition affects location and investment decisions and encourages MNEs to manipulate transfer prices in order to minimise tax liabilities.

2. Tax jurisdiction

The basis of jurisdiction varies between countries making it difficult to determine and collect taxes on the activities of MNEs.

3. Tax evasion

While each country has the means to enforce its own tax laws, standards of tax compliance vary widely between countries.

Tax harmonisation or at least some degree of international co-operation between tax authorities with respect to international trade would lead to greater efficiency, but no progress has been made at an international level, and within Europe the process is slow.

The single European market

While the UK was a signatory to the European Free Trade Area under the Stockholm Convention in 1960, it did not become a member of the European Community until 1 January 1973. The main objectives for establishing a European Common Market were laid down in the Treaty of Rome in 1957, Article 2, stating:

> **'It shall be the aim of the Community, by establishing a Common Market and progressively approximating the economic policies of member states, to promote throughout the Community the harmonious development of economic activities, a continuous and balanced expansion, an increased stability, an accelerated raising of the standard of living and closer relations between its member states.'**

The Treaty envisaged a Europe with no internal trade barriers in order to promote the free movement of goods and services, labour and capital across member states, and common policies with regard to trade outside Europe.

By the mid 1980s, progress in the European Community seemed to have come to a halt and, as a means of stimulation, the Treaty of Rome was amended in the Single European Act 1986 in the hope of achieving the original objectives laid down in 1957.

The Single European Act called for progress to be made towards economic, social and political union by establishing a single European market (SEM) by the end of 1992.

The introduction of the SEM on 1 January 1993 demonstrated the commitment to achieve economic and social integration within Europe which will require the removal of the distortions caused by different social, economic and political policies among member states. Full integration implies European laws, standards and taxes culminating in monetary union. Progress in these areas is slow for as more and more decisions are transferred to Brussels it is seen as a surrender of national sovereignty.

The removal of trade barriers to achieve a SEM requires a tax system that does not distort choice between member states. The free movement of goods and services requires the harmonisation of indirect taxation and, while some progress has been made in this area, differences in rates still exist sufficiently to cause some distortion, e.g. cross-frontier shopping to take advantage of lower rates of tax. However, it is believed that differences in corporate taxation are responsible for economic distortion to a much greater extent.[1]

The harmonisation of corporate taxation in Europe

Corporate taxes affect investment decisions and large tax differences cause economic distortion influencing the international mobility of capital. Economic efficiency in the SEM would require the system of corporate taxation to be neutral between member states. The harmonisation of corporate taxation within the SEM would provide for the free movement of capital and 'encourage the interplay of competition in such a way that integration and economic growth . . . may be achieved'.[2]

In the reduction of trade barriers corporate tax differences are of prime importance. These differences amount to:

1. Differences in tax rates

Although differences in tax rates may encourage companies to locate in areas of low tax jurisdiction, harmonisation of tax rates alone is insufficient to promote economic efficiency if other substantial differences exist. It is also interesting to note that there is a weak tendency for rates of corporation tax to converge, for although there are a few exceptions, many European corporation tax rates fall within a relatively narrow band between 30–37 per cent.

2. Differences in tax systems

Six out of the 16 members of the SEM operate a classical system of corporation tax, these are Luxembourg, Holland, Austria and Sweden, with Belgium and Denmark having reverted back to a classical system after having changed to an imputation system for several years. Even among those members who apply the imputation system there are vast differences.

As far as the harmonisation of corporate tax systems goes, the SEM is less harmonised now than it was several years ago. Harmonisation of tax systems may reduce distortions but even if the SEM adopted only one system there may still be distortions between assets, activities and sources of finance.

3. Differences in the tax base

Taxation, inflation rates and interest rates all affect the cost of capital but differences in tax rules between member states have a profound effect. Differences in the tax base encourage:

- tax avoiding behaviour, which may be inefficient;
- companies to locate in areas with the most favourable tax regime;
- MNEs to manipulate transfer prices; and
- investment into those areas where tax incentives are the greatest.

There are substantial differences in the tax rules of member states regarding:

- stock valuation;
- bad debt provision;
- exchange gains and losses;
- tax accounting and commercial accounting e.g. the tax base is more liberal than the accounting rules require in some countries, such as the UK and Holland, whereas in France there are strict tax rules in the calculation of taxable profits; and
- tax incentives.

Harmonisation of the tax base would reduce distortions with regard to:

- the scale of activities;
- investment decisions; and
- financing methods.

Harmonising the tax system and rates of tax is insufficient if there are huge discrepancies in the rules for determining a company's taxable profits. The most important areas for harmonising the tax base are as follows:

- depreciation allowances;
- treatment of losses;
- stock valuation;
- foreign exchange gains and losses; and
- withholding taxes.

The harmonisation of corporate taxes within Europe has been extremely slow to develop since the Neumark Report was published in 1962:

(a) The Neumark Report 1962

This regarded that the different systems of corporation tax presented the main barrier to the free movement of capital between member states and recommended that members adopt a split rate system of corporation tax, however this proposal was rejected by the member countries.

(b) Van den Tempel Report 1970

This report concentrated on harmonising the systems and rates of corporation tax, recommending a classical system and a single common rate. These proposals were rejected by the European Commission which instead published its own draft directive in 1975.

(c) The European Commission draft directive 1975

The draft directive proposed that member states should adopt:

- an imputation system of corporation tax;
- a common system of withholding tax; and
- a rate between 45–55 per cent.

The draft was rejected by the European Parliament on the grounds that harmonisation of tax systems and rates alone would be ineffective if there were large variations in the tax base.

(d) The European Commission draft directive 1988

This draft directive proposed the harmonisation of the tax base. On the basis that the tax burden is a function of the tax rate and the tax base, if the base is harmonised, the harmonisation of rates would be easier to achieve.

(e) The Ruding Committee Report 1992

The Committee under the chairmanship of Onno Ruding was established by the European Commission in 1990 and published the following recommendations in 1992:

(a) there should be maximum and minimum rates of corporation tax;

(b) there should be an arm's length approach to transfer prices;

(c) there should be harmonisation of the tax base especially regarding:
- depreciation
- leasing
- stock valuation
- bad debts
- foreign currency gains/losses
- capital gains.

The aims and requirements of harmonisation

A report carried out in 1989[3] proposed that a programme of harmonisation should take into account the following:

1. Economic efficiency

Corporate taxes affect the following:

- location decisions;
- investment decisions; and
- financing methods.

A neutral tax system would not affect these decisions.

(a) Location decisions

In the absence of taxes, firms would choose to locate where production is cheapest. If the existence of taxation makes the investment more expensive in one country than another, the firm will locate in the country providing the highest after tax profit. A neutral system of taxation would require that companies must face the same effective tax rate wherever it locates. This is known as *capital export neutrality* (CEN).

(b) Investment decisions

In the absence of taxes, only the most efficient firms would exist. If the tax system discriminates between companies, then a less efficient firm may end up undertaking a project because the more efficient firm is more heavily taxed. A neutral tax system would require that all companies able to produce a good must face the same effective tax rate regardless of the country in which the company is established. This is known as *capital import neutrality* (CIN).

2. Political acceptability

This is concerned with the degree to which countries are willing to give up national sovereignty in tax matters:

(a) *Sovereignty of the source country* – concerns the right to tax activities taking place in a country.

(b) *Sovereignty of the resident country* – concerns the right to tax the residents of a country who produce and make profits in another country.

(c) *Domestic sovereignty* – concerns the right to tax residents who operate only at a national level.

Of all these, domestic sovereignty is the most difficult to give up. Therefore, reforms affecting only international activities should be easier to achieve than reforms affecting all activities in each country.

3. Administration and compliance costs

These costs should be minimised and changes should not result in increases.

4. Transfer pricing

Any proposals should aim to eliminate or reduce transfer pricing problems.

5. Mergers within Europe

Any proposals should not discourage mergers with Europe.

Devereux and Pearson suggested six possibilities for reform:[4]

1. Single European corporation tax

This is the most extreme form of harmonisation and unlikely to be achieved as countries are generally not prepared to relinquish national sovereignty with regard to tax policy. A fully harmonised CT would require the following:

- a harmonised tax base;
- harmonised tax rates;
- harmonised tax systems;
- the abolition of withholding taxes; and
- groups of companies would be taxed on their European profits, this however would require some method of allocating profits between the relevant countries.

The advantages of a fully harmonised system would be that:

- it promotes economic efficiency;
- administrative and compliance costs would be lower;
- transfer pricing problems are avoided; and
- it encourages European mergers.

2. Corporation tax in location of shareholder residence

This type of reform would achieve CEN and CIN and would not require harmonised rates or a harmonised base, but full credit for foreign tax paid would need to be given. The effects of this type of reform are:

- higher administration and compliance costs; and
- the loss of some sovereignty by the source and residence countries of the company.

3. Corporation tax in location of parent company residence

The parent company would receive a full tax credit for any tax paid in the country where the subsidiary resides with the result that governments do not have to give up much sovereignty, and transfer pricing and merger problems would disappear as CEN is achieved but not CIN.

4. Corporation tax mainly in location of parent company residence

Tax would be charged on European profits and credit relief for foreign tax paid would be given, i.e. as the credit relief given in the UK as present.

The effects of this type of CT are:

- the source country retrieves some sovereignty;
- capital export neutrality is lost creating transfer pricing problems; and
- higher administrative and compliance costs.

5. A unitary system of taxation

Each country would tax all the companies operating, residing or distributing in that country on a proportion of its European profits using a formula. The problem with this system is that if all the countries concerned used the same formula, then in effect there would be a single European CT with all the associated disadvantages. Where different formulae are used, the advantages are reduced and administrative and compliance costs would increase. Under a unitary system, sovereignty is more complex and depends on what base the formula is calculated.

6. Corporation tax in location of production

This type of CT would require withholding taxes to be abolished. The system would be administratively simple and maintain CIN, however, CEN would be lost and so the system would affect location decisions, with the result that transfer pricing problems will arise.

Under this type of CT, the residence country would lose sovereignty, making this system unacceptable.

Conclusions

In July 1990 the Council of Ministers reached agreement after many years of consultation on three proposals dealing with transnational co-operation between firms:

(a) A common system of taxation should apply to parent companies and subsidiaries from different member states, in order to eliminate the double taxation of dividends received by the parent company due to a non-recoverable withholding of tax in the country where the subsidiary is established. To achieve this the parent company could either:
  - exempt the dividend from corporation tax; or
  - deduct the tax already paid in the country in which the subsidiary is established.

(b) A common system of taxation applicable to mergers by deferring capital gains arising from a merger until the gain is actually realised.

(c) Arbitration procedures with respect to transfer pricing problems, designed to eliminate the double taxation that would occur if an adjustment is made in one member state that is not accompanied by a corresponding adjustment in the country in which the associated business is established.

It is intended that these proposals for directives should be adopted by the SEM alongside an emphasis of co-operation among member states rather than rigid harmonisation.

Both in Europe and on the international level there are therefore three main options for the future:

1. Full harmonisation

This is unlikely to be achieved in Europe in the foreseeable future and even less likely internationally as countries are unwilling to give up their sovereignty in tax matters.

2. Competition

Competition between nations may cause tax policies to converge and indeed over the last few years tax reforms in many countries have been on the same track. However, competition alone may result in tax policies that are damaging to some smaller economies, as countries strive to attract economic activity by introducing incentives.

3. Co-ordination

This third option is the most feasible and least damaging as co-ordination of international tax policy would promote economic efficiency, encouraging the mobility of capital without undermining national sovereignty.

It would appear that the only way forward is increased co-ordination between member states to reduce favourable tax regimes that inevitably influence location decisions. In December 1997, the EU Commission agreed on a code of conduct to tackle the problem of harmful tax competition between member states. The two basic components of the code are, firstly, EU members should not introduce tax measures that would harm competition between member states, and, secondly, they should examine their existing tax laws, and, where these prove to be harmful to competition, they should be removed by 1 January 2003. For example, the Irish 10 per cent rate for certain companies is to be phased out by 2002; however, this seems rather futile when consideration is given to the fact that the Irish government has also received clearance from the Commission to reduce its general CT rate to 12.5 per cent in stages between 1999 and 2003. Political support has been given to the code of conduct, despite the fact that it is not legally binding, and a Working Party was set up to consider which tax measures are likely to harm competition between countries, which submitted its final report in November 1999. Two other matters were considered by the Working Party: a proposal sponsored by Germany requiring EU states to deduct a 20 per cent withholding tax on interest paid to individuals from another EU state, or to provide information to the relevant tax authority in order to counter tax avoidance and evasion. (Such measures, however, may have the effect of transferring investment to other countries, such as Switzerland and the USA, rather than to EU member states). Finally, a draft directive was also considered concerning the treatment of interest and royalty payments made between associated companies, which effectively face double taxation because they are taxed in more than one country when they cross national frontiers.

The European Commission has also expressed concern that corporate taxation is too low in relation to taxes on labour, and a reversal of this trend may have the effect of reducing unemployment. However, a systematic lowering of CT rates and the simultaneous broadening of the tax base has been the trend in many countries since the mid 1980s. Unusually in countries where CT rates are high, e.g. Germany, CT revenues fell between 1988 and 1997, whereas, in countries which cut CT rates, revenues have increased, illustrating the fact that mobile activities are increasingly difficult to tax with the consequential shifting of taxation from mobile inputs, such as capital, to less mobile inputs, such as labour.

Whatever progress is made in the future remains to be seen, but for now it would appear that 30 years of negotiation and debate in this area have been less than fruitful.

REFERENCES

1 Kay, J.A. and King, M.A. (1990) *The British Tax System* (5th edn), Oxford University Press.
2 The Neumark Committee Report (1962), International Bureau of Fiscal Documentation, Amsterdam.
3 Devereux, M. and Pearson, M. (1989) 'Corporate tax harmonisation and economic efficiency', *Institute of Fiscal Studies Report Series*, No. 35.
4 Devereux, M. and Pearson, M. *op. cit.*, Chapter 4.

FURTHER READING

Bond, S., Chennells, L., Devereux, M.P., Gammie, M. and Troup, E. (2000) *Corporate Tax Harmonisation in Europe: A Guide to the Debate,* Institute of Fiscal Studies, May.

Devereux, M. (1992) 'The Ruding committee report: an economic assessment', *Fiscal Studies*, Vol. 13, No. 2, pp. 96–107 .

Devereux, M. and Pearson, M. (1989) 'Corporate tax harmonisation and economic efficiency', *Institute of Fiscal Studies Report Series*, No. 35.

Gammie, M. (1992) 'The harmonisation of corporate income taxes in Europe: the Ruding committee report', *Fiscal Studies*, Vol. 13, No. 2, pp. 108–21.

Keen, M. (1993) 'The welfare economics of tax co-ordination in the EC: a survey', *Fiscal Studies*, Vol. 14, No. 2, pp. 15–36.

Owens. J. (1993) 'Globalisation: the implications for tax policies', *Fiscal Studies*, Vol. 14, No. 3, pp. 21–44.

Vanistendael, F. (1992) 'The Ruding committee report: a personal view', *Fiscal Studies*, Vol. 13, No. 2, pp. 85–95.

PRACTICE QUESTIONS

1. Discuss how the need for taxation arises.

2. What criteria would you use to evaluate a modern tax system? Indicate to what extent you consider that the UK tax system conforms to these criteria.

3. 'A progressive system of taxation is required if equity is to be adequately maintained.' Discuss.

4. Discuss the extent to which taxes on income create disincentive effects.

5. Discuss the main objectives for including capital in the UK tax base.

6. What changes, if any, would you make to the present system of capital taxation in order to increase its effectiveness?

7. 'The UK system of capital taxation is inefficient and ineffective and should be abolished.' Discuss.

8. Discuss the extent to which direct taxation in the UK provides for equity and the redistribution of income and wealth.

9. What are the advantages and disadvantages of an indirect tax such as VAT compared with an income tax?

10. What is the rationale for imposing a separate tax on companies?

11. Discuss the various systems of corporation tax, commenting on their effectiveness.

12. Tax reform since the mid 1980s has emphasised the importance of fiscal neutrality. Comment on the effectiveness of these reforms with regard to the investment decisions of individuals and companies.

13. To what extent do taxes on income and taxes on spending create an excess burden for the taxpayer?

14. Widespread avoidance and evasion reduce the efficiency of a tax. Discuss the problem of avoidance and evasion in the present UK tax system.

15. Evaluate the various tax bases used in the present UK tax system and comment on their effectiveness in achieving the objectives and principles of taxation.

16. Discuss the advantages and disadvantages of replacing income tax with:
    (a) a direct expenditure tax;
    (b) a comprehensive income tax;
    (c) an annual wealth tax.

17. Do international tax differentials cause major distortion with regard to investment and competition?

18. Discuss the need for international tax co-operation and suggest possible ways in which a degree of harmonisation may be achieved.

PART 2

Income tax

CHAPTER 9

Introduction to income tax

Income tax was first introduced in the UK by William Pitt in 1799, as a temporary measure to help fund the war with France. Pitt's income tax of 1799 was an unpopular tax and when Addington, Pitt's successor, re-enacted income tax in 1803 it embodied two principles that still exist in today's income tax, namely, the schedules of income tax and the deduction of tax at source.

Income tax was last introduced by Robert Peel in 1842, again, as a temporary tax, and remains as such today, and for this reason it has to be reimposed each year by Parliament *via* the Finance Act.

The main statutory charging provisions for income tax are contained in the Income and Corporation Taxes Act (ICTA 1988). This chapter examines the basic framework of income tax.

Outline of the income tax system

Income tax is levied for a fiscal year, which runs from 6 April to 5 April of the following year, i.e. the fiscal year 2002/03 runs from 6 April 2002 to 5 April 2003. The fiscal year may also be referred to as the tax year, or the year of assessment. Because income tax remains a temporary tax, it must be reintroduced each year *via* the Finance Act. This is generally achieved in three stages:

1. Budget speech

Each year the Chancellor will set out the new tax proposals in his Budget speech.

2. Finance Bill

The Finance Bill sets out the new tax proposals in detail, which are then debated and may be amended before being passed by Parliament.

3. Finance Act

When the Finance Bill receives Royal Assent, it then becomes law, i.e. the Finance Act. Section 820 of the ICTA 1988 provides for the continuity of income tax in a new tax year until the Finance Bill is given Royal Assent.

Individuals, partnerships and trusts that are resident in the UK during a fiscal year are liable to UK income tax on their *worldwide* income; non-residents are only liable to UK income tax on their UK income, ordinary residence and domicile can also affect the tax liability. Residence, ordinary residence and domicile are considered fully in Chapter 18.

Certain persons, however, are specifically exempt from income tax, namely:

- representatives of overseas countries, and their staff, e.g. ambassadors;
- UK registered charities (provided the income is used for charitable purposes);
- trade unions;
- friendly societies;
- approved pension funds; and
- members and staff of visiting overseas armed forces.

Besides certain persons being exempt from income tax, certain types of income are also exempt from the tax as follows:

1. Social security payments

Many social security payments are exempt from income tax, the main ones being:

- disability living allowance;
- invalidity benefit;
- attendance allowance;
- maternity allowance;
- death grants;
- child benefit;
- Working Families Tax Credit (WFTC);
- Christmas bonuses for pensioners;
- war disability pensions; and
- war widows' pensions.

Note: State retirement pension and jobseeker's allowance are *taxable* social security payments.

Since coming to power in 1997, the government has been committed to its 'Welfare-to-Work' programme, in an attempt to make working more worthwhile than claiming benefits. Many of the new work-related benefits, such as the Working Families Tax Credit (WFTC) and the Disabled Person's Tax Credit (DPTC), have been integrated into the tax system; employers are now responsible for paying WFTC and DPTC, together with the recovery of student loans (CSL) through the PAYE system, where the Revenue directs them to do so (*see* Chapter 44).

2. Interest

Certain payments of interest are exempt from income tax such as:

- the first £70 of interest on a National Savings Bank (NSB) ordinary account;
- interest and bonuses on National Savings Certificates;
- interest and bonuses on SAYE schemes;
- interest on damages for personal injury;

- interest on ISAs; and
- interest on certain government securities payable to persons not ordinarily resident in the UK.

3. Payments from employment

Certain payments arising from employment are exempt from income tax, e.g.:

- statutory redundancy payments;
- the first £30 000 of termination payments.

4. Miscellaneous exempt income

Other exempt payments include:

- scholarship and educational grants;
- lump sums received under approved pension schemes;
- capital portion of a life annuity;
- gambling and lottery winnings;
- premium bond prizes.

The schedular system of income tax

There is no definition of income in the tax legislation, instead sources of income are identified, and if an individual has income from any one of these sources, then it is taxed according to the rules of the particular source of income. These sources of income are known as the *Schedules of income tax*.

The legislation lays down the rules for calculating the tax liability for each of the schedules with regard to:

- the basis of assessment;
- expenses available; and
- loss relief available.

The Schedules of income tax are as follows:

Schedule A

Taxes the income from the ownership of land in the UK.

Schedule B

Abolished.

Schedule C

Abolished.

Schedule D

Schedule D is divided into six cases and taxes the following income:

Case I   Taxes the income from trading in the UK.

Case II   Taxes the income from professions and vocations carried on in the UK.

Case III   Taxes interest received gross and taxed interest on non-trading loans.

Case IV   Taxes the income from foreign securities.

Case V   Taxes the income from foreign possessions.

Case VI   Taxes the income not falling under any other case or Schedule.

Schedule E

Schedule E taxes the income from employment.

Schedule F

Taxes dividends and other distributions received from UK companies.

Banks and building societies

Interest received from banks and building societies is not included under any of the Schedules of income tax, and is usually paid net of 20% income tax to individuals. Non-taxpayers, however, can elect to have the interest paid gross, provided that they can certify in advance that they are non-taxpayers.

Note: Companies receive interest from banks and building societies gross, and as such it is taxed under Schedule D Case III.

Collection of income tax

Income tax is collected by either:

- deduction at source; or
- by direct assessment.

1. Deduction of income tax at source

Certain types of income have tax deducted at source, i.e. the tax is collected from the person paying the source of income rather than from the person receiving the income.

This feature was first introduced in the UK in Addington's income tax of 1803 and has two main advantages:

- it is administratively efficient; and
- it lowers the risk of tax revenue being lost through bad debts.

Income received net of basic rate income tax

- Income received under a deed of covenant
- Patent royalties
- Income portion of a purchase life annuity.

Income received net of 20 per cent income tax

- Bank deposit interest*
- Building society interest*
- Debenture interest
- Interest on government securities.

  * unless a claim has been made by a non-taxpayer to receive the income gross.

Dividend income

The tax credit on dividend income was reduced from 20 per cent to 10 per cent from 6 April 1999, and non-taxpayers are no longer be able to reclaim the tax credit.

It must be emphasised that the deduction of income tax at source does not necessarily extinguish the individual's liability to tax on that source of income, it merely acts as a payment on account, the gross amount of the income must be included in the tax computation, and further tax may be due from a higher rate taxpayer.

Pay as you earn

Tax is also deducted at source on Schedule E income under the PAYE system, and is covered fully in Part 6.

2. Direct assessment

Income not taxed at source is self assessed from 1996/7 onwards. The mechanism for self assessment is that two equal payments on account of the income tax due are made on 31 January and 31 July with the balancing payments being due on the annual filing date, i.e. 31 January in the following year.

EXAMPLE

The liability to self assessed tax for 2002/03 is paid as follows:

31 January 2003 – First payment on account of income tax for 2002/03
31 July 2003   – Second payment on account of income tax for 2002/03
31 January 2004 – Annual filing date for the return of income and gains for 2002/03 together with any balancing payment plus the first payment on account of income tax for 2003/04.

Self assessment is covered fully in Part 6 of this book.

CHAPTER 10

Business income

Individuals resident in the UK are charged to income tax under Schedule D on the annual profits arising from any trade (Case I), profession or vocation (Case II).

This chapter considers what constitutes a trade, profession and vocation, and then goes on to examine the rules for determining the taxable profits of unincorporated businesses, the basis of assessment under Schedule D Cases I and II, and the tax treatment of partnership income.

Determination of trading

Annual profits or gains not arising from a trade and not falling under any other Schedule or Case will be liable to income tax under Schedule D Case VI or possibly capital gains tax. Therefore, it is important to establish whether or not a trade is being carried on, as the rules for Schedule D Case I are essentially very different from the rules for Schedule D Case VI and capital gains tax.

The distinction as to whether an asset has been acquired as an investment or for the purposes of trade is of fundamental importance, as the profits/gains on an investment may be subject to capital gains tax. Goods that give personal enjoyment from ownership, or produce an income, such as shares, are more likely to have been acquired as an investment. There is less incentive these days to prefer a capital gain rather than extra income, since individuals now pay capital gains tax at their marginal rate of income tax. Nevertheless, individuals can still benefit from the annual exemption limit, making a capital gain preferable to extra income. 'Trade' is not adequately defined in the tax legislation. Section 832 of the ICTA 1988 states that 'trade' includes 'every trade, manufacture, adventure or concern in the nature of trade'.

This definition of 'trade' is very wide and implies that even a one off isolated transaction can be construed as trading and liable to income tax under Schedule D Case I.

What constitutes trading has been the subject of much case law. The *Report of the Royal Commission on the Taxation of Profits and Income* (1954) concluded that there was no single test in deciding whether or not a trade was being carried on but suggested that there are certain features that may indicate trading. These objective tests are known as *the badges of trade*.

The badges of trade

1. Subject matter

>'While almost any form of property can be acquired to be dealt in, those forms of property, such as commodities or manufactured articles, which are normally the subject of trading, are only very exceptionally the subject of investment. Again property which does not yield to its owner an income or personal enjoyment merely by virtue of its ownership is more likely to have been acquired with the object of a deal than property that does.' (Royal Commission, 1954)

Therefore, the courts will look at the subject matter of the transaction as an indication of trading. The purchase and resale of 1 million toilet rolls in a single transaction was held to be trading, since they were unlikely to have been acquired for the individual's own use, or as an investment – *Rutledge* v *CIR* (1929) 14 TC 490. Similarly, 44 million yards of aircraft linen purchased and resold was held to be trading – *Martin* v *Lowry (HMIT)* (1927) 11 TC 297.

2. Length of ownership

>'Generally speaking property meant to be dealt in is realised within a short time after acquisition.' (Royal Commission, 1954)

Where an item is purchased and immediately resold, or sold within a short time, the courts are more likely to hold that the transaction is an adventure in the nature of trade – *Wisdom* v *Chamberlain* (1968) 45 TC 92.

3. Frequency of transactions

>'If realisations of the same sort of property occur in succession over a period of years or there are several such realisations at about the same date a presumption arises that there has been dealing in respect of each.' (Royal Commission, 1954)

This badge does not negate the fact that a single isolated transaction can be trading; it merely strengthens the possibility that a trade is being carried on. Transactions which in isolation are likely to be of a capital nature can however be regarded as trading in nature where frequency indicates trading – *Pickford* v *Quirke (HMIT)* (1927) 13 TC 251.

This, however, does not apply where individuals frequently deal in quoted securities.

4. Supplementary work

>'If the property is worked up in any way during the ownership, so as to bring it into a more marketable condition, or if any special exertions are made to find or attract purchasers, such as the opening of an office or large scale advertising, there is some evidence of dealing.' (Royal Commission, 1954)

The way in which the asset is handled may help to determine whether it is trading or not. Additional work to make the asset more saleable has been regarded as evidence of trading – *Cape Brandy Syndicate* v *IR Commrs* (1921) 12 TC 358.

5. Circumstances of sale

The reason for the transaction may serve to weaken any other evidence that may support trading, for example, if the circumstances force a sale – *Taylor* v *Good* (1974) 49 TC 277.

6. Motive

A profit motive is often regarded as a relevant factor in establishing that the transaction is trading.

While the profit motive is relevant, it is not decisive in itself, because the test is not simply dependent on profit, but on what is actually done, i.e. the test is objective and the absence of profit does not preclude the finding of a trade being carried on.

No single test is decisive in establishing trading, and in the case of *Marson* v *Morton* (1986) 59 TC 381 the judge reviewed and broadened the badges to some degree as follows:

- Has the taxpayer undertaken a similar transaction?
- Is the transaction related to the trade which the taxpayer otherwise carries on? *Kirkby* v *Hughes* [1993] STC 76.
- How was the transaction financed?
- Was the item normally the subject of trading?
- Was the transaction typical of the trade in an item of that nature?
- Was work carried out on the item for the purposes of resale?
- Was the item sold as it was bought, or broken down into saleable lots?
- Did the item provide enjoyment, pride of possession or produce an income?
- What was the taxpayer's intention when the item was purchased?

The judge summed up the issue as follows: 'was the taxpayer investing money or was he doing a deal?'

The fact that the trade is illegal does not prevent the profits being chargeable to income tax under Schedule D case I – *IRC* v *Aken* [1990] STC 497.

Personal service businesses

Intermediaries, such as service companies, can be set up to provide clients with the services of an individual, such that, were it not for the existence of the service company, the individual would be an employee of the client. This allows the individual to extract funds from the company in the form of dividends, rather then a salary, which are not liable to NICs, resulting in the individual benefitting from paying less in NICs than either employed or self-employed persons, as well as from tax advantages. The Chancellor in the 1999 Budget announced measures to counter tax avoidance through the provision of personal services (IR35), to ensure that people working through intermediaries, such as personal service companies, in what is really employment, face the same tax burdens as someone employed directly. The provisions will use existing tests in determining whether the individual is employed or self-employed (*see* Chapter 14).

From 6 April 2000, the intermediary will be regarded as the individual's employer and as such will be responsible for the PAYE and NICs. The intermediary will be liable even if all the payments the intermediary receives are not passed on to the individual. For NIC purposes, the worker will be treated as having an annual earnings period in the same way as directors (*see* Chapter 14).

The legislation sets out the criteria to identify intermediaries to which the news rules apply as follows:

1. If the intermediary is a company and the worker has a material interest in the company, or the worker has no material interest but receives income from the company which is not a salary but nevertheless represents earnings.

2. If the intermediary is a partnership and:
   - the worker is entitled to 60 per cent or more of the profits; or
   - most of the profits are from a single client together with their associates; or
   - income received from the partnership under the profit sharing agreement by any of the partners is based on income generated by that partner under contracts to which this legislation applies.

3. If the intermediary is an individual and payments are made to the worker which are not salary, but nevertheless represent earnings.

The legislation will not apply to payments made to foreign entertainers and sportsmen visiting the UK, as provisions already exist to prevent tax leakage through this source.

Tax and NICs due are payable on 5 April, the first payment being on 5 April 2001 calculated as follows:

1. Take the relevant amounts received by the intermediary, including benefits in kind. As an allowance for the costs of running the intermediary, this amount is reduced by 5 per cent.

2. Benefits in kind provided for the worker or his family that are not taxable under Schedule E are included if they are taxable benefits for Schedule E purposes.

3. Expenses paid by the intermediary are allowed if they are allowable under Schedule E.

4. Deduct capital allowances if they would have been allowed under Schedule E.

5. Deduct contributions paid by the intermediary to an approved pension scheme for the benefit of the worker.

6. Deduct employer's Class 1 and Class 1A paid on salary and benefits in kind provided to the worker.

7. Deduct any amounts of salary and benefits in kind subject to Schedule E tax and Class 1 and Class 1A NICs, unless they have already been deducted at 3 above.

8. If at this stage the result is nil or negative, then no further tax and NICs will be due. If the result is positive, the employer's NICs payable on the deemed payment are also deductible, so calculate the amount which, together with the employer's NICs on it, equals the result in 7 above. This is the amount of the deemed payment.

Individuals falling within the ambit of the 'IR 35' legislation qualify for business mileage under the Approved Mileage Allowances Payments Scheme from 6th April 2002.

Profession or vocation

The annual profits/gains of professional persons in self-employment are liable to income tax under Schedule D Case II, as is the income tax from a vocation, meaning the way one spends one's life, e.g. artists, authors, etc. The dividing line between profession and vocation is very narrow and irrelevant for tax purposes.

The rules relating to Schedule D Cases I and II are exactly the same and so the distinction is academic and unimportant for practical purposes, and as such Schedule D cases I and II will be treated as one and no distinction will be made.

Adjustment of profits

Accounts for tax purposes should be prepared using accepted principles of accounting.

However, the accounting profit is unlikely to be the same as the taxable profit as some items of expenditure are not allowed for tax purposes and must therefore be added back to the accounting profit.

In adjusting the profits of a business, you must start by taking the net profit as shown in the accounts and make the following adjustments:

	£	£
Net profit as per accounts		X
Add back:		
(1) Capital items of expenditure	X	
(2) Appropriations of profit	X	
(3) Items specifically disallowed by statute	X	
(4) Expenditure not incurred wholly and exclusively for business purposes	X	
(5) Income taxable under Schedule D Cases I/II but not included in the accounts	X	X
		X
Deduct:		
(1) Items not taxable as income e.g. capital receipts	X	
(2) Items taxable under another Schedule of income tax	X	
(3) Expenditure deductible but not charged in the accounts	X	(X)
Adjusted Schedule D Cases I/II profits		X

Some of these adjustments need a more detailed explanation as follows:

1. The capital/revenue distinction

An expense will only be deductible in arriving at the taxable profits if the expense is a revenue expense. Items of capital expenditure must be added back to the accounting profit. Therefore, a deduction will be allowed for repairs, but not for improvements – *Law Shipping Co Ltd* v *IRC* (1923) 12 TC 62.

The *Law Shipping* case applies where expenditure is required to make the asset commercially viable. Compare this case with *Odeon Theatres Ltd* v *Jones (HMIT)* (1971) 48 TC 257 where a different rule applies where the asset is already commercially viable. When examining the distinction between revenue items of expenditure which are allowable and capital items which are disallowable for Schedule D Cases I/II purposes, consideration should be given to the following:

(a) Fixed/circulating capital

The fixed capital of any business relates to capital items of expenditure on fixed capital items incurred in order to make a profit, and as such is disallowed for Schedule D Cases I/II. Whereas, the circulating capital, or stock in trade, are items bought and sold in the course of the business, and represent revenue items which are allowable. For example, a machine bought by the business in order to manufacture goods for sale will be a capital item and must be added back to the accounting profit. However, a machine bought for resale by a business trading in machinery is part of the circulating capital of that business and represents a revenue item which is allowable.

(b) Once and for all expenditure

Once and for all expenditure on a capital asset to make it more valuable will be a capital expense and not a revenue expense – *Tucker (HMIT)* v *Granada Motorway Services Ltd* (1979) 53 TC 92.

(c) Enduring benefit

In the case of *British Insulated and Helsby Cables Ltd* v *Atherton (HMIT)* (1925) 10 TC 155 Viscount Cave said: 'when expenditure is made not only once and for all but with a view to bringing into existence an asset or advantage for the enduring benefit of the trade, I think that there is very good reason . . . for treating such an expenditure as properly attributable not to revenue, but to capital'.

(d) Identifiable asset

The enduring benefit test has been said to concentrate too much on the reason for the expenditure rather than on the subject matter and the courts will often apply the identifiable asset test, i.e. can a capital asset be identified for which the payment was made.

The expense will be treated as capital if it is made in regard to an enduring capital asset, even if the profits of the business are increased as a result of the payment for the capital asset – *Whitehead (HMIT)* v *Tubbs (Elastic) Ltd* (1984) 57 TC 472.

(e) Capital receipts

Capital receipts are not taxable as income. Where these have been included in the accounts, the profit has been increased by amounts that may be liable to capital gains tax, rather than income tax, and so they must be deducted from the accounts when making the adjustments.

Basically there are two important questions to be asked in determining whether a receipt is income or capital:

1. Does the receipt relate to assets of a permanent nature (enduring benefits)?
2. Does the receipt relate to fixed or circulating capital?

Despite these general rules, there are certain situations where the distinction may be blurred and we must look to the case law when applying the above rules.

(f) Compensation

Where a trader receives compensation for the loss of a beneficial contract or some other loss or damage, the basic principle is that a **payment for a loss of profit is a trading receipt.**

(a) Sterilisation of assets

Compensation that is paid because a fixed asset can no longer be used will be a capital receipt, because the compensation relates to fixed capital of a permanent nature – *Glenboig Union Fireclay Co Ltd* v *CIR* (1922) 12 TC 427.

The real test is whether the item in respect of which the taxpayer has received compensation is the depreciation of a capital asset or a restriction of trading opportunities – *Burmah Steamship Co Ltd v CIR* (1930) 16 TC 67.

(b) Cancellation of contracts

If the compensation relates to the whole structure of the profit making apparatus, the compensation will be treated as a capital receipt – *Van der Berghs Ltd v Clark (HMIT)* (1935) 19 TC 390.

However, where the compensation is merely a payment for loss of profit, it will be treated as a trading receipt – *Kelsall Parsons & Co v IRC* (1938) 21 TC 608.

It is, however, often difficult to distinguish a contract as one merely created in the ordinary course of business and one that relates to the profit making structure.

(c) Restrictive covenants

Compensation paid for entering into a restrictive covenant will generally be treated as a capital receipt – *Higgs (HMIT) v Oliver* (1952) 33 TC 136.

In general, lump sums paid for exclusivity agreements will be treated as income/capital by the Revenue according to the intention of the payer; if the amount is repayable and written off over the life of the agreement, which is usual, then income items are treated as revenue received when they are written off.

Fig 10.1 summarises the distinction between capital and revenue.

Money going out
(1) enduring benefit (is it capital?)
(2) identifiable asset (fixed/circulating capital)
(3) once and for all expenditure

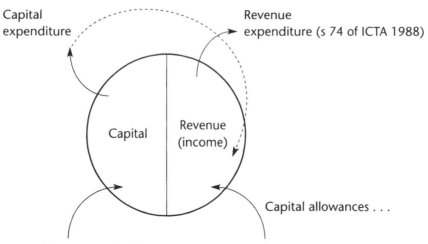

Money coming in
(1) is it a surragatum for loss of profit? (Revenue)
(2) is it part of the profit making apparatus? (Capital)

Fig 10.1 Summary capital/revenue distinction

2. Appropriations of profit

Appropriations of profit are not deductible, they must be added back for tax purposes. Appropriations of profit include the following:

(a) Any item(s) which could be classed as drawings by the proprietor, for example:

- salary taken by proprietor;
- expenses for private use of assets;
- stock for own use; must be added back at market value *Sharkey (HMIT)* v *Wernher* (1955) 36 TC 275; and
- partnership salaries and interest on capital.

(b) Income tax and National Insurance contributions paid on behalf of the proprietor and deducted from the accounts must be added back for tax purposes as they amount to an appropriation of profit. However, VAT paid by a non-registered trader is allowed as a deduction.

Note: Income tax and National Insurance contributions deducted under PAYE in respect of employees is allowable as it forms part of the wages charged.

(c) Transfers to general provisions and reserves are disallowed. Transfers to specific reserves may be allowable, e.g. provisions for specific bad debts written off, whereas general provisions for bad debts are disallowed. A provision for depreciation may be considered to be either a specific provision against capital, or a general provision for the replacement of assets, either way depreciation is specifically disallowed for tax purposes.

The treatment of bad debts and depreciation with regard to adjustment of profits are considered in more detail later in this chapter.

3. Expenditure specifically disallowed by statute

An expense will be disallowed if its deduction is specifically prohibited by statute. Deductions specifically disallowed include:

(a) Entertainment

Business entertainment is specifically disallowed under s 577 of the ICTA 1988. The one exception being that staff entertainment is allowed, provided the amount is reasonable. The Revenue take reasonable to mean not more than £75 per head. If the amount is greater than £75 per head, the whole of the expense is disallowed and not just the excess (ESC A70).

(b) Gifts

Gifts are disallowed unless:

- the cost does not exceed £50; and
- the gift is not food or drink or tobacco, or vouchers exchangeable for goods; and
- the gift carries a conspicuous advertisement for the business.

Note: The restrictions on allowable gifts do not apply to charities.

(c) Losses and expenses

Losses and expenses that are recoverable under insurance contracts – s 74(1), ICTA 1988.

(d) Other payments

Any payment which constitutes a criminal offence by the payer.

(e) Annual charges

Annual payments, such as patent royalties and deeds of covenant, that have been deducted in the accounts must be added back in arriving at the Schedule D Cases I/II profit. Although these payments are tax effective, relief is not given as a deduction from profits, but as a charge against income.

4. Wholly and exclusively for the purpose of trade

Section 74 of the ICTA 1988 provides that an expense will only be deductible in arriving at the taxable profits under Schedule D Cases I/II, provided that it is incurred wholly and exclusively for the purpose of trade, profession or vocation.

If the expense is too remote from the trade or there is a duality of purpose, then generally the expense is disallowed.

● The remoteness test

The expenditure should not be too remote from the trade if it is to be allowable. Expenses incurred by a trader in a capacity other than the capacity as a trader will be disallowed – *Strong & Co of Romsey Ltd* v *Woodifield* [1906] STC 215.

● The duality test

Wholly and exclusively will deny deduction where the expense has a duality of purpose, i.e. expenditure partly for business purposes and partly for personal purposes will be disallowed – *Caillebotte* v *Quin* (1975) 50 TC 222, *Mallalieu* v *Drummond* (1983) 57 TC 330.

The duality rule can be harsh and applies even where there is only incidental personal benefit. The taxpayer's motive in incurring the expenditure often has to be determined.

However, despite the duality of purpose rule, in practice the Revenue allow an apportionment of expenses that are partly for private use – e.g. motor expenses, accommodation expenses, telephone expenses, etc. – where a reasonably accurate apportionment can be made. Generally the Revenue will accept two-thirds business use for such expenditure but business use of more than two-thirds will have to be supported with evidence, e.g. logged mileage for motor expenses.

Some of the above adjustments need a more detailed explanation as follows:

(a) Legal and professional expenses

Legal and professional expenses incurred on capital transactions are disallowed, whereas those incurred on revenue items are allowable, e.g. legal and professional expenses incurred for debt recovery would be allowable.

Legal expenses in connection with leases can cause problems. Where legal fees are incurred in taking out a new lease, the expense is deemed to be in relation to a capital transaction and is therefore disallowed. However, the renewal of a short lease (50 years or less) is considered to be in relation to a revenue transaction and is therefore allowable.

(b) Depreciation

Depreciation is not allowed for tax purposes and must be added back to the accounting profit. What the business receives instead are capital allowances which is a standardised method of depreciation for tax purposes.

Lease amortisation is another form of depreciation and must be added back to the accounting profit.

However, where a premium is paid on the grant of a lease for business purposes, the amount of Schedule A assessed on the grantor can be deducted from the business profits, evenly over the life of the lease.

EXAMPLE

Mr Green paid a premium of £10 000 for the grant of an eight-year lease of his shop.

Amount chargeable to Schedule A

	£
Premium	10 000
less 2% (8 – 1) × £10 000	(1 400)
Schedule A assessment on grantor	8 600

Relief available to Mr Green

$$\frac{£8600}{8} = £1075 \text{ pa}$$

The £1075 is allowed as a deduction in adjusting the trading profits for tax purposes.

(c) Hire charges

Part of the rental charge is disallowed on hired cars costing more than £12 000 when new. The disallowable amount is calculated as:

$$\text{Amount charged in A/Cs} \times 50\% \times \frac{(\text{retail price} - £12\,000)}{\text{retail price}}$$

EXAMPLE

Car costing £16 000 with annual rental charge of £3200. The disallowable amount is:

$$£3200 \times 50\% \times \frac{(£16\,000 - £12\,000)}{£16\,000} = £400$$

This restriction will not apply to low emission cars from 17th April 2002.

(d) Bad and doubtful debts

Specific bad trading debts are allowable. General provisions for bad debts are disallowable. Loans to employees written off will be disallowable unless the trade is in the business of making loans.

Adjustments:

- *add back* any creation or increase in the provision for bad debts;
- *add back* staff loans written off (unless it is the normal business to make loans);
- *deduct* any decrease in the general provision for bad debts; and
- *deduct* any staff loans recovered and previously written off.

EXAMPLE

Bad and doubtful debts A/C

2001	£	2001	£
31 December		1 January b/f	
Bad debts written off:		Specific provision	462
Trade	625	General provision	575
Staff	135		
		Recoveries – trade	58
Bal c/down:			
Specific provision	485	Profit & loss A/C	645
General provision	495		
	1740		1740

Adjustments needed	£
Add back:	
Staff loan written off	135
less Decrease in general provision:	
(£575 – £495)	(80)
Net amount added back	55

Check	£
Allowable amount:	
Trade debts written off	625
Increase in specific provision:	
(£485 – £462)	23
	648
less Trade debts recovered	(58)
Allowable	590

	£
Profit and Loss A/C	645
less Amount added back	(55)
	590

(e) Travelling expenses

Travelling expenses incurred on journeys from home to place of business will only be allowed if the business is run from home – *Horton* v *Young* (1971) 47 TC 60.

(f) Removal expenses

Removal expenses will be disallowed if the move is a result of business expansion. If the expense is disallowed, the expense of removing plant and machinery can be added to the capital cost for capital allowance purposes.

(g) Defalcations

The misuse of property or funds by a proprietor or director is disallowed, but any such misappropriation by a subordinate is allowed, provided that it is not covered by insurance. This is because it is part of the normal risk of employing people.

(h) Fines

Fines imposed for breaking the law are disallowed. However, motoring fines incurred by employees whilst they are undertaking business activities are normally allowed.

(i) Subscriptions and donations

Applying the wholly and exclusively test, subscriptions and donations are disallowed if they are not for the benefit of the trade, therefore trade subscriptions would be allowable as would donations made for the benefit of employees.

Donations to political parties are disallowed.

Research and development (R&D)

Generally R&D expenditure is deducted as a revenue expense in the year that it is incurred, firms unable to make the deduction, because there are insufficient taxable profits, carry forward the expenditure against future profits.

The FA 2000 saw the introduction of R&D tax credit for qualifying small and medium-sized businesses from April 2000. The tax credit is 150 per cent of current R&D expenditure, i.e. a £150 deduction will be available for every £100 spent on R&D. Strictly, it is not a credit but a deduction from taxable profits, except that it was also proposed that the credit be partially refundable to those firms not making taxable profits. To be eligible the firms must satisfy the following conditions:

- they must spend at least £25 000 per annum on R&D; and
- the annual turnover must not be more than £25 million.

Note: R&D tax credits only apply to companies (see Chapter 31).

Allowable expenses

Some items of expenditure are specifically allowed, even though they may appear to be disallowable by applying the above rules. The main ones that you are likely to meet are as follows:

(a) Cost of applications for patents and trademarks, s 83 of ICTA 1988.

   Note: Patent royalties are paid under the deduction of income tax, therefore relief is allowed as a charge on income and not a deduction from profits.

(b) Non-statutory redundancy payments, provided that they do not exceed three times the statutory payment on a cessation of business, s 90 of ICTA 1988.

(c) Pre-trading expenditure, provided that the expense would have been allowed had the trade commenced, and it was incurred not more than seven years before commencement, s 401 of ICTA 1988.

(d) Payments made in consideration of a restrictive covenant are allowable in computing the payer's profits, s 73 of FA 1988.

(e) *Ex-gratia* payments.

(f) Salary and related expenses where an employee is temporarily seconded to a charity, s 86 of ICTA 1988.

(g) Contributions to approved profit sharing schemes.

(h) Contributions to pension funds, s 590 of ICTA 1988.

(i) Expenditure on providing security services to improve personal security after 5 April 1989, s 111 of FA 1989.

(j) Incidental costs of obtaining loan finance, s 77 of ICTA 1988.

(k) Preparation and restoration of waste disposal sites, s 91 of FA 1990.

(l) Bank interest, hire purchase interest, credit card interest and bank overdraft interest incurred wholly and exclusively for the purpose of trading is allowed.

Note: Annual charges and annuities are payable under the deduction of income tax and are allowed as a charge on income and not as a deduction from profits.

Tax relief for British qualifying films

Following the recommendations of the Advisory Committee on Film Finance, set up in 1996 under the chairmanship of Sir Peter Middleton, the first Labour Budget in July 1997 announced changes to the tax relief available for British qualifying films, to be effective as from 2 July 1997.

Generally a film will be classed as a British qualifying film if the company producing it is registered, managed and controlled in the UK or other EU member state, and it is produced mainly in UK studios.

Prior to 2 July 1997 British filmakers could write off expenditure either:

(a) as the film generated income; or

(b) at a flat rate of 33⅓ per cent per year after the film was completed.

For British films costing £15 million or less to produce, the new proposals accelerate the rate at which relief can be obtained by increasing the flat rate relief to 100 per cent on the following expenditure:

(a) production expenditure incurred after 1 July 1997; and

(b) acquisition expenditure on films completed and acquired after that date regardless of when the film was started.

Note: The 100 per cent write off does not apply to audio tapes and disks or non-qualifying films.

Mobile phone licences and IRUs

Generally, expenditure on acquiring capacity on submarine telecommunication cables, known as indefeasible rights of use (IRUs), is a capital expense, and so would not be allowed as a revenue item for Schedule D Case I purposes, nor would it qualify for capital allowances. However, from 21 March 2000, these costs will now be allowed as a revenue expense, spread evenly over the life of the asset.

A similar proposal was made in the 1999 Budget for the costs of acquiring licences to operate third-generation mobile communication services, that is to be legislated for in 2001, whereby intellectual property will be allowed as a revenue expense over the life of the asset in the same way as IRUs.

Basis of assessment

The FA 1994 introduced legislation to change the basis of assessment under Schedule D Case I from a prior year basis to a current year basis, in preparation for the introduction of self assessment from 1996/97.

Prior year basis

Under a prior year basis (PYB), the assessable profit for a year of assessment is the Schedule D Case I adjusted profit for the accounting period ending in the previous fiscal year.

Current year basis

Under a current year basis (CYB), the assessable profit for a fiscal year is the Schedule D Case I adjusted profit for the accounting period ending in that year of assessment.

EXAMPLE

Fred is a self-employed electrician preparing accounts for calendar years:

PYB: Under a PYB Fred would be assessed in 1997/98 on the profits he earned in the previous fiscal year 1996/97, i.e. the adjusted Schedule D Case I profit for the accounting period ending 31 December 1996.

CYB: Under a CYB Fred would be assessed in 1997/98 on the profits he earned in the current fiscal year 1997/98, i.e. the adjusted Schedule D Case I profit for the accounting period ending 31 December 1997.

Businesses that were established before 6 April 1994 continued to be assessed on a PYB up to and including the fiscal year 1995/96, the CYB being applied in the 1997/98 fiscal year. The transition from PYB to CYB was achieved in 1996/97 by taking an average of the profits falling into the 'gap' between the final PYB in 1995/96 and the first CYB in 1997/98.

EXAMPLE

The following results related to a business established in 1985:

	£
YE 31/12/94	10 000
YE 31/12/95	12 000
YE 31/12/96	13 000
YE 31/12/97	14 600

1995/96 (Final PYB)	£
YE 31/12/94	10 000

1997/98 (First CYB)	
YE 31/12/97	14 600

The 'gap' runs from 1/1/95 – 31/12/96. The transitional assessment for 1996/97 is an average of these profits calculated as:

$$\text{Profits for period of 'gap'} \times \frac{12}{\text{no. of months in 'gap'}}$$

$$\text{i.e. YE } 31/12/95 + \text{YE } 31/12/96 \times \frac{12}{24}$$

$$= \frac{12\,000 + 13\,000}{2} = \underline{\underline{£12\,500}}$$

The transitional rules also provide that profits that are assessed in 1997/98 that fall before 6 April 1997 are to be treated as overlap profits which are deducted once in the year of cessation or possibly on a change of accounting date. In the example above the 1997/98 assessment is based on the profits for the period 1/1/97 – 31/12/97. The portion of these profits earned before 6 April 1997 will be treated as overlap profits, i.e. 1/1/97 – 5/4/97:

$$\frac{95}{365} \times £14\,600 = \underline{\underline{£3800}}$$

Note 1: For businesses established before 6 April 1994 overlap relief is known as transitional overlap relief, and is calculated using the profit before any adjustment is made for capital allowances and balancing charges.

Note 2: Strictly the overlap profits should be calculated in days as above but for examination purposes it may be permitted to work in months.

EXAMPLE

The following information relates to Helen, who has been trading for many years, preparing accounts to 30 June each year:

	£
YE 30/6/93	16 000
YE 30/6/94	15 500
YE 30/6/95	18 000
YE 30/6/96	21 000
YE 30/6/97	18 250

For the years 1994/95 and 1995/96 Helen would have been assessed on a PYB, 1996/97 was the transitional year with 1997/98 being assessed on a CYB.

Year	Assessment (£)
1994/95 (PYB) YE 30/6/93	16 000
1995/96 (PYB) YE 30/6/94	15 500

1996/97 (Transitional year)

$$\text{YE } 30/6/95 + \text{YE } 30/6/96 \times \frac{12}{24}$$

$$\frac{18\,000 + 21\,000}{2} \qquad\qquad 19\,500$$

1997/98 (CYB)
YE 30/6/97   18\,250

Overlap profits:

1997/98
1/7/96 – 30/6/97

Overlap: 1/7/96 – 5/4/97

$$= \frac{279}{365} \times £18\,250 \qquad\qquad £13\,950$$

The CYB of assessment came into effect immediately for businesses established on or after 6 April 1994, the assessments being calculated as follows:

Year one

Based on the actual profits from the date of commencement to 5 April in the first fiscal year.

Year two

The basis of assessment in the second year is affected by the length of the first period of account as follows:

(a) If the accounting period ending in the second fiscal year is for at least 12 months, the basis period is 12 months to the accounting date.

(b) If the accounting period ending in the second fiscal year is less than 12 months, the basis period is the first 12 months trading.

(c) If there is no accounting period falling in the second fiscal year because the first set of accounts is a long period of account, the basis period is the actual profits during the second fiscal year.

Year three

The basis of assessment in the third year depends on whether there was an accounting date in year two or not:

(a) If there was an accounting date in year two, then normal CYB applies.

(b) If there was no accounting date in the second fiscal year because there was a long period of account, the basis period is 12 months to the accounting date in the third year.

Year four and subsequent years will be assessed on the normal CYB.

EXAMPLE 1

Business commenced 1 July 1997 with the following results:

	£
YE 30/6/98	12 775
YE 30/6/99	19 000
YE 30/6/2000	22 000

1997/98 (YR1)   (£)
Assessed on the actual profits from 1/7/97 – 5/4/98:

$$\frac{279}{365} \times £12\,775$$ 9765

1998/99 (YR2)
As there is an accounting date in 1998/99 for exactly
12 months, the basis of assessment is YE 30/6/98   12775

1999/00 (YR3)
As there was an accounting date in year two, normal
CYB applies: YE 30/6/99   19000

2000/01
YE 30/6/00   22000

Under the CYB for new businesses, any profits that are taxed more than once in the early years, i.e. overlap profits, are deducted once in the year of cessation or possibly on a change of accounting date. In the last example the profits for YE 30/6/98 have been assessed more than once to the extent of:

$$\frac{279}{365} \times £12\,775 = £9\,765$$

EXAMPLE 2

Business commences 1 January 1997 with the following results:

	£
6 months to 30/6/97	10860
YE 30/6/98	24000
YE 30/6/99	25000

1996/97 (YR1)   £
Assessed on the actual profits from 1/1/97 – 5/4/97

$$\frac{95}{181} \times £10\,860$$ 5700

1997/98 (YR2)   (£)
As the accounting date in 1997/98 is for
a period less than 12 months the basis of
assessment is the first 12 months trading:
6 months to 30/6/97 + 6/12 × £24000
£10860 + £12000   22860

1998/99 (YR3)
As there was an accounting date in 1997/98
normal CYB applies:
YE 30/6/98   24000

1999/00
CYB: YE 30/6/99   25 000

Overlap profits:
Profit for the period to 30/6/97 and the YE 30/6/98 have been assessed to tax more than once; the overlap profits being:

$(95/181 \times £10\,860) + (6/12 \times £24\,000) =$ £17 700

EXAMPLE 3

Business commences 1 January 1995 with the following results:

	£
16 months to 30/4/96	24 300
YE 30/4/97	26 000
YE 30/4/98	30 000

1994/95 (YR1)   (£)
Assessed on the actual profits from 1/1/95 – 5/4/95:

$\dfrac{95}{486} \times £24\,300$ 4 750

1995/96 (YR2)
As there is no accounting date falling in the
1995/96 fiscal year, the basis of assessment is
the actual profits between 6/4/95 and 5/4/96

$\dfrac{12}{16} \times £24\,300$ 18 225

1996/97 (YR3)
As there is no accounting date in the second
fiscal year, the basis of assessment is 12 months
to the accounting date in the third year:
12 months to 30/4/96

$\dfrac{12}{16} \times £24\,300$ 18 225

1997/98 (YR4)
CYB: YE 30/4/97   26 000

1998/99
YE 30/4/98   30 000

Overlap profits:
Profit for the 16 months to 30/4/96 has been assessed to tax more than once, the overlap profits being:

$(95/461 \times £24\,300) + (8/16 \times £24\,300) =$ £16 900

Basis of assessment on cessation

Under the CYB, the normal basis of assessment for the final year of trading runs from the end of the basis period in the previous year to the last day of trading.

EXAMPLE

Business commenced 1 May 1994 and ceased trading on 30 September 1999, with accounts being prepared on the following dates:

YE 30/4/95
YE 30/4/96
YE 30/4/97
YE 30/4/98
YE 30/4/99
Five months to 30/9/99

The basis periods for all the years concerned are as follows:

1994/95
1/5/94 – 5/4/95
$\dfrac{340}{365} \times$ YE 30/4/95

1995/96
YE 30/4/95

1996/97
YE 30/4/96

1997/98
YE 30/4/97

1998/99
YE 30/4/98

1999/2000 (final year)
1/5/98 – 30/9/99, i.e. YE 30/4/99
Plus five months to 30/9/99.

The assessment in the final year is then reduced by any overlap profits from the early years. These rules apply in the following situations:

(a) all cessations of businesses established after 6 April 1994; and

(b) cessations taking place on or after 6 April 1999 in the case of businesses established before 6 April 1994.

EXAMPLE 1

Gabriel commenced in business on 1 June 1994 and ceased trading on 28 February 1999. The adjusted Schedule D Case I profits for all the years were as follows:

	£
Four months to 30/9/94	8 000
YE 30/9/95	16 425
YE 30/9/96	18 000
YE 30/9/97	15 500
YE 30/9/98	12 000
Five months to 28/2/99	7 300

Year		Assessment
	(£)	(£)

1994/5
1/6/94 – 5/4/95

	(£)	(£)
1/6/94 – 30/9/94	8 000	
1/10/94 – 5/4/95 (187/365 × £16 425)	8 415	16 415

	(£)	(£)

1995/96

YE 30/9/95		16 425

1996/97

YE 30/9/96		18 000

1997/98

YE 30/9/97		15 500

1998/99
Final basis of assessment runs
from 1/10/97 – 28/2/99

	(£)	(£)
1/10/97 – 30/9/98	12 000	
1/10/98 – 28/2/99	7 300	
	19 300	
less Overlap profits*	(8 415)	10 885

* Overlap profits are calculated as:

$$\frac{187}{365} \times £16\,425 = £8\,415$$

EXAMPLE 2

Matthew ceased trading on 31 May 1999. The results of the last few years had been as follows:

	£
YE 31/10/94	31 000
YE 31/10/95	32 000
YE 31/10/96	28 000
YE 31/10/97	18 980
YE 31/10/98	14 000
Seven months to 31/5/99	9 500

As the business was established before 6/4/94, the first year under the CYB is 1997/98. The assessments for all the years concerned are as follows:

Year	(£)	Assessment (£)
1995/96 (PYB)		
YE 31/10/94		31 000
1996/97 (Transitional year)		
$1/11/94 - 31/10/96 \times \dfrac{12}{24}$		
$(32\,000 + 28\,000) \times \dfrac{12}{24}$		30 000
	(£)	(£)
1997/98 (CYB)		
YE 31/10/97		18 980
1998/99		
YE 31/10/98		14 000
1999/2000		
1/11/98 – 31/5/99	9 500	
less Overlap profits*	(8 112)	1 388

* Overlap profits for businesses established before 6/4/94 are calculated by taking the assessment for 1997/98, the first year for CYB, and determining how much of those profits were earned before 6/4/97:

1997/98
Assessed on the profits earned from 1/11/96 – 31/10/97. Profits from 1/11/96 – 5/4/97 are overlap profits, i.e.

$$\frac{156}{365} \times £18\,980 = £8\,112$$

If the assessment in the final year is insufficient to absorb the overlap profits, the assessment for that year is nil and the excess is available for loss relief. Suppose that in the last example Matthew's profits for the seven months to 31 May 1999 had been £5500. The assessment for 1999/2000 would then have been as follows:

Year	(£)	Assessment (£)
1999/2000		
1/11/98 – 31/5/99	5500	
less Overlap profits	(8112)	nil
Available for loss relief	(2612)	

Farmers' averaging

Profits arising from agricultural businesses have a tendency to fluctuate from one year to the next. To smooth out these fluctuations any individual who carries on a farming or market gardening business in the UK, either alone or in partnership, can claim to have the profits of two consecutive years averaged provided that certain conditions are met. There are two forms of averaging relief available:

(a) Full averaging

Full averaging is available for two consecutive years where one year's profit is 70 per cent or less of the other year. Where a loss is incurred the assessment will be nil and loss relief is not affected by an averaging claim.

EXAMPLE

A farmer, trading for many years, had the following recent Schedule D Case I assessments:

	£
1998/99	2 000
1999/00	30 000
2000/01	nil (loss £7 500)

The assessment for 1998/99 can be averaged with the assessment for 1999/00 as the lower profit satisfies the 70 per cent test:

1998/99	£
£2000 + £30 000 ÷ 2	16 000

1999/00	£
£2000 + £30 000 ÷ 2	16 000

The 1998/99 assessment becomes fixed but 1999/00 can be averaged with 2000/01 as the lower profit satisfies the 70 per cent test:

1999/00	£
£16 000 + nil ÷ 2	8 000

2000/01	£
£16 000 + nil ÷ 2	8 000

Again, 1999/00 becomes fixed but the 2000/01 assessment could possibly be averaged with 2001/02, provided that the 70 per cent test is satisfied.

The final assessments are then:

	£
1998/99	16 000
1999/00	8 000

(b) Marginal averaging

Marginal averaging is available where the lower profit is more than 70 per cent but less than 75 per cent of the higher profit calculated as:

$$3 (H - L) - \tfrac{3}{4} H$$

where H = higher profit
L = lower profit

The amount calculated is deducted from the higher profit and added to the lower profit.

EXAMPLE

A market gardener, in business for many years, had the following recent Schedule D assessments:

	£
1996/97	12 200
1997/98	7 800
1998/99	13 900
1999/00	15 500

The assessment for 1996/97 can be averaged with the assessment for 1997/98 as the lower profit satisfies the 70 per cent test:

1996/97	£
£12 200 + £7800 ÷ 2	10 000

1997/98	£
£12 200 + £7800 ÷ 2	10 000

The 1996/97 assessment is fixed, the 1997/98 assessment of £10 000 is more than 70 per cent, but less than 75 per cent of the 1998/99 assessment so marginal averaging is available:

$$3 (£13 900 - £10 000) - (\tfrac{3}{4} \times £13 900)$$
$$£11 700 - £10 425 = £1275$$

1997/98	£
£10 000 + £1275	11 275

1998/99	£
£13 900 - £1275	12 625

As the profit for 1998/99 is more than 75 per cent of the profit for 1999/00, no averaging is available. The final assessments are:

	£
1996/97	10 000
1997/98	11 275
1998/99	12 625

It is possible for the 1999/00 assessment to be averaged with 2000/01, provided that the 70 per cent or 75 per cent test is satisfied.

A claim for averaging is not available in the first and final year of a business.

The claim for averaging must be made within 22 months after the end of the latest fiscal year for which the claim is made.

These averaging rules are to be extended to authors and creative artists, the first years available for averaging being 2000/01 and 2001/02, provided that the profits of the lower year are less than 75 per cent of the higher year.

Change of accounting date

From 6 April 1997, a change of accounting date is recognised for tax purposes if the following conditions are met:

1. the accounting period to the new accounting date is not more than 18 months;
2. the Revenue are informed of the change by 31 January following the first fiscal year in which the accounts are prepared to the new accounting date;
3. there has not been a change of accounting date in the previous five years, or the taxpayer can demonstrate that the change has been made for *bona fide* commercial reasons.

The rules are complex and the change may result in overlap profits being generated, or the overlap profits from the early years may be relieved depending on:

- the length of the period of account to the new accounting date; and
- the fiscal year in which the new accounting date ends.

There are four possible situations as follows:

1. Accounting period less than 12 months

(a) Arising in the same fiscal year as the old accounting date

The basis period in this case runs from the end of the basis period in the previous year to the new accounting date in the current year, and will therefore always be for more than 12 months.

In this situation some or all of the overlap profits generated previously may be relieved. The amount to be relieved being calculated as:

$$\text{Total overlap profits} \times \frac{\text{no. of days in basis period} - 365^* \text{ days}}{\text{no. of days in overlap period}}$$

* 366 days for a leap year

EXAMPLE

George commenced his business on 1 January 1995 with the following results:

	£
Six months to 30/6/95	10 860
YE 30/6/96	23 725
YE 30/6/97	28 000

Year	(£)	Assessment (£)
1994/95 (YR1)		
1/1/95 – 5/4/95		
95/181 × £10 860		5 700

1995/96 (YR2)
Accounting period in current year
is less than 12 months so basis of
assessment is first 12 months trading:
1/1/95 – 31/12/95

	(£)	Assessment (£)
1/1/95 – 30/6/95	10 860	
1/7/95 – 31/12/95:		
184/365 × £23 725	11 960	22 820

1996/97 (YR3)
CYB:

		Assessment (£)
YE 30/6/96		23 725

Overlap profits:	£
1/1/95 – 5/4/95: 95/181 × £10 860	5 700
1/7/95 – 31/12/95: 184/365 × £23 725	11 960
Total overlap profits	17 660

Number of days in overlap period = 95 + 184 = 279 days

During 1997/98 George changed his accounting date by preparing accounts for eight months to 28/2/98, notice of the change being given to the Revenue by 31/1/99. The fiscal year of the change therefore is 1997/98. The accounts are prepared for a period of less than 12 months and there has already been an old accounting date during 1997/98, so the basis of assessment for 1997/98 runs from the end of the basis period in the previous year to the new accounting date:

1/7/96 – 28/2/98 (608 days)

The overlap profits that can be relieved against this long basis period are calculated as:

$$£17 660 \times \frac{608 - 365}{279} = £15 381$$

£17 660 – £15 381 = £2279 of overlap profits can be carried forward. The accounts for the period 1/7/97 to 28/2/98 show a profit of £17 500. The assessment for 1997/8 is therefore:

1997/98	£	£
1/7/96 – 30/6/97	28 000	
1/7/97 – 28/2/98	17 500	
	45 500	
less Overlap profit	(15 381)	30 119

(b) Arising in fiscal year following the year of assessment in which accounts are last prepared to the old accounting date

The basis period in this case is 12 months to the new accounting date, and as some profits will therefore be assessed more than once, overlap profits are generated.

EXAMPLE

Freda commenced in business on 1 November 1994 with the following results:

	£
YE 31/10/95	17 885
YE 31/10/96	20 000
YE 31/10/97	21 535

Year	Assessment (£)
1994/95 (YR1)	
1/11/94 – 5/4/95	
156/365 × £17 885	7 644
1995/96 (YR2)	
YE 31/10/95	17 885
1996/97	
YE 31/10/96	20 000
1997/98	
YE 31/10/97	21 535

Overlap profits:

156/365 × £17 885 =	£7 644

During 1998/99 there was a valid change of accounting date to 30 June. The accounts prepared to 30/6/98 show a profit of £15 000. The accounting period is less than 12 months and there is no old accounting date during 1998/99, so the basis period is 12 months to the new accounting date in the current year, i.e. 12 months to 30/6/98. This means that some of the profits assessed in 1997/98 will be taxed again, generating overlap profits:

1998/99	£
12 months to 30/6/98	
1/7/97 – 31/10/97: 123/365 × £21 535	7 257
1/11/97 – 30/6/98	15 000
	22 257

Overlap profits generated on the change of accounting date are £7257 which can be added to the overlap profits generated on commencement of £7644, so that £14 901 of overlap profits are carried forward for relief in the future.

2. Accounting period more than 12 months

(a) Ending in the fiscal year following the year in which accounts were prepared to the old accounting date

In this case the basis period is the accounting period in the current year which will be for more than 12 months and so overlap profits generated previously can be used to reduce the assessment.

EXAMPLE

Oliver commenced in business on 1 July 1994 with the following results:

	£
18 months to 31/12/95	16 470
YE 31/12/96	23 500

Year	Assessment (£)
1994/95 (YR1)	
1/7/94 – 5/4/95	
279/549 × £16 470	8 370
1995/96 (YR2)	
12 months to 31/12/95	
365/549 × £16 470	10 950
1996/97 (YR3)	
CYB:	
YE 31/12/96	23 500
Overlap profits:	
95/549 × £16 470 =	£2 850

Number of days in overlap period = 95 days.

From 31/12/96 there was a valid change of accounting date by preparing accounts for 14 months to 28/2/98. As the new accounting date falls in the next fiscal year, the basis period runs from the end of the basis period in the previous year to the new accounting date, i.e. from 1/1/97 to 28/2/98 (424 days). If the profit for the 14 month period to 28/2/98 was £26 000, the assessment for 1997/98 is calculated as:

1997/98	£	£
1/1/97 – 28/2/98	26 000	
less Overlap profits*	(1 770)	24 230

*Overlap profits to be relieved are calculated as:

$$\text{Total overlap profits} \times \frac{\text{no. of days in basis period} - 365}{\text{no. of days in overlap period}}$$

$$£2850 \times \frac{424 - 365}{95} = £1770$$

£2850 – £1770 = £1080 of overlap profits can then be carried forward for relief in the future.

(b) Ending in the next fiscal year but one from the last old accounting date

The fiscal year following the year in which the accounts were prepared up to the last accounting date will have no accounts. The basis period in this case for the next two fiscal years is taken as the 12 months to the new accounting date in that year. This means that some profits will be taxed more than once and so overlap profits will be generated.

EXAMPLE

Leroy commenced in business on 1 July 1994 with the following results:

	£
6 months to 31/12/94	5 000
YE 31/12/95	11 680
YE 31/12/96	15 330

Year	(£)	Assessment (£)
1994/95		
1/7/94 – 5/4/95		
1/7/94 – 31/12/94	5 000	
1/1/95 – 5/4/95:		
95/365 × £11 680	3 040	8 040
1995/96		
YE 31/12/95		11 680
1996/97		
YE 31/12/96		15 330
Overlap profits:		
95/365 × £11 680 =		£3 040

There is a valid change of accounting date after 31/12/96 by preparing accounts for 16 months from 1/1/97 – 30/4/98 (485 days) showing a profit of £19 400.

Year	(£)	Assessment (£)
1997/98		
12 months to 30/4/97		
1/5/96 – 31/12/96		
245/365 × £15 330	10 290	
1/1/97 – 30/4/97		
120/485 × £19 400	4 800	15 090
1998/99		
12 months to 30/4/98		
1/5/97 – 30/4/98		
365/485 × £19 400		14 600

Overlap profits to carry forward:

(a) 245/365 × £15 330		10 290
(b) generated on commencement		3 040
Total overlap profits to carry forward		13 330

Partnerships

The tax legislation does not provide a statutory definition of a partnership, however, s 1 of Partnership Act 1890 states that a partnership is 'the relation which subsists between persons carrying on business in common with a view to profit'. The Revenue take the view that a partnership does not exist merely because the individuals concerned state that a partnership is in existence; in the same way, the absence of a written agreement does not preclude the existence of a partnership. What the individuals concerned actually do is what matters, i.e. the Revenue look at the substance of the arrangement rather than the legal form.

The CYB of assessment has radically changed the way in which partnership profits are assessed and came into effect immediately for partnerships established on or after 6 April 1994 and for all partnerships from 1997/98. The partnership adjusted profits are calculated in the same way as sole traders and then divided between the partners according to the profit sharing arrangements in force during the accounting period and not the fiscal year. Partners are liable to income tax on their share of the partnership profits as if it was a separate business carried on by the partners on their own accounts.

EXAMPLE

Rosemary and Basil commenced business in partnership on 1 July 1996, preparing accounts to 31 December each year with the following results:

	£
Six months to 31/12/96	16 710
YE 31/12/97	38 690

Salaries were arranged as follows:

Period to 31/12/96

Rosemary	£4000 pa
Basil	£4000 pa

YE 31/12/97

Rosemary	£5000 pa
Basil	£4000 pa

The partners are entitled to interest on their fixed capital accounts at 10 per cent pa:

Rosemary:	fixed capital £7400
Basil:	fixed capital £8000

The balance of profits and losses are shared in the ratio of 60 per cent for Rosemary and 40 per cent for Basil for both periods. Each partner's share of the partnership profits is calculated as:

Six months to 31/12/96	Rosemary (£)	Basil (£)	Total (£)
Salary (6/12)	2 000	2 000	4 000
Interest (6/12)	370	400	770
Balance (60%:40%)	7 164	4 776	11 940
	9 534	7 176	16 710

YE 31/12/97	Rosemary (£)	Basil (£)	Total (£)
Salary	5 000	4 000	9 000
Interest	740	800	1 540
Balance (60%:40%)	16 890	11 260	28 150
	22 630	16 060	38 690

The individual partners are liable to income tax on these profits as if they were sole traders:

(a) Rosemary

Year		(£)	Assessment (£)
1996/7 (YR1)			
1/7/96 – 5/4/97			
1/7/96 – 31/12/96		9 534	
1/1/97 – 5/4/97			
95/365 × 22 630		5 890	15 424

Year	Assessment
1997/98	(£)
YE 31/12/97	22 630

Rosemary's overlap profits to be deducted in the year the partnership ceases or when she leaves the partnership are calculated as:

95/365 × £22 630 = £5890

(b) Basil

Year	(£)	Assessment (£)
1996/97		
1/7/96 – 5/4/97		
1/7/96 – 31/12/96	7 176	
1/1/97 – 5/4/97		
95/365 × £16 060	4 180	11 356
1997/98		
YE 31/12/97		16 060

The overlap profits to be deducted in Basil's final year are calculated as:

95/365 × £16 060 = £4180

The CYB rules mean that a partnership change has no effect on existing partners, they continue to be liable for income tax on their share of the partnership profits:

1. Admission of a new partner

A new partner joining the partnership is subject to income tax under the commencement rules in the same way as sole traders.

EXAMPLE

Suppose that on 1 January 1998 Rosemary and Basil admitted Miss Lavender as a junior partner, being paid a salary of £2000 pa and partnership sharing ratios being changed to:

Rosemary	40%
Basil	40%
Miss Lavender	20%

Assuming that Rosemary's and Basil's salaries and interest remain unchanged for the YE 31/12/98 and the adjusted profit for that period is £42 690, each partner's share of the partnership profit is calculated as:

YE 31/12/98	Rosemary (£)	Basil (£)	Miss Lavender (£)	Total (£)
Salary	5 000	4 000	2 000	11 000
Interest	740	800	–	1 540
Balance (40%:40%:20%)	12 060	12 060	6 030	30 150
	17 800	16 860	8 030	42 690

The individual partners are treated as if they are sole traders:

(a) Rosemary

Year	Assessment (£)
1998/99	
YE 31/12/98	17 800

(b) Basil

Year	Assessment (£)
1998/99	
YE 31/12/98	16 860

(c) Miss Lavender

Year	Assessment (£)
1997/98 (YR1)	
1/1/98 – 5/4/98	
95/365 × £8 030	2 090
1998/99 (YR 2)	
YE 31/12/98	8 030

Miss Lavender's overlap profits to be deducted in her final year are calculated as:

$$95/365 \times £8030 = £2090$$

2. Partner leaving the partnership

When a partner leaves the partnership, it has no effect on the existing partners. The partner leaving is liable to income tax under the normal cessation rules for sole traders and overlap relief is available in the final year.

EXAMPLE

Suppose that Basil leaves the partnership on 31 December 1999, all other information remaining the same and the adjusted Schedule D Case I profit for YE 31/12/99 was £41 340.

YE 31/12/99	Rosemary (£)	Basil (£)	Miss Lavender (£)	Total (£)
Salary	5 000	4 000	2 000	11 000
Interest	740	800	–	1 540
Balance (40%:40%:20%)	11 520	11 520	5 760	28 800
	17 260	16 320	7 760	41 340

(a) Rosemary

Year	Assessment (£)
1999/2000	
YE 31/12/99	17 260

(b) Basil

Year	Assessment (£)
1999/2000	
1/1/99 – 31/12/99	16 320
less overlap profits	(4 180)
	12 140

(c) Miss Lavender

Year	Assessment (£)
1999/2000	
YE 31/12/99	7 760

Notional profit/loss

If, because of partnership salaries, one partner ends up with a net profit allocation when the partnership as a whole has incurred a loss this notional profit is allocated to the other partners in the ratios of the net loss initially allocated to them.

EXAMPLE

Park, Hill and Dale share profits and losses in the ratio of 40%:40%:20% respectively after receiving the following salaries:

	£
Park	15 000 pa
Hill	5 000 pa
Dale	5 000 pa

For the YE 31/12/01 the partnership incurred a loss of £(7000).

2001/02	Park (£)	Hill (£)	Dale (£)	Total (£)
Salaries	15 000	5 000	5 000	25 000
Balance (40%:40%:40%)	(12 800)	(12 800)	(6 400)	(32 000)
	2 200	(7 800)	(1 400)	(7 000)

The notional profit of £2200 is reallocated to Hill and Dale in the ratio of 7800:1400

	Park	Hill	Dale	Total
	(£)	(£)	(£)	(£)
Original allocation	2200	(7800)	(1400)	
Ratio 7800:1400	(2200)	1865	335	
Final allocation	nil	(5935)	(1065)	(7000)

The same procedure is followed if one partner has a notional loss when the partnership as a whole has made an overall profit. There is no question of a partner with a notional loss claiming loss relief.

EXAMPLE

Black, White, Brown and Green share profits and losses equally after receiving the following salaries:

	£
Black	15 000 pa
White	15 000 pa
Brown	3 000 pa
Green	12 000 pa

The Schedule D Case I adjusted profit for YE 30/4/02 was £25 000.

2002/03	Black	White	Brown	Green	Total
	(£)	(£)	(£)	(£)	(£)
Salaries	15 000	15 000	3 000	12 000	45 000
Balance	(5 000)	(5 000)	(5 000)	(5 000)	(20 000)
Original allocation	10 000	10 000	(2 000)	7 000	25 000

The notional loss of £2000 is reallocated to Black, White and Green in the ratio of 10 000:10 000:7000.

	Black	White	Brown	Green	Total
	(£)	(£)	(£)	(£)	(£)
Original alloc	10 000	10 000	(2 000)	7 000	
Ratio 10:10:7	(741)	(741)	2 000	(518)	
Final allocation	9 259	9 259	nil	6 482	25 000

Partnerships established before 6 April 1994

From 1997/98, all partnerships are assessed on a CYB. The transition from PYB taking place during 1996/97 in the same way as for sole traders. Under the new rules, care must be taken identifying overlap profits where a partnership was established before 6 April 1994 but a new partner was admitted after 6 April 1997.

EXAMPLE

Wax and Wayne had been in partnership for many years sharing profits equally. On 1 June 1997 Moon was admitted into the partnership and the profit sharing ratio was 3:3:2. Wax and Wayne receive salaries of £6000 pa and Moon receives a salary of £3600 pa. The adjusted Schedule D Case I profits are as follows:

	£
YE 31/12/97	44530
YE 31/12/98	43800

YE 31/12/97 – partnership allocation:

	Wax	Wayne	Moon	Total
1/1/97 – 31/5/97 (151 days)	(£)	(£)	(£)	(£)
Salary (5/12)	2500	2500	–	5000
Balance (151/365)	6711	6711		13422
	9211	9211	nil	18422
1/6/97 – 31/12/97 (214 days)				
Salary (7/12)	3500	3500	2100	9100
Balance (214/365)	6378	6378	4252	17008
(ratio 3:3:2)	9878	9878	6352	26108
Total allocation YE 31/12/97 (1997/98)	19089	19089	6352	44530

YE 31/12/98 – partnership allocation

	Wax	Wayne	Moon	Total
	(£)	(£)	(£)	(£)
Salary	6000	6000	3600	15600
Balance (3:3:2)	10575	10575	7050	28200
Allocation YE 31/12/98	16575	16575	10650	43800

Partner	Year			Assessment
			(£)	(£)
(a) Wax	**1997/98** (CYB)			
	YE 31/12/97			19089
	1998/99 (CYB)			
	YE 31/12/98			16575
(b) Wayne	**1997/98** (CYB)			
	YE 31/12/97			19089
	1998/99 (CYB)			
	YE 31/12/98			16575

(c) Moon	**1997/98** (YR1)			
	1/6/97 – 5/4/98:			
	1/6/97 – 31/12/97	6352		
	1/1/98 – 5/4/98			
	95/365 × £10 650	2772		9124
	1998/99 (YR2)			
	YE 31/12/98			10650

Overlap profits

As Wax and Wayne were in business before 6 April 1994 their overlap profits are identified as the profits earned before 6 April 1997 that are assessed in 1997/8, i.e. the 1997/98 assessment is based on YE 31/12/97, i.e. profits earned between 1 January 1997 and 31 December 1997, of these profits 95/365 days are overlap:

$$1/1/97 – 5/4/97 \ (95 \ days) \ 95/365 \times 19\,089 = £4968$$

Wax and Wayne can each carry forward £4968 overlap profits to be relieved in the year of cessation or potentially on a change of accounting date.

Moon, on the other hand, commenced in business on 1 June 1997 and so his overlap profits are identified in the opening years, part of the profits for YE 31/12/98 (£10 650) have been taxed more than once as part of these profits were taxed in 1997/98:

$$95/365 \times £10\,650 = £2772$$

Moon therefore carries forward £2772 of overlap profits to be relieved in the year of cessation, or potentially on a change of accounting date.

SELF ASSESSMENT QUESTIONS

10.1 Charlotte commenced in business on 1 January 2001. Accounts prepared for the 16-month period ending on 30 April 2002 showed the following results:

	£	£
Gross profit		41 250
Rental income		6 000
Building society interest		1 200
		48 450
less Expenses:		
Rent and rates	8 500	
Motor expenses (note 1)	3 690	
Drawings	12 000	
Depreciation	1 800	
General expenses (note 2)	2 870	
Legal and professional fees (note 3)	1 250	

Advertising	350	
Lease written off (note 4)	5000	(35 460)
Net profit		12 990

Notes:

(1) Charlotte uses her car 60% for business purposes.

(2) General expenses include: £

subscription to trade association	500
telephone	684
postage and stationery	298
general administration costs	738
subscription to health club	650
	2870

(3) Legal and professional fees comprise: £

accountancy fees	700
legal fees in connection with new lease	550
	1250

(4) Charlotte took out a ten-year lease on premises from 1 May 2001 for a premium of £30 000.

(5) Capital allowances for the 16-month period to 30/4/02 are calculated at £1302.

REQUIRED:

(a) Calculate the Schedule DI figure for the 16-month period ended on 30 April 2002.

(b) Calculate the Schedule DI assessments for 2000/01, 2001/02 and 2002/03, identifying any overlap profits that have been generated.

10.2 George commenced trading on 1 July 1996 and ceased trading on 30 September 2001. The adusted Schedule DI profits were as follows:

	£
6 months to 31/12/96	13 135
YE 31/12/97	25 300
YE 31/12/98	30 000
YE 31/12/99	28 000
YE 31/12/00	26 600
9 months to 30/9/01	10 000

REQUIRED:

Calculate the Schedule DI assessments for all the years concerned.

CHAPTER 11

Capital allowances

We learned in Chapter 10 that the capital/revenue distinction is important in calculating the Schedule D Case I profit, as capital items of expenditure are not allowed as a deduction against the revenue of the business; depreciation of capital assets charged in the accounts must also be added back for tax purposes. The capital expenditure may, however, qualify for capital allowances.

The capital allowance system is a standardised method of depreciation for tax purposes, available on certain items of capital expenditure.

The main statutory provisions for capital allowances are contained in the Capital Allowance Act 2001 (CAA 2001). This chapter examines the capital allowance system.

General rules

The capital allowances are deducted as a trading expense for a period of account during which:

- a business is being carried on; and
- there is a balance of qualifying expenditure.

Capital allowances may also be claimed against income from:

- Schedule E on plant and machinery purchased and used by employees in their employment; and
- Schedule A on assets used for the maintenance and repair of the property.

The chapters covering Schedule A and Schedule E will make this point, and this chapter is concerned with capital allowances available against business income.

Capital expenditure included

Capital expenditure is included in the capital allowance computation for a period of account, if the expense has been incurred during that period. The expense is generally deemed to be incurred when the obligation to pay becomes unconditional, however, if payment is actually required more than four months later, then the expenditure is deemed to be incurred when payment is actually made.

Pre-trading capital expenditure is deemed to have been incurred on the first day of trading.

Hire purchase agreements

Where capital items are acquired under a hire purchase agreement, the capital allowances are claimed on the cash price of the asset, any interest payments being allowed as a revenue deduction.

Value added tax

A person who is not registered for VAT will include all the VAT as part of the capital cost, whereas a registered person will only include VAT that is irrecoverable through the VAT system, e.g. motor cars.

Qualifying expenditure

The categories of expenditure qualifying for capital allowances are as follows:

- plant and machinery
- industrial buildings
- hotels
- dwelling houses let on assured tenancies
- buildings in an enterprise zone
- agricultural buildings and works
- patents
- know-how
- scientific research
- mineral extraction
- dredging
- information and communication technology.

The rest of this chapter will examine each of these areas in more detail.

The definition of plant

Prior to the FA 1994, plant and machinery were not defined in the legislation, and so were given their everyday meanings. Machinery rarely presented any practical problems; plant, on the other hand, has caused many problems over the years, as the huge body of case law in this area would indicate.

The provisions of s 117 of the FA 1994 apply to expenditure incurred after 30 November 1993, and was an attempt to codify existing case law decisions up to that date, by first of all identifying assets treated as part of a building.

Table 1, Schedule AA1 to s 117 of the FA 1994 is divided into two columns (*see* Table 11.1); column one lists items treated as part of a building and so cannot be treated as plant, and column two lists items which, while they constitute part of a building, may qualify as plant on the basis of existing case law. Therefore, while the statutory definitions establish parameters on the meaning of plant, case law is still of importance.

Table 11.1 FA 1994, s 117, Sch AA1, Table 1

(1) Assets included in the expression 'building'	(2) Assets so included, but expenditure on which is unaffected by the Schedule
A. Walls, floors, ceilings, doors, gates, shutters, windows and stairs.	1. Electrical, cold water, gas and sewerage systems (a) provided mainly to meet the particular requirements of the trade, or (b) provided mainly to serve particular machinery or plant used for the purposes of the trade. 2. Space or water heating systems; powered systems of ventilation, air cooling or air purification; and any ceiling or floor comprised in such systems.
B. Mains services, and systems, of water, electricity and gas.	3. Manufacturing or processing equipment; storage equipment, including cold rooms; display equipment; and counters, checkouts and similar equipment. 4. Cookers, washing machines, dishwashers, refrigerators and similar equipment; washbasins, sinks, baths, showers, sanitary ware and similar equipment; and furniture and furnishings.
C. Waste disposal systems.	5. Lifts, hoists, escalators and moving walkways. 6. Sound insulation provided mainly to meet the particular requirements of the trade.
D. Sewerage and drainage systems.	7. Computer, telecommunication and surveillance systems (including their wiring or other links). 8. Refrigeration or cooling equipment.
E. Shafts or other structures in which lifts, hoists, escalators and moving walkways are installed.	9. Sprinkler equipment and other equipment for extinguishing or containing fire; fire alarm systems. 10. Burgular alarm systems. 11. Any machinery (including devices for providing motive power) not within any other item in this column.
F. Fire safety systems.	12. Strong rooms in bank or building society premises; safes. 13. Partition walls, where moveable and intended to be moved in the course of the trade. 14. Decorative assets provided for the enjoyment of the public in the hotel, restaurant or similar trades. 15. Advertising hoardings; and signs, displays and similar assets. 16. Swimming pools (including diving boards, slides and structures on which such boards or slides are mounted).

The body of case law in relation to capital allowances stems from the case of *Yarmouth* v *France* (1887) 19 QBD 647, where a horse was held to be plant. This case was not in fact a tax case, but an employers' liability case. In order for the employee to receive compensation for injury caused by the horse in the course of his employment, the horse had to be plant. In this case Lindley LJ defined plant as follows:

- it must be apparatus;
- it must be used by the claimant in carrying on his business; and
- it must be kept for permanent use in the business.

Although the courts looked for permanence in the business, there needed only to be a measure of durability – *Hinton* v *Maden & Ireland Ltd* (1959) 38 TC 391.

By its restrictions to goods and chattels, Lindley LJ's test was not helpful where the courts had to decide whether a permanent structure was plant or simply mere setting, i.e. place where the business is carried on – *Benson* v *Yard Arm Club* [1979] STC 266.

However, the two categories need not be mutually exclusive – *Jarrold* v *John Good & Sons* (1962) 40 TC 681.

A structure was more likely to be plant if it was not passive but part of the apparatus used by the business – *Cooke* v *Beach Station Caravans Ltd* [1974] STC 402.

As case law developed, the courts have generally applied the function versus setting test, i.e. does the item perform a function in the business, in which case it is more likely to be plant, or is it just part of the setting in which the business is carried on, in which case it will probably not be classed as plant – *Dixon* v *Fitches Garage Ltd* [1975] STC 480; *Cole Bros* v *Phillips* [1982] STC 308.

However, later cases have put some doubt on the decision in Fitches Garage – *CIR* v *Scottish & Newcastle Breweries* [1982] STC 296; *Wimpey International Ltd* v *Warland* [1988] STC 273; *Hunt* v *Henry Quick Ltd*; *King* v *Bridisco Ltd* [1992] STC 633.

In the Wimpey case, Hoffman J set out the important questions to be asked in deciding whether an item was plant or not. *See* Fig 11.1.

For example, in Table 11.1 walls are in column 1(A) and so generally not allowable as plant, however, moveable partition walls may be treated as plant if column 2(13) applies – *Jarrold* v *John Good & Sons Ltd* (1962) 40 TC 681.

Lighting systems are included in column 1(B) and so initially would not be eligible as plant unless it also fell within 2(1) – *Cole Bros* v *Phillips*; *CIR* v *Scottish & Newcastle Breweries Ltd*; *Wimpey International Ltd* v *Warland*; *Hunt* v *Henry Quick Ltd*; *King* v *Bridisco Ltd*.

However, just because an item falls within column 2, it will not automatically be treated as plant, the decision must be made by examining the facts of the particular case in the light of existing case law.

Table 2, Schedule AA1 to s 117 of the FA 1994, again, is divided into two columns (*see* Table 11.2), this time with regard to structures and assets: column one identifying structures that cannot qualify as plant, and column two listing those structures which may qualify as plant on the basis of existing case law.

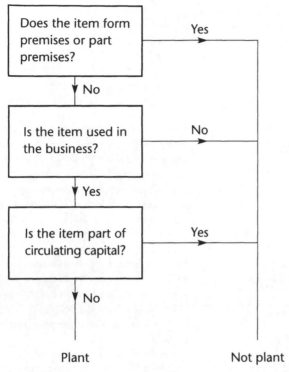

Fig 11.1 Questions to determine whether or not an item is plant

For example, in Table 11.2 any dock is excluded by column 1(E), however, a dry dock may qualify as plant under column 2(2), provided that it is performing a function in the business – *CIR* v *Barclay Curle & Co Ltd* (1969) 45 TC 221.

In the same way, a silo may be excluded under column 1(G) but may be eligible under column 2(7) – *Schofield* v *R&H Hall Ltd* [1975] STC 353.

Besides the items listed in Tables 1 and 2 of s 117 of the FA 1994, other statutory provisions allow the following items of expenditure to qualify as plant:

- alterations to buildings incidental to the installation of plant;
- heat insulation of industrial buildings;
- computer software;
- films, tapes and discs;
- expenditure to comply with fire regulations;
- expenditure on sports grounds to comply with safety regulations; and
- expenditure on security assets.

The provisions of FA 1994 s117 have now been incorporated into ss 21–23, CAA 2001.

Table 11.2 FA 1994, s 117, Sch AA1, Table 2

(1) Structures and assets	(2) Expenditure which is unaffected by the Schedule
A. Any tunnel, bridge, viaduct, aqueduct, embankment or cutting.	1. Expenditure on the alteration of land for the purpose only of installing machinery or plant.
B. Any way or hard standing, such as a pavement, road, railway or tramway, a park for vehicles or containers, or an airstrip or runway.	2. Expenditure on the provision of dry docks.
	3. Expenditure on the provision of any jetty or similar structure provided mainly to carry machinery or plant.
C. Any island navigation, including a canal or basin or a navigable river.	4. Expenditure on the provision of pipelines or underground ducts or tunnels with a primary purpose of carrying utility conduits.
	5. Expenditure on the provision of towers provided to support floodlights.
D. Any dam, reservoir or barrage (including any sluices, gates, generators and other equipment associated with it).	6. Expenditure on the provision of any reservoir incorporated into a water treatment works or on the provision of any service reservoir of treated water for supply within any housing estate or other particular locality.
E. Any dock.	7. Expenditure on the provision of silos provided for temporary storage or on the provision of storage tanks.
	8. Expenditure on the provision of slurry pits or silage clamps.
F. Any dike, sea wall, weir or drainage ditch.	9. Expenditure on the provision of fish tanks or fish ponds.
G. Any structure not within any other item in this column.	10. Expenditure on the provision of rails, sleepers and ballast for a railway or tramway.
	11. Expenditure on the provision of structures and other assets for providing the setting for any ride at an amusement park or exhibition.
	12. Expenditure of the provision of fixed zoo cages.

Plant and machinery

A general pool of expenditure is maintained for plant and machinery, the basic computational layout being as follows:

	Pool (£)	Allowances (£)
Balance of expenditure b/fwd	X	
plus Additions for period of account not qualifying for first year allowance (FYA)	$\underline{X}$	
	X	

	Pool (£)	Allowances (£)
less Disposals during period of account	(X)	
	X	
less Writing down allowance	(X₁)	X₁
	X	
Additions qualifying for FYA	X	
less FYA	(X₂)	X₂
	X	
Balance of expenditure c/fwd	X	X₍₁₊₂₎

We will now examine the component parts of this computation:

1. Additions not qualifying for FYA

Expenditure incurred during the period of account on qualifying plant and machinery (not eligible for FYA), is added to the balance of expenditure brought forward from the last period of account, provided that the expense was incurred wholly and exclusively for the purpose of the trade. For expenditure incurred prior to April 1998, the expenses on which capital allowances could be claimed had to be notified within two years. This requirement to notify was abolished retrospectively in the FA 2000 for expenditure from April 1998 where notification falls due on or after April 2000 (1/4/00 for corporation tax, 6/4/00 for income tax). Capital allowances are available for the period in which the expense was incurred, even if the asset has not been brought into use in that period.

2. Disposals

If plant is disposed of during the period, the sale proceeds are deducted from the pool of expenditure. However, as we cannot take out of the pool more than was originally put in, the amount deducted is restricted to the original cost of the asset.

3. Writing down allowance

A maximum of 25 per cent writing down allowance (WDA) is given for a period of account, on a reducing balance basis:

25% × n/12 (where n is the number of months in the period of account)

Capital allowances on plant and machinery with an expected working life of 25 years or more will be reduced from 25 per cent to 6 per cent for groups of companies or businesses spending more than £100 000 per year (long life assets).

The legislation which takes effect for assets purchased after 26 November 1996 excludes the following:

- ships and railway assets purchased before the year 2010; and
- expenditure incurred before the year 2000 under contracts entered into before 26 November 1996.

4. First year allowance

If an item is eligible for a FYA, then it is dealt with in the computation after the WDA has been calculated on the balance of expenditure, and any balance of the expense not claimed as FYA is added to the balance of the pool to carry forward to the next period of account. This is because FYA and WDA on plant and machinery cannot both be claimed in the same year.

The FA 1997(No. 2) introduced a 50 per cent FYA on plant and machinery (12 per cent where long life asset rules apply) for expenditure incurred between 2 July 1997 and 1 July 1998 for small and medium-sized businesses. In the FA 1998 the availability of a FYA on plant and machinery was extended at a rate of 40 per cent for expenditure incurred between 2 July 1998 and 1 July 1999. This 40 per cent FYA was further extended in the FA 1999 and made permanent in the FA 2000. For this purpose, a business is a small or medium business if it satisfies two of the following criteria:

1. turnover not more than £11.2 million
2. assets not more than £5.6 million
3. maximun of 250 employees.

For small and medium-sized businesses acquiring assets that are to be used in Northern Ireland, the FYA is increased to 100 per cent on expenditure incurred between 12 May 1998 and 11 May 2002.

In order to be eligible for the increased allowance, a business must be classed as a small or medium business in the year that the expenditure is incurred.

Historically motor cars have never qualified for a FYA. However from 17th April 2002 expenditure on new low emission cars for use in a business, and equipment for refuelling vehicles with natural gas or hydrogen fuel is eligible for enhanced allowances by all businesses. Expenditure on a new car qualifies for 100% FYA if it is registered after 17th April 2002 and is either electrically propelled or the CO_2 emissions figure on the registration document is no greater than 120gm/km.

EXAMPLE

William commenced trading on 1 January 1995 with the following trading results:

	£
18 months to 30 June 1996	49 500
YE 30 June 1997	40 000
YE 30 June 1998	42 000

During this time he incurred the following expenditure:

		£
1 January 1995	Second hand plant	5 000
1 May 1995	Lorry	7 000
31 July 1996	New plant	10 000
10 November 1996	Office equipment	1 500
31 May 1997	Machinery	3 000
6 June 1997	New lorry	12 750

On 31 October 1996, he sold the second hand plant for £6000, and on 6 June 1997 he sold the old lorry for £5750.

		Pool (£)	Allowances (£)
1/1/95–30/6/96			
Additions:			
Plant (1/1/95)		5 000	
Lorry (1/5/95)		7 000	
		12 000	
WDA 25% × 18/12		(4 500)	4 500
	C/fwd	7 500	
1/7/96–30/6/97			
Additions:			
Plant (31/7/96)		10 000	
Office equipment (10/11/96)		1 500	
Machinery (31/5/97)		3 000	
Lorry (6/6/97)		12 750	
		34 750	
Disposals:			
Plant			
(restricted original cost)		(5 000)	
Lorry		(5 750)	
		24 000	
WDA 25%		(6 000)	6 000
	C/fwd	18 000	
1/7/97–30/6/98			
WDA 25%		(4 500)	4 500
	C/fwd	13 500	

	Profits	less	CA	=	Net Schedule D Case I
1/1/95–30/6/96					
	£49 500	–	£4 500	=	£45 000
1/7/96–30/6/97					
	£40 000		£6 000	=	£34 000
1/7/97–30/6/98					
	£42 000		£4 500	=	£37 500

	Assessments (£)
1994/95	
1/1/95–5/4/95	
3/18 × £45 000	7 500
1995/96	
12/18 × £45 000	30 000

1996/97
12/18 × £45 000   30 000

1997/98
YE 30/6/97   34 000

1998/99
YE 30/6/98   37 500

Note: overlap profits to be deducted in year of cessation 9/18 × £45 000 = £22 500.
FYAs were not available until 2/7/97.

EXAMPLE

George has been in business for many years, and prepares accounts to 31 December each year. At 1 January 2001 he had the following capital allowance balances brought forward:

	£
Pool plant and machinery	16 000
Motor car (60% business use)	11 000

On 30 September 2001 George bought a new machine for £10 000.

YE 31/12/01		Pool (£)	Car (£)	Allowance (£)
b/f		16 000	11 000	–
WDA 25%		(4 000)		4 000
WDA 25%			(2 750) × 60%	1 650
Addition qualifying FYA:				
30/9/01	10 000			
FYA (40%)	(4 000)	6 000		4 000
c/f		18 000	8 250	
Total allowances				9 650

Balancing adjustments

A balancing charge is a negative allowance and is added to the trading profit for tax purposes. A balancing charge will occur where the disposal proceeds are greater than the balance of qualifying expenditure in the pool.

A balancing allowance on the other hand occurs where the disposal proceeds are less than the balance of qualifying expenditure and the item(s) in the pool are disposed of. For the main pool of expenditure this will only generally occur on a cessation when all the items are disposed of, but for items kept in separate pools, then a balancing adjustment can occur at any time.

Separate pools

Separate pools of expenditure must be maintained for the following assets:

1. Assets with any private use

Where an asset is used partly for private purposes the capital allowance available is restricted to the business use.

EXAMPLE

Alfred has been in business for many years, preparing accounts to the 31 December each year. On 1 June 1997, he bought a machine costing £6000 that was to be used 75 per cent for business use and 25 per cent for private use. The balance of expenditure on the main pool brought forward at 1 January 1997 was £6200. There were no other additions or disposals during the year.

Because of the private use, the asset cannot be added to the main pool of expenditure, it must be kept in a separate pool, and the allowance restricted to the business use:

YE 31/12/97	Pool (£)	Asset with private use (£)	Allowances (£)
b/f	6200	–	
Addition		6000	
	6200	6000	
WDA 25%	(1550)		1550
WDA 25%		(1500) × 75%	1125
C/fwd	4650	4500	2675

Suppose that during YE 31/12/98 Alfred sold the machine for:

(a) £5500
(b) £3500

The asset in the separate pool is disposed of giving rise to a balancing adjustment:

(a) YE 31/12/98	Asset with private use (£)	Allowances (£)
b/f	4500	
Disposal	(5500)	
	(1000)	
Balancing charge	1000	
BC 75% × £1000 =	£750	

(b) YE 31/12/98	Asset with private use (£)	Allowances (£)
b/f	4500	
Disposal	(3500)	
	1000	
Balancing allowance	(1000) × 75%	750

2. Motor cars

(a) Cars costing over £12000

Cars costing over £12000 are regarded as expensive cars and each car in this category must be kept in a separate pool, as the WDA is restricted to a maximum of £3000 per year (i.e. 25% × £12 000).

NB : From 17th April 2002 this restriction does not apply to new low emission cars.

(b) Company cars costing less than £12000 each

Prior to April 2000 cars provided for employees were pooled in what was known as the FA 1980 car pool, provided they were not expensive cars. No restriction of allowances is made on the employer, even if the employee has private use. Private use of the car by the employee may be taxable as a benefit in kind under Schedule E, if the employee is higher paid (see Chapter 13). The FA 2000 abolished the FA1980 car pool for chargeable periods including 1 April 2000 for corporation tax, or 6 April 2000 for income tax, any brought forward balance being added to the general pool of expenditure, with the option to delay for one year, i.e. until the start of the chargeable period that includes 1 April 2001 for corporation tax, or 6 April 2001 for income tax.

(c) Cars with private use

Cars with private use must be kept in a separate pool, even if they are not expensive cars, as with any other asset used partly for private purposes.

3. Short life assets CAA 2001, ss 83–89

Assets with a short life, defined as four years from the end of the period in which the expense was incurred, may be pooled separately provided an election is made within two years after the period in which the expense was incurred.

The rules do not apply to the following assets:

- ships
- motor cars
- assets leased to non-traders
- assets not used wholly for business purposes.

The effect of the de-pooling election is that if the asset is disposed of within the four years a balancing adjustment arises.

EXAMPLE

Sally has traded for many years preparing accounts to 30 June each year. On 31 May 1997 she purchased a computer for £9000 and elected for de-pooling. Suppose the computer was sold during YE 30/6/00:

(a) For £2000
(b) For £4500

	SLA (£)	Allowances (£)
YE 30/6/97		
Computer	9000	
WDA 25%	(2250)	2250
C/fwd	6750	
YE 30/6/98		
WDA 25%	(1688)	1688
C/fwd	5062	

YE 30/6/99

WDA 25%	(1266)	1266
C/fwd	3796	

(a) YE 30/6/00

Disposal	(2000)	
	1796	
Balancing allowance	(1796)	1796
	nil	

(b) YE 30/6/00

b/f	3796	
Disposal	(4500)	
	(704)	
Balancing charge	704	

If the asset is not disposed of within four years after the end of the year in which it was acquired, then the tax written down value is transferred to the general pool.

In the last example, suppose the computer was not disposed of until after 30 June 2001, then the tax written down value at 30 June 2001 (4 years after year of acquisition) is transferred to the general pool:

	SLA	Allowances
YE 30/6/00	(£)	(£)
b/f	3796	
WDA 25%	(949)	949
C/fwd	2847	
YE 30/6/01		
WDA 25%	(712)	712
	2135	
Transferred to general pool	(2135)	
	nil	

COMPREHENSIVE EXAMPLE

Oliver has been in business for many years preparing accounts to 31 December each year. The balances brought forward from 2000/01 were as follows:

	£
General pool of plant	18 750
Car (25% private use)	11 000
(sold 6 August 2001)	

During the year ended 31 December 2001 Oliver made the following purchases:

	£
20 March car for employee	8 000
10 April plant	12 000
16 June office equipment	5 000
20 June computer	10 000
25 June Oliver replaced his car with new car	16 000
27 June plant	3 000

He also made the following disposals:

	£
6 August car	9 000
12 October plant (original cost £8000)	6 000
11 November plant (original cost £2500)	3 000

Oliver elects for de-pooling of the computer. Calculate the maximum capital allowances available for 2001/02.

	Main pool £	Car (1) £	Car (2) £	SLA pool £	Allowances £
2001/02					
YE 31/12/01					
b/f	18 750	11 000			
Additions:					
20/3/01	8000				
25/6/01			16 000		
Disposals:					
6/8/01		(9 000)			
		2 000			
Balancing allowance		(2 000) × 75%			1 500
12/10/01	(6 000)				
11/11/01	(2 500)				
	18 250	nil	16 000	nil	
WDA (25%)	(4 563)				4 563
WDA (restricted)					2 250
			(3 000) × 75%		
C/fwd	13 687	nil	13 000	nil	8313

b/f						£
		13 687	nil	13 000	nil	8313
FYA:	£					
Plant	12 000					
Equip.	5 000					
Plant	3 000					
	20 000					
FYA	(8 000)	12 000				8 000
SLA	10 000					
FYA	(4 000)				6 000	4 000
c/fwd		25 687	nil	13 000	6 000	20 313

Industrial buildings

An industrial building is defined by CAA 2001 as any building or structure used for the following qualifying purposes:

1. Mills, factories or other buildings used for the manufacture or processing of goods, i.e. the building must be used for manufacturing purposes.
2. Drawing offices connected with manufacturing industries.
3. Canteens provided for the employees of manufacturing industries.
4. Storage of goods or materials provided they are:

    (a) used in the manufacture of other goods or materials; or

    (b) subject to any process; or

    (c) manufactured goods or processed goods not yet sold; or

    (d) import warehouses.

    Note: Wholesale or retail warehouses will not qualify, the building being used for storage must be connected with the manufacturing of those goods.

5. Toll roads.
6. Buildings provided for staff welfare in manufacturing industries.
7. Sports pavillions used by the employees of any trade.

Note: The restriction to manufacturing trades does not apply to sports pavillions.

Specifically excluded are:

(a) dwelling houses

(b) retail shops

(c) showrooms

(d) offices.

Qualifying expenditure

The capital expenditure qualifying for an industrial buildings allowance (IBA) is the cost of construction of the building, including architects' fees, plus the cost of preparing the land, e.g. levelling, cutting, foundations, but *not* the cost of the land itself or any legal fees incurred in connection with the acquisition.

Where the building includes a non-industrial part, e.g. offices, then provided that the excluded part is 25 per cent or less of the total cost (excluding the cost of the land), no restriction will be made; however, if the non-industrial part is greater than 25 per cent, the non-industrial part will not qualify for allowances.

EXAMPLE

David incurred the following expenditure in the construction of a factory:

	£
Cost of land	35 000
Legal fees	5 000
Architect's fees	10 000
Preparing land	30 000
Construction of factory	110 000
Construction of offices	55 000
Construction of canteen	45 000

Qualifying expenditure:	£
Architect's fees	10 000
Preparing land	30 000
Cost of construction	210 000
	250 000

As the building is an industrial building to be used for manufacturing purposes, the canteen will be allowable. The offices will be allowable provided the cost does not exceed 25% of the total cost:

$\dfrac{55\,000}{250\,000}$ = 22%, therefore the qualifying expenditure is £250 000.

If the offices had represented more than 25% of the total cost, then the qualifying expenditure would be £250 000 – £55 000, i.e. £195 000.

The allowances available

There is no pooling of industrial buildings; allowances for each building are calculated separately.

Writing down allowance

An industrial building is assumed to have a tax life of 25 years and so a writing down allowance (WDA) of 4 per cent is available on a straight line basis, provided that the building has been brought into use during the period. This contrasts with the WDA on plant and machinery where there is no requirement for the asset to be actually brought into use, provided it was purchased during the period of account, the WDA is available for plant and machinery.

First year allowance

Prior to March 1984, a 75 per cent first year allowance (FYA) was available on qualifying expenditure on an industrial building. This was phased out over the two-year period to 31 March 1986, and expenditure incurred after this date qualified only for a WDA.

Again, as an incentive to stimulate investment, a 20 per cent FYA was available for expenditure incurred on an industrial building between 1 November 1992 and 31 October 1993.

The FYA was available in the period that the expense was incurred and the WDA available if the building had been brought into use, so if the building was brought into use during the same period as the expenditure was incurred, both the FYA and the WDA were available in the same year, unlike plant and machinery where both allowances are not available in the same year.

Balancing adjustments

If the industrial building is sold during its tax life, then no WDA is available in the year of disposal, and there will be a balancing adjustment on the vendor. The balancing adjustment is calculated by comparing the sale proceeds with the tax written down value (WDV):

(a) Proceeds > WDV

A balancing charge will arise where the sale proceeds are greater than WDV. However, the balancing charge cannot be greater than the allowances previously given.

(b) Proceeds < WDV

Where the sale proceeds are less than the WDV, the vendor will be entitled to a balancing allowance.

Allowances available to purchaser

The allowances available to the purchaser of a second-hand industrial building during its tax life are based on the building's remaining tax life and not 4 per cent of the cost, calculated as follows:

$$\frac{\text{WDV} + \text{BC} (- \text{BA})/\text{Purchase price (whichever is lower)}}{\text{Remaining tax life}}$$

EXAMPLE

Livingstone Ltd prepares accounts to 31 December each year. On 6 June 1996 Livingstone bought a new factory with a qualifying cost of £200 000, bringing it into immediate use. On 6 June 2001 he sold the factory to Stanley Ltd for:

(a) 250 000
(b) 150 000

Livingstone would have received the following allowances:

	Factory (£)	Allowances (£)
YE 31/12/96		
Cost	200 000	
WDA (4%)	8 000	8 000
C/fwd	192 000	
YE 31/12/97		
WDA (4%)	(8 000)	8 000
C/fwd	184 000	

YE 31/12/98

WDA (4%)	(8 000)	8 000
C/fwd	176 000	

YE 31/12/99

WDA (4%)	(8 000)	8 000
C/fwd	168 000	

YE 31/12/00

WDA (4%)	(8 000)	8 000
C/fwd	160 000	

YE 31/12/01

Building sold during this period
no WDA available. WDV   160 000

Total allowances given to date   40 000

(a) If the building is sold for £250 000 then a balancing charge will arise:

Proceeds > WDV = BC
£250 000 – £160 000 = £90 000

However, the balancing charge is restricted to the allowances previously given, i.e. £40 000 is clawed back as a balancing charge.

The allowances available to Stanley Ltd are calculated as:

$$\frac{WDV + BC}{\text{remaining life}}$$

Remaining tax life = 25 years less 5 years = 20 years

$$\frac{£160\,000 + £40\,000}{20} = £10\,000 \text{ pa for 20 years}$$

(b) If the building was sold for £150 000 then a balancing allowance would arise:

Proceeds < WDV = BA

£150 000 – £160 000 = £10 000 BA

In this case the allowances available to Stanley Ltd are calculated as:

$$\frac{WDV - BA}{\text{remaining life}}$$

$$\frac{£160\,000 - £10\,000}{20} = £7500 \text{ pa for 20 years}$$

Non-industrial use

If the building is not in industrial use at the end of a period of account, the balance of expenditure is reduced by a notional WDA, but no allowance is available to the taxpayer.

If such a building is sold during its tax life, the balancing adjustment is calculated by first comparing the sale proceeds with the original cost:

(a) Proceeds > original cost

Where the sale proceeds are greater than the original cost then a balancing charge arises, restricted to the allowances previously given.

(b) Proceeds < original cost

If the sale proceeds are less than the original cost then the capital allowances given must be compared with the adjusted net cost of the building, i.e. the cost adjusted for industrial use:

$$\text{Adjusted net cost} = (\text{original cost} - \text{sale proceeds}) \times \frac{\text{Period of industrial use}}{\text{Total period of use}}$$

CA > adjusted net cost = BC
CA < adjusted net cost = BA

The allowances available to the purchaser are calculated in the normal way, i.e.:

$$\frac{\text{Tax WDV} + \text{BC} (- \text{BA})}{\text{remaining life}}$$

EXAMPLE

West Ltd prepares accounts to 31 December each year. On 1 June 1995 a qualifying building was purchased at a cost of £250 000 and brought into immediate use. The building was used for industrial purposes until 31 May 1997. From 1 June 1997 until 31 May 1999 it was used for non-industrial purposes. From 1 June 1999 it was used for industrial purposes again until it was sold on 31 May 2001 for:

(a) £300 000
(b) £175 000
(c) £220 000

Capital allowances given to date:

YE 31/12/95	£	£
Cost	250 000	
WDA (4%)	(10 000)	10 000
C/fwd	240 000	
YE 31/12/96		
WDA (4%)	(10 000)	10 000
C/fwd	230 000	

YE 31/12/97

Notional WDA (4%)	(10 000)	
C/fwd	220 000	

YE 31/12/98

Notional WDA (4%)	(10 000)	
	210 000	

YE 31/12/99

WDA (4%)	(10 000)	10 000
C/fwd	200 000	

YE 31/12/00

WDA (4%)	(10 000)	10 000
C/fwd	190 000	

YE 31/12/01

Building sold 31/5/01	Allowances given	40 000

Remaining tax life = 25 years – 6 years = 19 years

(a) Proceeds greater than original cost, therefore there is a balancing charge restricted to the allowances previously given, i.e. £40 000

Allowances available to purchase:

$$\frac{WDV + BC}{\text{remaining life}} = \frac{£(190\,000 + 40\,000)}{19}$$

$$= £12\,105 \text{ pa}$$

(b) Proceeds less than original cost, therefore the adjusted net cost must be compared with the allowances previously given:

Adjusted net cost $= (250\,000 - 175\,000) \times \frac{4}{6} = £50\,000$

CA = £40 000, i.e. less than adjusted net cost of £50 000, therefore there is a balancing allowance of £10 000

Allowances available to purchaser:

£190 000 – £10 000 = £180 000 restricted to purchase price

$$\frac{£175\,000}{19} = £9\,210 \text{ pa}$$

(c) Again, the proceeds are less than the original cost and so the capital allowances given must be compared with the adjusted net cost:

$(250\,000 - 220\,000) \times 4/6 = £20\,000$

CA given = £40 000, i.e. more than the adjusted net cost, therefore there is a balancing charge of £20 000

Allowances available to purchaser:

$$\frac{£(190\,000 + 20\,000)}{19} = £11\,053 \text{ pa}$$

Leased property

If the property is leased, it is usually the lessor, i.e. the person with the relevant interest in the property, who claims the allowances.

However, where a long lease is granted, i.e. one for 50 years or more, then the lessor and the lessee can make a joint claim to have the grant of a long lease treated as if it were a transfer of interest, for proceeds equivalent to the premium paid, so that the lessee can then obtain the relevant allowances.

EXAMPLE

Barton Ltd is a property investment company preparing its accounts to 31 December each year. On 1 July 1991 Barton Ltd purchased a building for £150 000 which was let out on a short lease from 1 July 1991 until 30 June 1996 for manufacturing purposes. From 1 July 1996 until 30 September 2000 the building was let on another short lease for non-industrial use. On 1 October 2000 Barton Ltd let the property on a 60-year lease to Grange Ltd, for industrial use, for a premium of £80 000. Both Barton Ltd and Grange Ltd made an election. Grange Ltd prepares accounts to 31 March each year.

First of all calculate the allowances to Barton Ltd:

	£	£
YE 31/12/91		
Cost	150 000	
WDA (4%)	(6 000)	6 000
YE 31/12/92	144 000	
WDA (4%)	(6 000)	6 000
YE 31/12/93	138 000	
WDA (4%)	(6 000)	6 000
YE 31/12/94	132 000	
WDA (4%)	(6 000)	6 000
YE 31/12/95	126 000	
WDA (4%)	(6 000)	6 000
YE 31/12/96	120 000	
Notional WDA (4%)	(6 000)	–
YE 31/12/97	114 000	
Notional WDA (4%)	(6 000)	
YE 31/12/98	108 000	
Notional WDA (4%)	(6 000)	
YE 31/12/99	102 000	
Notional WDA (4%)	(6 000)	
	96 000	

Building let to Grange Ltd	£
1/10/00	
an election is made	
Allowances given	30 000

The building has had periods of non-industrial use, so any balancing adjustment is calculated by comparing the capital allowances given and the net adjusted cost of the building:

Total use: 1/7/91 until 30/9/00 = 9 years 3 months
Industrial use: 1/7/91 until 30/6/98 = 5 years

$$\text{Adjusted net cost} = (£150\,000 - £80\,000) \times 5/9.25$$
$$= £37\,838$$

The CA given were £30 000, so there is a balancing allowance of £7838 available to Barton Ltd.

To calculate the allowances available to Grange Ltd, first of all establish the remaining life of the building: 25 years less 9 years 3 months, i.e. 15 years and 9 months, divided into the lower of:

- (WDV – BA) = £96 000 – 7838 = £88 162

or

- deemed proceeds = £80 000

From YE 31/3/01 to 31/3/2015 inclusive, i.e. 15 years, Grange Ltd will be entitled to WDA of:

$$\frac{£80\,000}{15.75} = £5080 \text{ per year and a balance of £3800 will be given in the YE 31/3/2016.}$$

Hotels

Qualifying hotels can claim capital allowances similar to IBA, i.e. 4 per cent WDA. A qualifying hotel is one which:

- has accommodation in buildings of a permanent nature;
- is open for at least four months in the season (from April to October);
- has at least ten letting bedrooms;
- provides a service for guests, including breakfast, evening meals, cleaning of rooms, etc.

Dwelling houses let on assured tenancies

An allowance similar to IBA, i.e. 4 per cent WDA, is available to approved bodies under the assured tenancy scheme under s 56 of the Housing Act 1980. The provisions were an attempt to encourage private investment in properties for rent under assured tenancies. The 4 per cent WDA is available against the letting income of all types of dwellings under the scheme on expenditure incurred between 10 March 1982 and 1 April 1992.

Buildings in an enterprise zone

Industrial and commercial buildings and qualifying hotels are eligible for 100 per cent allowances on expenditure incurred within ten years of the area becoming a designated enterprise zone. If the taxpayer does not wish to claim the full 100 per cent in the year of the expenditure, a maximum of 25 per cent, on a straight line basis, may be claimed. The sale of a building during its first 25 years will give rise to balancing adjustments in the same way as for industrial buildings.

Fixtures and fittings

Where the building includes fixtures and fittings the vendor and purchaser can make a joint election as to the amount attributable to fixtures and fittings on expenditure incurred after 24 July 1996.

Agricultural buildings allowance

Agricultural buildings allowances (ABAs) are available to persons having a major interest in the agricultural land, e.g. owner or tenant farmers. At the time the expenditure is incurred the agricultural land must be used for the intensive farming of animals or fish, or for the production of food for human consumption, carried out on a commercial basis.

The allowances do not apply to any expenditure that is incurred on the acquisition of the land, or rights over the land, but to the cost of construction of the following:

- farmhouses (maximum $\frac{1}{3}$);
- farm buildings;
- farm cottages;
- fences and other works;
- drainage, sewerage, water and electricity installations; and
- greenhouses (market gardeners).

The current system of ABAs which came into effect for expenditure after 1 April 1986, is similar to the allowances available on industrial buildings:

- 4 per cent WDA on a straight line basis;
- for expenditure incurred between 1 November 1992 and 31 October 1993, a FYA of 20 per cent was available in the same way as an industrial building.

Balancing adjustments however, are not treated in exactly the same way as industrial buildings. When a building is sold during its tax life, the balance of allowances automatically passes to the purchaser. The vendor will be entitled to a pro-rata WDA in the year of disposal, and correspondingly the purchaser can claim a pro-rata WDA in the year of acquisition.

EXAMPLE

James commenced in business as a market gardener on 1 July 1997 and prepares accounts to 30 June each year. On 1 July 1997 he purchased a new greenhouse for £30 000 on which he claimed ABAs.

On 1 May 1999 he sold the greenhouse to Dora for £20 000. Dora is also a market gardener and prepares accounts to 31 December each year.

		Allowances
YE 30/6/98	(£)	(£)
(1/7/97 – 30/6/98)		
Cost	30 000	
WDA (4%)	(1 200)	1 200
C/fwd	28 800	

YE 30/6/99		
(1/7/98 – 30/6/99)		
James disposes of the greenhouse		
so the ABA is split pro-rata between		
James and Dora. James owned it		
until 30/4/97, i.e. 10 months.		
WDA 4% × 10/12	(1 000)	1 000
Balance transferred to Dora	27 800	
Allowances given		2 200

As Dora produces accounts to 31 December each year, the acquisition on 1/5/99 falls into the accounting period ending 31/12/99 which form the basis of assessment for 1999/00:

		Allowances
YE 31/12/99	(£)	(£)
Balance of cost transferred	27 800	
WDA 4% × 8/12		
(ABA split pro-rata)	(800)	800
	27 000	
For the next 22 years she will		
receive WDA of 4% on cost		
each year, i.e. 22 years × £1200	(26 400)	26 400
C/fwd	600	
YE 31/12/2022		
WDA	(600)	
		600
	nil	27 800

If both the vendor and the purchaser make a joint election, rules can be avoided, and balancing adjustments will accrue to the vendor in the same way as they do for industrial buildings.

If in the last example, James and Dora make a joint election, there will be a balancing adjustment on James as follows:

The balancing adjustment is calculated by comparing the sale proceeds with the tax written down value.

1999/00	£	£
C/fwd WDV	28 800	
Sale proceeds	(20 000)	
Balancing allowance	8 800	8 800

Allowances available to Dora:

$$\frac{WDV - BA}{\text{remaining life}} =$$

$$\frac{£28\,800 - 8800}{23\text{ years 2 months}} = £863 \text{ pa for 23 years}$$

$$£151 \text{ in final year}$$

Patent rights and know-how

For expenditure on or after 1 April 1986, patent rights and know-how qualify for a WDA of 25 per cent on a reducing balance in the same way as plant and machinery.

Balancing adjustments may arise on the disposal of patent rights. The disposal proceeds are restricted to original cost in the capital allowance computation as is the case for plant and machinery.

Where there is a gain on disposal, i.e. sale proceeds are greater than the original cost, the excess is chargeable to income tax under Schedule D Case VI.

EXAMPLE

Brindle Ltd prepares accounts to 31 December each year and has acquired the following patent rights:

Patent	Date acquired	Period	Cost (£)
X	1/7/96	15 years	12 000
Y	1/9/97	8 years	15 000
Z	1/5/98	3 years	25 000

On October 1 1998 the patent rights of X were sold for £8000 and the patent rights of Y are sold for £21 000 on 1 September 2000. The expenditure on patent rights is pooled in the same way as the general pool on plant and machinery.

	Pool (£)	Allowances (£)
YE 31/12/96		
Cost (X)	12 000	
WDA 25%	(3 000)	3000
	9 000	
YE 31/12/97		
Addition (Y)	15 000	
	24 000	
WDA 25%	(6 000)	6000
	18 000	
YE 31/12/98		
Addition (Z)	25 000	
Disposal (X)	(8 000)	
	35 000	
WDA 25%	(8 750)	8750
	26 250	
YE 31/12/99		
WDA 25%	(6 563)	6563
	19 687	
YE 31/12/00		
Disposal (Y)		
(restricted to cost)	(15 000)	
	4 687	
WDA 25%	(1 172)	1172
	3 515	
YE 31/12/01		
Patent Z lapse		
Balance allowance	(3 515)	3515
	nil	

The lapse of the last patent gives rise to a balancing allowance. The gain on patent Y of £6000 is assessable under Schedule D Case VI in six annual instalments of £1000 commencing 2000, i.e. the period in which the sale occurred.

Know-how is treated in exactly the same way as patent rights except that disposal proceeds are not restricted to original cost but deducted in full.

Scientific research

Capital expenditure on scientific research for the purpose of trading is eligible for 100 per cent capital allowances in the year the expense is incurred, e.g. laboratories, computer rooms, plant and machinery, prototypes, etc., but excludes the cost of land and dwelling houses. However, if a dwelling house forms part of a larger building used for research and the cost is less than 25 per cent of the whole building, it may be ignored for this purpose. This is a similar rule to non-qualifying expenditure as regards industrial buildings.

Note: Payments made to universities, colleges and research institutes for any research related to the taxpayer's trade are allowable deductions from trading profits.

Mineral extraction

Where the taxpayer is in the trade of mineral extraction, e.g. mines, oil wells, capital allowances are available on expenditure incurred on or after 1 April 1986 on the following:

- mineral exploration and access;
- acquisition of a mineral asset;
- construction of works that will have little or no value after the extraction;
- construction of works in connection with a foreign concession that will have no value to the trader when the commission ends; and
- provision of buildings and common services for employees where the mineral extraction is overseas.

The WDA of 25 per cent is available except that the following items only attract a WDA of 10 per cent:

- expenditure on the acquisition of a mineral asset; and
- pre-trading expenditure.

If the assets are disposed of, balancing adjustments will arise. If the expenditure includes the acquisition of an interest in land, then any undeveloped market value of the land is not included in the qualifying expenditure.

Note: There may be an overlap with IBAs and capital allowances on plant and machinery or scientific research, in which case a claim for mineral extraction allowances prohibits other allowances.

Dredging

For expenditure incurred on or after 1 April 1986 on dredging for trades engaged in maintaining or improving the navigation of a harbour, estuary or waterway, a WDA of 4 per cent on a straight line basis is available.

Information and communication technology

In order to encourage increased use of information and communication technology, the Chancellor announced in the Budget 2000 that a 100 per cent FYA will be available to small businesses investing in computer technology, i.e. hardware and software, and Internet-enabled mobile telephones in the three years ended 31 March 2003. For this purpose, a business is small if it satisfies two of the following criteria:

1. turnover not more than £2.8 million;
2. assets not more than £1.4 million;
3. maximum of 50 employees.

Additional 100 per cent FYA

The FA 2001 introduced 100% FYAs for the following expenditure:

- Energy saving plant and machinery defined in the Energy Technology List. This allowance was extended to assets for leasing in the Budget 2002.
- Renovation or conversion of space above commercial premises in order to provide flats for rent.

SELF ASSESSMENT QUESTIONS

11.1 Gordon commenced in business on 1 January 1997 and prepared his first set of accounts for the 18-month period to 30 June 1998 and thereafter to 30 June each year. Between 1 January 1997 and 30 June 2000 he incurred the following expenditure:

		£
1 January 1997	second hand plant	7 000
1 January 1997	car for Gordon's use	10 000
12 June 1997	lorry	10 000
1 September 1998	new plant	8 000
10 November 1998	office equipment	4 000
15 May 1999	machinery	12 000
20 May 1999	new car for Gordon	15 000
30 September 1999	new lorry	20 000

During the same periods he disposed of the following items:

	£
31 October 1998 sold the second hand plant	8 000
20 May 1999 sold the car acquired 1/1/97	5 000
30 September 1999 sold the lorry acquired 12/6/97	6 599

Gordon uses his car 60% for business purposes.

REQUIRED:

Calculate the maximum capital allowances available to Gordon for each of the periods ending 30/6/98, 30/6/99 and 30/6/2000.

11.2 Browning Ltd, a manufacturing company, prepares accounts to 31 December each year, and incurred the following expenditure constructing a new factory:

	£
	£
Cost of land	20 000
Legal fees	7 000
Architect's fees	8 000
Preparing land	10 000
Construction of factory	120 000
Construction of offices	50 000
Construction of canteen	60 000

Browning Ltd brought the building into use on 1 September 1996. On 1 September 2001 Browning Ltd sold the factory to Keats Ltd for £300,000. Keats Ltd is also a manufacturing company and prepares accounts to 31 March each year.

REQUIRED:

(a) Calculate the maximum IBAs that Browning Ltd was entitled to during the period of ownership.
(b) Calculate the balancing adjustment on Browning Ltd when the building is sold.
(c) Calculate the allowances available to Keats Ltd.

CHAPTER 12

Relief for trading losses

If, overall, a business incurs a trading loss, i.e. the adjusted profit calculation produces a negative amount, the Schedule D Case I assessment for that period will be nil, with tax relief available for the trading loss. This chapter examines the various ways in which unincorporated businesses may obtain tax relief for trading losses.

Carry forward the loss to a subsequent accounting period
(ICTA 1988, s 385)

A trading loss may be carried forward against profits of the same trade without time limit – *Gordon & Blair Ltd* v *IRC* (1962) 40 TC 358.

The loss must be deducted from the first available profit before the deduction of personal allowances.

EXAMPLE

Mr Apple has been trading as a greengrocer since 1 July 1998 with the following results:

	£
YE 30/6/98 loss	(8000)
YE 30/6/99 profit	4000
YE 30/6/00 profit	8000

Mr Apple has no other income and in the three years prior to commencing in business he did not pay income tax. Relief is claimed under the ICTA 1988, s 385.

	Schedule D Case I assessment (£)		Loss memo (£)
1998/99			
1/7/98 – 5/4/99		YE 30/6/99	(8000)
9/12 × £(8000)	nil		
1999/00			
YE 30/6/99			
£(8000)	nil		

	Schedule D Case I assessment (£)		Loss memo (£)
2000/01			
YE 30/6/00	4000		
s 385	(4000)		4000
	nil	C/fwd	(4000)
2001/02			
YE 30/6/01	8000		
s 385	(4000)		4000
	4000		

The claim for relief under s 385 must be made within five years from 31 January in the tax year following the year of the loss, i.e. loss incurred YE 31/12/98 is in the 1998/99 tax year and so relief must be claimed within five years from 31 January 2000.

The disadvantages of using s 385 are:

- relief is not immediate and the loss may not be relieved for several years;
- personal allowances may be wasted; and
- the relief is only against future trading income and not against general income.

Set off against general income (ICTA 1988, s 380)

The loss can be relieved against the taxpayer's statutory total income in the year that the loss was made and the previous tax year. The legislation gives no priority of set off except that relief for losses in a current year take priority over a loss carried back. A claim for relief under the ICTA 1988, s 380 must be made by 31 January, within 22 months after the end of the tax year in which the loss was incurred, i.e. if a loss is incurred during 2002/03 a claim for relief under the ICTA 1988, s 380 must be made by 31 January 2005.

Partial claims are not allowed and the loss must be set off in full against statutory total income, even if personal allowances are wasted. The main advantage of s 380 over s 385 is that relief is given at once and is not dependent on profit. Relief under s 380 however, is only available provided that the business is conducted on a commercial basis with a view to profit: ICTA 1988, s 384. There is also a restriction on farming and market gardening businesses in that if there have been losses in each of the five years prior to the current year loss, relief under s 380 is denied unless it can be shown that there is a reasonable expectation of profits in the near future. The restriction of relief under the ICTA 1988, s 384, however, does not prevent the loss being carried forward under the ICTA 1988, s 385.

The taxpayer may include a further claim under the FA 1991, s 72 to have any unrelieved loss set off against net capital gains for that year *before* deducting taper relief and the annual exemption. Any loss still unrelieved under these provisions may be carried forward under ICTA 1988, s 385.

EXAMPLE

Mr Allen, a single man, prepares accounts for calendar years. For the years ending 1998 and 1999 the business showed the following Schedule D Case I profit/loss:

	£
YE 31/12/98 Profit	12000
YE 31/12/99 Loss	(15000)

Mr Allen has investment income of £6000 for each of the two years, and claims relief under ICTA 1988, s 380. As the legislation gives no priority of set off, Mr Allen can claim relief for 1998/99 and then 1999/00 or vice versa. However, if 1998/99 had also produced a loss, then the loss of a current year takes priority over a loss carried back. Mr Allen therefore has the following alternatives:

1. Claim for 1998/99 priority

	Assessment (£)		Loss memo (£)
1998/99		YE 31/12/99	(15000)
Schedule D Case I	12000		
Investment income	6000		
	18000		
s 380 (prior year claim)	(15000)		15000
	3000		
PA (restricted)	(3000)		
Taxable income	nil		
1999/00			
Schedule D Case I	nil		
Investment income	6000		
	6000		
PA	(4335)		
Taxable income	1665		

2. Claim for 1999/00 priority

	Assessment (£)		Loss memo (£)
1999/00		YE 31/12/99	(15000)
Schedule D Case I	nil		
Investment income	6000		
s 380	(6000)		6000
Taxable income	nil		(9000)

.

	Assessment (£)	Loss memo (£)
1998/99		(9000)
Schedule D Case I	12 000	
Investment income	6 000	
	18 000	9 000
s 380	(9 000)	
	9 000	
PA	(4 195)	
Taxable income	4 805	

It is therefore preferable for the s 380 claim to be given priority to 1998/99. If priority had been given to 1999/00, personal allowances would have been wasted.

Note: If a loss had been incurred in 1998/99, it would take priority over a loss carried back.

Losses in the early years

When a business first commences, accounts may have to be aggregated in order to arrive at the Schedule D Case I assessment, for example a business commenced 1 May 1998 and produced accounts as follows:

		£
Five months to 30 September 1998	Loss	(4 000)
YE 30 September 1999	Profit	15 000

1998/99	£	Assessment (£)
1/5/98 – 5/4/99:		
1/5/98 – 30/9/98	(4 000)	
1/10/98 – 5/4/99		
7/12 × £15 000	8 750	
		4750

Although there is no statutory provision which deals with this situation, a loss relieved in aggregation as above is deemed to have been relieved. Where there is an overlap in the early years, because the same loss is used in the assessment for two successive years, then loss relief is only available for the first year. For losses incurred in the early years and not relieved in aggregation, relief may be claimed under s 380 and s 385 as for established businesses.

There is, however, a further relief available for losses incurred in any of the first four fiscal years of a new business under the ICTA 1988, s 381, provided that a claim is made within 22 months after the end of the fiscal year in which the loss was made, i.e. if a loss is incurred during 1999/00, a claim for relief under ICTA 1988, s 381 must be made by 31 January 2002.

A claim under s 381 is only available to individuals; there is no similar relief for a company and this may be an important factor in considering the choice of business medium. Partial claims are not allowed under s 381; the loss must be set off in full against the individual's statutory total income even if personal allowances are wasted. If the loss is not fully relieved, claims may also be made under s 380 or s 385. In the same way as s 380, relief under s 381 is restricted unless the business is conducted on a commercial basis with a view to profit. Under s 381 the loss is carried back for three years and set off against the individual's statutory total income, taking the earliest year first.

EXAMPLE

Gerrard commenced business on 1 January 1998 and prepared accounts to 31 March each year with the following results:

		£
Three months to 31/3/98	Profit	2 700
YE 31/3/99	Loss	(24 000)
YE 31/3/2000	Profit	12 000

Gerrard is single and had the following income for 1995/96 and 1996/97:

	1995/96 (£)	1996/97 (£)
Schedule E	10 000	7 250
Investment income	2 000	2 000

He had no other income and claims relief for the loss under ICTA 1988, s 381.
   The assessments will be as follows:

	Assessment £
1997/98	
1/1/98 – 5/4/98	2 700
1998/99	
YE 31/3/99	nil
1999/00	
YE 31/3/2000	12 000

The loss can be carried back under s 381 as follows:

	1995/96 (£)	1996/97 (£)	1997/98 (£)	1998/99 (year of loss) (£)
Schedule E	10 000	7 250	nil	nil
Schedule D Case I	nil	nil	2 700	nil
Investment income	2 000	2 000	nil	nil
	12 000	9 250	2 700	nil
s 381	(12 000)	(9 250)	(2 700)	–
Taxable income	nil	nil	nil	nil

There will be repayment of tax for each of the three years and the balance of the loss can be carried forward under s 385:

	Loss memo	
	(£)	
YE 31/3/99	(24 000)	
s 381 1995/96	12 000	
	(12 000)	
s 381 1996/97	9 250	
	(2 750)	
s 381 1997/98	2 700	
	50	c/fwd s 385

Pre-trading expenditure ICTA 1988, s 401

Expenditure incurred within seven years before trading commences is allowed, provided that the expenditure would have been allowed had the trade commenced. For unincorporated businesses, pre-trading expenditure is treated as a trading loss in the first year of assessment and relief may be claimed under s 380, s 381 or s 385 of the ICTA 1988. Pre-trading expenditure is kept separate from any other trading loss and must be claimed separately.

Transfer of a business to a company (ICTA 1988, s 386)

The general rule is that relief is personal to the taxpayer and cannot be carried forward when the business is transferred: ICTA 1988, s 385. However, ICTA 1988, s 386 provides that where a sole trader or partnership is transferred to a company, any unrelieved losses of the unincorporated business can be set off against income received from the company by the former proprietor during any year in which the shares are owned and during which the company continues to trade. The relief is given primarily against earned income, i.e. remuneration, and then against unearned income, i.e. dividend income received from the company.

For s 386, ICTA 1998 to apply, the consideration for the transfer must be mainly or wholly shares in the newly formed company, and at least 80 per cent of the shares must still be held by the person during any tax year in which relief under s 386 is claimed.

Terminal loss relief (ICTA 1988, s 388)

A trading loss incurred in the final 12 months of trading can be carried back and set off against the available income of the three years prior to closure taking the latest year first. The available income is the net Schedule D Case I assessment and the final 12 months is made up as follows:

(a) period from 6 April to date of cessation; and

(b) trading results to make (a) up to 12 months.

If either (a) or (b) is a net profit, then the figure is ignored in calculating the terminal loss.

EXAMPLE

Business commenced 1 July 1996 with the following results:

		£
Six months to 31/12/96	profit	20 000
YE 31/12/97	profit	15 000
YE 31/12/98	profit	3 000
Nine months to cessation 30/9/99	loss	(18 000)

Step 1: Identify the fiscal year of cessation, i.e. 1999/00.

Step 2: Calculate the available income for the previous three years, i.e. 1996/97, 1997/98 and 1998/99:

		Assessment
	£	£
1996/97		
1/7/96 – 5/4/97:		
1/7/96 – 31/12/96	20 000	
1/1/97 – 5/4/97		
3/12 × £15 000	3 750	23 750
1997/98		
YE 31/12/97		15 000
1998/99		
YE 31/12/98		3 000
1999/00 (Year of cessation)		
1/1/98 – 30/9/99	(18 000)	
Overlap profits:		
(3/12 x £15 000)	(3 750)	
Loss in 1999/00	(21 750)	

Step 3: Calculate the terminal loss:

		£	£
(1)	Period 6/4/99 – 30/9/99:		
	6/9 × £(21 750)		(14 500)
(2)	Period 1/10/98 – 5/4/99:		
	1/10/98 – 31/12/98		
	3/12 × £3000	750	
	1/1/99 – 5/4/99		
	3/9 × £(21 750)	(7 250)	(6 500)
	Terminal loss		21 000

Step 4: Set off the terminal loss:

	1996/97	1997/98	1998/99
Net Schedule D Case I	23 750	15 000	3 000
s 388	(3 000)	(15 000)	(3 000)
Schedule D Case I	20 750	nil	nil

There will be a repayment of income tax for the three years prior to cessation.

Loss memo

£	
(21 000)	Terminal loss
3 000	s 388 1998/99
(18 000)	
15 000	s 388 1997/98
(3 000)	
3 000	s 388 1996/97

SELF ASSESSMENT QUESTIONS

12.1 Sammy Smart, a single man, has been in business for several years, preparing accounts to 30 June each year. Recent results show the following Schedule D Case I profit /(loss):

		£
YE 30/6/01	profit	15 000
YE 30/6/02	loss	(20 000)

Sammy has investment income of £7000 each year and wishes to claim loss relief under s 380, ICTA 1988.

REQUIRED

Show the most tax efficient claim for loss relief under s 380, ICTA 1988.

12.2 Emily commenced in business on 1 January 1999, preparing her first set of accounts for the 15-month period to 31 March 2000, and thereafter to 31 March each year, with the following results:

		£
15 months to 31/3/00	profit	5 000
YE 31/3/01	(loss)	(36 000)
YE 31/3/02	profit	18 000

Before commencing in business, Emily had worked as a secretary and had the following income for 1997/98 and 1998/99:

	1997/98	1998/99
	£	£
Schedule E	13 000	10 000

She also had £1200 of investment income each year.

REQUIRED

(a) Show the Schedule DI assessments for all the tax years from 1998/99 to 2001/02 inclusive, before any claim for loss relief is made.
(b) Show the effect of a claim for loss relief under s 381, ICTA 1988.
(c) Show how any loss unrelieved under s 381 can be used in the most tax efficient manner.

CHAPTER 13

Income from employment

Having considered the income tax liability from self-employment, we now turn our attention to income arising from employment, which is charged to tax under Schedule E, and generally collected under the pay as you earn (PAYE) system. There are three cases of Schedule E, which are applied according to the residency status of the person and whether the duties are performed in the UK or overseas. Cases II and III are concerned with overseas aspects and are considered in Chapter 18. Income arising from duties performed in the UK, by UK resident and ordinarily resident persons are charged to income tax under Schedule E Case I.

The charge to tax under Schedule E

Emoluments arising from employment, pensions and certain social security benefits, are all charged to income tax under Schedule E. We will examine each of these items in more detail:

1. Emoluments

Emoluments includes salaries, wages, bonuses, fees, commissions, and payments in kind.

To be taxable under Schedule E, the general rule is that the payment or benefit must be a reward for services, past, present or future. Salaries, wages, fees and commissions are obvious emoluments, but the following items require more clarification:

(a) Gifts, awards, prizes

Gifts will not be exempt if they are given as a reward in exchange for past, present or future services. Gifts, awards, bonuses etc. are more likely to be 'tax free' if they amount to a one-off payment – *Moore* v *Griffiths (HMIT)* (1972) 48 TC 475; *Ball (HMIT)* v *Johnson* (1971) 47 TC 155.

Long service awards
ESC A22 exempts long service awards provided that the following conditions are met:

(a) the award is no more than £20 for each year of service;

(b) the award is made to recognise at least 20 years service; and

(c) the person receiving the award has not had a similar award in the previous ten years.

Staff suggestion schemes

ESC A57 provides that awards for staff suggestion schemes are not taxable emoluments.

Prizes and non-cash awards

Some employers may offer prizes as incentives to their employees. Such items would normally form part of the employee's taxable emoluments as payments in kind. Where employers provide such incentives they can operate what is known as the taxed award scheme provided they make prior arrangements with the Revenue. Under the *taxed award scheme* the employer pays the tax due on the grossed up value of the award, so that the amount of the incentive is not reduced in the hands of the employee.

(b) Tips

Tips are treated as part of an employee's taxable income. Sometimes tips account for a substantial part of an employee's wages, and where the particular occupation normally involves tips the Revenue include estimated amounts to prevent them from escaping the charge to income tax.

(c) Restrictive covenants

Section 313(1) and (2) of the ICTA 1988 provides that payments made for entering into a restrictive covenant by persons who held, hold or are about to hold employment, are to be treated as emoluments for the purposes of Schedule E, and charged to tax in the year that the payment is made. Payments caught by this charge are treated as allowable business expenses.

(d) Golden hellos

Payments made as an inducement to take up employment are taxable if they represent an advance of salary – *Shilton* v *Wilmshurst (HMIT)* [1991] STC 88.

Where the amounts are treated as taxable, because they amount to a payment for future services, they are deemed to be received in the first year of employment.

(e) Golden handshakes (termination payments)

Income payments received on the termination of employment, and their tax treatment, are quite complex and summarised as follows:

1. Payments made to employees on the termination of employment are taxable under the normal rules of Schedule E, in the year in which they are received, where the payment amounts to a reward for services.

2. Section 148 of the ICTA 1988 specifically provides that income payments made to compensate persons for the loss of employment, whether they are paid voluntarily or not, are charged to income tax under Schedule E in the year that they are received, with the proviso that the first £30 000 of any such payment is exempt, any excess payment over the £30 000 being charged to tax in full as if it were the top slice of income.

Statutory redundancy payments while being exempt under the normal rules of Schedule E are potentially chargeable under s 148, as are payments made in lieu of notice that do not amount to a payment for services rendered, and as such will form part of the £30 000 exemption limit, i.e. such payments are deducted from the £30 000 exemption.

Note: Prior to the FA 1993, out placement counselling provided to redundant employees fell within the charge to tax under s 148 but is now exempt for expenditure incurred after 16 March 1993.

EXAMPLE

Charles was made redundant on 6 October 2002. He had been employed on a salary of £29 000 pa and received the following redundancy package:

	£
Statutory redundancy payment	3 500
Ex-gratia lump sum payment	25 000
Payment in lieu of notice	2 500

Charles had no other income or charges in 2002/03. Assuming that the payment in lieu of notice does not amount to remuneration for work done, the taxable termination payment is calculated as follows:

	£	£
Lump sum (s 148)		25 000
Payment in lieu (s 148)		2 500
		27 500
Exempt amount	30 000	
less Statutory redundancy	(3 500)	(26 500)
Taxable portion of termination package		1 000
		£
Salary (6/12)		14 500
Taxable termination package		1 000
Statutory total income 2002/03		15 500

If the payment in lieu was payment for services rendered, then it would be taxable under the normal Schedule E rules and not under s 148, therefore it would not be part of the package eligible for the £30 000 relief:

	£	£
Lump sum (s 148)		25 000
Exempt amount	30 000	
less Statutory redundancy	(3 500)	
	26 500	
restricted to		(25 000)
Taxable		nil

	£
Salary (6/12)	14 500
Payment in lieu	2 500
Statutory total income 2002/03	17 000

3. Section 188 of the ICTA 1988 specifically provides that the following termination payments are not taxable:

(a) payments made on the termination of employment due to the injury, disability or death of the employee;

(b) lump sums paid under personal pension plans, retirement annuities or approved superannuation schemes; and

(c) grants and annuities paid to retiring members of the armed forces.

Prior to 6 April 1996, continuing benefits provided on the termination of employment were taxed in the year the employment terminated. Following consultations, as a temporary measure, for redundancies between 6 April 1996 and 5 April 1998 the ex-employee could elect for the benefits to be taxed when they were actually received. To ensure a fairer tax treatment for continuing benefits, the FA 1998 introduced legislation to provide that where termination packages provide for benefits to continue after termination, they will now only be taxed in the year they are received.

(f) Benefits in kind

Payments in kind may form part of the employee's taxable income and are examined in detail under 'benefits in kind' below.

2. Pensions

State pensions, personal pensions and any pension or annuity derived from employment are charged to income tax under Schedule E.

3. Social security benefits

The following social security benefits form part of an individual's taxable income for Schedule E purposes:

- jobseeker's allowance;
- income support (on means tested basis);
- statutory sick pay;
- statutory maternity pay;
- invalid care allowance;
- widow's pension;
- invalidity allowance paid with retirement pension;
- incapacity benefit (over 28 weeks); and
- industrial death benefit.

From April 2000, employers will be responsible for paying WFTC and DPTC through the PAYE system.

Basis of assessment

Following the FA 1989, assessment under Schedule E is on a receipts basis, i.e. on emoluments received during the fiscal year.

The receipt of emoluments is taken to be the earlier of the following events:

- the payment/payment on account; or
- the entitlement to payment/payment on account.

In the case of directors, the receipt of the emoluments is taken to be the earlier of the following events:

- when the amounts are credited to the director in the company accounts;
- the end of the accounting period to which they relate if the amounts have been determined; or
- when the amount is determined if this is after the end of the accounting period to which they relate.

Expenses

The legislation provides that the following types of expenditure are allowed as a deduction from the employee's gross emoluments for Schedule E purposes:

1. Professional subscriptions (ICTA 1988, s 201)

Subscriptions to Revenue approved professional bodies are allowed as a deduction provided that they are relevant to the employment.

2. Payroll giving scheme (ICTA 1988, s 202)

Prior to April 2000 under the payroll giving scheme (GAYE), payments to approved charities up to a maximum of £1200 pa were tax efficient, provided that the payment was made through an approved deduction scheme operated by the employer. From April 2000, this maximum limit has been abolished and an additional 10 per cent government contribution will be available until 2003 in order to encourage charitable giving.

Tax efficient charitable giving can also be achieved by deed of covenant and the gift aid scheme (*see* Chapter 17).

3. Provision for retirement (ICTA 1988, s 592)

Contributions to an approved occupational pension, personal pension, or retirement annuity scheme are an allowable deduction, subject to the statutory maximum amount. Pensions are considered fully in Chapter 15.

Besides these specific deductions, other expenses are only allowable provided that they fall within the ambit of s 198.

Section 198 (1) of the ICTA 1988 states:

> '**If the holder of an office or employment is necessarily obliged to incur and defray out of the emoluments of that office or employment the expenses of travelling in the performance of the duties of that office or employment, or of keeping and maintaining a horse to enable him to perform those duties,**

or otherwise to expend money, wholly, exclusively and necessarily in the performance of those duties, there may be deducted from the emoluments to be assessed the expenses so necessarily incurred and defrayed.'

The wording of this section is strictly applied in practice and, like Schedule D Case I, 'wholly and exclusively' means there can be no duality of purpose, so that expenditure incurred for personal use, e.g. food and clothing, is, as a general rule, disallowed unless the clothing relates to protective or special clothing, in which case it would be allowable. The Revenue, however, do sometimes allow a proportion of the expenditure, and in this respect set allowances have been negotiated with the Revenue for various occupations for such items as clothing, food, tools, etc.; insurance agents, for example, have set allowances that may be claimed for a number of items such as wear and tear of clothing, meals, use of home as office, etc. However, the criteria are much more stringent under s 198 than the legislation requires for self-employment under Schedule D Case I, where an expense will generally be allowed where it has been incurred wholly and exclusively for the purpose of business (s 74, ICTA 1988). In s 198 it is the additional wording 'necessarily' and 'in the performance of the duties' that makes claims for expenses under s 198 less generous than those under Schedule D Case I.

1. Travelling expenses

As the legislation states that travelling expenses will only be allowed where they are necessarily incurred in the performance of the duties, it follows that any travelling expenses incurred before the duties commence, or after the duties terminate, cannot be allowed as a deduction for Schedule E purposes, therefore travelling to and from work is not generally an allowable expense – *Ricketts* v *Colquhourn* (1926) 10 TC 118.

For travelling expenses to be allowable under Schedule E, they must be incurred while carrying out the duties of the employment, e.g. if there are two places of work, expenses incurred travelling between two places may be allowable – *Owen* v *Pook (HMIT)* [1970] AC 244.

Despite the general rules discussed above, there are a number of exemptions and concessions as follows:

(a) travel to and from work, including subsistence, when public transport is disrupted (ESC A58);
(b) travel to and from work for the severely disabled (ESC A59);
(c) travel to and from the mainland for offshore oil rig and gas workers (ESC A65);
(d) travel to and from work when employees have to work late (ESC A66); and
(e) travel leave facilities for the armed forces (s 141, ICTA 1988).

In all these situations the expenses are allowable, and where the employer bears the cost they are not regarded as taxable emoluments.

The FA 1997 simplifies the relief for travel and subsistence available for triangular travel when an employee works 'on site', away from the normal place of work. From 6 April 1998 the cost of travelling over and above the cost of the normal journey from home to the usual place of work will be allowed.

In order to encourage environmentally friendly travel to work, there will be no taxable benefit on the following transport facilities provided by employers:

- works buses seating 9 or more;
- subsidies for public bus services;
- bicycles and cycling safety equipment; and
- workplace parking for bicycles and motorcycles.

In addition to these provisions, employees can claim capital allowances on a proportion of the capital cost of the bicycle and a tax free mileage rate of 12 pence per mile will be available; i.e. if the employer makes the payment of 12 pence per mile, there will be no taxable benefit on the employee, or if the employer either makes no payment or makes a payment of less than 12 pence per mile then the employee can claim tax relief of up to a maximum of 12 pence per mile. For motorcycles the rate is 24 pence per mile.

ESC 66 is also to be extended to encourage employers to support car sharing arrangements by employees.

From April 2002 there will be no tax or National Insurance liability where an employer provides free or subsidised travel using a local bus company.

2. Round sum expense allowances/reimbursed expenses

Where an employee is given a round sum expense allowance or the employer reimburses the employee for expenses incurred, these amounts form part of the employee's emoluments for Schedule E purposes; it is then up to the employee to claim any legitimate business expenses under the ICTA 1988, s 198.

3. Entertaining

Generally, entertaining is disallowed, and where employees bear the cost of such expenses they cannot then claim them as an expense against income. However, if the employee is given a round sum entertainment allowance or is reimbursed by the employer, these amounts will form part of the employee's emoluments but they will also be entitled to claim legitimate business entertainment that was wholly, exclusively and necessarily incurred as above.

Note: The company paying the entertainment allowance will not have been allowed to deduct the amount in arriving at the Schedule D Case I profits – ICTA 1988, s 577.

4. Incidental overnight expenses

Where the employer pays the employee incidental overnight expenses while working away from home, from 1995/96 such expenses will not form part of the employee's emoluments provided they do not exceed:

- £5 per night in the UK; or
- £10 per night overseas.

5. Liability insurance

The costs of defending liability claims or the cost of insuring against liabilities arising from the employment are an allowable expense from 1995/6. Similarly, if the employer bears the cost then the amount is not treated as part of the employee's emoluments.

6. Capital allowances

Capital allowances are available where the employee provides capital items that are wholly, exclusively and necessarily incurred for the performance of the duties of the employment.

Since the FA 1990, the word 'necessarily' was dropped with respect to cars provided by employees for use in the performance of the duties of the employment. Where a car, in this case, is used partly for private purposes, the allowances are restricted by the private use in the same way as for Schedule D Case I.

7. Other expenses

To be allowable, the expense must be incurred wholly, exclusively and necessarily in the performance of the duties of the employment.

The expense may qualify because it is necessarily incurred, but fail to be allowable because it is not incurred in the performance of the duties of the employment – *Fitzpatrick* v *IRC* [1994] STC 237.

To be allowable, the expense must be imposed by the duties of the employment and not merely a condition of the employment – *Brown* v *Bullock (HMIT)* (1961) 40 TC 1.

Finally, it is amusing to note that ICTA 1988, s 198 refers specifically to 'keeping and maintaining a horse to enable him to perform his duties', despite the fact that horses have long since ceased to be a common mode of transport.

Benefits in kind

Payments in kind for money's worth, i.e. benefits that can be converted into cash, are included in the definition of emoluments. The legislation also provides that certain benefits which are not convertible are to be included in the charge to Schedule E.

The assessment of benefits in kind is further complicated by the legislation providing for two distinct classes of employee:

1. Higher paid employees

Employees whose total emoluments, including the benefits, are greater than £8500 pa. This group are also known as P11D employees.

2. Lower paid employees

Employees whose total emoluments, including the benefits, are less than £8500 pa. This group are also known as P9D employees.

Directors

There are special rules regarding directors. A director will be classed as a P11D employee in the following situations:

(a) where the director is a full-time working director, and together with his associates, he controls a material interest in the company (more than 5 per cent), regardless of the level of emoluments; or

(b) where the director is a full-time working director and even though he has no material interest in the company his total emoluments are greater than £8500 pa.

A director will therefore only be classed as a P9D employee in rare circumstances, when the following conditions are met:

(a) the director's emoluments are less than £8500 pa; and

(b) the director is a full-time working director with no material interest in the company.

or

(c) the company is a charity or non-profit making organisation.

In calculating these total emoluments, the only expenses that are allowed as a deduction are pension contributions; benefits and reimbursed expenses must be included:

	£
Salary, fees, commissions, etc.	X
Benefits in kind	X
	X
Reimbursed expenses	X
less Pension contributions	(X)
Total emoluments	Y
less s 198 expenses	(X)
Net Schedule E emoluments	Z

Y is then the figure that determines whether an individual is a P11D or P9D employee.

We will now examine the manner in which benefits in kind are assessed to income tax.

1. Benefits assessable on all employees

For some benefits no distinction is made between the two classes of employee. The following benefits are taxable on all employees:

(a) Non-cash vouchers

A taxable benefit arises on all employees where they are provided with vouchers that can be exchanged for goods or services. The assessable benefit is the cost to the employer less any contribution that the employee makes towards this cost.

Luncheon vouchers fall into this category but by concession will be exempt from the charge provided they are:

- non-transferable;
- used only for meals;
- available to lower paid employees; and
- limited to 15 pence per day.

If the value of the luncheon vouchers is more than 15 pence per day, any excess is taxable as a benefit in kind. The time at which the benefit is assessed to tax is the later of:

- the year in which the employer incurred the expense; or
- the year in which the voucher is redeemed.

(b) Cash vouchers

A taxable benefit arises if the employee is provided with vouchers that can be exchanged for cash. The assessable benefit is the redemption value, less any contribution made by the employee.

(c) Credit cards

Where an employee obtains goods or services on a credit card provided by the employer, then a taxable benefit arises when the goods or services obtained, not when the employer settles the liability. The assessable benefit is the cost of the goods or services obtained, less any contribution made by the employee, and does not include any interest or charges made on the employer in respect of the credit card.

(d) Discharge of employee's liabilities

Where the employer pays any bills for which the employee is contractually liable, a taxable benefit arises at the cost to the employer, less any contribution made by the employee.

(e) Accommodation

Living accommodation provided by the employer is an assessable benefit on all employees. The basic charge is calculated as the higher of the following:

(a) *Gross annual value (GAV)*. This is the gross rateable value of the property, but since rates have been replaced by the council tax, newer properties will require an estimated rateable value to be placed on them; or

(b) *Rent paid by employer*. In situations where the employer does not own the property and rents a property for the employee's use.

The benefit is reduced by any rent paid by the employee.

EXAMPLE

Robert's employers, Grange Ltd, provide him with a house; the following details are available:

	£
GAV	1000
Rent paid by Grange Ltd	2500
Rent paid by Robert	1200

The benefit is calculated as:

	£
higher of: GAV/Rent paid by Grange Ltd	2500
less Robert's contribution	(1200)
Taxable benefit	1300

Expensive accommodation

There is an additional charge made where the cost of the accommodation is greater than £75 000 calculated as:

(cost − £75 000) × official rate of interest at the beginning of the fiscal year

The 'cost' is the cost of the accommodation to the employer including any enhancement expenditure before the beginning of the tax year less any capital contributions made by the employee.

EXAMPLE

Alice has the use of a company house that cost £80 000 in 1996. The gross rateable value of the house is £1800 and the company carried out improvements on the property as follows:

	£
October 1999	15 000
June 2000	8 000

Alice contributed £5000 towards the cost of the improvements in October 1999 and £2000 towards the costs in June 2000, and pays £1000 pa rent to the company.

Assuming an official rate of interest of 7.5 per cent, the additional charge for 2000/01 is calculated as:

	£
Cost of property	80 000
Enhancement October 1999	15 000
	95 000
less Capital contribution	(5 000)

$$[£90\,000 - £75\,000] \times 7.5\%$$

$$= £1\,125$$

Note: The improvements in June 2000 are not included in the 2000/01 charge as they were incurred after the beginning of the fiscal year. The total accommodation benefit for Alice for 2000/01 is as follows:

	£
Basic charge (GAV)	1800
Additional charge	1125
	2925
less Employee's contribution	(1000)
Taxable benefit	1925

If the employer has owned the property for more than six years before it is made available to the employee, the market value of the property at the time it is first occupied by the employee is substituted for the original cost.

EXAMPLE

Ambleside Ltd acquired a property in 1987 for £70 000 and have spent the following amounts on improving the property:

	£
June 1997	10 000
September 1999	6 000

Clive, an employee, has had the use of the property rent free since June 1999 when the property was valued at £79 000. The GAV of the accommodation is £1200 pa. Assuming an official rate of interest of 7.5 per cent, the assessable benefit on Clive for 2002/03 will be:

	£
Basic charge (GAV)	1200
Additional charge:	
$[(79\,000 + 6\,000) - 75\,000] \times 7.5\%$	750
Taxable benefit	1950

Note: The enhancement expenditure in June 1997 will be reflected in the June 1999 valuation.

No assessable benefit will arise on the employee where the accommodation is deemed to be job related, i.e.:

(a) it is necessary in order for the employee to perform his duties, e.g. lighthouse keeper;

(b) it is necessary for the better performance of the employee's duties and it is customary to provide accommodation, e.g. clergy;

(c) the employer is an individual providing accommodation in the normal course of events, e.g. domestic servant;

(d) it is necessary where there is a threat to the employee's safety and the accommodation is provided as part of special security arrangements, e.g. the prime minister.

Where the accommodation is job related, no benefit will arise under the basic charge or the additional charge.

Note: Job-related accommodation can only apply to directors with a material interest in the company if it is provided for security purposes.

Ancillary benefits

Any benefits provided in connection with the accommodation, e.g. services, furniture, etc. are assessable under the general rules applicable to the class of employee, i.e. P9D or P11D, and will be considered under these headings.

2. Benefits assessable on lower paid employees (P9D)

The general rule is that lower paid employees are only assessable on benefits that can be converted into cash, i.e. they can be disposed of to a third party, in which case the benefit is assessed at the second hand value rather than the cost to the employer, less any contribution by the employee.

EXAMPLE

Janice is employed on a salary of £7500 pa. Her employers provide her with two new suits each year at a cost of £200 each. She has no other emoluments. The cost of the suits to the employer is £400, but as Janice is lower paid, the assessable benefit will be something less than £400, being the second hand value of the suits.

If the benefit provided is not transferable or has no second hand value, then no assessable benefit arises.

EXAMPLE

Board and lodging provided to hotel staff is not transferable and has no second hand value and so no taxable benefit will arise in respect of lower paid employees. The same rule will apply to any item that is provided for the use of lower paid employees where they are not free to dispose of the item.

Ancillary benefits

Benefits provided in connection with accommodation follow the same general rule and are only assessable if they can be converted into money. Where the accommodation is job related no taxable benefit arises.

Note: It is not effective where, for example, the employer reimburses the employee for the electricity bill – the employer must be contractually liable, i.e. the employer's name must be on the account. If the employee is contractually liable, it amounts to a discharge of the employee's liabilities, in which case the benefit arising is the cost to the employer (*see* 'benefits assessable on all employees', p. 156).

3. Higher paid employees and directors (P11D)

For P11D employees the general rule is that the employee is assessed on the benefit at the cost to the employer less any contribution made by the employee.

(a) Gift of used goods

Where the item given as a gift to the employee is not new, the cost to the employer is taken to be the market value at the date of the gift.

(b) Facilities provided

Where the benefit is the provision of facilities that are shared with others, e.g. cheap school fees for employee's children, the cost to the employer of such 'in house' benefits is to be taken as the marginal cost. This fact was established by the House of Lords in *Pepper (HMIT)* v *Hart* [1992] STC 898.

(c) Loan of an asset

Where the employee has the use, but not the ownership, of an asset, the cost to the employer is taken to be:

$$20\% \times \text{cost}$$

EXAMPLE

Brian's employers provide him with the use of a television and video which cost the company £900. The benefit chargeable on Brian is calculated as:

$$20\% \times £900 = £180 \text{ pa}$$

If instead of buying the equipment, the company had rented it for £20 per month, then Brian's taxable benefit would be the higher of:

		£
(a)	$20\% \times £900$	180
or		
(b)	$12 \times £20$	240

The taxable benefit would therefore be £240 (the cost to the employer).

If an asset is transferred to an employee that was previously on loan to him, the benefit is calculated as the higher of:

	£
(a) The market value at disposal	X
less Any contribution by employee	(X)
	X

or

(b) Original cost   X
  less Benefits to date   (X)
  less Contribution by employee (X)
            X

EXAMPLE

In 1999/00 George had the use of television, video and hi-fi equipment that had cost his company £2400 in total. In 2002/03 the equipment was transferred to him for a payment of £300. The market value of the equipment when it was transferred was £800. The taxable benefit in 2002/03 is calculated at the higher of:

		£
(a)	Market value on disposal	800
	less Contribution	(300)
		500

or

		£	£
(b)	Original cost		2 400
	less Benefits to date:		
	1999/00 (20% × £2 400)	480	
	2000/01 (20% × £2 400)	480	
	2001/02 (20% × £2 400)	480	(1 440)
			960
	less Contribution		(300)
			660

The taxable benefit is therefore £660.

Ancillary benefits

Benefits provided in connection with accommodation are taxable as follows:

(a) *Non job-related accommodation.* Where the accommodation is not job related, ancillary benefits are taxable following the general rules for P11D employees, i.e. on the cost to the employer.

(b) *Job-related accommodation.* Where the accommodation provided is job related, the taxable ancillary benefits cannot exceed 10 per cent of the employee's net emoluments, excluding the ancillary benefits, less any contribution made by the employee.

EXAMPLE

Brian is employed on a salary of £22 000 pa. His company provides him with a house that cost £120 000 and has a GAV of £2500. The company also pays the following expenses:

	£
Electricity	650
Council tax	850
Gardener	1040

Brian has other taxable benefits of £2000 and pays £1500 pa into a personal pension scheme. On the assumption that the official rate of interest is 7.5%, the accommodation benefit, assuming:

(a) the accommodation is not job related;
(b) the accommodation is job related;

is calculated as follows:

(a)	£	£
Accommodation:		
Basic charge		2 500
Additional charge:		
(120 000 – 75 000) × 7.5%		3 375
		5 875
Ancillary benefits:		
Electricity	650	
Council tax	850	
Gardener	1 040	2 540
Other benefits		2 000
Total taxable benefits		10 415

(b)	£	£
Accommodation:		
Basic charge (exempt)		nil
Additional charge (exempt)		nil
Ancillary benefits	2 540	
restricted to:		
10% net emoluments	2 250	2 250
Other benefits		2 000
Total taxable benefits		4 250

Working – Net emoluments:

	£
Salary	22 000
Other benefits	2 000
	24 000
less Pension	(1 500)
	22 500

10% × £22 500   = £2 250

Ancillary benefits restricted to £2250.

(d) Medical insurance

Where the employer provides medical insurance for the employee, a taxable benefit arises under the general rules, i.e. cost to the employer less any contributions made by the employee. The exception to this rule is where medical insurance is provided for business travel overseas.

(e) Cars

1. Cars with an element of private use

From 6th April 2002 the taxable benefit on company cars will be linked to carbon dioxide(CO_2) emissions; the discounts previously available for business mileage and the age of the car are abolished from this date.

From the 6th April 2002 the taxable benefit is calculated as follows:

(a) Calculate the list price for tax purposes.

The list price is not necessarily the price advertised by a garage but is taken to be:

(a) manufacturer's list price including major accessories when the car was first registered; *plus*

(b) the cost of optional extras in excess of £100 (excluding telephones) fitted after the employee receives the car.

The list price used in the calculation is subject to a maximum of £80 000. For existing cars the Revenue will accept either:

- manufacturer's list price plus major accessories; or
- published price guides where the manufacturer's list price is unavailable.

A Revenue Press Release of 27 September 1993 states that where an employer cannot find the price of an existing car, then they should provide their tax office with an estimated price including major accessories.

From 6 April 1995, accessories fitted for use by a disabled person are not to be taken into account, provided that they are designed for the sole use of the disabled person or they hold a disabled badge.

There are special rules regarding classic cars, being defined as at least 15 years old and worth at least £15 000 at the end of the tax year. If at the end of the tax year the market value of the car is higher than the original list price, then the market value is used in calculating the taxable benefit. The limit of £80 000 and capital contribution reduction applies. If the employee makes a capital contribution towards the car, then it is deducted from the list price before the benefit is calculated. The maximum capital contribution allowed is £5000.

(b) Find the CO2 emissions figure

For cars registered in the UK after 1st March 2001 the CO_2 emissions figure will be shown on the vehicle registration document. For cars registered between 1st January 1998 and 28th February 2001 the information can be obtained from the Society of Motor Manufacturers and Traders free of charge under an agreement with the Inland Revenue.

(c) Calculate the percentage charge

If the CO_2 emissions figure does not end in 0 or 5, then it is rounded down to the nearest 5gm/km, e.g. CO_2 emissions figure of 183gm/km is rounded down to 180gm/km. Where the figure is below the minimum level, then use the minimum percentage.(see Appendix 2 for full details).

Cars registered before 1st January 1998 will not have a CO_2 emissions figure; for these cars the engine size will determine the percentage to be used as follows:

Engine size cc	Registered before 1/1/98	Registered after 1/1/98
0–1400	15%	15%
1401–2000	22%	25%
over 2000	32%	35%

(d) Add supplements or apply discounts

A supplement of 1% to 3% is added where the car runs solely on diesel. Discounts are also available for cars that run on alternative fuels and technologies. (see Appendix 2)

(e) Calculate the taxable benefit

List price × percentage charge

(f) Adjust the benefit where the car has not been available for the whole of the fiscal year.

(g) Deduct any contributions made by the employee

EXAMPLE

Petrol car with an approved CO_2 emissions figure of 187gm/km and a list price of £17,000.
    The emissions figure is rounded down to 185gm/km, the percentage charge being 19% for 2002/03 therefore the basic charge for 2002/03 is:

£17,000 × 19% = £3,230.

If the car was a diesel car a 3% supplement would be added and the basic charge would then be calculated as:

£17,000 × 22% = £3,740

2. Second cars

From April 2002 there are no special rules for second cars; they will be taxed like the main car.

3. Chauffeur

Where an employee is provided with a chauffeur, an additional benefit arises under the general rules, i.e. cost to the employer. When a chauffeur is used for journeys that are necessary for the performance of the duties of the employment, the employee is entitled to make a claim under the ICTA 1988, s 198 for the expense of the chauffeur in respect of these business journeys.

4. Vans

Since 1993/4, the private use of a company van (3500 kg or less) is treated as a benefit and assessed at a flat rate of £500 pa, reduced to £350 pa if the van is over four years old at the end of the tax year, less any contribution that the employee makes towards the running costs.

If the van is shared by at least two employees, then each employee is assessed on his share of the benefit, up to a maximum of £500 pa; alternatively the employee can elect to be assessed at the rate of £5 for each day the van is available for his use, up to a maximum of £500 pa.

EXAMPLE

A company has four vans, three of which are new, the other is over four years old. The vans are shared by Adam, Bill, Charlie and David, except that for 105 days in the year Adam had the exclusive use of one of the newer vans, and did not use a shared van on any of these days.

The total amounts to be shared are:

	£
Two new shared vans @ £500 each	1000
Older van	350
Van shared for 260 days (260/365 × £500)	356
	1706

	A (£)	B (£)	C (£)	D (£)
Share of aggregate	426	426	426	426
Standard charge:				
105/365 × £500	144	–	–	–
	570	426	426	426
less Excess over £500 pa	(70)	–	–	–
Benefit for use of van	500	426	426	426

Any of the employees could claim the alternative of £5 for each day the van is available for his use, up to a maximum of £500 pa.

Vans not available for the whole of the fiscal year are reduced proportionately in the same way as company cars.

5. Pool cars / vans

Pooled cars/vans do not give rise to a taxable benefit, provided they satisfy the following conditions:

- the private use is incidental to the business use;
- the vehicle is used by several employees; and
- the vehicle is not normally kept at/near the employee's home (in this respect the Revenue take 60 per cent of the time to be normal).

6. Company car fuel benefit

Fuel provided for private motoring is a taxable benefit and charged in accordance with the following scale rates based on engine size:

	2002/03		2001/02	
	Petrol engines (£)	Diesel engines (£)	Petrol engines (£)	Diesel engines (£)
up to 1400 cc	2 240	2 850	1 930	2 460
1401 cc – 2000 cc	2 850	2 850	2 460	2 460
over 2000 cc	4 200	4 200	3 620	3 620

If the fuel is only provided for business motoring, or if the employee pays for private petrol, there is no benefit, but if the employee contributes towards the cost of private fuel then there is no deduction in the way there is for other employee contributions.

From 6 April 1999, where an extra cost has been incurred in order to convert company cars to road fuel gases, then that cost will be ignored when calculating the taxable benefit.

Note: The fuel scale charge does not apply to company vans; the flat rate charge is fully inclusive.

7. Mileage allowance / fixed profit car scheme (FPCS)

Sometimes employers pay their employees a fixed rate per mile for using their own car for company business. These payments form part of the individual's emoluments with expenses necessarily incurred being claimed under the ICTA 1988, s 198.

EXAMPLE

	£		
Petrol	2600	Business miles	6 000
Road tax	140	Private miles	9 000
Insurance	560	Total miles	15 000
Repairs	625		
Breakdown cover	75		
Total motoring costs for year	4000		

$$\frac{6000}{15\,000} \times £4000 = £1600 \text{ claim for business expenses under s 198.}$$

This makes it necessary for employees to keep detailed records of costs and logged mileage. To simplify matters, the FA 1990 introduced the FPCS which gives a tax free mileage rate based on engine size and number of business miles travelled:

	First 4000 miles	Next 4000 miles
up to 1500 cc	40p	25p
over 1500 cc up to 2000 cc	45p	25p
over 2000 cc	63p	36p

Any excess over these rates paid by the employer is taxable, but shortfalls in the amount the employer pays can be claimed as an allowable expense under the ICTA 1988, s 198.

Note: Relief for interest on loans taken out to purchase the vehicle is not included in the FPCS rates.

(f) Beneficial loans

Loans granted to employees or members of their families that are either interest free or charged interest at a rate lower than the official interest rate (sometimes referred to as 'soft' loans) give rise to an assessable benefit on P11D employees, except in the following circumstances:

(a) where the loan is made in the ordinary course of business on the same terms as loans made to the general public;

(b) where the aggregate amount of any such loans granted to an employee is less than the *de minimus* limit of £5000;

(c) where the loan is granted to a member of the employee's family and the employee can show that no personal benefit was derived from it.

Where a loan is written off, the amount written off will be an assessable benefit on the employee, regardless of whether or not it was a 'soft' loan, except where the loan is written off on the death of the employee or where the employee can show that no benefit was derived.

There are two methods of calculating the assessable benefit:

(a) *The standard method.* The benefit is calculated by applying the official rate of interest, less any interest actually paid by the employee, to the average amount of the loan outstanding during the tax year:

Average loan outstanding × (official rate interest – interest rate charged)

(b) *The alternative method.* The average method above is the normal practice for calculating the assessable benefit but the alternative method, which calculates the benefit on a more accurate daily basis, can be substituted by either the tax-payer or the Revenue:

$$\text{Amount of loan} \times \frac{\text{no. of days}}{365} \times (\text{official rate of interest} - \text{interest rate paid})$$

EXAMPLE

George is employed on a salary of £40 000 pa. On 6 April 2002 his employers grant him a loan of £25 000 at 2.5 per cent interest. On 6 January 2003 George repays £15 000 of the loan, so that the amount outstanding on 5 April 2003 is £10 000. Assume the official rate of interest is 7.5 per cent.

Standard method:

$$\text{Average amount of loan} = \frac{25\,000 + 10\,000}{2}$$

$$= £17\,500$$

$$£17\,500 \times (7.5\% - 2.5\%) = £875$$

Alternative method:

6/4/99 – 5/1/00 = 275 days
6/1/00 – 5/4/00 = 90 days

	£
$25\,000 \times \dfrac{275}{365} \times (7.5\% - 2.5\%)$	942
$10\,000 \times \dfrac{90}{365} \times (7.5\% - 2.5\%)$	123
	1065

Because a large amount was paid off towards the end of the fiscal year, the average method will produce a lower benefit. The alternative method means that tax avoidance, by paying off large sums just before the end of the fiscal year can be controlled. Where the difference is not significant, the Revenue will not use the alternative method. The taxpayer can also elect for the alternative method and would do so if this produced a lower figure than the standard method.

(g) Director's tax paid by employer

If the company does not deduct tax under PAYE but accounts to the Revenue for the tax after 5 April 1983, the amount of any tax not reimbursed by the director is treated as part of his emoluments.

(h) Scholarships

The general rule is that scholarships provided for employee's children after 14 March 1983 are treated as a benefit in kind on P11D employees except where it can be shown that:

(a) the scholarship is not a result of the employment;

(b) no more than 25 per cent of the scholarships (by value), are provided as a result of the employment, i.e. to children of employees; and

(c) the 25 per cent figure includes scholarships awarded to the children of lower paid employees, i.e. the scholarships should not be restricted to the children of P11D employees.

4. Benefits not assessable

The following benefits provided by employers are 'tax free' to all employees:

(a) Canteen facilities

Canteen facilities and subsidised meals are not a taxable benefit provided that the facility is available to all employees.

(b) Luncheon vouchers

Vouchers up to 15p a day are not taxable. Any excess over this amount is a taxable benefit.

(c) Pensions

Employer contributions to approved pension schemes and retirement benefit schemes are not taxable.

(d) Sports facilities

From 6 April 1993 sports and recreational facilities provided by employers in-house or managed by an outside firm will not amount to a taxable benefit, provided that the facilities are available to all employees.

(e) Workplace nurseries

From 6 April 1990 the provision of childcare facilities at the workplace for children of P11D employees is no longer a taxable benefit.

Note: Employer subsidised nursery facilities not provided at the workplace remain a taxable benefit on P11D employees at the cost to the employer. P9D employees, however, would not be taxable as the facility is not transferable.

In order to encourage employers to provide childcare facilities for employees, in the FA 2000 the Chancellor proposed to keep childcare provided as a benefit in kind free from Class 1A NICs (*see* Chapter 14).

(f) Protective / industrial clothing

(g) Miners' coal benefit

By concession (ESC A6) miners' free coal or cash received in lieu of free coal does not form part of the employee's taxable emoluments.

(h) Staff entertaining

Extra-statutory concession A70 provides that the following benefits do not constitute taxable emoluments:

(a) gifts made by third parties to employees, provided that the cost is not more than £150 in any tax year; and

(b) social functions, Christmas parties, etc. are not taxable benefits, provided that the cost is reasonable, i.e. not more than £75 per head.

(i) Clergy

Section 132 of the ICTA 1988 provides that reimbursed or settled council tax and other statutory amounts for members of the clergy are not taxable benefits, provided that the accommodation is owned by the charity or organisation. By concession (ESC A61) reimbursed ancillary expenses are not taxable benefits for lower paid members of the clergy.

Note: For P9D employees generally, ancillary expenses will only be exempt where the employer is contractually liable.

(j) Relocation expenses

From 5 April 1993, relocation expenses up to a maximum of £8000 are not taxable. Section 190 of the ICTA 1988 also provides that resettlement payments made to individuals ceasing to be MPs or MEPs are not taxable.

(k) Security assets / services

The FA 1989, in ss 50–52, provides that expenditure incurred or reimbursed on the provision of assets or services to improve personal security is exempt from the Schedule E charge.

Pay as you earn system

Income tax under Schedule E is generally collected under the PAYE system. While employees are responsible for making a return of their income chargeable to tax, the main responsibility for operating the system, and collecting tax and National Insurance contributions, falls on the employer.

The employer's main duties include:

(a) deduction of income tax and National Insurance contributions from employees' pay;

(b) keeping records of pay, National Insurance contributions and tax;

(c) making an end of year return for each employee (form P14);

(d) completing an end of year summary (form P35);

(e) supplying each employee with end of year details (form P60);

(f) complying with the requirements when an employee leaves or joins the firm (form P45);

(g) completing a return of benefits, expenses, etc. for directors and higher paid employees (form P11D);

(h) completing a return of benefits, expenses, etc. for lower paid employees (form P9D).

The PAYE system is onerous, especially for smaller businesses, and places heavy demands on employers, particularly in respect of expenses and benefits in kind. This burden has been further exacerbated with the inclusion of tax credits and recovery of student loans being made through the PAYE system from April 2000.

The operation of the PAYE system is considered in more detail in Part 6 of this book.

Incentive schemes

The offer of financial incentives to improve performance is not a new idea, e.g. bonuses, however, the following schemes carry with them tax advantages for the employee:

1. Profit sharing schemes

Generally shares given as a gift to employees would amount to a taxable emolument. Approved profit sharing schemes allow shares to be allocated to employees without incurring a Schedule E charge, provided that certain conditions are met. The tax relief does not extend to income tax on the dividends or capital gains tax on disposal. The value of the shares that can be appropriated to the employee is the higher of:

- £3000; or
- 10 per cent of salary (excluding benefits) up to a maximum of £8000.

Eligible employees

Employees eligible for inclusion in a profit sharing scheme must satisfy the following conditions:

1. they must be resident or ordinarily resident in the UK when the shares are allocated;
2. they must have been directors/employees for the last five years;
3. within the previous 12 months they must not have had a material interest in a close company whose shares are involved.

Mechanism of scheme

1. The company allocates money to a trust. This will be an allowable deduction for Schedule D Case I purposes.
2. The trustees then purchase shares in the employing company for the benefit of the employees.
3. The shares are allocated to the employees.

The tax benefit to the employee is that there is no Schedule E charge on the receipt of the shares provided they are retained for a period of three years from the date they were acquired by the trustees (prior to the FA 1996, the shares had to be retained for a period of five years).

If the shares are disposed of within three years, there is a potential Schedule E charge, depending on the circumstance surrounding the disposal. The percentage of the original value liable to income tax is as follows:

	Death	Redundancy/injury or retirement	Other
	Circumstances of disposal		
Disposal within three years	nil	50%	100%

Note: Where the original value is greater than the market value at the date of disposal, the market value on disposal is used to calculate the Schedule E charge.

Awards of shares under such a scheme are only available until 5/4/02.

2. Share option schemes

Generally, employees who are granted an option to purchase shares in their company of employment will be liable to income tax under Schedule E on the difference between the value of the shares on the date the option is exercised and the price paid by the employee. On the disposal of the shares, there would be a capital gains tax liability but the Schedule E charge when the option was exercised would be an allowable deduction. This liability to income tax can be avoided if the option is granted under an approved share option scheme as follows:

(a) Schemes linked to save as you earn schemes

A SAYE scheme can be linked to the option to purchase shares in the employing company. Employees enter into a contract to have the savings deducted from their salary until sufficient money has been saved to exercise the option. The minimum amount that can be saved under such a scheme is £5 per month and the maximum amount is £250 per month. Approved schemes must meet the following criteria:

1. the scheme must be open to all eligible employees (as defined for profit sharing schemes above);
2. the option price must not be less than 80 per cent of the market value of the shares when the option was granted;
3. the date at which the option can be exercised must be fixed when the option is granted and can be for three, five or seven years;
4. contributions to the SAYE scheme must continue for a minimum of three years;
5. at the end of the term a bonus is added to the savings but the value of the shares acquired must not be greater than the amount the employee is entitled to from the scheme.

If all the conditions are satisfied and the employee retains the shares for at least three years, the charge to income tax under Schedule E is avoided.

(b) Share option schemes not linked to SAYE

These schemes are often referred to as executive share option schemes because they need not be made available to all eligible employees as is the case with previous schemes. Because these schemes are more ambitious, they are usually only made available to key executives. To be eligible the employee must be either a full-time director (minimum 25 hours per week) or an employee working at least 20 hours per week, but persons owning at least 10 per cent of the ordinary shares of a close company are excluded.

For options granted after 17 July 1995, no charge under Schedule E will accrue to the employee on the grant or exercise of options to a maximum of £20 000, provided that:

- the option is not granted at a significant discount; and
- the option is exercised between three and ten years after it was granted.

From 6 April 1998, share options that can be excercised more than 10 years after the date the option was granted will be liable to income tax if the market value, when the option was granted, is greater than the option price.

Proposals for a new all employee share scheme were put forward in the 1999 Budget, and introduced in the FA 2000. The main features for the scheme are as follows:

- employees can buy employer shares out of pre-tax income up to the value of £1500 per year, known as 'partnership shares', free of tax and NICs;
- employers can give up to £3000 of shares each year, free of tax and NICs;

- where employees have purchased 'partnership shares', the employers can give two free shares for every 'partnership share' held;
- employers can deduct costs in excess of employees' contributions for corporation tax purposes;
- shares held in the scheme for five years will be free of income tax and NICs;
- shares held in the scheme for at least three years will only be liable to income tax and NICs on the initial value of the shares;
- shares held in the scheme until they are disposed of will not be liable to capital gains tax.

3. Enterprise management incentives (EMIs)

Tax advantaged share options can be granted to reward a company's key employees, provided the following conditions were met under FA 2000:

1. the company is an independent trading company with assets not exceeding £15 million;
2. up to 15 key employees can benefit from the share options up to a maximum of £100 000 at the time that the option was granted.

To allow small, high-risk and growing companies to take advantage of an EMI, the following changes were announced in the FA 2001:

- the limit of 15 employees is removed;
- the value of options increased from £1.5 million to £3 million;
- time limit for notification increased from 30 days to 92 days;
- no prior approval required for alteration to share capital.

If the conditions apply, the tax advantages are as follows:

- no tax liability arises on the grant of the option;
- no income tax or NICs are payable by the employee at the time the option is exercised;
- no NIC liability arises for the employer;
- on disposal, the taper is calculated from the date the option was granted.

4. Vocational training

In the FA 1999 the government introduced the notion of Individual Learning Accounts (ILAs) in order to encourage vocational training.

The idea behind the scheme is that the individual is responsible for his/her own training programme. Contributions made by employers to ILAs held by their employees will be tax deductible and will be free of tax and National Insurance contributions for the employee. Relief on ILAs will be available at 20 per cent on training costs up to a maximum of £500 pa.

The ILAs are to have effect from the tax year 2001/02 when vocational training relief will be abolished.

SELF ASSESSMENT QUESTIONS

13.1 Charles is employed on a salary of £28000 pa. His employers provide him with the following benefits for 2002/03:

(a) A 1998 cc petrol motor car which had been purchased new in August 2001 for £18000, and he was provided with all his private fuel. The approved CO_2 emissions are 192 gm/Km.

(b) Two new suits each year, at a cost to his employer of £300 each. The suits are technically on loan to Charles and he must return them to the company when they are replaced.

(c) Subscription to BUPA at a cost of £500 pa.

(d) Charles and his family live in a house owned by his employers. The gross annual value of the property is £3600 pa; the house had been purchased by Charles' employers for £120000 in 1998. Assume an official rate of interest of 7 per cent.

REQUIRED

Calculate Charles' Schedule E emoluments for 2002/03.

13.2 Amos has the use of a company house that cost £75000 in 1999. The gross annual value of the property is £2000 pa, and his employers carried out improvements to the property as follows:

	£
October 2001	12000
June 2002	7000

REQUIRED

Assuming an official rate of interest of 7 per cent, calculate Amos' taxable benefit for 2002/03.

13.3 Jenny is employed on a salary of £30000 pa. Her company provides her with the following benefits:

(a) A company car that runs on diesel that had been purchased by the company for £15000. She pays for all her private fuel, and approved CO_2 emissions are 182 gm/Km.

(b) A house that cost the company £130000 in 1998. The gross annual value of the property is £3000 pa and the company pays the following expenses:

	£
Electricity	600
Council tax	900
Gardener	1560

Jenny pays £2000 qualifying contribution into a personal pension scheme. The accommodation is not job related. Assume an official rate of interest of 7 per cent.

REQUIRED

(a) Caculate Jenny's Schedule E emoluments for 2002/03.

(b) Calculate the accommodation benefit if the property had been job related.

CHAPTER 14

National Insurance contributions

The social security system can be divided into two distinct parts:

1. Non-contributory scheme

Entitlement to receive state benefits is not linked to National Insurance contributions but based on some other measure, e.g. means tested benefits such as income support.

2. Contributory scheme

Entitlement to receive state benefits is dependent on the individual having paid the relevant National Insurance contributions, e.g. state retirement pension.

National Insurance contributions (NICs) are payable on an earnings related basis and paid into the National Insurance fund to help meet the costs of contributory benefits and make a small contribution (approximately 12 per cent of the fund) to the National Health Service, despite the fact that national healthcare is not dependent on NICs.

Current NICs are mainly used to finance current state pensions and the small contribution towards the cost of the National Health Service, the balance of social security expenditure being paid for from general taxation.

The National Insurance scheme (NIS) is administered by the Department of Social Security (DSS), which was reorganised in 1991 and split into the following agencies:

- Benefits Agency;
- Information Technology Services Agency; and
- Contributions Agency.

The Contributions Agency was transferred to the Inland Revenue in April 1999, in the hope that the move would both improve customer service and reduce administration costs.

The Contributions Agency is responsible for the contributions made to the NIS. The state benefits that are linked to NICs, i.e. contributory benefits are as follows:

- incapacity benefit;
- jobseeker's allowance;
- maternity allowance;
- widow's pension; and
- retirement pension.

National Insurance contributions are based on earnings and payable by employers, employees and self-employed persons. There are four classes of NICs, each with a different contribution rate, and entitlement to the contributory benefits depends on the class of NIC paid.

Generally persons under 16 years of age and over retirement age do not have to pay NICs. The liability under each class depends on whether the individual is employed or self-employed, therefore, the distinction between a *contract of service* (employment) and a *contract for service* (self-employment) is important not only for income tax purposes, but also for NIC liability.

The rest of this chapter considers the distinction between employment and self-employment and examines the liability to NICs under each of the four classes of contribution. The main charging provisions are contained in the Social Security Contributions and Benefits Act 1992 (SSCBA 1992).

Employment *v* self-employment

It is important to distinguish between a contract of service, amounting to employment, and a contract for services, which would be classed as self-employment. The correct categorisation of employment or self-employment is significant with regard to the following:

1. Employment protection law

Unfair dismissal claims can only be brought by employed persons – *Massey* v *Crown Life Insurance Company* [1978] 1 WLR 676.

2. Income tax

Employed persons are liable to income tax under Schedule E, while self-employed persons are liable to income tax under Schedule D Case I, which is often more generous regarding expenses, etc.

3. NICs

The contributions payable by self-employed individuals are significantly lower than the class 1 contributions payable in respect of employed persons.

The legislation defines a contract of service as 'any contract of service or apprenticeship whether written or oral, and whether express or implied': s 122, SSCBA 1992. It is unclear whether a contract of service is a question of law or a question of fact and the courts will look to the agreement made between the parties to the contract where the distinction between employment and self-employment is blurred.

Whether a person is employed or self-employed is usually self evident, however, in some instances the categorisation is not always clear cut, in which case tests or 'badges' can be useful to indicate whether the contract is likely to be a contract of service (employment) or a contract for services (self-employment) – *see* Table 14.1.

No one test is conclusive in itself, they are merely indicators and the final outcome will depend on the particular facts of the case in much the same way as the badges of trade (*see* Chapter 10). With regard to NICs, the DSS have the power to alter a person's NIC status where they have been incorrectly categorised; more often than not the recategorisation is from self-employment to employee status. Since 6 April 1987, written decisions on categorisation, provided that all the material facts have been disclosed, will be binding on both the DSS and the IR. Where an individ-

Table 14.1 Employment/self-employment categorisation

Test	Contract of service (employment)	Contract for services (self-employment)
1 Mutual obligation	The employer is obliged to provide work and the employee is obliged to carry out the work provided.	There is no mutual obligation between a self-employed person and clients.
2 Is the work performed an integral part of the organisation?	The work performed is an integral part of the business.	The work is not an integral part of the business and alternative suppliers of the service can be used by the client.
3 Remuneration and hours of work	An employee usually has to work specific hours and is paid on a regular basis.	Self-employed persons work the hours they choose and receive payment on the basis of work done and invoices submitted.
4 Economic reality	Employed persons take no financial risk and receive payment regardless of profit, and are usually provided with tools, equipment, etc. by the employer.	Self-employed persons take financial risks by supplying their own capital, and making financial decisions – they can hire and fire and provide their own equipment, tools, etc.
5 Control, i.e. is there a master/servant relationship?	Employers control the work undertaken by employees; the employee cannot choose how and when the work will be undertaken, i.e. there is a master/servant relationship.	A self-employed person can choose which work to undertake and how and when the work will be performed, i.e. the self-employed person is his /her own master.

ual has been incorrectly categorised, the procedure followed by the DSS depends on whether the recategorisation is from self-employment to employment or vice versa:

(a) Self-employed recategorised as employed

The DSS implement the change immediately and the date of the change can be made retrospective. In theory, the DSS can go back without time limit, but in practice do not go back before 6 April 1975. With a retrospective recategorisation to class 1 NICs, the procedure is as follows:

1. Class 2 contributions paid while the individual was classed as self-employed are reallocated to primary class 1 NICs.

2. The balance of primary class 1 and the secondary class 1 NICs are requested from the employer.

3. The IR refund class 4 NICs overpaid.

(b) Employed recategorised to self-employed

The DSS treat this has having effect from the date of the decision and do not tend to make it retrospective, thereby preventing the repayment of class 1 NICs paid. The choice not to make the change retrospective may be challenged on the grounds that the individual has been found to be self-employed during the period in which class 1 NICs were paid.

Class 1 contributions

Class 1 NICs which are collected under the PAYE system are earnings related and payable by both the employee and the employer:

1. Employee class 1 contributions

Primary class 1 contributions are payable by all employed persons under pensionable age and over 16 years of age. The deduction is based on a percentage of earnings for a contribution period, provided that they are over a specified lower limit; once earnings are above this lower limit the whole of the earnings up to a specified upper limit are liable to primary class 1 NICs.

The SSCBA 1992 refers to earnings as 'remuneration' or 'profit', which are not further defined by the legislation and so are to be given their ordinary meanings. For social security purposes, 'earnings' has a fairly narrow meaning in comparison to the tax legislation; there is no definition of payments in kind except that the regulations state that payment in kind; the provision of board and lodgings or services or other facilities are excluded from earnings. This fact presented a 'loophole' in that a favourite way of avoiding class 1 NICs was for directors to be paid in gilts. However, since 1988 the regulations closed this loophole, and payments in kind will be classed as earnings for NIC purposes where:

- the benefit can be surrendered for cash;
- the employer discharges a liability of the employee.

The contribution period, or earnings period, is generally weekly or monthly, this being the shortest interval between the regular receipt of earnings. For example, if an employee receives a monthly salary, a quarterly commission and an annual bonus, the earnings period would be monthly.

The contributions payable for an earnings period are not calculated on a cumulative basis, as is the case for income tax under PAYE, so that if an employee has particularly high earnings in one earnings period, NICs will be deducted on the earnings for that period even if in the next earnings period the employee's earnings are below the specified lower limit. There is, however, an exception to this general rule where directors' remuneration is concerned. Because there is a ceiling on primary class 1 NICs, company directors could potentially receive all their earnings in one contribution period, which would amount to an under payment of NICs. To prevent this type of abuse, class 1 NICs for directors are calculated on an annual earnings period. This means that, unlike other employees, directors' NICs are deducted on a cumulative basis.

The limits for primary contributions are fixed for a fiscal year:

	2002/03 £	2001/02 £
Lower earnings limit:		
weekly	75	72
monthly	325	312
annual (directors)	3 900	3 744
primary threshold (per week)	89	87
Upper earnings limit:		
weekly	585	575
monthly	2 535	2 492
annual (directors)	30 420	29 900

The FA 1998 introduced radical changes to the system of NICs, to be effective from April 1999. Up until 1999, if the employee's income for the income period was above the lower earnings limit (LEL), then an initial rate of 2 per cent applied to earnings below the LEL, with a standard rate of 10 per cent being applied to the excess, up to the upper earnings limit (UEL). The standard rate of 10 per cent is reduced to 8.4 per cent where the employee is contracted out of the State Earnings Related Pension Scheme (SERPS). From April 1999, the 2 per cent initial rate applied to earnings up to and including the LEL is abolished; for earnings in excess of the LEL, the primary contribution is charged at 8.4 per cent for employees contracted out of SERPS, and 10 per cent for employees not contracted out of SERPS, up to the UEL.

EXAMPLE

Employee earns £250 per week gross throughout the whole of 1998/99 and 1999/00.

1998/99

(a) non-contracted out
   52 (£64 × 2%) + (£186 × 10%) = £1033.76

(b) contracted out
   52 (£64 × 2%) + (£186 × 8.4%) = £879.01

1999/00

(a) non-contracted out
   52 (250 – 66) × 10% = £956.80

(b) contracted out
   52 (250 – 66) × 8.4% = £803.71

It is the government's intention to raise the lower level in line with the income tax personal allowance in the same way as the secondary threshold. However, to do this in one step would mean that some people would be outside the scope of primary contributions, with the consequence that they would lose their entitlement to benefits. To preserve these benefits, earnings between the lower level and the primary threshold will effectively be liable to NICs at 0 per cent, and only those earnings between the primary threshold and the upper earnings level will be liable to a positive rate of NICs.

EXAMPLE

An employee earns £100 per week in non-contracted out employment for the whole of 2002/03.

52 (100 – 89) × 10% = £57.20

2. Employer class 1 contributions

Employers are liable for the following contributions:

(a) Secondary class 1 contributions

Secondary class 1 NICs are payable by employers in respect of all employees over the age of 16. From April 1999, a lower earnings threshold was introduced for secondary contributions in line with the income tax personal allowance. Employers will not pay secondary contributions unless the employee's earnings exceed the threshold for a contribution period. The rates and limits for secondary contributions are fixed for a fiscal year but there is no upper limit with respect to the employer's contribution.

	2002/03	2001/02
Lower earnings limit (per week)	£89	£87
Rate (non-contracted out SERPS)	11.8%	11.9%

Reduced rates apply where the employee is contracted out of SERPS, depending on the type of scheme:

Salary-related schemes   8.3% (2002/03)

Money-purchase schemes   10.8% (2002/03)

EXAMPLE

Employee earns £600 per week in non-contracted out employment for the whole of 2002/03.

Primary contributions (employee)
52 (585 – 89) × 10% = £2579.20

Secondary contributions (employer)
52 (600 – 89) × 11.8% = £3135.50

(b) Class 1A NICs

Although benefits that cannot be converted into cash do not form part of an employee's earnings for NIC purposes, certain benefits are charged to class 1A contributions on the employer. Employers are liable to pay a class 1A contribution at the maximum employers' rate on the value of the benefit assessed on an employee with regards to motor cars (not vans) and fuel, for years to 1999/00 and for other benefits in kind from April 2000.

EXAMPLE

Brian is provided with a 1800 cc car by his employers. The car was purchased new in 2000 for £21 000 and Brian is provided with all his petrol. The CO_2 emission is 205gm/km.

	£
Car benefit:	
£21 000 × 23%	4830
Fuel benefit	2850
Taxable benefit	7680
Class 1A NICs on employer:	
£7680 × 11.8%	906.24

From April 2000, employers' NICs were extended to include all taxable benefits in kind. The exceptions to this being as follows:

- qualifying beneficial loans;
- general welfare counselling provided by an employer;
- provision of childcare;
- small amounts of private use of items provided by the employer for the employee's work.

The payment of class 1 NICs entitles the employee to all the contributory benefits. The high rates of class 1 NICs for both employees and employers compared with the class 2 and class 4 liabilities for unincorporated businesses, makes NICs an important consideration in deciding on the choice of business medium when starting up a business.

Class 2 contributions

Self-employed persons, under pensionable age and over 16 years old are liable to the flat rate class 2 contribution. The individual must be ordinarily resident in the UK and if not ordinarily resident must have been resident for at least 26 weeks in the preceding 52 contribution weeks, and must be physically present in the UK during the week in which the contribution is paid.

The flat rate class 2 contribution is fixed for a fiscal year:

2001/02	£2.00 per week
2002/03	£2.00 per week

Payment of class 2 NICs entitles the self-employed person to the basic state retirement pension and all other contributory benefits except the jobseeker's allowance. The onus is on the self-employed person to notify the DSS in writing with regard to the following matters:

- on the commencement of self-employment;
- on the cessation of self-employment; and
- on a change of address.

Exemption from class 2 NICs

Exemption from class 2 contributions is mandatory where the person is incapacitated, i.e. where for any contribution week the earner is:

- receiving maternity allowance
- receiving incapacity benefit
- in legal custody or imprisoned throughout the whole week
- receiving invalid care allowance
- incapable of work during the whole week.

Exemption can also be claimed where the individual's earnings for a fiscal year are below a prescribed limit. The small earnings limit is fixed for a fiscal year:

2002/03	£4025
2001/02	£3955

Unless the trader produces accounts to 5 April, this will involve apportioning two sets of accounts.

EXAMPLE

A trader prepares accounts to the 31 December each year with the following results:

	£
YE 31/12/01	3800
YE 31/12/02	4000
YE 31/12/03	2500

In order to see if the profits fall within the small earnings limit, the actual profits for the fiscal year need to be determined:

2001/02	£	£
6/4/01 – 5/4/02		
6/4/01 – 31/12/01		
9/12 × £3800	2850	
1/1/02 – 5/4/02		
3/12 × £4000	1000	3850

2002/03
6/4/02 – 5/4/03

6/4/02 – 31/12/02		
9/12 × £4500	3375	
1/1/02 – 5/4/02		
3/12 × £2500	625	4000

In this case the trader can claim small earnings exemption for 2000/01 and 2001/02. Once the DSS approve the claim, they issue a certificate of small earnings exemption (form CF17) which applies to the tax year concerned.

However, if the claim is made, the trader will not be making the relative class 2 contributions and this will affect the individual's contribution record, which may result in the loss of future benefit entitlement.

The payment options for class 2 contributions are as follows:

1. Quarterly billing

Fourteen days after the end of the quarter (13 weeks) the self-employed earner receives a written notice stating:

- the number of weeks of liability
- the weekly rate
- the formal date of notification.

The account must be settled within 28 days of the formal date of notification.

2. Direct debit

Payments are deducted from the individual's bank account on the second Friday in every month for each of the contribution weeks in the preceding tax month.

3. Deduction at source

It may be possible to have contributions deducted at source from certain state benefits, e.g. war disablement pension.

Failure to pay class 2 NICs when they are due renders the individual liable to a fine of up to £1000 on summary conviction for each offence.

Class 3 contributions

Class 3 NICs are flat rate voluntary contributions that can only be paid where no liability arises under the other classes in order to preserve long-term contributory benefits. The flat rate class 3 contribution is fixed for a fiscal year:

2002/03	£6.85 per week
2001/02	£6.75 per week

Payment of class 3 NICs entitles the individual to claim long-term basic benefits, such as the state retirement pension and widow's benefits, and are likely to be made by non-employed persons or those whose earnings are below the thresholds of other NICs.

Class 3 contributions are normally paid on or before 5 April following the tax year in which NICs were deficient, although a period of six years may be allowed. The payment options for class 3 contributions are as follows:

- quarterly billing
- monthly direct debit
- annual payment by cheque.

Because the payments are voluntary, there are no rules for enforcement and no penalty regime.

Class 4 contributions

Self-employed persons are liable to class 4 contributions as well as class 2 contributions on the basis of Schedule D Case I profits for the fiscal year in question. There will be no class 4 liability, however, if the individual is:

- over pensionable age at the beginning of the fiscal year; or
- under 16 years of age at the beginning of the fiscal year, provided that an application is made for exception.

Class 4 contributions do not entitle the payer to any contributory benefits even though they are included in the NI Fund, and they are not collected by the DSS but are the responsibility of the IR. The contributions are collected along with the Schedule D Case I income tax liability and as such the Schedule D Case I requirements and penalty regime apply equally to class 4 NICs. As there is no benefit entitlement in respect of class 4 contributions, the DSS do not generally keep records of class 4 NICs unless there is an application for deferment.

The charge to class 4 is calculated as a percentage of profits between upper and lower limits. These limits are fixed for a fiscal year:

	Upper limit	*Lower limit*	%
2001/02	£29 900	£4535	7
2002/03	£30 420	£4615	7

EXAMPLE

Calculate the class 4 contribution on the following Schedule D Case I profits for 2002/03 and 2001/02: (a) £4000, (b) £16 230 and (c) £32 000

2002/03
(a) No class 4 liability as the Schedule D Case I profit is below £4615.

(b) £ (16 230 − 4615) × 7% = £813.05

(c) £ (30 420 − 4615) × 7% = £1 806.35

2001/02
(a) No liability

(b) £ (16 230 − 4535) × 7% = £818.65

(c) £ (29 900 − 4535) × 7% = £1775.55

The Schedule D Case I profit on which class 4 NICs are charged is the Schedule D Case I profit for income tax purposes, after deducting any loss relief. Trading losses that are relieved against general income under the ICTA 1988, s 380 can, however, be carried forward for class 4 purposes.

Maximum NICs

There is a ceiling on the amount of contributions that an individual must pay in any one fiscal year for each class of NIC.

Note: There is no annual maximum liability with regard to employers' secondary class 1 contributions.

Where an individual is either employed or self-employed or has more than one employment, there are maximum amounts that the individual must pay in aggregate.

(a) Maximum class 1 and class 2

The annual maximum amount of class 1 and class 2 contributions is calculated as:

53 × maximum standard class 1 weekly rate

Payments made in excess of this are repayable. The order in which the repayments are made are as follows:

- class 2
- class 1 not contracted out
- class 1 contracted out.

EXAMPLE 1

Marco is employed on a salary of £35 000 pa and is paid monthly. He also runs a part-time business and the Schedule D Case I profits were £4500 for 2002/03. He pays primary class 1 contributions at the non-contracted out rate.

	£
Class 1 contributions paid:	
12 (2535 – 386) × 10%	2578.80
Class 2 contributions paid:	
52 × £2.00	104.00
	2682.80
The maximum class 1 and class 2:	
53 × (585 – 89) × 10%	(2628.80)
Repayable	54.00

EXAMPLE 2

Freda had two jobs during 2002/03 which were paid as follows:

Job 1: £400 per week and is not contracted out
Job 2: £1750 per month contracted out on a salary related scheme.

Class 1 contributions paid:	£
Job 1	
52 (400 – 89) × 10%	1617.20
Job 2	
12 (1750 – 386) × 8.4%	1374.91
	2992.11
Maximum class 1	(2628.80)
Repayable	363.31

The repayment would be made from job 1, i.e. the non-contracted out employment. The repayments must be claimed within six years from the end of the fiscal year concerned.

(b) Maximum class 4

Where an individual is liable for class 1, 2 and 4, the class 4 liability cannot exceed:

(The maximum class 2 and 4) *less* (class 1 and 2 paid)

Maximum class 2: (2002/03)	£
53 × £2.00	104

Maximum class 4 (2002/03)	
£(30 420 – 4615) × 7%	1806.35

EXAMPLE

Malcolm is self-employed and the Schedule D Case I profit for 2002/03 is £26,750. He is also employed earning £250 per week not contracted out:

	£	£
Maximum class 2		104.00
Maximum class 4		1806.35
		1910.35
less:		
Class 1 paid:		
52 (250 – 89) × 10%	837.20	
Class 2 paid:		
52 × £2.00	104.00	(941.20)
Maximum class 4		969.15
Class 4 paid:		£
£(26 750 – 4615) × 7%		1549.45
Maximum class 4		(969.15)
Class 4 repayment due		580.30

Deferment

Where it is likely that the individual will pay more than the maximum NICs, an application can be made for a deferment of NICs in the following order:

- class 4
- class 2 and/or
- class 1.

(a) Class 4 deferment

The application for deferment must be made on form CF 359 to the DSS Deferment Group and the applicant must provide the DSS with any relevant information and evidence they require. If the deferment is approved, the DSS issue a certificate of deferment until such time as all the relevant information is available, and the IR do not collect the contributions. If the deferred contributions ultimately become payable, responsibility for collecting them rests with the DSS and not the IR.

(b) Class 2 deferment

In situations where an individual is both employed and self-employed and likely to pay more than the annual maximum contributions, the DSS may agree to defer class 2 NICs until the liabilities can be determined with accuracy.

(c) Class 1 deferment (primary contributions)

In situations where an individual has more than one employment and it is likely that maximum class 1 NICs will be payable in one of the employments, the DSS may agree to defer class 1 primary contributions in the other employments rather than the individual having to make a repayment claim for excess class 1 NICs. The DSS will always defer primary class 1 NICs at standard rate in priority to contracted out primary class 1 contributions.

Note: Deferment has no effect on the secondary class 1 contribution payable by the employer.

If as a result of the deferment further class 1 NICs remain payable, they are collected by direct assessment.

SELF ASSESSMENT QUESTIONS

14.1 Employee is paid £400 per week gross in non-contracted out employment for the whole of 2002/03.

REQUIRED

Calculate the primary and secondary class 1 contributions.

14.2 Julie is employed on a salary of £35 000 pa. She also runs a part-time business; Schedule DI profits were £4500 for 2002/03. Julie pays class 1 contributions at the non-contracted out rate.

REQUIRED

Calculate the maximum NICs payable, and any contributions repayable for 2002/03.

CHAPTER 15

Provision for retirement

Pensions are given favourable tax treatment in the legislation compared with other types of savings and investments, and as such they are an important aspect of tax planning. All individuals who have paid sufficient class 1 or class 2 NICs are entitled to receive the basic state pension on their retirement. National Insurance legislation was radically reformed in 1978 with the introduction of the State Earnings Related Pension Scheme (SERPS); individuals who have paid class 1 NICs at the higher contracted in rate are entitled to receive an additional pension based on their average lifetime earnings. SERPS, however, gives no tax advantage to the individual as the scheme makes no provision for a tax free lump sum on retirement and NICs are not tax deductible, although the employer's NIC costs are an allowable business expense. However, with people generally living much longer it became apparent quite soon after its introduction that the cost of SERPS into the next century would continue to escalate.

Following the Social Security Act 1986, the tax legislation regarding pensions was overhauled with more choices being made available for 'topping up' the basic state retirement pension in an attempt to relieve the government of its future pension liabilities. This chapter examines the alternative pension strategies available outside the state system under the present tax regime.

Occupational pension schemes (ICTA 1988, ss 590–612)

Occupational pension schemes or superannuation schemes are set up by employers for the benefit of their employees. These schemes are also known as retirement benefit schemes and may be either:

(a) *Final salary schemes* – based on defined benefits, i.e. based on earnings at or near the time of retirement; or

(b) *Money purchase schemes* – based on defined contributions, i.e. the value of the fund at retirement.

Occupational pensions may be contracted out of SERPS, provided that the scheme is Revenue-approved by the Pension Schemes Office (PSO). To be approved, the scheme must fulfil the following conditions:

(a) The scheme is established for the benefit of employees on retirement between the ages of 60–75, or to the employee's widow/widower or dependants in the event of the employee's death.

(b) The employer must make a contribution to the scheme.

(c) The pension provided on retirement is calculated as $\frac{1}{60}$ of final salary for each year of service up to a maximum of 40 years and the final salary is subject to an 'earnings cap' of £97 200 for 2002/03.

(d) A tax free lump sum may be payable calculated as $\frac{3}{80}$ of the final salary for each year up to a maximum of 40 years, subject to the 'earnings cap' of £97 200.

(e) The scheme allows the above fractions to be increased where employees do not have 40 years of working life before retirement age.

(f) The amount payable to a widow/widower/dependant does not exceed $\frac{2}{3}$ of the pension payable to the employee, and any lump sum payable on death before retirement cannot exceed four times the final salary.

Approved company pension schemes provide an efficient means of saving for retirement as they receive the following tax benefits:

(a) Employee contributions are an allowable deduction from Schedule E income up to a maximum of 15 per cent of remuneration, subject to the 'earnings cap' of £97 200.

(b) Employer's contributions are an allowable trading expense and are not treated as a benefit in kind on employees.

(c) Income and gains arising in the scheme are exempt from tax.

(d) Lump sums payable on retirement/death are tax free.

(e) Approved schemes may be contracted out of SERPS, in which case employee and employer class 1 contributions are reduced but no SERP is paid on retirement.

Additional voluntary contributions

Employees contributing to an occupational pension scheme can make additional voluntary contributions, provided that they are within the 15 per cent limit, in order to enhance their pensions on retirement. This can be done by either:

(a) making additional voluntary contributions (AVCs) to the existing scheme to provide an increased pension; or

(b) making free-standing additional voluntary contributions (FSAVCs) to a separate scheme to provide an extra pension in addition to the occupational pension.

Where employers operate an occupational pension scheme, they can also set up 'top up' schemes, but as they will be unapproved schemes, they carry no tax benefits but enable employers to provide more generous benefits as they are not subject to the conditions for approved schemes.

Personal pension schemes (ICTA 1988, ss 630–55)

In order to increase the choice available to individuals in providing for their retirement outside the state system, personal pension schemes (PPSs) were introduced with effect from 1 July 1988. Approved PPSs receive favourable tax treatment and are offered by a variety of financial institutions and may be taken out by:

- self-employed persons;
- employed persons in non-pensionable employment; and
- employed persons opting out of their employer's occupational pension scheme.

Provided that the scheme is Revenue-approved, the individual can contract out of SERPS and pay the lower rate of class 1 NICs; as it is anticipated that benefits under SERPS will be reduced for persons retiring after March 2000, a personal pension could be a beneficial retirement strategy to embark on for those individuals due for retirement in the 21st century.

Benefits under a PPS can be taken as:

- an annuity commencing between the ages of 50 and 75; and
- a lump sum payable on retirement provided that it does not exceed 25 per cent of the value of the fund.

Approval of PPSs is broadly similar to occupational pension schemes and the Revenue will generally check that they only provide for a pension payable to the individual or their spouse in the event of death. Schemes that enable the individual to assign the pension or obtain a lump sum in excess of an agreed percentage will generally not gain Revenue approval.

Approved PPSs receive the following tax benefits:

- income and gains arising in the fund are exempt from tax;
- lump sums payable on retirement are exempt from tax;
- the scheme can be contracted out of SERPS; and
- contributions are allowed as a deduction from the individual's net relevant earnings at the rates shown in Table 15.1.

Table 15.1 PPS contributions rate

Age at beginning of tax year	Percentage of net relevant earnings
up to 35	17.5%
36 – 45	20%
46 – 50	25%
51 – 55	30%
56 – 60	35%
over 61	40%

Five per cent of the allowed percentage can be used to provide a lump sum payable on death, and the net relevant earnings are subject to a ceiling of £97 200 (2002/03).

Employees

The net relevant earnings for PPS purposes are the Schedule E emoluments less any allowable deductions.

EXAMPLE

Henry, who was born on 2 March 1955 is employed on a salary of £16 000 pa in non-pensionable employment. Total benefits for 2002/03 amount to £5800 and he pays £200 pa in professional subscriptions allowable under the ICTA 1988, s 201. Henry's relevant earnings are:

	£
Salary	16 000
Benefits	5 800
	21 800
less s 201	(200)
Net relevant earnings	21 600

As Henry is 47 years old at the beginning of the tax year the maximum contribution into a PPS eligible for tax relief is calculated as:

$25\% \times £21\,600 = £5400$

Where the employer makes a contribution to the employee's PPS, the total contribution eligible for relief is subject to the above limits.

EXAMPLE

George, who was born on 5 May 1944, is employed on a salary of £13 000 pa. His employers contribute £750 pa into George's PPS. As George is 57 years old at the beginning of 2002/03, the maximum amount qualifying for relief is calculated as:

$35\% \times £13\,000 = £4550$

Therefore, the maximum contribution that George can make that is eligible for tax relief is:

$£4550 - £750 = £3800$

Employed persons paying premiums into a PPS pay the amount net of basic rate income tax. As the contribution eligible for relief is deducted gross in the computation, the basic rate tax deducted at source must be added back to the tax liability.

EXAMPLE

Adrian, a single man, is 32 years old and employed on a salary of £17 000 pa, with no other income for 2002/03. During the year he paid £2464 (net) into a PPS.

The maximum gross contribution eligible for relief is calculated as:

$$17.5\% \times £17\,000 = £2975$$

Pension paid (gross) $2464 \times 100/78 = £3159$ therefore tax relief restricted to £2975.

	£
Salary	17 000
less Pension	(2 975)
	14 025
less PA	(4 615)
Taxable income	9 410

1920 × 10%	192
7490 × 22%	1648
	1840

Add back basic rate tax deducted on pension £(2975 × 22%)	654
Tax liability	2 494

Gross amount of contribution (£2464 × 100/78)	3 159
Gross amount eligible for relief	(2 975)
Contribution not eligible for relief	184

Self-employed

As self-employed persons do not pay class 1 contributions, they do not contribute to SERPS and so cannot contract out. The net relevant earnings for PPS purposes are the Schedule D Case I/II income less business charges and loss relief.

EXAMPLE

Lucy has a Schedule D Case I adjusted profit of £26 000 for 2002/03 and trading losses brought forward of £4000. During the year she paid business charges of £750.

	£
Schedule D Case I	26 000
less Loss relief	(4 000)
less Trade charges	(750)
Net relevant earnings	21 250

The percentages depending on age are applied in the same way as employed persons in order to calculate the maximum contributions eligible for tax relief. Self-employed persons paying contributions into a PPS generally make the payments gross and so no adjustment is needed as is the case for employees.

Contributions carried back (ICTA 1998, s 641)

The taxpayer can elect to have all or part of the contributions paid in a particular tax year carried back to the previous tax year, or, if there are no relevant earnings in the previous year, to the year before that, provided there is surplus capacity. This election can be useful where there are excess contributions paid in the current year, or the individual's marginal rate of tax was higher in the previous year and there is surplus capacity in the previous year to absorb the relief. The election must be made by the 31 January following the tax year in which the contribution was paid, i.e. by the normal annual filing date for the return of income and gains for that tax year, e.g. a claim to carry back contributions paid in 2002/03 would have to be made by 31 January 2004, which is the annual filing date for the return of income and gains for 2002/03.

EXAMPLE

Mr Patel, who was born on 5 September 1953, is self-employed and pays £4000 (gross) each year into an approved PPS. His net relevant earnings for the last three years have been:

	£
1999/00	24 000
2000/01	16 000
2001/02	13 000

Year	Net relevant earnings	% eligible for relief	Maximum PPS relief	PPS relief used	Unused PPS relief
1999/00	24 000	20%	4800	4000	800
2000/01	16 000	25%	4000	4000	nil
2001/02	13 000	25%	3250	3250	nil

In 2001/02, therefore, Mr Patel has £750 of excess contributions. An election can be made to carry back the excess contributions to 1999/00, as there are no relevant earnings in 2000/01 to absorb the contributions. Mr Patel will therefore be entitled to a repayment of income tax on the £750 at his marginal rate of tax for 1999/00.

Unused relief carried forward (ICTA 1988, s 642)

If the contribution made to a PPS is less than the amount eligible for tax relief, the unused amount can be carried forward for up to six years. Unused relief carried forward is used on a FIFO basis to relieve excess contributions in future years where the maximum relief has been used in full.

EXAMPLE

Samantha, who was born on 11 November 1963, has been self-employed since 1996/97 with the following net relevant earnings:

	£
1996/97	12000
1997/98	15000
1998/99	16000
1999/00	20000
2000/01	18000
2001/02	20000

She has paid £2000 gross contributions each year into an approved PPS. In 2001/02 Samantha paid an extra £5000 into her pension fund.

Year	Net relevant earnings (£)	% eligible for relief	Maximum PPS relief (£)	PPS relief used (£)	Unused PPS relief (£)	Unused relief c/fwd (£)
1996/97	12000	17.5%	2100	2000	100	100
1997/98	15000	17.5%	2625	2000	625	725
1998/99	16000	17.5%	2800	2000	800	1525
1999/00	20000	17.5%	3500	2000	1500	3025
2000/01	18000	20%	3600	2000	1600	4625
2001/02	20000	20%	4000	7000	nil	1625

Samantha's contribution of £2000 pa qualifies in full each year for tax relief. The £5000 extra contribution paid in 2001/02 also qualifies for full relief as follows:

2001/02	£
Maximum PPS relief	4000
PPS paid	(7000)
Excess contribution	(3000)

The excess contribution can be relieved by using brought forward unused relief from earlier years on a FIFO basis:

	£
1996/97	100
1997/98	625
1998/99	800
1999/00	1475
	3000

The unused relief of £1625 can be carried forward and used within six years of the year in which the excess arose:

	Unused relief (£)	Carry forward to
1999/00	25	2005/06
2000/01	1600	2006/07

As there is unused relief each year, Samantha could have made a claim to have had part of the contributions carried back to the previous year. The decision of whether or not to carry forward unused relief or relate back contributions to the previous year depends on the marginal rate of income tax for the years concerned and so should be considered carefully to gain the maximum benefit.

The FA 1995 introduced provisions to enable individuals to defer the purchase of an annuity and make income withdrawals on schemes approved after 1 May 1995 (s 58 and Schedule II to the FA 1995).

Where the provisions apply, individuals may defer purchasing an annuity at the pension date until the age of 75 and withdraw income during the deferral period equal to the amount of annuity the fund would have produced, provided the individual is at least 50 years old. This may be useful in situations where annuity rates are low when the individual is approaching retirement.

These provisions do not affect the individual's right to a tax free lump sum at pension date.

Retirement annuity contracts (ICTA 1988, ss 618–29)

Retirement annuity contracts (RACs) were replaced by PPS from 1 July 1988 but existing contracts are allowed to continue under the RAC provisions unless they have been transferred to a PPS. Prior to 1 July 1988, a RAC could be taken out by:

- self-employed persons;
- employed persons in non-pensionable employment; and
- employed persons opting out of their employer's occupational pension scheme.

Provided that the RAC was Revenue-approved, the individual could deduct the qualifying premium from their net relevant earnings at the following rates:

Age at beginning of tax year	% of net relevant earnings
under 51	17.5%
51 – 55	20%
56 – 60	22.5%
over 61	27.5%

Revenue approval was the same for RACs as it is for PPSs and the net relevant earnings are calculated in the same way. The facility to carry back excess premiums or carry forward unused relief is available to RACs in the same way as PPSs. There is no 'earnings cap' with regard to RACs but contracts taken out after 17 March 1987 imposed a limit of £150 000 on the lump sum payment at pension date. Where an individual pays a premium into an approved RAC, they may also obtain tax relief for contributions paid into a PPS provided the PPS limit is not exceeded, i.e. the premium paid into the RAC is deducted from the PPS limit.

EXAMPLE

Sally, who was born on 10 July 1955, and has net relevant earnings of £14 000, pays a premium of £1000 into an approved RAC in 2001/02. Assuming that there is no unused relief brought forward, the maximum PPS contribution eligible for tax relief in 2001/02 is calculated as:

	£
Maximum RAC premium = £14 000 × 17.5%	2450
Maximum PPS contribution = £14 000 × 20%	2800

Therefore, maximum PPS contribution eligible for tax relief is: (£2800 − £1000) = £1800

Although RACs are no longer available, it may be worth maintaining existing contracts where the individual is a higher rate taxpayer. This is because there is no 'earnings cap' with regard to RACs as there is for PPSs, even though the percentage of contributions attracting tax relief is higher for contributions to a PPS.

EXAMPLE

Edward, who was born on 10 January 1968, has net relevant earnings of £105 000 for 2002/03, and has both a PPS and RAC. Assuming that there is no unused relief brought forward, the maximum amounts eligible for tax relief are as follows:

	£
Maximum RAC premium = £105 000 × 17.5%	18 375
Maximum PPS contribution = £97 200 (max) × 17.5%	17 010

If Edward pays £12 000 premium into the RAC, the maximum PPS contribution that would attract tax relief is:

(£17 010 − £12 000) = £5010

If he paid £12 000 into the PPS, the maximum RAC premium would also be £5010 as the RAC premium is deducted from the PPS limit. However, Edward could pay £18 375 into the RAC, but as this exceeds the maximum PPS contribution limit, no contribution into the PPS can attract tax relief.

The FA 1998 introduced changes to the pension legislation in order to tighten control over small Revenue-approved schemes and counter tax avoidance.

(a) Small self-administered schemes

The intention behind the reforms, which have been effective since 17 March 1998, was to bring these schemes more in line with occupational pension schemes:

- the independent trustee approved by the Revenue, i.e. the pensioneer trustee, cannot be removed without an immediate replacement;
- the pensioneer trustee must be a co-signatory to bank accounts;
- the pensioneer trustee must be a registered owner of scheme assets;
- the scheme administrator will have to maintain specified records, and make them available for inspection if required;
- there will be restrictions on the type of investments and financial transactions that will be allowed.

(b) Tax avoidance

From 17 March 1998, a 40 per cent tax charge will be made on the value of assets in schemes ceasing to be Revenue-approved in order to curtail the abuse of tax reliefs by certain pension schemes transferring their assets to an off-shore trust when they cease to be Revenue-approved.

Stakeholder Pensions

Stakeholder pensions were introduced from 6 April 2001 through which the government hopes to encourage more people to save for their retirement. Stakeholder pensions can be taken out whether or not the individual is employed or not, making the system more flexible than in the past when pension contributions could only be made from earned income to be tax efficient. From 6th April 2001, everyone can save £3600 per year, tax free, in a stakeholder pension.

From October 2001, employers with five or more staff will have to offer access to a pension scheme

SELF ASSESSMENT QUESTION

15.1 Robin Batty has been in business for many years. His net relevant earnings (NRE) over the last six years have been as follows:

	NRE £
1996/97	13 000
1997/98	17 000
1998/99	18 000
1999/00	25 000
2000/01	20 000
2001/02	16 000

Robin was born on 11 November 1962 and contributes £2200 pa (gross) into an approved PPS. In 2001/02 Robin paid an extra £2000 into his pension fund.

REQUIRED

Show how the pension payments can qualify for tax relief, and indicate any additional payment Robin can contribute to the fund to make use of all of the relief available to date.

CHAPTER 16

Investment income

Historically the distinction between earned income and investment income was important for many reasons, for example, an investment income surcharge was levied at 15 per cent on investment incomes in excess of £7000 (1983/4), however, investment income surcharge was abolished by the FA 1984, effective from 6 April 1984.

Also, prior to the introduction of independent taxation in 1990/91, spouses' incomes were aggregated for tax purposes, but a married woman could claim to be taxed separately on her earned, but not her unearned income, this remained part of her husband's income for tax purposes. Where a separate taxation of wife's earnings election was not in force, the distinction was important for calculating the wife's earned income relief, available to a married man.

Despite changes in the tax laws, making the above rules redundant, the distinction is still important in determining relevant income for calculating maximum personal pension premiums and in respect of jointly held property by spouses.

The most usual types of investment income are interest, dividends and rents.

This chapter examines the tax treatment of these various types of investment income and considers tax efficient savings and investments for individuals resident in the UK.

Schedule A

Rent and other income arising from property and land in the UK is assessed to income tax under Schedule A. However, the ICTA 1988, s 55 specifically provides that income from the following sources is treated as trading income and taxed under Schedule D Case I:

- mines and quarries;
- ironworks, gasworks;
- canals, docks;
- markets, fairs, toll bridges, ferries; and
- railways.

The FA 1995 radically changed the way in which income from land is assessed on individuals. The legislation refers to a 'Schedule A business', and the income treated as if it were a business even where the income merely involves the letting of a single property.

Examples of common sources of Schedule A incomes include:

- rents under leases;
- ground rents;
- rent charges;
- hunting and fishing rights;
- letting of caravans on fixed sites and house boats on fixed moorings; and
- furnished accommodation (prior to the FA 1995, furnished accommodation was taxed under Schedule D Case VI and not Schedule A).

Schedule A profit/loss

All sources of Schedule A income of the taxpayer are pooled together and allowable expenses deducted to produce a Schedule A profit or loss, which should be prepared on an accruals basis as if it were a business.

The allowable expenses for a 'Schedule A business' follow the principles that apply to Schedule D Case I. Under the new Schedule A however, only a strict statutory fiscal year basis will apply, and so accounts must be prepared for fiscal years. Capital allowances are available on plant and machinery used in the maintenance, repair or management of the property and are given as a Schedule A expense.

For furnished lettings there is an additional concessional relief available for fixtures and fittings calculated on either:

(a) *a renewals basis* – on a renewals basis no relief is given for the original cost, but the cost of renewing an item is treated as an expense;

or more usually:

(b) *wear and tear allowance* – the wear and tear allowance is calculated as 10 per cent (rents minus any rates paid by the landlord).

Interest on loans to buy or improve property for letting on a commercial basis is allowed as a deduction in computing the Schedule A profits. Losses of a 'Schedule A business' are carried forward and set off against the first available Schedule A income.

Despite the income under Schedule A being calculated as if it were a business, the income remains *investment income* and *not earned income*. The only exception to this is in relation to furnished holiday accommodation which will be considered separately.

Premiums

When a landlord grants a lease to a tenant for a period of time, the landlord still retains an interest in the property; whereas on the assignment of a lease, the entire interest in the property is sold and there is a liability to capital gains tax.

Premiums paid on the grant of a long lease (over 50 years) are charged to capital gains tax; where a premium is paid on the grant of a short lease (not exceeding 50 years), the premium is partly charged to capital gains tax and partly charged to income tax under Schedule A as rent. The part of the premium assessable under

Schedule A takes account of the maximum tax life of the lease, i.e. 50 years (100% ÷ 50 = 2%), and is calculated as the premium receivable less 2 per cent for every year of the lease except the first 12 months:

	£
Premium receivable	X
less 2% (n – 1) × premium	(Y)
Assessable under Schedule A	Z

where n = number of complete years of lease.

EXAMPLE

Adrian grants a seven-year lease to Sally on 6 April 2002. The rent is £3000 per annum payable in advance on the 6th day of each month, and a premium of £5000 is charged. The amount assessable to Schedule A for 2002/03 is as follows:

	£	£
Rent		3000
Premium	5000	
less 2% (7 – 1) × £5000	(600)	4400
Schedule A assessment		7400

Where a person carries on a trade, profession or vocation, and pays a premium on the lease of business premises, then the amount assessed to Schedule A on the landlord may be treated as a business expense spread evenly over the term of the lease.

EXAMPLE

Penelope grants a six-year lease of business premises to Ben for a premium of £5000 on 1 July 2002.

	£
Premium	5000
less 2% (6 – 1) × £5000	(500)
Assessable to Schedule A 2002/03 (on Penelope)	4500

If Ben prepares accounts to 31 December each year, then for his accounts to 31 December 2002 he could claim a deduction of:

$$\frac{£4500}{6} \times 6/12 = £375$$

He could then claim a deduction of £750 for the next five years with a final claim of 6/12 (£375) in the last year of the lease.

A similar relief is available where a tenant, having paid a premium on a lease, then grants a sub-lease.

The relief is calculated as follows:

$$\frac{\text{Full duration of sub-lease}}{\text{Full duration of head lease}} \times \text{Chargeable premium for head lease}$$

EXAMPLE

Charles granted a lease to Edward on 6 April 1992 for 30 years, for a premium of £30 000. On 6 April 2002 Edward granted a sub-lease to George for seven years for a premium of £16 000.

Charles' Schedule A liability:

	£
Premium	30 000
less:	
2% (30 – 1) × £30 000	(17 400)
Schedule A assessable 1992/93 (on Charles)	12 600

Edward's Schedule A liability:

	£
Premium	16 000
less:	
2% (7 – 1) × £16 000	(1 920)
	14 080
less Sub-letting relief:	
7/30 × £12 600	(2 940)
Schedule A assessable 2002/03 (on Edward)	11 140

The relief available for a sub-lease cannot create a loss. Any unrelieved premium will be allowed against the net rents over the term of the lease.

EXAMPLE

John grants a 25-year lease on business premises to Pauline on 6 July 1998 at a premium of £30 000 and an annual rental of £2500 paid quarterly in advance. On 6 July 2002 Pauline grants a sub-lease to Alan for 15 years for a premium of £12 000 and an annual rental of £3500 payable in advance on the 6th of each month.

Pauline's assessment for 2002/03 would be:

	£
Premium	12 000
less:	
2% (15 – 1) × £12 000	(3 360)
	8 640
Sub-letting relief	
15/25 × £15 600 *	(9 360)
Assessable premium	nil

	£
Unrelieved premium	720
Rent received 9/12 × £3500	2625
Rent paid	(2500)
	125
Relief £720/15 × 9/12	(36)
Schedule A	89

£720/15 = £48 will be allowed against net rents in future years.

* Premium	30 000
less 2% (25 – 1) × £30 000	(14 400)
Schedule A on head lease	15 600

Section 34 of the ICTA 88 contains provisions to deal with specific situations that may otherwise lead to avoidance of income tax under Schedule A.

The main anti-avoidance provisions are:

1. Premiums in the form of work done

Where the terms of the lease impose an obligation on the tenant to carry out improvement work on the premises the cost will be treated as if it were a premium received by the landlord.

EXAMPLE

David granted a five-year lease on 1 September 2002 for an annual rental of £1440 payable monthly in advance on the 1st of each month. Under the terms of the lease, in 2002 the tenant was required to build an extension which cost £6000.

The extension will be treated as if David received a premium of £6000 in 2002/03.

Schedule A assessment 2002/03

	£	£
Rent (8 × £120)		960
Premium (deemed)	6000	
less:		
2% (5 – 1) × £6000	480	5520
Schedule A		6480

2. Lump sum rents

Where a sum becomes payable by the tenant instead of the whole or part of the rent for any period, the sum paid is deemed to be a premium.

EXAMPLE

Geraldine grants a 21-year lease on 1 July 1995. The terms of the lease provide that she can demand £20 000 after seven years instead of the rent for the remainder of the lease.

Deemed premium is £20 000 for a lease of 14 years (21 – 7).

	£
Premium	20 000
less:	
2% (14 − 1) × £20 000	(5 200)
Schedule A 2002/03	14 800

3. Payments to vary the terms of the lease

Where a sum becomes payable by the tenant, other than rent, in consideration for varying the terms of the lease, the sum is deemed to be a premium in the year when the contract providing for the variation was entered into.

EXAMPLE

Susan grants a lease of 21 years. The terms of the lease state that the tenant has an option to take further term, provided that the conditions of the lease are fulfilled. If the tenant fails to do so after ten years have elapsed but then pays £15 000 to waive Susan's right to object to a further term being taken, the sum paid of £15 000 would be treated as a premium on an 11-year, lease i.e. (21 − 10).

	£
Premium	15 000
less:	
2% (11 − 1) × £15 000	(3 000)
Assessable to Schedule A	12 000

Rent a room relief (FA 1992 (No. 2), s 59 and Sch 10)

Available to owner/occupiers and tenants who let furnished rooms in their homes. Gross annual rents which do not exceed £4250 are exempt from income tax. Where rents exceed this amount, the taxpayer can choose between either paying tax on the excess without any deduction for expenses or on the actual profit in the normal way.

Furnished holiday accommodation

The letting of furnished accommodation did not constitute trading even in cases where considerable managerial duties were involved as would be the case with a boarding house, for example. This fact was established in *Griffiths* v *Jackson* [1983] STC 184.

Occasionally, however, case law is overturned by new legislation and following the case of *Griffith* v *Jackson* in 1983 new legislation was passed to make furnished holiday accommodation, while still assessable under Schedule A (prior to 6 April 1995, furnished holiday accommodation was taxed under Schedule D Case VI), for all intents and purposes to be treated as a trade provided certain conditions are satisfied.

Conditions (ICTA 88, ss 503 and 504)

The accommodation must:

(a) be let on a commercial basis with a view to profit;

(b) be available for letting as holiday accommodation for at least 140 days a year;

(c) be actually let for at least 70 days a year; and

(d) not be let to the same tenant for more than 31 days consecutively in a period of seven months, not necessarily continuous, in a year.

The year would normally be a year of assessment except that in the first year of letting it will be 12 months from the commencement of the letting. If the 70 days actual letting criteria is met on some lettings but not on others, the taxpayer can elect for an averaging treatment specifying the properties to which it is to apply. Provided that the conditions are met, the income is treated as trading income even though it remains assessable under Schedule A.

The fact that it is treated as trading income brings with it several advantages:

(a) the income is regarded as earned income and so constitutes relevant earnings for pension relief;

(b) trading loss provisions apply; and

(c) for capital gains tax purposes, roll-over relief and retirement relief are available.

If the property is used partly for private purposes, then the expenses are reduced proportionately.

EXAMPLE

Emily owns two cottages in Wales which she lets as holiday accommodation. The two cottages, Ivy Cottage and Holly Cottage, are both available for letting throughout the year except that they are both used for two weeks during the summer by Emily and her family for their annual holiday.

The income and expenditure for both cottages for 2002/03 are as follows:

	Ivy		Holly	
	£	£	£	£
Rent		5400		3900
Council tax	416		416	
Advertising	175		135	
Cleaning	300		300	
Insurance	250		220	
Repairs	92		115	
Electricity	200		175	
Gas	250		230	
Central heating installation	1875		–	
		(3558)		(1591)
		1842		2309

Wear and tear allowance has been agreed at 10 per cent of rents less council tax.

The Schedule A assessment for 2001/02 will be as follows:

	Ivy £	Ivy £	Holly £	Holly £
Rent		5400		3900
Council tax	416		416	
Cleaning	300		300	
Insurance	250		220	
Repairs	92		115	
Electricity	200		175	
Gas	250		230	
	1508 × 50/52	(1450)	1456 × 50/52	(1400)
		3950		2500
less Advertising		(175)		(135)
less Wear and tear:				
10% [5400 – (416 × 50/52)]		(500)	10% [3900 – (416 × 50/52)] (350)	
		3275		2015

Investment income received gross under Schedule D Case III

Investment income received gross is taxable under Schedule D Case III and includes:

(a) discounts on Treasury Bills;

(b) income from deep discount securities;

(c) interest on:
  - National Savings Bank accounts (*Note*: The first £70 interest on a National Savings Bank ordinary account is exempt);
  - government securities held on the National Savings stock register;
  - $3\frac{1}{2}$ per cent war loans;
  - certificates of tax deposit;
  - quoted Eurobonds; and
  - loans between individuals.

There are no allowable expenses deductible from Schedule D Case III income. From 1997/98 tax is charged under Schedule D Case III on the interest arising in the current year.

Deep discount and deep gain securities

A deep discount security is a redeemable security that is not:

- a share;
- convertible into a share; or
- an indexed linked security

and the security is issued at a discount of either:

- 15 per cent or more of the amount payable on redemption; or
- 0.5 per cent pa until the earliest redemption date.

By purchasing at a discount, these securities were used as a method of avoiding income tax by converting potential income into capital until legislation was passed to close this loophole in 1984.

The discount is treated as income over the life of the security and when it is disposed of, or reaches maturity the income element is charged to income tax under Schedule D Case III in the year of disposal.

The income element is calculated as:

$$(A \times B / 100) - C$$

where A = the issue price plus any previous income elements
       B = % yield to maturity
       C = annual interest payable on the security

If the security is disposed of during an income period, the income element is apportioned accordingly:

$$\text{Income element for period} \times \frac{\text{Portion of income period}}{\text{Total length of income period}}$$

EXAMPLE

Security issued at 200p on 1 April 1995 and is redeemable at 264p on 1 April 2000. Interest of 4 per cent is paid on 1 April each year. The yield to maturity is 7.5 per cent. Assuming that:

(1) the security is held until maturity;

(2) the security is sold on 1 September 1998;

the income elements would be as follows:

	(1) pence	(2) pence
1/4/95 – 31/3/96 $(200 \times 7.5 / 100) - C$	11.00	11.00
1/4/96 – 31/3/97 $(211 \times 7.5 / 100) - C$	11.83	11.83
1/4/97 – 31/3/98 $(222.83 \times 7.5 / 100) - C$	12.71	12.71
1/4/98 – 31/3/99 $(235.54 \times 7.5 / 100) - C$	13.67	
1/4/98 – 31/8/98 $13.67 \times 5/12$		5.70
1/4/99 – 31/3/00 $(249.21 \times 7.5 / 100) - C$	14.69	
Income element per unit to maturity	63.90	
Income element per unit to disposal 1/9/98		41.24

While some securities cannot be classified as deep discount securities when they are issued, they may, however, yield a deep gain on redemption. The FA 1989 introduced the concept of a deep gain security, which is a security issued at a discount as for deep discount securities, but also includes at least one variable element, e.g. the redemption value may be uncertain at the time the security is issued. Where a deep gain security is disposed of after 14 March 1989, there are no CGT consequences, but the 'gain' (proceeds less cost) is charged to income tax under Schedule D Case III.

Investment income taxed at source

Most types of investment income have tax deducted at source, rather than the person receiving the income gross. In order to ensure that the correct amount of tax is paid, the income must be included gross in the individual's tax computation, and the tax already paid, the tax credit, is deducted from the final tax bill.

Dividends received from UK companies

Income from UK dividends is taxed under Schedule F on the actual income received during the fiscal year. Prior to 6 April 1999, dividends were received net of 20 per cent tax, i.e. the shareholder received 80 per cent of the gross dividend with a 20 per cent tax credit. This was because the rate of advance corporation tax (ACT) was related to the lower rate of income tax (lower rate income tax prior to 1999/00 was 20 per cent):

$$\text{ACT} = \frac{\text{lower rate income tax}}{100 - \text{lower rate income tax}} = \frac{20}{80} = \frac{1}{4}$$

The ACT paid by the company was equal to the tax credit imputed to the shareholder. The net amount was grossed up in the individual's tax computation, the gross dividend being referred to as franked investment income (FII).

EXAMPLE

Dividend of £160 received during 1998/99.

£160 × $\frac{100}{80}$ = £200 gross with a tax credit of £40

- a non-taxpayer could reclaim the £40 tax credit;
- a standard rate taxpayer had no further tax liability on the dividend;
- a higher rate taxpayer paid tax at 40 per cent, with the tax credit of £40.

The dividend income was treated as the top slice of income and taxed at 20 per cent or 40 per cent, depending on the individual's marginal rate of tax.

EXAMPLE

Trevor, a single man, had a salary of £24 000 and received dividend income of £6000 for 1998/99.

	Non-savings income £	Savings income £	Tax Credit £
Salary	24 000		
Dividends		7 500	1 500
	24 000	7 500	1 500
less Personal allowance	(4 195)	–	
Taxable income	19 805	7 500	

Trevor's taxable income was in excess of the lower and basic rate bands of £27 100 for 1998/99. First calculate the amount chargeable to tax at 40 per cent:

	£
Taxable income	27 305
Higher rate threshhold	(27 100)
Taxable at 40%	205

As the dividend was treated as the top slice of income and it was taxed at 20 per cent or 40 per cent, next calculate how much of the dividend is taxed at 20 per cent:

	£
Dividend	7 500
40% tax	(205)
20% tax	7 295

Non-savings	£
£4300 × 20%	860
£15 505 × 23%	3 566

Savings	£
£7295 × 20%	1 459
£205 × 40%	82
	5 967
less Tax credit	(1 500)
Tax payable	4 467

The FA 1998 introduced radical changes to the tax credit regime, to be effective from 2 July for most companies and pension providers, with the above system remaining in force for other shareholders until 5 April 1999, after which date significant changes to the taxation of dividend income came into effect.

From 6 April 1999, the rate of tax credit is reduced to 10 per cent and non-taxpayers will no longer be able to reclaim tax credits on dividends.

The rate of income tax payable on dividend income from 6 April 1999 will be reduced to 10 per cent, known as the Schedule F ordinary rate, for lower and basic rate taxpayers, so that the tax credit extinguishes their liability to income tax on the dividend. For higher rate taxpayers the rate of tax payable on dividend income will be 32.5 per cent, known as the Schedule F upper rate, so that they are no worse off as a result of the change:

	Up to 5/4/99		From 6/4/99	
	£		£	
Dividend received	900		900	
Tax credit	225	(20%)	100	(10%)
Gross dividend	1125		1000	
Tax	(450)	(40%)	(325)	(32.5%)
After tax income	675		675	

The dividend continues to be treated as the top slice of savings income for these purposes.

EXAMPLE 1

Sandra has a salary of £12 600 and received dividends of £4500 for 2002/03.

	Non-savings income	Dividend income	Tax credit
	£	£	£
Salary	12 600		
Dividends		5 000	500
less Personal allowance	(4 615)		
Taxable income	7 985	5 000	500

Non-savings	£
£1920 × 10%	192
£6065 × 22%	1 334
Dividends	
£5000 × 10%	500
	2 026
less Tax credit	(500)
Tax payable	1 526

Because Sandra is a standard rate taxpayer, her liability to tax on the dividend is satisfied by the tax deducted at source.

EXAMPLE 2

Mark, a single man, has a salary of £30 000 and received dividend income of £6750 for 2002/03.

	Non-savings income £	Dividend income £	Tax credit £
Salary	30 000		
Dividends		7 500	750
	30 000	7 500	750
less Personal allowance	(4 615)	–	
Taxable income	25 385	7 500	

Mark's taxable income is higher than the basic and lower rate bands of £29 400, so part of his dividend will be liable to income tax at the Schedule F upper rate:

	£		£
Taxable income	32 885	Dividends	7 500
Higher rate threshold	(29 900)	Schedule F upper rate	(2 985)
Schedule F upper rate	2 985	Schedule F ordinary rate	4 515

Non-savings	£
£1920 × 10%	192
£23 465 × 22%	5 162

Dividends	
£4515 × 10%	452
£2985 × 32.5%	970
	6 776
less Tax credit	(750)
Tax payable	6 026

From 6 April 1999, the following shareholders are no longer able to reclaim tax credits on dividend income:

- personal equity plan holders
- venture capital trusts
- individuals with no tax liability*
- charities.**

* These shareholders will be able to switch to the new Individual Savings Account (ISA), introduced from 6 April 1999.

** To compensate charities for the loss of tax credits, they will receive compensation from the Revenue, calculated as a percentage of the dividend received for five years from 6 April 1999 as follows:

- 1999/00   21%
- 2000/01   17%
- 2001/02   13%
- 2002/03   8%
- 2003/04   4%

Bank and building society interest

Interest received from banks and building societies is not included under any of the Schedules of income tax, and from 6 April 1996 is paid net of 20 per cent income tax to individuals. Non-taxpayers can elect to have the interest paid gross, provided that they make an application on form R85 (1990) certifying that they are non-tax-payers. From 6 April 1999, savings income is taxed at 10 per cent if it falls within the 10 per cent starting rate limit, 20 per cent if it is within the basic rate band, and 40 per cent where the savings income is above the basic rate limit.

NB: savings income is not liable to income tax at 22 per cent, even where it is within the basic rate band.

Note: Companies receive bank and building society interest gross and as such it is taxed under Schedule D Case III.

Income from the following is received net of lower rate income tax from 1996/7:

- Government securities – Gilt-edged securities, or 'gilts' as they are often known, are fixed interest securities that usually have a fixed redemption date. The interest on such securities is paid net of lower rate income tax.
- Debenture and loan stock interest from UK companies.

Income from the following is received net of basic rate tax:

- patent royalties
- income from covenants
- income element of a purchased life annuity
- income from trusts.

Note: Income received from a discretionary trust will have been subjected to income tax at 34 per cent and so such income will be received net of 34 per cent income tax.

NB From April 2001 companies can pay interest and charges gross where the recipient is within the charge to Corporation Tax.

Miscellaneous income – Schedule D Case VI

Schedule D Case VI is the 'mopping up' case of Schedule D, taxing profits/gains not falling to be taxed under any other Schedule or Case. In this way Case VI taxes income that would otherwise escape tax. To be assessable under Case VI, the profit must be:

- of an income nature and not of a capital nature; and
- the same type of income taxed under Cases I–V of Schedule D.

Income received from isolated transactions or speculative activities may be charged under Schedule D Case I if it can be established that a trade is being carried on (*see* 'badges of trade', Chapter 10). This will be decided on the particular facts of the particular Case and if no trade can be established the profits may fall to be taxed under Schedule D Case VI – *Hobbs* v *Hussey (HMIT)* (1942) 24 TC 152.

Note: Speculative activities that amount to gambling do not fall within the ambit of Case VI and are not assessable profits.

Besides this general charge under Case VI, certain other sources of income, and deemed income, associated with anti-avoidance provisions, are charged specifically under Case VI including:

(a) sale of patent rights

(b) post cessation receipts

(c) artificial transactions in land

(d) premiums paid to someone other than the landlord

(e) sale and leaseback of property – on the sale of a short lease, i.e. 50 years or less, and a leaseback of that lease for 15 years or less, part of the consideration is taxed under Case VI where the person paying the rent and receiving the consideration does not do so as part of a trade. The amount assessable is calculated as:

$$\frac{16 - \text{Duration of leaseback (in years)}}{15} \times \text{Consideration}$$

Note: If the person engages in the sale and leaseback in the course of business, the amount is taxed under Schedule D Case I.

(f) chargeable 'gains' on non-qualifying insurance policies

(g) income assessable under the accrued income scheme (bond washing).

In order to prevent the avoidance of income tax by converting income into capital by selling securities cum interest, i.e. the right to receive the next payment of interest, ss 713–15 of the ICTA 1988 provide that the accrued interest up to the date of transfer is apportioned to the vendor, and assessed to income tax under Schedule D Case VI. The accrued interest is calculated pro-rata as follows:

$$\frac{\text{Number of days in interest period (including day of transfer)}}{\text{Total length of interest period}} \times \frac{\text{Interest payable on}}{\text{next interest date}}$$

The purchaser will receive the whole of the next interest payment but the accrued interest up to the date of acquisition will be deducted from the Schedule D Case III liability. Where a security is disposed of ex-interest, i.e. the security is disposed of without interest accruing, the vendor will have received all the interest for the interest period, and any interest accrued from the date of transfer to the end of the interest period will be allowed as a deduction from the Schedule D Case III liability. The purchaser in this case will be charged income tax under Schedule D Case VI on the same amount.

EXAMPLE

On 1 July 2001 Amy bought £50 000 12 per cent Treasury stock. Interest payments are made on 31 January and 31 July each year and the stock goes ex-interest on 31 December and 30 June each year. On 1 November 2002 she sold the stock.

The interest periods are:

1 August – 31 January
1 February – 31 July

The interest payable for each period on Amy's holding is:

$$12\% \times £50\,000 \times 6/12 = £3000$$

When Amy acquired the stock on 1 July 2001, it was ex-interest and so the following amount would be assessed on Amy under Schedule D Case VI:

$$\frac{1 \text{ July} - 31 \text{ July}}{1 \text{ February} - 31 \text{ July}} \times £3000 \quad = \frac{31}{182} \times £3000$$
$$= £511$$

The transferor would be able to deduct the amount of the accrued interest from their Schedule D Case III assessment.

Amy would receive £3000 interest payments on each of 31 January 2002 and 31 July 2002. On 1 November 2002 she disposes of the stock cum interest and, again, will be assessed under Schedule D Case VI on the accrued interest:

$$\frac{1 \text{ August } 2002 - 1 \text{ November } 2002}{1 \text{ August } 2002 - 31 \text{ January } 2003} = \frac{93}{184}$$

$$\frac{93}{184} \times £3000 = £1516.30$$

The purchaser will receive the whole of the interest payment on 31 January 2003 but the accrued interest up to 1 November can be deducted from the Schedule D Case III liability.

The accrued income scheme applies to loan stock or securities on disposals after 27 February 1986, whether issued by a UK body or not, but does not apply to:

- shares
- certificates of deposit
- National Savings certificates
- stock on which no interest is payable but which is redeemable at more than issue price.

The following persons are also exempt from the scheme:

- individuals and personal representatives where the nominal value of the securities held is £5000 or less;
- traders where the transaction is part of the trade; and
- persons neither resident nor ordinarily resident in the UK during the period in which the transfer takes place.

The accrued interest under the provisions of the scheme is treated as arising at the end of the interest period in which the transfer takes place and not the date of the transfer. From 6 April 1998, the charge to tax under the accrued income scheme is reduced from basic rate to 20%.

Tax efficient savings and investments

The government encourages saving and investment by conferring tax advantages on certain investments in the UK.

1. National Savings

National Savings certificates produce tax free income, which may be particularly attractive to higher rate taxpayers. Also the first £70 of interest on a National Savings Bank *ordinary* account is exempt from income tax, £140 on a joint account.

2. Save as you earn schemes

There is no income tax or capital gains tax liability on any interest, bonuses or other sums paid on a qualifying SAYE scheme.

3. Premium bonds

Premium bonds do not attract interest but the serial numbers enter the monthly draw for cash prizes, which are tax free. The maximum permitted holding is £20 000 and the bonds can be purchased in multiples of £100 at post offices. Premium bonds can be cashed for their face value at any time.

4. Tax exempt special savings accounts

Tax exempt special savings accounts (TESSAs) were first introduced in January 1991, and all the interest on a TESSA is tax free over the life of the TESSA, which is five years. The following rules apply to TESSA accounts:

(a) individuals aged 18 or over may have *one* TESSA;

(b) a maximum of £3000 may be invested in the first year, then up to £1800 per annum but the total amount invested over five years cannot exceed £9000;

(c) withdrawals can be made without losing the tax advantage provided that they do not reduce the balance below the sum of:

- all the sums invested, and
- any interest credited plus the tax credit at the time the interest was credited. If this condition is broken, all the interest credited to date is taxable in the year it is withdrawn;

(d) after five years the account ceases to be a TESSA; and

(e) if the taxpayer dies, the balance on the TESSA is paid to the estate with no income tax liability.

The first TESSAs matured in 1996 and interest earned after maturity becomes taxable. Individuals investing in a second TESSA can invest the amount of capital held in the first TESSA up to a maximum of £9000, provided that the second TESSA is opened within six months of the maturity of the first TESSA.

Individuals investing less than £9000 in the first year of a second TESSA will be able to invest in the TESSA over the next four years, within the current limits of £1800 per annum and £9000 in total. For individuals who invested less than £3000 in the first TESSA, the first year limit in a second TESSA remains at £3000.

A TESSA could be taken out up until 5 April 1999 and will continue to receive the tax benefits over the life of the investment. From 6 April 1999, however, they have been withdrawn and replaced with the new Individual Savings Accounts (ISAs).

5. Personal equity plans

Any individual over the age of 18, who is resident or ordinarily resident in the UK, can invest up to £6000 per fiscal year in a personal equity plan (PEP). An individual can invest in only one ordinary PEP per year regardless of the amount invested; however, an individual may also invest up to £3000 in a *corporate PEP*, i.e. one that invests in the shares of only one company.

The tax reliefs available are:

- the PEP is exempt from capital gains tax on the disposal of the shares; therefore gains are not chargeable and losses are not allowable;
- all dividends and interest payments are exempt from income tax. The tax credits are reclaimed by the plan manager.

PEPs are most beneficial to those who pay higher rate income tax and fully utilise the annual exemption for capital gains tax.

Similarly to a TESSA, a PEP cannot be taken out after 5 April 1999. Existing PEPs will also continue to receive the tax benefits over the life of the investment but are, again, replaced by the new ISAs.

6. Enterprise investment scheme

The enterprise investment scheme (EIS) was introduced by the FA 1994 to replace the business expansion scheme (BES), which was abolished in December 1993, and applies to shares issued after 1 January 1994. Up to £100 000 per tax year could be invested in a qualifying company with relief being given at 20 per cent, as a tax reducer. Eligible shares that are held for five years are exempt from all tax; however, under the EIS scheme losses on disposal will qualify for relief. A qualifying company is one that:

- is unquoted; and
- trades in the UK.

Qualifying companies could raise £1 million per year prior to 6 April 1998 under the EIS. The individual could also claim to have 50 per cent of the amount invested in the first half of the tax year, i.e. 6 April – 5 October, carried back to the previous year up to a maximum of £15 000, before April 1998.

The FA 1998 introduced legislation to combine the tax benefits of the EIS and the capital gains tax reinvestment relief to create a unified scheme in order to increase the incentive for investing in venture capital in unquoted trading companies, to be effective from 6 April 1998.

The main changes for investors are:

- the limit qualifying for relief is increased from £100 000 to £150 000;
- chargeable gains reinvested in qualifying shares by individuals and trustees can obtain unlimited deferral;
- the maximum amount that can be carried back to the previous year for investments made between 6 April and 5 October is increased from £15 000 to £25 000.

The main changes to companies issuing shares under the new EIS are:

- the £1 million limit on the amount that can be raised each year has been abolished;
- only companies with gross assets of less than £15 million before and no more than £16 million after the investment will be eligible.

The FA 1999 provides that CGT taper relief cumulatively for reinvestment from one EIS company to another, to encourage serial entrepreneurs and other investors in EIS companies, and will be effective where the shares in the first EIS company were issued after 5 April 1998 and disposed of after 5 April 1999.

For shares issued on or after 6 April 2000, the minimum holding period is reduced to three years.

7. Venture capital trusts

A venture capital trust (VCT) is a quoted company investing in unquoted companies. The FA 1995 introduced provisions to give favourable tax treatment to individuals investing in companies qualifying as VCTs with effect from 6 April 1995. The tax benefits of investing in a VCT are as follows:

- 20 per cent relief is given as a tax reducer in the year the money is invested;
- dividends are free of income tax; and
- disposal of shares is exempt from capital gains tax, i.e. gains are not chargeable, and losses not allowable.

The maximum investment in a VCT for tax purposes is £100 000 per individual, over the age of 18 years, in any tax year.

To maintain the tax benefits, the shares must be kept for at least five years; if the shares are disposed of within five years, the reliefs may be lost. For shares issued on or after 6 April 2000, the minimum holding period is reduced to three years.

The FA 1997 introduced new measures to make it easier for VCTs and EIS companies to obtain capital from potential investors. From 27 November 1996, the group as a whole is considered rather than each individual group member, which enables a parent company to qualify, despite the fact that some group members may carry on non-qualifying activities, provided that qualifying activities are mainly carried on by the group as a whole.

For accounting periods ending on or after 2 July 1997, the following amendments apply:

- exclusion of guaranteed loans from VCTs;
- VCTs must comply with a minimum of 10 per cent ordinary non-preference share content in the investment;
- for shares issued after 2 July 1997, investors will not qualify for EIS reliefs where they are protected from the normal risks involved when investing in unquoted companies, for example, third party guarantees;
- property based trades including farming, market gardening, forestry, timber production, property development, operating and managing hotels, guest houses, nursing homes and residential care homes are excluded trades under the EIS, for shares issued on or after 17 March 1998, and for VCTs from 17 March 1998 in determining whether their investments qualify, but will not apply to a VCT funded by money raised before 17 March 1998.

The FA 2000 introduced the following changes to EIS and VCTs to make them more attractive to investors:

- protection of tax relief under the schemes if the company goes into receivership by extending the rules available to companies in liquidation;
- the definition of control has been changed so that companies are not prevented from investing in EIS, provided that they do not control the affairs of the company;
- generally companies that receive most of their income in the form of licence fees or royalties are excluded from the scheme except where they are derived from films or research and development. For shares issued after 6 April 2000, companies will be able to receive licence fees and royalty income from intangible assets that have largely been created by the company.

Following the FA 2001, relief will not be denied if the company becomes quoted, provided that it was unquoted, and there were no arrangements to become quoted when the EIS shares were issued. From 17th April 2002 VCTs can retain tax approval on merging.

8. Individual savings accounts

From 6 April 1999, individual and PEP investors can invest in the new individual saving accounts (ISAs) through which the goverment intends to extend the principles of TESSAs and PEPs to encourage long-term savings.

ISAs come into effect from 6 April 1999, initially for a period of 10 years, but they will be reviewed after seven years.

Individuals can invest £5000 pa in an ISA, of which £1000 can be cash and £1000 can be life assurance. For the first year that ISAs come into effect, i.e. 6 April 1999 to 5 April 2000, the limit is increased to £7000, and the cash limit increased to £3000. This limit was extended to 2005/06 in the Budget 2001.

The main benefits and features of the new ISAs are:

- investments in ISAs are free of income tax and capital gains tax, and, for the first five years, i.e. until 5 April 2004, a 10 per cent tax credit will be paid on dividends received from UK companies;

- tax relief will not be affected by withdrawals;

- there is no cumulative lifetime limit;

- PEPs held at 5 April 1999 can continue outside ISAs, without any loss of tax benefits;

- TESSAs can be opened until 5 April 1999 under the existing rules for the five-year term. Capital from maturing TESSAs can be transferred into the cash element of the ISA;

- subscriptions to TESSAs over the five-year term and maturing capital from TESSAs do not count against the annual limit for ISAs.

9. Life assurance policies

Policies taken out before 13 March 1984 enjoyed 15 per cent relief on premiums paid. This relief was withdrawn by the FA 1984 on new policies taken out after 13 March 1984, but existing policies continue to receive relief at $12\frac{1}{2}$ per cent. However, qualifying policies still benefit from a tax exemption on maturity or surrender. A policy is qualifying if:

(a) it is taken out on the policy holder's, or spouse's, life;

(b) the company involved trades in the UK;

(c) the policy secures a capital sum on death, earlier disability, or a date not before the tenth anniversary;

(d) the premiums are reasonably even and payable annually or at shorter intervals; and

(e) a certain capital sum is assured of 75 per cent of premiums payable in respect of endowment policies, and 75 per cent of premiums payable up to the age of 75 years for whole life policies.

If a qualifying policy is surrendered before the tenth anniversary and in a period less than $\frac{3}{4}$ of the term of the policy, any 'gain' on surrender is taxed as if it were a non-qualifying policy. Non-qualifying policies are often advertised as investment or property bonds. The 'gain' on the surrender or maturity of non-qualifying policies are taxable. However, partial surrenders will not incur an immediate tax liability provided that it does not exceed 5 per cent per annum of the premium, taken on a cumulative basis.

EXAMPLE

£20 000 single premium investment bond was purchased in 1996. In 2002 a partial surrender can be effected, without incurring an immediate tax liability of:

£20 000 × 5% × 6 years = £6000

Personal portfolio bonds

A personal portfolio bond is a type of insurance policy where the policy holder possesses nearly all the benefits of direct personal investment. They are generally held with non-UK insurers and designed primarily for tax avoidance.

In an attempt to curtail tax avoidance using such bonds, an additional tax charge will be imposed on a deemed 'gain' of 15 per cent of the sum of the total premiums paid up, to the end of each policy year, and the total deemed 'gains' from previous years. A deemed 'gain' will also arise when the policy terminates, or any other chargeable event occurs. The charge on the deemed 'gain' is in addition to the normal charge which would arise on a chargeable event.

This provision was introduced in the FA 1998 and will apply to policy years ending after 6 April 1999; this time lag gave the policy holders of such bonds the opportunity to surrender them before the additional charge came into effect.

Policies held in trust

'Gains' arising on policies held in trust will generally be taxable on the settlor. In situations where the settlor is dead, or non-UK resident, at the time of the chargeable event, no one is actually liable for any tax due on the 'gain'. To remedy this defect in the legislation, from 6 April 1998 'gains' on policies held in trust, where the settlor is deceased, or non-UK resident, will be taxable on a UK resident trustee, or a UK resident beneficiary of the trust.

SELF ASSESSMENT QUESTIONS

16.1 Susan inherited a property on 1 March 2002. She rented out the property on a five-year lease from 1 July 2002 for a premium of £4000 and a rental of £300 per month, payable in advance on the first of each month. Expenses for 2002/03 were £480.

REQUIRED

Calculate Susan's Schedule A assessment for 2002/03.

16.2 Ben granted a lease to Colin on 6 April 1997 for 25 years for a premium of £35 000 and an annual rental of £4000 pa, paid quarterly in advance. On 6 July 2002 Colin granted a sub-lease to Elsie for 12 years for a premium of £10 000 and an annual rental of £6000 pa, payable in advance on the 6th of each month.

REQUIRED

Calculate Colin's Schedule A assessment for 2002/03.

CHAPTER 17

The unified tax computation

Income tax is either deducted at source or raised by direct assessment under the various Schedules of income tax. In order to establish that the correct amount of tax has been paid for a particular fiscal year, all the different sources of income are aggregated together in the individual's personal tax computation using the following layout:

	Non-savings income (£)	Savings income (£)	Dividend income (£)
Non-savings income:			
e.g. Schedule D Case I	X		
less s 385/s 388 loss relief	(X)		
	X		
less Pension contributions	(X)		
	X		
Schedule E *less* contributions	X		
Other non-savings, e.g. Schedule A	X		
Trust income	X		
Savings income:			
e.g. Dividends			X
Building society interest		X	
Bank interest		X	
	X	X	X
less Charges on income	(X)	(X)	(X)
Statutory total income	X	X	X
less s 380/s 381 loss relief	(X)	(X)	(X)
	X	X	X
less Personal allowances	(X)	(X)	(X)
Taxable income	X_1	X_2	X_3

Tax is then calculated at lower, basic and higher rates as appropriate on X_1. Depending on the individual's level of income, dividend income is taxed at the Schedule F ordinary rate of 10 per cent for basic rate taxpayers and the Schedule F upper rate of 32.5 per cent for higher rate taxpayers. Tax on X_2 is calculated at 10 per cent, 20 per cent or 40 per cent, depending on the individual's level of income.

The following adjustments are then made to ascertain the income tax payable or repayable:

	£	£
Tax on X_1:		
at lower rate (10%)	X	
at basic rate (22%)	X	
at higher rate (40%)	X	X
Tax on X_2:		
at starting rate (10%)	X	
at lower rate (20%)	X	
at higher rate (40%)	X	X
		X
Tax on X_3:		
at ordinary rate (10%)	X	
at upper rate (32.5%)	X	X
		X
less Tax reducers		(X)
Income tax borne		X
add back Basic rate tax deducted		
on charges paid		X
Tax liability		X
less Tax deducted at source		(X)
Income tax payable (repayable)		X

This chapter now continues by explaining charges on income and the personal allowance system.

Charges on income

Once each source of the taxpayer's income has been determined, in accordance with the particular rules for each source of income, the next step in the computation is to deduct any annual charges that have been paid, to arrive at the individual's statutory total income (STI).

A charge on income is an annual recurring liability on the taxpayer that is recognised by the Revenue. Section 347 of the ICTA 1988 sets out those annual payments that are allowed as a charge against the taxpayer's total income.

There are two main classes of charge to consider:

1. Payments made gross

(a) Eligible interest on loans used for the following qualifying purposes:

1. Purchase of plant and machinery (ICTA 1988, s 359)

Section 359 allows, as a charge on income, the interest paid on loans taken out to purchase plant or machinery for use in the taxpayer's partnership or employment, provided that the borrower is entitled to capital allowances on the equipment, and the loan interest is paid within three years of obtaining the loan. The relief is adjusted to take account of any private use.

2. Purchase of interest in a close company (ICTA 1988, s 360)

Interest on money borrowed to purchase ordinary shares in, or make a loan to, a close company is allowed as a charge on income provided that the borrower:

- owns more than 5 per cent of the ordinary share capital; or
- owns ordinary shares and has worked for the greater part of his time (more than 50 per cent) in the management of the company.

3. Purchase of interest in a co-operative or employee-controlled company (ICTA 1988, s 361)

Interest paid on loans to acquire shares in, or make a loan to, a co-operative is allowed as a charge on income provided that the borrower has worked for the greater part of his time (more than 50 per cent) in the co-operative or a subsidiary of the co-operative. An employee-controlled company is one where the employees own at least 50 per cent of the voting rights. Interest on loans used to purchase shares in an employee-controlled company is treated as a charge on income, provided that:

- the company is an unquoted trading company;
- the shares are acquired within 12 months of the company becoming employee controlled; and
- the borrower is employed full-time by the company since purchasing the shares.

4. Purchase of interest in a partnership (ICTA 1988, s 362)

Interest paid on a loan taken out to buy a share in a partnership, or to make a loan to the partnership to be used wholly for the purpose of the partnership business is treated as a charge on income provided that the borrower is not a limited partner.

5. Payment of inheritance tax (ICTA 1988, s 364)

Interest on loans taken out by personal representatives to pay inheritance tax before probate is obtained is treated as a charge on income for up to 12 months from the date of the loan.

(b) Copyright royalties

2. Payments made net

The following payments are allowed as a charge on income but are usually paid net of basic rate tax:

(a) Deeds of covenant

A deed of covenant is a legally binding agreement where the payer agrees to make payments for which nothing is received in return, i.e. there must be an element of bounty. The covenanted payment is treated as a charge on income provided the deed is:

- irrevocable;
- not in favour of one's own unmarried children under the age of 18 years;
- not given for a consideration; and
- capable of exceeding six years for covenants to individuals taken out before 15 March 1988 or three years in the case of charitable covenants.

Non-charitable deeds of covenant taken out after 15 March 1988 are no longer tax effective but a covenant in existence that was executed before 15 March 1988 is allowed as a charge on income provided that the above conditions apply, but does not attract relief at the higher rate. Charitable deeds of convenant on the other hand attract relief at the higher rate provided the above conditions apply. From 31 July 1990, the deed must be signed in the presence of at least one witness.

(b) Patent royalties

All charges on income are deducted *gross* from the taxpayer's total income in the year that they are paid. However, where a charge is paid net of tax then the amount of tax retained by the taxpayer must be added back to the income tax borne, otherwise relief is being obtained twice.

EXAMPLE

Max, a single man, has a salary of £35 000 and pays £1560 (net) charitable covenant in 2002/03.

	£
Salary	35 000
less Charges (£1560 × $\frac{100}{78}$)	(2 000)
Statutory total income	33 000
less Personal allowance	(4 615)
Taxable income	28 385

	£
£1920 × 10%	192
£26 469 × 22%	5 822
	6 014 Tax borne
add back Tax retained at source on covenant (22% × £2000)	440
	6 454 Tax liability

If there is insufficient taxed income to cover the charge, an extra assessment is raised under the ICTA 1988, s 350.

(c) Other payments

Certain other payments are either deducted from total income or the relief is given as a tax reducer, i.e. the tax relief is deducted from the final tax bill.

1. Gift aid

One-off charitable donations of cash made by individuals are treated as a charge on income and relief is available at the higher rate. The payment is made net of basic rate tax and the tax retained by the payer must be added to the income tax borne. Prior to April 2000, the amount of the gift had to be at least £250 (net). This minimum amount was abolished in the Finance Act 2000. From 6/4/02 tax relief is available on gifts of land or buildings to a charity by an individual or company, and also from this date an individual can make a claim to carry back higher rate tax relief (18%) on Gift Aid to the prior year.

2. Maintenance payments (prior to 6 April 2000)

From 6 April 2000, maintenance relief is withdrawn, except where one of the parties to the agreement was over the age of 65 years, at 6/4/00 relief is available at 10 per cent on a maximum amount of £2110, for 2002/03.

The personal allowance system

Once the statutory total income has been established, the next step in the tax computation is to deduct personal allowances that attract relief at the individual's marginal rate of income tax to arrive at the taxable income. The only reliefs that are presently deducted from statutory total income are as follows:

(a) Personal allowance (£4615 for 2002/03)

The basic personal allowance (PA) is available to all taxable individuals resident in the UK, and nationals of all European Economic Area states, under the age of 65 years, regardless of marital status, including children. Any unused PA for a fiscal year is wasted; PA cannot be carried forward, transferred to another individual or used to reduce taxable income below zero.

EXAMPLE

Mr and Mrs Wren earn £15000 and £3500 respectively in the 2002/03 fiscal year, and have no other sources of income.

	Mr Wren (£)	Mrs Wren (£)
Salary	15000	3500
PA	(4615)	(3500) (restricted)
Taxable income	10385	nil

Mrs Wren has unused PA of £1115, which cannot be transferred to Mr Wren or carried forward, and so is lost.

(b) Personal age allowance

Increased allowances, personal age allowance (PAA), are available to individuals attaining the age of 65 years and 75 years at any time during the fiscal year:

	£
Age 65–74 years	6100 (2002/03)
Age 75 and over	6370 (2002/03)

However, where the individual's statutory total income exceeds £17900 for 2002/03, the increased allowance is restricted by £1 for every £2 over the limit but cannot fall below the basic PA.

EXAMPLE

Three individuals, all single and over the age of 65 years, but under 75 years, have the following statutory total incomes for 2002/03:

(a) £14 600
(b) £18 100
(c) £22 600

		(a) (£)	(b) (£)	(c) (£)
STI		14 600	18 100	22 600
PAA:				
(a)		(6 100)		
(b)	6 100			
less $\frac{1}{2}$(£18 100 – £17 900)	(100)		(6 000)	
(c)	6 100			
less $\frac{1}{2}$(£22 600 – £17 900)	(2 350)			
	3 750			
cannot fall below	4 615			(4 615)
Taxable income		8 500	12 100	17 985

(c) Blind person's allowance (£1480 for 2002/03)

This additional allowance is available to any individual who is registered blind. If both husband and wife are registered blind, they are entitled to £1480 each. Any excess allowance can be transferred between spouses whether the spouse receiving the transferred allowance is blind or not.

EXAMPLE

Mr and Mrs Magpie have statutory total incomes of £5000 and £20 000 respectively for 2002/03. Mr Magpie is registered blind.

	Mr Magpie (£)	Mrs Magpie (£)
STI	5 000	20 000
PA	(4 615)	(4 615)
BPA (part)	(385)	
BPA transferred:		
(£1480 – £385)		(1 095)
Taxable income	nil	14 290

The following personal reliefs are given as tax reducers:

(a) Married couples' age allowance

The married couples' age allowance is available where *either* spouse was 65 years old at 5 April 2000:

Age 65–74 years	£5465 (2002/03)
Age 75 and over	£5535 (2002/03)

Again, there is a restriction where the *husband's* statutory total income exceeds £17 900. The married couples' age allowance (MCAA) is restricted by £1 for every £2 over the limit but cannot fall below £2110 for 2002/03, unless the couple have not been married for the whole of the fiscal year.

EXAMPLE

Mr Kingfisher is 66 years old and his wife is 68 years old at 5 April 2000, and they have statutory total incomes of £21 000 and £18 000 respectively, from pension income, for 2002/03.

Restriction of allowances:

Mr Kingfisher
$\frac{1}{2}$ (21 000 − 17 900) = £1550

Total allowances restricted by £1550 but not to fall below the basic allowances:

	£
PAA	6100
less Restriction	(1485)
PA cannot fall below this amount	4615

	£
MCAA	5465
less Restriction (£1550 − £1485)	(65)
MCAA available at 10%	5400

Mrs Kingfisher
$\frac{1}{2}$ (£18 000 − £17 900) = £50

	£
PAA	6100
less Restriction	(50)
PAA available	6050

Note: The wife's income does not affect the level of MCAA.

	Mr Kingfisher (£)	Mrs Kingfisher (£)
STI	21 000	18 000
Less PAA (restricted)	(4 615)	(6 050)
Taxable income	16 385	11 950

	£		£
£1 920 × 10%	192	£1920 × 10%	192
£14 465 × 22%	3 182	£10 030 × 22%	2 207
Tax borne	3 374	Tax borne	2 399

less MCA:	
£5400 × 10%	(540)
Tax liability	2 834

(b) Childrens' Tax Credit

From 6 April 2001, individuals can claim the Childrens' Tax Credit (CTC) where:

- they have a child who lives with them for the whole or part of the fiscal year;
- the child is under 16 years of age in the tax year.

Only one CTC is available irrespective of the number of qualifying children. As the claim can be made for any child under the age of 16, it is logical to make a claim for the youngest child, so that the credit can be given for the longest length of time without having to make a claim.

Where custody is shared, the CTC can also be shared. Married couples and couples living together as husband and wife can also share the CTC, provided that neither of them pays income tax at the higher rate, and the partner with the larger income must claim the credit.

Where one or both of the partners is a higher rate tax payer, the credit is reduced by £1 for every £15 of income taxed at the higher rate.

For 2002/03 the CTC is £5290 given as a tax reducer at 10 per cent.

SELF ASSESSMENT QUESTIONS

17.1 Mr Pink is employed on a salary of £27 000 pa. Mr Pink also runs a part-time business; Schedule DI profits for the year ended 30 June 2002 are £6500. Mr Pink's other income for 2002/03 was as follows:

	£
Building society interest received	1 200
Bank interest received	60
Dividends received	2 880
Rental income	5 200
National Savings Bank (NSB) (ordinary a/c)	180

Mr Pink also made the following payment for 2002/03:

£500 (gross) under a deed of covenant to a charity.

Income tax deducted under PAYE was £6100.

REQUIRED

Calculate Mr Pink's income tax liability for 2002/03 on the assumption that Mr Pink has no children and is 42 years old.

17.2 Rebeckah, who is 42 years old, has the following income for 2002/03. She has no children.

	£
Salary	27 865
Dividends received	5 400
Building society interest received	1 020
NSB (investment a/c)	250

REQUIRED

Calculate Rebeckah's income tax liability for 2002/03.

17.3 Arnold, a single man aged 67 years, received the following income for 2002/03:

	£
Part-time salary	7 000
Pensions	8 500
Dividends received	1 890
Bank interest received	980

REQUIRED

Calculate Arnold's income tax liability for 2002/03.

EXAMPLE

Peter is a married man whose wife is not employed, and they have a five year old son.
His taxable income for 2002/03 is £30 995.

	£
CTC 2002/03	529 (£5 290 × 10%)
Less:	
$(£30\,995-£29\,900) = \dfrac{£1\,095}{15}$	(73)
	456 CTC 2002/03

Losing £1 for every £15 of income taxed at the higher rate equates to losing £2 of the credit for every £3 of income taxed at the higher rate, i.e.:

	£	
	5 290	(2002/03)
less: $\dfrac{£1\,095 \times 2}{3}$	(730)	
	4 560	@ 10% = £456 CTC 2002/03

CHAPTER 18

Overseas aspects of income tax

It is generally accepted that a country's tax jurisdiction cannot extend beyond its national boundaries; the liability to income tax is therefore affected by the individual's residency status. This chapter considers the overseas aspects of income tax with regard to UK resident and non-resident individuals.

Residence, ordinary residence and domicile

Generally, UK resident individuals are liable to income tax on their worldwide income, while non-residents are only liable to UK income tax on income arising in the UK. However, an individual's ordinary residence and domicile can affect their tax position, although for income tax purposes residence is more significant than domicile, domicile being more important for inheritance tax purposes. The terms residence, ordinary residence and domicile are now considered in more detail.

1. Residence

Residence is not defined in the tax legislation and so is to be given its ordinary meaning:

> **'To dwell permanently, or for a considerable time, to have one's usual or settled abode, to live in or at a particular place'.** (*Oxford English Dictionary*)

In deciding whether or not an individual is resident in the UK, the Revenue consider the following tests:

(a) Individuals are considered to be resident if they are present in the UK for more than 182 days in any fiscal year. Generally, for this purpose days of arrival and departure are ignored.

(b) Where the individual concerned makes regular and substantial visits to the UK, residency status may be established. For this purpose, the Revenue consider three months each year to be substantial and regularity is established after visits in four successive years. If this is proved, residence would generally commence from the beginning of the fifth year unless the individual has been informed that the visits establish residence status before this time.

Prior to 6 April 1993, maintaining a place to live in the UK, regardless of the length of the visits, was another test applied by the Revenue. Although this was withdrawn from 6 April 1993, accommodation can still be a factor in determining whether (a) and (b) apply.

2. Ordinary residence

Ordinary or usual residence has a narrower meaning than residence and usually indicates a greater degree of permanence. For example, a Frenchman who is usually resident in Paris and works in the UK for two years will be resident in the UK but ordinarily resident in France: *IRC v Lysaght* (1928) 13 TC 511.

3. Domicile

While individuals may have dual residence, they can only have one domicile at any one time which may be:

(a) Domicile of origin

Domicile is usually acquired at birth, a child taking the domicile of the father or legal guardian.

(b) Domicile of choice

Individuals may take a domicile of choice, provided that they are over 16 years of age. However, in this case the intention of the individual must be proven, i.e. that they sever all ties with their domicile of origin and their actions demonstrate the intention to settle permanently in the domicile of choice.

Ordinary residence and domicile affects the liability to income tax under Schedule D Cases IV and V, and Schedule E. Individuals who are resident but not ordinarily resident or domiciled in the UK are affected as follows:

- they are liable to income tax under Schedule D Cases IV and V on a remittance basis;
- they are not liable to tax in respect of certain government securities; and
- the charge to tax under Schedule E is affected.

Residence for tax purposes is a question of fact and generally determined for a fiscal year. However, by concession (ESC A11) the Revenue apply the following rules:

- (a) individuals arriving in the UK on a permanent basis are treated as resident from the date of arrival;
- (b) individuals leaving the UK on a permanent basis are treated as resident up to the date of departure;
- (c) individuals who leave the UK to work abroad for more than one year are treated as resident up to the date of departure and from the date they return to the UK.

Schedule E

Schedule E taxes the income from employment and is divided into three cases; liability to income tax under each Case of Schedule E depends on:

- the residence status of the individual; and
- whether the duties of the employment are performed in the UK or overseas.

Non-UK residents

Individuals who are not resident in the UK, or who are resident but not ordinarily resident, are liable to income tax under Schedule E Case II on the income from employment if the duties are performed in the UK. Individuals who are resident, but not ordinarily resident in the UK are liable to income tax under Schedule E Case III on the income that is remitted to the UK in respect of duties performed overseas.

If the employment requires individuals to carry out their duties partly in the UK and partly overseas, then the income from the employment will be apportioned usually on a time basis in order to assess the liability under Schedule E Cases II and III.

UK residents

Individuals who are resident and ordinarily resident in the UK are liable to tax on their worldwide income, and as such are liable to income tax under Schedule E Case I on the income from employment, whether the duties are performed in the UK or overseas.

The 365-day rule

Prior to 17 March 1998, a 100 per cent deduction was allowed in respect of duties performed outside the UK where the individual was absent from the UK for 365 days. This was sometimes referred to as the foreign earnings deduction. If the individual concerned made return visits to the UK, the 100 per cent deduction was not affected provided that the return visits fulfilled the following conditions:

- no one visit should be for more than 62 days; and
- the UK visits in total were less than $\frac{1}{6}$ of the total period of absence, calculated immediately before every return visit to the UK.

From 17 March 1998, the general foreign earnings deduction was withdrawn. The deduction available to seafarers, however, is maintained, allowing them UK visits of up to one half of the qualifying period (including visits of up to 183 consecutive days).

Allowable expenses

Expenses paid or reimbursed by employers are generally included in the employee's taxable emoluments, with the employees claiming a deduction for allowable expenses. Besides the normal Schedule E expenses allowed under the ICTA 1988, s 198, where employees perform their duties overseas the following expenses paid, or reimbursed by the employer, are allowed as a deduction from the employee's Schedule E emoluments:

(a) travelling expenses from the UK to the overseas employment;

(b) travelling expenses back to the UK when the overseas employment has terminated;

(c) the cost of board and lodging provided outside the UK;

(d) the cost of a maximum of two return journeys in each fiscal year are allowed for the employee's spouse and children under the age of 18, provided that the employee is engaged on duties overseas for a period of at least 60 days; and

(e) the cost of medical insurance while the employee is overseas.

Table 18.1 Summary of Schedule E liability

Case	Residence status	Place duties performed	Tax treatment
Case I	Resident and ordinarily resident	UK duties and overseas duties	Taxed in full on a receipts basis
Case II	Resident but not ordinarily resident or non-resident	UK duties	Taxed in full on a receipts basis
Case III	Resident but not ordinarily resident	Overseas duties	Taxed on the amount remitted to the UK

Schedule D Cases IV and V

Foreign income is charged to income tax under Schedule D Cases IV and V as follows:

Schedule D Case IV

Taxes the interest from overseas investments, i.e. foreign securities such as debentures (but not stocks and shares).

Schedule D Case V

Taxes the income from foreign possessions:

- dividends received from overseas companies;
- foreign pensions;
- profits from overseas trades; and
- rent in respect of overseas property.

Remittance basis

For individuals who are resident in the UK, but are not ordinarily resident or not domiciled in the UK, the liability under Schedule D Cases IV and V is limited to the amount of income remitted to the UK.

UK residents

Individuals who are resident and ordinarily resident in the UK are liable to income tax on foreign income under Schedule D Cases IV and V. From 1997/98, all Schedule D income is liable to tax on a current year basis. The various sources of foreign income will now be examined.

1. Foreign pensions

Overseas pensions paid to UK resident and domiciled individuals are taxed under Schedule D Case V on a current year basis, subject to a deduction of 10 per cent, in other words only 90 per cent of the pension is taxable.

2. Rents

Rent received from properties situated overseas are taxed under Schedule V on a current year basis. The ICTA 1988, s 65(1) provides that income not received in the UK will nevertheless be subject to the same deductions and allowances that would have been allowed had the income been received in the UK. Therefore, deductions for expenses that are allowed for a 'Schedule A business' are applicable, e.g. rates, agents fees, wear and tear allowances, etc.

NB: Interest on loans taken out to purchase an overseas property is NOT an allowable deduction.

3. Dividends from overseas companies

Dividends received from overseas companies are taxed under Schedule D Case V. The overseas dividend will have suffered foreign tax but must be grossed up in the individual's tax computation and relief given for double taxation.

4. Overseas trades

The profit arising from trading in the UK is liable to income tax under Schedule D Cases I and II, trades carried on overseas are liable to income tax under Schedule D Case V. Despite the fact that the liability arises under Schedule D Case V, the profits are computed in exactly the same way as they are under Schedule D Cases I and II except that losses arising under Schedule D Case V can only be relieved against other Schedule D Case V income either:

- in the current year; or
- carried forward against future Schedule D Case V income.

Deductions are allowed against Schedule D Case V trading income for expenses incurred for travelling and board and lodging, in the same way as for Schedule E purposes, provided that the expense is incurred wholly and exclusively for the purpose of the business.

The profits are charged to Schedule D Case V where the trade is carried on wholly overseas; if this is not the case, the profits are liable to Schedule D Case I or II. In determining where the business is 'carried on', this is where the central management and control is excercised.

Double tax relief

UK resident individuals are liable to income tax on their worldwide income; any income received from overseas will usually have suffered foreign tax, so effectively the income is taxed twice. To mitigate the effect of this double taxation, relief is available. There are two main types of double tax relief (DTR):

1. Double tax treaties

Relief under double tax treaties may be given by either:

(a) treaty exemption – where certain categories of income are wholly or partially exempt from tax in one country or the other; or

(b) tax credit – where tax charged in one country may be allowed as a credit in the other country.

2. Unilateral relief

Where no double tax treaty exists, or where the treaty does not provide for the particular circumstances, unilateral credit relief is available, calculated as the lower of:

- the foreign tax paid; or
- the UK tax on the foreign income.

It should be noted that in calculating the DTR available the foreign income is treated as if it was the top slice of income in order to maximise the relief available, however, when calculating the individual's tax liability, savings income is treated as the top slice of income before considering DTR.

EXAMPLE

George, a married man aged 48 years, has the following income for 2002/03:

	£
Gross salary (PAYE deducted £5800)	28 000
Building society interest (BSI) received	700
Schedule A income (net of expenses)	6 000
Schedule D Case V income:	
(a) rent from overseas property	4 400
(net of 20% foreign tax)	
(b) foreign dividends received	750
(net of 25% foreign tax)	

2002/03:	Non-savings (£)	Savings (£)	Tax credits (£)
Salary	28 000		5 800
BSI (£700 × 100/80)		875	175
Schedule A	6 000		
			5 975
Schedule D Case V:			
(a) rents (£4400 × 100/80)	5 500		
(b) dividends (£750 × 100/75)	1 000		
	40 500	875	
less PA	(4 615)	–	
Taxable income	35 885	875	

The building society interest is treated as the top slice of income and falls entirely in the 40 per cent band.

Non-savings:	£
£1920 × 10%	192
£27 980 × 22%	6156
£5985 × 40%	2 394
	8 742

Savings:	
£875 × 40%	350
	9 092
less DTR*	(1 350)
	7 742
less Tax credits	(5 975)
Tax payable	1 767

* DTR is calculated as the lower of the foreign tax or the UK tax paid:

	UK tax (£)	Foreign tax (£)
(a) Rents:		
£5500 × 40%; 20%	2 200	1 100
(b) Dividends:		
£1000 × 32.5%; 25%	325	250

Note: In calculating DTR, the Schedule D Case V income is treated as if it were the top slice.

From 17 March 1998, where a claim for DTR proves to be excessive because all or part of the overseas tax has been repaid, then the taxpayer must notify the Revenue, in writing, of any adjustment to foreign tax on which DTR has been claimed. The notification must be made within 12 months of any such adjustment. Failure to notify the Revenue will result in a maximum financial penalty equal to the excess amount of DTR claimed.

CHAPTER 19

Taxation of estate income

In the event of death, the deceased person's tax affairs need to be settled up to the date of death and the estate administered and passed to the legatees. This chapter examines the responsibilities and income tax position of personal representatives during the year of death and throughout the administration period, the tax treatment of the legatees and concludes by considering the tax treatment of foreign estates.

Personal representatives

There are two types of personal representatives (PRs) that may be appointed to deal with the deceased person's estate:

1. Executors

A valid will generally names the persons who are to act as executors of the will, to obtain probate and distribute the assets under the terms of the will, authority to act as PR in this case being derived from the will.

2. Administrators

Administrators are appointed where a person dies intestate, or where no executors are named in the will, under the Administration of Estates Act 1925; in this case, authority to act as PR is derived from the court.

The PRs are treated as a single body, and if all the PRs are resident or ordinarily resident in the UK, they are liable to income tax on the worldwide income of the estate, whereas if all the PRs are neither resident nor ordinarily resident in the UK, they are only liable to income tax on the UK estate income.

In the case of mixed residency, the FA 1989, s 111 provides that the residency of the deceased will determine the residency of the PRs. In situations where there is at least one PR who is non-UK resident, therefore, the estate will be treated as resident if the deceased was resident, ordinarily resident or domiciled in the UK at the date of death.

The PRs are responsible for:

- settling the tax liabilities of the deceased taxpayer; and
- settling the tax liabilities arising during the administration period.

We will now examine each of these in turn.

Income tax in the year of death

The tax liability of the taxpayer on income *receivable* up to the date of death, should be settled by the PRs. The deceased is entitled to the full amount of personal allowances in the year of death, i.e. no apportionment is made.

EXAMPLE

James was 68 years old when he died on 10 October 2002. He had been married for many years and had the following income up to 10 October 2002:

	£
Rental income	6 000
Pension	7 000

		£
Schedule E		7 000
Schedule A		6 000
		13 000
less PA		(6 100)
	Taxable income	6 900

	£
£1920 × 10%	192
£4980 × 22%	1 095
	1 287

less MCAA:		
(5465 × 10%)	(547)	
	740	Tax liability in year of death to be settled by PRs

There are special time limits for raising assessments in respect of deceased persons. These are considered fully in Part 6.

Income tax during the administration period

1. Income tax position of PRs

Before the residue of the estate is determined, i.e. during the course of administration of the estate, the PRs are liable to income tax on the income arising during the administration period, where this has not already been deducted at source.

Personal representatives, not being individuals, are not entitled to personal allowances, and do not pay income tax at the higher rate. In calculating the income tax liability, administration expenses are not allowed as a deduction from estate income, i.e. they are paid out of taxed income, thereby reducing the residuary income available to the legatees.

EXAMPLE

The following information relates to Henry, who died on 10 January 2002 aged 58 years. He had been married for many years and left a widow aged 56 years:

Income from 6/4/01 – 10/1/02

	£
Salary	20 665
Dividends received	4 500
Rental income	8 000

PAYE deducted on the salary was £2 300.

Income for 2002/03

	£
Dividends received	6 300
Rental income	12 000

The administration was not complete by 5 April 2003. The tax position of the PRs is as follows:

(a) Year of death (2001/02)

	Non-savings (£)	Dividends (£)	Tax paid (£)
Schedule E	20 665		2 300
Schedule A	8 000		
Dividends (4500 × 100/90)		5 000	500
STI	28 665	5 000	2 800
less PA	(4 535)		
Taxable income	24 130	5 000	

Non-savings:	£
£1880 × 10%	188
£22 250 × 22%	4895

Dividends:	
£5000 × 10%	500

	5583
less Tax paid	(2800)
	2783

2783 Tax liability in year of death to be settled by PRs.

(b) Income tax during course of administration (2002/03)

PRs do not pay income tax at the higher rate:

	Non-savings (£)	Tax (£)	Dividends (£)	Tax (£)
Schedule A	12 000	nil		
Dividend (£6300 x 100/90)			7 000	700
Taxable income	12 000		7 000	700

The liability to tax on the dividend has been deducted at source. The PRs are responsible for income tax on the rental income at 22%:

$$12\,000 \times 22\% = £\,2\,640$$

	Gross (£)	Net (£)	Tax (£)
Schedule A	12 000	9 360	2 640
Dividends	7 000	6 300	700
	19 000	15 660	3 340

Any administration expenses are deducted from taxed income which will reduce the amount of income available to the legatees. The expenses of administering the estate are paid from savings income first. If in the example above the PRs incurred administration expenses of £300 in 2002/03, the amount of income available for the legatees would be:

	£
Dividend income (net)	6 300
less Expenses	(300)
	6 000
Schedule A income (net)	9 360
Residuary income 2002/03	15 360

Although administration expenses are deducted from taxed income, certain charges on income are allowed in arriving at the PRs' income tax liability:

(a) Interest on loans to pay inheritance tax (ICTA 1988, s 364)

Interest paid on loans taken out to pay inheritance tax is treated as a charge on income for up to 12 months from the date of the loan. Any interest that cannot be relieved during the year it is paid can first be carried back and deducted from income of the previous year, and then be deducted from the following year.

(b) Annuities

The terms of the will may provide for an annuity to be paid to a legatee, e.g. £1000 pa for life. An annuity is treated as a charge on income, the gross amount of the annuity being deducted from the estate income, the PRs then pay the annuity to the legatee (the annuitant) net of basic rate tax.

EXAMPLE

Charles died on 1 October 2001. For 2002/03 the gross income was £10 000 derived from property rentals. The terms of the will provide for an annuity of £3000 pa to be paid to Mary, Charles' sister, for life. The position of the PRs is as follows:

	£
Schedule A	10 000
less Charge on income (annuity)	(3 000)
Taxable income	7 000
Tax at 22% × £7 000	1 540
add Basic rate tax deducted on charge	660
Income tax payable by PRs	2 200

The annuity is paid to Mary net of basic rate income tax, i.e. £2340, but she will be liable for tax on the gross amount of the annuity and can set off the tax credit of £660 against her income tax liability. The PRs must give Mary a certificate showing the tax deducted:

	Gross (£)	Tax (£)	Net (£)
Annuity	3000	660	2340

If there is insufficient income to pay the annuity, the will may provide for any shortfall to be met from capital. If this is the case, the basic rate tax on the amount not covered by the estate income is assessed on the PRs under the ICTA 1988, s 350, as is the usual procedure where there is insufficient income to cover the basic rate tax on the charge.

EXAMPLE

In the example above, if the estate income had only been £2500 and the shortfall was met from capital the position of the PRs would be as follows:

	£
Schedule A	2500
less Charge	(2500)
Taxable income	nil
Shortfall of charge met from capital	500
Tax at 22% of income	nil
add Basic rate tax deducted on charge £2500 × 22%	550
add s 350 assessment: £500 × 22%	110
Tax liability of PRs	660

Mary's position remains unchanged.

Sometimes the will provides for an annuity to be payable 'tax free', in which case the annuity needs to be grossed up, e.g. £1000 pa for life 'free of tax':

$$£1000 \times 100/78 = £1282 \ (2002/03)$$

2. Income tax position of legatees

During the course of administration, the specific tax treatment of the legatees will depend on the particular legacies provided for in the will.

(a) Specific legacies of non-income producing assets

Non-income producing assets have no income tax effect as no income is generated, e.g. pieces of furniture. If a specified sum of money is bequeathed, again, there is no income tax effect but the legatee may be entitled to interest if the money is not paid within 12 months of the death. Such interest is paid gross and liable to income tax under Schedule D Case III in the hands of the legatee.

(b) Specific legacies of income producing assets

Legatees are entitled to the income received from the asset from the date of death, and forms part of their taxable income, despite the fact that the PRs are liable for income tax during the administration period, and as such the PRs must issue a tax deduction certificate to the legatee so that he/she can claim a tax credit for the tax paid by the PRs.

(c) Residuary legacies

The residue of the estate – after taking account of all the payments properly chargeable to the estate, e.g. annuities, administration expenses, specific legacies, funeral expenses, etc. – is then available to the residuary legatees.

The residuary legatees may have a limited or absolute interest in the residue:

(a) Limited interest
A person with a limited interest in the residue is entitled to the income but not the capital of the whole or part of the residue. A life interest is a limited interest.
Amounts paid during the administration period are grossed up at the applicable rate and treated as income of the legatee in the year it is receivable. The PRs must issue the legatee with a tax deduction certificate for any payments made, so that if the individual is a non-taxpayer a repayment of the tax paid by the PRs is available.

(b) Absolute interest
A person with an absolute interest in the residue is entitled to both the income and capital of the whole or part of the residue. Amounts paid to an individual with an absolute interest in the residue are grossed up and treated as income of the legatee in the year that the payment was made, together with a tax credit for the tax paid by the PRs. Payments made during the administration period in respect of absolute interests are deemed to be paid out of income, provided that it does not exceed the residuary income for the year.

Extra-Statutory Concessional (ESC) A14 provides that residuary legatees who are neither resident nor ordinarily resident in the UK are treated as if the income had arisen directly to them, thus only UK income will be liable to UK income tax.

The amounts paid to residuary legatees during the administration period will require adjustments when the administration is completed and the final residue ascertained:

(i) Limited interests

For administrations completed after 5 April 1995, any amounts due to the legatee are treated as income for the year in which the administration was completed, unless the limited legatee died before the estate was finally administered, in which case it is treated as income received during the year in which the interest ceased.

(ii) Absolute interests

For administrations completed after 5 April 1995, the residuary income entitlement is calculated and compared with amounts paid during the administration period, and adjustments made giving rise to an additional assessment or claim for relief. Where the legatee has been paid less than the amount he/she is entitled to, the balance is treated as being paid immediately before the administration was completed.

Foreign estates

Section 701(9) and (10) of the ICTA 1988 provides that a UK estate is one where all the income is subject to income tax either by deduction at source or by direct assessment on the PRs because they are classed as resident or ordinarily resident in the UK.

All estates which are not UK estates under the provisions of the ICTA 1988, s 701 are foreign estates. Income received from a foreign estate by a UK resident legatee is assessed to income tax under Schedule D Case IV.

SELF ASSESSMENT QUESTION

19.1 William Harvey died on 5 October 2001 aged 58 years, leaving a wife and two grown up children. William had been employed on a salary of £38 000 pa. He was also a director in Appollo plc, earning £2000 per month. William owned 5000 shares in Appollo plc and a dividend of 16 pence per share was paid on 30 September 2001. Up to the date of his death, £4900 had been deducted under the PAYE system.

REQUIRED:

Calculate the income tax payable by the PRs in respect of William's income in the year of his death.

CHAPTER 20

Income tax on trusts

A trust, or settlement, is a legal device whereby the trustees of the settlement hold assets such as shares, cash, property, etc. for the benefit of other individuals, known as the beneficiaries of the trust. Section 681(4) of the ICTA 1988 provides that a settlement includes any disposition, trust, covenant, agreement or arrangement, but will only exist where there is an element of bounty involved – *CIR* v *Plummer* [1979] STC 793; *Copeman* v *Coleman* (1939) 22 TC 594.

Once the settlor has set up the trust, the trustees have the legal ownership of the property, which they hold for the benefit of the beneficiaries of the trust, for example the beneficiaries may be entitled to the income from the trust. A trust can be set up during the settlor's lifetime or under the terms of their will on death, but either way the income tax treatment is the same.

This chapter classifies the various types of trust and examines the income tax treatment of express private trusts with regard to the trustees and beneficiaries of the trust, and considers the situations where the settlor may be liable to the tax on the income arising from the trust, which essentially relates to the legislation enacted to prevent the use of trusts merely to avoid tax, and concludes by considering foreign trusts.

Classification of trusts

Trusts can be classified as follows:

Express trusts

(a) Private

A trust expressly created by the settlor for certain individuals (beneficiaries).

(b) Charitable

A trust established for the benefit of a charitable purpose, which must be legally charitable.

(c) Public non-charitable

A trust that benefits the public at large or some section of the general public.

Trusts imposed by equity

Trusts are imposed by equity in circumstances where a person having legal title to property should not be allowed to benefit from it, e.g. where there is money left in a trust after the purposes of the trust have been achieved.

Trusts imposed by statute

Trusts may be imposed by statute, for example, where a minor becomes entitled to property in an estate, the PRs may hold the assets in trust until the minor is 18 years of age.

The rest of this chapter is concerned with the following main types of express private trusts.

1. Interest in possession trusts

These trusts are also known as fixed interest trusts. With this type of trust the income of the trust, or the right to use trust property, belongs to one or more of the beneficiaries, for example, the terms of the trust may grant a beneficiary the right to live in a house for life. Where a beneficiary is entitled to trust income or the use of trust property for life, they are known as the *life tenant* of the trust. On the death of a life tenant, another life interest may be created in the assets of the trust, or the remainder may pass absolutely to the beneficiaries.

2. Non-interest in possession trusts

These may further be categorised as:

(a) Discretionary trusts

With this type of trust the income of the trust must be distributed among the beneficiaries but the trustees have the discretion as to how the distribution is made.

(b) Accumulation and maintenance trusts

With an accumulation and maintenance trust (A&M), the trustees are given the following discretionary powers:

- whether or not to distribute trust income; and
- if the income is to be distributed, how that distribution is to be made.

Trustees

If all the trustees are UK resident, then the trust is treated as a UK resident trust and liable to income tax on worldwide income; whereas if all the trustees are neither resident nor ordinarily resident in the UK, they are only liable to UK income tax on the UK income of the trust.

In the case of mixed residency, the FA 1989, s 110 provides that the residency of the settlor will determine the residency of the trust. Therefore, in situations where at least one trustee is non-UK resident, the trust will be considered UK resident if the settlor was resident, ordinarily resident or domiciled in the UK when the settlement was created or funds added to it. In the case of trusts created on death, the above rules apply if at the time of death the settlor was resident, ordinarily resident or domiciled in the UK. Foreign trusts are considered under 'Foreign Trusts' below.

The trustees receive income of the trust for the benefit of the beneficiaries and not in a personal capacity, and so they are not entitled to personal allowances, nor do they benefit from the general lower rate band or pay income tax at the higher rate. The trustees of non-interest in possession trusts are liable to income tax at 34 per cent on discretionary income. Whatever the source of the trust income, it can never be treated as earned income, for example, for pension contribution relief.

In calculating the trustees' liability to income tax, administration expenses are not allowed as a deduction from trust income, i.e. they are paid from taxed income thereby reducing the income available for distribution to the beneficiaries. The expenses are treated as being paid from investment income with the lowest rate first, in the same way as estate administration expenses.

1. Charges on income

Charges on income, such as an annuity, are paid to the beneficiaries net of basic rate income tax and deducted from the trust income gross in the same way as for individuals, the basic rate tax on the annuity being paid to the Revenue.

EXAMPLE

An interest in possession trust has gross Schedule A income of £6500 for 2002/03. The terms of the trust provide that an annuity of £2000 (gross) is paid to Mary each year and the rest of the income paid to Adam.

Trustees' income tax liability 2002/03

	£
Schedule A income	6500
less Annuity	(2000)
STI	4500
Tax @ 22% × £4500	990
add Basic rate tax deducted at source on annuity	440
Trustees basic rate tax liability	1430

Mary

Mary will receive £1560, however, £2000 will be included in her income tax computation with a tax credit of £440 attached to it.

	Gross (£)	Tax (£)	Net (£)
Annuity	2000	440	1560

Adam
The income available for Adam:

	£
Schedule A income	6500
less Tax liability	(1430)
less Annuity paid	(1560)
Available for Adam	3510

Adam will receive £3510, however, £4500 will be included in his income tax computation with a tax credit of £990 attached to it:

Gross	Tax	Net
(£)	(£)	(£)
4500	990	3510

If there is insufficient income to pay the annuity, the beneficiary is assessed on the gross amount of the annuity received.

EXAMPLE

Suppose in the last example there had only been £1000 of Schedule A income:

	£
Schedule A income	1 000
less Annuity	(1 000)
STI	nil

Trustees' income tax liability:

Tax on annuity deducted at source £1000 × 22% = £220

Mary
Mary would receive £780 (net):

Gross	Tax	Net
(£)	(£)	(£)
1000	220	780

In this situation there would be no income available for Adam.

The terms of the trust may, however, provide that any shortfall is paid out of capital, in which case the beneficiary is liable to income tax on the gross amount of the annuity with the corresponding tax credit attached to it, and the trustees will be liable to income tax under the ICTA 1988, s 350 on the capital payment.

EXAMPLE

Suppose that in the previous example the trustees have the power to make up the annuity from capital.

	£
Schedule A income	1000
less Annuity	(1000)
STI	nil
Shortfall from capital	1000

Trustees' income tax liability:

	£
Tax on annuity paid from income:	
22% × £1000	220
add ICTA, s 350 tax on capital payment:	
22% × £1000	220
Total tax payable	440

Sometimes the terms of the trust provides that the annuity should be paid free of tax, in which case the annuity must be grossed up accordingly.

EXAMPLE

Ivan is entitled to a tax free annuity of £1950 pa from a trust set up by his uncle. Ivan is a single man aged 58 years whose only other income for 2002/03 was building society interest received of £1420:

gross annuity = £1950 × 100/78 = £2500

	£	£ Tax
Annuity	2500	550
BSI (£1420 × 100/80)	1775	355
	4275	905
less PA (restricted)	(4275)	
	nil	

Ivan will be due a tax repayment of £905.

2. Self assessment

The basic rules for the self assessment of income and gains apply equally to trustees, i.e. due dates for filing returns, enquiry procedures, etc. However, self assessment introduces the concept of the 'relevant trustee' defined as:

(a) a person who is a trustee at the time the income arises or becomes a trustee subsequently; and

(b) in respect of chargeable gains, a person who is a trustee in the year the chargeable gains arise, or who becomes a trustee subsequently.

Any relevant trustee can be responsible for the tax obligations of the body of trustees, for example:

- notifying chargeability;
- making a return of income and gains; and
- dealing with an enquiry.

The Revenue can also take action against any relevant trustee, except that no penalty or surcharge can be demanded from a person who did not become a relevant trustee until after the penalty or surcharge arose.

The rules for relevant trustees, which apply from 1996/97 (the first year of self assessment), provide for tax obligations to pass to new trustees when changes take place, e.g. on the death or retirement of a trustee.

These general rules apply to all trustees regardless of the type of trust. Consideration will now be given to the specific income tax treatment for each type of trust.

Interest in possession trusts

'**An interest in possession in settled property exists where a person having the interest has immediate entitlement to income as it arises, after expenses and outgoings properly chargeable to income. Any discretion or power to withhold the income from that person, makes it impossible for an interest in possession to exist.'** (IR Press Release, 12 February 1996)

The trustees of an interest in possession trust are liable to income tax at 20% on savings income, 10% on dividend income, and basic rate on all other income.

EXAMPLE

An interest in possession trust has the following income for 2002/03:

	£
Schedule A income (gross)	6500
Schedule A expenses	375
Buildings society interest received	2320
Trust administration expenses	400

The terms of the trust provide that the income from the trust is payable to Robert for life. The trust expenses are deducted from savings income in priority to basic rate income:

	£
BSI (net)	2320
less Trust expenses	(400)
Net savings income available for Robert	1920

Tax has been deducted at source on the savings and no further tax is payable by the trustees in respect of this income. The trustees are liable to income tax at basic rate on the Schedule A income:

	£
Schedule A (gross)	6500
less Schedule A expenses	(375)
Taxable at 22%	6125
Net schedule A income	6125
less Tax at 22%	(1347)
Schedule A income available for Robert	4778

Total income tax liability of trustees:

	£
Tax on savings income used for expenses	100
(£400 × 100/80) × 20%	
Tax on rest of savings income	480
(£1920 × 100/80) × 20%	
Tax on Schedule A income	1347
Total tax liability	1927

Net income available for Robert:

	£
Savings income	1920
Schedule A income	4778
	6698

The trustees must issue Robert with a tax deduction certificate R 185 E:

	Net (£)	Tax (£)	Gross (£)
Savings income	1920	480	2400
(20% tax deduction)			
Other income	4778	1347	6125
	6698	1827	8525

The gross amount will appear in Robert's income tax computation with the corresponding tax credit of £1827, so that if Robert has no other income his tax position would be as follows:

	Non-savings (£)	Savings (£)	Tax (£)
BSI		2400	480
Schedule A	6125		1347
less PA	(4615)	–	1827
Taxable income	1510	2400	

Non-savings	£
1510 × 10%	151
Savings	
410 × 10%	41
1990 × 20%	398
Tax liability	590
less Tax credits	(1827)
	(1237)

Robert would be due for a repayment of £1237. Although annuity income is treated as arising from the trust itself, other income paid from an interest in possession trust is deemed to arise from its original source. This is often referred to as 'looking through' the trust, so that the beneficiary is entitled to the tax credits and reliefs relating to the income as if the beneficiary had owned the income, i.e. in the example above the savings income is taxed at 20 per cent or 40 per cent depending on Robert's marginal rate of income tax, the savings income being treated as the top slice of income. This 'looking through' a trust also means that non-UK residents can claim any reliefs available to them on the particular source of income, e.g. interest on government securities are free of tax to non-UK residents.

Non-interest in possession trusts

The difference between this type of trust and an interest in possession trust arises from the fact that the trustees have the discretion of how to distribute the income between the beneficiaries of the trust. This fact could mean that the trustees may if they wish divert income away from higher rate taxpayers so that the income arising in the trust is liable to the lower rates of income tax in the hands of the beneficiaries. To counteract this, the ICTA 1988, s 686 provides that discretionary income in such trusts is liable to income tax at 34 per cent. From April 1995, discretionary trusts receive bank and buildings society interest net of tax.

The discretionary income is the trust income less:

● charges on income;
● income treated as belonging to the settlor (*see* 'anti-avoidance legislation' below);
● trust expenses; and
● capital receipts treated as income, e.g. lease premiums.

Non-interest in possession trusts may be either:

1. Discretionary trusts

The trustees have the discretion of how to distribute the income of the trust among the beneficiaries, and so they will be liable to income tax on the discretionary income at 34 per cent.

EXAMPLE

A discretionary trust has the following income for 2002/03:

	£
Schedule A income (net of expenses)	8600
Lease premium assessable	2000
Annuity payable to named beneficiary	1900 (gross)

Trustees' income tax liability:

	£
Schedule A	8600
Lease premium	2000
	10600
less Annuity	(1900)
STI	8700

Tax liability of trustees:

	£
Tax at 22% on premium	440
Tax at 34% on discretionary income:	
£6700 × 34%	2278
Tax on annuity (£1900 × 22%)	418
Total tax liability	3136

Tax liability of annuitant:

The annuitant will receive £1482, however, £1900 will be included in the individual's tax computation with a tax credit of £418 attached to it:

Gross	Tax	Net
(£)	(£)	(£)
1900	418	1482

The income available for distribution:

	£
Schedule A income	8600
Lease premium	2000
	10600
less Annuity	(1900)
	8700
less Tax liability	(3136)
Available for distribution	5564

If the income is distributed, the beneficiaries are deemed to have received the income net of 34 per cent tax, in which case the trustees must have paid sufficient tax on the discretionary income. If there has been insufficient tax paid, an additional liability arises on the trustees under the ICTA 1988, s 687.

EXAMPLE

A discretionary trust has discretionary income of £4620 for 2001/02 and £3300 for 2002/03. For each year it makes a discretionary payment of £2046. None of the income is dividend income.

Section 687 of ICTA 1988 tax pool:

2001/02		£
Tax on discretionary income:		
34% × £4620		1571
less Tax on discretionary payment:		
£2046 × 34/66		(1054)
	c/fwd	517

2002/03		£
Tax on discretionary income:		
34% × £3300		1122
		1639
less Tax on discretionary payment:		
£2046 × 34/66		(1054)
	c/fwd	585

If the tax in the pool is insufficient to cover the discretionary payment, the trustees are liable for the shortfall under the ICTA 1988, s 687.

EXAMPLE

Suppose that the discretionary payment in the last example for 2002/03 had been £3960.

2002/03		£
	b/fwd	517
Tax on discretionary income:		
34% × £3300		1122
		1639
less Tax on discretionary payment:		
£3960 × 34/66		(2040)
		(401)
Trustees' tax liability under s 687		401

2. Accumulation and maintenance trusts

Accumulation and maintenance (A&M) trusts are usually set up for the benefit of children, with the trustees having the discretion to use the income of the trust for the maintenance, education or benefit of the beneficiaries until they reach a specified age. In respect of trusts set up for children, the Trustee Act 1925, s 31 is significant as it applies to all trusts, unless the terms of the trust specifically exclude it, or are in conflict with it in which case the trust would override s 31. Section 31 of Trustee Act 1925 provides the following:

(a) The trustees can use the income of the minor beneficiaries' share of the trust for their maintenance, education or benefit. Any income not used for this purpose must be added to the capital that will pass to the beneficiaries when the trust comes to an end.

(b) On reaching 18 years of age, beneficiaries are entitled to the income from their share of the trust, i.e. the beneficiary becomes entitled to an interest in possession.

For example, the trust may provide that the property is held in trust for the beneficiaries until they reach 25 years of age, in which case the trustees will have the discretion to provide for the maintenance, education or benefit of the beneficiaries up to the age of 18 years, after which the beneficiaries will become absolutely entitled to the income from their share of the trust, i.e. beneficiaries will have an interest in possession of their share of the trust income, and on reaching the age of 25 years the beneficiary will be entitled to the property itself.

Because the trustees of an A&M trust have discretionary powers regarding the distribution of trust income, they are liable to income tax at 34 per cent on the discretionary income. If none of the beneficiaries are entitled to an interest in possession, because they are all under 18 years of age, the tax treatment is exactly the same as discretionary trusts. Where the trust provides for several beneficiaries, each beneficiary will become entitled to an interest in possession on reaching 18 years of age. Where some of the beneficiaries are entitled to an interest in possession and some are not, i.e. a mixed A&M trust, the interests in possession are deducted from the calculation of the liability to tax at 34 per cent.

EXAMPLE

An A&M trust has the following income and expenses for 2002/03:

	£
Income received net of basic rate tax	1170
BSI received	2440
Trust expenses	400

The terms of the trust provide that the beneficiaries are entitled to receive the capital of the trust when they reach their twenty-fifth birthday. The beneficiaries of the trust are:

John (aged 19 years)
Michael (aged 13 years)
Wendy (aged 11 years)

As John is over 18 years, he is entitled to an interest in possession of $\frac{1}{3}$ of the trust income:

John	Savings income		Other income	
Taxed income	£	£ Tax	£	£ Tax
(£1170 × 100/78) × 1/3			500	110
BSI:				
[(£2440 – 400) 100/80] × 1/3	850	170		
	850	170	500	110

The trust expenses are deducted from taxed income. The trustees must provide John with a certificate of tax deduction R 185 E:

	Gross (£)	Tax (£)	Net (£)
BSI	850	170	680
Taxed income (22%)	500	110	390
	1350	280	1070

John will receive £1070 from the trustees but £1350 will appear in John's income tax computation, so that if John has no other income, he can reclaim the tax credit of £280.

Trustees' income tax liability under s 686:

Taxed income	£	£ Tax
(£1170 × 100/78) × 2/3	1000	220
BSI:		
[(£2440 – 400) 100/80] × 2/3	1700	340
	2700	560

Tax @ 34% × £2700	918
less Tax credits	(560)
Tax to be paid by trustees	358

Trustees receive income net of income tax in the same way as individuals, i.e. dividends are received net of a 10 per cent tax credit, savings net of 20 per cent, and non-savings income net of basic rate tax. As trust expenses are deducted from taxed income, the trust expenses must be grossed up at 10 per cent, 20 per cent or 22 per cent, depending on the type of income used to cover the trust expenses. Trust expenses are deducted from taxed income in the following order:

1. dividend income
2. savings income
3. other income.

EXAMPLE

A discretionary trust receives the following income for 2002/03:

	£
Schedule A	6000
Dividends (net)	180
BSI (net)	132

The administration expenses were £546.

The expenses will be matched as follows:

	Net £	Gross £
1. Dividend income	$180 \times \dfrac{100}{90}$	200
2. BSI	$132 \times \dfrac{100}{80}$	165
3. Non-savings	$234 \times \dfrac{100}{78}$	300
	546	665

Because it is a discretionary trust, any income not matched with expenses will be liable to income tax at 34 per cent:

	£
$200 \times 10\%$	20
$165 \times 20\%$	33
$300 \times 22\%$	66
$5700 \times 34\%$	1938
Income tax liability	2057

From 6 April 1999, the tax treatment of dividends was substantially altered, the tax credit on dividends being reduced from 20 per cent to 10 per cent, and a new Schedule F tax rate of 10 per cent being applicable to basic rate taxpayers (*see* Chapter 16). In order to compensate for the reduction in the tax credit, for trustees who are liable to income tax at 34 per cent, i.e. trustees of accumulation and discretionary trusts, a Schedule F trust tax rate of 25 per cent will be applied to the dividend income of such trusts.

EXAMPLE

A discretionary trust has the following income for 2002/03:

	£
Dividends (net)	9000
Schedule A	5200

Trust expenses were £540.

The expenses are deducted from dividend income:

	£
Dividends (net)	9000
Less expenses	(540)
	8460

Trustees income tax liability:

	£
Dividend income used for expenses $540 \times \dfrac{100}{90}$ @ 10%	60

Rest of dividend income at the Schedule F trust rate:

$(9000 - 540) \times \dfrac{100}{90}$ @ 25%	2350
Schedule A @ 34%: $5200 \times 34\%$	1768
	4178

Anti-avoidance legislation

1. Revocable settlements

Where a settlement can be revoked, and as a result of the revocation the settlor can benefit in some way, the arrangement will not be effective for tax purposes:

(a) Income settlements

A revocable income settlement is one where the settlor is liable to make annual payments but either the settlor/spouse can reduce the payments, or stop making the payments at some future date. A revocable income settlement, e.g. a covenant, will not be allowed as a deduction for income tax purposes unless the power to revoke the payments cannot be exercised for *three years* from the first payment with respect to charitable covenants, or *six years* with respect to individuals. However, covenants made to individuals after March 1988 are ineffective in any case.

(b) Capital settlements

A revocable capital settlement is one where anyone has the power to revoke the settlement once the funds have been provided by the settlor, and as a result of the revocation the settlor or spouse can receive any of the capital or income arising from the settlement. This also includes the power to reduce the property in the settlement. Where there is a revocable capital settlement, any income arising is deemed to be income of the settlor unless the power cannot be exercised for *six years* from the time the property was settled, in which case the income will not be treated as the settlor's income until the power can be exercised.

2. Settlements where settlor retains an interest

If any of the income or capital in a settlement can be applied for the benefit of the settlor or spouse, then any undistributed income in the trust is treated as the settlor's income.

3. Settlements in favour of settlors' minor child(ren)

When parents create settlements for their child(ren), any income paid to any child who is unmarried and under the age of 18 years is treated as income of that parent for any year that they are resident in the UK.

Prior to 9 March 1999, a bare trust of income set up by a parent for the benefit of a minor child was effective for income tax purposes, i.e., the income was treated as the child's income and not the parent's, provided that none of the income was actually used for the child's benefit, and any tax repayments that were obtained were retained in the trust. However, with effect from 9 March 1999, the income arising from bare trusts set up for children after 9 March 1999, or from funds added after 9 March 1999 to existing bare trusts, will be treated as income of the parent, subject to a *de minimus* amount of £100.

Foreign trusts

1. Trustees' UK income tax liability

The trustees of a non-UK resident trust are only liable to UK income tax on the UK income. However, where the trust is a non-interest in possession trust, the trustees are liable to income tax at 34 per cent on the UK income. Trust expenses are deducted pro-rata from the overseas and UK income.

EXAMPLE

A non-UK resident discretionary trust has the following income and expenses for 2002/03:

	£
Overseas income (gross)	5000
UK dividends (net)	6300
Expenses	600

Trustees' UK tax liability

	UK income (£)	Overseas income (£)
Dividends (£6300 × 100/90)	7000	
Overseas income		5000
	7000	5000

Expenses apportioned to UK income:

$$£600 \times \frac{7000}{7000 + 5000} = £350$$

	Gross income (£)	Tax credits (£)
Dividends (£6300 − £350) × 100/90	6611	661

Trustees' UK tax liability:

	£
£6611 × 34%	2248
less Tax credits	(661)
Tax payable by trustees	1587

2. UK resident beneficiaries liability

(a) Interest in possession trusts

The income is treated as if the original source belonged to the beneficiary under the principle of 'looking through' the trust, so that the individual is entitled to the tax credits and can claim credit relief for overseas tax paid.

(b) Non-interest in possession trusts

The income is taxable under Schedule D Case V. Tax credits for overseas tax paid will be allowed by concession provided that the trustee's UK tax affairs are up to date.

EXAMPLE

Suppose that in the last example £3000 is paid to a UK beneficiary. The payment is apportioned as follows:

$$£3000 \times \frac{6611}{6611 + 5000} = £1708$$

£1708 is therefore attributable to UK income and the corresponding tax credit calculated as:

$$£1708 \times \frac{34}{66} = £880$$

SELF ASSESSMENT QUESTIONS

20.1 An interest in possession trust has the following income for 2002/03:

	£
Schedule A (net of expenses)	7650
Trust administration expenses	500
Building society interest received	2320

The terms of the trust provide that the income of the trust is payable to Mary for life.

REQUIRED

(a) Calculate the income available to Mary in 2002/03

(b) Calculate the total income tax liability of the trustees for 2002/03.

20.2 An accumulation and maintenance trust has the following income and expenses for 2002/03:

	£
Building society interest received	4600
Income received net of basic rate tax	3465
Trust administration expenses	400

The terms of the trust provide that the beneficiaries are to receive the capital of the trust on reaching their 25th birthdays. The beneficiaries are:

Amy (aged 20 years)
Jo (aged 16 years)
Beth (aged 14 years)

During 2002/03 no discretionary payments were made.

REQUIRED

(a) Calculate the income Amy is entitled to receive in 2002/03.

(b) Calculate the trustees' income tax liability under s 686 for 2002/03.

PRACTICE QUESTIONS

1. Penelope commenced in business on 1 January 2001. The adjusted Schedule D Case I figure for the 6 months ended on 30 June 2001 was £14 600. The accounts have been prepared for the year ended 30 June 2002 and show the following:

Year ended 30/6/02	£	£
Gross profit		60 000
Dividends received		1 960
Bank interest received		800
		62 760
less Expenses		
General expenses (note 1)	12 050	
Legal and professional fees (note 2)	1 130	
Drawings	6 000	
Depreciation	2 500	
Premium on lease (note 3)	15 000	
Motor expenses (note 4)	2 650	
Rent	6 000	
Heat and light	1 250	
Telephone	750	(47 330)
Net Profit		15 430

Notes:
(1) General expenses include the following:

Postage and stationery	£600
Office wages	£10 000
Subscription to political party	£500
Subscription to chamber of trade	£200
Subscription to health club	£750
	£12 050

(2) Legal and professional fees include:

Debt collection	£150
Accountancy fees	£400
Legal fees re new lease	£580
	£1 130

(3) Penelope took over leased premises on 1 July 2001 for a premium of £15 000 and annual rent of £6000 pa on a nine-year lease.

(4) It has been agreed that Penelope uses her car 60 per cent for business purposes.

The balance of capital expenditure brought forward at 1 July 2001 was:

General pool	£11 000
Car	£9 000

During the year ended 30 June 2002, Penelope had the following acquisitions and disposals:

1/8/01	bought office equipment	£2200
30/11/01	bought plant	£5000
30/11/01	sold equipment (original cost £3000)	£3200
12/1/02	bought fax machine	£1200

You are required to:

(a) calculate the maximum capital allowances available for the year ended 30 June 2002;

(6 marks)

(b) calculate the Schedule D Case I adjusted profit figure for the year ended 30 June 2002; and

(13 marks)

(c) show the Schedule D Case I assessments for 2000/01, 2001/02 and 2002/03 and identify any overlap profits.

(6 marks)
(Total: 25 marks)

2. Harry Hudson Ltd, a bicycle manufacturer, makes up annual accounts to 31 December and has been trading for several years. On 1 July 1998 the company purchased a new building, which qualified as an industrial building, and which was brought into use immediately. The building, which was not in an enterprise zone, cost £150 000 and was used as an industrial building until 31 March 2000. Between 1 April 2000 and 30 June 2001, the factory was leased for non-industrial use as a keep fit club because of a downturn in bicycle sales. On 1 July 2001 production of bicycles recommenced and continued until 30 June 2002 when the building was sold for £140 000 to Tommy Turpin Ltd. The purchaser company has been a manufacturer of refrigerators since 1981 and immediately commenced production in the factory. Tommy Turpin Ltd's accounting date is 30 September.

You are required to calculate:

(a) the industrial buildings allowance given to Harry Hudson Ltd for all relevant years;

(5 marks)

(b) the balancing adjustment on Harry Hudson Ltd on the sale of the building in 2002; and

(3 marks)

(c) the future industrial buildings allowance claimable by Tommy Turpin Ltd following its purchase of the building.

(3 marks)
(Total: 11 marks)
(Source: ACCA, Dec 91)

3. (a) Max has been a sheep farmer for many years. His adjusted trading results are as follows:

	£
Year ended 31 December 2000	14 000 profit
Year ended 31 December 2001	44 000 profit
Year ended 31 December 2002	(6 000) loss

You are required:

(i) to state the nature of the election which Max can make to reduce his liability to income tax; and

(1 mark)

(ii) to calculate the assessments for all the relevant years following such an election.

(3 marks)

(b) Geoffrey, a farmer, had erected a new barn costing £10 000 in one of his fields on 1 July 2000. On 1 July 2002 Geoffrey sold the field and the barn to Thomas, another farmer. The barn was sold for £9500. Geoffrey has always made up accounts to 31 December and Thomas to 30 June.

You are required to calculate the capital allowances for all relevant years on the assumption that:

(i) no election is made by Geoffrey and Thomas on the sale of the building; and

(5 marks)

(ii) an election is made by Geoffrey and Thomas on the sale of the building.

(2 marks)
(Total: 11 marks)
(Source: ACCA, Dec 91)

4. Robert Alfreton had been in business as a grocer for many years, but he ceased trading on 31 March 2003 because of increasing competition from supermarkets.

(a) His profits and losses adjusted for income tax were:

		£
Year ended 30 June 1998	Profit	15 000
Year ended 30 June 1999	Profit	14 000
Year ended 30 June 2000	Profit	11 000
Year ended 30 June 2001	Profit	12 000
Year ended 30 June 2002	Loss	(2 500)
Period to Cessation on 31 March 2003	Loss	(12 500)

(b) Capital allowances were:

	£
1999/00	1 700
2000/01	1 500
2001/02	1 000
2002/03	1 200

(c) Robert has no other income.

You are required to calculate the amount of loss relief which can be claimed and to show how this will be relieved.

(11 marks)

(Source: ACCA, June 90)

5. Mr K is chairman and chief executive of AD Ltd.

He received a salary of £45 000 per annum and during the income year 2002/03 he is provided with the following benefits:

The company has provided him with the use of a Jaguar motor car costing £26 000 from 6 April 2002. The distributor's list price was £26 700 at that time; approved CO_2 emissions were 233gm/km.

On 31 July 2002, he was involved in a serious road accident and the car was written off. He was charged with dangerous driving and the company met his legal costs of £2000.

When he resumed on 1 October 2002, he was provided with a Mercedes car costing £30 000 (list price £30 450) and the use of a chauffeur. This car is used solely for business purposes; approved CO_2 emissions were 245gm/km.

While he had use of the Jaguar, he contributed £120 being 50 per cent of the cost of his private fuel.

Throughout the year, his wife, who is not employed by the company, has been provided with the use of a BMW car costing £15 000, the list price, four years ago; the company meets all running costs and fuel bills. Approved CO_2 emissions were 226 gm/km.

He occupies a house which had cost the company £80 000 when purchased in 1984 and on which expenditure of £40 000 on improvements had been incurred prior to being first occupied by Mr K in 1996 when its market value was £140 000. Its annual value is agreed at £3600. Mr K pays no rent but does meet all running costs.

He is provided with the use of two suits which had been purchased by the company at a cost of £800 in total.
All the cars were petrol driven with engine sizes greater than 2000cc.

You are required to:

(a) compute the total amount of benefits in kind assessable on Mr K for the income tax year 2002/03;

(12 marks)

(b) compute any additional costs which will be borne by the company as a result of providing the above benefits.

(3 marks)

Assume an official rate of interest of 8 per cent.

(Total: 15 marks)

(Source: CIMA, Nov 92)

6. John and Hilda Brown have been married for many years. The company that John works for is streamlining its operations and planning a number of redundancies before the end of 2002/03. John, who is 55 years old, is being made redundant on 31 January 2003, and for 2002/03 was employed on a salary of £30 000 pa. The company also provided him with a car (1988 cc) that cost £18 000 when it was new in October 1999. John paid £200 in 2002/03 towards the running cost of the car. He was also provided with all his petrol, including private petrol. CO_2 emissions were 238 gm/km. John's compensation package agreed by the company was as follows:

	£
Lump sum *ex gratia* payment	35 000
Statutory redundancy payment	6 000
Payment in lieu of notice	1 500

He was also allowed to keep his company car which had a value of £8200 on 31 January 2003.

Hilda works as a secretary on a salary of £12 000 pa (PAYE deducted 2002/03 was £1750).

John Brown had £5880 tax deducted under PAYE for 2002/03.

The couple also had the following investment income for 2002/03:

	John (£)	Hilda (£)
Building society interest received	612	740
Bank interest received	720	300
Dividends received	3840	1420
Rental income (net of expenses)	nil	6000

You are required to:

(a) calculate John's income tax liability for 2002/03 and calculate any further tax payable by John.

(14 marks)

(b) calculate Hilda's income tax liability for 2002/03 and calculate any further tax payable by Hilda.

(7 marks)

(c) Hilda is thinking of having the rented property improved as she thinks this might reduce her tax liability on the property. Briefly explain to Hilda how the improvements on the property will be treated for tax purposes.

(4 marks)
(Total: 25 marks)

7. Joshua Wrekin retired from his job as technical director with Wenlock Engineers Ltd on 30 April 2002, his 65th birthday. He received an *ex-gratia* payment from his employers of £25 250 plus his company car which was valued at £6500. The Revenue accept that this is a termination payment (assessable under s 148) and not a payment under an unapproved retirement benefit arrangement.

His monthly salary, payable on the last day of the month was £2275. The car was a 2500 cc BMW costing £18 500 with CO_2 emissions of 240 gm/km. The running costs of the car as shown on the P11D form were £400 including approximately half of the petrol used for Joshua's private motoring. Wenlock Engineers Ltd paid Joshua's subscription to BUPA, a private health insurance company, costing £42 for the month of April 2002.

Joshua decided to use his engineering skills and business contacts as a self-employed consultant. He commenced on 1 May 2002 and made up his first accounts to 30 April 2003. His summarised accounts for the first period of trading were:

	£	£	£
Consultancy fees			27 510
Reference books (note 1)		300	
Wife's wages as secretary (note 2)		4 200	
Car expenses (note 3)			
Depreciation	1 600		
Petrol and oil	1 500		
Servicing	200		
AA subscription	60		
Replacement tyres	150		
Insurance	1 000		
		4 510	
Depreciation of furniture and equipment		250	
Rent of office		7 000	
Premium payment for lease (note 4)		2 500	
Office running costs		1 500	
			(20 260)
Net profit			7 250

Notes:
(1) The reference books were purchased in May 2002.

265

(2) Wife's wages of £350 were paid on the last day of the month and accepted by the Revenue as being at a commercial rate.

(3) The BMW was used in the business. Joshua's business mileage in the period covered by the first set of accounts was 20 000 and his private mileage was 2000. This proportion is expected to apply for future periods.

(4) The lease was for 10 years from 1 May 2002.

(5) Capital purchases were made as follows:

		£
May 2002	Office furniture	1000
May 2002	Computer/word processor	1500
November 2002	Photocopier	920
June 2003	New telephone and fax system	2174

No election was to be made to treat any of the assests purchased as 'short-life' assets.

Joshua estimates that the profits adjusted for tax purposes, for the years ending 30 April 2004 and 2005 will be £10 000 and £15 000 respectively.

Joshua's wife, Brenda, had purchased a life annuity from an insurance company on her 65th birthday during 1999 which paid her £100 a month. The income element has been agreed with the Revenue at £50. She received £1200 interest from the Northern Shires Building Society on 31 December 2002 and paid £900 (net) to a national charity under a four-year deed of covenant on 1 January each year.

Joshua received National Insurance Retirement Pension of £4842 for the year 2002/03 and both he and Brenda began paying private medical insurance of £40 each (gross) per month on 1 July 2002.

You are required to:

(a) calculate the Schedule D Case II assessments for the first three years in respect of Joshua's business;

(13 marks)

(b) calculate the income tax payable by Joshua for 2002/03; and

(9 marks)

(c) calculate the income tax liability of Brenda for 2002/03.

(8 marks)
(Total: 30 marks)
(Source: ACCA, Dec 91)

8. There are many factors to be considered which may not individually point in the direction of employment or self-employment. The following factors will, however, be the ones which the Inland Revenue and, ultimately, the courts will consider when reaching a decision. Matters which are special to a particular case will, of course, be given due attention.

   You are required to discuss the factors to be taken into consideration when deciding whether a person is employed or self-employed for the purpose of income tax.

   (11 marks)
   (Source: ACCA, Dec 91)

PART 3

Capital gains tax

CHAPTER 21

Introduction to capital gains tax

When a person makes a profit on the sale of a capital asset, they may be liable to capital gains tax (CGT). There may also be a liability when an asset is lost or destroyed, or when it is disposed of by way of a gift.

Capital gains tax was introduced in the Finance Act 1965, in an attempt to achieve a greater degree of equity in the British tax system. In his Budget speech of that year, James Callaghan said 'Yield is not my main purpose . . . The failure to tax capital gains is . . . the greatest blot on our system of direct taxation . . . This new tax will provide a background to equity and fair play.'

There have, however, been many changes made since the tax was first introduced in 1965. The statutory charging provisions for CGT are contained in the Taxation of Chargeable Gains Act 1992 (TCGA 1992) which consolidated previous CGT legislation.

There is a charge to CGT when a *chargeable person makes a chargeable disposal of a chargeable asset.*

This chapter examines each of these aspects in detail.

Chargeable person

Persons chargeable to CGT are individuals resident and ordinarily resident in the UK, including trustees and personal representatives.

Note: Companies do not pay CGT as such, even though they are classed as a 'person' in law. Instead companies pay corporation tax on their chargeable gains, *see* Chapter 32.

Section 2(1) of the TCGA 1992 provides that a person is chargeable to CGT in respect of worldwide gains accruing in a year of assessment, during any part of which that person is resident or ordinarily resident in the UK.

Overseas domiciled individuals are liable to CGT on the disposal of UK assets at any time they are resident or ordinarily resident in the UK, but assets disposed of overseas are only liable on the amount of gain remitted to the UK.

Residence, ordinary residence, and domicile are discussed fully in Part 2, Chapter 18.

A. Individuals

Individuals are entitled to an annual exemption of £7700 for 2002/03; only chargeable gains in excess of this amount are taxable.

Prior to 6 April 1999, CGT was charged at the individual's marginal rate of income tax, the gain being treated as if it were the top slice of income for this purpose.

EXAMPLE 1

Charles, a single man, has a salary of £6300 and chargeable gains of £35 000 for 1998/99:

Income tax	£
Salary	6 300
PA	(4 195)
Taxable income	2 105

The taxable income falls entirely in the 20 per cent band (1998/99):

£2105 × 20% = £421 income tax due.

Capital gains tax	£
Chargeable gain	35 000
less Annual exemption (98/99)	(6 800)
Taxable gain	28 200

	£
Unused lower rate band (£4300 – £2105)	2 195
Basic rate band	22 800
Higher rate	3 205
	28 200

Therefore, the CGT was charged as follows:

	£
£2195 × 20%	439
£22 800 × 23%	5 244
£3205 × 40%	1 282
	6 965 CGT due

An added complication used to arise out of the fact that savings income is not liable to income tax at the basic rate. This affected the CGT rate in cases where an individual's non-savings income was below the limit for the lower rate band. When this happened, the chargeable gains were first appropriated to utilise the lower rate band as follows:

EXAMPLE 2

Amy, a single woman, has a total income of £27 195 and chargeable gains of £20 000 for 1998/99.

Income tax	£
Total income (earned)	27 195
PA	(4 195)
Taxable income	23 000

	£
£4300 × 20%	860
£18700 × 23%	4401
	5161 Income tax due

Capital gains tax

	£
Chargeable gains	20000
less Annual exemption	(6800)
Taxable gains	13200

There are £4100 left in the basic rate band for 1998/99, and so the CGT liability is calculated as follows:

	£
£4100 × 23%	943
£9100 × 40%	3640
	4583 CGT due

Suppose, however, that Amy's total income for 1998/99 included savings income of £21000.

	£
Taxable income	23000
less Savings income	(21000)
Other income	2000

Therefore, £4300 – £2000 = £2300 of the lower rate band was not used by income other than savings income; £2300 of the gain can then in this case be charged at 20 per cent to use up the lower rate band.

Capital gains tax	£
Chargeable gains	20000
less Annual exemption	(6800)
Taxable gains	13200

	£
£2300 × 20%	460
£(4100 – 2300) × 23%	414
£9100 × 40%	3640
	4514 CGT due 1998/99

The 1999 Budget removed this complication, and simplified the way in which gains are charged to tax, by treating gains in the same way as savings income, i.e. by taxing gains at 20 per cent or 40 per cent, depending on the individual's marginal rate of income tax, again, gains being treated as the top slice.

EXAMPLE 3

Julie has a salary of £26 335 and chargeable gains of £18 000 for 2002/03.

Income tax	£
Salary	26 335
PA	(4 615)
Taxable income	21 720

	£	
£1920 × 10%	192	
£19 800 × 22%	4 356	
	4 548	Income tax due

As Julie has £8180 left in the basic rate band, i.e. £29 900 – £21 720, the first £8180 of taxable gain will be charged at 20 per cent and any taxable gain in excess of this amount will be liable to CGT at 40 per cent.

Capital gains tax	£
Chargeable gains	18 000
less Annual exemption	(7 700)
Taxable gains	10 300

	£	
£8180 × 20%	1 636	
£2120 × 40%	848	
	2 484	CGT due

For 1999/00, therefore, gains could not be subject to the 10 per cent rate, even in situations where the individual could not utilise the 10 per cent band. This situation was rectified in the FA 2000; gains will still continue to be taxed at 20 per cent where they fall within the basic rate band and at 40 per cent where they fall above the basic rate limit, but from 6 April 2000, taxable gains falling below the starting rate are liable to CGT at 10 per cent.

NB: Gains are not liable to tax at the basic rate.

EXAMPLE 4

Susan, aged 55 years, has savings income of £4385 (gross), and a chargeable gain of £10 000 for 2002/03.

Income tax	£
Savings income	4385
PA (restricted)	(4385)
Taxable income	nil

However, as Susan has not used any of the 10 per cent band, the first £1920 of any taxable gain will be taxed at 10 per cent.

Capital gains tax

	£
Chargeable gain	10 000
less Annual exemption	(7 700)
Taxable gain	2 300

	£
Taxable gain	2 300
less Unused starting rate	(1 920)
Remaining gain	380

As the remaining taxable gain falls entirely in the basic rate band, CGT is charged as follows:

	£	
£1920 x 10%	192	
£380 x 20%	76	
	268	CGT due

EXAMPLE 5

James, aged 36, has a salary of £25 580 and a chargeable gain of £20 000 for 2002/03.

Income tax	£
Salary	25 580
PA	(4 615)
Taxable income	20 965

	£	
£1920 x 10%	192	
£19 045 x 22%	4 190	
	4 382	income tax

As James has £8935 left in the basic rate band, i.e. £29 900 – £20 965, the first £8935 of taxable gain will be charged at 20 per cent and any taxable gain in excess of this amount will be liable to tax at 40 per cent.

Capital gains tax	£
Chargeable gain	20 000
less Annual exemption	(7 700)
Taxable gain	12 300

Therefore, CGT is charged as follows:

	£
£8935 x 20%	1 787
£3365 x 40%	1 346
	3 133 CGT due

B. Partnerships

A partnership is merely a collection of individuals, so each partner is assessed on his share of the gains accruing on the disposal of partnership assets. The size of the share is determined by the partnership agreement.

The taxation of partnership gains is considered more fully in Chapter 28.

C. Personal representatives

Personal Representatives (PRs) are liable to CGT at 34 per cent, and are eligible for an annual exemption for the year of death, and the following two years.

Estates and CGT are considered in more detail in Chapter 30.

D. Trustees

Trustees generally receive half the annual exemption available to individuals. Where there is a group of settlements, the annual exemption available is the higher of:

(a) $\dfrac{£3850}{\text{No. of settlements in the group}}$

or

(b) $\frac{1}{10}$ of the annual exemption available to individuals (i.e. £770 for 2002/03).

However, where the trust is for a mentally disabled person in receipt of an attendance allowance, then the full amount of annual exemption available to individuals is given.

Trustees are charged CGT at 34 per cent as for PRs.

Trusts and settlements for CGT are considered in more detail in Chapter 30.

Table 21.1 Summary of tax rates and annual exemptions

Person	Annual exemption (£)	Rate
(1) Individuals	7700	Gains are treated as if they were the top slice of income and taxed at 10%, 20% or 40%
(2) Personal representatives	7700 for the year of death and the following two years	34%
(3) Trustees (a) general trusts (b) trusts for the mentally disabled	 3850 7700	34%

Note: Companies do not pay CGT but pay corporation tax on their gains at their marginal rate of corporation tax. There is no annual exemption for companies.

Exempt persons

Certain 'persons' are, however, generally exempt from CGT:

(a) local authorities

(b) health service bodies

(c) public institutions, etc.

(d) scientific research associations (provided that they are approved by the Secretary of State)

(e) consular officials and foreign diplomats

(f) Lloyd's underwriters:

  – gains or losses on assets in premium trust funds or special reserve funds are subject to income tax from 1992/93; before this they were subject to CGT.

    Other fund assets are subject to CGT in the normal way. Since 1994, members can participate in syndicates through a 'Members Agent Pooling Arrangement' (MAPA), allowing members access to a wide range of syndicates in order to spread the risk. In 1995 Lloyd's changed the rules to allow syndicate capacity to be bought and sold with the result that members could realise gains and losses on their disposals. Prior to 1999, the Revenue allowed the deferral of most of these small gains and losses until such time as the member leaves the syndicate. The FA 1999 legislated for this practice to allow roll-over relief to all syndicate capacity, whether held through a MAPA or directly. This will have the effect of reducing the number of computations that would otherwise become necessary.

    Note: these rules do not apply to corporate members of Lloyd's.

(g) pension funds:

  – gains on the disposal of investments held in superannuation schemes, personal pension schemes, etc. (provided that they are Revenue approved) are exempt from CGT;

  – from 26 July 1990 this was extended to cover gains arising from dealings in future contracts and options by occupational or personal pension schemes, etc.

(h) charities:

  – charities are exempt from CGT on their gains (provided that any such gains are used for charitable purposes);

  – trustees under a will are not exempt from CGT even though the beneficiaries include charities. However, there is no charge to CGT where a charity becomes absolutely entitled to settled property.

    When property ceases to be held for charitable purposes, there is a chargeable deemed disposal at market value.

Chargeable disposal

Because disposal is not specifically defined, it is given its general meaning of transfer of ownership. The legislation does, however, extend this meaning, and a disposal for CGT purposes includes:

- the sale of an asset;
- the sale of part of an asset;
- the gift of an asset;
- the gift of part of an asset;
- the loss/destruction of an asset;
- the loss/destruction of part of an asset;
- the transfer of assets into a settlement; and
- the receipt of a capital sum resulting from the ownership of an asset.

Date of disposal

Generally, the date of disposal of an asset for CGT purposes is the date that title to the asset passes to the new owner. However, disposals under contract and hire purchase agreements have special rules:

(a) Disposals under contract (TCGA 1992, s 28)

Where an asset is disposed of under a contract, the date of disposal is the date of the contract, which may be different from the date the asset is transferred to its new owner.

EXAMPLE

James disposed of his country cottage in 2001/02. Contracts were exchanged on 10 August 2001 and completion took place on 2 October 2001. For CGT purposes, the date of disposal is 10 August 2001, the date of the contract, and not 2 October 2001 when title to the cottage passed to the new owner. If the contract is conditional, then the disposal date is the date that the contract becomes unconditional.

EXAMPLE

William exchanged contracts for the sale of his holiday home on 6 June 2002. The contract was conditional on a boundary dispute being settled. The dispute was settled on 16 November 2002 and completion took place on 10 January 2003.

For CGT purposes, the date of disposal is 16 November 2002, when the conditional contract became unconditional.

(b) Hire purchase agreements (TCGA 1992, s 27)

Where an asset is disposed of under a hire purchase agreement, the beginning of the hire period is the date of disposal for CGT purposes – *Lyon* v *Pettigrew* [1985] STC 107.

Exempt disposals

The following disposals are exempt from CGT:

- transactions liable to income tax
  - income tax prevails over CGT so where a transaction is charged to income tax, it cannot also be charged to CGT;
- transfers of assets on death (TCGA 1992, s 62);
- transfers of assets as security for a mortgage or loan;
- gifts for national heritage; and
- gifts to charities.

There are other disposals which, while they are not specifically exempt, are treated as being transferred on a no gain/no loss basis:

- disposals between spouses; and
- intra-group disposals.

Chargeable assets (TCGA 1992, s 21)

Section 21 of the TCGA 1992 provides that all forms of property are assets for CGT purposes, whether or not they are situated in the UK, unless they are specifically exempted.

Property for this purpose includes anything capable of being owned such as freehold or leasehold land, shares, securities and other tangible and intangible assets. The definition in s 21 is very wide and includes:

- acquired assets, whether purchased or inherited;
- created assets, e.g. goodwill;
- shares;
- options;
- debts;
- leases;
- trademarks;
- copyrights;
- currency other than sterling.

Exempt assets

Certain assets are exempt from CGT:

- chattels sold for £6000 or less (TCGA 1992, s 262);
- chattels that are wasting assets (provided that they are not eligible for capital allowances) (TCGA 1992, s 45);
- motor cars including vintage cars (TCGA 1992, s 263);
- National Saving certificates (TCGA 1992, s 121);
- foreign currency purchased for personal use (TCGA 1992, s 269);
- principal private residence (TCGA 1992, s 222);
- life assurance policies (TCGA 1992, s 210);
- decorations for valour (unless acquired for money/money's worth) (TCGA 1992, s 268);
- gambling winnings (TCGA 1992, s 51);
- compensation for personal injury (TCGA 1992, s 51);
- gilt-edged securities and qualifying corporate bonds (TCGA 1992, s 115).

CHAPTER 22

The computation of gains and losses

As CGT was first introduced by the FA 1965, only gains accruing from 6 April 1965 were chargeable to CGT. There have, however, been many changes to CGT since it was first introduced in 1965. An indexation allowance was first introduced by the FA 1982, so that CGT was not being charged on inflationary gains; this was extended by FA 1985 so the indexation allowance could be used to increase or create a loss. The FA 1988 saw the rebasing of assets to their value at 31 March 1982 so that, effectively, gains accruing before 31 March 1982 were not chargeable on disposals after 6 April 1988. The FA 1993 again restricted the indexation allowance, so for disposals made on or after 30 November 1993, it cannot be used to increase or create a loss. Fundamental changes to the system of CGT were introduced in the FA 1998, replacing the indexation allowance with a taper for disposals made by individuals, trustees and PRs after 6 April 1998. The FA 1999 and 2000 also made changes to the rates at which CGT is calculated with respect to individuals.

Despite these many changes, the basic calculation arrived at by deducting allowable expenditure from the disposal proceeds has changed little over the years, allowable and disallowable items of expenditure being generally limited by statute.

This chapter examines the basic CGT computation for individuals, trustees and PRs, the rules for rebasing, assets held on the 6 April 1965 and the rules for part disposals. It then goes on to consider the tax treatment of capital losses and the special rules for husband and wife and connected persons.

The basic computation

	£	£
Gross sale proceeds (or market value)		X
less Incidental costs of sale		(X)
less Relevant allowable expenditure:		X
Acquisition costs	X	
Incidental cost of acquisition	X	
Enhancement expenditure	X	
		(X)
Unindexed gain/(loss)		X
less Indexation allowance to April 1998		(X)
Gain eligible for taper relief		X
less Taper relief		(X)
Chargeable gain		X

We will now examine in detail the components parts of the CGT computation:

1. Gross sale proceeds

The gross sale proceeds is the price paid for the acquisition of the asset.

EXAMPLE

Penelope sold an antique desk at auction for £16 000 on which she had to pay the auctioneer a 10 per cent commission. The gross sale proceeds are therefore £16 000. The £1600 auctioneer's fees are Penelope's costs of sale.

Deferred consideration

Where an asset is acquired by paying the full purchase price in instalments, no allowance is taken of this fact in computing the CGT liability of the person making the disposal; the computation is based on the full purchase price, even though it has not all been received at the time of disposal. If any part of the consideration proves to be irrecoverable at a later date, an appropriate adjustment is made at that time.

However, the TCGA 1992, s 280 does provide that if the taxpayer can prove that the above treatment will cause hardship, then the CGT due on the disposal may be paid in instalments.

Consideration received in a foreign currency

Where an asset is acquired or disposed of for a currency other than sterling, the foreign currency must be translated into sterling *before* the gain/loss is calculated. The gain/loss *cannot* be calculated in the foreign currency and then translated into sterling – *Bentley* v *Pike (HMIT)* (1981) 53 TC 590.

Market value (TCGA 1992, s 17)

There are certain transactions where market value is substituted for the gross sale proceeds:

- by way of a gift;
- where the consideration cannot be valued;
- where the transaction is between connected persons;
- by way of transfer into a settlement; and
- in connection with loss of employment.

The market value is the amount which could reasonably be expected if the asset was sold on the open market (TCGA 1992, s 272).

1. Quoted shares and securities (TCGA 1992, s 272(3))

These are valued using the Stock Exchange Daily Official List and for CGT purposes the market value is the lower of:

(a) $\frac{1}{4}$ *up rule* – the lower of the two quoted prices plus $\frac{1}{4}$ of the difference between the two prices on that date; or

(b) *average bargain* – the average of the highest and lowest prices of the recorded bargains at that date.

EXAMPLE 1

Shares quoted at 160p and 168p. The highest and lowest marked bargains on that date were 158p and 168p.

(a) $\frac{1}{4}$ up

168p
160p
8p *difference*

$\frac{8}{4}$ + 160p = 162p

(b) *Average bargain*

158p
168p
326p ÷ 2 = 163p

Therefore, the market value for CGT purposes is 162p.

EXAMPLE 2

Shares quoted at 200p and 212p. The highest and lowest marked bargains on that date were 200p and 204p.

(a) $\frac{1}{4}$ up

212p
200p
12p *difference* $\frac{12p}{4}$ + 200p = 203p

(b) *Average bargain*

200p
204p
404p ÷2 = 202p

Therefore, the market value for CGT purposes is 202p.

2. Unquoted shares and securities (TCGA 1992, s 273)

The valuation of unquoted shares must be agreed by the Inland Revenue's Shares Valuation Division for CGT purposes.

Section 273, TCGA 1992 provides that the market value at any time is the price they would fetch in the open market where the prospective purchaser has all the information that a prudent purchaser might reasonably require if he were proposing to purchase the asset from a willing vendor by private treaty and at arm's length.

Shares and securities dealt in on the Unlisted Securities Market (USM) are not listed in the Stock Exchange Daily Official List and so for CGT purposes are treated as unquoted securities. However, there will be evidence of bargains on or near the date of disposal to assist in the valuation.

3. Unit trusts (TCGA 1992, s 272 (5))
These are valued using the lowest buying price published on that day or the latest date before.

2. Incidental costs of sale

Includes items such as:

- valuation fees;
- auctioneer/estate agency fees;
- costs of advertising; and
- legal costs.

These are deducted from the gross sale proceeds because, while they are an allowable deduction, they *do not* rank for an indexation allowance, up until April 1998.

Note: According to IR Tax Bulletin, February 1994, p. 118, allowable costs of sale do not include any costs incurred in negotiating the value.

3. Acquisition costs

The cost of originally acquiring the asset, or in the case of created rather than acquired assets, expenditure wholly and exclusively incurred in providing the asset.

4. Incidental costs of acquisition

Those will be the same type of costs as the incidental costs of sale, the difference being that these costs *do* rank for an indexation allowance, up until April 1998.

5. Enhancement expenditure

Expenditure wholly and exclusively incurred in enhancing the value of the property is allowed, e.g. central heating, provided that it is reflected in the state of the asset at the date of disposal.

NB: *It does not include repairs or maintenance.* Enhancement expenditure does not include the estimated labour costs of the taxpayer: *Oram (HMIT) v Johnson* [1980] 1 WLR 558.

Other allowable expenditure

(a) Expenditure incurred in establishing, preserving or defending title to, or right over, the asset.

(b) Value added tax (VAT) where the VAT is not recoverable by the purchaser.

(c) Where legatees or beneficiaries dispose of an asset to which they became absolutely entitled, expenditure incurred by the legatees, or beneficiaries, the PRs or trustees in transferring the asset to them is an allowable deduction for CGT.

EXAMPLE

Morris bought a country cottage as a second home for £40 000, his acquisition costs being £2000. He installed central heating and a bathroom costing £2500 and £3500 respectively. He also spent £4000 in legal fees for defending a boundary dispute. He later sold the cottage for £85 000, the cost of sale being £1850.

	£	£
Gross sale proceeds		85 000
less Costs of sale		(1 850)
Net sale proceeds		83 150
less Allowable expenses:		
Acquisition cost	40 000	
Costs of acquisition	2 000	
Enhancement expenditure	6 000	
Legal costs	4 000	(52 000)
unindexed gain		31 150

6. Indexation allowance

To prevent taxpayers from being charged CGT on inflationary gains, relief is given by adjusting the allowable expenditure for increases in the Retail Price Index (RPI).

For disposals after 6 April 1998, the indexation allowance is restricted to April 1998, and cannot be used to increase or create a loss.

The indexation allowance is arrived at by applying the indexation factor to the item of allowable expenditure.

The indexation factor is calculated by using the following formula:

$$\frac{R_D - R_1}{R_1}$$

where R_D = figure in the month of disposal or 6/4/98 whichever is earlier

R_1 = figure in month of acquisition or March 1982 whichever is later.

Indexation cannot go back before March 1982 as this is when it was first introduced. The resulting figure must then be rounded to three decimal places and then applied to the allowable expenditure.

EXAMPLE 1

Calculate the indexation factors between the following dates:

(a) January 1982 and January 1998
(b) April 1985 and June 1997
(c) February 1987 and October 1996
(d) September 1990 and March 1997
(e) December 1991 and September 1996

(a) $\dfrac{\text{RPI January 1998} - \text{RPI later of January 1982/March 1982}}{\text{RPI later of January 1982/March 1982}}$

$\dfrac{159.5 - 79.4}{79.4} = 1.0088161$

Indexation factor = 1.009

(b) $\dfrac{\text{RPI June 1997} - \text{RPI April 1985}}{\text{RPI April 1985}}$

$\dfrac{157.5 - 94.8}{94.8} = 0.6613924$

Indexation factor = 0.661

(c) $\dfrac{\text{RPI October 1996} - \text{RPI February 1987}}{\text{RPI February 1987}}$

$\dfrac{153.8 - 100.4}{100.4} = 0.5318725$

Indexation factor = 0.532

(d) $\dfrac{\text{RPI March 1997} - \text{RPI September 1990}}{\text{RPI September 1990}}$

$\dfrac{155.4 - 129.3}{129.3} = 0.2018561$

Indexation factor = 0.202

(e) $\dfrac{\text{RPI September 1996} - \text{RPI December 1991}}{\text{RPI December 1991}}$

$\dfrac{153.8 - 135.7}{135.7} = 0.1333824$

Indexation Factor = 0.133

Separate indexation factors need to be calculated where allowable expenditure is incurred on different dates.

7. Taper relief

For disposals after 6 April 1998, the indexation is replaced by a taper relief. The taper effectively reduces the chargeable gain depending on how long the asset has been held for periods after 5 April 1998, business assets receiving more favourable relief than non-business assets.

Prior to 6 April 2000, business assets were defined as:

- assets used for trading purposes; or
- holdings of at least 5 per cent of the voting shares, where the individual is an employee; or
- holdings of at least 25 per cent of the voting shares, where the individual is not an employee.

285

Business assets 1999/00

No. complete yrs after 5/4/98 for which asset is held	*Taper relief*
0	nil
1	7.5%
2	15%
3	22.5%
4	30%
5	37.5%
6	45%
7	52.5%
8	60%
9	67.5%
10 or more	75%

For disposals made after 6 April 2000:

1. Business assets are now defined as:

- assets used for trading purposes; or
- shareholdings in unquoted trading companies; or
- shareholdings held by employees in quoted trading companies; or
- shareholdings in quoted trading companies of at least 5 per cent of the voting shares, where the individual is not an employee;
- shareholdings held by employees without a material interest (10%) in a non-trading company;
- assets disposed of by trustees that have been used in a trade carried on by a partnership in which the trustee is a member.

NB: Where shareholdings only qualify as a business asset from 6 April 2000 (as a result of the change in definition), any subsequent gain on the disposal of those shares will need to be apportioned so that the correct taper applies.

2. The holding period for business assets was reduced from ten to four years and again from four to two years for disposals after 6/4/02 as follows:

No. years after 5/4/98 for which the asset is held	*Taper relief from 6/4/00*
0 – 1	nil
1 – 2	12.5%
2 – 3	25%
3 – 4	50%
Over 4	75%

Whole years asset held	*Taper relief from 6/4/02*
Less than one	nil
One	50%
Two or more	75%

3. The deemed additional year for assets held at 5 April 1998 is no longer available for business assets.

Non-business assets

No. complete yrs after 5/4/98 for which asset is held available   *Taper relief*

0	nil
1	nil
2	nil
3	5%
4	10%
5	15%
6	20%
7	25%
8	30%
9	35%
10 or more	40%

No changes were made to the taper available on non-business assets and the additional year for assets owned at 5 April 1998 continues to apply.

The taper is applied *before* the annual exemption is applied but *after* deducting:

- current year losses and brought forward losses;
- holdover reliefs.

EXAMPLE

Adrian bought a business asset in July 1998 for £12 000 and sold it in September 2001 for £25 000. Adrian had no other gains or losses during 2001/02 and no losses brought forward.

	£
Proceeds	25 000
less Cost	(12 000)
Gain eligible for taper relief	13 000
Taper relief:* 50% × £13 000	(6 500)
Chargeable gain	6 500

*Asset held for 3 to 4 years after 5 April 1998.

When calculating the taper relief available, an additional year is given for assets held at Budget day 1998, in respect of non-business assets.

EXAMPLE

Asset aquired on 1 November 1997 and disposed of on 6 May 2001 will be treated as being held for four years, i.e. three complete years after 5 April 1998 plus one additional year.

For assets held at 5 April 1998, indexation continues to be available for periods up until April 1998.

EXAMPLE

Percy bought a painting for £4000 in April 1986 which he sold in May 2002 for £25 000.

	£
Proceeds	25 000
less Cost	(4 000)
Unindexed gain	21 000

less Indexation: (up to April 1998)

$$\frac{162.5 - 97.7}{97.7} = 0.664 \times £4000 \qquad (2\,656)$$

Gain eligible for taper relief	18 344

The asset will be treated as having been held for 5 years, i.e. 4 complete years since 5 April 1998 plus an additional year because the asset was owned at 5 April 1998:

	£
Gain eligible for relief	18 344
less Taper: 15% × £18 344	(2 752)
Chargeable gain	15 592

Rebasing

The Finance Act 1988 changed the base date for CGT from 6 April 1965 to 31 March 1982. The effect of this is that:

(a) for disposals after 5 April 1988, only gains or losses accruing from 31 March 1982 will be charged to CGT; and

(b) for assets held on 31 March 1982, rebasing means that the asset is deemed to have been sold and reacquired at its market value (MV) on 31 March 1982.

Rebasing is mandatory except for the following:

(a) if rebasing produces a larger gain then the original gain will stand;

(b) if rebasing produces a larger loss then the original loss will stand; and

(c) if rebasing produces a gain and original cost a loss, or vice versa, it will be treated as being a no gain/no loss disposal.

Two computations must therefore be prepared, indexation being computed on the higher of:

- value on 31 March 1982; and
- original cost.

EXAMPLE 1

Barry bought a painting in 1970 for £7000, which he sold in May 2002 for £28000. The value of the painting on 31 March 1982 was £12500.

	Cost	Rebasing
	£	£
Proceeds	28 000	28 000
less Cost/MV 31/3/82	(7 000)	(12 500)
	21 000	15 500

less Indexation to April 1998:

$$\frac{162.6 - 79.4}{79.4} = 1.048 \times £12\,500$$

	Cost	Rebasing
	(13 100)	(13 100)
Gain eligible for taper relief	7 900	2 400

The untapered gain is £2400 under the rebasing rules, as this produces the lower gain. Indexation up until April 1998 is applied to the higher of cost or market value.

EXAMPLE 2

Geoffrey bought a non-business asset for £10 000 in 1980, which he sold for £22 000 in October 2002. The market value of the asset on 31 March 1982 was £12 000.

	Cost	Rebasing
	£	£
Proceeds	22 000	22 000
less Cost /MV	(10 000)	(12 000)
	12 000	10 000

less Indexation to April 1998:

$$\frac{162.6 - 79.4}{79.4} = 1.048 \times £10\,000$$

	Cost	Rebasing
	(10 480)	(10 000)
Gain eligible for taper relief	1 520	nil

As the original cost produces a gain and rebasing is restricted to nil, there is no gain/no loss. Indexation cannot be used to create a loss.

Global rebasing election (i.e. election for 31 March 1982 valuation on all assets)

The taxpayer can elect for capital gains and losses on *all* assets held at 31 March 1982 to be calculated on the market values on 31 March 1982, without any reference to original cost. This does away with the need for the taxpayer to keep pre-1982 records and simplifies the computations as there is no need to compute the gain or loss on the basis of original cost. Generally, if all assets held have a greater value at

31 March 1982 than original cost, the election will be advantageous. However, the election will require careful consideration if there are some chargeable assets with original costs in excess of the March 1982 value.

The election (TCGA 1992, s 35(5))

The election, which is irrevocable, must be made by notice in writing, before 6 April 1990 *or* within *two years* after the end of the tax year in which the first disposal of assets held at 31 March 1982 was made.

COMPREHENSIVE EXAMPLE

Christopher made the following disposals during 2001/02:

1. In 1970 he had bought a country cottage as a weekend retreat from his city home. The cottage had cost £35 000 and acquisition costs had been £850. He had made the following improvements to the property:

	£
April 1980 central heating	3 000
June 1984 extension	8 000

   He had spent £1000 in legal costs defending a boundary dispute in September 1992. In 2001 he sold the cottage for £120 000. Contracts were exchanged in September 2001 and completion took place in November 2001. The cost of disposal was £700. The market value of the property was £46 000 on 31 March 1982.

2. He disposed of an antique table for £12 000 in September 2001. The table had cost him £5000 in 1981 and was valued at £4500 on 31 March 1982.

3. He sold a painting in October 2001 for £12 000. He had bought the painting in 1980 for £4000. The market value of the painting on 31 March 1982 was £7000.

   Calculate Christopher's taxable gain for 2001/02.

(1)	£	Cost (£)	Rebasing (£)
Gross proceeds		120 000	120 000
Cost of sale		(700)	(700)
Net proceeds		119 300	119 300
less Cost:			
Original cost	35 000		
Acq. cost	850		
Pre-1982 expenditure	3 000	(38 850)	
MV 31/3/82			(46 000)
		80 450	73 300
less Extension (1984)		(8 000)	(8 000)
Legal costs (1992)		(1 000)	(1 000)
Unindexed gain c/f		71 450	64 300

	£	Cost (£)	Rebasing (£)
b/f		71 450	64 300

less Indexation to April 1998:

(a) $\dfrac{162.6 - 79.4}{79.4}$

		Cost (£)	Rebasing (£)
1.048 × £46 000		(48 208)	(48 208)
(MV 31/3/82 is higher)		23 242	16 092

(b) *Extension*

$\dfrac{162.6 - 89.2}{89.2}$

		Cost (£)	Rebasing (£)
0.823 × £8000		(6 584)	(6 584)
		16 658	9 508

(c) *Legal costs*

$\dfrac{162.6 - 139.4}{139.4}$

	Cost (£)	Rebasing (£)
0.166 × £1000	(166)	(166)
Gain eligible taper relief	16 492	9 342
Taper relief (10%)	1 650	935
Chargeable gain	14 842	8 407

↑
chargeable gain

(2)

	Cost (£)	Rebasing (£)
Gross proceeds	12 000	12 000
less Cost : MV 31/3/82	(5 000)	(4 500)
Unindexed gain	7 000	7 500

less Indexation to April 1998:

$\dfrac{162.6 - 79.4}{79.4}$

	Cost (£)	Rebasing (£)
1.048 × £5000	(5 240)	(5 240)
Gain eligible taper relief	1 760	2 260
Taper relief (10%)	(176)	(226)
Chargeable gain	1 584	2 034

↑
chargeable gain

(3)	Cost (£)	Rebasing (£)
Gross proceeds	12 000	12 000
less Cost : MV 31/3/82	(4 000)	(7 000)
	8 000	5 000

less Indexation to April 1998:

$$\frac{162.6 - 79.4}{79.4}$$

	Cost (£)	Rebasing (£)
$1.048 \times £7000$	(7 336)	
Restricted to:		(5 000)
(disposal after 30/11/93)		
	664	nil

There is no gain/no loss.

2001/02	£
(1) Gain on cottage	8 407
(2) Gain on table	1 584
(3) Gain on painting	nil
Total chargeable	9 991
Annual exemption	(7 500)
Taxable gain	2 491

Assets held on 6 April 1965

Since CGT was first introduced by the FA 1965, only gains accruing from that date can be brought into charge. With the introduction of rebasing for disposals after 6 April 1988, the rules are becoming less significant, but nevertheless still need to be known.

There are two rules for assets held on 6 April 1965, set out in Schedule 2 to the TCGA 1992, depending on the type of asset involved:

1. Assets other than quoted shares and land with a development value

For assets other than quoted shares and land with a development value acquired before 6 April 1965 the gain is computed on three bases:

- under the rebasing rules;
- based on original cost with time apportionment (TAB);
- based on the value at 6 April 1965 (sometimes known as budget day value – BDV).

The time apportionment basis assumes that the gain has accrued evenly over time and so the chargeable gain under time apportionment is calculated as:

$$\text{Overall gain (after indexation)} \times \frac{\text{Period of ownership since } 6/4/65}{\text{Total period of ownership}} = \text{Time apportioned gain}$$

Time apportionment is applied *after* the deduction of the indexation allowance – *Smith (HMIT)* v *Schofield* [1993] BTC 147.

When considering the total period of ownership, the Revenue only go back 20 years before CGT was introduced, so any asset acquired before 6 April 1945 is deemed to have been acquired on that date.

If the figure calculated using BDV is to stand, then the taxpayer must actually elect for this basis within *two years* from the end of the tax year in which the disposal takes place. If no election is made for BDV, then the chargeable gain, or allowable loss, is the lower of:

- the figure calculated under rebasing; or
- the figure based on time apportionment.

If the election is made for BDV, the indexation allowance is computed on the asset's value on 6 April 1965 if this is higher.

EXAMPLE

Harry purchased an asset in 1944 for £5000. The value on 31 March 1982 was £12000. He sold the asset on 6 April 2002 for £32500.

	Tab (£)	Rebasing (£)
Proceeds	32 500	32 500
less Cost : MV 31/3/82	(5 000)	(12 000)
	27 500	20 500

less Indexation to April 1998:

$$\frac{162.6 - 79.4}{79.4} = 1.048$$

1.048 × £12 000	(12 576)	(12 576)
	14 924	7 924

$$\frac{6/4/65 - 6/4/02}{6/4/45 - 6/4/02} = \quad \frac{37}{57} \times £14\,924$$

$$= \quad £9\,687$$

The calculation under rebasing produces the lower gain so this is the gain that will stand. Suppose, however, that the value of the asset on 6 April 1965 had been £13 000 and Harry makes an election for BDV.

	BDV (£)
Proceeds	32 500
less BDV	(13 000)
	19 500
less Indexation:	
1.048 × £13 000	(13 642)
Gain eligible taper relief	5 876

For the lower gain of £5876 to stand, Harry needs to make the election within two years, i.e. before 5 April 2005. If the election is not made, the untapered gain on the disposal will be £7924.

If the election produces a loss, that loss is allowable, assuming that it is less than the loss under rebasing, unless:

(a) The computation by reference to cost *before the time apportionment* produces a smaller loss, in which case this is allowable. If *no election is made, the loss by reference to cost must be time apportioned*.

(b) The computation by reference to cost produces a gain, in which case there is no gain/no loss. Again, for this to apply, the election must be made.

EXAMPLE

Alice had bought an asset for £5000 on 6 June 1955 and sold it on 6 October 2002 for £26 000. The asset was valued at £15 000 on 6 April 1965 but on 31 March 1982 it was only worth £12 000.

	Tab (£)	Rebasing (£)
Proceeds	26 000	26 000
less Cost : MV 31/3/82	(5 000)	(12 000)
	21 000	14 000

less Indexation to April 1998:

$$\frac{162.6 - 79.4}{79.4}$$

$1.048 \times £12 000$	(12 576)	(12 576)
	8 424	1 424

$\dfrac{6/4/65 - 6/10/02}{6/6/55 - 6/10/02} =$	$\dfrac{450}{568} \times$	£8424
	$=$	£6 674

Without an election for BDV, the untapered gain is the lower gain, i.e. £1424.

	BDV (£)
Proceeds	26 000
less BDV	(15 000)
	11 000

less Indexation:
$1.048 \times £15 000$	(11 000) (restriction)
	nil

As the calculation under BDV is nil if the election is made, the disposal is treated as a no gain/no loss disposal.

2. Quoted shares and land with a development value

The rules for these assets are based on the fact that the value on 6 April 1965 should be readily available from Stock Exchange Daily Official Lists or from the District Valuer. Therefore, there is no need for time apportionments to be made; the shares or land concerned are deemed to have been disposed of and reacquired at the market value on 6 April 1965.

The detailed tax treatment of these assets is considered in Chapters 25 and 26.

Part disposals

The disposal of some part of an asset is a disposal for CGT purposes. Where there is a part disposal, the cost of the whole of the asset must be apportioned between the part of the asset disposed of and the part of the asset retained. The apportionment of the allowable cost is made using the following formula:

$$\frac{A}{A+B} \times \text{allowable expenditure}$$

where A = value of the disposed part
B = value of the part retained.

EXAMPLE

Sandra bought six Chippendale chairs for £40 000 in January 1987 and incurred acquisition costs of £1500. She sold two of the chairs at auction in June 2002 for £30 000, auctioneers' fees being 10 per cent. The market value of the four remaining chairs is £75 000.

	(£)
Proceeds	30 000
less Disposal costs	(3 000)
	27 000

less Cost of part sold:

$\dfrac{30\,000}{30\,000 + 75\,000} \times (£40\,000 + £1\,500)$	(11 857)
Unindexed gain	15 143

less Indexation to April 1998:

$$\frac{162.6 - 100}{100}$$

$0.626 \times £11\,857$	(7 423)
Gain eligible taper relief	7 720

The allowable expenditure for the four remaining chairs on a future disposal is:

	£
Allowable cost of six chairs	40 000
Acquisition costs	1 500
	41 500
less Apportioned cost on disposal in January 1994	(11 857)
Allowable cost of remaining chairs	29 643

Where the asset was held at 31 March 1982, both original cost and market value on 31 March 1982 must be apportioned.

Suppose in the last example that Sandra had bought the chairs in June 1981, and the market value of the six chairs had been £45 000 on 31 March 1982, with all other facts remaining the same.

	Cost (£)	Rebasing (£)
Proceeds	30 000	30 000
less Disposal costs	(3 000)	(3 000)
	27 000	27 000

less Cost of part sold:

$$\frac{30\,000}{30\,000 + 75\,000} \times £41\,500 \qquad (11\,857)$$

$$\frac{30\,000}{30\,000 + 75\,000} \times £45\,000 \qquad\qquad\qquad (12\,857)$$

	15 143	14 143

less Indexation:

$$\frac{162.6 - 79.4}{79.4}$$

$1.048 \times £12\,857$

	(13 474)	(13 474)
	1 669	669

↑
gain eligible taper relief

The untapered gain will be the lower gain of £669. The market value of the four remaining chairs will be:

	£
	45 000
	(12 857)
Allowable MV of remaining chairs	32 143

EXAMPLE

Paul bought a piece of land in 1970 for £30 000. He sold part of it in July 1981 for £20 000 when the value of the part retained was £80 000. The land was valued at £100 000 on 31 March 1982. In June 1990 he disposed of another part of the land for £50 000 when the value of the part retained was £75 000. What is the base cost of the remaining land for any future disposal?

	Original cost (£)	MV 31/3/82 (£)
Cost in 1970	30 000	
less Part disposal 1981:		
$\dfrac{20\,000}{20\,000 + 80\,000} \times £30\,000$	(6 000)	
	24 000	
MV 31/3/82		100 000
less Part disposal 1990:		
$\dfrac{50\,000}{50\,000 + 75\,000} \times £24\,000$	(9 600)	
$\dfrac{50\,000}{50\,000 + 75\,000} \times £100\,000$		(40 000)
Cost : MV remaining	14 400	60 000

Capital gains tax losses

Losses of the current year must be set off in full against current year gains, even if this means wasting the annual exemption. Net losses are carried forward to be set off against future gains. Taper relief is applied *before* deducting the annual exemption but *after* deducting losses of the current year and brought forward losses.

EXAMPLE

Amy realised the following untapered gains and losses during the year 2000/01:

	£
Gain on business asset (taper relief 25%)	25 000
Loss on painting	(5 000)

Amy also had a brought forward loss of £12 000

	£
Gain	25 000
less Current year loss	(5 000)
	20 000
less B/fwd loss	(12 000)
	8 000
less Taper (25%)	(2 000)
	6 000
less AE taxable gain (restricted)	(6 000)
	nil

The benefit of the taper is significantly reduced because of this order of set off. Therefore, where an individual incurs losses and gains during a fiscal year, the loss should be set off against gains in such a way as to preserve the value of the taper, i.e. the loss should be set off where possible against those gains attracting the least amount of taper relief.

EXAMPLE

John made the following untapered gains and losses in 2002/03:

	£
Gain on business asset (taper available 50%)	9 000
Gain on non-business asset (taper available 10%)	12 000
Losses	(8 000)

The loss should be set off against the gain on the non-business asset in priority to the business asset in order to preserve the value of the taper:

	£
Non-business asset	12 000
less Loss	(8 000)
	4 000
less Taper (10%)	(400)
Chargeable gain	3 600

	£
Business asset	9 000
less Taper relief (50%)	(4 500)
Chargeable gain	4 500

	£
Total gains	8 100
less AE	(7 700)
Taxable gain	400

If the loss had been applied to the business asset, the value of the taper would have been reduced and, therefore, the taxable gain would have been higher:

	£
Business asset	9 000
less Loss	(8 000)
	1 000
less Taper (50%)	(500)
Chargeable gain	500

	£
Non-business asset	12 000
less Taper (10%)	(1 200)
Chargeable gain	10 800

	£
Total gains	11 300
less AE	(7 700)
Taxable gain	3 600

Year of death

Generally, a capital loss can only be carried forward and set against net chargeable gains in a future year. The exception to this is where there are losses in the year of death and remain unrelieved at the date of death. In this situation the loss can be carried back for three years on a LIFO basis, without wasting the annual exemption. *This is the only occasion in which capital losses may be carried back.*

Losses to connected persons

A loss on disposal to a connected person can only be set off against any gains in the same or future years *to the same connected person*.

Connected persons (TCGA 1992, s 286)

The following persons are considered to be connected for CGT purposes:

1. Individuals

Most of an individual's relatives are connected for CGT purposes, namely:

(a) the individual's brothers, sisters, ancestors and lineal descendants, and their spouses;

(b) the individual's spouse; and

(c) brothers, sisters, ancestors and lineal descendants of the individual's spouse, and their spouses.

2. Trustees

A trustee is connected with the settlor, and anyone connected with the settlor, but not necessarily the beneficiaries.

3. Partnerships

Partners and their relatives are connected unless assets are disposed of and acquired in *bona fide* commercial transactions.

4. Companies

A company is connected with:

- the person who controls the company;
- other companies under the same control.

Disposals between connected persons are deemed to be disposed of at market value, to prevent avoidance of CGT, as they are not considered to be disposals at arm's length.

Transfers between the following, however, are not chargeable disposals:

- husband and wife (TCGA 1992, s 58);
- UK resident companies within the same 75 per cent group (TCGA 1992, ss 170(2), 171);
- personal representatives and legatee (TCGA 1992, s 62(4)).

Disposals in a series of transactions (TCGA 1992, ss 19, 20)

For disposals after 19 March 1985, legislation was introduced to prevent the avoidance of CGT by disposing of assets in a series of linked transactions to a connected person. Obvious areas for abuse are majority shareholdings and 'sets' of antiques. Where separate disposals to a connected person are made within six years of each other, after 19 March 1985 the market value will be adjusted if it was less than it would have been if the assets had been disposed of together.

EXAMPLE

George makes the following disposals of shares in his family company to his grandchildren:

(a) 400 shares on 1 June 1996
(b) 200 shares on 1 July 1998
(c) 250 shares on 1 October 2000
(d) 250 shares on 1 September 2002

The following transactions will be treated as a series of linked transactions:

1.   (a) + (b)
When transaction (b) is made, the value of the shares will be adjusted if the value of the 600 shares is greater than the value of the 400 shares in (a) and 200 in (b) considered separately.

2. (a) + (b) + (c)

When transaction (c) is made, comparison between the adjusted values of (a) + (b) above plus the value of (c) and the market value of 850 shares, will be made as if they had been disposed of together.

3. (b) + (c) + (d)

When transaction (d) is made, the market value of 700 shares together will be compared with the market value of the individual transactions.

Note: (a) and (d) cannot be considered as they are more than six years apart.

Husband and wife

Since 6 April 1990, married couples have been taxed separately; the CGT consequences of independent taxation are:

(a) each spouse is entitled to an annual exemption;

(b) the capital losses of one spouse cannot be set off against the other spouse's capital gains; and

(c) any unused exemption cannot be transferred between spouses.

Jointly owned assets

Where assets are held jointly by a husband and wife, the following rules apply:

(a) gains are split between husband and wife in the same proportion as the beneficial interest in the asset at the date of disposal;

(b) where the beneficial interest of each spouse is not clear, they will be deemed to own the asset in equal shares; and

(c) if a declaration has been made regarding the proportions of ownership for income tax purposes, then the same proportions will apply for CGT.

Transfers between husband and wife

When assets are transferred between husband and wife, they are deemed to be transferred at cost plus indexation to the date of transfer, i.e. so that the transfer produces neither a gain/nor a loss.

EXAMPLE

Trevor bought a painting in June 1985 for £12000. He transferred it to his wife Sandra in October 1993.

	£
Cost to Trevor	12000
Indexation to date of transfer:	

$$\frac{141.8 - 95.4}{95.4}$$

$0.486 \times £12000$	5832
Deemed cost to Sandra	17832

On the transfer of an asset between spouses, any taper relief available on a subsequent disposal after 6 April 1998 will be calculated on the combined period of ownership.

SELF ASSESSMENT QUESTIONS

22.1 During 2002/03 Eve Treasure disposed of the following assets:

(a) In August 2002 she sold part of a plot of land for £50 000, when the value of the land retained was £70 000. She had acquired the land in April 1986 for £45 000.

(b) In September 2002 she sold her country cottage for £66 000. She had bought the cottage in 1970 for £20 000. The property had been valued at £40 000 on 31 March 1982. The cottage had never been Eve's main residence.

(c) In November 2002 she disposed of a business asset for £25 000. She had acquired the asset in June 1990 for £10 000.

REQUIRED

Calculate Eve's taxable gains for 2002/03.

22.2 Mark disposed of an investment property for £400 000 on 16 July 2002. Mark had bought the property for £100 000 in June 1980 and spent £50 000 on permanent improvements in June 1990. The market value of the property on the 31 March 1982 was £130 000. The property is a non-business asset.

REQUIRED

Calculate Mark's chargeable gain on the disposal of the property.

CHAPTER 23

Chattels and wasting assets

A chattel is defined as tangible, moveable property, i.e. an asset that can be touched, moved and seen.

Assets that have a short useful life are referred to as wasting assets.

Because of the nature of chattels and wasting assets, there are special rules for calculating the gains on the disposal of these assets. Most personal belongings are chattels and many personal belongings do not have a particularly high value, for this reason the legislation exempts chattels that cost less than £6000 and are sold for less than £6000.

Assets, other than chattels, of a depreciating nature (wasting assets) also have special rules, as generally, the allowable cost is deemed to waste away over the life of the asset.

Chattels that also have a short useful life are known as wasting chattels and are generally exempt from CGT, although there are exceptions.

This chapter examines the special rules for calculating the gains on the disposal of chattels and wasting assets.

Chattels

Chattels are tangible, moveable assets, e.g. antiques, works of art, etc.

Certain chattels are specifically exempt in the legislation, e.g. motor cars (TCGA 1992, s 263). Section 262 of the TCGA 1992 provides that any chattel sold for £6000 or less is exempt from CGT. This provision effectively exempts most personal belongings apart from very valuable antiques, works of art, jewellery, etc.

EXAMPLE

Robert bought a stamp collection in May 1987 for £2000 and sold it in May 2002 for £5800.

As the proceeds and cost are less than £6000, the disposal is exempt from CGT.

Marginal relief

A form of marginal relief is available where a chattel is sold for more than £6000. In this situation the untapered gain cannot exceed:

$\frac{5}{3}$ (gross sale proceeds less £6000)

EXAMPLE

Pauline bought an antique brooch for £1500 in April 1988. She sold the brooch at auction in September 2002 for £9000, the auctioneer's fees being 10 per cent.

	£
Gross proceeds	9 000
less Cost of sale	(900)
Net proceeds	8 100
less Cost	(1 500)
	6 600

less Indexation to April 1998:

$$\frac{162.6 - 105.8}{105.8}$$

$0.537 \times £1500$	(806)
Indexed gain	5 794

But cannot exceed:
$$\frac{5}{3}(9000 - 6000) = \underline{£5000}$$

Therefore, the untapered gain is £5000 as this is lower than the gain as calculated.

Loss restriction

As chattels sold for £6000 or less are not chargeable to CGT, there is also a restriction on allowable losses where the asset was acquired for more than £6000 and disposed of for less than £6000. In this situation the allowable loss is restricted by substituting actual disposal proceeds by a deemed selling price of £6000, thereby restricting the loss.

EXAMPLE

Jane bought a desk in June 1985 for £10 000, believing it to be a genuine antique. It was later discovered that the desk was a reproduction and she sold it in September 2002 for £2000.

The actual proceeds of £2000 are substituted for deemed sale proceeds of £6000:

	£
Deemed proceeds	6 000
less Cost	(10 000)
Unindexed loss	(4 000)
Indexation	nil
(cannot be used to increase the loss)	
Allowable loss	(4 000)

Anti-avoidance provisions

The chattel provision cannot be exploited by breaking up a set of articles and selling the individual items to the same person, e.g. a set of antique chairs. This situation is covered by the rules relating to a series of transactions, and would treat the transactions as if it was a disposal of one asset (*see* Chapter 22).

Nor can the £6000 chattel exemption be exploited by disposing of part of an asset (without being caught under the series of transactions provisions). In this case, only if the combined value of the part disposed of and the part remaining is less than £6000 will the disposal be exempt.

EXAMPLE

Brian bought a set of four antique books in March 1989 for £8000. He sold one of the books for £3000 in September 2002, when the value of the remaining three was £12 000.

		£
£6000 test:	Value of part disposed of	3 000
	Value of part remaining	12 000
	Combined value	15 000

Therefore, the sale of the book is a chargeable chattel as the combined value is greater than £6000.

	£
Proceeds	3 000
less Cost:	

$$£8000 \times \frac{3000}{3000 + 12000}$$ (1 600)

| Unindexed gain | 1 400 |

less Indexation to April 1998:

$$\frac{162.6 - 112.3}{112.3}$$

| 0.448 × £1600 | (717) |
| Untapered gain | 683 |

Marginal relief is also available where the combined value is marginally over £6000, so that the untapered gain on a part disposal cannot exceed:

$$\tfrac{5}{3}(\text{combined value less } £6000) \times \frac{A}{A + B}$$

where A = value of the disposed part
       B = value of the part remaining

EXAMPLE

Florence had bought a set of six antique chairs for £1500 in March 1989. She sold two of the chairs in September 2002 for £3000 when the value of the four remaining chairs was £7000.

£6000 test: £3000 + £7000 = £10 000, therefore it is a chargeable chattel.

305

	£
Proceeds	3000
less Cost:	

$$£1500 \times \frac{3000}{3000 + 7000}$$

	£
	(450)
Unindexed gain	2550

less Indexation:

$$\frac{162.6 - 112.3}{112.3}$$

	£
$0.448 \times £450$	(202)
Untapered gain	2348

However, the gain cannot exceed:

$$\tfrac{5}{3} (£10\,000 - £6000) \times \frac{3000}{3000 + 7000}$$

$$= £2000$$

Therefore, the untapered gain is restricted to £2000.

Wasting assets

A wasting asset is one with a predictable useful life of 50 years or less at the time of acquisition. Freehold land and buildings are never classed as wasting assets, whereas plant and machinery are always classed as wasting assets. Because of the depreciating nature of these assets, comparing the usual disposal proceeds with original cost would be unsound for taxation purposes.

The nature of wasting assets means that special rules are required for CGT purposes.

The legislation deals with the various types of wasting asset as follows:

1. General rule for wasting asset (e.g. copyrights)

The general rule for wasting assets is that the allowable expenditure is deemed to waste away over the asset's predictable life on a straight line basis. There may or may not be a residual scrap value at the end of the asset's life.

EXAMPLE 1

Rebekah paid £30 000 for the copyright of a book on 1 May 1990, when it had 20 years left to run. She sold the copyright to a publisher for £22 000 on 1 May 2002. Assume an indexation factor of 60 per cent.

	£
Proceeds	22 000
less Cost:	

$$£30\,000 \times \frac{\text{length of copyright at sale}}{\text{length of copyright at start}}$$

		£
	b/f	22 000

$£30\,000 \times \dfrac{8}{20}$ (12 000)

Unindexed gain   10 000

less Indexation:

$0.6 \times £12\,000$ (7 200)

Untapered gain   2 800

EXAMPLE 2

Charles bought a wasting asset (which is neither a chattel nor eligible for capital allowances) on 6 July 1990 for £15 000, when it had a predictable life of 20 years and an estimated residual scrap value of £500. He sold the asset on 6 July 2002 for £12 000. Assume indexation of 70 per cent.

	£
Unexpired cost:	
Cost July 1990	15 000
less Scrap value	(500)
	14 500

less Amount written off:

$£14\,500 \times \dfrac{12}{20}$ (8 700)

         5 800

add back Scrap value   500

Unexpired value   6 300

	£
Proceeds	12 000
less Unexpired cost	(6 300)
Unindexed gain	5 700

less Indexation to April 1998:

$70\% \times £6300$ (4 410)

Untapered gain   1 290

2. Short leases of land

A short lease, i.e. one with an unexpired life of 50 years or less, is a wasting asset. However, the gain on the disposal of a short lease is calculated using the percentage table for short leases to be found in Schedule 8, TCGA 1992.

The reason for the special depreciation table for short leases is that a short lease is deemed to depreciate more in the later years than in earlier years, unlike general wasting assets which are deemed to depreciate evenly over the life of asset.

The detailed computation for the disposal of a short lease is considered fully in Chapter 25 of this book.

3. Options

An option is the right to purchase something at a set price within a defined time period. Generally options are treated as wasting assets and the precise tax treatment depends on whether the option is exercised, abandoned or sold.

(a) Exercise of an option

If the option is exercised then the granting of the option, and the subsequent disposal of the asset over which the option is created, is treated as a single transaction taking place when the option is exercised.

EXAMPLE 1

Amos bought a plot of land in June 1988 for £15 000. He grants an option to George for £1200 in August 1999 to sell the land for £30 000 at any time George chooses before 31 July 2003. George exercises his option in July 2002. Assume indexation of 75 per cent.

The disposal proceeds are the proceeds from the grant of the option plus the proceeds from the disposal of the asset:

	£
Proceeds (£1200 + £30 000)	31 200
less Cost	(15 000)
	16 200
less Indexation:	
0.75 x £15 000	(11 250)
Indexed gain	4 950

George's base cost for a future disposal will be £31 200, i.e. the cost of the land plus the cost of the option.

EXAMPLE 2

In July 1980 White acquired an option to buy a property before 1986 for £1500. The option was valued at £2500 on 31 March 1982. White exercised his option in July 1985 at a cost of £27 500. In July 2002 White sold the property for £60 000.

		Cost (£)	Rebasing (£)
Proceeds		60 000	60 000
less Cost (£1500 + £27 500)		(29 000)	
less MV (£2500 + £27 500)			(30 000)
Unindexed gain	c/f	31 000	30 000

		Cost (£)	Rebasing (£)
	b/f	31 000	30 000

less Indexation:

1. *Option*

$$\frac{162.6 - 79.4}{79.4}$$

$1.048 \times £2500$ (2 620)   (2 620)

2. *On exercise consideration*

$$\frac{162.6 - 95.2}{95.2}$$

$0.708 \times £27\,500$ (19 470)   (19 470)

Indexed gain   8 910   7 910

The indexed gain will be the lower gain of £7910.

(b) Abandonment of an option

If an option is abandoned, the person granting the option is treated as having made a disposal when the option was granted. The grant of an option is the disposal of an asset (the option) rather than a part disposal of the asset over which the option is created. The person acquiring the option, acquires a chargeable asset, but there will only be a disposal if the abandoned option falls into one of the following categories:

- quoted options to subscribe for shares in a company
- a traded option or financial option
- an option to acquire assets for the purposes of a trade.

EXAMPLE

John grants Jane an option to buy a plot of land for £20 000, for which Jane paid £2000. Jane decides not to exercise the option.

John: The proceeds of £2000 are a chargeable gain; there is no indexation allowance as the option had no cost.

Jane: Abandonment of the option in this case does not constitute a disposal, because the land does not fall into any of the above categories (assuming that Jane is not a trader acquiring the land for business purposes). As there is no disposal, there is no allowable loss.

The abandonment of an option falling into the above categories does, however, constitute a disposal and, as such, can give rise to an allowable loss.

(c) Sale of an option

The disposal of an option to a third party is a disposal for CGT purposes. The rules for calculating the chargeable gain or allowable loss depend on the type of asset for which the option is granted.

Where the option is:

- a quoted option to subscribe for shares in a company
- a traded option, or financial option
- an option to acquire assets for the purposes of a trade

the CGT computation is based on the difference between disposal proceeds and cost, less indexation allowance, i.e. normal CGT computation.

Where the option is for assets other than the above, the chargeable gain or allowable loss is calculated using the normal rules for wasting assets.

EXAMPLE

Green holds an option to purchase some shares in 15 years' time. The option cost him £3000 on 1 June 1991. He sells the option on 1 June 2002 for £2000. It is neither a quoted nor a traded option.

	£	£
Proceeds		2 000
less: Cost	3 000	
less Depreciation:		
$\frac{11}{15} \times £3000$	(2 200)	(800)
		1 200
less Indexation:		
$\dfrac{162.6 - 134.1}{134.1}$		
$0.213 \times £800$		(171)
Indexed gain		1 029

Wasting chattels

A wasting asset that is also a chattel is exempt from CGT, e.g. yacht, racehorse, etc.

Note: Motor cars are specifically exempt under the TCGA 1992, s 263, even though they would be generally exempt because they are wasting chattels.

There is, however, one exception to wasting chattels being generally exempt from CGT, and this is where they have been used in a business, and have had, or could have had, capital allowances claimed on them, i.e. plant and machinery qualifying for capital allowances, sold for more than £6000 and more than original cost. If the plant or machinery is sold for less than £6000, then the exemption for chattels sold for £6000 or less will apply, irrespective of its trade use.

EXAMPLE

Boris has been in business for many years, preparing accounts to 31 December each year. He bought a machine for £12 000 in April 2000 and sold it for £14 000 in September 2002. The income tax and CGT position is:

Capital allowances

(assuming no previous pool of expenditure)

YE 31/12/00	£	*£ Allowances*
Cost	12 000	
40% FYA	(4 800)	4 800
c/f	7 200	
YE 31/12/01		
WDA (25%)	(1 800)	1 800
c/f	5 400	
YE 31/12/02		
Disposal	(12 000)	
(restricted to original cost)		
	(6 600)	
Balancing charge	6 600	

This is to say, on sale of machine all allowances previously given are clawed back by way of a balancing charge.

CGT	£
Proceeds	14 000
less Cost	(12 000)
Unindexed gain	2 000

Where there is a loss on disposal, the loss is restricted by the available capital allowances, i.e. the difference between the disposal value and the capital cost of the asset.

EXAMPLE

Plant was purchased for £40 000 in July 1994, for use in a business, and sold for £20 000 in September 2000. Assume indexation of 30 per cent.

	£
Proceeds	20 000
less Cost	(40 000)
	(20 000)
less Restriction:	
(£40 000 – £20 000)	20 000
	nil
Indexation allowance	
30% × £40 000 (restricted)	nil
Allowable loss	nil

SELF ASSESSMENT QUESTIONS

23.1 During 2002/03 Rebeckah disposed of the following assets:

(a) In June 2002 she sold an antique brooch for £5800. She had bought the brooch in March 1985 for £3000.
(b) In July 2002 she sold a painting at auction for £15 000, the auctioneer's fee being 10 per cent. Rebeckah had bought the painting in September 1990 for £5000.
(c) In September 2002 she sold an antique table for £7000. She had bought the table for £2000 in July 1994.

REQUIRED:

Calculate Rebeckah's chargeable gains for 2002/03.

23.2 Colin disposed of the following assets during 2002/03.

(a) He sold a painting in September 2002 for £8000. He had bought the painting for £5000 in December 1992.
(b) He sold a business asset for £80 000 in November 2002. The asset had cost him £20 000 in May 1980 and its market value on 31 March 1982 was £25 000.

REQUIRED:

Calculate Colin's chargeable gains for 2002/03.

CHAPTER 24

Compensation and insurance money

The loss or destruction of a chargeable asset, and compensation received in respect of chargeable assets is treated as a chargeable disposal, even if the asset does not change hands.

Section 22(1) of the TCGA 1992 provides that the following events will be treated as disposals for CGT:

- capital sums received as compensation for the loss of, or damage to assets;
- capital sums received under an insurance policy for the loss of, or damage to assets;
- capital sums received for a forfeiture of rights, or for refraining from exercising rights in an asset;
- capital sums received as consideration for the use or exploitation of assets.

Note: Compensation received for personal injury or wrong suffered by an individual is specifically exempt from CGT (TCGA 1992, s 51).

This chapter examines the CGT treatment, and reliefs available to the recipients of compensation and insurance money.

Assets not completely destroyed

If an asset is damaged but not completely destroyed, then there is a deemed part disposal of the asset on the date the capital sum is received.

EXAMPLE

Eric bought a painting in June 1989 for £15 000. It was damaged in July 1993 causing its value to fall to £12 500. Insurance proceeds were received in February 1994 for £3500. Eric did not restore the painting but sold it in October 2002 for £18 500.

February 1994

On receipt of the insurance proceeds, there is a deemed part disposal of the painting:

	£
Insurance proceeds	3 500
less Cost:	

$$£15\,000 \times \frac{3\,500}{3\,500 + 12\,500}$$

(3 281)

| Unindexed gain | 219 |

less Indexation:

$$\frac{142.1 - 115.4}{115.4}$$

| 0.231 × £3281 (restricted) | (219) |
| Allowable loss/chargeable gain | nil |

Disposal 2002

	£
Proceeds	18 500
less Cost (£15 000 – £3281)	(11 719)
Unindexed gain	6 781

less Indexation to April 1998:

$$\frac{162.6 - 115.4}{115.4}$$

| 0.409 × £11 719 | (4 793) |
| Gain eligible taper relief | 1 988 |

If the compensation money is used to restore the asset, the taxpayer can make a claim under s 23(1) of the TCGA 1992, so there is no immediate CGT assessment and the capital sum is 'rolled over', which will effectively increase the gain on a future disposal of the asset.

Section 23(1), TCGA 1992 can be claimed where:

(a) the capital sum is wholly applied in restoring the asset (s 23(1)(*a*)); or

(b) at least 95 per cent of the capital sum is used to restore the asset (s 23(1)(*b*)); or

(c) the capital sum is small in relation to the value of the asset, i.e. not greater than 5 per cent of the assets value (s 23(1)(*c*)).

If s 23(1) is elected, the receipt is deducted from cost or market value, thereby increasing the gain on a future disposal.

Where s 23(1) is claimed and the capital sum has been deducted from the allowable expenditure, and indexation applies, the indexation allowance is calculated in stages:

(a) on cost/market value – this is deducted from the unindexed gain;

(b) on restoration costs – this is deducted from the unindexed gain;

(c) on capital sum received – this is *added* to the unindexed gain.

EXAMPLE 1: TCGA 1992, s 23(1)(a)

Charles bought an asset in June 1980 for £50 000. It was damaged in September 1988. Immediately before the damage it was valued at £60 000. The asset was restored in October 1988 at a cost of £20 000, and this amount was received from the insurance company in December 1988. Charles sold the asset for £130 000 on 16 October 2002. The value of the asset on 31 March 1982 was £54 000.

As Charles used all the insurance proceeds to restore the asset, he can make a claim under s 23(1)(a), TCGA 1992 for the capital sum to be 'rolled over', so there is no deemed disposal for 1988/9 when the proceeds are received in December 1988.

Disposal in October 2002

	Cost (£)	Rebasing (£)
Proceeds	130 000	130 000
less Cost : MV 31/3/82	(50 000)	(54 000)
	80 000	76 000
less Restoration costs (Oct 1988)	(20 000)	(20 000)
	60 000	56 000
s 23(1)(a) 'roll over' (December 1988)	20 000	20 000
Unindexed gain	80 000	76 000

less Indexation to April 1998:

(1) On cost: MV from 31/3/82

$$\frac{162.6 - 79.4}{79.4}$$

$1.048 \times £54\,000$	(56 592)	(56 592)

(2) On restoration costs from October 1988

$$\frac{162.6 - 109.5}{109.5}$$

$0.485 \times £20\,000$	(9 700)	(9 700)

(3) *add* Indexation on 'rolled over' amount from December 1988

$$\frac{162.6 - 110.3}{110.3}$$

$0.473 \times £20\,000$	9 460	9 460
Gain eligible taper relief	23 168	19 168

The gain eligible for taper relief is the lower gain of £19 168.

EXAMPLE 2: TCGA 1992, s 23(1)(b)

Suppose that in Example 1 Charles had only spent £19 000 on restoring the asset in October 1988. As Charles has applied at least 95 per cent of the capital sum in restoring the asset, he can make a claim under s 23(1)(b) to have the capital sum 'rolled over', therefore there will be no deemed part disposal in December 1988.

Disposal 2002

	Cost (£)	Rebasing (£)
Proceeds	130 000	130 000
less Cost : MV 31/3/82	(50 000)	(54 000)
	80 000	76 000
less Restoration costs	(19 000)	(19 000)
(October 1988)	61 000	57 000
s 23(1)(b) 'roll over'		
December 1988	20 000	20 000
Unindexed gain	81 000	77 000

less Indexation:

(1) On cost : MV
   $1.048 \times £54\,000$ — (56 592) — (56 592)

(2) On restoration
   $0.485 \times £19\,000$ — (9 215) — (9 215)

(3) *add* Indexation
   on 'roll over'
   $0.473 \times £20\,000$ — 9 460 — 9 460

| Gain eligible taper relief | 24 653 | 20 653 |

The gain eligible for taper relief is the lower gain of £20 653.

EXAMPLE 3: TCGA 1992, s 23(1)(c)

Mohammed bought an asset for £10 000 in April 1986. The asset was damaged by fire and in August 1988 he received insurance proceeds of £500, when the asset was worth £12 000. He sold the asset in September 2002, without repairing the damage, for £17 500.

As the capital sum that Mohammed received of £500 is less than 5 per cent of the asset's value of £12 000, he can claim to have the capital sum 'rolled over' under s 23(1)(c) and so there will be no deemed part disposal in August 1988.

Disposal September 2002

		£
Proceeds		17 500
less Cost		(10 000)
		7 500
s 23(1)(c) 'roll over'		500
Unindexed gain	c/f	8 000

		£
b/f		8 000

less Indexation to April 1998:

(1) on cost from April 1986

$$\frac{162.6 - 97.7}{97.7}$$

0.664 × £10 000		(6 640)

(2) *add* Indexation on rolled over amount from August 1988

$$\frac{162.6 - 107.9}{107.9}$$

0.507 × £500		254
Gain eligible taper relief		1 614

These rules apply whether the capital sum is received in respect of damage to, forfeiture of rights in, or exploitation of assets.

Partial application of capital sum (TCGA 1992, s 23(3))

Where only part of the capital sum is used in restoration of the asset and relief cannot be claimed under the TCGA 1992, s 23(1), the taxpayer can make a claim under TCGA 1992, s 23(3) to have the amount spent on restoration 'rolled over'. The part not spent must be treated as a part disposal when the capital sum is received.

EXAMPLE

Higgins bought an asset in July 1984 for £60 000. It was damaged by fire in October 1987. In December 1987 £7000 was spent on restoration out of agreed insurance proceeds of £12 000, which were received in July 1988. Higgins sold the asset for £120 000 in May 2002. The market value after restoration in December 1987 was £75 000.

There is a deemed part disposal in July 1988, but if Higgins makes a claim under s 23(3), only the amount not used will be assessed to CGT in 1988/89. He cannot make a claim under s 23(1) because less than 95 per cent of the proceeds have been used to restore the asset.

Part disposal July 1988

		£
Capital sum not used (£12 000 − £7000)		5 000

less Part of original cost:

£60 000 × $\dfrac{5000}{5000 + 75 000}$		(3 750)
		1 250

less Part of restoration cost:

£7000 × $\dfrac{5000}{5000 + 75 000}$		(438)
Unindexed gain	c/f	812

	£
b/f	812

less Indexation:

(1) On cost from July 1984

$$\frac{106.7 - 89.1}{89.1}$$

$0.198 \times £3750$ (743)

(2) On restoration cost
from December 1987

$$\frac{106.7 - 103.3}{103.3}$$

$0.033 \times £438$ (15)

Chargeable gain 54

There is a chargeable gain in 1988/89 of £54, the £7000 used to restore the asset is 'rolled over' until the asset is disposed of in 2002/03.

Disposal May 2002

	£
Proceeds	120 000
less Balance of cost (£60 000 – £3750)	(56 250)
	63 750
less Balance of restoration cost (£7000 – £438)	(6 562)
	57 188
s 23(3) 'roll over'	7 000
Unindexed gain	64 188

less Indexation:

(1) On cost from July 1984 to April 1998

$$\frac{162.6 - 89.1}{89.1}$$

$0.825 \times £56 250$ (46 407)

(2) On restoration costs from December 1987 to April 1998:

$$\frac{162.6 - 103.3}{103.3}$$

$0.574 \times £6562$ (3 767)

c/f 14 014

		£
	b/f	14014

(3) *add* Indexation on
rolled over sum from July 1988

$$\frac{162.6 - 106.7}{106.7}$$

	£
0.524 × £7000	3668
Gain eligible taper relief	17682

The reliefs available under s 23 do not apply to wasting assets.

Assets completely lost or destroyed

In general, on the entire loss or destruction of an asset, there is a deemed disposal for CGT purposes, whether or not compensation is received.

If there is no compensation, there will be an allowable loss for CGT purposes.

EXAMPLE

Charlotte buys an asset (not a chattel) for £20000 in May 1986. In December 2002 it is completely destroyed by fire and has no residual value. Charlotte had failed to insure the asset.

2002/03	£
Proceeds	nil
less Cost	(20000)
Unindexed loss	(20000)
less Indexation:	
restricted as cannot increase a loss	(nil)
Allowable loss	(20000)

It must be remembered that where a chattel is disposed of for less than £6000 and its original cost was more than £6000, the allowable loss will be restricted by substituting deemed proceeds of £6000 for actual proceeds.

If, therefore, Charlotte's asset had been a chattel the allowable loss would have been:

	£
Deemed disposal proceeds	6000
less Cost	(20000)
Unindexed loss	(14000)
less Indexation (restricted)	nil
Allowable loss	(14000)

Where there is no compensation received, the date of disposal is the date the asset was lost or destroyed.

If compensation is received, then the date of disposal is the date that the capital sum is received.

EXAMPLE

Doris lost a diamond necklace that had cost £6000 in December 1988. The necklace was insured for £12 000 and she received the insurance money on 16 April 2002.

Deemed disposal April 2002

	£
Proceeds	12 000
less Cost	(6 000)
Unindexed gain	6 000

less Indexation to April 1998

$$\frac{162.6 - 110.3}{110.3}$$

0.474 × £8000	(2 844)
Gain eligible taper relief	3 156

If the compensation is used to buy a replacement asset within 12 months, the CGT assessment can be 'rolled over' into the cost of the replacement asset, provided that a claim is made under the TCGA 1992, s 23(4). The effect of the election is to treat the deemed disposal on the loss of the asset as taking place on a no gain/no loss basis. Although the legislation states that the replacement asset must be acquired within 12 months, the time limit is in practice negotiable and the Inspector may allow a longer period.

EXAMPLE

Ivan bought an asset for £6000 in January 1987, which was destroyed by fire in July 2002. The asset was insured and Ivan received £16 000 in October 2002, and the asset had a scrap value of £600. A replacement asset was purchased in December 2002 for £18 000.

The effect of a claim under s 23(4), TCGA 1992 is that the disposal is deemed to be at no gain/no loss:

	£
Cost of asset	6 000
Indexation to April 1998:	

$$\frac{162.6 - 100}{100}$$

0.626 × £6000	3 756
Deemed disposal proceeds (no gain/no loss)	9 756

The base cost of the replacement asset for a future disposal is calculated by deducting the difference between the insurance proceeds plus any scrap value and the deemed disposal proceeds, from the cost of the replacement asset, that is:

	£	£
Cost of replacement		18 000
Insurance proceeds	16 000	
add Scrap value	600	
	16 600	
less Deemed		
consideration (old asset)	(9 756)	(6 844)
Base cost of replacement asset		11 156

If a claim had not been made under s 23(4), TCGA 1992, the chargeable gain in October 2002 would have been:

	£
Proceeds	16 000
less Cost:	

$$6000 \times \frac{16\,000}{16\,000 + 600}$$ (5 783)

(part disposal as there is a residual value of £600)

	£
Unindexed gain	10 217
less Indexation:	
$0.626 \times £5783$	(3 621)
Gain eligible for taper relief	6 596

If a claim is not made, the base cost of the new asset is £18 000.

If the asset was held at 31 March 1982 and destroyed before 6 April 1988, only 50 per cent of the amount 'rolled over' is deducted from the cost of the replacement asset.

EXAMPLE

Asset bought in 1980 for £6000 and suffered fire damage in May 1987. Insurance proceeds of £16 000 were received in July 1987. The scrap value of the asset was £600, and a replacement asset was purchased for £18 000 in September 1987:

	£
Cost of asset	6 000
Indexation:	

$$\frac{101.8 - 79.4}{79.4}$$

	£
$0.282 \times £6000$	1 692
Deemed disposal proceeds	7 692
(no gain/no loss)	

Base cost of replacement asset:

	£	£
Cost of replacement		18 000
Insurance proceeds	16 000	
add Scrap value	600	
	16 600	
less Deemed disposal (old asset)	(7 692)	
	8 908 × 50%	(4 454)
Base cost of replacement asset		13 546

If all the compensation is not used to replace the asset, then the amount not used for the replacement will give rise to a chargeable gain, and the taxpayer can make a claim under the TCGA 1992, s 23(5) to have the balance of the gain deferred.

EXAMPLE

Asset bought in January 1987 for £6000. The asset was destroyed in July 2001. Insurance proceeds of £16 000 were received in October 2001. A replacement asset was purchased in February 2002 for £15 000.

	£	£
Proceeds		16 000
less Cost		(6 000)
Unindexed gain		10 000

less Indexation to April 1998:

$$\frac{162.6 - 100}{100}$$

0.626 × £6000		(3 756)
Indexed gain		6 244
less Roll-over relief:		
Chargeable gain	6 244	
Proceeds not used	(1 000)	(5 244)
Indexed gain		1 000

Base cost of replacement asset:

	£
Cost	15 000
less Roll-over relief	(5 244)
Base cost of replacement asset	9 756

Relief under s 23(4) and (5) of the TCGA 1992 is not available in respect of wasting assets.

Assets becoming negligible in value

Where an asset, wasting or non-wasting, becomes worthless, the taxpayer can make a negligible value claim under the TCGA 1992, s 24(2). Provided that the inspector is satisfied that the value of the asset has become negligible, the taxpayer is deemed to have disposed of the asset and immediately reacquired it at its negligible value, so establishing an allowable loss.

The Revenue take the view that negligible is considerably less than 5 per cent.

Land and buildings

By extra-statutory concession (ESC D19), buildings can be treated as separate assets from the land on which they are built for the purposes of a claim under the TCGA 1992, s 23.

If a building is the subject of a negligible value claim, it is also treated as being a separate asset from the land on which it stands, however, the land must also be treated as disposed of for its market value: TCGA 1992, s 24(3).

SELF ASSESSMENT QUESTIONS

24.1 Paul bought an asset in July 1990 for £20 000. In August 1994 it was damaged, causing its value to fall to £16 000. Insurance proceeds of £5000 were received in March 1995. Paul did not restore the asset but sold it in October 2002 for £30 000. The asset was not a business asset.

REQUIRED

Calculate the effect for CGT purposes as a result of the above events.

24.2 Susan had acquired an asset in January 1989 for £8000. The asset was destroyed in July 2001. Insurance proceeds of £20 000 were received in November 2001, and a replacement asset was purchased in February 2002 for £18 000. The asset was not a business asset.

REQUIRED

Calculate Susan's chargeable gain for 2001/02 and state the base cost of the replacement asset assuming all relevant claims are made.

CHAPTER 25

Land and property

Land is a chargeable asset for CGT purposes, and so the disposal of land or an interest in land has CGT consequences.

With regard to leases, the precise tax treatment depends on both the length of the lease, i.e. whether it is a short or a long lease, and whether there is an assignment or grant of that lease.

This chapter examines the special CGT rules for leases, part disposals of land, and land held at 6 April 1965, and concludes by considering the exemption from CGT of an individual's principle private residence.

The assignment of a lease

The assignment of a lease is a complete disposal of the entire interest in the property. The manner in which the chargeable gain is calculated on the assignment of a lease, depends on whether the lease is a short lease, or a long lease.

1. The assignment of a short lease

A short lease is one with 50 years or less left to run at the date of disposal. Although a short lease is a wasting asset, the cost is not deemed to depreciate evenly over the life of the lease, as is the general rule for wasting assets. A short lease is deemed to depreciate more in the later years than in the earlier years. The gain on the assignment of a short lease is calculated using the percentage depreciation table for short leases found in Schedule 8 of the TCGA 1992.

The allowable cost on the assignment of a short lease is calculated as:

$$\text{Cost} \times \frac{\%\text{ of remaining life on disposal}}{\%\text{ of remaining life on acquisition}}$$

Or, where the lease was acquired before 31 March 1982, the allowable expenditure is calculated as:

$$\text{Market value} \times \frac{\%\text{ of remaining life on disposal}}{\%\text{ of remaining life on 31/3/82}}$$

Table 25.1 Percentage depreciation table for short leases (Schedule 8, TCGA 1992)

Years	Percentage	Years	Percentage
50 (or more	100	24	79.622
49	99.675	23	78.055
48	99.289	22	76.399
47	98.902	21	74.635
46	98.490	20	72.770
45	98.059	19	70.791
44	97.595	18	68.697
43	97.107	17	66.470
42	96.593	16	64.116
41	96.041	15	61.617
40	95.457	14	58.971
39	94.842	13	56.167
38	94.189	12	53.191
37	93.497	11	50.038
36	92.761	10	46.695
35	91.981	9	43.154
34	91.156	8	39.999
33	90.280	7	35.414
32	89.354	6	31.195
31	88.371	5	26.722
30	87.330	4	21.983
29	86.226	3	16.959
28	85.053	2	11.629
27	83.816	1	5.983
26	82.496	0	0
25	81.000		

EXAMPLE

Lease acquired on 31 March 1980 for £50 000 with 35 years to run. It was assigned on 31 March 1999 for £85 000. The market value of the lease on 31 March 1982 was £55 000.

Remaining life on acquisition is 35 years
Lease expires on 31/3/15
Remaining life on disposal, i.e. 31/3/99 is 16 years
Remaining life on 31/3/82 is 33 years

From the percentage tables:

16 years = 64.116
33 years = 90.280
35 years = 91.981

The allowable expenditure on original cost:

$$\text{Cost} \times \frac{\% \text{ remaining life on disposal (16 years)}}{\% \text{ remaining life on acquisition (35 years)}}$$

$$£50\,000 \times \frac{64.116}{91.981} = \underline{\underline{£34\,853}}$$

The allowable expenditure on 31/3/82 value:

$$31/3/82 \text{ value} \times \frac{\% \text{ remaining life on disposal (16 years)}}{\% \text{ remaining life on 31/3/82 (33 years)}}$$

$$£55\,000 \times \frac{64.116}{90.280} = \underline{\underline{£39\,061}}$$

The gain is then calculated as:

	Cost (£)	MV 31/3/82 (£)
Proceeds	85 000	85 000
less Cost : MV 31/3/82	(34 853)	(39 061)
	50 147	45 939

less Indexation to April 1998:

$$\frac{162.6 - 79.4}{79.4}$$

1.048 × £39 061	(40 936)	(40 936)
	9 211	5 003

The gain eligible for taper relief is the lower gain of £5003.

If the remaining life on the acquisition or disposal is not an exact number of years, the percentage is calculated as follows:

(a) take the percentage figure for the whole number of years, and then *add*

(b) $\frac{1}{12}$ of the difference between the percentage in (a) above and the next higher percentage for each month. Any odd 14 days or more are counted as one month.

So for $17\frac{1}{2}$ years, take the percentage figure for 17 years (66.470) and then add to this $\frac{6}{12}$ of the difference between the figure for 18 years (68.697) and the figure for 17 years (66.470), that is:

$$(68.697 - 66.470) \times 6/12 = 1.114$$

Therefore, the percentage figure for $17\frac{1}{2}$ years is (66.470 + 1.114) = $\underline{67.584}$

EXAMPLE

Suppose that in the first example the lease had been assigned on 15 December 1998 instead of 31 March 1999:

Remaining life on acquisition = 35 years
Remaining life on 31/3/82 = 33 years
Remaining life on disposal 15/12/98 = 16 years three months and 16 days

From percentage tables:

16 years = 64.116
17 years = 66.470
33 years = 90.280
35 years = 91.981

The percentage on disposal is calculated as:

$$64.116 + [(66.470 - 64.116) \times 4/12] = 64.901$$

Allowable expenditure on cost:

$$£50\,000 \times \frac{64.901}{91.981} = £35\,280$$

Allowable expenditure on 31/3/82 value:

$$£55\,000 \times \frac{64.901}{90.280} = £39\,539$$

The gain is then calculated as:

	Cost (£)	MV 31/3/82 (£)
Proceeds	85 000	85 000
less Cost : MV 31/3/82	(35 280)	(39 539)
	49 720	45 461
less Indexation to April 1998:		
$\dfrac{162.6 - 79.4}{79.4}$		
1.048 × £39 539	(41 437)	(41 437)
	8 283	4 024

The gain eligible for taper relief is the lower gain of £4024.

2. The assignment of a long lease

A long lease is one with more than 50 years to run at the date of disposal. A long lease is not a wasting asset and so the normal CGT rules apply.

EXAMPLE

Lease assigned with 70 years to run in March 2002 for £60 000; it had been acquired in June 1979 for £20 000. The market value on 31 March 1982 was £30 000. Assume indexation of 80 per cent.

	Cost (£)	Rebasing (£)
Proceeds	60 000	60 000
less Cost : MV 31/3/82	(20 000)	(30 000)
	40 000	30 000
80% × £30 000	(24 000)	(24 000)
	16 000	6 000

The gain eligible for taper relief is the lower gain of £6000.

The grant of a lease

On the grant of a lease, the grantor still retains an interest in the property and as such it amounts to a part disposal for CGT purposes. Where there is a grant of a short lease, the part disposal calculation is further complicated by the fact that, where a premium is received on the grant of a short lease, a portion of the premium is chargeable to income tax, as rent, under Schedule A (*see* Part 2, Chapter 16) and this must be taken into account when calculating the gain.

The method of calculating the chargeable gain on the grant of a lease differs according to whether the lease being granted is:

- a long lease out of a freehold or long sub-lease out of a long head lease;
- a short lease out of a freehold or short sub-lease out of a long lease; or
- a short sub-lease out of a short head lease.

We will now examine the methods for calculating the chargeable gain in each of the three situations:

1. The grant of a long lease out of a freehold, or a long sub-lease out of a long head lease

There are no Schedule A implications on the grant of a long lease. The chargeable gain is calculated using the normal part disposal rules, i.e. the allowable expenditure is calculated using the part disposal formula:

$$\frac{A}{A + B}$$

where A = value of the disposed part (i.e. premium received)
B = value of the part retained (i.e. the reversionary interest)

EXAMPLE

A freehold property was acquired in February 1984 for £100 000. In June 2002 a 60-year lease was granted for a premium of £250 000, when the reversionary interest was valued at £120 000. Assume indexation of 80 per cent.

	£
Proceeds	250 000
less Cost:	
$£100\,000 \times \dfrac{£250\,000}{£250\,000 + £120\,000}$	(67 568)
	182 432
£67 568 × 80%	(54 055)
Gain eligible taper relief	128 377

2. The grant of a short lease out of a freehold, or a short sub-lease out of a long head lease

When a short lease is granted for a premium, part of the premium is assessed as rent under Schedule A. The amount of the premium not chargeable to Schedule A is charged to CGT as a part disposal. The part disposal formula used to calculate the allowable expenditure is modified slightly to take account of the Schedule A assessment as follows:

$$\frac{a}{A + B}$$

where a = value of disposed part *less* Schedule A assessment
    (i.e. premium received *less* Schedule A assessment)
  A = value of the disposed part (i.e. premium received)
  B = value of the part retained (i.e. reversionary interest)

EXAMPLE

A long lease with 80 years to run was acquired in October 1988 for £50 000. In July 2002 a 21-year lease was granted for a premium of £85 000, when the value of the reversionary interest was £55 000. Assume indexation of 75 per cent to April 1998.

The grant of the 21-year lease is a short lease (less than 50 years), so part of the premium will be charged to income tax under Schedule A:

	£
Premium	85 000
less 2% (21 − 1) × £85 000	(34 000)
Schedule A assessment	51 000

The amount not charged to income tax i.e. £34 000 is charged to CGT as follows:

	£
Premium not treated as rent	34 000
less Allowable cost:	

$$£50\,000 \times \frac{£34\,000}{£85\,000 + £55\,000}$$

	(12 143)
	21 857
less Indexation:	
£12 143 × 75%	(9 107)
Gain eligible taper relief	12 750

3. The grant of a short sub-lease out of a short head lease

Although this is again a part disposal for CGT purposes, the calculation of the chargeable gain is complicated by the following:

(a) Part of the premium received on the grant of the sub-lease will be liable to income tax under Schedule A.

(b) There will be relief deducted from the Schedule A assessment for any premium paid on the headlease, given by:

$$\frac{\text{Full duration of sub-lease}}{\text{Full duration of head lease}} \times \text{Chargeable premium on head lease}$$

(c) The head lease being a short lease is a wasting asset

The gain is calculated using the percentage depreciation table for short leases, and then the gain is reduced by any Schedule A assessments.

The allowable cost is given by the formula:

$$\frac{X - Z}{Y}$$

where X = % remaining life head lease when sub-lease is granted
  Z = % remaining life of head lease when sub-lease terminates
  Y = % remaining life of head lease at date of acquisition or 31 March 1982

EXAMPLE

A 45-year lease was granted on 6 April 1992 for a premium of £60 000. On 6 April 2002 a sub-lease was granted for 20 years for a premium of £100 000. Assume indexation of 75 per cent to April 1998.

Schedule A assessment

	£	£
Premium of sub-lease		100 000
less 2% (20 − 1) × £100 000		(38 000)
c/f		62 000

	£	£
	b/f	62 000

less Relief for premium
paid on head lease:

Premium	60 000	
less 2% (45 − 1) × £60 000	(52 800)	
Chargeable premium on head lease	7 200	
relief: $\dfrac{20}{45} \times 7200$		(3 200)
Schedule A assessment		58 800

Remaining life on acquisition of head lease = 45 years
Remaining life on grant of sub-lease   = 35 years
Remaining life on termination of sub-lease = 15 years

X = % 35 years = 91.981
Z = % 15 years = 61.617
Y = % 45 years = 98.059

CGT	£	
Premium received on sub-lease	100 000	

less Allowable cost:

$\dfrac{(91.981 - 61.617)}{98.059} \times £60\,000$	(18 579)
	81 421
less Indexation: £18 579 × 75%	(13 934)
	67 487
less Schedule A assessment	(58 800)
Gain eligible taper relief	8 687

Note: When deducting the Schedule A assessment, it cannot increase or create a loss.

If there is a loss on the Schedule A assessment, this amount is allowed against rent received; if a loss then occurs on the grant of the sub-lease, the loss is reduced by the Schedule A relief given against the rents.

EXAMPLE

A 40-year lease was acquired for £20 000 on 6 April 1992. On 6 April 2002 a sub-lease was granted for ten years for a premium of £1000. Assume indexation of 75 per cent.

Schedule A

	£	£
Premium on sub-lease		1 000
less 2% (10 − 1) × £1 000		(180)
c/f		820

	£		£
		b/f	820

less Relief for premium
paid on head lease:

Premium	20 000	
less 2% (40 − 1) × £20 000	(15 600)	
Chargeable premium	4 400	
On head lease		

Relief: $\dfrac{10}{40} \times £4400$

		(1 100)
Allowable against rent received		(280)

CGT

Remaining life on acquisition of head lease = 40 years
Remaining life on grant of sub-lease   = 30 years
Remaining life on termination of sub-lease = 20 years

X = % 30 years = 87.330
Z = % 20 years = 72.770
Y = % 40 years = 95.457

	£
	1 000

Premium received on sub-lease
less Allowable cost:

$$\dfrac{(87.330 - 72.770)}{95.457} \times £20\,000$$

	(3 051)
	(2 051)

less Indexation:
75% × £3051
= £2288   restricted to:

	nil
	(2 051)
Deduct loss allowed under Schedule A	280
Allowable loss	(1 771)

Finally, if the rent for the head lease is less than the rent for the sub-lease and the premium is smaller than it should otherwise have been, the allowable cost is reduced by:

$$\dfrac{\text{Premium received}}{\text{Premium receivable with same rent as head lease}}$$

EXAMPLE

On 1 April 1990 a 45-year lease was acquired for £20 000. On 1 April 2003 a sub-lease was granted for 15 years at a higher rent than the head lease rent for a premium of £10 000. The premium that would have been payable at the head lease rent was £15 000. Assume indexation of 80 per cent.

Remaining life on acquisition of head lease = 45 years
Remaining life on grant of sub-lease = 32 years
Remaining life on termination of sub-lease = 17 years

X = % 32 years = 89.354
Z = % 17 years = 66.470
Y = % 45 years = 98.059

	£
Premium	10 000

less Allowable cost:

$$£20\,000 \times \frac{(89.354 - 66.470)}{98.059}$$

$$= £4667$$

restricted to $£4667 \times \dfrac{10\,000}{15\,000}$	(3 111)
	6 889

less Indexation:

0.8 × £3111	(2 489)
Gain eligible taper relief	4 400

Table 25.2 Summary of CGT rules for leases

	Type of lease	Tax treatment
1. Assignment of a lease		
The assignment of a lease amounts to a complete disposal	(a) long lease (i.e. > 50 years)	(a) Whole gain chargeable
	(b) short lease (i.e. ≤ 50 years)	(b) Gain chargeable using percentage depreciation table for leases
2. Grant of a lease		
On the grant of a lease the grantor retains an interest in the property	(a) long lease (i.e. > 50 years)	(a) Normal part disposal rules
	(b) short sub-lease (i.e. ≤ 50 years) out of freehold or long lease	(b) Part disposal rules – premium being reduced by any Schedule A assessment
	(c) short sub-lease (i.e. ≤ 50 years) out of short head lease	(c) Gain chargeable using percentage depreciation table for leases and then reduced by any Schedule A assessment

Part disposals of land

Where there is a part disposal of land, the taxpayer can make an election under the TCGA 1992, s 242, provided that certain conditions are met, to have the proceeds from the part disposal deducted from the CGT base cost of the land. This has the effect of deferring the liability to CGT.

Conditions:
(a) The disposal proceeds must be no more than 20 per cent of the total value of the land before the part disposal, and no more than £20 000.

(b) The proceeds from the part disposal, plus any other disposals of land made by the taxpayer in the same fiscal year must be no more than £20 000 in total.

If s 242, TCGA 1992 is claimed by the taxpayer, on a subsequent disposal of the land, indexation is calculated in two stages:

(a) the indexation allowance on the higher of either cost or market value on 31 March 1982 is deducted;

(b) the indexation of the part disposal proceeds is added back.

EXAMPLE

Twelve acres of land were acquired in May 1987 for £40 000. Part of the land was sold in July 1994 for £6000, when the value of the 12 acres prior to the part disposal was £80 000. No other disposals of land were made in 1994/95. In October 2002 the remaining land was sold for £100 000.

Part disposal in 1994/95
There is a part disposal of the land in 1994/95. However, the disposal proceeds are less than 20% ($\frac{6000}{80\,000}$ = 7.5%), and the total value of disposals of land in 1994/95 are less than £20 000. As the conditions for s 242, TCGA 1992 apply, the taxpayer can make the election to have the gain deferred, so there is no chargeable disposal in 1994/95. The disposal proceeds of £6000 are deducted from the base cost of the land, reducing the allowable expenditure on a future disposal, thus:

	£
Cost of land	40 000
less Disposal proceeds 1994/95	
(TCGA 1991, s 242)	(6 000)
Allowable expenditure for	
a future disposal of the land	34 000

Disposal 2002/03

	£
Proceeds	100 000
less Allowable cost:	
i.e. original cost less part disposal proceeds	
(£40 000 – £6000)	(34 000)
	66 000

Indexation to April 1998:

(1) *less* Indexation on
original cost:

$$\frac{162.6 - 101.9}{101.9}$$

0.596 × £40 000	(23 840)
	42 160

(2) *add* Indexation on
part disposal proceeds:

$$\frac{162.6 - 144}{144}$$

0.129 × £6000	774
Gain eligible for taper relief	42 934

If the part disposal of land is due to a compulsory purchase, the TCGA 1992, s 243 provides a similar relief, provided that the proceeds do not exceed 5 per cent of the total value of the land before the part disposal.

The relief under s 243 will be available on a compulsory purchase, even if the proceeds exceed £20 000, provided that the taxpayer has not shown an intent to sell the land prior to the compulsory purchase, e.g. by advertising the land for sale.

Where a small part disposal of land falls within s 242 or s 243, and the consideration is greater than the allowable expenditure for the whole of the land, an election can be made under s 244, TCGA 1992 to deduct the total cost of the land when calculating the immediate chargeable gain on the part disposal. This means, however, that on a future disposal of the remaining land there will be no allowable expenditure to carry forward.

By concession (SP D1), the Revenue will allow the part disposal of land to be calculated as if the part being disposed of is a separate asset from the land retained. This simplifies the computation as there is no need to determine the market value of the remaining land on the part disposal. The total allowable expenditure in this case being allocated between the land disposed of and the land remaining on some reasonable basis.

Note: If the above reliefs do not apply to the disposal, the gain is calculated using the normal part disposal rules.

Land with a development value held on 6 April 1965

Land with a development value is land situated in the UK that has been either:

(a) disposed of for an amount greater than its current use value; or

(b) where there has been some change in the nature, state or use of the land.

There are special rules for the disposal of land with a development value after 17 December 1973. The taxpayer is deemed to have disposed of the land and immediately reacquired it at its market value on 6 April 1965.

On the disposal of land with a development value after 17 December 1973, two computations were necessary:

- on original cost without time apportionment;
- on the value on 6 April 1965 (BDV).

For disposals after April 1988, a third computation is prepared under the rebasing rules.

Method for calculating the gain:

1. Compute the gain on cost without time apportionment and the April 1965 value (BDV). If one computation produces a gain and the other a loss, the disposal is a no gain/no loss disposal.

2. If the computations under cost and BDV both produce a gain, or both produce a loss, the computation under rebasing is prepared and the results compared as follows:

   (a) *gain/gain/gain under rebasing* – the chargeable gain is the smallest gain;

   (b) *loss/loss/loss under rebasing* – the allowable loss is the smallest loss;

   (c) *gain/gain/loss under rebasing;* or

   (d) *loss/loss/gain under rebasing* – the disposal is treated as a no gain/no loss disposal.

These rules also apply to quoted securities held on 6 April 1965.

Principal private residence exemption

The gain arising on the sale of residential accommodation is exempt from CGT, provided that throughout the period of ownership it has been the individual's only or main residence (TCGA 1992, s 223(1)). If it can be shown that the property was acquired for the purpose of realising a gain on disposal, the relief is denied (TCGA 1992, s 224).

The exemption applies to the main building, and any other relevant buildings adjoining it, such as a garage (TCGA 1992, s 222(1)). It may also be extended to cover buildings occupied for the purpose of the main residence, e.g. residential accommodation for staff – *Batey* v *Wakefield* [1981] STC 521.

Whether the staff accommodation forms part of the main residence for tax purposes would appear to be strongly influenced by the size of the accommodation in relation to the main house – *Markey* v *Sanders* [1987] STC 256; *Lewis* v *Rook* [1992] STC 171.

A caravan has been held to be eligible for relief under s 222(1) where mains services were supplied to the caravan – *Makins* v *Elson* [1977] STC 46. The absence of such services would seem to be an important factor in deciding whether a caravan falls within the ambit of s 222(1) – *Moore* v *Thompson* [1986] STC 170.

The exemption covers gardens and grounds of up to half an hectare, but the Revenue may allow a larger area, depending on the size and character of the house (TCGA 1992, s 222(1), (2)). Where a house is sold with only part of the gardens, and then the retained land is sold at a later date, the exemption will not apply to the disposal of the retained land – *Varty* v *Lynnes* [1976] STC 508.

Restriction of the relief

If the house has not been occupied throughout the period of ownership, only the gain relating to the period of occupation is exempt:

$$\text{Exempt gain} = \frac{\text{Period of occupation}}{\text{Period of ownership}} \times \text{Total indexed gain}$$

Periods prior to 31 March 1982 are ignored in this calculation.

In determining the period of occupation, certain periods of absence are deemed to be periods of occupation as follows:

(a) any period during which the owner or spouse is working abroad;

(b) any period(s) of absence totalling four years because the owner or spouse is working elsewhere in the UK;

(c) any period(s) of absence totalling three years, for any reason; and

(d) the final three years of ownership.

The final three years of ownership are always treated as deemed occupation, but in (a)–(c) above the periods of absence will only be treated as periods of deemed occupation if the house was actually occupied at some time both before and after the absence. However, by concession (ESC D4), the requirement to occupy the house *after* the period of absence is ignored in the case of (a) and (b) if the individual is prevented from returning to the house because of the employment.

A similar concession applies where an individual purchases a house but does not move in immediately because work is being carried out on the property. Provided that the repairs are completed within 12 months, the period is regarded as a period of occupation.

EXAMPLE

Jane bought a house on 6 January 1982 for £50 000. The house needed repairs and redecoration and Jane finally moved into the house on 1 July 1982, when the repairs were completed. She lived there until 31 December 1984 when she went to work abroad. She returned to the UK on 31 December 1987 when she immediately took up employment in another part of the UK that required her to live nearby, so she was unable to return to her house. She moved back to the house on 1 January 1993 and lived there until 31 December 1994 when she moved back to her parents' home. Jane finally sold the house on 1 July 1999 for £130 000. The house was valued at £55 000 on 31 March 1982. Assume indexation of 90 per cent, for period to April 1998.

The periods of actual and deemed occupation are:

Date	Reason	Exempt years	Chargeable years
6/1/82 – 31/3/82	Ignore (Prior to 31/3/82)	–	
1/4/82 – 30/6/82	Deemed occupation by concession	$\frac{3}{12}$	
1/7/82 – 31/12/84	Actual occupation	$2\frac{6}{12}$	
1/1/85 – 31/12/87	Deemed occupation working abroad	3	
1/1/88 – 31/12/92	Deemed occupation four years working elsewhere in the UK and one year for any reason	5	
1/1/93 – 31/12/94	Actual occupation	2	
1/1/95 – 30/6/96	Non-occupation not followed by a period of residence		$1\frac{6}{12}$
1/7/96 – 30/6/99	Deemed occupation final three years	3	
		$\overline{15\frac{9}{12}}$	$\overline{1\frac{6}{12}}$

Total period of ownership since 1/4/82:
1/4/82 – 30/6/99 = 17 years $\frac{3}{12}$

Gain on disposal:

	Cost (£)	Rebasing (£)
Proceeds	130 000	130 000
less Cost : MV 31/3/82	(50 000)	(55 000)
	80 000	75 000
less Indexation:		
90% × £55 000	(49 500)	(49 500)
Indexed gain	30 500	25 500

less Exempt:

$$\frac{15 \text{ years } 9/12}{17 \text{ years } 3/12}$$

$\frac{189}{207} \times £30\,500 : 25\,500$		
	(27 848)	(23 283)
	2 652	2 217

The asset is deemed to have been held for two years after 5 April 1998, i.e. one complete year plus the additional year, because the asset was held at 5 April 1998, therefore the taper relief available is nil and the chargeable gain is £2217, the lower gain.

Letting relief

If at any time during the period of ownership the house is let as residential accommodation the chargeable gain is reduced by the lower of:

- £40 000; or
- the amount of the exempt gain.

The letting relief, however, cannot be used to create a loss.

The relief applies to property that is let as residential accommodation: *Owen* v *Elliot* [1990] STC 469.

EXAMPLE

On 6 May 1992 Giles bought a house for £60 000. He occupied the house until 5 May 1993 and then let it as residential accommodation until 5 May 1999. The house then remained unoccupied until he sold it on 6 May 2002 for £150 000. Assume indexation of 80 per cent to April 1998:

```
6/5/92 – 5/5/93  actual occupation
6/5/93 – 5/5/99  let as residential accommodation
6/5/99 – 5/5/02  deemed occupation final three years
```

Total period of ownership is 10 years.
Actual + deemed occupation is 4 years.

		£
Proceeds		150 000
less Cost		(60 000)
	c/f	90 000

		£
b/f		90 000

less Indexation:

£60 000 × 80%	(48 000)
Total indexed gain	42 000
less Exempt gain 4/10 × £42 000	(16 800)
less Letting relief:	25 200

Lower of:
(a) £16 800; *or*

(b) £40 000	(16 800)
Untapered gain	8 400

If only part of the accommodation is let and the owner continues to occupy part of the property, the exemption will apply to the part he occupies.

EXAMPLE

Suppose, in the last example, that from 6 May 1993 to 5 May 1999 Giles had only let one-third of the house, occupying the other two-thirds himself:

	£	£
Total indexed gain		42 000
less Exemption for principle residence:		
4/10 × £42 000	16 800	
6/10 × £42 000 × 2/3	16 800	(33 600)
		8 400

less Letting relief:
lower of:
(a) £33 600; *or*
(b) £40 000

However, relief cannot be used to create a loss so restricted to	(8 400)
	nil

Note: No chargeable gain arises under the 'rent-a-room' scheme, nor when the owner takes in a lodger sharing the living accommodation.

Job-related accommodation

Where a person is living in job-related accommodation, relief is available on a house owned by that individual, provided that it is intended to be that person's main residence at some time in the future, e.g. on retirement.

House used partly for business

Where part of an individual's home is used exclusively for business purposes, the gain arising on the business portion will be chargeable to CGT. The portion of the gain attributable to the business use is made on some reasonable basis, e.g. area, or the proportion of household expenses that are treated as a business expense.

Dependent relative relief

Relief is also available on a house provided rent-free to a dependent relative before 6 April 1988.

Note: In the FA 1988 this relief was withdrawn for houses provided after 6 April 1988.

Second homes

Where a person owns more than one home, notification must be made in writing to the Inspector stating which house is intended to be the individual's main residence. The nomination must be made within two years of acquiring the second home.

SELF ASSESSMENT QUESTIONS

25.1 On 31 October 2002 Abigail sold the lease on a property for £150 000. She had aquired the lease on 31 October 1998 for a term of 30 years for £80 000.

REQUIRED

Calculate the gain on the disposal of the lease.

25.2 Cyril granted a 40-year lease to Penelope on 6 April 1993 for a premium of £50 000. On 6 April 2002 Penelope granted a sub-lease to Linda for 20 years for a premium of £80 000.

REQUIRED

Calculate Penelope's gain on the grant of the sub-lease in 2002/03.

CHAPTER 26

Shares and securities

There are special CGT rules for shares and securities, mainly because of the need to identify the cost of shares, where they have been acquired and/or disposed of at different times.

This chapter examines the treatment of shares and securities for CGT purposes with regard to disposals made by individuals, trustees and PRs, after 5 April 1998.

Matching rules

When shares are disposed of from a holding that has been acquired at different times, there has to be a method of identifying which shares have been sold, in order to allocate the allowable cost, calculate the indexation allowance (up until April 1998), and apply the correct taper relief.

Up until April 1998, shares of the same class were held in 'pools', according to when they were acquired.

For disposals after 6 April 1998, shares are matched in the following order:

(a) shares acquired on the same day;

(b) shares acquired in the previous 30 days;

(c) shares acquired after 5 April 1998 on a LIFO basis;

(d) shares held in the FA 1985 new holding pool;

(e) shares held in the FA 1982 frozen pool; and

(f) pre-1965 shares on a LIFO basis.

Prior to 6th April 2002, where an individual acquires shares under different employee share schemes, on the same day, and then disposes of some of them, they are treated as having acquired all the shares in one transaction. The disposal is treated as being made pro-rata from each acquisition, e.g. 1000 shares acquired under one scheme and 500 shares acquired under another followed by a disposal of 600 shares is treated as having disposed of 400 shares from the first scheme and 200 shares from the second scheme. For disposals on, or after 6th April 2002, the individual can elect that priority be given to those shares producing the smaller gain.

The FA 1985 pool

The FA 1985 pool consists of shares of the same class, that have been acquired between 6 April 1982 and 5 April 1998.

The pool is first set up at 6 April 1985 with all the shares that have been acquired between 6 April 1982 and 5 April 1985. These shares are then indexed from the date of acquisition to 6 April 1985, the indexation factor being calculated to three decimal places in the normal way.

After 6 April 1985, each time there is a transaction on the pool, i.e. an acquisition or a disposal, first of all the indexed rise is calculated, but after 6 April 1985 the indexation factor is not taken to three decimal places, as is the usual procedure, but instead it is kept in the calculator and applied to the amount in the indexed column of the pool, i.e.

$$\frac{R_T - R_L}{R_L} \times \text{indexed pool}$$

where R_T = RP1 figure at date of transaction
$\quad\quad R_L$ = RP1 figure at date of last indexation

After the indexed rise has been calculated, the pools are adjusted for the transaction.

EXAMPLE

On 10 August 2002 Helen sold 2000 shares in Troy Ltd for £22 000. She had acquired the shares as follows:

	No. of shares	(£)
10 April 1983	500	2250
5 May 1984	1000	5200
10 June 1986	1500	8100
30 September 1992	1000	5500

As all the shares were acquired between 6 April 1982 and 5 April 1998, they are all in the FA 1985 pool. The pool is first constructed with all the shares acquired between 6 April 1982 and 6 April 1985, i.e. the shares acquired in April 1983 and May 1984, as follows:

	No. of shares	Unindexed pool (£)	Indexed pool (£)
Pool starts 6/4/85			
10/4/83	500	2250	2250
5/5/84	1000	5200	5200
	1500	7450	7450

Indexation:

(1) $\dfrac{94.8 - 84.3}{84.3}$

$0.125 \times £2250$ — 282

(2) $\dfrac{94.8 - 89.0}{89.0}$

$0.065 \times £5200$ — 338

| Pool at 6/4/85 | 1500 | 7450 | 8070 |

From now on, transactions are dealt with by first calculating the indexed rise, without rounding to three decimal places, and then adjusting for the transaction, thus:

	No. of shares	Unindexed pool (£)	Indexed pool (£)
Pool at 6/4/85	1 500	7 450	8 070
June 1986			
$\dfrac{97.8 - 94.8}{94.8} \times £8\,070$			256
Acquisition	1 500	8 100	8 100
	3 000	15 550	16 426
September 1992			
$\dfrac{139.4 - 97.8}{97.8} \times £16\,426$			6 987
Acquisition	1 000	5 500	5 500
	4 000	21 050	28 913
August 2002			
$\dfrac{162.6 - 139.4}{139.4} \times £28\,913$			4 812
	4 000	21 050	33 725
Disposal	(2 000)	(10 525)	(16 863)
Bal. at 10/8/02	2 000	10 525	16 862

Helen's gain	£
Proceeds	22 000
less Cost	(10 525)
Unindexed gain	11 475
less Indexation:	
(16 863 – 10 525)	(6 338)
Gain eligible for taper relief	5 137

The FA 1982 'frozen pool'

The FA 1982 pool consists of all the shares of the same class that have been acquired between 6 April 1965 and 5 April 1982. The normal rules for rebasing and indexation apply.

EXAMPLE

In October 2002 Joan sold 2000 shares in Arc Ltd for £20 000. She had acquired the shares as follows:

	No. of shares	Cost (£)
March 1966	500	1 500
June 1975	400	1 400
April 1980	600	2 160
January 1982	1 000	3 800

The market value of the shares on 31 March 1982 was £4.00 each. Joan has not made a global election in respect of assets held at 31 March 1982. As all the shares were acquired between 6 April 1965 and 5 April 1982 they are all held in the FA 1982 frozen pool, comprising the total number of shares at cost and market value on 31 March 1982, thus:

	No. of shares	Cost (£)	MV 31/3/82 (£)
March 1966	500	1 500	2 000
June 1975	400	1 400	1 600
April 1980	600	2 160	2 400
January 1982	1 000	3 800	4 000
	2 500	8 860	10 000

Joan disposes of 2000 of the shares from the pool in October 2002; the 2000 shares and the pro-rata cost and market value are deducted from the 1982 pool, thus:

	No. of shares	Cost	MV 31/3/82
Balance of pool	2 500	8 860	10 000
Disposal October 2001	(2 000)	(7 088)	(8 000)
Balance c/f	500	1 772	2 000

The gain is calculated using the normal CGT rules for rebasing and indexation:

	Cost (£)	MV 31/3/82 (£)
Proceeds	20 000	20 000
less Cost : MV 31/3/82	(7 088)	(8 000)
	12 912	12 000

less Indexation:

$$\frac{162.6 - 79.4}{79.4}$$

1.048 × £8000	(8 384)	(8 384)
	4 528	3 616

↑
Indexed gain

The indexed gain is £3616, the lower gain; £8000 is used to calculate the indexation allowance as this is higher than cost.

Pre-1965 securities

Pre-1965 securities are matched on a LIFO basis. The exact CGT treatment depends on whether the securities are unquoted or quoted:

1. Unquoted securities

For unquoted securities acquired before 6 April 1965 the gain is calculated on three bases:

- on original cost with time apportionment (TAB)
- on rebasing (MV 31 March 1982)
- on market value 6 April 1965 (BDV).

The chargeable gain is the lowest of the three figures, however, if the BDV results in the smallest figure then the taxpayer must actually elect for this basis within two years from the end of the year of assessment in which the disposal takes place. If the election is not made, the chargeable gain will be the lower of rebasing and TAB. These are the rules that apply to all pre-1965 assets, other than quoted securities and land with a development value, and are considered in detail in Chapter 22.

EXAMPLE

Shares in White Ltd were acquired on 6 April 1958 for £10 000. The shares were valued at £15 000 and £12 000 on 6 April 1965 and 31 March 1982 respectively. The shares were sold for £40 000 on 30 September 2002:

If no election is made for BDV, the gain will be:

	Cost (£)	Rebasing (£)
Proceeds	40 000	40 000
less Cost : MV 31/3/82	(10 000)	(12 000)
	30 000	28 000

less Indexation to April 1998:

$$\frac{162.6 - 79.4}{79.4}$$

$1.048 \times £12\,000$	(12 576)	(12 576)
	17 424	15 424

$$\frac{6/4/65 - 30/9/02}{6/4/58 - 30/9/02} = \frac{37\frac{1}{2}\ \text{years}}{44\frac{1}{2}\ \text{years}}$$

$$\frac{450}{534} \times £17\,424 = \qquad\qquad £14\,683$$

(in months)

The indexed gain is £14 683 as this is the lower gain. However, if BDV is elected, the indexed gain will be:

	BDV
	(£)
Proceeds	40 000
less BDV	(15 000)
	25 000
less Indexation:	
1.048 × £15 000	(15 720)
Indexed gain	9 280

Provided that the election is made, the indexed gain will be £9280 as this is the lower gain.

2. Quoted securities

The TAB is not considered for quoted securities held at 6 April 1965, as the 1965 value is readily available.

On a disposal of quoted securities after 6 April 1965, two computations are necessary:

- on cost without time apportionment
- on BDV.

Method for calculating gain

(1) Compute the gain on cost and BDV as above. If one produces a gain and the other a loss, there is no need to consider rebasing and the disposal is treated as a no gain/no loss disposal.

(2) If the above does not apply, calculate the gain under the rebasing rules and compare the results of the three computations as follows:

    (a) *gain/gain/gain* – take the smallest gain

    (b) *loss/loss/loss* – take the smallest loss

    (c) *gain/gain/loss on rebasing* or *loss/loss/gain on rebasing* – the disposal is treated as being made for no gain/no loss.

If the calculations being compared are original cost and rebasing, indexation is computed on the higher of:

- original cost; or
- market value 31 March 1982.

However, if the calculations being compared are BDV and rebasing, the indexation is computed on the higher of:

- BDV; or
- market value 31 March 1982.

EXAMPLE

3000 shares were acquired in XYZ plc in 1960 for £15 000. The market value of the shares on 6 April 1965 and 31 March 1982 was £45 000 and £30 000 respectively. The shares were sold on 16 July 2002 for £95 000.

(1) First calculate the gain under original cost and BDV:

	Cost (£)	BDV (£)
Proceeds	95 000	95 000
less Cost : BDV	(15 000)	(45 000)
Unindexed gain	80 000	50 000

less Indexation to April 1998:

$$\frac{162.6 - 79.4}{79.4}$$

1.048 × £30 000	(31 440)	
(higher of cost and MV 31/3/82)		
1.048 × £45 000		
(higher of BDV and MV 31/3/82)		(47 160)
Indexed gain	48 560	2 840

(2) As both calculations produce a gain, the gain is recalculated under the rebasing rules:

	£
Proceeds	95 000
less MV 31/3/82	(30 000)
Unindexed gain	65 000
less Indexation:	
1.048 × £45 000	(47 160)
(higher of BDV and MV 31/3/82)	
Indexed gain	17 840

All three computations produce a gain and so the indexed gain is the smallest gain, i.e. £2840 under BDV.

Schedule 2 to the TCGA 1992

The taxpayer can make an election to have pre-1965 securities incorporated into the 1982 'frozen pool' at the market value on 6 April 1965. Separate elections are needed for each class of security held in a company, and once the election is made it is irrevocable.

EXAMPLE

Alice sold 2000 shares in RST plc for £20 000 in July 2002. She had acquired the shares as follows:

	No. of shares	Cost (£)
June 1961	5 000	10 000
June 1972	5 000	17 500

The shares were valued at £3.00 and £4.00 on 6 April 1965 and 31 March 1982 respectively. Alice has made an election under Schedule 2, TCGA 1992 to have her pre-1965 shares included in the FA 1982 'frozen pool'.

1982 Pool

	No. of shares	Cost (£)	MV 31/3/82 (£)
June 1961	5 000	15 000*	20 000
June 1972	5 000	17 500	20 000
	10 000	32 500	40 000
July 2001	(2 000)	(6 500)	(8 000)
Bal. of pool c/f	8 000	26 000	32 000

* The pre-1965 shares are incorporated into the 1982 pool at their market value on 6 April 1965.

	Cost (£)	Rebasing (£)
Proceeds	20 000	20 000
less Cost : MV 31/3/82	(6 500)	(8 000)
Unindexed gain	13 500	12 000

less Indexation to April 1998:

$$\frac{162.6 - 79.4}{79.4}$$

$1.048 \times £8000$	(8 384)	(8 384)
	5 116	3 616
		↑
		Indexed gain

The indexed gain is the lower gain of £3616.

COMPREHENSIVE EXAMPLE

Yasmin owned shares in West plc which she had acquired as follows:

	No. of shares	Cost (£)
16 July 1960	1 000	2 000
30 April 1963	1 000	1 800
10 September 1970	500	1 375
1 July 1972	1 500	4 500
10 May 1981	800	2 400
16 June 1982	200	800
23 August 1984	500	2 125
12 March 1992	1 000	4 300
17 February 1999	500	2 100
30 September 2002	500	2 875

The shares were valued at £2.50 and £3.75 on 6 April 1965 and 31 March 1982 respectively. On 7 October 2002 Yasmin sold 6 500 shares for £52 000.

Calculate the chargeable gain on the sale of the shares in 2001/02 on the assumption:

(1) that Yasmin had made an election under Schedule 2, TCGA 1992; and

(2) that no election for pooling had been made.

The shares will be matched as follows:

	No. of shares
(1) 1. Shares bought in previous 30 days	500
2. Shares acquired after 5/4/98	500
3. FA 1985 pool	1 700
4. FA 1982 pool	3 800
Total shares sold	6 500

Workings:

FA 1982 Pool

	No. of shares	Cost (£)	MV 31/3/82 (£)
16/7/60	1 000	2 500*	3 750
30/4/63	1 000	2 500*	3 750
10/9/70	500	1 375	1 875
1/7/72	1 500	4 500	5 625
10/5/81	800	2 400	3 000
	4 800	13 275	18 000
Disposal October 2002	(3 800)	(10 510)	(14 250)
Balance of 1982 pool	1 000	2 765	3 750

* Election under Schedule 2, TCGA 1992 incorporates pre-1965 shares at the market value on 6 April 1965.

Shares bought in the previous 30 days, and shares acquired after 5 April 1998, are matched first and so these cannot be included in the FA 1985 pool.

FA 1985 pool

	No. of shares	Unindexed (£)	Indexed (£)
Pool starts 6/4/85:			
16/6/82	200	800	800
23/8/84	500	2125	2125
	700	2925	2925

Indexation:

(1) $\dfrac{94.8 - 81.9}{81.9}$

$0.158 \times £800$ → 127

(2) $\dfrac{94.8 - 89.9}{89.9}$

$0.055 \times £2125$ → 117

Pool at 6/4/85	700	2925	3169

March 1992

$$\frac{136.7 - 94.8}{94.8} \times £3169$$
→ 1401

Acquisition	1000	4300	4300
	1700	7225	8870

October 2002

$$\frac{162.6 - 136.7}{136.7} \times £8870$$
→ 1681

	1700	7225	10551
Disposal	(1700)	(7225)	(10551)
	nil	nil	nil

Indexed gain:

	£	£	Indexed gain £

(1) *Previous 30 days:*

Proceeds: $\dfrac{500}{6500} \times £52000$ → 4000

less Cost → (2875) → 1125

→ 1125

(2) *Shares acquired after 5/4/98:*

Proceeds: $\dfrac{500}{6500} \times £52000$ → 4000

less Cost → (2100)

untapered gain 1900

351

(3) *FA 1985 pool:*

Indexed gain
(£)

Proceeds: $\dfrac{1700}{6500} \times £52\,000$

13 600

less Cost

(7 225)

6 375

less Indexation:
(10 551 – 7 225)

(3 326)

untapered gain

3 049

(4) *FA 1982 pool:*

	Cost (£)	MV 31/3/82 (£)	b/f
Proceeds:			
$\dfrac{3800}{6500} \times £52\,000$	30 400	30 400	
less Cost : MV 31/3/82	(10 510)	(14 250)	
	19 890	16 150	

less Indexation to April 1998:

$\dfrac{162.6 - 79.4}{79.4}$

$1.048 \times £14\,250$	(14 934)	(14 934)
	4 956	1 216

↑
Untapered gain

The taper must be calculated for each component part of the calculation, by calculating how long that part of the asset has been held since 5 April 1998, including the additional year for assets owned at 5 April 1998 for non-business assets.

Total chargeable gain:	£	£
(1) Previous 30 days:		
Indexed gain	1 125	
less Taper	nil	1 125
(2) Post 5/4/98 shares:		
Indexed gain	1 900	
less Taper 5%	(95)	1 805
(3) FA 1985 pool:		
Indexed gain	3 049	
less Taper 15%	(458)	2 591
(4) FA 1982 pool:		
Indexed gain	1 216	
less Taper 15%	(183)	1 033
Total chargeable gain		6 554

(2) If no election for pooling had been made, the shares will be matched as follows:

	No. of shares
1. Previous 30 days	500
2. Shares acquired after 5/4/98	500
3. FA 1985 pool	1 700
4. FA 1982 pool	2 800
5. Pre-1965 shares on LIFO basis:	
30/4/63	1 000
No. of shares sold	6 500

1000 shares remaining from 16 July 1960 purchase.

Workings

FA 1982 pool

	No. of shares	Cost (£)	MV 31/3/82 (£)
10/9/70	500	1 375	1 875
1/7/72	1 500	4 500	5 625
10/5/81	800	2 400	3 000
	2 800	8 275	10 500
Disposal	(2 800)	(8 275)	(10 500)
Bal. 1982 pool	nil	nil	nil

FA 1985 pool
  as before

Previous 30 days and post 5/4/98 acquisition
  as before

1982 pool

	Cost (£)	MV 31/3/82 (£)
Proceeds:		
$\frac{2800}{6500} \times £52\,000$	22 400	22 400
less Cost : MV 31/3/82	(8 275)	(10 500)
	14 125	11 900
less Indexation:		
1.048 × £10 500	(11 004)	(11 004)
	3 121	896

Indexed gain

Pre-1965 shares

	Cost (£)	BDV (£)	Rebasing (£)
Proceeds: $\frac{1000}{6500} \times £52\,000$	8 000	8 000	8 000
Cost : BDV : MV 31/3/82	(1 800)	(2 500)	(3 750)
	6 200	5 500	4 250
less Indexation:			
$1.048 \times £3750$	(3 930)	(3 930)	(3 930)
	2 270	1 570	320

The indexed gain is £320, the lower gain.

Total chargeable gain:	£	£
(1) Previous 30 days:		
Indexed gain	1 125	
less Taper	(nil)	1 125
(2) Post 5/4/98 shares:		
Indexed gain	1 900	
less Taper	(95)	1 805
(3) FA 1985 pool:		
Indexed gain	3 049	
less Taper	(458)	2 591
(4) FA 1982 pool:		
Indexed gain	896	
less Taper	(135)	761
(5) Pre-1965 shares:		
Indexed gain	320	
less Taper	(48)	272
Total chargeable gain		6 554

The reorganisation of share capital

A company may alter its share capital in several ways, e.g. there may be a bonus issue, or a rights issue, or there may be a takeover involved in the reorganisation.

For CGT purposes, when a reorganisation takes place, the new securities are deemed to have been acquired at the time of the original holding, i.e. it is not treated as a disposal of the 'old' securities and an acquisition of the 'new' securities.

In each case, because the shareholder's original holding will have changed in some way, there needs to be special CGT rules in order to allocate the original cost of the holding, to the holding after the reorganisation.

1. Bonus issues of the same class

When a company issues bonus shares, it is assumed that they were acquired on the same day as the holding to which they relate. A bonus issue of the same class of security simply increases the number of shares held, and so reduces the unit cost. It has no effect on indexation as nothing has been paid for the bonus issue.

EXAMPLE

Brian purchased 3000 ordinary shares in Towers Ltd for £8600 in July 1986. In December 1987 the company makes a one for three bonus issue of ordinary shares:

The shares will be held in the FA 1985 pool as follows:

	No. of shares	Unindexed pool (£)	Indexed pool (£)
July 1986	3 000	8 600	8 600
December 1987			
Bonus issue 1 for 3			
Indexed rise:			
$\dfrac{103.3 - 97.5}{97.5} \times £8600$			512
Bonus issue	1 000	–	–
Balance of pool December 1987	4 000	8 600	9 112

If Brian sold the shares in October 2002 for £18 000, the gain would be:

	No. of shares (£)	Unindexed pool (£)	Indexed pool (£)
Pool December 1987	4 000	8 600	9 112
October 2002			
$\dfrac{162.6 - 103.3}{103.3} \times £9112$			5 231
	4 000	8 600	14 343
Disposal	(4 000)	(8 600)	(14 343)
Pool balance	nil	nil	nil

	£
Proceeds	18 000
less Cost	(8 600)
Unindexed gain	9 400
less Indexation (14 343 – 8600)	(5 743)
Indexed gain	3 657

The rules apply to both quoted and unquoted securities. Where securities have been acquired at different times, and as such are in different 'pools', the bonus issue will increase each 'pool' and on a subsequent disposal the normal matching rules will be used.

EXAMPLE

Marco acquired ordinary shares in Polo plc as follows:

Date		No. of shares	Cost (£)
10 April 1970	bought	800	1800
10 April 1976	bought	800	2000
17 June 1983	bought	1000	3000
24 October 1986	bought	200	750

The market value of the shares on 31 March 1982 was £2.75 per share.

In December 1988 there was a one for four bonus issue of the same class of share. In September 2002 Marco sold 1750 shares for £10 500.

The shares purchased in 1970 and 1976 will be in the FA 1982 frozen pool and the shares bought in 1983 and 1986 will be in the FA 1985 pool. The pool balances after the bonus issue in 1988 will be as follows:

FA 1985 pool

	No. of shares	Unindexed pool (£)	Indexed pool (£)
Pool starts 6/4/85:			
17/6/83	1000	3000	3000
Indexation:			
$\dfrac{94.8 - 84.8}{84.8}$			
$0.118 \times £3000$			354
Pool at 6/4/85	1000	3000	3354
October 1986			
$\dfrac{98.5 - 94.8}{94.8} \times £3354$			131
Acquisition	200	750	750
	1200	3750	4235
December 1988			
Bonus issue one for four indexed rise:			
$\dfrac{110.3 - 98.5}{98.5} \times £4235$			508
Bonus issue	300	–	–
Pool in December 1988	1500	3750	4743

FA 1982 pool

	No. of shares	Cost (£)	MV 31/3/82 (£)
10 April 1970	800	1800	2200
10 April 1976	800	2000	2200
	1600	3800	4400
December 1988 Bonus issue one for four	400	–	–
Pool balance in December 1988	2000	3800	4400

On the disposal of 1750 shares in September 2002, the shares will be matched as follows:

	No. of shares
1. FA 1985 pool	1500
2. FA 1982 pool	250
	1750

FA 1985 pool

	No. of shares	Unindexed pool (£)	Indexed pool (£)
Balance in December 1988	1500	3750	4743

September 2002
Indexed rise to April 1998

	No. of shares	Unindexed pool (£)	Indexed pool (£)
$\dfrac{162.6 - 110.3}{110.3} \times £4743$			2249
	1500	3750	6992
Disposal	(1500)	(3750)	(6992)
Balance	nil	nil	nil

FA 1982 pool

	No. of shares	Cost (£)	MV 31/3/82 (£)
Bal. December 1988	2000	3800	4400
Disposal 2002	(250)	(475)	(550)
Balance of pool	1750	3325	3850

Marco's indexed gain 2002/03:

FA 1982 pool

	Cost (£)	MV 31/3/82 (£)
Proceeds: $\dfrac{250}{1750} \times £10\,500$	1500	1500
less Cost : MV	(475)	(550)
	1025	950

c/f

	Cost (£)	MV 31/3/82 (£)
b/f	1025	950

less Indexation:

$$\frac{162.6 - 79.4}{79.4}$$

$1.048 \times £550$	(577)	(577)
	448	373

↑
Indexed gain

FA 1985 pool

£

Proceeds: $\frac{1500}{1750} \times £10\,500$	9000
less Cost	(3750)
	5250
less Indexation (£6992 − £3750)	(3242)
Indexed gain	2008

Taper relief is available on the indexed gains.

2. Rights issue of the same class

When there is a rights issue, the shareholder has the choice of taking up the rights or selling the rights without making a payment. If the rights are taken up, the new securities relate to the original holding as with a bonus issue, but as there is a price for the rights issue the indexation is calculated from when the rights were issued and not from the date that the original holding was acquired.

EXAMPLE

On 6 May 1986 Christopher acquired 5000 shares in Columbus plc for £12 500. In November 1988 there was a one for five rights issue at £2.25 per share. Christopher took up the rights and in August 2002 he sold £3000 shares for £15 000.

The shares are held in the FA 1985 pool:

	No. of shares	Unindexed pool (£)	Indexed pool (£)
May 1986	5 000	12 500	12 500
November 1988 Rights issue Indexed rise:			
$\frac{110 - 97.8}{97.8} \times £12\,500$			1 560
			14060

	No. of shares	Unindexed pool (£)	Indexed pool (£)
b/f			14 060
Rights issue one for five at £2.25 each	1 000	2 250	2 250
Balance of pool November 1988	6 000	14 750	16 310

Disposal of 3000 shares in 2002:

	No. of shares	Unindexed pool (£)	Indexed pool (£)
Balance November 1988	6 000	14 750	16 310

August 2002
Indexed rise to April 1998:

	No. of shares	Unindexed pool	Indexed pool
$\dfrac{162.6 - 110.0}{110.0} \times £16\,310$			7 800
	6 000	14 750	24 110
Disposal	(3 000)	(7 375)	(12 055)
Balance of pool	3 000	7 375	12 055

Indexed gain:

	£
Proceeds	15 000
less Cost	(7 375)
Unindexed gain	7 625
less Indexation (12 055 – 7 375)	(4 680)
Indexed gain	2 945

If the rights issue occurred between 6 April 1982 to 6 April 1985, care must be taken with indexation when setting up the 1985 pool.

EXAMPLE

Solomon acquired 3000 shares in Grundy Ltd for £5700 in January 1983. In December 1984 there was a one for three rights issue at £1.80 per share, and Solomon took up the rights.

In June 2002 he sold 1000 shares for £5750.

	No. of shares	Unindexed pool (£)	Indexed pool (£)
Pool starts 6/4/85:			
January 1983	3 000	5 700	5 700
December 1984			
Rights issue one for three			
at £1.80 each	1 000	1 800	1 800
	4 000	7 500	7 500

Indexation:

(1) $\dfrac{94.8 - 82.6}{82.6}$

$0.148 \times £5700$ ... 844

(2) $\dfrac{94.8 - 90.9}{90.9}$

$0.043 \times £1800$ ... 78

	No. of shares	Unindexed pool	Indexed pool
Pool at 6/4/85	4 000	7 500	8 422

June 2002
Indexed rise to April 1998:

$\dfrac{162.6 - 94.8}{94.8} \times £8422$

			6 024
	4 000	7 500	14 446
Disposal	(1 000)	(1 875)	(3 612)
Balance of pool	3 000	5 625	10 834

Indexed gain:

	£
Proceeds	5 750
less Cost	(1 875)
	3 875
less Indexation (3 612 – 1 875)	(1 737)
Indexed gain	2 138

As with bonus issues, where the rights relate to a holding in the FA 1982 pool, the rights go into that pool. Care must be taken with the indexation when a rights issue affects the FA 1982 pool. On a subsequent disposal, a proportion will be from the original holding and a proportion from the rights issue when calculating the indexation allowance.

EXAMPLE

Gerald acquired ordinary shares in Ace Ltd as follows:

		No. of shares	Cost
Date			*(£)*
June 1979	bought	3000	4000
July 1986	bought	2000	6000

In August 1987 there was a one for four rights issue at £4.20 per share, and Gerald took up the rights. In September 2002 Gerald sold 6000 of the shares for £48 000. The shares were valued at £2.60 per share on 31 March 1982.

The shares purchased in 1979 will be held in the FA 1982 pool and the shares purchased in 1986 will be held in the FA 1985 pool.

The pool balances after the rights issue will be as follows:

FA 1985 pool	No. of shares	Unindexed pool (£)	Indexed pool (£)
July 1986	2 000	6 000	6 000
August 1987 Indexed rise:			
$\dfrac{102.1 - 97.5}{97.5} \times £6000$			283
Rights issue of one for four at £4.20 per share	500	2 100	2 100
Pool balance August 1987	2 500	8 100	8 383

FA 1982 pool	No. of shares	Cost (£)	MV 31/3/82 (£)
June 1979	3 000	4 000	7 800
August 1987 Rights issue of one for four at £4.20 each	750	3 150	3 150
Pool balance August 1987	3 750	7 150	10 950

On the disposal of 6000 shares in September 2002, the shares will be matched as follows:

	No. of shares
1. FA 1985 pool	2 500
2. FA 1982 pool	3 500
Total disposal	6 000

1985 pool	No. of shares	Unindexed pool (£)	Indexed pool (£)
Balance August 1987	2 500	8 100	8 383
September 2002 Indexed rise to April 1998 $\dfrac{162.6 - 102.1}{102.1} \times £8383$			4 968
c/f	2 500	8 100	13 351

	No. of shares	Unindexed pool (£)	Indexed pool (£)
b/f	2 500	8 100	13 351
Disposal	(2 500)	(8 100)	(13 351)
Pool balance	nil	nil	nil

Indexed gain:

$$\text{Proceeds: } \frac{2500}{6000} \times £48\,000$$

	£
Proceeds	20 000
less Cost	(8 100)
	11 900
less Indexation (13 351 – 8100)	(5 251)
Indexed gain	6 649

FA 1982 pool

	No. of shares	Cost (£)	MV 31/3/82 (£)
Balance August 1987	3 750	7 150	10 950
Disposal September 2002	(3 500)	(6 673)	(10 220)
Balance of pool	250	477	730

The indexation must be split between the original holding and the rights issue on the disposal. Although the rights are deemed to have been acquired when the original holding was acquired, the rights shares will only attract indexation from August 1987, when they were taken up. The disposal of the 3500 shares from the 1982 pool will be deemed to be:

2800	shares acquired June 1979
700	rights taken August 1987
3500	

The indexation for the 2800 shares will be based on the higher of cost or market value, thus:

Cost

$$\frac{2800}{3000} \times £4000 = £3733$$

MV 31/3/82

$$\frac{2800}{3000} \times £7800 = £7280$$

The indexation for the 700 rights shares will be based on the cost of those rights in August 1987, that is:

$700 \times £4.20 = £2940$

Indexed gains:

	Cost (£)	MV 31/3/82 (£)
Proceeds: $\dfrac{3500}{6000} \times £48\,000$	28 000	28 000
less Cost : MV 31/3/82		
Original holding	(3 733)	(7 280)
Rights (2940)	(2 940)	(2 940)
	21 327	17 780

less Indexation:

(1) From March 1982 – April 1998

$\dfrac{162.6 - 79.4}{79.4}$

$1.048 \times £7280$	(7 630)	(7 630)

(2) From August 1987 – April 1998

$\dfrac{162.6 - 102.1}{102.1}$

$0.593 \times £2940$	(1 744)	(1 744)
	11 953	8 406

                                      ↑
Indexed gain

Rights sold nil paid

If the shareholder does not take up the rights, but sells them to a third party without having paid anything for them, then for CGT purposes, it is effectively a part disposal. The allowable cost is calculated using the normal part disposal formula:

$$\frac{A}{A + B}$$

, where A is the value of the disposed part – the proceeds, and B is the value of the part retained – the market value of the holding.

EXAMPLE

In February 1986 Ferdinand bought 500 shares in Allgoods Ltd for £1200. There was a one for two rights issue at £2.80 per share in November 1988 when the shares were worth £3.00 per share. Ferdinand sold the rights nil paid for £100. In June 2002 he sold the shares for £3750.

	No. of shares	Unindexed pool (£)	Indexed pool (£)
February 1986	500	1200	1200

November 1988

$$\frac{110 - 96.6}{96.6} \times £1200$$

			167
	500	1200	1367

Disposal of rights:

$$\frac{100}{100 + 1500} \times 1200 : 1367$$

	–	(75)	(86)
	500	1125	1281

Gain on sale of rights:

	£
Proceeds	100
less Cost	(75)
	25
less Indexation:	
(86 – 75)	11
Chargeable gain	14

Disposal 2002

	No. of shares	Unindexed pool (£)	Indexed pool (£)
Balance November 1988	500	1125	1281

June 2002
Indexed rise to April 1998:

$$\frac{162.6 - 110.0}{110.0} \times £1281$$

			613
	500	1125	1894
Disposal	(500)	(1125)	(1894)
Balance	nil	nil	nil

Indexed gain:

	£
Proceeds	3750
less Cost	(1125)
	2625
less Indexation:	
(1894 – 1125)	(769)
Indexed gain	1856

However, where the consideration is 'small', i.e. less than 5 per cent of the value of the holding to which the rights relate, the gain can be deferred until a subsequent disposal by deducting the proceeds from the indexed and unindexed pools in the FA 1985 pool, or cost and market value in the FA 1982 pool. This is the small capital distribution rule found in the TCGA 1992, s 122.

EXAMPLE

Alice acquired 1000 shares in Oak Ltd for £3000 in January 1987. In November 1988 there was a rights issue of one for one at £1.40 when the shares were worth £1.50 per share. Alice sold the rights for £50 nil paid. In May 2002 she sold her shares for £7000.

The proceeds of the sale of rights of £50 is less than 5 per cent of the holding at that time i.e. 1000 shares @ £1.50 per share and so there is no disposal at the time the rights are sold, the £50 is deducted from the indexed and unindexed pools:

	No. of shares	Unindexed pool (£)	Indexed pool (£)
January 1987	1000	3000	3000
November 1988 Indexed rise:			
$\frac{110-100}{100} \times £3000$			300
	1000	3000	3300
Disposal of rights (TCGA 1992, s 122)		(50)	(50)
	1000	2950	3250
May 2002 Indexed rise to April 1998			
$\frac{162.6-110.0}{110.0} \times £3250$			1554
	1000	2950	4804
Disposal	(1000)	(2950)	(4804)
Balance	nil	nil	nil

	£
Proceeds	7000
less Cost	(2950)
	4050
less Indexation (4804 – 2950)	(1854)
Indexed gain	2196

Where the rights relate to shares held in both the FA 1985 pool and the FA 1982 pool, the amount is apportioned between them. For example, if in the last example 500 shares had been in the FA 1985 pool and 500 in the FA 1982 pool, then £25 would have been deducted from each pool on the sale of the rights. On a subsequent disposal of shares from the 1982 pool, indexation is calculated in two stages:

(1) indexation on higher of cost/MV 31 March 1982; *less*

(2) indexation on the rights proceeds.

The rules for rights issues, like bonus issues, apply equally to quoted and unquoted securities.

Bonus issues of a different class

Where the bonus issue is a different class of security from the original holding, the original cost must be apportioned between the different classes of security. How the cost is apportioned depends on whether the new securities are quoted or unquoted.

1. Quoted

Where the new securities are quoted on a recognised stock exchange within three months of their issue, the original cost is apportioned according to the market values of the securities after the reorganisation.

EXAMPLE

In August 1986 Penelope bought 2000 ordinary 25p shares in Lane plc, a quoted company, for £16 000. In July 1988 there was a bonus issue of five 50p preference shares for two ordinary shares held in the company. Immediately after the bonus issue the shares were quoted at:

	£
25p ordinary shares	9.60
50p preference shares	0.80

In June 2002 Penelope sold all the preference shares for £6000.

Holdings after bonus issue:

	£
2000 ordinary 25p shares @ £9.60 each	19 200
5000 preference shares @ £0.80 each	4 000
	23 200

Deemed cost of holdings: £

(1) *Ordinary shares*

$$\frac{19\,200}{23\,200} \times £16\,000 \qquad 13\,241$$

(2) *Preference shares*

$$\frac{4\,000}{23\,200} \times £16\,000 \qquad 2\,759$$

The preference shares are deemed to have been acquired in August 1986 when the original holding was acquired. As the issue was a bonus issue indexation is not affected.

Preference shares	No. of shares	Unindexed pool (£)	Indexed pool (£)
August 1986	5 000	2 759	2 759
June 2002			
$\frac{162.6 - 97.8}{97.8} \times £2759$			1 828
	5 000	2 759	4 587
Disposal	(5 000)	(2 759)	(4 587)
Balance	nil	nil	nil

Indexed gain:

	£
Proceeds	6 000
less Cost	(2 759)
less Indexation (4587–2759)	(1 828)
Indexed gain	1 413

The pool of ordinary shares will be as follows:

	No. of shares	Unindexed pool (£)	Indexed pool (£)
August 1986			
	2 000	13 241	13 241

When there is another transaction on the pool of ordinary shares, the indexed rise will be calculated from August 1986 to the date of the transaction.

2. Unquoted
If the securities are not quoted, the acquisition cost of the new holding is calculated using the market values of the securities at the date of a subsequent disposal.

EXAMPLE
Basil purchased 2000 ordinary shares in Yarrow Ltd for £16 000 on 14 June 1985. In August 1988 there was a bonus issue of one preference share for every two ordinary shares held. Basil sold 800 of the preference shares on 10 September 2002 for £800.

The value of the shares on 10/9/02 were:

Ordinary shares	£4.50 each
Preference shares	£1.00 each

Value of shares on 10/9/02:

	£
2000 ordinary shares @ £4.50 each	9 000
1000 preference shares @ £1.00 each	1 000
	10 000

Deemed cost of holdings:

Ordinary shares:

$$\frac{9\,000}{10\,000} \times £16\,000 = £14\,400$$

Preference shares:

$$\frac{1\,000}{10\,000} \times £16\,000 = £1600$$

The preference shares are deemed to have been acquired in June 1985 when the original holding was acquired.

Preference share pool

	No. of shares	Unindexed pool (£)	Indexed pool (£)
June 1985	1000	1600	1600
September 2002 Indexed rise to April 1998:			
$\dfrac{162.6 - 95.4}{95.4} \times 1600$			1127
	1000	1600	2727
Disposal 800 shares	(800)	(1280)	(2182)
Balance of pool	200	320	545

	£
Proceeds	800
less Cost	(1 280)
Unindexed loss	(480)
less Indexation (restricted to nil)	–
Allowable loss	(480)

The pool of ordinary shares will stand as follows:

	No. of shares	Unindexed pool (£)	Indexed pool (£)
June 1985	2000	14400	14400

When a transaction occurs on the ordinary share pool, the indexed rise will first be calculated from June 1985 to the date of the transaction, restricted to April 1998.

Rights issues of a different class

Where the rights issue is a different class of security from the original holding, the rules are exactly the same as for bonus issues of a different class. However, with a rights issue the amount paid for the rights is treated separately for indexation purposes, as it is for rights issues generally.

Convertible securities

A conversion of securities, e.g. from loan stock to shares, is not treated as a disposal of the 'old' security and an acquisition of a 'new' security. The new holding is deemed to have been acquired on the same day as the old holding.

If there is a consideration of money received on the conversion, there is a part disposal of the original holding. However, the small capital distributions rule can be used where the amount of cash received is 'small', i.e. less than 5 per cent in relation to the value of the securities.

EXAMPLE

Janice bought £5000 of 8 per cent convertible loan stock in Orion plc for £4600 in January 1986. The loan stock is converted to 3750 £1 ordinary shares in December 1997 together with a cash premium of £500. The market value of the shares in December 1997 was £3.00 per share.

Value of shares $3750 \times £3.00 = £11\ 250$

$$\frac{500}{11\ 250} = 4.4\%$$

As the cash premium is small, less than 5 per cent, in relation to the value of the convertible securities, the small capital distribution rule can be applied, so there is no part disposal in December 1997, the premium received is deducted from the pool.

	No. of shares	Unindexed pool (£)	Indexed pool (£)
January 1986	5000	4600	4600
December 1997 *Indexed rise:*			
$\dfrac{160 - 96.2}{96.2} \times £4600$			3051
	5000	4600	7651
Cash received		(500)	(500)
		4100	7151
Conversion to shares	3750		
Balance of pool December 1997	3750	4100	7151

Takeovers

Where there is a takeover bid, the CGT liability depends on whether the consideration is cash, shares, or a mixture of cash and shares.

1. Consideration in cash

Where the consideration in a take-over is entirely for cash, the shareholder is deemed to have made a chargeable disposal when the offer is accepted.

2. Share for share exchange

No CGT liability arises on a share for share exchange. The shareholder is deemed to have acquired the new shares at the date when the original shares were acquired.

EXAMPLE

John purchased 1000 ordinary shares in Pluto Ltd in January 1984 for £1200. The company is taken over by Venus Ltd in February 1997, with shareholders receiving five shares in Venus Ltd for every share held in Pluto Ltd. John would receive 5000 shares in Venus Ltd that are deemed to have been acquired for £1200 in January 1984.

If the exchange is for different classes of security, the original cost is apportioned using the market values as for bonus and rights issues.

3. Consideration in cash and shares

If part of the consideration is cash, then a liability to CGT will arise on the cash element of the takeover bid. However, the small capital distribution rule will apply if the cash element is no more than 5 per cent or £3000, whichever is the higher.

EXAMPLE

Jennifer owns 2000 ordinary shares in Saturn Ltd which had cost her £4500 in July 1984. In June 2002 Saturn Ltd is taken over by Mercury Ltd on the following terms:

For every 500 shares in Saturn Ltd the shareholder receives:
- (1) £50 cash
- (2) 200 ordinary shares in Mercury Ltd
- (3) 100 preference shares in Mercury Ltd.

The market values are:
ordinary shares £5.75 each
preference shares £1.20 each.

Jennifer's consideration:

	£
Cash: £50 × 4	200
Ordinary shares: 800 × £5.75	4600
Preference shares: 400 × £1.20	480
	5280

The original cost of the 2000 shares in Saturn Ltd is apportioned between the various elements of the consideration:

	£
(1) Cash $\dfrac{200}{5280} \times £4500$	170
(2) Ordinary shares $\dfrac{4600}{5280} \times 4500$	3921

(3) Preference shares

$$\frac{480}{5280} \times £4500 \qquad\qquad \underline{409}$$

$$\underline{\underline{4\,500}}$$

As the cash element is less than 5 per cent, the small capital distributions rule will apply.

Certain debentures received in exchange for shares/securities on a corporate reconstruction are treated as securities for certain CGT purposes. For disposals after 6th April 2001, and for holding periods from 6th April 1998 these deemed securities will be treated as securities for taper relief purposes, with the effect that they can qualify for business asset relief applying to shares and securities.

Gilt-edged securities and qualifying corporate bonds

Gilt-edged securities are government securities.

Qualifying corporate bonds (QCB) are securities that:

- represent a normal commercial loan;
- are not convertible into shares;
- are expressed in sterling and not convertible or redeemable in another currency;
- do not carry the right to excessive interest.

Section 115 of the TCGA 1992 provides that the disposal of gilt-edged securities and QCBs are exempt from CGT. The disposal of options and futures in such securities are also exempt.

Because of these exemptions, if a QCB is converted to other securities, or vice versa, on a reorganisation there are special CGT rules; the new asset is not treated as having been acquired when the old asset was acquired, but as being acquired on the date of the reorganisation for the market value of the old asset immediately before the reorganisation. This value is increased or decreased by any amount paid by, or received by, the holder of the securities.

Where 'old' asset is a QCB

If at the time of the reorganisation the gain would be exempt because the asset disposed of is a QCB, then the reorganisation is treated as a disposal of the old asset and no gain will accrue.

Where 'old' asset is not a QCB

The reorganisation is not treated as a disposal of the old asset. The gain or loss is calculated as if the asset was disposed of immediately before the reorganisation but it does not crystallise until the new asset is disposed of. If the new asset is a QCB, the exemption under the TCGA 1992, s 115 does not cover this deferred gain or loss.

From 26 November 1996, the conversion of a security from a non-qualifying corporate bond to a QCB will give rise to a gain calculated at the date of conversion which will crystallise when the bond is disposed of. The rules apply to companies but with new rules regarding loan relationships from 31 March 1996 it is unlikely to affect many companies.

Anti-avoidance

Specific legislation exists to prevent tax avoidance of CGT with respect to shares and securities.

Bed and breakfasting

The FA 1998 introduced legislation to counter the 'bed and breakfasting' of shares by individuals and trustees. For disposals on, or after 17 March 1998, any shares sold and repurchased within a 30-day period will be matched so that the gain, or loss which would have arisen by reference to the shares already held will not be realised.

Value-shifting

Sections 29 and 30 of the TCGA 1992 provide that adjustments may be made to a chargeable gain or allowable loss where the value of an asset is reduced prior to its disposal, so as to create a loss or reduce the gain, simply to avoid CGT, or confer a tax free benefit on the person making the disposal or any connected person.

If the anti-avoidance provisions apply, the gain or loss is calculated using deemed disposal proceeds that the Revenue considers to be just and reasonable.

Appeals against such adjustments are made initially to the Commissioners of the Inland Revenue.

SELF ASSESSMENT QUESTIONS

26.1 Thomas sold 10 000 shares in Appollo plc for £80 000 in August 2002. He had acquired the shares as follows:

	No. of shares	Cost
		£
June 1986	4 000	18 000
March 1990	3 000	15 000
January 1998	4 000	20 000

In August 1989 Thomas had taken up a one for four rights issue at £4 per share.

REQUIRED

Calculate the chargeable gain on the disposal of the shares.

26.2 Rose Bloom had purchased 15 000 shares in Lavender plc for £40 000 in April 1990. In November 2002 Jasmine plc acquired all the shares in Lavender plc. Under the terms of the takeover, shareholders in Lavender plc received two ordinary shares and one preference share in Jasmine plc plus £5 cash for every three shares held in Lavender plc. Immediately after the takeover the ordinary shares in Jasmine plc are quoted at £3.60 and the preference shares in Jasmine plc are quoted at £1.80.

REQUIRED

Calculate the chargeable gain on Rose Bloom for 2002/03 as a result of the takeover, and calculate the base cost of the shares in Jasmine plc held by her.

26.3 On 12 September 2002 Harvey Moon sold 2000 of his shares in Saturn Ltd for £17 200. He had acquired the shares as follows:

	No. of shares	Cost
		£
March 1984	1 000	2 600
June 1993	500	1 600
September 1995	1 000	3 600
July 1998	1 500	4 500

REQUIRED

Calculate the untapered gain on the sale of the shares.

CHAPTER 27

Capital gains tax reliefs

There are a number of exemptions from CGT which have already been discussed in previous chapters. These can be summarised as follows:

- annual exemption (Chapter 21)
- exempt persons (Chapter 21)
- exempt disposals (Chapter 21)
- exempt assets (Chapter 21)
- wasting chattels (Chapter 23)
- chattels sold for £6000 or less (Chapter 23)
- principal private residence exemption (Chapter 25).

Exemption from CGT may also be achieved by treating a disposal in such a way that it produces neither a gain nor a loss, as in the case of transfers between spouses (Chapter 22).

Besides exemptions, there are a number of CGT reliefs available. The main effect of these reliefs is to defer the charge to CGT until some subsequent event or disposal, provided that certain conditions are met. For example, we saw in Chapter 24 that when compensation is received for the damage, loss or destruction of an asset, the CGT can be deferred if the money is used to restore or replace the asset, provided certain conditions are met. This type of 'roll over' relief is also available to landlords on the compulsory purchase of land, when the consideration for the disposal is applied in acquiring other land (Chapter 25).

This chapter examines the reliefs available from CGT that have not already been considered in previous chapters.

Retirement relief

The disposal of a business or business assets is a chargeable disposal for CGT. Where the disposal is on retirement, the individual may be eligible for retirement relief on the gains arising from the disposal of business assets or from shares in the individual's personal company.

A company is an individual's personal company if the individual is a full-time working officer or employee owning at least 5 per cent of the voting shares.

Prior to 16 March 1993, retirement relief was only available on the disposal of shares in a 'family company', provided the individual was a full-time working director and held at least 25 per cent of the voting rights. If the 25 per cent requirement was not fulfilled, the individual could still be eligible for relief, provided that 5 per cent was held by the individual, and together with his relatives they held over 50 per cent. Relatives, for this purpose, include brothers, sisters, an ancestor or lineal descendents, spouses and their relatives. Therefore, prior to 16 March 1993, there was no relief available to employees.

The relief

The maximum relief available is £50 000 *plus* one-half of any gain in excess of this figure up to £200 000 (2002/03).

	£
	50 000
Plus 50% per cent (200 000 − 50 000)	75 000
Maximum relief available	125 000

The maximum relief is based on a qualifying period of ten years' ownership. Where the business has been owned for less than ten years, the limits are reduced proportionately, i.e. 10 per cent for each complete year up to the maximum of 100 per cent where the ten-year period is satisfied, part years are taken into account, e.g. where the business had been owned for three years and three months then $32\frac{1}{2}$ per cent of the limits would be used in calculating the relief except that there is no relief where the relevant period is less than 12 months.

EXAMPLE

If an individual aged 50 years had owned a business for the last seven years the maximum relief would be:

70% × £50 000 = £35 000
70% × £20 000 = £140 000

Therefore, maximum relief is £35 000 *plus* 50% of any gain in excess of this up to a maximum of £140 000.

	£
	35 000
plus 50% (£140 000 − £35 000)	52 500
Maximum relief if qualifying period is seven years	87 500

Suppose that, in the example above, the person concerned had a realised gain of £85 000, the maximum relief would be:

	£
	35 000
plus 50% (£85 000 − £35 000)	25 000
Maximum relief available	60 000

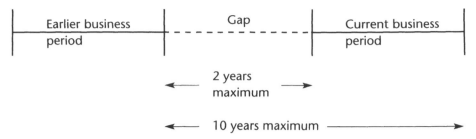

Fig 27.1 An individual owning separate businesses

If the individual concerned has owned separate businesses in the qualifying period, aggregation of the business periods will be allowed, provided that the 'gap' between them is no more than two years, and the earlier business period ended within ten years of the disposal of the current business, as shown in Fig 27.1.

Section 163(1) of the TCGA 1992 provides that retirement relief is given on a 'material disposal of business assets', made by a person eligible for relief at the time of the disposal, either:

(a) because the person is 50 years old (60 years for disposals before 19 March 1991, 55 years for disposals between 19 March 1991 and 28 November 1995); or

(b) because the person has retired on the grounds of ill health below the age of 50 years.

If the individual is retiring on the grounds of ill health, a claim for retirement relief must be submitted together with medical evidence supporting the claim. The Revenue will generally seek advice from the Regional Medical Service of the Department of Social Security, and the individual may be required to be examined by the Regional Medical Officer.

If the individual is 50 years old, retirement relief is *mandatory*, and no claim is needed. Furthermore, the individual need not actually retire and can still work in the business.

Retirement relief may be available in the following situations:

- the disposal of whole or part of a business;
- the disposal of assets which were used in a business which has ceased;
- the disposal of shares in a personal company which is a trading company or the holding company of a trading group;
- the disposal of assets held for the purpose of the individual's employment.

1. The disposal of whole or part of a business

If only part of the business is disposed of, it must be a material part of the business and not just a business asset to be eligible for relief – *McGregor (HMIT)* v *Adcock* [1977] STC 206.

The courts will look to see if there is a material change in the business and not just in its assets.

EXAMPLE

Rose owned a flower shop and in May 2001, at the age of 58, she sold the business realising a gain of £250 000. She had owned the business for eight years. Rose continued to work part-time under a service contract with the new owners.

Retirement relief

	£
80% × £50 000	40 000
80% × £200 000	160 000

	£
	40 000
plus 50% (£160 000 – £40 000)	60 000
Maximum relief available to Rose	100 000

	£
Realised gain	250 000
less Retirement relief	(100 000)
Gain eligible for taper	150 000

Retirement relief is only available in respect of business assets, if the business holds chargeable assets as investments, these will not qualify for relief and will be chargeable in full.

EXAMPLE

George is aged 52 years and he disposed of his business in May 2002. The gains on disposal are:

	£
Goodwill	35 000
Freehold factory	165 000
Shares in quoted companies	25 000
	225 000

If George had owned his business for 20 years, his retirement relief would be:

	£
Gains eligible for retirement relief:	
Goodwill	35 000
Factory	165 000
	200 000

The shares are not chargeable business assets and so do not qualify for relief. As George has owned the business for at least ten years, he is entitled to retirement relief as follows:

	£
	50 000
plus 50% (£200 000 – £50 000)	75 000
Maximum relief	125 000

If George had only owned the business for six years, his relief would be:

60% × £50 000 = £30 000
60% × £200 000 = £120 000

	£
	30 000
plus 50% (£120 000 – £30 000)	45 000
Maximum relief	75 000

	£
Total gains	225 000
less Retirement relief	(75 000)
Indexed gain (eligible taper)	150 000

2. The disposal of assets after cessation

Where a business ceases and prior to the cessation the individual was 50 years old or retired on the grounds of ill health, retirement relief can be extended to the disposal of privately owned assets that were used in the business. The individual must have reached 50 years or retired on ill health grounds before the business ceased and not merely before the asset was disposed of. Retirement relief will be available on the disposal of any such assets within 12 months of the cessation of the business, although the Revenue may allow a longer period.

3. The disposal of shares in a personal company

Retirement relief is given on the sale of shares in an individual's personal company, provided that the usual conditions are satisfied. Relief is restricted to the gains on the chargeable business assets. If the company holds chargeable assets that are not business assets, e.g. quoted investments, the gain eligible for relief is restricted as follows:

$$\text{Total gain (after indexation)} \times \frac{\text{Chargeable business assets}}{\text{Chargeable assets}}$$

Chargeable assets includes goodwill, land, buildings, plant and machinery (provided that they do not fall within the chattel exemptions) but excludes stock, debtors, cash, etc. Chargeable business assets refers to assets used for the purposes of the business and specifically excludes chargeable assets merely held as investments.

EXAMPLE

George held 50 per cent of the shares in XYZ Ltd. He had bought the shares on 6 October 1987 for £200 000, and had been a full-time working director of the company since that date. George, who is 55 years old, sold his shares on 6 October 2002 for £800 000 when he retired from the company. The company's net assets on 6 October 2002 were:

	£
Goodwill	50 000
Plant*	70 000
Quoted investments	100 000
Factory	980 000
Net current assets	400 000
	1 600 000

* Made up of items with a value in excess of £6000.

STEP 1 – calculate the gain on the disposal.

	£
Proceeds	800 000
less Cost	(200 000)
	600 000

Indexation to April 1998:

$$\frac{162.6 - 102.9}{102.9} = 0.580$$

0.580 × 200 000	(116 000)
Indexed gain	484 000

STEP 2 – calculate the gain eligible for retirement relief.

	£
Goodwill	50 000
Plant	70 000
Factory	980 000
Chargeable business assets	1 100 000
Investments	100 000
Total chargeable assets	1 200 000

$$\text{Gain eligible for business reliefs} = \frac{1\,100\,000}{1\,200\,000} \times £484\,000 = £443\,667$$

STEP 3 - calculate the maximum retirement relief.

	£
	50 000
plus 0.5 (200 000 – 50 000)	75 000
Maximum retirement relief	125 000

Retirement relief is given *after* any indexation up until April 1998 but *before* any taper relief is given.

Step 4 – calculate the gain eligible for taper relief.

	Business assets £	Non-business assets £	Total £
Gain	443 667	40 333	484 000
less Retirement relief	(125 000)	(nil)	(125 000)
Gain eligible for taper relief	318 667	40 333	359 000

Step 5 – calculate the taxable gain.

	£
Gain eligible for taper relief	359 000
less Taper 75%	(269 250)
Chargeable gain	89 750
less AE	(7 700)
Taxable gain	82 050

NB: The business rate of taper relief will apply to the gain on the company shares regardless of the use of the chargeable assets held by the company, even though the gain on the non-business assets does not qualify for retirement relief.

If there is a disposal of shares in a holding company, the fraction of the gain eligible for retirement relief must take into account assets held as investments by the entire group. Shares held in subsidiaries are ignored to prevent double counting.

EXAMPLE

Alfred has owned 20 per cent of his personal holding company, B Ltd, for the last 12 years. At the age of 58 he retires, selling his shares and realising a gain of £190 000.

B Ltd owns 80 per cent of C Ltd, 60 per cent of D Ltd and 100 per cent of E Ltd. The group's chargeable assets and chargeable business assets are as follows (ignoring shares in subsidiaries):

	Chargeable business assets (£)	Other chargeable assets (£)
B Ltd	–	200 000
C Ltd	400 000	200 000
D Ltd	300 000	–
E Ltd	300 000	300 000

	£
C Ltd 80% × £400 000	320 000
D Ltd 60% × £300 000	180 000
E Ltd 100% × £300 000	300 000
Chargeable business assets	800 000
C Ltd 80% × £600 000	480 000
D Ltd 60% × £300 000	180 000
E Ltd 100% × £600 000	600 000
Chargeable assets	1 260 000

Retirement relief is restricted to:

$$\frac{800\,000}{1\,260\,000} \times £190\,000 = \underline{\underline{£120\,635}}$$

4. The disposal of assets held for the purpose of the individual's employment

Retirement relief can also be extended to the disposal of personally owned assets used by the individual's personal company or partnership, provided that the asset is disposed of after the individual has disposed of his shares or interest in the partnership, and that they are entitled to retirement relief under the main legislation.

Note: There is no relief available if the asset is sold prior to disposing of the shares or partnership interest.

The relief is also available if rent has been charged for the use of the assets. If the rent had been at a commercial rate, no relief would be allowed, otherwise relief is given on a reasonable basis.

Earlier disposals

As maximum retirement relief is only given once during a lifetime, the maximum amount of relief that is available on a qualifying disposal is reduced by any retirement relief that has been given on an earlier disposal.

Husband and wife

Where a business has been transferred from a spouse either during a lifetime or on death, the taxpayer can elect to 'step into the shoes' of the transferor spouse when considering the relevant period for retirement relief.

EXAMPLE

Joe Bloggs ran a business for 15 years and then gave the business to his wife. She continued to run the business for a further six years and then sold it realising a gain of £400 000 when she was 60 years old. She had not previously claimed any retirement relief.

If she does not elect to have the qualifying period extended by reference to Joe's earlier period of ownership, her maximum retirement relief would be:

2002/03

	£
60% × £50 000	30 000
60% × £200 000	120 000

	£
	30 000
plus 50% (£120 000 – £30 000)	45 000
Maximum retirement relief	75 000

If she made the election, on the assumption that Joe had not previously claimed retirement relief, her maximum relief would be calculated as if she had owned the business from the time that Joe had owned it.

As the period of ownership is greater than ten years, maximum relief is available:

	£
	50 000
plus 50% (£200 000 − £50 000)	75 000
Maximum relief	125 000

Clearly in this situation she would be better off making the election.

On the other hand, if Joe had previously claimed retirement relief of £70 000, her position would be:

	£
Maximum relief on disposal	125 000
less Previous retirement relief	(70 000)
Maximum relief	55 000

Care must therefore be taken in deciding whether or not an election should be made. In this example, because of Joe's previous retirement relief, she would have been better off not making the election.

Retirement relief is to be phased out from 6 April 1999, as it will become unnecessary when the benfits derived from taper relief become more substantial in a few years time. For tax years 1998/99 onwards, the relief will be gradually reduced as the value of the taper becomes more significant, the relief being fully withdrawn by the years 2003/04 as follows:

Tax year	Lower limit £	Upper limit £
1998/99	250 000	1 000 000
1999/00	200 000	800 000
2000/01	150 000	600 000
2001/02	100 000	400 000
2002/03	50 000	200 000
2003/04	nil	nil

During the phasing out of the relief, the methods of calculation will remain unchanged, the relief being given *after* any indexation up until April 1998, but *before* any taper relief is given.

Gift relief

Disposals by way of a gift, or sales at an undervalue, i.e. not a bargain at arm's length, between persons resident or ordinarily resident in the UK between 1980 and 1989 were eligible for gift relief, i.e. the gain on disposal could be 'held over' until the asset was subsequently sold.

General gift relief was introduced in order to avoid double taxation, because under capital transfer tax (CTT) lifetime gifts were chargeable to CTT. When inheritance tax (IHT) was introduced in 1986, the charge on most lifetime transfers was removed. As a result of this, gift relief was being used merely to avoid tax. Consequently, general gift relief was withdrawn by the FA 1989, but retained for certain qualifying assets provided:

(a) the claim is made on a disposal not at arm's length, i.e., gift or sale at an undervalue, within six years from the date of transfer;

(b) the transferee is resident or ordinarily resident in the UK; and

(c) the claim is made by both the transferor and transferee except that only the transferor makes a claim where the transferees are trustees of a settlement.

The result is that the transferor's gain is not chargeable at the time of disposal and the amount of the held-over gain is deducted from the transferee's base cost for a future disposal.

The following assets qualify for gift relief:

1. Where the transfer is immediately chargeable to IHT (TCGA 1992, s 260)

Lifetime transfers into or from a discretionary trust are immediately chargeable to IHT, and gift relief may be claimed under s 260 to hold over the gain if:

- the disposal is made by an individual or the trustees of a discretionary trust; and

- the disposal is made to an individual or the trustees of a discretionary trust.

It makes no difference that no IHT is actually payable because it falls within the nil rate band; it is still chargeable, but at 0 per cent, and so is eligible for gift relief.

2. Where the assets transferred are business assets (TCGA 1992, s 165)

The following business assets are eligible for gift relief:

(a) assets used in a trade, profession or vocation carried on by the transferor or his personal company (defined as for retirement relief);

(b) agricultural property; and

(c) shares and securities of the transferors personal company (as defined for retirement relief) or the shares are unquoted and not dealt with on the unlisted securities market.

3. Transfers to political parties

4. Transfers of heritage property

5. Transfers to heritage maintenance funds

Gift relief on the transfer of shares and securities to a company is withdrawn for transfers on or after 9 November 1999.

The relief

The gain can be held over in full where:

(a) there is no consideration for the transfer, e.g. gifts and most transfers into trusts; or

(b) any consideration paid is less than the allowable expenditure available to the transferor, e.g. transfers at an undervalue to a connected person.

EXAMPLE 1

On 6 June 2002, James transfers a non-business asset worth £100 000 into a discretionary trust. James had bought the asset in June 1987 for £40 000. Assume indexation of 70 per cent to April 1998:

	£
Market value	100 000
less Cost	(40 000)
Unindexed gain	60 000
less Indexation:	
70% × £40 000	(28 000)
Indexed gain*	32 000
Gift relief (s 260)	(32 000)
Chargeable gain	nil

Trustees base cost:	£
Market value June 2002	100 000
less Held-over gain	(32 000)
Base cost	68 000

EXAMPLE 2

George sells a business asset to his son Geoffrey for £6000 in September 2002. George had bought the asset for £8000 in 1980 and it was valued at £14 000 on 31 March 1982. In September 2002 the asset was worth £40 000. Assume indexation of 80 per cent.

September 2002	Cost (£)	Market value (£)
Market value September 2002	40 000	40 000
less Cost : MV 31/3/82	(8 000)	(14 000)
Unindexed gain	32 000	26 000
less Indexation:		
80% × £14 000	(11 200)	(11 200)
Indexed gain	20 800	14 800

	£
Indexed gain	14 800
less Gift relief	(14 800)
Chargeable gain	nil

Geoffrey's base cost for any future disposal will be:

	£
Market value September 2002	40 000
less Held-over gain	(14 800)
Base cost	25 200

Gift relief is deducted before taper relief.

Where the allowable expenditure is less than the consideration received for the asset, only part of the gain can be held over; the amount chargeable is the cash gain.

EXAMPLE

John sold a business asset to his nephew for £60 000 in May 2002. He had bought the asset for £40 000 in September 1985. The market value of the asset in May 2002 was £100 000. Assume that the indexation allowance to April 1998 is £15 000 and gift relief is claimed.

May 2002	£
Market value	100 000
less Allowable expenditure	(40 000)
	60 000
less Indexation	(25 000)
Indexed gain	35 000
less Chargeable gain (60 000 – 40 000)	(20 000)
Gain eligible gift relief	15 000
less Gift relief	(15 000)
	nil

John's indexed gain on the disposal is £20 000, i.e. the difference between the sale proceeds and the allowable cost, and claims hold-over relief on £15 000. The £20 000 indexed gain is eligible for taper relief.

The base cost of the shares to John's nephew will be:

	£
Market value	100 000
less Held-over gain (s 165)	(15 000)
Base cost	85 000

If during the period of ownership the asset has been used for non-business purposes, the portion of the gain relating to the non-business use cannot be held over.

In the same way, where there is a disposal of shares in a company that owns non-business assets, the amount of the gain that can be held over is restricted as for retirement relief. The amount of the gain qualifying for gift relief is calculated as:

$$\text{Gain} \times \frac{\text{Chargeable business assets}}{\text{Chargeable assets}}$$

Where retirement relief and gift relief are available, retirement relief is given first and the balance is available for gift relief.

EXAMPLE

In November 2002, Mary, aged 55 years, retired and handed over her business to her son. Mary had bought the business in 1985 and realised an indexed gain of £270 000 on the disposal, in respect of goodwill and business premises. The market value of the business in November 2002 was £350 000.

As Mary had owned the business for over ten years, maximum retirement relief is available:

	£
	50 000
plus 50% (£200 000 – £500 000)	75 000
Maximum retirement relief	125 000

As all the assets are business assets, gift relief is also available, provided an election is made within six years:

	£
Indexed gain	270 000
less Retirement relief	(125 000)
	145 000
less Gift relief	(145 000)
Chargeable gain	nil

Base cost for a future disposal:

	£
Market value	350 000
less Gift relief	(145 000)
Base cost	205 000

Where the chargeable assets are not all chargeable business assets, only the gain attributable to business assets can be rolled over since 1989.

EXAMPLE

Mrs Diamond had been a director of Gems Ltd since she bought the entire share capital for £70 000 in 1985. She retired in July 2001 at the age of 52 years and sold all her shares to her nephew for £190 000. The value of the shares in July 2001 was £460 000.

The assets of Gem Ltd and the values in July 2001 were:

	£
Freehold premises	250 000
Goodwill	80 000
Quoted investments	50 000
Stock	30 000
Debtors	40 000
Cash	10 000
	460 000

Assume indexation of 50 per cent to April 1998:

	£
Market value	460 000
less Cost	(70 000)
	390 000

less Indexation:	
50% × £70 000	(35 000)
Indexed gain	355 000

Gain attributable to business assets:

$$£355\,000 \times \frac{330\,000}{380\,000} = £308\,290$$

Maximum retirement relief:

	£
	100 000
plus 50% (£308 290 – £100 000)	104 145
	204 145

	Business assets £	Non-business assets £	Total £
Gain	308 290	46 710	355 000
less Retirement relief	(204 145)	(nil)	(204 145)
	104 145	46 710	150 855
less Gift relief	(104 145)	(nil)	(104 145)
Untapered gain	nil	46 710	46 710

Maximum gift relief:

	£
Gain	355 000
less Excess proceeds (190 000 – 70 000)	(120 000)
	235 000

Resticted to:

$$£235\,000 \times \frac{330\,000}{380\,000} = £204\,078$$

This is restricted to the amount eligible for business reliefs, after deducting the retirement relief, i.e. £104 145.

The base cost of the shares to the nephew:

	£
Market value July 2001	460 000
less Gift relief	(104 145)
Base cost for future disposal	355 855

Replacement of business assets

When a business asset is disposed of and the proceeds are reinvested in a replacement asset, roll-over relief may be available. The assets eligible for relief must be within the following groups of assets, although the old asset and the replacement asset need not be both from the same group:

(a) land and buildings occupied for trading purposes (*Note*: land held by a dealer in land as trading stock is not eligible for relief);

(b) fixed plant and machinery which does not form part of a building; moveable plant is not eligible – *Williams* v *Evans (HMIT)* [1982] STC 498;

(c) ships, aircraft, hovercraft;

(d) satellites, space stations, spacecraft;

(e) goodwill; and

(f) milk and potato quotas and, from 1 January 1993, ewe and suckler cow premium quotas.

From the 1st April 2002 purchases of goodwill and quotas will no longer qualify as acquisitions for the purpose of capital gains roll-over relief, following the new rules introduced for expenditure incurred on the creation, acquisition, enhancement and maintenance of intangible assets (see chapter 31).

The following conditions must also be met:

(a) Both the old asset and the replacement asset must be used for business purposes by the person claiming relief, or his personal company (as defined for retirement relief), carried on concurrently or successively, provided that the length of time between the trades is not more than three years. The successive trades do not have to be the same; e.g. if a greengrocer sells his business and then buys a sports shop with the proceeds, the gains arising from the disposal of qualifying assets from the greengrocery business can be rolled over into qualifying assets in the sports shop.

(b) The reinvestment should be made within a period commencing 12 months before and ending 36 months after the disposal of the old asset. However, the Revenue do have the discretion to allow a longer period if necessary, e.g. where there is intention to replace the old asset and the delay is outside the taxpayer's control.

(c) Once the replacement asset has been acquired, there should not be a significant delay in bringing the asset into use in the business – *Campbell Connelly & Co Ltd* v *Barnett* [1994] STC 50.

If all the conditions are met, a claim for relief must be made within six years from the end of the year of assessment in which the disposal of old asset occurs.

Relief is also given by extra statutory concession in the following circumstances:

(a) where the disposal proceeds are used to enhance the value of existing assets (ESC D 22);

(b) where the disposal proceeds are used to acquire a further interest in an existing asset, e.g. extension of a leasehold (ESC D 25);

(c) where the same asset is sold and repurchased, provided that the transaction is for *bona fide* commercial reasons (ESC D 16);

(d) division of land on the dissolution of a partnership (ESC D 23);

(e) where the replacement asset is not brought into use immediately because capital work on the asset is being carried out, provided that on completion of this work the asset is then brought into use by the business (ESC D 24).

The effect of the relief is to defer the gain on disposal, the amount deferred being deducted from the cost of the replacement asset.

The FA 1999 introduced legislation to be effective from 9 March 1999, to ensure that tax deferred under a concession is duly paid.

Proceeds wholly invested in the replacement asset

The entire gain on the old asset can be deferred where the sale proceeds are wholly reinvested, provided the new asset is not a depreciating asset.

EXAMPLE

A trader bought a freehold factory on 6 August 1987 for £80 000 and sold it for £180 000 on 6 July 2002. He bought a new factory on 6 May 2002 for £200 000. Assume indexation of 80 per cent to April 1998.

As all the proceeds of sale, £180 000 are reinvested the whole of the gain can be rolled over into the cost of the new factory.

	£
Proceeds	180 000
less Cost	(80 000)
	100 000
less Indexation	
80% × £80 000	(64 000)
Indexed gain	36 000
less Roll-over relief	(36 000)
Chargeable gain	nil

The base cost of the new factory is reduced by the amount rolled over for any future disposal:

	£
Cost of new factory	200 000
less Rolled-over gain	(36 000)
Base cost	164 000

Proceeds not wholly invested in the replacement asset

If the entire proceeds are not reinvested in a non-depreciating asset, part of the gain on disposal will be chargeable. The chargeable gain is the lower of:

(a) the proceeds not reinvested; and

(b) the gain on the old asset.

EXAMPLE

A trader bought an asset for £30 000 and sold it for £60 000. Suppose a replacement non-depreciating asset was bought for:

(a)   £30 000
(b)   £40 000
(c)   £55 000

Assume the indexation allowance was £3000.

First calculate the gain on the asset:

	£
Proceeds	60 000
less Cost	(30 000)
	30 000
less Indexation	(3 000)
Gain on asset (1)	27 000

Calculate the amount not reinvested:

	£	£	£
	(a)	(b)	(c)
Proceeds	60 000	60 000	60 000
Cost of new asset	(30 000)	(40 000)	(55 000)
Amount not reinvested (2)	30 000	20 000	5 000

The chargeable gain is the lower of (1) and (2).

	(a)	(b)	(c)
Chargeable gain	27 000	20 000	5 000

Roll-over relief:

	(a)	(b)	(c)
Gain	27 000	27 000	27 000
less Chargeable gain	(27 000)	(20 000)	(5 000)
Gain rolled over	nil	7 000	22 000

Base cost of new asset:

	(a)	(b)	(c)
Cost	30 000	40 000	55 000
less Roll-over relief	(nil)	(7 000)	(22 000)
Base cost	30 000	33 000	33 000

If the asset has not been used for the purpose of trade throughout the period of ownership, only that part of the gain relating to the business use can be rolled over.

EXAMPLE

Charles had bought a shop in June 1985 for £30 000 from which he ran his greengrocery business. The shop had private accommodation agreed to be $\frac{1}{3}$. In November 2002 he sold the shop for £75 000 and in December 2002 bought a newsagents shop for £60 000, which had no private accommodation. Assume indexation to be 70 per cent.

	£	£
	Business ($\frac{2}{3}$)	Private ($\frac{1}{3}$)
Proceeds	50 000	25 000
less Cost	(20 000)	(10 000)
	30 000	15 000
less Indexation:		
70% × £20 000 : £10 000	(14 000)	(7 000)
Indexed gain	16 000	8 000

As all the proceeds from the business portion, i.e. £50 000 are reinvested in the new shop, Charles can claim roll-over relief on the whole of the gain relating to the business portion:

	£
Gain ($\frac{2}{3}$)	16 000
less Roll-over relief	(16 000)
Untapered gain	nil

Base cost of newsagents shop for a future disposal:

	£
Cost December 2002	60 000
less Rolled-over gain	(16 000)
Base cost	44 000

NB: In all these cases consideration should be given to the value of the taper available in order to achieve the best outcome:

	Business	Non-business	Total
	£	£	£
indexed gain	16 000	8 000	24 000
less taper (75%/15%)	(12 000)	(1 200)	(13 200)
	4 000	6 800	10 800
		less AE	(7 700)
		Taxable	3 100

The base cost in this case would remain at £60 000.

Replacement with a depreciating asset

Special rules apply where the replacement asset is a depreciating asset. In this case the gain on the old asset is deferred until the earliest of the following events:

(a) the replacement asset is disposed of;

(b) the replacement asset ceases to be used for the purpose of trade; or

(c) ten years have elapsed since the replacement asset was acquired.

When any one of the above events occurs, the held-over gain crystallises.

EXAMPLE

Martin purchased a freehold factory in June 1982 for £60 000 and sold it in June 1992 for £120 000. On 20 April 1992 he had acquired a 40-year lease on a replacement factory for £130 000. Martin still holds the lease on 20 April 2002. Assume indexation between June 1992 and June 1982 to be 40 per cent.

Disposal June 1992

	£
Proceeds	120 000
Cost	(60 000)
	60 000
less Indexation:	
40% × £60 000	(24 000)
Indexed gain	36 000

Martin reinvests the proceeds in a depreciating asset, i.e. the 40-year lease, and so the gain of £36 000 can be held over until the earliest of:

- the disposal of the lease; or
- the lease ceasing to be used for trade; or
- 20 April 2002;

at which point the gain crystallises. Therefore, the held-over gain crystallises on 20 April 2002 and becomes chargeable in 2002/03.

If, however, during this period a non-depreciating asset is acquired, the held-over gain may be rolled over into the new non-depreciating asset in the usual way.

EXAMPLE

Henry bought a freehold factory in May 1994 for £15 000 which was used wholly for business purposes. In May 1997 he sold the freehold for £30 000 and in June 1997 bought fixed machinery for £35 000. In June 2000 he bought another freehold for £28 000. Assume indexation of 30 per cent between May 1994 and May 1997.

Disposal May 1997

	£
Proceeds	30 000
less Cost	(15 000)
	15 000
less Indexation:	
30% × £15 000	(4 500)
Indexed gain	10 500

As Henry invested the proceeds in a depreciating asset, the gain of £10 500 can be held over until the earliest of the three events occurs. However, if before any of the three events a non-depreciating asset is acquired, then the held-over gain can be rolled over into the new non-depreciating asset, making the usual adjustments for proceeds not reinvested.

June 2000
The held-over gain can be rolled over:

	£
Held-over gain	10 500
less Proceeds not reinvested	
(£30 000 – £28 000)	(2 000)
Gain rolled over	8 500

The amount not rolled over, i.e. £2000, continues to be held over until the earliest of the three events at which point it becomes chargeable. The base cost of the freehold acquired in June 2000 will be:

	£
Cost of freehold	28 000
less Rolled-over gain	(8 500)
Base cost	19 500

Where roll-over relief has been claimed, the taper on a subsequent disposal is calculated by reference of the holding period of the replacement asset, and not the asset which it replaced.

Reinvestment relief

The FA 1993 introduced a form of relief that allowed the gains realised on unquoted shares in qualifying companies to be rolled over into the cost of replacement shares in a qualifying unquoted company.

This was extended by the FA 1994, for disposals on or after 30 November 1993, by allowing reinvestment relief to be claimed against the gains of any chargeable assets that are reinvested in unquoted shares in a qualifying company, within a period commencing 12 months before and ending 36 months after the disposal.

Note: Reinvestment relief is available where the *gain* is reinvested, unlike roll-over relief, which is available when the *proceeds* are reinvested.

The relief is available to individuals resident or ordinarily resident in the UK, and the reinvestment must be for ordinary shares in an unquoted trading company which is not involved in any of the following excluded trades:

● dealing in land, commodities, futures or shares;
● dealing in goods other than for ordinary wholesale or retail distribution;
● banking, insurance and other financial activities;
● leasing;
● legal and accountancy services;
● farming;
● property development.

Clawback of relief

Relief may be clawed back if within three years of the reinvestment in the shares any of the following occurs:

- the shares cease to be ordinary shares;
- the company ceases to be a qualifying company;
- the taxpayer ceases to be resident or ordinarily resident in the UK.

For investments after 26 November 1996, the rules for reinvestment relief are to be modified by including investment in groups that include non-UK subsidiaries, provided that the funds are invested in a trade which is carried on mainly in the UK and 80 per cent of its activities are qualifying. Clearance procedures for reinvestment relief are to be introduced to assist those companies looking to attract potential investors.

EXAMPLE

Mr Granger, who is 56 years old, has been a full-time working director in Fields Ltd since September 1985. He retired in February 2003 when he sold his shares in Fields Ltd, which he had held since December 1985, realising a gain of £350 000. In July 2003 he purchased ordinary shares in an unquoted company for £400 000.

Mr Granger qualifies for both retirement relief and reinvestment relief. Reinvestment relief of £350 000 could be claimed as the whole of the gain is reinvested, but this would have the effect of reducing the base cost of his shares to:

	£
Cost of shares	400 000
less Reinvestment relief	
(i.e. rolled-over gain)	(350 000)
Base cost	50 000

As retirement relief is available the maximum would be:

	£
	50 000
plus 50% (200 000 – 50 000)	75 000
Maximum retirement relief	125 000

If Mr Granger claims reinvestment relief to cover that part of the gain which would otherwise be chargeable, there is no immediate charge to CGT, and only £100 000 is rolled over into the cost of the new shares:

	£
Gain	350 000
less Retirement relief	(125 000)
	225 000
less Reinvestment relief	(225 000)
Chargeable gain	nil

Base cost of new shares:

Cost of shares	400 000
less Rolled-over (reinvestment relief)	(225 000)
Base cost	175 000

The FA 1998 introduced legislation to combine the benefits of the EIS and CGT reinvestment relief to create a unified scheme, whereby chargeable gains reinvested in qualifying shares by individuals and trustees can obtain unlimited deferral (*see* Chapter 16).

Transfer of a business to a company

When an unincorporated business is transferred to a company, there is a potential CGT liability on the disposal of the business assets to the newly formed company. Because this may have the effect of discouraging incorporation, reliefs are available. On the transfer of a business to a company, relief may be obtained in the following ways:

1. Reinvestment relief

For disposals after 30 November 1993, reinvestment relief may be used in order to defer the gain arising on the disposal of business assets to the company. This relief is considered fully under 'reinvestment relief' above.

2. Roll-over into shares

Provided that the consideration received by the taxpayer is wholly or partly for shares in the company, the gain on the disposal of the business assets to the company can be rolled over into the cost of the shares under the provisions of the TCGA 1992, s 162. This has the effect of deferring the gain until the shares are subsequently disposed of.

The conditions necessary for s 162 to apply are:

(a) the business must be transferred as a going concern;

(b) the consideration for the transfer is wholly or partly in exchange for shares in the company; and

(c) all the assets, other than cash, must be transferred to the company.

Relief under s 162 is given automatically and so no claim is necessary provided that *all* the assets of the unincorporated business are transferred. Because of this fact s 162 can be avoided by not transferring a non-cash asset.

Incorporation relief under S162 will not apply for businesses incorporated on, or after 6th April 2002 provided a claim is made within two years of the 31st January following the end of the year of assessment in which the business was transferred.

The amount of the gain that can be rolled over is calculated as:

$$\text{Indexed gain} \times \frac{\text{Market value of shares}}{\text{Market value of whole consideration}}$$

EXAMPLE

Mr Preston, who had traded for many years, transferred his business to a company on 1 May 2002 in exchange for 45 000 £1 ordinary shares and £20 000 cash. The assets and liabilities transferred were:

	Cost (£)	MV 31/3/82 (£)	MV 1/5/02 (£)
Freehold building	10 000	18 000	40 000
Equipment	5 000	6 000	3 000
Goodwill	nil	5 000	20 000
Debtors	nil	2 000	4 000
Creditors	nil	(1 000)	(2 000)
			65 000

Assume indexation to be 80 per cent.

Freehold building

	Cost £	MV 31/3/82 £
MV 1/5/02	40 000	40 000
less Cost : MV 31/3/82	(10 000)	(18 000)
	30 000	22 000
less Indexation:		
80% × £18 000	(14 400)	(14 400)
Indexed gain	15 600	7 600

Indexed gain (smaller)

Goodwill

	Cost (£)	MV 31/3/82 (£)
MV 1/5/02	20 000	20 000
less Cost : MV 31/3/82	nil	(5 000)
	20 000	15 000
less Indexation:		
80% × £5000	(4 000)	(4 000)
Indexed gain	16 000	11 000

Indexed gain (smaller)

Equipment – exempt under chattel rules

Total gains on disposal:	£
Building	7 600
Goodwill	11 000
	18 600

	£
Total gains	18 600
less Gain deferred:	
$\dfrac{45\,000}{65\,000} \times £18\,600$	(12 877)
Indexed gain	5 723

The base cost of Mr Preston's shares for any subsequent disposal will then be:

	£
Value shares 1/5/02	45 000
less Deferred gain	(12 877)
Base cost of shares	32 123

3. Roll-over into assets (TCGA 1992, s 165)

Relief under s 165 was considered under 'gift relief' above. The gain on disposal of an asset is rolled over into the cost of the asset in the company, so deferring the gain until the company subsequently disposes of the asset. Relief under s 165 would have to be applied for each asset transferred to the company, but note that this relief is not automatic and the conditions for s 165 relief set out under 'gift relief' must apply.

The effect of using s 165 rather than s 162 is that any subsequent gain will accrue to the company and will not affect the shares. Another important point is that relief under s 165 allows some assets to be retained outside of the company, whereas if s 162 was used, all the assets of the unincorporated business would have to be transferred to the company. Where retirement relief is available as well as roll-over relief, the retirement relief is given in priority so that the roll-over relief can be taken against that part of the gain not covered by retirement relief.

After rebasing was introduced in 1988, the FA 1988 provides that where a liability to CGT has been deferred between 31 March 1982 and 6 April 1988, then only 50 per cent of the held-over gain is deducted from the base cost of the asset.

SELF ASSESSMENT QUESTIONS

27.1 On 25 September 2002 George sold all his shares in his company for £480 000. George, who is 60 years old, has been a full-time working director of the company since he acquired the shares for £60 000 in August 1980. The market value of the shares on 31 March 1982 had been £80 000. The market value of the company's assets on 25 September 2002 was as follows:

	£
Land and buildings	250 000
Goodwill	85 000
Plant and machinery*	80 000
Investment property	50 000
Net current assets	15 000
	480 000

* All items of plant and machinery had a value in excess of £6000.

REQUIRED

Calculate the chargeable gain for 2002/03 arising from the sale of the shares, assuming all possible reliefs are claimed.

27.2 Raymond sold a business property on 14 October 2002 for £150 000. The property had been acquired in July 1988 for £70 000, using all the proceeds from the sale of a property in June 1988. The property that had been sold in June 1988 had cost £30 000 in 1970, and its market value on 31 March 1982 had been £40 000.

REQUIRED

Calculate the chargeable gain arising on the sale of the property in October 2002.

CHAPTER 28

Partnership gains

When a partnership incurs a capital gain, it is not treated as a gain on the firm, but a proportionate gain made by each individual partner in the business.

The special case of partnerships is not dealt with specifically in the legislation, except that the TCGA 1992, s 59 provides that each partner is treated as owning a share in the partnership assets according to the capital sharing arrangements in the partnership agreement. In the absence of capital sharing arrangements, it may be necessary to look at the accounts in order to establish how capital profits and losses are allocated between the partners. If there is no evidence in the accounts, and no capital sharing ratio, then the ordinary profit sharing arrangements will be used as the basis for allocating the individual partner's share of any partnership gains. The proportion of the individual partner's capital input to the business is irrelevant.

Because the legislation does not deal with partnership gains in detail, the Revenue have issued a statement of practice (SP D12), which sets out current Revenue practice regarding the treatment of partnership gains. This chapter examines the main aspects of SP D12.

Partnership assets

When a partnership acquires an asset, the acquisition cost is apportioned between the partners, on the basis of the capital profit sharing ratio. If the asset is sold to a third party, each partner is treated as disposing of a fraction of the asset.

EXAMPLE

Rosemary and Basil set up in partnership in 1980, both contributing equal amounts of capital. They share profits and losses equally and the capital sharing ratio is 60 per cent and 40 per cent respectively. In April 1986 the partnership acquired a property for £55 000, and sold it in December 2002 for £90 000. Assume indexation of 60 per cent to April 1998.

	Total (£)	Rosemary (£)	Basil (£)
Proceeds	90 000	54 000	36 000
less Cost	(55 000)	(33 000)	(22 000)
Unindexed gain	35 000	21 000	14 000
less Indexation:			
£55 000 × 60%	(33 000)	(19 800)	(13 200)
Indexed gain	2 000	1 200	800

The gain is allocated in accordance with the capital profit and loss sharing ratio. If a partnership asset is sold to one of the partners as opposed to a third party, then each partner is treated as disposing of their share in the asset, as in the last example, but the gain on the partner acquiring the asset does not become chargeable at that time, but is 'rolled over' and deducted from the base cost of that asset, so reducing the allowable cost on a future disposal of that asset. The gains accruing to the other partners are chargeable at the time of disposal.

EXAMPLE

Brown, White and Green have been in partnership for many years, sharing capital profits and losses equally. On 10 September 2002 Brown acquired a partnership asset for its then market value of £21 000. The asset had been bought in April 1987 for £6000. Assume indexation of 50 per cent to April 1998.

	Total	Brown	White	Green
	(£)	(£)	(£)	(£)
Proceeds	21 000	7 000	7 000	7 000
less Cost	(6 000)	(2 000)	(2 000)	(2 000)
Unindexed gain	15 000	5 000	5 000	5 000
less Indexation:				
£6 000 × 50%	(3 000)	(1 000)	(1 000)	(1 000)
Indexed gain	12 000	4 000	4 000	4 000

Brown's gain of £4000 is not chargeable in 2002/03 but is 'rolled-over' until such time as the asset is disposed of by reducing Brown's base cost of the asset:

	£
Market value 10/9/02	21 000
less Apportioned gain	(4 000)
Base cost for any future disposal by Brown	17 000

The same rules apply if a partnership asset is transferred to one of the partners. The asset in this case will be deemed to have been disposed of at its market value. This will crystallise a chargeable gain on the partners at the date of disposal, but the partner receiving the asset will not incur a chargeable gain at the time of disposal. Again, the gain will be deducted from the market value of the asset at the date of transfer, and this will form the base cost of the asset for any future disposal.

EXAMPLE

Bream, Roach, and Carp have been in partnership for many years sharing capital profits and losses in the ratio 50 per cent; 25 per cent; 25 per cent respectively. On 16 July 2002 the partnership transferred a partnership asset to Carp, when its market value was £15 000. The partnership had bought the asset in October 1988 for £3000. Assume indexation of 40 per cent for period to April 1998.

	Total (£)	Bream (£)	Roach (£)	Carp (£)
Deemed proceeds	15 000	7 500	3 750	3 750
less Cost	(3 000)	(1 500)	(750)	(750)
Unindexed gain	12 000	6 000	3 000	3 000
less Indexation:				
£3000 × 40%	(1 200)	(600)	(300)	(300)
Indexed gain	10 800	5 400	2 700	2 700

Carp's gain is 'rolled over' into the base cost of the asset:

	£
Market value 16/7/02	15 000
less Apportioned gain	(2 700)
Base cost (for any future disposal by Carp)	12 300

If the disposal results in a loss, the same rules apply, the loss being added to the market value for any future disposal by the partner acquiring the asset.

EXAMPLE

Larch, Oak and Beech, bought a partnership property in March 1983 for £55 000. This was transferred to Beech in July 2002. The property, however, had badly deteriorated over the years and was valued at £50 000 in July 2002. The partners share capital profits and losses in the ratio of 40 per cent; 40 per cent; 20 per cent respectively.

	Total (£)	Larch (£)	Oak (£)	Beech (£)
Deemed proceeds	50 000	20 000	20 000	10 000
less Cost	(55 000)	(22 000)	(22 000)	(11 000)
Unindexed loss	(5 000)	(2 000)	(2 000)	(1 000)
less Indexation:				
Restricted to nil	(nil)	(nil)	(nil)	(nil)
Allowable loss	(5 000)	(2 000)	(2 000)	(1 000)

Beech's base cost for a future disposal will be:

	£
Market value July 2002	50 000
add Allowable loss	1 000
Base cost	51 000

Provided that the transaction is a *bona fide* commercial transaction, the loss relief will not be restricted as a loss to a connected person.

Revaluation of assets in the accounts

The revaluation of assets in the accounts is not a chargeable occasion for CGT. Therefore, a revaluation of assets alone does not give rise to a chargeable gain or an allowable loss, nor is the base cost of the concerned assets altered to reflect this revaluation.

Changes in profit-sharing arrangements

Any change in the allocation of capital profits or losses is effectively a disposal by the partner decreasing his share and an acquisition by the partner whose share is increased. This situation will also arise where there is a change in the partners, i.e. when a partner joins or leaves the partnership.

The way in which changes are dealt with for CGT purposes depends on whether there has been a revaluation of the assets or not prior to the change, and whether there has been any payment made outside of the accounts. We will now examine the three possible situations in turn.

1. No revaluation and no payment made outside of the accounts

Where no payment is made and there has not been a revaluation of the assets prior to the change in sharing arrangements, the disposal is treated as being made on a no gain/no loss basis.

EXAMPLE

Black and White have been in partnership for many years sharing capital profits and losses equally. In June 2002 Gray was admitted to the partnership and from then on capital profits and losses were shared in the ratio of 40 per cent; 40 per cent; 20 per cent respectively. The main partnership asset is a freehold building which cost £105 000 in July 1991. There has been no revaluation of the building in the accounts and no payment is made outside the partnership. Assume indexation of 20 per cent.

Before Gray is admitted to the partnership, Black and White are deemed to own their fractional shares of the asset as:

	Total (£)	Black (£)	White (£)
Original cost	105 000	52 500 (50%)	52 500 (50%)

At this point, Black and White each have a base cost of £52 500 as regards the building.

On Gray's admittance to the partnership in June 2002, Black and White are each deemed to have disposed of 10 per cent of their interest in the building for a consideration of £10 500 each, so that:

	Total (£)	Black (£)	White (£)	Gray (£)
Original cost	105 000	42 000 (40%)	42 000 (40%)	21 000 (20%)

However, as the asset has not been revalued and there is no payment outside the partnership, the transaction is treated as being made for no gain/no loss, thus:

	Total	Black	White
Original cost of disposed part:			
£105 000 × 20%	21 000	10 500	10 500
Indexation:			
£21 000 × 20%	4 200	2 100	2 100
Deemed consideration	25 200	12 600	12 600

Black and White are treated as disposing of 10 per cent each for £10 500 plus indexation and Gray is deemed to have acquired 20 per cent for £21 000 plus indexation, therefore, no gain or loss has arisen.

Where the partnership asset was owned at 31 March 1982 and a partner acquires his share on a no gain/no loss basis after 31 March 1982, then on any disposal of the asset after 5 April 1982 he is treated as if he owned the asset on 31 March 1982 and as such is entitled to rebasing.

2. Changes in profit-sharing arrangements following a revaluation of assets

The situation is somewhat different if there is a change in profit-sharing arrangements following a revaluation. There will be an assessment on any partners whose share has decreased on their share of the change in value. Partners whose shares have increased will have their base costs increased by the amount of the deemed consideration of the disposed fractional share.

EXAMPLE

Hill and Dale have been in partnership since 1983, sharing capital profits and losses equally. The partnership owns a property that had been purchased in October 1989 for £60 000. The property was revalued on 18 July 1999 to £125 000. From 1 January 2003 the partners agreed to change the capital profit sharing ratio to 60 per cent and 40 per cent respectively.

The revaluation itself on 18 July 1999 has no CGT consequences. However, on the change in profit sharing arrangements on 1 January 2003 Hill's share has increased by 10 per cent and Dale's share has decreased by 10 per cent. Therefore, Hill's base cost will need to be adjusted to reflect this increase and Dale will incur a CGT assessment to reflect his disposal of 10 per cent. Assume indexation of 30 per cent.

Dale's chargeable gain:

	£
Deemed proceeds	
(10% × £125 000)	12 500
less Cost	
(10% × £60 000)	(6000)
Unindexed gain	6 500
less Indexation:	
£6000 × 30%	(1800)
Indexed gain	4700

Hill's base cost:

50% × £60 000	30 000
add Deemed consideration	
on 1/1/03	12 500
Revised base cost	42 500

Note: On any future disposal the £30 000 will be indexed from October 1989.

3. Payments made outside the partnership accounts

Any payment on a change of profit-sharing arrangements that is made outside the partnership accounts is included as part of the disposal proceeds.

If the partnership assets have been revalued beforehand, any payment made in respect of those assets is added to the consideration of the partner whose share has been reduced.

If the partnership assets have not been revalued beforehand, the disposal by the partner whose share has been reduced will be treated as taking place on a no gain/no loss basis, and any payment that is made means that a gain will accrue equal to the amount of the payment.

EXAMPLE

Holly, Ivy and Rose have been in partnership since 1985, sharing capital profits and losses in the ratio of 50 per cent; 25 per cent; 25 per cent respectively. On 1 January 2003 Marigold was admitted to the partnership and capital profits and losses were then shared in the ratio of: 30 per cent; 30 per cent; 30 per cent; 10 per cent. Marigold paid Holly £20 000 outside of the accounts for the goodwill. The goodwill had been purchased in July 1985 for £10 000 and revalued in July 1999 at £60 000.

Following Marigold's admission to the partnership on 1 January 2003, Holly is treated as having disposed of 20 per cent of her share in the partnership assets, 10 per cent to Marigold and 5 per cent each to Ivy and Rose. The revaluation in 1999 has no CGT consequences at that time, but on the later change in ratios a chargeable gain will accrue to Holly and the partners whose share has increased. They must have their base costs revised to reflect the increase. As Marigold made a payment of £20 000 to Holly outside the partnership accounts, this must be added to the disposal proceeds:

Assume indexation of 60 per cent.

Holly's gain:

	£
Proceeds (20% × £60 000)	12 000
add Payment	20 000
	32 000
less Cost (20% × £10 000)	(2000)
	30 000
less Indexation:	
£2000 × 60%	(1 200)
Indexed gain	28 800

Base costs:

	Total (£)	Holly (£)	Ivy (£)	Rose (£)	Marigold (£)
Original cost	10 000	5 000	2 500	2 500	–
1/1/03 (20%)	12 000	–	3 000	3 000	6 000
Cost of share sold	(2 000)	(2 000)	–	–	–
Base costs	20 000	3 000	5 500	5 500	6 000

Suppose, however, that there had been no revaluation of the goodwill in 1999. In this case the change in profit-sharing arrangements means that the disposal is treated as taking place for no gain/no loss. If the £20 000 is then added to the disposal proceeds, a gain equal to the £20 000 will accrue to Holly:

Deemed consideration:

	£
Original cost 20% × £10 000	2000
add Indexation:	
£2000 × 60%	1 200
Deemed consideration	3 200

Holly's gain

	£
Deemed proceeds	3 200
add Payment	20 000
	23 200
less Cost	(2 000)
	21 200
less Indexation	(1 200)
Indexed gain	20 000

Connected persons and partnerships

Although partners are generally connected persons, the TCGA 1992, s 286(4) provides that if the acquisition and disposal of partnership assets is a *bona fide* commercial transaction, the special rules for connected persons will not apply. So that where there is a change in profit-sharing ratios and no payment is made, it will be treated as a *bone fide* commercial transaction, provided that the partners are not otherwise connected, e.g. father and daughter, and that no payment would have been made had they not been so connected. If, on the other hand, the daughter had been admitted to the partnership on favourable terms, i.e. payment would have been made had she not been the partner's daughter, then the connected person's rule applies, and the transfer of a share in the partnership assets will be treated as though the market value was paid outside of the accounts.

Mergers

Where there is a partnership merger, the CGT treatment is the same as for changes in profit-sharing arrangements as above. Where gains arise, it will be possible to claim roll-over relief, as there will be a disposal of business assets in the old partnerships and the acquisition of new assets in the merged partnership.

Pensions for retired partners

When a partner retires, if he is paid his share of the partnership assets, it will be a disposal for CGT purposes. In the same way, a purchased life annuity will also be liable to CGT.

However, if the partnership pays a retired partner a pension, it will only be liable to CGT if the capitalised value is excessive. Provided that the individual had been a partner for at least ten years, the annual payment will not be considered excessive if it is not more than two-thirds of the partner's average share of the profits, before capital allowances and charges, in the best three out of the last seven years.

Where the period is less than ten years, the fractional amount that is considered reasonable is as follows:

Table 28.1 Fractional amount of pension for retired partners

Complete years in partnership	Fraction
1–5	1/60 for each year
6	8/60
7	16/60
8	24/60
9	32/60
10 and above	2/3

CHAPTER 29

Overseas aspects of CGT

Whether there is a charge to CGT depends on whether the person making the disposal is resident, ordinarily resident or domiciled in the UK or not. The precise meaning of residence, ordinary residence and domicile are considered more fully in Part 2, Chapter 18.

This chapter examines the charge to CGT where there is a foreign element involved in the disposal.

Persons resident, ordinarily resident and domiciled in the UK

Persons who are resident , ordinarily resident and domiciled in the UK are liable to CGT on their *worldwide* gains.

By concession (ESC D2), persons taking up residence in the UK on or after 6 April 1998, will only be liable to CGT on gains arising after their arrival in the UK, provided that they have not been resident, or ordinarily resident, in the UK at any time during the *five* fiscal years immediately prior to the year of arrival in the UK.

By the same concession, persons leaving the UK on or after 17 March 1998, will not be liable to CGT on gains from disposals made after the date of departure, provided that they were not resident, or ordinarily resident, in the UK for the whole of at least *four* out of the previous *seven* fiscal years immediately prior to the year of departure from the UK.

ESC D2 was revised in 1998 in order to prevent tax avoidance by selling assets during a period of temporary absence from the UK.

Note: Concessions will not be granted by the Revenue if it appears to them that it is being used solely for tax avoidance – *R v IRC ex-p Fulford-Dobson* [1987] STC 344.

Double taxation relief (DTR) is available where foreign tax has been charged on assets situated overseas. Relief for foreign tax paid on gains may be given either under a double tax agreement or by unilateral credit relief. The DTR given, however, cannot be more than the CGT on the disposal (TCGA 1992, s 277).

Section 278 of the TCGA 1992 also provides that the foreign tax paid can be used instead as a deduction in calculating the gain on disposal, if this would be more advantageous to the taxpayer than DTR; e.g. if the taxpayer is claiming 'roll-over relief' on the asset, s 278 would be more tax efficient, as the gain being 'rolled over' would be less, making the base cost for the replacement asset higher in the event of any future disposal.

If, due to circumstances beyond the taxpayer's control, the proceeds of any overseas gains cannot be remitted to the UK, the taxpayer can claim to have the chargeable gain deferred until such time as the proceeds can be transferred to the UK (TCGA 1992, s 279).

Persons resident, ordinarily resident *but not* UK domiciled

Persons resident, or ordinarily resident, but not domiciled in the UK are liable to CGT on any UK gains on an arising basis, but any gains made on assets situated outside the UK, are only liable to CGT if the gain is remitted to the UK.

As UK resident and domiciled persons are taxed on their worldwide gains, the location of assets is only significant when considering the tax liability of a foreigner on a remittance basis. Tangible property presents no difficulties: assets, such as land and chattels, are obviously located in the place where they are physically situated at the time of disposal. The location of intangible assets, such as goodwill and debts, is not so obvious. Section 275 of the TCGA 1992 sets out the rules for determining the location of assets for CGT purposes as follows:

Table 29.1 Location of assets for CGT purposes

Asset	Location
1. Tangible moveable property (chattels)	Physical location at the time of disposal
2. Tangible immovable property (e.g. land)	Physical location
3. Debts (secured and unsecured)	Wherever the creditor is resident
4. Government securities	The country of that government
5. Shares and securities	Country where the share register is kept
6. Goodwill	Where the business is carried on
7. Trademarks and patents	Where they are registered
8. Judgment debts	Where the judgement is recorded
9. Ships and aircraft	Only considered to be situated in the UK if the owner is resident in the UK

Overseas losses, however, cannot be remitted to the UK, and so are not allowable losses for CGT purposes.

EXAMPLE

Franco, who is resident in the UK but domiciled overseas, has the following gains and losses for 2002/03.

	£
Gain on overseas property	15 000
Gain on UK chattel	3 200
Gain on UK shares	9 000
Loss on overseas shares	(5 000)

The overseas property was sold for £40 000 and Franco remitted £8 000 to the UK from the proceeds during 2002/03.

Part of gain remitted to the UK	$\dfrac{£\,8\,000}{£40\,000} \times £15\,000 = £3\,000$

The loss on the overseas shares is not allowable for CGT purposes, i.e. it cannot be remitted to the UK.

Franco's chargeable gain 2002/03:

	£
UK shares	9 000
UK chattel	3 200
Gain remitted	3 000
	15 200
less Annual Exemption (AE)	(7 700)
Taxable gain	7 500

Non-UK resident persons

Generally persons not resident in the UK are not liable to CGT, even on assets situated in the UK. There are, however, two exceptions to this general rule:

(a) where the non-resident person is carrying on a business in the UK through a branch or agency; and

(b) in certain circumstances the gains of non-resident companies may be apportioned to UK shareholders who are resident and ordinarily resident in the UK (and domiciled in the case of individuals).

We will now examine each of these situations:

Carrying on a UK business through a branch or agency (TCGA 1992, s 10)

Although non-UK residents are not normally liable to CGT, there will be a charge on the disposal of any UK assets that have been used in, held or acquired for the purposes of the branch or agency.

The non-UK resident cannot avoid a charge to CGT by exporting the assets prior to disposal. In this case the TCGA 1992, s 25 provides that the non-resident is deemed to have disposed of the asset at its market value immediately prior to its export from the UK. Similarly, if there is a cessation of the branch or agency before disposing of the assets, the assets used in the business are deemed to have been disposed of, for their market value, immediately before the cessation.

Note: ESC D2 does not apply to gains on UK branch assets in the year of departure.

Because of the EU directive on cross-border mergers and transfers, any gain accruing because of the above provisions will be deemed to take place for no gain/no loss where a trade carried on in the UK is transferred from a company resident in one member state to a company resident in another member state, provided that certain conditions are met.

Conditions:
- both companies must make a claim;
- the transfer is wholly in exchange for shares;
- the transfer is for *bona fide* commercial reasons;
- the transferee company would be liable to UK tax on the assets transferred if they were disposed of immediately.

Both companies can seek advance clearance from the Revenue.

CHAPTER 30

Capital gains tax on estates and trusts

Capital gains tax on estates

Death itself is not a chargeable occasion for CGT. The personal representatives (PRs) are deemed to have acquired the assets at their market value at the date of death (TCGA 1992, s 62(1)).

EXAMPLE

Henry dies on 15 February 2003. His estate includes 2000 shares in Allgoods Ltd which Henry had purchased in September 1988 for £1500. The probate value of the shares is £4750. The PRs are deemed to have acquired the shares for £4750 in February 2003. This will be the PRs' base cost if they dispose of the shares at a later date.

Any assets passed on to a legatee under the terms of the will are not subject to CGT, the legatee is deemed to have acquired them at market value at the date of death (TCGA 1992, s 62(4)).

EXAMPLE

James died on 2 March 2001. His estate included shares in XYZ Ltd that he had bought in October 1983 for £6000. The probate value of the shares was £14 000. The shares were transferred to Sally on 8 September 2002 when the administration of the estate was completed. The shares were valued at £16 000 on 8 September 2002. The PRs are deemed to have acquired the shares at their market value at the date of death, i.e. £14 000. When the asset was passed to the legatee, Sally is deemed to have acquired them for a base cost of £14 000 (not £16 000), the value of the asset when it was transferred to her. The PRs' acquisition is deemed to be the legatee's acquisition.

Therefore, in both these instances, the assets are in effect subject to a 'free' tax uplift at the date of death.

A legatee may disclaim the entitlement so that the assets pass to the next person who would be entitled under the terms of the will. The disclaimer must be made in writing within two years of the death, and must not be made for a consideration.

Legatees may also make a deed of variation. With a deed of variation the legatee directs who should benefit, unlike a disclaimer. The deed of variation must be made in writing within two years of the death, and must not be made for a consideration. With a deed of variation the legatee must also elect for the variation to apply, within six months of the date of the variation.

A disposal of assets by the PRs to persons other than the legatees is liable to CGT in the normal way. For gains realised on or after 6 April 1998, PRs are liable to CGT at 34 per cent, (previously PRs were only liable to CGT at the basic rate). The PRs are also entitled to an annual exemption for the year of death, and the following two years, or, if earlier, until the estate is finally administered.

EXAMPLE

Barbara died on 18 May 2002. Her estate included some antique furniture that she had acquired in 1970 for £10 000. The probate value of the furniture was £25 000. The PRs sold the furniture to an unconnected third party for £32 000 in January 2003.

The PRs are deemed to have acquired the furniture for £25 000 in May 2002, and are treated as having made an unindexed gain of £7000 in 2002/03. The PRs are entitled to an annual exemption for the year of death, and the following two years, as it can often take a long time before the administration is completed.

In calculating the CGT liability, the PRs can set off the costs of obtaining probate, etc. relating to the asset – *IRC* v *Richards Exors* (1971) 46 TC 626.

Because it is sometimes difficult to apportion these costs, the Revenue have issued a scale of allowable expenses in establishing title, which is contained in a statement of practice (SP 7/81) and shown in Table 30.1.

For estates greater than £400 000, allowable expenditure is negotiated between the Inspector and the taxpayer.

The Revenue will accept computations based either on the scale shown in Table 30.1 or on the actual expenditure incurred.

Table 30.1 Scale of allowable expenses in establishing title

Gross value of estate	Allowable expenditure
A. up to £20 000	1.5% of the probate value of the assets sold by the PRs
B. £20 001 – £30 000	A fixed amount of £300 to be divided between all the assets in the estate in proportion to their probate values, and allowed in those proportions on assets sold by the PRs
C. £30 001 – £150 000	1% of the probate value of the assets sold by PRs
D. £150 001 – £200 000	A fixed amount of £1500 to be divided as in (B) above
E. £200 001 – £400 000	$\frac{3}{4}$ % of the probate value of the assets sold by PRs

Capital gains tax on UK resident trusts

The trustees of a trust are treated as a single and continuing body of persons (TCGA 1992, s 69(1)). This means that a change in the trustees will not amount to a chargeable disposal for CGT purposes.

There are, however, a number of events that give rise to a disposal or deemed disposal of trust assets; in some instances there is a deemed disposal but no charge to CGT. It is important, therefore, to understand when a liability to CGT will arise and when the deemed disposal does not give rise to an immediate charge to CGT.

Transfer of assets into a trust

The charge to CGT on the transfer of assets into a trust depends on whether the trust is created during the settlor's lifetime, or whether it is created under the terms of a will on the death of the settlor.

Trusts created on death

Where a trust is created on death, no chargeable disposal takes place. The trustees are treated as having acquired the assets at their market value at the date of death, as is the case for any other beneficiary under the terms of a will, i.e. the base cost of the asset(s) is uplifted at the date of death.

Trusts created during settlor's lifetime

Where a trust is created during the settlor's lifetime, the transfer of the assets into the trust is treated as a chargeable disposal by the settlor of the whole of the property, even if the settlor retains an interest in that property.

As the settlor and the trustees of a settlement are connected persons, the disposal is deemed to be at market value at the date of disposal. Gift relief may be available on the transfer of assets into a trust, e.g. where the assets transferred are business assets. Gift relief is considered fully in Chapter 27.

EXAMPLE

James set up a trust in September 2002 with an asset that he had acquired in June 1986 for £20 000. The asset was valued at £50 000 in September 2002.

There is a chargeable disposal by James in September 2002 when the trust is created. The deemed disposal proceeds are £50 000, the market value of the asset at the date of disposal.

	£
Deemed proceeds	50 000
less Cost	(20 000)
Unindexed gain	30 000
less Indexation to April 1998:	

$$\frac{162.6 - 97.8}{97.8}$$

0.663 × £20 000	(13 260)
Indexed gain	16 740

The base cost of the asset for the trustees would be £50 000.

If the gain had been eligible for gift relief, James could have elected to hold over the gain, so there would be no immediate charge to CGT in 2002/03, but the base cost of the asset for the trustees would be reduced by the gain held over:

	£
Market value at date of disposal	50 000
less Held-over gain	(16 740)
Base cost of asset for trustees if gift relief is claimed	33 260

Sale of assets by trustees to third parties

The disposal and acquisition of trust assets by trustees are subject to the normal CGT rules. The trustees are entitled to an annual exemption equal to one-half of the annual exemption available to individuals, however, if the trust is for the benefit of a mentally disabled person, the full amount of the annual exemption available to an individual is available. If there is a group of settlements, i.e. several trusts set up by the same settlor, the annual exemption available is the higher of:

(a) $\frac{\text{50\% annual exemption available to individuals}}{\text{No. of settlements in the group}}$

or

(b) $\frac{1}{10}$ of the annual exemption available to individuals

For gains realised on or after 6 April 1998, trustees are liable to CGT at 34 per cent, regardless of the type of trust; previously only gains accruing to accumulation and maintenance trusts, and discretionary trusts were charged to CGT at 34 per cent, other trusts were only liable to tax at the basic rate.

Termination of life interest

The exact CGT treatment depends on the circumstances of the termination:

Death of the life tenant

On the death of the life tenant, whether the interest terminates or remains settled property, there is a deemed disposal and reacquisition at market value of the deceased's interest, uplifting the base cost of the asset(s) at the date of death. However, there is no liability to CGT unless when the assets were transferred into the settlement gift relief had been claimed, in which case the chargeable gain is the smaller of the gain at the date of death or the gain held over when the assets were transferred into the trust.

EXAMPLE

In May 1987 William settled shares on trust for Amy for life, then on Bernard for life, with the remainder to Charles absolutely. William had acquired the shares in May 1984 for £12 000. The shares had been worth £20 000 in May 1987. Amy died in September 2001 when the shares were valued at £35 000.

William makes a chargeable disposal when he transfers the shares into the trust in May 1987:

May 1987

	£
Market value of shares	20 000
less Cost	(12 000)
Unindexed gain	8 000
less Indexation:	
$\dfrac{101.9 - 89.0}{89.0} \times £12\,000$	(1 740)
Chargeable gain	6 260

William would have incurred a chargeable gain of £6260 in 1987/88 and the trustees' base cost of the shares would be £20 000. On Amy's death the trustees are deemed to sell and reacquire the assets at the market value in September 2001, i.e. £35 000. The shares remain settled property for Bernard for life; there is no charge to CGT and £35 000 is the new base cost of the shares.

However, if William had claimed gift relief in 1987, on Amy's death a chargeable gain would crystallise. The gain chargeable would be the lower of:

(1) the gain on Amy's death;

or

(2) the gain held over in 1987.

On Amy's death:

	£	£
Market value of shares		35 000
Base cost of shares	20 000	
less Held-over gain	(6 260)	(13 740)
		21 260
less Indexation to April 1998:		
$\dfrac{162.6 - 101.9}{101.9} \times £13\,740$		(8 185)
Gain on Amy's death		13 075

However, the chargeable gain is restricted to the settlor's held-over gain of £6260.

During life of person entitled

There are no CGT consequences when a life interest terminates other than on death and the property remains settled property, and so on this occasion there is no increase in the base cost of the asset(s).

If a beneficiary disposes of an interest in a settlement, there are no CGT consequences, provided that the interest was not acquired for money or money's worth. However, if the interest had been acquired for money or money's worth, there will be a chargeable disposal, the base cost being the amount of the consideration.

Beneficiary becoming absolutely entitled to trust property

A person may become absolutely entitled to trust property in the following situations:

(a) when trustees make a payment out of capital to the beneficiaries of a discretionary trust;

(b) when the beneficiaries of an accumulation and maintenance trust become entitled to the capital. For example, beneficiaries entitled to capital when they reach 25 years of age: on reaching 25 years the beneficiaries are absolutely entitled to their share of the trust property;

(c) when the life tenant of a trust dies and the remainder man becomes absolutely entitled to the trust property.

When a beneficiary becomes absolutely entitled to trust property, the trustees are deemed to dispose of the property and immediately reacquire it at its market value at the date the person becomes absolutely entitled. This gives rise to a chargeable disposal on the trustees, although gift relief may be available. The trustees then merely hold the property as bare trustees until it is passed to the beneficiary. Any unrelieved losses relating to such property that the trustees are unable to utilise may be passed to the beneficiary who becomes absolutely entitled to that property.

If the CGT assessed on the trustees, on a person becoming absolutely entitled, is not paid within six months of the due date, the Revenue can make the assessment on the beneficiary within two years from when the tax was due (TCGA 1992, s 69(4)).

Note: Where a person becomes absolutely entitled to trust property on the death of a life tenant, the deemed disposal and reacquisition applies, i.e. there is a tax uplift of the assessed base cost, but there is no charge to CGT.

Trust gains assessed on the settlor

To prevent tax avoidance by sheltering assets in a trust to take advantage of the fact that the rates of tax for trustees are less than the top rate of tax for individuals, s 77 of the TCGA 1992 provides that where a settlor, or spouse of the settlor, is able to benefit from the trust, i.e. they have an interest in the income or property of the trust, then any trust gains are treated as if they were gains for the settlor. This does not apply, however, in the year the settlor dies.

COMPREHENSIVE EXAMPLE

Mr Smith died on 10 December 1998. Under the terms of his will, the family home which he solely owned was transferred into a will trust and his widow granted a life interest. In addition, a portfolio of shares worth £100 000 was settled to provide funds for the upkeep of the house. The reversionary interest was held in equal shares by Mr Smith's sons, Mark and John. Mark subsequently got into financial difficulties and sold his reversionary interest to John for its full market value on 1 July 1999.

On 10 April 2002 Mrs Smith died. The trust was formally wound up and all the assets were passed to the reversionary interest on 1 July 2002. The following market values have been ascertained:

	10/12/98 (£)	1/7/99 (£)	10/4/02 (£)	1/7/02 (£)
House:				
Tenanted	150 000	175 000	200 000	210 000
Vacant	450 000	500 000	525 000	530 000
Portfolio	100 000	110 000	95 000	15 000
Reversionary interest (in total)	275 000	300 000	N/A	N/A
Retail Price Index	164.4	165.1	174.8(e)	175.9(e)

(ATII November 1988, Updated)

1. Creation of the trust in December 1998

As the trust was created on the death of Mr Smith, no chargeable disposal takes place. The trustees are deemed to have acquired the assets at their market value on 10 December 1998.

2. Mark's disposal of his reversionary interest in July 1999

As Mark's interest in the trust was not acquired for money or money's worth, the disposal of his reversionary interest in July 1999 is exempt.

3. Mrs Smith's death on 10 April 2002

On Mrs Smith's death, her life interest terminates and John, as remainder man, becomes absolutely entitled to the trust property. The trustees are deemed to dispose of the property and immediately reaquire it as bare trustees for John.

Because John becomes absolutely entitled on the death of Mrs Smith, the deemed disposal and reaquisition applies, but there is no charge to CGT.

Half of John's reversionary interest was purchased from Mark, and as such gives rise to a chargeable disposal. The deemed proceeds is half the trust property and John's allowable cost is the amount paid for Mark's share. John's original half does not give rise to a chargeable disposal as he became absolutely entitled on the death of the life tenant.

Deemed disposal of John's purchased half share:

10/4/02

	£
Deemed proceeds:	
1/2 House (vacant)	262 500
1/2 Portfolio	47 500
	310 000
less Cost:	
1/2 × £300 000	(150 000)
Untapered gain	160 000

In the FA 2000, the Chancellor announced a package of anti-avoidance measures in order to prevent the tax leakage that occurs when individuals exploit the tax rules for trusts, to be effective from 21 March 2000, as follows:

1. Schemes where money is borrowed against the assets of a trust and then advanced to a second trust, known as a 'flip-flop scheme', the settlor then severing his interest in the first trust in order to avoid a charge to CGT when the assets are disposed of, will no longer be effective. Trustees in debt who transfer funds to another person will be treated as making a disposal and reacquisition of the property, unless the money was borrowed for normal trust purposes.

2. It will no longer be possible to offset gains on assets which have been transferred to a trust using Gift Relief in situations where the transferor, or a connected person, has acquired an interest in the trust for a consideration. The purpose of this legislation is to prevent individuals with large potential capital gains from buying their way into trusts with capital losses, or potential capital losses that would then be used to offset their gains when the assets are subsequently disposed of.

3. Where an interest in a trust is disposed of for a consideration and the settlor has an interest in the trust, any assets to which the interest relates are deemed to be disposed of and reacquired by the trustees at their market value, the resulting gain being assessed on the settlor and Gift Relief will not be available. The purpose of this legislation is to prevent individuals from placing assets in a trust in which they retain an interest, and then effectively selling assets to third parties tax free.

Capital gains tax on non-UK resident trusts

As only persons resident and ordinarily resident in the UK are liable to CGT, it follows that generally non-UK resident trusts are outside the scope of CGT.

A trust is treated as non-UK resident where the trustees, or the majority of them, are neither resident nor ordinarily resident in the UK, and the general administration of the trust is carried on overseas (TCCA 1992, s 69(1)).

A trust is also treated as being non-UK resident where it is managed by UK resident professional trustees, but the settlor was not resident, ordinarily resident or domiciled in the UK when the settlement was made (TCGA 1992, s 69(2)).

Nevertheless, legislation exists to prevent tax avoidance by the use of overseas resident trusts where the settlor was domiciled and resident, or ordinarily resident, in the UK when the gains were made, or when the settlement was created.

Emigration of trusts

The rules relating to the export of a UK resident trust were changed substantially by the FA 1991.

Export of a UK resident trust before 19 March 1991

Where a UK resident trust became non-UK resident prior to 19 March 1991 by virtue of the conditions in s 69(1), TCGA 1992, if the trustees still held any assets that had previously had gift relief claimed on them, then the held-over gain crystallised immediately prior to the trust becoming non-UK resident.

Because the gain originally held over crystallised, the trustees then held the assets at the market value at the date they were settled (FA 1980, s 79).

Export of a UK resident trust after 18 March 1991

Where a UK resident trust ceases to be UK resident after 18 March 1991 by virtue of the conditions in s 69(1), TCGA 1992, the trustees are deemed to dispose of the trust assets at market value and reacquire them immediately before the trust is exported (TCGA 1992, s 80).

Section 80 of the TCGA 1992 does not apply to assets situated in the UK and used by the trustees to carry on a business through a UK branch or agency. This is because s 10, TCGA 1992 brings such assets within the scope of CGT.

Because the definition of a non-UK resident trust stipulates that where the majority of trustees are non-resident and the administration is carried on overseas, the death of a trustee can, inadvertently, cause a UK resident trust to become non UK resident. If a trust becomes non-UK resident because of the death of a trustee and then the trust reverts to being UK resident within six months, a TCGA 1992, s 80 charge will only apply to those assets disposed of while the trust was non-UK resident.

Gains assessed on the settlor

The FA 1991 introduced legislation to prevent tax avoidance by the use of non-UK resident trusts.

Section 86 of the TCGA 1992 provides that where the settlor has an interest in the trust, and he is domiciled and resident or ordinarily resident in the UK at some time during the year, any trust gains realised on assets provided by the settlor, are treated as if they were the settlor's own gains.

Section 86, TCGA 1992 will apply where:

(1) the trust was created after 18 March 1991; or

(2) if the trust was created before 19 March 1991 and either:

    (a) funds are added to the trust by the settlor,

    (b) the beneficiaries are changed to include persons connected with the settlor,

    (c) persons connected with the settlor benefit from the trust after 18 March 1991 but are not named beneficiaries.

For disposals on or after 6 April 1999, the rules under s 86 are extended to include all trusts created before 19 March 1991. However, the charge on the settlor will be excluded when the only persons connected to the settlor who can benefit from the trust are:

- minor children (under 18 at 5 April 1999);
- unborn children;
- future spouse of settlor;
- future spouses of settlor's children.

The settlor charge will also apply to trusts that are created after 17 March 1998, where the beneficiaries are the settlor's grandchildren, their spouses or the companies they control, or grandchildren of the settlor's spouse, their spouses, or the companies they control.

If the trust was created before 17 March 1998, the above rules will apply if after 17 March 1998 either:

- funds are added to the trust by the settlor;
- the beneficiaries are changed to include the connected persons above;
- persons connected with the settlor benefit from the trust after 17 March 1998, but are not named beneficiaries;
- a resident trust becomes an offshore trust.

Note: If, in a year of assessment, trust expenses exceed trust income, the settlor can safely add funds to cover these expenses without affecting his CGT position with regard to s 86.

If trust gains are assessed on the settlor, they are treated as the top slice of gains. The settlor's annual exemption can be used against any gains assessed under the TCGA 1992, s 86 and the tax may be recovered from the trustees. However, a charge under s 86 will not be made in the year the settlor dies.

From 2003/04 the settlor will set personal losses against personal gains and then against any attributable amounts. The amounts attributed in this way will normally be in respect of untapered gains of the trustees, i.e. after trust losses have been deducted, and the taper relief that would have been applied by the trustees will be applied to the net attributed amounts. The settlor can elect for these provisions to apply for the tax years 2000/01 to 2002/03, provided that a joint election is made by 31st January 2005.

Trust gains assessed on beneficiaries

Prior to 17 March 1998, the gains of a non-UK resident trust may be assessed on the beneficiaries of the trust if they receive capital payments from the trust, and the settlor was domiciled and resident, or ordinarily resident, in the UK at the time the gains were made, or when the settlement was created (TCGA 1992, s 87). For gains realised after 17 March 1998, the charge on such beneficiaries will apply, regardless of the residency status of the settlor at the time the trust was created, or when the capital payments were made.

Any gain assessed under s 87 cannot be more than the capital payments received and CGT is only chargeable on those beneficiaries who are domiciled and resident, or ordinarily resident, in the UK. The gains on non-resident trusts for the purposes of s 87 are calculated as if the trust had been UK resident.

EXAMPLE

A non-UK resident discretionary trust has the following gains and capital payments to beneficiaries:

	1999/00 (£)	2000/01 (£)	2001/02 (£)
Gains	8 625	18 000	25 000
Capital payments:			
Alice	2 500	5 000	2 000
Bernard	3 000	5 000	1 000
Charles	1 500	15 000	1 500

		Beneficiaries		
1999/00	*Trustees:*	**A**	**B**	**C**
	(£)	(£)	(£)	(£)
Gains	8 625			
Capital payments		2 500	3 000	1 500
Matched 1999/00	(7 000)	(2 500)	(3 000)	(1 500)
Excess gains c/f	1 625			
2000/01				
Gains	18 000			
Capital payments		5 000	5 000	15 000
Matched 1999/00*		(325)	(325)	(975)
Matched 2000/01	(18 000)	(3 600)	(3 600)	(10 800)
Capital payments c/f		1 075	1 075	3 225
2001/02				
Gains	25 000			
Capital payments		2 000	1 000	1 500
Total capital payments		3 075	2 075	4 725
Matched 2001/02	(9 875)	(3 075)	(2 075)	(4 725)
Excess gains c/f	15 125			

Gains are matched to capital payments on a FIFO basis. If, in a year, capital payments made to beneficiaries exceed the trust gains, then the gains are allocated in proportion to the capital payments, any excess capital payments are then carried forward.

In the example for the year 2000/01, the capital payments exceed the trust gains so the gains are apportioned as follows:

Total capital payments 2000/01 £25 000
Total gains 2000/01 £18 000

A: $\dfrac{5\,000}{25\,000} \times £18\,000 = £3600$

B: $\dfrac{5\,000}{25\,000} \times £18\,000 = £3600$

C: $\dfrac{15\,000}{25\,000} \times £18\,000 = £10\,800$

* There were excess capital gains brought forward at the end of 1999/00 of £1625; this amount is allocated in the same proportions:

A: $\dfrac{5\,000}{25\,000} \times £1\,625 = \underline{\underline{£325}}$

B: $\dfrac{5\,000}{25\,000} \times £1\,625 = \underline{\underline{£325}}$

C: $\dfrac{15\,000}{25\,000} \times £1\,625 = \underline{\underline{£975}}$

Summary:

	1999/00 (£)	2000/01 (£)	2001/02 (£)
A:	2 500	3 925	3 075
B:	3 000	3 925	2 075
C:	1 500	11 775	4 725

Provided that the beneficiaries are UK domiciled and resident, the gains will be added to their own personal gains for each year and charged to CGT. If any of the beneficiaries are not domiciled in the UK, the gains are still apportioned to them but there is no charge to CGT.

Where capital payments are made after April 1992 and the capital payment is matched with gains made in an earlier period, there is a supplementary charge made of 10 per cent pa for each year that the gains are not distributed, up to a maximum of six years (TCGA 1992, s 91). The supplementary charge is treated as additional CGT, but the total CGT charged in such circumstances can never exceed the amount of the capital payment. The supplementary charge only applies where gains from an earlier period are matched with capital payments, i.e. if a capital payment is matched with gains made in the same year there is no additional charge. For example, if trust gains were made during 1996/97 and not attributed until 1999/00, the supplementary charge would run from 31 January 1998 (the normal due date for CGT for 1996/97), until the day before CGT is due for 1999/00, i.e. 31 January 2001.

In the last example, trust gains made in 1993/94 but not allocated until 1994/95 would carry 10 per cent charge from 1 December 1994 to 30 November 1995. Where capital payments are paid out of gains realised in several disposals, the capital payments are matched with gains on a FIFO basis.

Note: The due date for CGT prior to self assessment in 1996/97 was 1 December following the year of assessment.

In order to clamp down CGT avoidance schemes using trusts, Gordon Brown announced a series of measures to be effective from 21 March 2000:

1. The tax-free uplift will be withdrawn in situations where an offshore trust with realised, but undistributed gains, comes onshore and then goes offshore again in order to benefit from the tax uplift.

2. It will no longer be possible to shelter gains using a trust and an offshore company. Where assets are held in an offshore company, owned by a non-resident trust, rather than being held in the trust, and the overseas country has a tax treaty exempting the gains arising to residents of the other country, then normally the UK-resident settlor, trustees or beneficiaries cannot be charged on the gains. From Budget day, however, gains will be attributed to the trustees in this situation, on the principle of 'looking through' the company to the trustees, as participators of the company.

PRACTICE QUESTIONS

1. (a) In April 1975, Ian bought some freehold land costing £50 000. In August 1986, part of the land was sold for £150 000 when the value of the remainder was £200 000. In June 2002 the remainder of the land was sold for £250 000. The value of all the land originally purchased was £175 000 on 31 March 1982.

No election has been made or will be made under s 35(6), TCGA 1992 to have all pre-31 March 1982 acquisitions re-based to 31 March 1982.

You are required to calculate, before annual exemption, the capital gain assessable on Ian for 2002/03.

(7 marks)

(b) In September 2002 Roy, who was then 60 years old, gave all his shares in his 'personal' company, Magic Motors Ltd, to his son Colin. At that time the shares had a market value of £500 000 and had been purchased by Roy in September 1979 for £100 000. The total value of the shares on 31 March 1982 was £80 000. Roy had been a full-time working officer in the company since September 1990. Roy and Colin made a joint claim for any capital gain to be held over. All chargeable assets of the company are chargeable business assets.

No election has been made or will be made under s 35(6), TCGA 1992 to have all pre-31 March 1982 acquisitions re-based to 31 March 1982.

You are required to calculate, before annual exemption, the capital gain assessable on Roy for 2002/03 and the cost which will be available to Colin to set against future disposals.

(6 marks)

(c) In January 1981, Philip acquired 1000 ordinary shares in Leisure Products plc, a quoted company, for £1500. In January 1988, when the price of the shares was £3 each, the company made a rights issue of 1 for 5 at a price of £2.00. Philip sold all his rights for 70p per share. Philip sold his original 1000 shares in August 2002 for £7500.

The share price on 31 March 1982 was £1.60 per share.

No election has been made or will be made under s 35(6), TCGA 1992 to have all pre-31 March 1982 acquisitions re-based to 31 March 1982.

You are required to calculate, before annual exemption, the capital gain assessable on Philip for 2002/03.

(5 marks)
(Total: 18 marks)
(Source: ACCA, Dec 91)

2. (a) Victoria held 20 000 shares in Forum Follies plc which she purchased in May 1989 for £50 000. In January 2003, Exciting Enterprises plc acquired all the share capital of Forum Follies plc. Under the terms of the takeover, shareholders in Forum Follies received three ordinary shares and one preference share in Exciting Enterprises plc plus £1 cash for every two shares previously held in Forum Follies plc. Immediately after the takeover the ordinary shares in Exciting Enterprises are quoted at £3 each and the preference shares at £1.50 each.

No election has been made or will be made under s 35(6), TCGA 1992 to have all pre-31 March 1982 acquisitions re-based to 31 March 1982.

You are required to calculate any gain assessable on Victoria (before annual exemption) for 2002/03.

(7 marks)

(b) Evelyn purchased shares in Dassau plc, a quoted company, as follows:

	No. of Shares	Cost (£)
December 1974	2 000	3 000
December 1986	1 000	2 000
April 1989, 1 for 2 rights issue		£2 per share

In November 2002, Evelyn sold 4 000 shares for £32 000.

The market value of the shares on 31 March 1982 was £1.75 each.

No election has been made or will be made under s 35(6), TCGA 1992 to have all pre-31 March 1982 acquisitions re-based to 31 March 1982.

You are required to calculate Evelyn's capital gain for 2002/03 (before annual exemption).

(12 marks)
(Total: 19 marks)
(Source: ACCA, June 91)

3. (a) James purchased a house in Oxford, 'Millhouse', on 1 July 1981 and took up immediate residence. The house cost £50 000. On 1 January 1983 he went to work and live in the United States where he stayed until 30 June 1985. On 1 July 1985 James returned to the UK to work for his United States employers in Scotland where it was necessary for him to occupy rented accommodation. On 1 July 1986 his mother became seriously ill and James resigned from his job to go and live with her. His mother died on 30 September 1987 leaving her house to James. James decided to continue to live in his mother's house and finally sold 'Millhouse' on 30 June 1999 for £200 000. The value of the house on 31 March 1982 was £75 000.

You are required to calculate, before annual exemption, the capital gain assessable on James for 1999/00.

No election has been made or will be made under s 35(6), TCGA 1992 to have all pre-31 March 1982 acquisitions re-based to 31 March 1982.

(7 marks)

(b) Adrienne bought 1000 ordinary £1 shares in Pokhara Ltd for £100 000 in March 1982. She sold her entire holding in December 2000 for £320 000.

She bought an investment on 1 June 2001 for £250 000.

You may assume that Adrienne's investment qualified for re-investment relief.

Adrienne made no other disposals in 2000/01.

You are required to calculate how much re-investment relief Adrienne will claim and the base cost of her new investment.

(7 marks)
(Total: 14 marks)
(Source: ACCA, June 90)

4. Gabriel, a single man, has the following income for 2002/03:

	£
Salary (gross)	18 265
Dividends received	5 400
Building society interest received	1 000
National savings bank interest (ordinary a/c)	150

Gabriel is provided with a company car that was first purchased by the company in 1998 for £18 000. No private fuel is provided by the company. CO_2 emissions were 240 gm/Km, and the car runs on petrol.

£4200 was deducted from Gabriel's salary under the PAYE system.

Gabriel is negotiating to buy a holiday home near the coast and to help finance this, he disposed of the following assets:

(i) In July 2002 he sold an antique table for £5800. He had bought the table for £2000 in 1980.

(ii) In August 2002 he sold a plot of land for £40 000. The land had been bought in 1980 for £6000 and the market value on 31/3/82 had been £7500.

(iii) In September 2002 he sold a painting at auction for £25 000. Auctioneer's fees were 10 per cent. Gabriel had bought the painting in August 1988 for £8000.

You are required to:

(a) calculate Gabriel's income tax liability for 2002/03 and calculate any repayment of tax that may be due to him;

(8 marks)

(b) calculate Gabriel's total chargeable gains for 2002/03;

(9 marks)

(c) calculate Gabriel's capital gains tax liability for 2002/03;

(3 marks)

(d) explain to Gabriel the income tax implications should he decide to rent out his holiday home when he is not using it himself.

(5 marks)
(Total: 25 marks)

5. (a) On 31 March 2003, her 58th birthday, Angela sold all her shares in Scott Stockings Ltd a manufacturing company.

(1) Holdings of ordinary shares in the company were as follows:

	%
Angela	15
Michael, Angela's husband	15
Martin, Angela's brother	15
Raquel, Michael's sister	10
Yvonne, Angela's cousin	15
Charles, Angela's uncle	15
David, Angela's uncle	15
	100%

(2) Angela had been a full-time working officer of the company for the last six years and had owned 15 per cent of the shares for the last eight years.

(3) The capital gain, after indexation, was £290 000.

(4) The market values of the company's assets on 31 March 2003 were:

	£ 000s
Land and buildings	2000
Plant and machinery*	1000
Goodwill	500
Investments in gilt-edged securities	250
Net current assets	1500
	5250

* All items of plant and machinery have a market value of more than £6000.

You are required to calculate Angela's assessable capital gain for 2002/03, assuming no other disposal of chargeable assets in the year.

(10 marks)

(b) Victor had the following transactions in the ordinary shares of Victorious Vulcanising plc a quoted company.

	No. of shares	Total amount £
1 August 1980 bought	600	7 200
1 April 1989 bought	1000	11 000
1 September 1991 (1 for 2 rights) bought	800	4 800
1 August 2002 sold	2100	30 100

The value per share on 31 March 1982 was £8.

You are required to calculate Victor's capital gain 2002/03 before the annual exemption.

(11 marks)
(Total: 21 marks)
(Source: ACCA, Dec 92)

6. Yasmin owned shares in East plc which she had acquired as follows:

Date	Number of shares	Cost
		£
10 September 1970	1000	2750
1 July 1972	1000	3000
10 May 1981	800	2400
16 June 1982	200	800
23 August 1984	500	2125
12 March 1989	1000	4300
17 February 1994	500	2100
6 July 1999	1500	8625
30 September 2002	500	3000

A few days after her last purchase, the shares escalated in value and she sold 6000 of the shares for £72 000 on 5 October 2002.

The value of the shares on 31 March 1982 had been £3.75 per share.

Yasmin's income for 2002/03 was as follows:

	£
Salary	16 365
Rental income	5 025

Yasmin also had other chargeable gains of £10 129 for 2002/03.

You are required to:

(a) set up the 1982 and 1985 share pools;

(8 marks)

(b) show how the disposal on 5 October 2002 will be matched with Yasmin's acquisitions of the shares in East plc;

(3 marks)

(c) calculate the total chargeable gain on the disposal of the 6000 shares in East plc.

(7 marks)

(d) calculate Yasmin's income tax liability for 2002/03.

(3marks)

(e) calculate Yasmin's capital gains tax liability for 2002/03.

(4 marks)
(Total: 25 marks)

PART 4

Corporation tax

CHAPTER 31

The charge to corporation tax

A separate tax on companies was first introduced in the UK by the FA 1965, under a classical system of corporation tax (CT). This was replaced in 1973 by an imputation system of CT, which alleviated the double taxation of dividends, a major criticism of the classical system.

The main statutory charging provisions for CT are contained in the Income and Corporation Taxes Act 1988 (ICTA 1988).

This chapter examines the basic charge to CT under the imputation system.

The profit chargeable to corporation tax

UK resident companies are liable to CT on their worldwide profits and gains for an accounting period.

Non-resident companies will only be charged to CT on the profit of any trading operations in the UK; the non-trading income of non-resident companies will be liable to income tax. Residence is covered fully in Chapter 37.

A company for CT purposes includes those incorporated under the Companies Act, by Royal Charter or Special Act of Parliament, and un-incorporated associations that are not partnerships or incorporated bodies, e.g. sports clubs.

The basic profit chargeable to corporation tax (PCTCT) is arrived at by aggregating all the company's income and chargeable gains for an accounting period, and then deducting charges on income that have been paid during the accounting period:

Basic CT computation:

	£
Schedule D Case I	X
Schedule D Case III	X
Schedule D Case IV and V	X
Schedule D Case VI	X
Schedule A	X
Taxed income	X
Chargeable gains	X
	X
less Charges on income paid (gross)	(X)
PCTCT	X

As indicated above, the Schedules and Cases for income tax are also applicable to CT, the income being calculated in accordance with the rules of the particular source of income:

Schedule D Case I

The company's trading income is calculated under the rules of Schedule D Case I, i.e. the accounting profit is adjusted for tax purposes in exactly the same way as it is adjusted for sole traders and partnerships under the income tax rules. Capital allowances are treated as a trading expense of the accounting period and are calculated as they are for income tax purposes (*see* Chapters 10 and 11).

Schedule D Case III

It should be noted that, unlike individuals, companies receive bank interest gross, and as such it is taxable under the rules of Schedule D Case III. Since 14 December 1992, building societies have been able to pay interest gross to companies, and so building society interest received by companies is also generally taxed under Schedule D Case III in the same way as bank interest.

Schedule D Case V

If a company has overseas income, it is assessed under Schedule D Cases IV and V. If the foreign income is received net of overseas tax, it must be grossed up in the CT computation and double tax relief given for the foreign tax paid. The overseas aspects of CT are considered fully in Chapter 37.

Schedule D Case VI

Miscellaneous income of the company is assessed under schedule D Case VI.

Rental income

Rents and other income derived from the ownership of land in the UK are generally assessed to tax under Schedule A.

However, the ICTA 1988, s 55 specifically provides that income from the following sources is chargeable under Schedule D Case I as trading income:

- mines and quarries
- ironworks, gasworks
- canals, docks
- markets, fairs, toll bridges and ferries
- railways.

Section 15(1) of the ICTA 1988 provides that tax under Schedule A shall be charged on the annual profits or gains arising in respect of land in the UK.

For the purpose of the taxes Acts, land includes: buildings and other structures, land covered with water and any estate, interest, easement, servitude or right over land. Examples of common sources of Schedule A income include:

- rents under leases
- ground rents
- rent charges
- hunting and fishing rights.

In the FA 1998 the corporation tax rules regarding property income were amended, with effect from 1 April 1998, to bring them more in line with the income tax rules, whilst preserving reliefs for corporate interest and management expenses:

- All UK rental income is pooled together, allowable expenses following the same principles that apply to Schedule DI income.
- The corporate interest rules in the FA 1996 remain in place (*see* 'Interest on loans' below).
- Capital allowances are available for Schedule A income with no special rules.
- Losses under Schedule A are treated in the same way as management expenses (*see* Chapter 33), i.e. first set against other income and gains of the current period; any excess can then be carried forward and set off against future income from all sources, or surrendered as group relief.

Premiums

When a company receives a premium on the grant of a lease, it forms part of the Schedule A assessment. The special rules regarding lease premiums are the same for companies as they are for individuals, and are covered fully in Part 2, Chapter 16.

Chargeable gains

Companies do not pay CGT, instead they pay CT on their net chargeable gains (current year gains less current year losses, less brought forward losses) for an accounting period, and there is no annual exemption for companies. The chargeable gains, or allowable losses, are calculated using the specific charging provisions contained in the TCGA 1992, and covered in detail in Part 3 of this book. However, when calculating the chargeable gains for CT purposes, the reforms contained in the FA 1998 do not apply, i.e.:

- the distinction between long-term and short-term gains is not applicable, i.e. *the taper does not apply to companies*;
- indexation is given in full; there is no cut-off point at April 1998 as there is for individuals, trustees and PRs.

The basic computation

	£	£
Gross		X
less Incidental cost of sale		(X)
less Allowable expenditure:		
Acquisition costs	X	
Incidental costs of acquisition	X	
Enhancement expenditure	X	(X)
Unindexed gain/(loss)		X
less Indexation allowance		(X)
Chargeable gain/(allowable loss)		X

EXAMPLE

Meridian Ltd disposed of an office block for £250 000 on 16 September 2000. The property had been acquired as an investment in June 1986 for £60 000 and £20 000 was spent on improvements in July 1990.

RPI:	June 1986	97.8
	July 1990	126.8
	September	174.6

	£	£
Gross sale proceeds		250 000
less Allowable expenditure:		
Cost	60 000	
Enhancement expenditure	20 000	(80 000)
Unindexed gain		170 000
less Indexation allowance:		

(1) on cost:

$$\frac{174.6 - 97.8}{97.8}$$

= 0.785 × £60 000		(47 100)

(2) on improvements:

$$\frac{174.6 - 126.8}{126.8}$$

= 0.377 × £20 000		(7 540)
Chargeable gain		115 360

Shares and securities

Because taper relief does not apply to companies, shares of the same class can be held in 'pools'. For corporate disposals of shares and securities after 1 April 1985, shares are matched in the following order:

(a) shares acquired on the same day;

(b) shares acquired in the previous nine days on the FIFO basis;

(c) shares from the FA 1985 new holding pool;

(d) shares from the FA 1982 frozen pool; and

(e) pre-1965 shares on a LIFO basis.

Note: (a) and (b) cannot qualify for the indexation allowance.

The disposal of shareholdings of 10% or more, in trading companies or holding companies of trading groups, made by trading companies and groups will be exempt from tax for disposals on or after 1st April 2002.

FA 1985 pool

The FA 1985 pool consists of shares of the same class that have been acquired since 1 April 1982. The pool is first set up at 1 April 1985 with all the shares that have been acquired between 1 April 1982 and 31 March 1985, in exactly the same way as for individuals (*see* Chapter 26).

FA 1982 pool

The FA 1982 pool consists of all the shares that have been acquired between 6 April 1965 and 31 March 1982, and calculated in exactly the same way as for individuals (*see* Chapter 26).

Bed and breakfasting

Bed and breakfasting is the disposal and repurchase of shares; the acquisition of additional shares before selling original shares is known as double banking. Legislation exists in order to prevent companies from entering into bed and breakfasting and double banking deals in order to crystallise an allowable loss.

Section 106, TCGA 1992 provides that where a company holds at least 2 per cent of the issued share capital of the shares dealt in, within six months before or after the transaction (one month for quoted shares), the disposal is identified with those shares acquired within six months before or after the disposal (one month for quoted shares).

The disposal is first matched with those shares acquired nearest to the date of disposal, taking the shares that were acquired before in preference to those acquired after the disposal.

Corporate venturing scheme

The government's rationale for this scheme is twofold:

- to encourage corporate venturing relationships; and
- to increase the amount of venture capital to small high-risk trading companies.

The corporate venturing scheme, to be introduced from 1 April 2000, provides tax incentives in establishing corporate venturing relationships in the same way as VCTs for individuals, provided that the following conditions are met:

- the small company must be unquoted;
- the shares must be held for three years;
- the corporate venturer must not control the small company in which it has invested;
- 20 per cent of the shares in the small company must be held by individuals;
- the corporate venturer must not hold more than 30 per cent of the shares in the small company.

NB: relief will not be denied if the small company becomes quoted within the three-year period, provided that the small company was unquoted when the shares were issued and the company had no plans at that time to seek a listing.

If the conditions are met, the benefits to the investing company are as follows: Corporation tax relief at 20 per cent is available on amounts invested in ordinary shares. Gains can be deferred provided they are reinvested in other shares under the scheme. Losses on disposal can be relieved against income.

Qualifying companies under the scheme are defined in the same way as for EIS and VCTs (*see* Chapter 16).

The Budget 2002 announced new rules to apply to intangible assets created or acquired on or after 1st April 2002 as follows:

- Companies can obtain tax relief on the cost of intangible assets, based on the amortisation in the accounts.
- For indefinite or longer life assets a fixed rate of 4% pa is available.
- The relief applies to the expenditure on their creation, acquisition or maintenance.
- Payments made for the use of intangibles are included, eg royalty payments.
- Disposals will be taxed on an income basis with a rollover relief available for reinvestment in new intangibles.
- Intangibles held at 1st April 2002 will generally be taxed under current law except that gains on disposal will qualify for rollover relief under the new rules.
- Disposals of goodwill and quotas held at 1st April 2002 will not qualify for capital gains rollover relief except where the reinvestment took place before 1st April 2002 and within 12 months prior to disposal.
- Purchases of goodwill and quotas after 1st April 2002 are no longer qualifying assets for capital gains rollover relief.

Charges on income

Charges on income are generally payments made by the company net of basic rate income tax. Although charges on income are paid net of basic rate income tax, the gross amount is deducted in arriving at the company's PCTCT. Only those charges actually paid in the accounting period are deductible. There is no relief for acrued charges. A charge on income by the paying company is taxed income for the receiving company and includes:

- patent royalties
- covenanted payments to charities
- donations under the gift aid scheme.

From 1 April 2001, royalties and annual payments can be paid gross, provided that the recipient is within the charge to CT.

Following the changes to the tax treatment of intangibles in the Budget 2002, the charge on income rules will no longer apply to royalty payments. Relief for royalty payments and receipts will follow the accounting treatment.

R&D tax credits

In the November 1999 pre-Budget report, the Chancellor announced the introduction of Research and Development (R&D) Tax Credits to be introduced from April 2000. Because the tax credit is a notifiable State Aid, the proposed scheme needed clearance from the European Commission before it could be brought into operation; this clearance was, however, received in February 2000, and so the tax credits are to be effective from 1 April 2000.

R&D tax credits are only available to small and medium-sized companies, i.e. individuals and partnerships DO NOT qualify for the relief. The definition of a small or medium-sized company for this purpose follows the European definition as follows:

- fewer than 250 employees
- annual turnover no more than euro 40 million (approx. £25 million)
- assets no more than euro 27 million (approx. £17 million).

The research does not have to be undertaken in the UK to attract relief, but if the whole or part of the project is funded by government grants, none of the expenditure qualifies for the R&D tax credit. The following conditions also apply:

- the company claiming the relief must be entitled to the ownership rights of any intellectual property arising from the R&D;
- the minimum expenditure must be £25 000;
- the expenditure must not have been met by another person.

If these conditions are satisfied the allowable expenditure includes:

- costs of staff directly involved in the R&D
- consumables used in the R&D effort
- certain costs where R&D is sub-contracted.

The new R&D tax credits have two components:

1. an increased deduction of 150 per cent of qualifying R&D expenditure, i.e. £150 for every £100 spent;
2. a *payable* R&D tax credit for companies with no taxable profits.

The 'loss' attributable to R&D can be surrendered to the Exchequer for a cash payment of £24 for every £100 spent on R&D. This payable credit, however, is limited to the *total* amount of class 1 NICs and PAYE, for *all* personnel, payable by the company for the accounting period.

Following the Budget 2002 R&D tax credits have been extended to large companies, including those who subcontract to universities, charities etc. For qualifying expenditure after 1st April 2002 large companies can deduct 125%, ie £125 for every £100 spent.

Interest on loans

From 1 April 2001, payments of interest can be paid gross, provided that the recipient of the interest is a company, within the charge of CT, however, payments made to individuals continue to be paid net of 20 per cent income tax, as was the situation prior to 1 April 2001.

1. Trading loan relationship

Where the loan relationship exists for the purpose of the trade, all the profits, losses and costs are treated as Schedule D Case I income or expenses.

2. Non-trading loan relationships

Where the loan relationship does not exist for trading purposes, the tax treatment is as follows:

(a) income is treated as Schedule D Case III income; and

(b) losses are treated as follows:

- set off against the total profit of the same accounting period after brought forward losses, but before any claims under s 393A (*see* Chapter 33);
- surrendered as group relief (*see* Chapter 36);
- carried forward as a loss against non-trading income and capital gains (*see* Chapter 33); or
- carried back against Schedule D Case III profit on non-trading loan relationships (*see* Chapter 33).

From 21 March 2000, companies can claim interest relief on loans where the interest rates are linked to profits, known as 'ratchet loans'. Prior to the Budget 2000, relief on these loans was denied where the creditor was not a UK company because the payments were treated as a distribution of profit.

Donation of medical supplies

From 1st April 2002 companies donating medical supplies and equipment to developing countries for humanitarian purposes will avoid the tax charge on market value as well as being able to deduct the transportation costs.

Taxed income

Income received net of lower or basic rate income tax must be grossed up in the CT computation at the appropriate rate. Any surplus income tax that has been deducted during the CT accounting period and not repaid can be used to reduce the company's CT liability. This is considered in more detail in Chapter 32.

EXAMPLE

ABC Ltd has the following income for the YE 31/3/03:

	£
Trading profit	150 000
Bank interest received	5 000
Building society interest received	2 000
Dividends received from UK companies	27 000
Debenture interest received from UK companies (gross)	14 000
Chargeable gains	35 000
Capital losses	(6 000)
Rental income (net of expenses)	10 000
Dividend received from overseas company (net of 10% withholding tax)	9 000

ABC Ltd had capital losses brought forward of £10 000 at 1 April 2002.
During the year ABC Ltd made the following payments:

	£
Dividends paid	18 000
Debenture interest paid (paid to individuals)	9 000
Charitable deed of covenant paid	936

Trading income: Assessed under Schedule D Case I.

Bank and building society interest: Received gross by the company and assessed under Schedule D Case III £5000 + £2000 = £7000.

Dividends from UK companies: The FII received by ABC Ltd is not liable to CT and is not included in the PCTCT.

Debenture interest received: From 1 April, payments of interest can be paid gross if the recipient, like ABC Ltd, is a company within the charge to CT.

Capital gains: The company's net chargeable gains are included in the PCTCT:

	£
Chargeable gains	35 000
less Allowable losses	(6 000)
Net gains YE 31/3/03	29 000
less Allowable losses b/f	(10 000)
Net chargeable gains	19 000

Rental income: Received gross and assessed under Schedule A.

Dividend received from overseas company: Foreign dividends are assessed under Schedule D Case V. It is received net of 10 per cent foreign tax, but must be shown gross in the PCTCT:

$$9000 \times \frac{100}{90} = £10\,000 \text{ (gross)}$$

Dividends paid: Dividends are paid out of post tax profits so are not deducted in the PCTCT.

Debenture interest paid: Debenture interest is paid net of lower rate income tax and the gross amount is allowed as a deduction from the trading profit, as the payments are made to individuals.

$$9000 \times \frac{100}{80} = \underline{\underline{£11\,250}} \text{ (gross)}$$

Deed of covenant: The charitable deed of covenant is paid net of basic rate income tax, assuming that the recipient is not within the charge to corporation tax, but the gross amount is deducted in the CT computation as a charge on income.

$$936 \times \frac{100}{78} = \underline{\underline{£1200}} \text{ (gross)}$$

The company's PCTCT is as follows:

	£	£
Trading profit	150 000	
less Debenture interest paid	(11 250)	
Schedule D Case I		138 750
Schedule D Case III		7 000
Schedule D Case V		10 000
Schedule A		10 000
Debenture interest		14 000
Chargeable gains		19 000
		198 750
less Charges on income		(1 200)
PCTCT		197 550

Calculation of gross corporation tax

A company's gross corporation tax (GCT) liability is calculated as:

GCT = PCTCT × CT rate applicable

The rates of corporation tax

Rates of CT are set for financial years. The financial year (FY) runs from 1 April to the following 31 March, and is identified with the April date, e.g. FY 1999 runs from 1 April 1999 to 31 March 2000. This contrasts with income tax where the rates are set for fiscal years, i.e. from 6 April to the following 5 April.

The rate at which CT is charged depends on whether the company is classed as a large company or a small company. This has nothing to do with the actual size of the company, it is determined by the size of its 'profits'. The definition of 'profit' for this purpose is as follows:

'Profits' = PCTCT *plus* FII

Table 31.1 Rates of corporation tax

FY	CT rate	Small company rate	Small company rate limits		10% starting rate (£)	0% starting rate (from FY 2002)
			Lower (£)	Upper (£)		
1993	33%	25%	250 000	1 250 000	–	–
1994	33%	25%	300 000	1 500 000	–	–
1995	33%	25%	300 000	1 500 000	–	–
1996	33%	24%	300 000	1 500 000	–	–
1997	31%	21%	300 000	1 500 000	–	–
1998	31%	21%	300 000	1 500 000	–	–
1999	30%	20%	300 000	1 500 000	–	–
2000	30%	20%	50 000–300 000	1 500 000	0–10000	
2001	30%	20%	50 000–300 000	1 500 000	0–10000	
2002	30%	19%	50 000–300 000	1 500 000	0–10000	

From 1 April 2000, a new starting rate of 10 per cent is available to companies with profits of up to £10 000; this starting rate is reduced to 0% for FY 2002.

It is important to understand that the company does not pay CT on its FII, the figure is merely added to the company's PCTCT in order to determine the level of profit for small companies rate.

For the FY 2002, a company with profits in excess of £1 500 000 is a large company and charged CT at 30 per cent on its PCTCT; a company with profits between £50 001 and £300 000 is a small company and charged CT at 19 per cent on its PCTCT; and for companies with profits below £10 000 the new CT starting rate of zero per cent applies.

The upper and lower limits are rateably reduced for accounting periods of less than 12 months.

If the company has associated companies, the limits are divided by the number of associated companies. An associated company for this purpose means over 50 per cent control. The limits are divided even if the company was not associated for the whole of the accounting period. If the associated company has been dormant for the whole of the accounting period, however, it is ignored for this purpose, but foreign resident associated companies are counted. For example, X Ltd has two 51 per cent subsidiaries Y Ltd and Z Ltd, therefore the three companies are associated and the limits must be divided as follows:

$$\text{upper limit} = \frac{1\,500\,000}{3} = \underline{\underline{£500\,000}}$$

$$\text{lower limit} = \frac{300\,000}{3} = \underline{\underline{£100\,000}} \,;\quad \frac{50\,000}{3} = £16\,667$$

$$\text{starting rate limit} = \frac{10\,000}{3} = £3333$$

EXAMPLE 1

A company has PCTCT of £104 000 for YE 31/3/03. During the year it received dividends of £18 000 from another UK company.

	£	
PCTCT	104 000	'Income'
add FII:		
£18 000 × 100/90	20 000	
	124 000	'Profit'

If the company has no associated companies, CT will be charged at 19 per cent as the 'profit' is between £50 001 and £300 000.

GCT = £104 000 × 19% = £19 760

EXAMPLE 2

A company has PCTCT of £1 350 000 for YE 31/3/03. During the year it received dividends of £180 000 from another UK company:

	£	
PCTCT	1 350 000	'Income'
add FII:		
£180 000 × 100/90	200 000	
	1 550 000	'Profit'

As the company's 'profit' is in excess of £1 500 000, it is charged to CT at the full rate of 30 per cent.

GCT = £1 350 000 × 30% = £405 000

EXAMPLE 3

A company has a PCTCT of £8000 for its YE 31/3/02, and during the year received dividends of £1800 from another UK company.

	£	
PCTCT	8 000	'Income'
add FII:		
£1800 × 100/90	2 000	
	10 000	'Profit'

As the company's profit does not exceed £10 000, CT is charged at 10 per cent on the

PCTCT:
GCT = £8000 x 10% = £800

For FY 2002 the starting rate is reduced to zero per cent.

Marginal relief (ICTA 1988, s 13)

Special rules apply to companies with 'profits' between the limits; CT is charged at 30 per cent/19 per cent on the PCTCT with a form of marginal relief, given by the following formula, which is deducted from the CT:

$$\text{Fraction} \times (\text{Upper limit} - \text{'Profits'}) \times \frac{\text{'Income'}}{\text{'Profits'}}$$

The fraction used in the marginal relief formula is as follows:

Table 31.2 Marginal relief fraction

FY	Marginal relief at 30% Fraction	Marginal relief at SCR Fraction
1993	1/50	N/A
1994	1/50	N/A
1995	1/50	N/A
1996	9/400	N/A
1997	1/40	N/A
1998	1/40	N/A
1999	1/40	N/A
2000	1/40	1/40
2001	1/40	1/40
2002	11/400	19/400

EXAMPLE 4

Planet Ltd had the following income for the YE 31/3/03.

	£
Trading profit	280 000
Bank interest	8 000
Chargeable gain	12 500
Rental income	15 000
Dividends received from UK company	27 000
Debenture interest paid (gross)	15 000
No associated companies	

	£	£
Trading profit	280 000	
less Debenture interest:		
	(15 000)	
Schedule D Case I		265 000
Schedule D Case III		8 000
Schedule A		15 000
Chargeable gain		12 500
PCTCT		300 500

	£	
PCTCT	300 500	'Income'
add FII:		
£27 000 × 100/90	30 000	
	330 500	'Profit'

Since the 'profit' is between £300 000 and £1 500 000, CT is charged at 30 per cent on the PCTCT and marginal relief is given:

	£
CT @ 30% × £300 500	90 150
less Marginal relief:	
11/400 (£1 500 000 − £330 500) × 300 500/330 500	(29 242)
GCT	60 908

EXAMPLE 5

Horizon Ltd had the following income for the YE 31/3/03:

	£
Schedule DI	20 000
Schedule DIII	4 000
Schedule A	10 000
Chargeable gains	2 000

During the year the company paid charges of £2000 (gross) and received dividends of £5400 from another UK company. Horizon Ltd has no associated companies.

	£	
Schedule DI	20 000	
Schedule DIII	4 000	
Schedule A	10 000	
Gains	2 000	
	36 000	
less Charges paid	(2 000)	
PCTCT	34 000	'Income'
add FII:		
£5400 x 100/90	6 000	
	40 000	'Profits'

Since the profit is between £10 000 and £50 000, CT is charged at 19 per cent and marginal relief given:

	£
£34 000 x 19%	6 460

less:

$$19/400 \times (50\,000 - 40\,000) \times \frac{34\,000}{40\,000}$$

	£
	(404)
GCT	6056

Corporation tax accounting periods

Companies pay CT on the actual income they receive during an accounting period, i.e. companies pay tax on a current year basis.

Long periods of account

A corporation tax accounting period (CTAP) can be for less than 12 months but cannot be for more than 12 months. Where there is a long period of account, it must be split for CT purposes into CTAPs not exceeding 12 months.

EXAMPLE

A company incorporated on 1 April 1980, produced accounts to the 31 March each year until 31 March 2000, after which it changed its accounting date to 30 June by preparing a 15-month set of accounts to 30 June 2001 and thereafter to 30 June each year. The accounting periods are:

YE	31/3/00
15 months	30/6/01
YE	30/6/02
YE	30/6/03

For CT purposes, the accounts are split into CTAPs not exceeding 12 months:

YE	31/3/00
12 months to	31/3/01
3 months to	30/6/01
YE	30/6/02
YE	30/6/03

Where there is a long period of account, it is split into two CTAPs, the first being for 12 months and the second being for however many months remain in the accounting period.

In order to allocate the income, gains and charges of a long accounting period, the following rules apply:

(a) trading income is calculated before deducting capital allowances and then apportioned on a time basis;

(b) the capital allowances are calculated for each of the CTAPs;

(c) schedule A income is allocated to the period when it is due;

(d) schedule D Case VI income is apportioned on a time basis;

(e) interest receivable is allocated to the period in which it is receivable;

(f) other income and chargeable gains are allocated to the CTAP in which they are received;

(g) charges on income are deducted in the CTAP in which they are paid.

EXAMPLE

Ambleside Ltd has no associated companies and prepared accounts for an 18-month period to 30 September 2002. The adjusted results were as follows:

	£
Trading profit (before capital allowances)	1 890 000
Bank interest received	205 000
Schedule A (receivable 31/3/02)	10 000
Debenture interest paid (due 30 June each year) (net)	36 000
Charge on income (paid 10/1/02) (net)	7 800
Dividends received from UK companies:	
31/7/01	180 000
31/7/02	45 000

The bank interest was credited as follows:

	£
30/9/01	85 000
31/3/02	60 000
30/9/02	60 000
	205 000

Allowable expenditure for plant and machinery brought forward at 1 April 2001 was £80 000 and no disposals or acquisitions took place in the period to 30 September 2002.

CTAPs: As the accounts have been prepared for an 18-month period this must be split into CTAPs of 12 months and six months as a CTAP cannot exceed 12 months:

period ended 31/3/02 (12 months)
period ended 30/9/02 (6 months)

Trading income: The trading income, before capital allowances, is apportioned on a time basis:

12 months to 31/3/02
$12/18 \times 1\,890\,000 \quad = \underline{£1\,260\,000}$

6 months to 30/9/02
$6/18 \times £1\,890\,000 \quad = \underline{£630\,000}$

Bank interest: This Schedule D Case III income is allocated to the period to which it relates.

Debenture interest: The debenture interest is deducted from the trading income on an accruals basis. The payment of £36 000 represents 24 months interest paid on 30 June each year. Therefore, only 18 months accrued interest is included in the CT computation.

$$31/3/02 \; £18\,000 \times \frac{100}{80} = £22\,500$$

$$30/9/02 \; £18\,000 \times \frac{100}{80} \times \frac{6}{12} = £11\,250$$

Capital allowances:

Period 31/3/02 (12 months)	*Pool* (£)	*Allowances* (£)
B/f	80 000	
WDA 25%	(20 000)	20 000
C/fwd	60 000	

Period 30/9/02 (6 months)		
WDA 25% $\times \dfrac{6}{12}$	(7500)	7500
	52 500	

Rates of CT: The rate at which CT is charged will depend on the level of profits for each period:

12 months to 31/3/02
All in the FY 2001:
upper limit £1 500 000
lower limit £300 000

6 months to 30/9/02
6/12 of FY 2002:
upper limit – 6/12 × £1 500 000 = £750 000
lower limit – 6/12 × £300 000 = £150 000

Charges paid: Charges actually paid are deducted gross in the period in which they are paid:

$$£7800 \times \frac{100}{78} = £10 000$$

Calculation of gross corporation tax:

	31/3/02 (12 months) (£)	30/9/02 (6 months) (£)	
Trading profit	1 260 000	630 000	
less:			
Capital allowances	(20 000)	(7500)	
Debenture interest	(22 500)	(11 250)	
Schedule D Case I	1 217 500	611 250	
Schedule D Case III	145 000	60 000	
Schedule A	10 000	–	
	1 372 500	671 250	
less Charges	(10 000)	–	
PCTCT	1 362 500	671 250	'Income'
c/f			

	31/3/02 (12 months) (£)	30/9/02 (6 months) (£)	
b/f	1 362 500	671 250	
add FII:			
£180 000 × 100/90	200 000		
£45 000 × 100/90		50 000	
	1 562 500	721 250	'Profits'

Period to 31/3/02 (12 months): The 'profit' for this period is greater than £1 500 000 so CT is charged at 30 per cent on the PCTCT:

	£
30% × £1 362 500	408 750
GCT = £408 750	

Period to 30/9/02 (6 months): As the 'profit' for this period is between £150 000 and £750 000, CT is charged at 30 per cent on the PCTCT and marginal relief is deducted:

	£
CT @ 30% × £671 250	201 375
11/400 (£750 000 − £721 250) × 671 250/721 250	(736)
GCT	200 639

Accounting periods straddling 31 March

If a company's accounting period falls into two financial years, and there has been a change in the rates, or small companies limits, the liability is calculated in two parts, e.g., YE 31/12/02 will fall into two financial years as follows:

1/1/02 – 31/3/02	3/12 in the FY 2001
1/4/02 – 31/12/02	9/12 in the FY 2002

EXAMPLE

Windamere Ltd had the following income for YE 30/9/02:

	£
Schedule D Case I	300 000
Chargeable gains	1 500
Bank interest	4 550
Taxed income (gross)	12 000

Windamere Ltd paid charges of £6 000 (gross) during the year:

	£	
Schedule D Case I	300 000	
Schedule D Case III	4 550	
Chargeable gains	1 500	
Taxed income	12 000	
	318 050	
less Charges paid	(6 000)	
PCTCT	312 050	'Income'

As the company received no FII for the YE 30/9/02, the 'income' and 'profit' figure is the same.

However, the period of account falls into two FYs:

1/10/01 – 31/3/02   6/12 FY 2001
1/4/02 – 30/9/02   6/12 FY 2002

As there was a change in the rates of corporation tax between FY 2001 and FY 2002, the GCT must be calculated in two parts:

FY 2001:

6/12 of PCTCT falls into FY 2001, i.e. $6/12 \times £312\,050 = £156\,025$

upper limit $= £1\,500\,000 \times 6/12 = £750\,000$
lower limit $= £300\,000 \times 6/12 = £150\,000$

As the company's profit is between £150 000 and £750 000, CT is charged at 30% per cent on £156 025, and marginal relief deducted:

	£
CT @ 30% × £156 025	46 807
Less:	
*1/40 (750 000–156 025)	(14 850)
GCT	31 957

* As there is no FII, 'Income' and 'Profits' are the same figure. Therefore, the 'Income'/'Profits' element of the marginal relief formula is ignored because it equals one.

FY 2002:

6/12 of PCTCT falls into FY 2002. The limits for the FY 2001 are the same as the FY 2002, however the rate for small companies and the starting rate did change with the consequence that the fractions for marginal relief changed between the two financial years.

	£
CT @ 30% × £156 025	46 807
less: 11/400 (£750 000 – £156 025)	(16 335)
GCT	30 472

Total GCT for YE 30/9/02 $= £31\,957 + £30\,472 = £62\,429$

SELF ASSESSMENT QUESTIONS

31.1 Wellbetter Ltd manufactures pharmaceutical products and the summarised accounts for the year ended 31/3/03 show the following results:

	£	£
Gross trading profit		1 400 000
Bank interest received		18 000
Dividends received from UK companies		160 000
Debenture interest received (gross)		35 000
Building society interest received		9 000
less:		1 622 000
Rent and rates	46 000	
Repairs and renewals	38 000	
Office expenses	116 000	
Bank interest paid	8 000	(208 000)
Net profit for year		1 414 000

Notes:
1. Office expenses include:

	£
Depreciation	60 000
Entertaining customers	6 000

2. Wellbetter Ltd paid debenture interest of £20 000 (gross) during the year.
3. Capital allowances were agreed at £38 750.
4. During the year Wellbetter Ltd disposed of the following assets:
    (a) In June 2002 the company disposed of investment property for £250 000. The property had been acquired in April 1988 for £90 000.
    (b) In November 2002 the company disposed of its entire holding of shares in Appollo Ltd for £85 000. The shares had been acquired as follows:

	No. of shares	Cost (£)
March 1984	2 000	5 600
June 1990	3 000	18 600

5. Wellbetter Ltd has no associated companies.
6. Repairs and renewals includes £20 000 for repairs to recently acquired plant.
7. During the year charges of £14 000 were paid gross.

REQUIRED

(a) Calculate the Schedule DI adjusted profit for the year ended 31/3/03.
(b) Calculate Wellbetter Ltd's chargeable gains for the year ended 31/3/03.
(c) Calculate the corporation tax payable for the year ended 31/3/03.

31.2 The following information relates to Kirkstone Ltd for its year ended 31/12/02.

	£
	£
Trading income	360 000
Chargeable gains	20 000
Bank interest received	7 000
Rental income	10 000
Debenture interest received (gross)	12 000
Trade Charges paid (gross)	8 000
Debenture interest paid (gross)	25 000
Charitable deed of covenant paid (gross)	2 000

Kirkstone Ltd has no associated companies and received £18 000 in dividends from a UK company during its year ended 31/12/02.

REQUIRED

Calculate Kirkstone Ltd's corporation tax liability for the year ended 31/12/02.

CHAPTER 32

Advance corporation tax and income tax

UK resident companies must account to the Revenue for the basic rate and lower rate income tax deducted on certain payments they make. Accounting for income tax is achieved by a system of quarterly accounting.

Prior to 6 April 1999, UK resident companies also had to account quarterly for advance corporation tax (ACT), payable when the company made a qualifying distribution. From 6 April 1999, however, ACT is abolished, and a system of 'shadow ACT' introduced to enable companies to relieve the surplus ACT accumulated at 6 April 1999.

This chapter explains the meaning of a qualifying distribution, the system of shadow ACT and quarterly accounting for income tax, and concludes by examining the treatment of shadow ACT and income tax in calculating a company's corporation tax liability.

Qualifying and non-qualifying distributions

A distribution includes the transfer of assets from a company. Sections 209–11 of the ICTA 1988 set out what is meant by a distribution. The definition of what constitutes a qualifying distribution is very wide and includes all payments made to shareholders other than repayments of capital, for example:

- dividends;
- excessive interest payments;
- the issue of redeemable shares or securities without consideration being received for the issue;
- distributions from a company's assets in respect of shares, other than capital repayments.

The following are non-qualifying distributions:

- bonus issues;
- repayments or reductions of capital;

    Note: If there is a bonus issue and a simultaneous repayment or reduction of capital, a qualifying distribution may arise.

- distributions in respect of share capital on a winding up;

- distributions in an approved demerger;

- purchase of a company's own shares, provided that the conditions of ss 219–29, ICTA 1988 apply;

- stock dividends, i.e. shares that are issued instead of the company paying a dividend.

The essential difference between a qualifying and non-qualifying distribution is that a qualifying distribution is a past or present transfer of assets as opposed to a non-qualifying distribution which amounts to a future transfer of assets, i.e. the company's assets will only be depleted at some time in the future. For example, if a company issues redeemable bonus shares, the bonus issue is a non-qualifying distribution, however, the redemption of those shares at some time in the future would amount to a qualifying distribution.

Shadow ACT

Prior to 6 April 1999, when a company paid a qualifying distribution (usually a dividend) it had to account to the Revenue for ACT. The ACT paid on the dividend was equal to the tax credit that was imputed to the shareholder, being 20 per cent for the tax years 1994/95 to 1998/99 inclusive. From 6 April 1999, the tax credit attaching to dividends is reduced to 10 per cent, with a corresponding reduction in the rate of tax on dividend income (*see* Chapter 16), with the company no longer being liable to pay ACT. ACT, as its name implied, was corporation tax paid in advance and, subject to certain restrictions, could be deducted from the company's gross corporation tax to arrive at the corporation tax payable. The maximum ACT that could be deducted for an accounting period was calculated as:

PCTCT × ACT rate

A company unable to relieve all the ACT paid in a period could either carry forward the surplus ACT, or carry it back for six years on a LIFO basis, again having regard for the maximum amount of ACT that could be off-set against its gross corporation tax. Companies with surplus ACT brought forward at 6 April 1999, when ACT is abolished, can relieve it through the system of shadow ACT, which will work as follows:

(1) Calculate the ACT that would have been paid on the dividends had ACT not been abolished; this is known as the 'shadow ACT'.

(2) Calculate the maximum ACT set-off under the rules prior to 6 April 1999, i.e.:

PCTCT × ACT rate

(3) The surplus ACT that can be relieved is the difference between the maximum ACT and the shadow ACT.

EXAMPLE

A company has surplus ACT of £90 000 brought forward at 1/4/99. During the year ending 31/3/2000 the company pays a dividend of £90 000, and has a PCTCT of £200 000.

Shadow ACT:

$$(£90\,000 \times \frac{100}{80}) \times 20\% = \underline{£22\,500}$$

Maximum ACT:

$$£200\,000 \times 20\% = \underline{£40\,000}$$

	£
Maximum ACT	40 000
less Shadow ACT	(22 500)
Maximum accumulated ACT to be set-off for YE 31/3/2000	17 500

Accumulated ACT carried forward at 1/4/2000 £72 500.

Where the company has also received FII during the accounting period, the FII is deducted from the FP in order to calculate the shadow ACT. However, because the tax credit on dividends is reduced from 20 per cent to 10 per cent from April 1999, the FII and the FP must be adjusted by $\frac{9}{8}$. This is because the shadow ACT is calculated as if ACT had not been abolished, i.e. as if the tax credit was 20 per cent.

EXAMPLE

	£
Dividend received	27 000
Dividend paid	90 000

$$\text{Franked payment} = £90\,000 \times \frac{100}{90} = £100\,000$$

$$\text{Franked Investment income} = £27\,000 \times \frac{100}{90} = £30\,000$$

Shadow ACT is calculated as follows:

	£
FP : £100 000 $\times \dfrac{9}{8}$	112 500
less FII: £ 30 000 $\times \dfrac{9}{8}$	(33 750)

Shadow ACT = 78 750 @ 20% = £15 750

This is the same ACT that would have been paid had ACT not been abolished:

$$\text{FP: £90 000} \times \frac{100}{80} \qquad \text{£} \atop 112\,500$$

$$\textit{less} \text{ FII: £30 000} \times \frac{100}{80} \qquad (33\,750)$$

ACT = 78 750 @ 20% = £15 750

The Shadow ACT, however, is easier to calculate using the net amounts:

Shadow ACT	£
Dividends paid	90 000
less Dividends received	(27 000)
	63 000

$$\text{Shadow ACT} = \text{£63 000} \times \frac{1}{4} = \underline{\text{£ 15 750}}$$

Quarterly accounting for income tax

When a company pays charges on income, the payment is made net of basic rate income tax and the company must account to the Revenue for the basic rate income tax deducted, the gross amount of the charge being known as an unfranked payment (UP).

Unfranked payment = Charge paid + Basic rate income tax

From 1 April 2001, however, the paying company is not required to deduct basic rate income tax where the recipient is a company within the charge to CT. Similarly, from 1 April 2001, companies are not required to deduct income tax at 20 per cent on payments of interest made to companies within the charge to CT. However, as these new rules do not apply in all situations, for example, where the recipient is an individual, quarterly accounting for income tax is not completely redundant. The following examples examine the situation prior to 1 April 2001, which will continue to apply where payments are not eligible to be paid gross.

Companies are required to make a return of their income tax position on the form CT 61 showing income tax payable and repayable, for each of the calendar quarters:

31 March

30 June

30 September

31 December

If the company's year end does not coincide with any of the above dates, a fifth return is needed at the company's year end. For example, a company whose year end is 31 July will have the following return periods:

30 September

31 December

31 March

30 June

31 July

The CT 61 form must be submitted within 14 days after the end of the return period, although a nil return is not required.

Where the tax suffered on income exceeds the tax deducted on payments, there is no carry forward facility: any overall income tax reclaimable at the end of an accounting period can be used to reduce the company's CT liability or, if there is no liability to CT, the income tax is repaid.

Note: For accounting periods ending after 31 March 1996, interest paid and received is dealt with in the CT computation on an *accruals basis*, while charges on income are dealt with in the CT computation on a *paid basis*. However, for the purposes of quarterly accounting for income tax, *all* payments and receipts, i.e. charges and interest, are dealt with under a *paid basis*. For this reason, care must be taken with interest payments to use the correct basis.

EXAMPLE 1

For the YE 31/12/01 Lark Ltd had the following transactions:

	£
1 March 2001 paid debenture interest (gross)	10 000
16 April 2001 received interest on debentures (gross)	12 000
25 September 2001 paid deed of covenant (gross)	1 000
16 November 2001 received interest on debentures (gross)	12 000

Return period	Tax on payments	Tax on income	Cumulative net	IT paid (repaid)	Due date
31/3/01	2 000 (20%)		2 000	2 000	14/4/01
30/6/01		2 400 (20%)	(400)	(2 000)	14/7/01
30/9/01	220 (22%)		(180)	–	14/10/01
31/12/01		2 400 (20%)	(2 580)	–	14/1/02

The net result is that over the accounting period an excess of income tax is suffered which is reclaimable either against CT liability or as a repayment.

	£
Tax on income	4 800
Tax on payments	(2 220)
Reclaimable	2 580

EXAMPLE 2

For the YE 30/6/01 Jay Ltd had the following transactions:

	£
16 July 2000 paid debenture interest (gross)	15 000
31 October 2000 received interest on Treasury Stock (gross)	10 000
16 January 2001 paid debenture interest (gross)	15 000
10 March 2001 paid deed of covenant (gross)	1 000
31 March 2001 received interest on Treasury Stock (gross)	10 000

Return period	Tax on payments	Tax on income	Cumulative net	IT paid (repaid)	Due date
30/9/00	3 000 (20%)	–	3 000	3 000	14/10/00
31/12/00	–	2 000 (20%)	1 000	(2 000)	14/1/01
31/3/01	3 000 (20%)				
	220 (22%)	2 000 (20%)	2 220	2 220	14/4/01
30/6/99	No return needed				

There will be no repayment of income tax as the tax on payments exceeds the tax on income:

	£
Tax on income	4000
Tax on payments	(6220)
Net tax payable	2220

Calculation of the corporation tax liability

1. ACT set off

Prior to 6 April 1999, ACT was payable when a company paid a dividend under a quarterly accounting system in the same way as income tax. ACT paid during an accounting period could then be deducted from the company's gross corporation tax, restricted to the maximum set off, i.e. PCTCT × ACT rate. From 6 April 1999, a company no longer has to pay ACT on its distributions; any surplus ACT accumulated at 6 April 1999 can, however, be deducted from the gross corporation tax under the shadow ACT regime.

EXAMPLE

Osprey Ltd had the following income for YE 31/3/02:

	£
Schedule DI	180 000
Chargeable gains	8 000
Bank interest received	3 000
Dividends received	18 000

During the year to 31/3/02 the following payments were made:

	£
Patent royalties (gross)	15 000
Dividends paid	80 000

Osprey had no associated companies. There was £60 000 of accumulated ACT brought forward at 1/4/01.

	£
Schedule DI	180 000
Schedule DIII	3 000
Chargeable gains	8 000
	191 000
less Charges	(15 000)
PCTCT	176 000

$$add \text{ FII: } £18\,000 \times \frac{100}{90}$$

	£
	20 000
'Profits'	196 000

The company is a small company as profits are between £50 000 and £300 000.

Shadow ACT:

	£
Dividends paid	80 000
less Dividends received	(18 000)
	62 000

$$\text{Shadow ACT} = £62\,000 \times \frac{1}{4} = £15\,500$$

ACT set off:

	£
Maximum ACT(PCTCT x 20%)	35 200
less Shadow ACT	(15 500)
Maximum set off	19 700

	£
GCT: £176 000 x 20%	35 200
less ACT set off	(19 700)
CT liability	15 500

Accumulated ACT c/f 1/4/02 = £40 300

2. Double tax relief

Another restriction in the set off of ACT can occur when the company has foreign income. Double tax relief is given before the ACT set off for accounting periods ending after 1 April 1984.

Because the double tax relief is deducted first, it may cause surplus ACT to be generated. Where double tax relief and ACT are involved, the maximum set off rule applies to each category of income (*see* Chapter 37).

Note: ACT is abolished from 6 April 1999.

3. Changes in ownership

As an anti-avoidance measure the ICTA 1988, s 245 provided that ACT set off is also restricted on a change of ownership of the business in the following circumstances:

(a) where there has been a change of ownership and there is a major change in the nature or conduct of the trade within a period of three years before the change or three years after the change; or

(b) where after the change of ownership there is a considerable increase in the activities of the trade, which at the time of the change had become negligible.

Although this anti-avoidance legislation was repealed when ACT was abolished, the essence of the provisions has been maintained in the 'Shadow ACT' regulations.

Income tax set off

There is no carry forward facility for income tax suffered in the quarterly accounting system. If there is excess income tax at the end of the accounting period, this excess can be deducted from the company's MCT liability.

EXAMPLE

The following information relates to Peacock Ltd for the YE 31/3/03.

	£
Schedule D Case I	1 600 000
Schedule D Case III	10 000
Taxed interest received (gross) (rec'd net)	30 000
Patent royalties paid (gross) (paid net)	15 000

	£
Schedule D Case I	1 600 000
Schedule D Case III	10 000
Taxed income	30 000
	1 640 000
less Charges paid	(15 000)
PCTCT	1 625 000

GCT is charged at 30 per cent because the company is a large company.

	£
GCT @ 30% × £1 625 000	487 500

	£
Tax on income (20% × £30 000)	6 000
Tax on payments (22% × £15 000)	(3300)
Reclaimable	2 700

	£
GCT	487 500
less Income tax	(2 700)
Corporation tax liability	484 800

If during the accounting period the tax on income is less than the tax on payments, there will be no deduction for income tax.

EXAMPLE

The following information relates to Magpie Ltd for YE 31/3/03:

	£
Schedule D Case I	170 000
Schedule D Case III	20 000
Taxed interest (gross) (rec'd net)	19 000
Charges paid (gross) (paid net)	35 000

Magpie Ltd has no associated companies.

	£
Schedule D Case I	170 000
Schedule D Case III	20 000
Taxed interest	19 000
	209 000
less Charges paid	(35 000)
PCTCT	174 000

GCT is charged at small companies rate because the PCTCT is between £50 000 and £300 000.

	£
GCT @ 19% × £174 000	33 060

There is no income tax set off as the tax on payments is greater than the tax on income.

Where the CT is insufficient to absorb the income tax due, a repayment is due from the Revenue.

EXAMPLE

The following information relates to Swan Ltd for YE 31/3/03:

	£
Schedule D Case I	50 000
Schedule D Case III	10 000
Schedule A	5 000
Taxed interest received (gross) (rec'd net)	90 000
Dividends paid	60 000
Charges paid (gross) (paid net)	15 000

Swan Ltd has accumulated ACT of £45 000 brought forward at 1/4/02.

Swan Ltd has no associated companies.

	£
Schedule D Case I	50 000
Schedule D Case III	10 000
Schedule A	5 000
Taxed interest	90 000
	155 000
less Charges paid	(15 000)
PCTCT	140 000

As the 'profits' are between £50 000 and £300 000, Swan Ltd is classed as a small company and charged to CT at small companies rate.

Shadow ACT YE 31/3/03

$$£60 000 \times \frac{1}{4} = £15 000$$

		£
Maximum ACT	Max. ACT	28 000
PCTCT × 20%	*less* Shadow ACT	(15 000)
£140 000 × 20% = £28 000	Max. accumulated ACT to set off YE 31/3/03	13 000

Income tax:

	£
Tax on interest (20%)	18 000
Tax on charges (22%)	(3 300)
Reclaimable	£14 700

	£
GCT @ 19% × £140 000	26 600
less Accumulated ACT set off	(13 000)
	13 600
less Income tax	(13 600)
Corporation tax liability	nil

Accumulated ACT c/f 1/4/03 = £32 000. £1 100 of income tax is reclaimable.

SELF ASSESSMENT QUESTIONS

32.1 Swallow Ltd received the following income for its year ended 31/3/03:

	£
Trading income	490 000
Chargeable gains	80 000
Bank interest received	20 000
Rental income	10 000
Debenture interest received (net)	20 000
Dividends received from UK companies	11 250

During the year it made the following payments:

	£
Patents royalties (net)	4 680
Debenture interest (net)	8 000
Charitable deed of covenant (net)	2 340
Dividends paid	42 750

Swallow Ltd has one associated company.

REQUIRED

Calculate Swallows Ltd's corporation tax liability for the year ended 31/3/03.

32.2 At 1/4/02 Sparrow Ltd had surplus ACT of £110 000 brought forward. During its year end to 31/3/03 it paid a dividend of £180 000. For the year ended 31/3/03 the PCTCT was £480 000, and the 'profit' for small companies rate purposes was £550 000. Sparrow Ltd has two associated companies.

REQUIRED

Calculate Sparrow Ltd's corporation tax liability for the year ended 31/3/03, and state how much ACT there is to carry forward at 1/4/03.

CHAPTER 33

Loss relief

Loss relief is available when a company incurs a loss. The type of relief available depends on whether the loss is a trading loss or a non-trading loss. Losses incurred as a result of trading activities receive more favourable tax treatment than non-trading losses, as it is considered that there is less likelihood of engineering a trading loss as opposed to other losses. This chapter examines the reliefs available to companies for trading and non-trading losses and concludes by looking at the corporation tax position when a company is in liquidation or receivership.

Relief for trading losses

The reliefs available are as follows:

1. Carry forward the trading loss to subsequent accounting periods (ICTA 1988, s 393(1))

Trading losses can be carried forward indefinitely and set off against the *first available trading income of the same trade.*

EXAMPLE

The following information relates to Arthur Ltd for the year ended 31 March 2002:

	£
Schedule D Case I	7 000
Taxed income (gross)	2 000
Schedule D Case III	900
Chargeable gains	1 200
Patent royalties paid (gross)	1 000
Losses brought forward under s 393(1)	(10 000)

Arthur Ltd has no associated companies.

	£	£
Schedule D Case I		7 000
s 393(1)	(10 000)	
Relieved	7 000	(7 000)
C/f s 393(1)	(3 000)	nil

	£	£
Taxed income		2 000
Schedule D Case III		900
Chargeable gains		1 200
		4 100
less Charges paid		(1 000)
PCTCT		3 100

GCT: £3100 × 10%   310

NB: The starting rate for FY 2002 is 0%.

2. Off set trading losses against total profits

The claim must be made within two years of the end of the accounting period in which the loss was incurred.

The company may set the trading loss against its other income and gains of the same period *before* deducting charges on income (ICTA 1988, s 393A(1)(*a*)). Any loss still unrelieved may be carried back and set off against the total profits for the 12 months prior to the accounting period in which the loss was incurred, *after* deducting *trade charges* (ICTA 1988, s 393A(1)(*b*)). The claim for the current year must be made first. No claim can be made unless the trade was carried on, on a commercial basis, with a view to profit (ICTA 1988, s 393(5)).

If the company is engaged in the trade of farming or market gardening, relief under this section is denied where the company has made losses in each of the five years prior to the year for which loss relief is claimed (ICTA 1988, s 397).

Note: The company may still carry forward the loss under (ICTA 1988, s 393(1)).

EXAMPLE

The following information relates to Merlin Ltd for the three years ending 31/3/03:

	Year ending 31 March		
	2001	*2002*	*2003*
	£	£	£
Schedule DI profit (loss)	15 000	(50 000)	16 000
Schedule A	10 000	10 000	10 000
Schedule DIII	4 000	5 000	2 000
Chargeable gains	nil	2 000	7 000

The loss of £50 000 in the year to 31/3/02 is relieved as follows:

(a) claim under s 393A for current year by 31/3/2004
(b) claim under s 393A for previous year by 31/3/2004
(c) any loss still unrelieved is carried forward under s 393(1).

Year ending 31 March

	2001 £	2002 £	2003 £
Schedule DI	15 000	nil	16 000
s 393(1)	–	–	(4 000)
	15 000	nil	12 000
Schedule A	10 000	10 000	10 000
Schedule DIII	4 000	5 000	2 000
Chargeable gains	nil	2 000	7 000
	29 000	17 000	31 000
s 393A(1)(a)	–	(17 000)	–
	29 000	nil	31 000
s 393A(1)(b)	(29 000)	–	–
PCTCT	nil	nil	31 000

Loss memo	£
YE 31/3/02	(50 000)
s 393A(1)(a) YE 2002	17 000
	(33 000)
s 393A(1)(b) YE 2001	29 000
	(4 000) c/f s 393 (1)
s 393(1) YE 2003	4 000

Losses incurred prior to 2 July 1997

Losses incurred prior to 2 July 1997 could be carried back and set off against the total profits for the 36 months prior to the accounting period in which the loss was incurred, on a LIFO basis, *after* deducting trade charges, under s 393A(1)(b). The FA 1997 reduced the carry back facility to 12 months, reverting to the situation that existed before 1991.

Although losses incurred before 2 July 1997 could be carried back for 36 months after a claim for the current year had been made, the method of computation was the same. The three-year carry back facility is, however, retained for losses incurred after 2 July 1997 in the following situations:

- losses due to 100 per cent allowances on the costs of decommissioning North Sea oil and gas installations; and
- trading losses incurred in the final 12 months before cessation (terminal loss relief).

Unrelieved charges on income (ICTA 1988, s 393(9))

The normal method of obtaining relief for charges paid is by deduction from total profits. Provided that there is sufficient income to relieve the charges in this way, there is no distinction made between business and non-business charges, e.g. patent royalties and covenanted charitable payments.

However, if there is insufficient income to deduct the charges paid, then the ICTA 1988, s 393(9) provides that *trade* charges may be carried forward as a loss and set off against the first available *trading income* under s 393(1), ICTA 1988.

The amount of trade charges to be carried forward in this way is the lower of:

- unrelieved charges
- trade charges paid.

EXAMPLE

The following relates to Hill Ltd and Park Ltd for the year to 31 March 2003.

	Hill Ltd (£)	Park Ltd (£)
Schedule D Case I	4 000	500
Chargeable gains	500	nil
Patent royalties paid (gross)	3 500	3 500
Covenanted payments to charity (gross)	2 000	2 000

	Hill Ltd (£)	(£)	Park Ltd (£)	(£)
Schedule D Case I		4 000		500
Chargeable gains		500		nil
Total income		4 500		500
Patent royalties paid	3 500		3 500	
Payments to charity	2 000		2 000	
Total charges	5 500		5 500	
Relieved	(4 500)	(4 500)	(500)	(500)
Unrelieved charges	1 000		5 000	
PCTCT		nil		nil

The amount of charges to be carried forward is:

	Hill Ltd (£)	Park Ltd (£)
The lower of:		
(a) unrelieved charges; or	1 000	5 000
(b) trade charges	3 500	3 500
Amount carried forward	1 000	3 500

Trade charges will often become unrelieved on a claim for loss relief under the ICTA 1988, s 393A(1)(*a*) as the relief is given *before* deducting charges.

When preparing loss relief computations, always calculate the PCTCT for the years concerned in the following order:

1. current year
2. previous years
3. subsequent years.

It is also useful to adopt the following format to ensure that relief is given against the correct income:

	£
Schedule D Case I	X
s 393(1)	X̲
	X
Schedule A	X
Schedule D Case III	X
Taxed income	X
Chargeable gains	X̲
	X
s 393A(1)(*a*)	(X̲)
	X
Trade charges	(X̲)
	X
s 393A(1)(*b*)	(X̲)
	X
Non-trade charges	(X̲)
PCTCT	X̲

Loss relief and ACT

Losses carried back to a previous accounting period can have a knock-on effect with regard to ACT. Although ACT was abolished from April 1999, losses carried back to a period before ACT was abolished may have the effect of generating surplus ACT where it had previously been relieved, and for periods after April 1999, the set off of accumulated ACT could be affected.

EXAMPLE

The following information relates to Tintagel Ltd for the year ended 31/3/99:

	£
Schedule DI	100 000
Schedule DIII	20 000
Chargeable gains	15 000
Dividends paid	60 000
Dividends received	20 000
Patent royalties paid (gross)	8 000

Tintagel Ltd's corporation tax liability for the year ended 31/3/99 would have been as follows:

	£
Schedule DI	100 000
Schedule DIII	20 000
Gains	15 000
	135 000
less Charges paid	(8 000)
PCTCT	127 000

$$add \text{ FII:} \left(20000 \times \frac{100}{80}\right)* \qquad 25000$$

'Profits'	152 000

*Tax credit for 1998/99 was 20%.

Assuming that Tintagel Ltd has no associated companies, the corporation tax liability is as follows:

	£
GCT @ 21% x £127 000	26 670
less ACT set off **	(10 000)
CT liability	16 670

** Maximum ACT = 127 000 x 20% = £25 400

ACT paid:	£
Dividends paid	60 000
less Dividends received	(20 000)
	40 000

$$40000 \times \frac{1}{4} = £10000$$

Suppose that Tintagel Ltd's results for the year ended 31/3/00 were as follows:

	£
Schedule DI loss	(140 000)
Schedule DIII	10 000
Patent royalties paid (gross)	8 000

Tintagel could relieve the loss in the current period and the previous 12 months as follows:

	YE 1999 £	YE 2000 £
Schedule DI	100 000	nil
Schedule DIII	20 000	10 000
Gains	15 000	nil
	135 000	10 000
less s 393A(1)(a)	–	(10 000)
	135 000	nil
less Trade charges	(8 000)	(nil)
	127 000	nil
less s 393A(1)(b)	(127 000)	(–)
PCTCT	nil	nil

Loss memo	£
YE 31/3/00	(140 000)
s 393A(1)(a)	10 000
	(130 000)
s 393A(1)(b)	127 000
C/f	(3 000)
Trade charges c/f	(8 000)
Total c/f	(11 000)

Tintagel Ltd will receive a repayment of corporation tax for the year ended 31/3/99. However, as the PCTCT is nil, the s 393A(1)(b) claim has the effect of generating surplus ACT for the year ended 31/3/99. Tintagel Ltd's accumulated ACT at 1/4/99 can be relieved under the shadow ACT rules in the year ended 31/3/01, assuming that the surplus ACT cannot be carried back to earlier accounting periods.

Suppose the results for YE 31/3/01 were as follows:

	£
Schedule DI	60 000
Schedule DIII	10 000
Chargeable gains	2 000
Patent royalties paid (gross)	8 000
Dividends paid	20 000
Dividends received	9 000

	£
Schedule DI	60 000
less s 393(1)	(11 000)
	49 000
Schedule DIII	10 000
Gains	2 000
	61 000
less Trade charges	(8 000)
PCTCT	53 000
add FII: 9000 x $\frac{100}{90}$	10 000
'Profits'	63 000

	£
GCT @ 20% × £ 53 000	10 600
less ACT set off ***	(7 850)
CT liability	2 750

***	£	£	£
Accumulated ACT b/f			10 000
Maximum ACT = 53 000 × 20%		10 600	
less Shadow ACT:			
Dividends paid	20 000		
Dividends received	(9 000)		
	11 000 × $\frac{1}{4}$	(2 750)	
Maximum set off		7 850	(7 850)
Accumulated ACT c/f			2 150

Restriction of relief

Under the provisions of the ICTA 1988, s 768 the right to carry forward the loss is lost if:

(a) within a period of three years there is both a change in the ownership of the company and a major change in the nature of the trade; or

(b) the state of activity of the company becomes negligible and there is a change of ownership before there is any considerable revival of the trade.

Also, for changes of ownership after 13 June 1991, the restriction also applies to the carry back of losses to previous accounting periods where (a) or (b) above applies, i.e. losses incurred after the change of ownership cannot be carried back to profits before the change.

The restrictions are designed to prevent tax avoidance where a company is bought and sold purely for its tax losses. The Revenue have issued a statement of practice (SP 10/91) setting out guidelines as to what it considers to be a major change in the nature or conduct of the business, giving consideration to the following factors:

- customers
- markets
- facilities
- methods of manufacture
- location
- pricing and purchasing policies
- management and staff.

However, changes that are made merely to increase efficiency or to keep abreast with technology will not be regarded as a major change for the purposes of the ICTA 1988, s 768. The statement includes the following examples of where the Revenue is prepared to draw the line:

'Examples where a change would not of itself be regarded as a major change:

(a) A company manufacturing kitchen fitments in three obsolescent factories moves production to one new factory (increasing efficiency).

(b) A company manufacturing kitchen utensils replaces enamel by plastic, or a company manufacturing timepieces replaces mechanical by electronic components (keeping pace with developing technology).

(c) A company operating a dealership in one make of car switches to operating a dealership in another make of car satisfying the same market (not a major change in the type of property dealt in).

(d) A company manufacturing both filament and fluorescent lamps (of which filament lamps form the greater part of the output) concentrates solely on filament lamps (a rationalisation of product range without a major change in the type of property dealt in).

Examples where a major change would be regarded as occurring:

(e) A company operating a dealership in saloon cars switches to operating a dealership in tractors (a major change in the services or facilities provided).

(f) A company owning a public house switches to operating a discotheque in the same, but converted, premises (a major change in the services or facilities provided).

(g) A company fattening pigs for their owners switches to buying pigs for fattening and resale (a major change in the nature of the trade, being a change from providing a service to being a primary producer).'

Terminal loss relief

The three-year carry back facility is still available where a company incurs a loss in its final year of trading. In this case the loss can be carried back for three years on a LIFO basis.

EXAMPLE

Camelot Ltd ceased trading on 31/3/03. The following information relates to the five years ending on 31/3/03:

Year ended 31 March

	1999	2000	2001	2002	2003
	£	£	£	£	£
Schedule DI	100 000	80 000	50 000	12 000	(100 000)
Trade charges	10 000	10 000	10 000	10 000	10 000
Non-trade charges	3 000	3 000	3 000	3 000	3 000

Terminal loss:

	£
Trading loss 12 months to 31/3/03	100 000
Unrelieved trade charges	10 000
Terminal loss	110 000

Year ended 31 March

	1999	2000	2001	2002	2003
	£	£	£	f	£
Schedule DI	100 000	80 000	50 000	12 000	nil
Trade charges	(10 000)	(10 000)	(10 000)	(10 000)	–
	90 000	70 000	40 000	2 000	nil
Terminal loss relief	nil	(68 000)	(40 000)	(2 000)	–
	90 000	2 000	nil	nil	nil
Non-trade charges	(3 000)	(2 000)	–	–	–
PCTCT	87 000	nil	nil	nil	nil

Notes:

(1) The non-trade charges for 2001, 2002 and 2003 are lost, as is £1000 of the non-charge in 2000.

(2) If Camelot could not have relieved the loss by 31/3/00, it could not have carried back the loss to 1999, as terminal losses can only be carried back for 36 months.

(3) Camelot Ltd will receive a repayment of corporation tax for the years ending 31/3/00, 31/3/01, and 31/3/02.

Loss memo

	£
Terminal loss	(110 000)
YE 2002	2 000
	(108 000)
YE 2001	40 000
	(68 000)
YE 2000	68 000

Loss surrendered as group relief ICTA 1988, s 402

Companies in the same 75 per cent group or consortia can transfer trading losses to the profit making companies in the group or consortia. This is known as group relief and is covered in detail in Chapter 36.

Relief for non-trading losses

1. Capital losses

Where a company incurs a capital loss, the loss is first used to reduce any capital gains in the same accounting period; any unrelieved loss being carried forward and set against the company's capital gains in a subsequent accounting period.

Capital losses cannot be carried back to a previous accounting period or set off against other income of the company.

2. Schedule A

Prior to 1 April 1998, Schedule A losses could only be carried forward and set off against future Schedule A income. However, in the FA 1998 the corporation tax rules regarding property income were amended, with effect from 1 April 1998, to bring them more in line with the income tax rules, whilst preserving relief for corporate interest and management expenses. From 1 April 1998, Schedule A losses are treated in the same way as management expenses, i.e. they are first set against other income and gains for the same period. This is significantly more generous than the income tax treatment of Schedule A losses. Any Schedule A loss still unrelieved can then be either:

- carried forward and set off against the total income of a subsequent accounting period, if the 'Schedule A business' is still being carried on in the accounting period in which relief is claimed; or
- surrendered as group relief.

3. Unrelieved interest on loans

The precise tax treatment depends on whether the loan is for trading or non-trading purposes:

(a) Trading loans

Interest paid on loans taken out for trading purposes is deducted from the Schedule D Case I results. If this creates or increases a loss, the resulting trading loss can be relieved under s 393, ICTA 1988.

(b) Non-trading loans

Interest and costs on non-trading loans are set against Schedule D Case III income. Where this results in a net loss, relief is available as follows:

- against the PCTCT in the same accounting period *after* brought forward trading losses under the ICTA 1988, s 393(1) have been relieved but *before* s 393A relief;
- against Schedule D Case III income of the previous 12 months on a LIFO basis;

- against future non-trading profits; and
- surrendered as group relief.

Relief for non-trading deficits must be made within two years and partial claims are allowed. In practice it is unlikely that companies will have non-trading loans and especially to the extent that interest payable could not be relieved immediately against other profits.

4. Schedule D Case V

Where a trade is taxed under Schedule D Case V because it is carried on and controlled overseas, any Schedule D Case V loss is carried forward and set off against the first available Schedule D Case V income.

Schedule D Case V losses cannot be carried back to a previous accounting period or set off against other income and gains of the company.

Note: Section 393(1)(*a*) and (*b*) only applies to Schedule D Case I *trading losses.*

5. Schedule D Case VI

Schedule D Case VI losses may be carried forward and set off against future Schedule D Case VI income. *Schedule D Case VI losses cannot be carried back to a previous accounting period or set off against other income and gains of the company.*

Receiverships

If a company becomes unable to pay its debts, the secured creditors can appoint a receiver to run the business as a going concern and/or sell the company's assets in order to pay off the secured loan. The appointment of a receiver does not affect the CT position of the company, the company's trade is continued, it is merely treated as a change in the management, any profits and gains are subject to CT for the normal accounting period and loss relief is available in the normal way.

When a company goes into receivership, it is not necessarily followed by a liquidation of the business, the receiver may sell the business as a going concern.

Hive downs (ICTA 1988, s 343)

Where a company is in receivership and likely to go into liquidation, another possibility is to effect a reconstruction without a change of ownership before a liquidator is appointed, as a portion of any tax losses may be carried forward to the transferee company provided that the conditions contained in the ICTA 1988, s 343 apply that is, provided that at least 75 per cent of the shares belong to the same persons *at some time within one year before* the transfer and at *any time* within *two years after* the transfer.

A reconstruction under s 343, ICTA 1988 provides for the following:

Capital allowances

On the transfer the capital allowance computations are not interrupted. This fact may actually work against the transferee company, as on a subsequent sale of the assets concerned there may be a liability for balancing charges. If the amounts involved are likely to be significant, a transfer of the trade outside s 343 may be more prudent.

Trading losses

Trading losses can be carried forward under the ICTA 1988, s 393(1). However, for hive downs after 19 March 1986, the amount of loss that can be carried forward by the transferee company is reduced by an amount equal to the difference between the transferor company's relevant liabilities and relevant assets immediately prior to the transfer.

Relevant liabilities

Liabilities outstanding and not transferred excluding share capital, reserves and loan stock.

Relevant assets

Assets held and not transferred *plus* the consideration paid by the transferee company.

Note: It should be remembered that the ICTA 1988, s 768 may prevent the use of the tax losses if there is a major change in the nature or conduct of the business (*see* SP 10/91).

Section 343, ICTA 1988 fails to deal with the following areas of corporation tax:

- ACT – unrelieved ACT is not carried forward to the transferee company;
- capital losses – unrelieved capital losses are not carried forward to the transferee company;
- chargeable assets – on a hive down chargeable assets are transferred on a no gain/no loss basis. However, if the hive down company is subsequently sold the gain crystallises.

EXAMPLE

Padley Ltd ceased trading on 1 January 2003. Its summarised balance sheet at that date was:

	£(000s)	£(000s)
Freehold factory		80
Freehold warehouse		40
Plant and machinery		30
Motor vehicles		30
		180
Current assets		
Stock	125	
Debtors	375	
Cash	1	
	501	

Current liabilities

Trade creditors	425	
Bank overdraft (unsecured)	375	
Hire purchase liabilities	31	
	831	
Net current liabilities		(330)
Creditors due after more than year:		
Loan secured on freehold warehouse		(35)
		(185)
Share capital		100
Profit and loss account		(285)
		(185)

The profit and loss account for the final year's trading comprised:

	£(000s)	£(000s)
Turnover		1 825
Opening stock	225	
Purchases	1 375	
	1 600	
Closing stock	125	
Cost of sales		(1 475)
Gross profit		350
less:		
Wages and salaries	(180)	
Depreciation	(30)	
Other overheads	(305)	
		(515)
Net loss for the year		(165)

You ascertain that there have been no additions or disposals of fixed assets during the year, and that the unrelieved expenditure brought forward at 1 January 2002 was £20 000 for the plant pool; none of the buildings qualified as an industrial building. It is accepted that book values approximate to the actual market values of fixed assets at 31 December 2002. No vehicles originally cost more than £12 000.

There were unrelieved trading losses at 1 January 2002 amounting to £290 000. The company has incurred substantial losses in each of the last three years.

Other overheads include an increase in the general bad debts provision of £75 000 and disallowable items of a capital nature of £5000.

A receiver was appointed by the bank at the request of the directors on 18 December 2002. A wholly owned subsidiary, Gill Ltd, was formed and on 1 January 2002 the assets and undertaking of Padley Ltd were hived down. All assets were transferred to Gill Ltd except the freehold warehouse which the receiver sold to a third party on 10 January 2003. No liabilities were transferred to Gill Ltd other than the hire purchase liabilities which relate entirely to plant and motor vehicles. The consideration for the trade transferred was the issue of shares in Gill Ltd which were quickly sold by the receiver to a third party for £475 000.

You are required to:

(1) calculate the losses available to Padley Ltd for the year ended 31 December 2002;

(2) indicate the amount of unrelieved trading losses which are available to be transferred to Gill Ltd.

(ATII, November 1987, Updated)

(1) Losses available for year to 31/12/02

	£(000s)	£(000s)
Net loss as per A/Cs		(165)
add back:		
Depreciation	30	
Bad debts prov.	75	
Capital items	5	110
		(55)
less CA (£20 000 × 25%)		(5)
Trading loss		(60)
Unrelieved losses at 1/1/02		290
Trading loss for YE 31/12/02		60
Unrelieved losses at 31/12/02		350

(2) Losses available to Gill Ltd:

Relevant assets:	£(000s)	£(000s)
Assets not transferred:		
Freehold warehouse		40
less Loan on warehouse		(35)
		5
Consideration received		475
		480

Relevant liabilities:		£(000s)
Current liabilities		831
less Liabilities transferred		(31)
		800

	£(000s)	£(000s)
Unrelieved losses		350
Relevant liabilities	800	
Relevant assets	(480)	(320)
Losses transferred to Gill Ltd		30

Liquidations

For corporation tax purposes an accounting period comes to an end:

- on the cessation of trading;
- at the commencement of liquidation;
- 12 months after the commencement of liquidation.

EXAMPLE

Faltering Ltd ceased to trade on 31 March 2001. It had previously prepared accounts for calendar years. A liquidator was appointed on 1 June 2001 and the company was wound up on 30 November 2002. The accounting periods for corporation tax purposes are:

YE 31/12/00	Normal year end
Period 1/1/01 – 31/3/01	Accounting period comes to an end when the company ceases to trade
Period 1/4/01 – 31/5/01	Accounting period ends when the liquidator is appointed
YE 31/5/02	Accounting period ends 12 months after appointment of liquidator
Period 1/6/02 – 30/11/02	Accounting period ends when company is wound up.

Although the cessation of trading normally marks the end of an accounting period, it is irrelevant if it occurs *after* winding up has commenced and does not bring about the end of an accounting period, as it would do if it took place *before* liquidation commenced.

EXAMPLE

Stumbling Ltd appointed a liquidator on 31 March 2000, having normally prepared accounts for calendar years. Trading continues until 31 August 2001 and the company was wound up on 10 December 2002. The corporation tax accounting periods are as follows:

YE 31/12/99	Company's normal year end
Period 1/1/00 – 31/3/00	Accounting period ends when liquidator is appointed
YE 31/3/01	Accounting period ends 12 months after liquidator is appointed
YE 31/3/02	Second 12-month period after appointment of liquidator
Period 1/4/02 – 10/12/02	Accounting period ends on winding up.

In this case, cessation of trading is irrelevant as it takes place after the liquidation has commenced.

Where there are substantial trading losses, the timing of a resolution to wind up a company can be significant.

EXAMPLE

Falling Ltd prepares accounts to 31 December each year. At 1 January 2002 it had a brought forward trading loss of £45 000. A liquidator was appointed on 30 September

2002 and losses in the period to 30 September 2002 were £75 000. The company suffered a further trading loss of £150 000 by 31 December 2002 when trading ceased. The freehold premises were sold realising a chargeable gain of £300 000 and a balancing charge of £90 000, and the company was wound up.

The corporation tax accounting periods are:

YE 31/12/01   Company's normal year end
1/1/02 – 30/9/02   Accounting period ends on the appointment of the liquidator
1/10/02 – 31/12/02   Accounting period ends when the company is wound up

The tax position would be:

Nine months to 30/9/02

	£	£
Schedule D Case I loss		(75 000)
Loss brought forward s 393(1)		(45 000)
Schedule D Case I loss c/f s 393(1)		(120 000)

Three months to 31/12/02

	£	£
Schedule D Case I loss	(150 000)	
Balancing charge	90 000	
Loss	(60 000)	
Chargeable gain	300 000	
s 393A(1)(*a*)	(60 000)	
Assessable profit	240 000	
Unrelieved losses	(120 000)	

The tax position could have been improved if the company could have delayed the appointment of the liquidator until after the property had been sold:

YE 31/12/01	£	£
Schedule D Case I loss c/f s 393(1)		(45 000)
YE 31/12/02		
Schedule D Case I loss b/f s 393(1)		(45 000)
Schedule D Case I loss	(225 000)	
Balancing charge	90 000	
	(135 000)	
Chargeable gain	300 000	
s 393A(1)(*a*)	(135 000)	
Assessable profit	165 000	
Unrelieved losses	(45 000)	

The sale of an industrial building will generally give rise to a balancing charge. If this occurs after the trade has ceased, the balancing charge is treated as if it were income assessable under Schedule A. However, by concession ESC B19, if the company has unused trading losses, these may be used to off set the balancing charge.

Once a liquidator is appointed, the assets are held in trust by the liquidator for the creditors and shareholders of the company. Where a parent company goes into liquidation, the degree of ownership will be affected which in turn will affect the reliefs available to groups. Group relationships and liquidations are considered in Chapter 36.

SELF ASSESSMENT QUESTIONS

33.1 The following information relates to XYZ Ltd for the three years ended 31/12/02:

	31 December		
	2000	*2001*	*2002*
	£	£	£
Schedule DI profit (loss)	60 000	(100 000)	100 000
Schedule A	15 000	15 000	15 000
Bank interest received	7 000	8 000	10 000
Chargeable gains	18 000	10 000	15 000
Allowable capital losses	(20 000)	(2 000)	(7 000)
Patent royalties paid (gross)	8 000	8 000	8 000
Charitable covenant paid (gross)	1 000	1 000	1 000

XYZ Ltd has no associated companies. There are £5000 trading losses brought forward at 1/1/00.

REQUIRED

Calculate the corporation tax liabilities for the three years.

33.2 RST Ltd commenced trading on 1/4/00. Results for the first three years are as follows:

	31 March		
	2001	*2002*	*2003*
	£	£	£
Schedule DI profit (loss)	10 000	35 000	(60 000)
Patent royalties received (gross)	8 000	8 000	8 000
Debenture interest received (gross)	12 000	12 000	12 000
Chargeable gains	10 000	nil	5 000
Trade charges paid (gross)	5 000	5 000	5 000
Charitable covenant paid (gross)	2 000	2 000	2 000

RST Ltd has no associated companies.

REQUIRED

Calculate the corporation tax liabilities for each of the three years assuming that loss relief is claimed as early as possible.

CHAPTER 34

Close companies

Companies controlled by a small number of shareholders and their associates are known as close companies. Very often these companies are small family businesses, where the shareholders and directors are usually the same people.

In addition to the general CT legislation, companies under close control are subject to close company legislation, which is essentially anti-avoidance legislation.

Since 1922, closely held UK companies have been singled out for special treatment, mainly because this form of organisation provides opportunities for the owners to manipulate the company's affairs in order to avoid paying higher rate income tax.

This chapter examines the conditions necessary for close company status and the tax consequences of being a close company.

Determination of close company status

Section 414 of the ICTA 1988 provides that a UK resident company will be a close company if it is under the *control* of:

(a) five or fewer *participators* together with their *associates*; or

(b) any number of participators who are also *directors*, together with their *associates*.

Within this definition of a close company, it is important to understand the precise meaning of the following:

Control

Section 416, ICTA 1988 provides that control is proved if the person owns or has the right to own the greater part, i.e. more than 50 per cent, of the company's:

- voting rights;
- share capital;
- distributable income; or
- assets in a winding up.

Participator

Section 417(1), ICTA 1988 describes a participator as any person with a financial interest in the company, i.e. shareholders and debenture holders. However, this does not include financial obligations incurred in the normal course of business such as trade creditors and banks operating in the UK.

Director

Section 417(5), ICTA 1988 provides that a director is any person who:

(a) acts as a director of the company, regardless of his title; and

(b) is involved in the management of the company's trade or business and controls at least 20 per cent of the ordinary share capital, whether on their own or together with their associates.

Associates

In establishing control, the interests of participators are taken together with their associates. Section 417(3) of the ICTA 1988 states that, for the purposes of close company status, associate includes:

(a) spouses;

(b) direct relatives, i.e. lineal ancestors and descendants, brothers and sisters but does *not* include uncles and aunts, nephews and nieces, or the spouse of relatives or children, i.e. sister-in-law or son-in-law;

(c) business partners; and

(d) trustees or personal representatives if the participator has an interest in the shares of a company which form part of the trust or estate.

EXAMPLE

Hardy Ltd has issued share capital of 45 000 £1 ordinary shares, and each share carries one vote. The shares are owned by the following:

	No. of shares held
David Elliot	6 750
Doris Elliot (David's wife)	4 000
Dora Dickens (Doris' sister)	1 850
Bob Pope	2 000
Charles Wilde	4 000
Charlotte Burns	2 000
Emily Lamb (Charlotte's business partner)	750
Trustees of a settlement created by Bob's deceased sister	1 000
30 other equal shareholders	22 650
	45 000

David and Doris Elliot are directors of Hardy Ltd and the only connections between the shareholders are as indicated.

The first step is to see if the company is controlled by directors and their associates owning at least 20 per cent of the share capital.

Directors and their associates:

David Elliot	6 750
Doris Elliot	4 000
Dora Dickens	1 850
	12 600

$$\frac{12\,600}{45\,000} = 28\%$$

As the directors and their associates do not control Hardy Ltd, at this point the company is not close.

The next step is to see whether the company is controlled by five or fewer participators, together with their associates:

(1)	David Elliot	6 750	
	Doris Elliot	4 000	
	Dora Dickens	1 850	12 600
(2)	Charles Wilde		4 000
(3)	Bob Pope	2 000	
	Trustees	1 000	3 000
(4)	Charlotte Burns	2 000	
	Emily Lamb	750	2 750
(5)	Any other shareholder		755
			23 105

$$\frac{23\,105}{45\,000} = 51.3\%$$

Therefore, the company is a close company as five participators exercise control. If Charlotte and Emily were not business partners, or the partnership ceased, the situation would be:

(1)	David Elliot	6 750	
	Doris Elliot	4 000	
	Dora Dickens	1 850	12 600
(2)	Charles Wilde		4 000
(3)	Bob Pope	2 000	
	Trustees	1 000	3 000
(4)	Charlotte Burns		2 000
(5)	Any other shareholder		755
			22 355

$$\frac{22\,355}{45\,000} = 49.7\%$$

In this case, control is not exercised by five participators and the company would not be a close company.

Despite these tests for establishing close company status, a company will not be considered to be close if the company is:

(a) not resident in the UK;

(b) a registered industrial and provident society or building society;

(c) controlled by a non-close company or companies and can only be regarded as close by including the non-close company as a participator;

(d) controlled by the Crown and could not be close if the Crown's interest was disregarded; and

(e) controlled by a non-UK resident company unless the controlling company would be considered to be close if it were UK resident.

Quoted companies and close company status

Quoted companies where at least 35 per cent of the voting power is owned by the public will not be considered to be close provided:

(a) the principal members own less than 85 per cent of the voting power; and

(b) the shares have been dealt in and quoted by a recognised stock exchange in the last 12 months.

The *principal members* are the *five* shareholders with the greatest voting power, (together with their associates) provided each principle member owns more than 5 per cent of the voting rights.

Where the principal members own more than 85 per cent of the voting power, the company will be a close company, even if 35 per cent is owned by the public.

EXAMPLE

Browning plc has issued share capital of 100 000 £1 ordinary shares carrying one vote per share, and is owned by the following shareholders:

	Shares	Percentage
Charles	20 000	20%
Peter	18 000	18%
Penelope	13 000	13%
Keats Ltd (a non-close company)	37 000	37%
Twelve individuals each owning 1% each	12 000	12%
	100 000	100%

As Browning plc is controlled by five or fewer participators, it would indicate the company is a close company:

(1) Charles	20%
(2) Peter	18%
(3) Penelope	13%
	51%

Because Browning plc is quoted company, we also need to consider whether:

(a) at least 35 per cent is owned by the public, which would make the company non-close; and

(b) at least 85 per cent owned by the principal members which overrules the 35 per cent public test.

Because Keats Ltd is a non-close company, the shares are deemed to be held by the public, and would suggest that Browning plc is not a close company. However, the overriding factor is whether 85 per cent of the voting rights are owned by the principal members. This presents a difficulty because Keats Ltd is both a principal member and owned by the public. For this purpose, a non-close company or an approved pension fund can be counted as both a principal member and owned by the public:

	Owned by public	Principal members
(1) Charles	–	20%
(2) Peter	–	18%
(3) Penelope	–	13%
(4) Keats Ltd	37%	37%
(5) 12 individuals	12%	–
	49%	88%

The 12 individuals cannot be considered to be principal members because they own less than 5 per cent each.

Even though the public own 49 per cent of the voting rights, Browning plc will be a close company because the principal members control more than 85 per cent of the voting rights.

This aspect need only be considered if the company in question is a quoted company.

Consequences of close company status

Close company legislation makes provisions to prevent participators extracting funds from the company in such a way as to avoid the tax that would have been due had it been a normal distribution. The legislation covers two main areas:

1. Benefits provided to a participator (ICTA 1988, s 418)

Any benefit provided for a participator, or associate, that does not fall within the Schedule E rules for benefits in kind, will be treated as if it were a distribution, i.e. it would be disallowed in computing the company's profits. Such payments are treated as income in the hands of the recipient and charged to tax at the appropriate rates.

2. Loans to participators (ICTA 1988, s 419)

If a close company makes a loan to a participator, or associate, the company is charged tax on the amount of the loan. For periods before 6 April 1999, the company must pay *notional* ACT on the amount of the loan. In this case, it is not treated as a distribution as such and so the *notional* ACT cannot be used to offset the CT liability, but if the loan is repaid, the company can then reclaim the *notional* ACT. If a close company makes such a loan after 6 April 1999, tax equal to 25 per cent of the loan is charged on the company, this being repaid if the loan is repaid.

These rules do not apply in the following situations:

(a) loans made in the normal course of business; and

(b) loans not greater than £15 000 made to a director of the company, provided that he is a full-time working director and together with his associates does not own more than 5 per cent of the ordinary share capital.

Where a company is closely held, or the Inspector believes it to be a close company, the Officer of the Board may give notice for the company to provide information deemed to be relevant within 30 days.

CGT taper relief

On the disposal of assets or shares that individuals own in a close company, they are entitled to taper relief. For any such disposals made by individuals on or after 17th April 2002, any periods of 'inactivity' from 6th April 1998 will not count for taper relief purposes.

CHAPTER 35

Investment companies

All companies are liable to CT on their profits for an accounting period, and basically investment companies are taxed like any other company. However, there are additional provisions that apply to investment companies concerning management expenses and the treatment of 'losses'.

This chapter examines the special rules applicable to investment companies.

Investment companies

Section 130 of the ICTA 1988 defines an investment company as one whose business consists wholly or mainly in making investments, and whose income or the main part of its income is derived from investments.

Such investment companies are not the same as companies who deal in investments. The difference depends on how realised profits on the sale of investments are dealt with. Profits arising from the sale of investments form part of the capital of an investment company, and as such can only be used for limited purposes, whereas a company dealing in investments may distribute such profits.

Because investment companies are not trading companies, they will not have Schedule D Case I income. The main sources of an investment company's PCTCT are likely to be Schedule D Case III, Schedule A and UII, remembering that if a company receives FII it does not form part of that company's PCTCT. Any expenses that the company incurs in running the business will either be deductible from the particular source of income, or they are classed as management expenses.

Management expenses

Management expenses will generally amount to office expenses that are not deductible under a particular Schedule of income, including the following items:

- office expenses such as rent, rates, stationery, etc.
- commissions
- wages and salaries
- employers' National Insurance contributions
- statutory redundancy payments
- incidental cost of obtaining loan finance

- payments to approved pension schemes
- discounts on bills of exchange
- certain training costs
- costs of annual general meeting
- valuation costs
- contributions to certain profit sharing schemes
- directors' remuneration.

Note: There may be some difficulty in deducting directors' remuneration that the Revenue considers to be excessive with regard to the directors effort in making and realising the investments – *LG Berry Investments Ltd* v *Attwooll* (1964) 41 TC 547. This situation rarely occurs regarding the level of remuneration for a director of a trading company.

Capital allowances

Capital allowances are available on plant and machinery used in the management of the business, and usually deducted from the source of income to which they relate. However, the company can elect to have its capital allowances, which are calculated in the normal way, deducted from its PCTCT.

EXAMPLE

Portfolio Ltd, an investment company with one associated company, had the following income and expenses for its year ended 31 March 2003:

	£
Taxed income (gross)	10 000
Dividends received from UK companies (gross)	20 000
Schedule A	55 000
Schedule D Case III	67 000
Chargeable gains	57 750
Interest on loan on rented property	9 000
Management expenses (all qualifying)	87 500

	£	£	
Schedule A	55 000		
less Loan interest	(9 000)	46 000	
Schedule D Case III		67 000	
Taxed income		10 000	
Chargeable gains		57 750	
		180 750	
less Management expenses		(87 500)	
PCTCT		93 250	'Income'
add FII		20 000	
		113 250	'Profits'

As 'profits' are between £25 000 and £150 000, the company will be charged to CT at 19 per cent on its PCTCT, i.e. £93 250 × 19% = £17 718.

Excess management expenses

If in an accounting period the investment company has more management expenses than income, it will have incurred a 'loss'. The 'loss' is referred to as excess management expenses, and can be relieved in the following ways:

1. Excess management expenses may be carried forward and set off against the PCTCT of a subsequent accounting period. This is one advantage that an investment company has over a trading company, where a trading loss can only be carried forward against trading income. However, there is no carry back facility for excess management expenses in the way that a trading company can carry back a loss for 12 months.

   Any unrelieved capital allowances and charges on income that have been incurred wholly and exclusively for the purpose of the business can be carried forward as surplus management expenses.

2. Excess management expenses and unrelieved capital allowances and charges may be surrendered as group relief. Investment companies must set its management expenses against its own profits first, and only excess management expenses can be surrendered as group relief (*see* Chapter 36).

The FA 1995 introduced provisions to deny the carry forward of excess management expenses where there has been a change of ownership and within three years before or after the change:

(a) there is a major change in the nature or conduct of the business; or

(b) the company's business revives having been negligible or small before the change.

The new rules also deny relief where:

(a) there is a significant increase in the company's capital in the year before, or three years after the change; and

(b) an asset is acquired from another group member and is disposed of outside of the group within three years of the change.

These rules bring excess management expenses in line with trading losses, capital gains and ACT.

Losses on unquoted shares in a trading company

Where an investment company incurs a loss on the disposal of ordinary shares in an unquoted trading company, a claim can be made under the ICTA 1988, s 573 to have the loss deducted from the company's income, rather than from its chargeable gains. The claim must be made within two years from the year in which the loss was incurred.

The loss is deducted from the income of the current year, and/or income of the previous 12 months, before deducting management expenses and charges, and before loss relief under the ICTA 1988, s 393(2) or s 402.

To be eligible for relief under s 573, ICTA 1988, the shares must be disposed of:

(a) for their full market value;

(b) as a distribution in a winding up; or

(c) under a negligible value claim (TCGA 1992, s 24(2)).

If the loss cannot be relieved in full under these provisions, the balance is available for capital gains purposes.

EXAMPLE

Equity Ltd, an investment company, has the following income and gains:

YE 31/3/01	£
Income	15 000

YE 31/3/02	
Income	10 000
Chargeable gains	6 000

During the YE 31/3/00 Equity Ltd disposed of shares in Downfall Ltd, an unquoted trading company at a loss of £30 000. The disposal qualifies for relief under ICTA 1988, s 573:

YE 31/3/02	£
Income	10 000
s 573, ICTA 1988	(10 000)
	nil

YE 31/3/01	£
Income	15 000
s 573, ICTA 1988	(15 000)
	nil

After utilising the loss against income of the current year and previous 12 months, £5000 remains unrelieved, and so the balance of the loss can be used in calculating chargeable gains:

YE 31/3/02	£
Chargeable gains	6 000
Allowable loss	(5 000)
Chargeable gain	1 000

Loss memo	£
Loss	(30 000)
s 573, YE 2002	10 000
s 573, YE 2001	15 000
Unrelieved loss	(5 000)
Available for relief against chargeable gains	5 000

Close investment companies

The FA 1989 introduced provisions to prevent the avoidance of tax by higher rate taxpayers using close companies to hold investments in order to benefit from small companies rate and marginal relief.

A close company will be considered to be a close investment company (CIC) unless it exists wholly or mainly for certain purposes, the main two being:

- carrying on a trade on a commercial basis;
- investing in land to be let out on a commercial basis.

Consequences of being a CIC

1. Small companies rate and marginal relief unavailable

For accounting periods after 31 March 1989, small companies rate and marginal relief are not available to CICs, so that the full rate of CT is charged regardless of the profit level.

2. Restriction of tax credits

Prior to 6 April 1999, where a UK resident individual receives a dividend from a CIC and circumstances are such that a repayment of the tax credit would be due to that individual then the inspector may restrict the tax credit where the main purpose of the payment was to obtain a tax advantage. Because the repayment of tax credits has been abolished from 6 April 1999, this provision no longer applies.

CHAPTER 36

Groups of companies

The taxation of companies must operate within the general framework of existing company law, and the tax regime must reflect the principles embodied in company law if anomalies are to be avoided. The general principle of company law, which was established in *Salomon* v *Salomon & Co. Ltd* [1987] AC 22, is that a registered company is a separate legal entity. However, the complex corporate group is now the typical form of business organisation.

Revenue law reflects the general principle of company law that each company is a separate legal entity in that it is taxed on its own profits/losses and there is no tax on group profits as such. However, the existence of groups poses problems in both company law and Revenue law, for while they are in law separate legal entities, as members of a group the commercial reality cannot be overlooked, and has caused much concern in the realms of insolvency law and the protection of creditors.

Where groups of companies exist, the separate legal entity principle can obscure the commercial reality and in certain respects company law recognises the economic entity in requiring group accounts to be published. Tax law to some extent recognises the commercial reality of groups of companies, but only within the framework of company law. For example, by sharing the upper and lower limits rates for small companies rate between associated companies in order to prevent tax avoidance. There are also a number of reliefs available to companies in a group situation. This chapter examines the main benefits available to companies which are members of a group.

Introduction

There are four situations where UK resident companies which are members of a group may defer or minimise their tax liabilities:

1. the payment of charges and interest without deducting income tax prior to 1/4/01;
2. the transfer of assets within a group without any immediate capital gains implications;
3. replacement of business assets within a group attracts roll-over relief as if the group was a single company;
4. trading losses may be relieved within the group.

The definition of a group varies significantly in each of these situations and some reliefs are also available to consortia. A company is owned by a consortium if 75 per cent or more of its ordinary shares are owned by UK resident companies, none of which has a holding of less than 5 per cent, the investing companies being called members of the consortium.

We will now examine these reliefs in detail taking care in each case to note:

- the definition of a group
- the direction of the relief.

Group interest and inter-company charges (ICTA 1988, ss 247–8)

Prior to 1st April 2001 51 per cent group members and consortia could jointly elect to pay charges and interest without deducting income tax. The paying company made the payment gross and did not enter the charge on the CT 61 return. The receiving company included the gross amount in its corporation tax computation in the normal way, but there was no income tax credit as the interest was not entered on the CT 61 return.

The relief could flow from holding company to subsidiary and vice versa in the case of 51 per cent subsidiaries, but relief for consortia could only flow from the subsidiary to consortium members as shown in Fig 36.1.

Note: Consortium members could not pay charges to the subsidiary without accounting for income tax.

Once an election was made it remains in force until it is revoked.

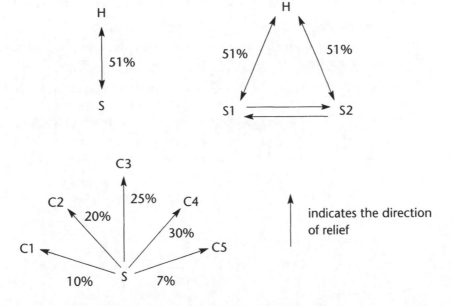

Fig 36.1 Flow of relief between holding company/consortium members and subsidiaries

The main advantage to be gained from this type of relief was a cash flow advantage.

Before April 1999, 51 per cent group members and consortia could jointly elect to pay dividends to the holding company/consortium members without accounting for ACT. This election became redundant in April 1999 when ACT was abolished, however, inter-company dividends, i.e. group income, is ignored when calculating the 'profit' for small companies rate purposes, i.e. it is not treated as part of the company's FII.

NB From 1 April 2001, interest and charges may be paid gross making this relief redundant (*see* Chapter 31).

Capital gains reliefs

Capital gains tax reliefs are available to the principal company and all its 75 per cent subsidiaries and their 75 per cent subsidiaries, i.e. directly and indirectly, *see* Fig 36.2. However, any 75 per cent subsidiary which is not an effective 51 per cent subsidiary of the principal company is not included.

Consider the group structure shown in Fig 36.3: H, S1, S2, S3 and S4 would be a capital gains group, S5 would not be included as it is not an effective 51 per cent subsidiary of the principal company H (45 per cent).

1. Inter-company transfer of assets (TCGA 1992, s 171)

Assets can be transferred between companies in a capital gains group without attracting an immediate capital gain. The asset is treated as being disposed of for an amount equal to the cost plus indexation allowance, i.e. it is transferred on a no gain/no loss basis. A chargeable gain will arise in the following situations:

(a) when the asset is disposed of outside the group; or

(b) when the company holding the asset leaves the group within six years of the date of transfer.

The relief under the TCGA 1992, s 171 is automatic and no claim is needed.

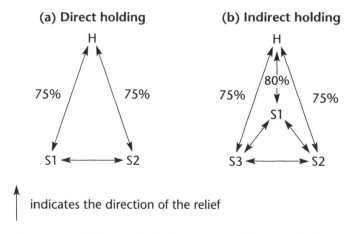

(a) Direct holding   **(b) Indirect holding**

↑ indicates the direction of the relief

Fig 36.2 Capital gains tax relief of a principal company and its subsidiaries for (a) direct holding, and (b) indirect holding

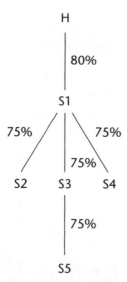

Fig 36.3 Sample capital gains group structure for a principal company and its subsidiaries

<u>EXAMPLE 1</u>

Pluto Ltd has a wholly owned subsidiary Jupiter Ltd. On 1 October 1996 Pluto Ltd transferred an asset to Jupiter Ltd that it had acquired on 1 April 1983 for £150 000, the asset was valued at £200 000 on 1 October 1996. In December 2002 Jupiter sold the asset to an unconnected third party for £400 000.

(Assume indexation to be 20 per cent from 1 October 1996 to December 2002.)

The transfer of the asset from Pluto Ltd to Jupiter Ltd, its wholly owned subsidiary, is transferred at no gain/loss to Pluto Ltd:

	£
Cost (1/4/83)	150 000
Indexation from 1/4/83 to 1/10/96:	

$$\frac{153.8 - 84.3}{84.3}$$

	£
0.824 × £150 000	123 600
Deemed cost to Jupiter Ltd	273 600

When Jupiter disposes of the asset outside the group, a chargeable gain arises on Jupiter calculated as follows:

	£
Proceeds	400 000
less Deemed cost	(273 600)
	126 400
less Indexation:	
20% × £273 600	(54 720)
Chargeable gain	71 680

EXAMPLE 2

Mercury Ltd owns 80 per cent of Venus Ltd. On 15 September 1998 Mercury Ltd transferred an asset to Venus Ltd when the asset had been worth £240 000. Mercury Ltd had acquired the asset in July 1983 for £80 000.

In May 2002 Venus Ltd left the group and still owned the asset on 1 January 2003. Both companies prepare accounts to 31 December each year. The transfer of the asset in September 1998 is treated as being transferred on a no gain/no loss basis as the two companies are a group for capital gains purposes:

	£
Cost (July 1983)	80 000
Indexation:	
(from July 1983 to September 1998)	

$$\frac{164.4 - 85.3}{85.3}$$

$0.927 \times £80\,000$	74 160
Deemed cost to Venus Ltd	154 160

If Venus Ltd had disposed of the asset outside the group, its allowable cost of £154 160 and indexation from September 1998 to the date of disposal would be deducted from the proceeds.

However, as Venus Ltd leaves the group within six years of the transfer still owning the asset, the gain will crystallise and become chargeable in the YE 31/12/02; i.e. the accounting period in which Venus Ltd leaves the group. The chargeable gain is calculated as if Venus Ltd had sold the asset and immediately reacquired it at the market value at the date of transfer:

	£
Deemed proceeds (MV September 1998)	240 000
less Deemed cost to Venus Ltd	(154 160)
Chargeable gain	85 840

There are, however, certain situations where relief under s 171, TCGA 1992 is denied. The following disposals are immediately chargeable:

- a disposal of an interest in shares in a group company, by way of a capital distribution from that company;

- where the disposal is in satisfaction of a debt;

- where the disposal is the redemption of redeemable shares;

- where an asset is appropriated to trading stock there is an immediate chargeable gain or allowable loss, calculated using the market value at the date the asset is appropriated, the cost for Schedule DI purposes being the market value at the date of the appropriation. The company can, however, make an election, within two years, to have the gain or loss ignored, in which case the Schedule DI cost is reduced by any gain or increased by any loss.

Conversely, when an asset is appropriated from trading stock for some other purpose, there is a deemed sale for Schedule DI purposes, at its market value at the date the asset was appropriated, this amount being the base cost of the asset for a future disposal.

Where a group acquires a company with capital losses, or assets that would generate capital losses, s 177A and Schedule 7A of the TCGA 1992 provide that these pre-entry losses are restricted to prevent tax avoidance by such 'loss buying'. When a company joins a group, that company's capital losses are identified as follows:

(1) losses generated *before* the company joined the group; and

(2) losses on disposals made *after* joining the group, on assets owned *before* joining the group, must be apportioned by calculating the pre-entry proportion of the loss.

Only losses arising *after* joining the group are allowable for group purposes after 6 March 1993, and this applies to losses of a company joining a group after 31 March 1987.

EXAMPLE

Mars Ltd acquired an asset on 1 September 1995 for £300 000, and spent a further £100 000 on improving the asset on I May 1997. The asset was valued at £280 000 on 1 July 2000, when Mars Ltd joined the Orion group. On 1 September 2001 Mars Ltd sold the asset for £200 000. Mars Ltd prepares accounts to 31 December each year.

Total loss on disposal:

	£	£
Proceeds		200 000
less Cost	300 000	
Improvements	100 000	(400 000)
Total loss		(200 000)

This loss must then be apportioned for each item of expenditure in order to calculate the value of the pre-entry loss as follows:

$$\text{Loss} \times \frac{\text{Cost of allowable expenditure}}{\text{Total allowable expenditure}} \times \frac{\text{Length of ownership before entry}}{\text{Total period of ownership}}$$

Cost:
Ownership before entry : 1/9/95–30/6/00, 4 years 10 months = 58 months
Total period of ownership: 1/9/95–31/8/01, 6 years = 72 months

Improvements:
Ownership before entry : 1/5/97–30/6/00, 3 years 2 months = 38 months
Total period of ownership: 1/5/97–31/8/01, 4 years 4 months = 52 months

Pre-entry losses:

	£	£
$200\,000 \times \dfrac{300\,000}{400\,000} \times \dfrac{58}{72}$	120 833	
$200\,000 \times \dfrac{100\,000}{400\,000} \times \dfrac{38}{52}$	36 538	157 371

The pre-entry loss of £1573 71 is restricted and can only be set against the following:

- assets disposed of before joining the group;
- assets acquired from a third party after joining the group, provided the assets had been used in the company's trade that was carried on before and after joining the group;
- assets owned before joining the group.

A company in this situation can, however, make a claim, within two years, to have the normal calculation set aside and the pre-entry loss calculated as the lower of:

(1) the actual loss on sale; or

(2) the loss that would have arisen had the company disposed of the asset at market value when it joined the group, gains being treated as nil.

In the example above this would be the lower of:

(1) £200 000, or

(2)	£	£
Deemed proceeds (MV 1/7/00)		280 000
less Cost	300 000	
less Improvements	100 000	(400 000)
		(120 000)

Because the pre-entry loss is restricted, the company needs the lowest pre-entry loss possible, so in this case Mars Ltd should make the election within two years of its year ending 31 December 2002.

Since the legislation restricting pre-entry losses was enacted, schemes using 'gain buying' have become more prevalent. In order to combat tax aviodance through capital gain buying by groups of companies, the FA 1998 introduced measures similar to those for loss buying, to be effective from 17 March 1998. Under the new rules the only losses that can be set off against pre-entry gains are:

- losses that arise before joining the group; and
- losses that arise after joining the group on assets held before joining the group.

The rules for capital gain buying are simpler than those for capital loss buying, and do not apply to accounting periods after the one in which the company joins the group.

The FA 2000 introduced legislation to reflect the globalisation of modern business: from 1 April 2000, assets can be transferred between members of a world-wide group, provided that any gains remain within the scope of UK corporation tax, for example, in the following situations:

1. assets can be transferred between two UK resident companies with a common non-resident parent company;

2. assets can be transferred between a UK resident company and a non-UK resident company within the same group, provided that the non-resident company is carrying on a trade in the UK through a branch or agency, and the asset remains within the charge to UK corporation tax.

The assets will no longer have to be moved in order to set off gains and losses on different assets held in the group; from 1 April 2000, an election can be made to have the disposal treated as made by a different group member.

2. Roll-over relief (TCGA 1992, s 175)

Members of a 75 per cent capital gains group are treated as if they were a single company for the purposes of roll-over relief. Therefore the gain on the disposal of an asset by one group member can be rolled over into the cost of a replacement asset acquired by another group member. The general conditions for replacement of business assets relief are considered fully in Chapter 27.

The FA 1990, however, denies relief where the replacement asset is acquired by a dual resident company and the replacement asset would be exempt from UK tax because of a double tax treaty.

Group relief (ICTA 1988, s 402)

The surrender of losses between members of a group is known as group relief and is available to 75 per cent groups and consortia. From 1 April 1998, the types of losses that may be surrendered under the group relief provisions fall into two categories:

1.
   - trading losses
   - excess capital allowances
   - non-trading deficit on a company's loan relationships.*

2.
   - unrelieved charges on income
   - Schedule A losses **
   - excess management expenses.

* Can only be surrendered as group relief provided a claim is made to treat it as eligible for group relief.

** The Schedule A business must be carried on on a commercial basis, and Schedule A losses carried forward from an earlier period cannot be surrendered as group relief.

Note: Capital losses cannot be surrendered.

A claim for group relief must be made by the claimant company, with agreement from the surrendering company within two years from the end of the accounting period in which the loss arose. Any payments made for surrendered relief are ignored for corporation tax purposes up to the amount of the relief surrendered.

1. 75 per cent groups

Trading losses can be transferred between members of a 75 per cent group in order to reduce the group's overall tax liability. Indirect 75 per cent groups are not eligible for group relief, i.e. the holdings must be direct holdings, *see* Fig 36.4. H and S are a 75 per cent group for group relief purposes. S1, S2, S3 and S4 are all at least 75 per cent subsidiaries of H and therefore all these companies form a group for group relief purposes, i.e., a loss in any company can be surrendered to any other group member. In Fig 36.5, H, S1 and S2 are all members of a 75 per cent group for group relief purposes. H, S3 and S4 *do not* form a 75 per cent group for group relief purposes, as H effectively only owns 56.25 per cent of S4 (75% × 75%). H and S3 are a 75 per cent group. S3 and S4 are a 75 per cent group.

Where a member of a 75 per cent group incurs a trading loss, it may surrender all or part of the loss to members of the same 75 per cent group. The company incurring the loss, the surrendering company, need not claim loss relief under s 393A before surrendering the loss.

The claimant company, however, must first deduct any losses and charges of the current year before deducting relief under s 402. The order of set off for the claimant company is therefore as follows:

(a) deduct s 393A(1)(*a*) claims for current year losses and s 393(1) brought forward losses in the claimant company;

(b) deduct current year charges;

(c) deduct s 402 relief; and

(d) deduct s 393A(1)(*b*) carry back loss claims.

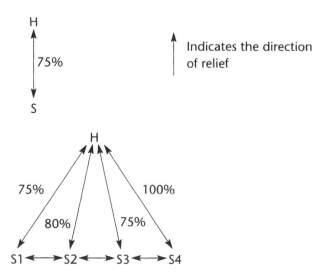

Fig 36.4 Holdings where members form a 75 per cent group

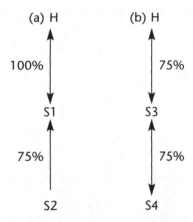

Fig 36.5 Comparison of holdings where members (a) form a 75 per cent group and (b) do not form a 75 per cent group

Only current year losses may be surrendered and used to relieve the claimant company's profits *for the same period*.

If the surrendering company and claimant company have different accounting periods, the loss must be apportioned between the claimant company's accounting periods, i.e. the loss to be set off against the profits of the corresponding accounting period is calculated as follows for accounting periods ending before 2 July 1997:

$$\text{Loss of surrendering company} \times \frac{\text{Common period}}{\text{Accounting period of the surrendering company}}$$

Similarly, only the profits that correspond to the period in which the loss arose can attract group relief, i.e. the profits against which the loss may be relieved is calculated as:

$$\text{Profits of claimant company} \times \frac{\text{Common period}}{\text{Accounting period of claimant company}}$$

The group relief available is limited to the lower of:

(a) the surrendering company's losses available for group relief; or

(b) the claimant company's profits available for group relief.

EXAMPLE

Saturn Ltd prepares accounts to 31 December each year. Its wholly owned subsidiary Jupiter Ltd prepares accounts to 30 June each year and for the year ended 30 June 1996 made a loss of £6 000 000. Saturn Ltd had the following profits for the two years ended 31 December 1996:

	£
YE 31/12/95	1 500 000
YE 31/12/96	3 000 000

There are no other companies in the group. Calculate the corporation tax liability of Saturn Ltd assuming maximum group relief is claimed.

As the accounting periods do not coincide, the profits of the corresponding accounting period must be calculated:

(1) *YE 31/12/95*

$$£1\,500\,000 \times \frac{1/7/95 - 31/12/95}{1/1/95 - 31/12/95} = £750\,000$$

(2) *YE 31/12/96*

$$£3\,000\,000 \times \frac{1/1/96 - 30/6/96}{1/1/96 - 31/12/96} = £1\,500\,000$$

The loss of the corresponding accounting period must also be calculated:

(1) $£6\,000\,000 \times \dfrac{1/7/95 - 31/12/95}{1/7/95 - 30/6/96} = £3\,000\,000$

(2) $£6\,000\,000 \times \dfrac{1/1/96 - 30/6/96}{1/7/95 - 30/6/96} = £3\,000\,000$

The maximum amount available for group relief is the lower of:

(1) £750 000 and £3 000 000, i.e. £750 000 YE 1995

(2) £1 500 000 and £3 000 000, i.e. £1 500 000 YE 1996

Saturn Ltd	*YE 31/12/95*	*YE 31/12/96*
	(£)	*(£)*
Trading profits	1 500 000	3 000 000
less s 402	(750 000)	(1 500 000)
PCTCT	750 000	1 500 000

As there are two companies in the group, the upper and lower limits for small companies rate are divided by two, and Saturn Ltd is a large company for both years concerned.

	£	£
GCT @ 33% × PCTCT	247 500	495 000

Because it was possible to exploit the amount of relief available by surrendering to, or claiming from, more than one company, the FA 1997 (No. 2) repealed the previous legislation, and for accounting periods ending after 2 July 1997 the amount of relief that can be surrendered or claimed by companies whose accounting dates do not co-incide is restricted, by limiting the aggregate of surrenders or claims for any part of an accounting period after 2 July 1997.

2. 75 per cent consortia

Group relief is also available to 75 per cent consortia, provided that the surrendering company and all the consortium members consent to the loss being surrendered. The relief is calculated in the same way as for 75 per cent groups except that there are the following differences:

(a) The amount of relief surrendered or claimed by the consortium company, or consortium members is restricted to the respective shareholdings, *see* Fig 36.6.

The maximum amount of relief that can be surrendered by S to the consortium members is:

C1 : 20% × £600 000 = £120 000
C2 : 25% × £600 000 = £150 000
C3 : 15% × £600 000 = £90 000
C4 : 30% × £600 000 = £180 000

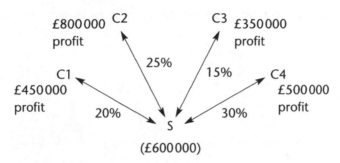

Fig 36.6 Relief surrendered by consortium company

The maximum relief that can be claimed by each company in this example would be:

C1 : 20% × £450 000 = £90 000
C2 : 25% × £800 000 = £200 000
C3 : 15% × £350 000 = £52 500
C4 : 30% × £500 000 = £150 000

Therefore, the maximum consortium relief would be:

C1 = £90 000
C2 = £150 000
C3 = £52 500
C4 = £150 000

If there are fluctuations during the surrendering company's accounting period, a weighted average percentage of the shareholding for the period is used.

(b) Relief must be claimed under s 393A(1)(*a*) for the current period before a loss is surrendered.

Following the decision in *ICI* v *Colmer* in the European Court of Justice, group relief has been available since February 1999, where the group is resident in Europe. The FA 2000 extended the group relief rules even further to reflect the globalisation of business activity. From 1 April 2000, group relief will be available regardless of the residence of the companies through which the group/consortia is established as shown in Figs 36.7, 36.8 and 36.9 overleaf.

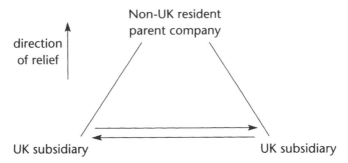

Fig 36.7 The two UK resident subsidiaries can claim and surrender group relief between them

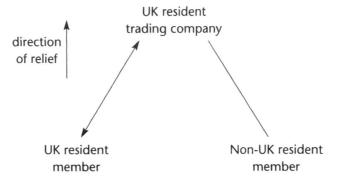

Fig 36.8 The UK consortium member and the UK trading company can claim and surrender group relief between them

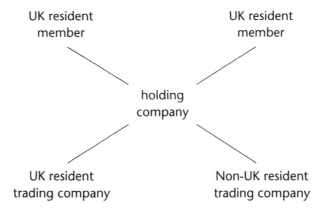

Fig 36.9 Consortium relief is available to the UK resident consortium members

From 1 April 2000, the rules will also be extended to branches as follows:

1. UK branches of overseas companies can claim losses surrendered by other group members to reduce its taxable profits, and surrender its losses as group relief to the extent that the loss cannot be relieved in the overseas country.

2. Overseas branches of UK companies can surrender losses incurred in the overseas branch, provided that they cannot be relieved in the overseas country.

Because companies in the marginal relief band pay an effective rate of CT higher than the full rate, this should be kept in mind when allocating a surrendered loss in order to maximise the tax benefits. The effective rate for FY 2002 for companies at the margin between SCR and Full rate is 32.75%

CALCULATION OF EFFECTIVE RATE AT THE MARGIN

Suppose a company with no associated companies had a profit of £400 000 for FY 2002:

	£
CT @ 30% × £400 000	120 000
less Marginal relief:	
11/400 (£1 500 000 – £400 000)	(30 250)
CT	89 750

A company with profits of £300 000 would pay CT @ 19 per cent:

	£
CT @ 19% × £300 000	57 000

So effectively the first company has suffered £32 750 extra CT for extra profits of £100 000:

$$\text{Effective rate} = \frac{32\,750}{100\,000} \times 100 = \underline{\underline{32.75\%}}$$

EXAMPLE

The following results for YE 31/3/03 relates to four companies that form a 75 per cent group for group relief purposes.

	Profit (loss) (£)
Alpha	(450 000)
Beta	60 000
Gamma	160 000
Delta	400 000

As there are four companies in the group, the upper and lower limits must be divided by four for small company purposes:

Upper limit: $\dfrac{£1\,500\,000}{4} = £375\,000$; $\dfrac{10\,000}{4} = £2\,500$

Lower limit: $\dfrac{£300\,000}{4} = £75\,000$; $\dfrac{£50\,000}{4} = £\,12\,500$

If no election is made for group relief, the CT liabilities would be as follows:

	YE 31/3/03			
	Alpha	Beta	Gamma	Delta
	(£)	(£)	(£)	(£)
Profits	nil	60 000	160 000	400 000
CT:				
@ 19%		11 400		
@ 30%			48 000	120 000
less Marginal relief:				
11/400 (£375 000 – £160 000)	—		(5 913)	—
GCT	nil	11 400	42 087	120 000

If group relief is claimed, the loss should be surrendered to marginal companies to bring their profits to the lower limit and then to companies paying CT at full rate, thus:

1. to Gamma
2. to Delta
3. to Beta.

	YE 31/3/02			
	Alpha	Beta	Gamma	Delta
	(£)	(£)	(£)	(£)
Profits	nil	60 000	160 000	400 000
less s 401		(40 000)	(85 000)	(325 000)
PCTCT	nil	20 000	75 000	75 000
CT:				
@19%		3 800	14 250	14 250

Loss memo

YE 31/3/03	(450 000)	
s 401	85 000	surrendered to Gamma
	(365 000)	
s 401	325 000	surrendered to Delta
	(40 000)	
s 401	40 000	balance of loss surrendered to Beta

From the financial year 2000, consideration must also be given to the 10 per cent starting rate.

EXAMPLE

Suppose that a company has a profit of £11 000, then as the profit is between £10 000 and £50 000, tax will be charged at 19 per cent and marginal relief given (2002 FY):

	£
CT @ 19% x £11 000	2090
less: 19/400 (50 000 – 11 000)	
	(1853)
GCT	237

A company with a profit of £10 000 would pay CT at zero per cent, i.e. CT £1000. The effective rate at the margin is therefore 23.7 per cent:

Effective rate = 237/1000 = <u>23.7%</u>

Other planning points to be considered when surrendering a loss are as follows:

(a) rate of tax saved when considering s 393A claims or group relief claims;

(b) cash flow when considering s 393A claims as opposed to group relief, i.e. s 393A claims would result in repayments of CT; and

(c) group relief could generate surplus ACT in the claimant company.

SELF ASSESSMENT QUESTIONS

36.1 H Ltd owns the following shares in A Ltd, B Ltd, and C Ltd:

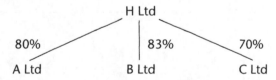

The following information relates to the year ended 31/3/03:

	H Ltd	A Ltd	B Ltd	C Ltd
	£	£	£	£
Schedule DI profit (loss)	170 000	(60 000)	90 000	(10 000)
Schedule A	10 000	20 000	nil	2 000
Taxed income (20%) gross	12 000	8 000	nil	5 000
Trade charges paid (gross)	8 000	nil	2 000	1 000

REQUIRED

(a) Calculate the CT liabilities for each of the above companies for the YE 31/3/03, assuming relief is claimed for the losses in the most tax efficient manner.

(b) State any amount to be carried forward at 31/3/03.

36.2 Wellington Ltd owns 85 per cent of Nelson Ltd. On 11 November 1998 Wellington Ltd transferred an asset to Nelson Ltd, when its market value was £200 000. Wellington had acquired the asset in August 1986 for £100 000. Both companies prepare accounts to 31 March each year. In June 2002 Nelson Ltd left the group but still owned the asset on 1 April 2003.

REQUIRED

Calculate the chargeable gain on Nelson Ltd, stating the year in which it becomes chargeable.

CHAPTER 37

Overseas aspects of corporation tax

The problems arising from increasing international trade are twofold; companies undertaking *bona fide* commercial activities and investment overseas need to be afforded some sort of relief if double taxation is to be avoided, while at the same time governments are increasingly concerned with the loss of tax revenue caused by channelling operations to areas with a low tax jurisdiction. This chapter considers the tax treatment of overseas activities and investment by UK resident companies, examining the types of double taxation relief available, current anti-avoidance legislation, and the factors that may influence the decision of whether to operate as a branch or subsidiary overseas.

Residence

Section 8 of the ICTA 1988 provides that UK resident companies are chargeable to CT on their worldwide income and gains. Section 66 of the FA 1988 widened the definition of residence as follows:

(a) UK or foreign companies that are incorporated in the UK are UK resident for tax purposes; and

(b) foreign incorporated companies are treated as resident in the country where the central management and control exists.

This principle, however, was first established in *De Beers Consolidated Mines* v *Howe* [1906] STC 198.

The effect of this is that a company incorporated overseas will be treated as UK resident if its central management and control are located in the UK.

For accounting periods beginning after 30 November 1993, s 249 of the FA 1994 provides that dual resident companies that are regarded as not being UK resident for the purposes of a double tax agreement by the two countries concerned will be treated as non-UK resident for all tax purposes.

Double taxation relief for companies (ICTA 1988, ss 788–816)

A UK resident company is charged to CT on its worldwide income and gains; any income received from overseas will usually have suffered foreign tax, so effectively the income is taxed twice. To mitigate the effect of this, double taxation relief is available. There are two main types of double tax relief (DTR):

1. Double tax treaties

The UK has entered into double taxation agreements with over 100 countries which may take the form of:

(a) Treaty exemption

The countries party to the treaty set out the categories of income that are to be partially or completely exempt from tax in one country or the other.

(b) Tax credit

The treaty may allow for the tax charged in one country to be allowed as a credit in the other country. For example, there are special arrangements with Eire, credit being given in the country of residence for tax payable in the country of origin (ICTA 1988, s 68).

2. Unilateral relief

Where no double tax treaty exists, or where a treaty exists but does not cover the particular circumstances, unilateral credit relief is given, calculated as the lower of:

(a) the foreign tax paid; or

(b) the UK tax on that income.

EXAMPLE

A company, with no associated companies, has the following income for YE 31/3/03:

	£
Schedule D Case I	5 000 000
Schedule D Case V received	
(net of 35% foreign tax)	104 000

The foreign income must be grossed up in the company's tax computation:

	£	£
Schedule D Case I		5 000 000
Schedule D Case V (£104 000 × 100/65)		160 000
PCTCT		5 160 000

	£	£
CT @ 30% × £5 160 000		1 548 000
less DTR:		
lower of:		
(a) Foreign tax paid:		
£160 000 × 35%	56 000	
or		
(b) UK tax on foreign income:		
£160 000 × 30%	48 000	(48 000)
GCT		1 500 000

Dividends received from overseas companies may be subject to a withholding tax and underlying tax:

(a) Withholding tax

Dividends received from foreign companies will usually have had tax deducted at source known as withholding tax. In the absence of a double taxation agreement, unilateral credit relief is available as in the above example.

(b) Underlying tax

Underlying tax refers to the foreign corporation tax, or equivalent, that has been paid on the profits from which the dividend has been paid. The DTR for underlying tax is available to companies (not individuals), provided that the UK resident company controls at least 10 per cent of the voting power of the overseas company paying the dividend, either directly or indirectly. The underlying tax available for DTR is calculated as:

$$\frac{\text{Gross amount of dividend}}{\text{After tax profits of foreign company}} \times \text{Tax paid by foreign company on its profits}$$

In other words, it is the proportion of foreign tax paid on the profits that relates to the gross amount of the dividend paid to the UK company.

EXAMPLE

H Ltd owns 20 per cent of S Ltd, an overseas subsidiary, and receives a dividend of £13 500 net of 25 per cent withholding tax. The overseas tax paid by S Ltd on its profits was £9000 and its after tax profits were £45 000.

The DTR available if H Ltd pays sufficient corporation tax is calculated as follows:

	£
Net dividend	13 500
Withholding tax @ 25%	4 500
Gross amount of dividend	18 000
Underlying tax:	
$\frac{£18\,000}{£45\,000} \times £9000$	£3 600
Schedule D Case V	£21 600

DTR is the lower of: £

(a) Foreign tax:

Withholding tax	4 500
Underlying tax	3 600
	8 100

or

£

(b) UK tax on dividend

£21 600 × 30%	6 480

(assuming the company pays CT @ 30%)

Any unrelieved foreign tax is wasted, it cannot be carried forward for relief in subsequent years.

As DTR is given on the lower of either foreign tax paid or the UK tax paid on the foreign income, then any deductions for charges on income and loss relief claims should be deducted where possible from UK income and gains before the foreign income in order to maximise the DTR available for set off.

EXAMPLE

Orion Ltd has four associated companies, and its results for YE 31/3/03 were as follows:

	£
Schedule D Case I	600 000
Schedule D Case V (foreign tax 40%)(gross)	250 000
Chargeable gains	100 000
Charges paid (gross)	30 000

The charges should be deducted from UK income where possible, in order to preserve the DTR and minimise the company's tax liability:

	UK income (£)	O/S income (£)	Total (£)
Schedule D Case I	600 000	–	600 000
Schedule D Case V		250 000	250 000
Gains	100 000		100 000
	700 000	250 000	950 000
less Charges	(30 000)	–	(30 000)
PCTCT	670 000	250 000	920 000

Because Orion Ltd has four associated companies, it is a large company, and charged to CT at 30 per cent:

	UK income (£)	O/S income (£)	Total (£)
CT @ 30%	201 000	75 000	276 000
DTR:			
lower of:			
(a) £75 000 or			
(b) £250000 × 40%			
= £100 000		(75 000)	(75 000)
GCT	201 000	nil	201 000

The foreign tax unrelieved is lost:

	£
Foreign tax paid	100 000
DTR given	(75 000)
Unrelieved	25 000

If the charges had been deducted from the foreign income, DTR would have been wasted and the company's overall tax liability would have been higher:

	UK income (£)	O/S income (£)	Total (£)
Schedule D Case I	600 000		600 000
Schedule D Case V		250 000	250 000
Gains	100 000		100 000
	700 000	250 000	950 000
less Charges	–	(30 000)	(30 000)
PCTCT	700 000	220 000	920 000
GCT @ 30%	210 000	66 000	276 000
less DTR:			
(a) £66 000 or			
(b) £100 000		(66 000)	(66 000)
GCT	201 000	nil	210 000

Charges should therefore be deducted from UK income and gains in priority to foreign income in order to maximise the DTR available and reduce the company's overall tax liability.

Where the UK income tax has been exhausted before all the charges and loss claims have been relieved and the company has more than one source of foreign income, the priority of set off should be against the foreign income bearing the lowest rate of foreign tax in order to maximise the DTR available.

EXAMPLE

Libra Ltd is part of a group of eight companies. Its results for YE 31/3/03 were as follows:

	£	
Schedule D Case I	10 000	
Schedule A	15 000	
Chargeable gain	3 000	
Schedule D Case V (foreign tax 35%)	250 000	(gross)
Schedule D Case V (foreign tax 40%)	187 000	(gross)
Charges paid	50 000	(gross)

The foreign tax paid on Schedule D Case V income:

	£
£250 000 × 35%	87 500
£187 000 × 40%	74 800
	162 300

In order to maximise the DTR available, loss reliefs and charges should be deducted in the following order:

1. from UK income
2. from foreign income with overseas tax of 35 per cent
3. from foreign income with overseas tax of 40 per cent.

	UK income	Overseas income (35%)	Overseas income (40%)	Total
	(£)	(£)	(£)	(£)
Schedule D Case I	10 000			10 000
Schedule A	15 000			15 000
Gains	3 000			3 000
Schedule D Case V		250 000	187 000	437 000
	28 000	250 000	187 000	465 000
less Charges	(28 000)	(22 000)	–	(50 000)
PCTCT	nil	228 000	187 000	415 000
CT @ 30%		68 400	56 100	124 500
less DTR (1)				
lower of:				
(a) Foreign tax:				
250 000 × 35%				
= £87 500				
or				
(b) UK tax:				
£250 000 × 30%				
= £75 000		(68 400)		(68 400)
c/f	nil	56 100	56 100	

	UK income	Overseas income (35%)	Overseas income (40%)	Total
	(£)	(£)	(£)	(£)
c/f		nil	56100	56100
less DTR (2)				
(a) Foreign tax:				
£187000 × 40%				
= £56100				
or				
(b) UK tax:				
£187000 × 30%				
= £56100			(56100)	(56100)
	nil	nil	nil	nil

CT = nil

If charges had been deducted from the overseas income bearing 40 per cent tax, DTR would have been wasted:

	UK income	Overseas income (35%)	Overseas income (40%)	Total
	(£)	(£)	(£)	(£)
Schedule D Case I	10000			10000
Schedule A	15000			15000
Gains	3000			3000
Schedule D Case V		250000	187000	437000
	28000	250000	187000	465000
less Charges	(28000)		(22000)	(50000)
PCTCT	nil	250000	165000	415000
CT @ 30%		75000	49500	124500
less DTR (1)				
lower of:				
(a) UK tax £75000				
or				
(b) Foreign tax £87500		(75000)		(75000)
less DTR (2)				
lower of:				
(a) UK tax £49500				
or				
(b) Foreign tax £74800				
restricted to amount				
available			(49500)	(49500)
MCT	nil	nil	nil	nil

Rather than claim credit relief, the company can claim expense relief under s 811 of the ICTA 1988. This allows the foreign tax to be deducted so that the company is only charged to tax on the net amount. This may be preferable where the company has incurred substantial trading losses so that no DTR is available. When considering this choice the following must be taken into account:

- the cash flow situation
- the rate of foreign tax
- the rate of corporation tax
- the availability of future profits.

EXAMPLE

Aquarius Ltd, a company with no associated companies, has the following results for its year ended 31 March 2003:

	£
Schedule D Case I loss	(30 000)
Schedule D Case V (net of 20% foreign tax)	12 000

Assuming that Aquarius Ltd cannot carry the loss back, the following alternatives are possible:

1. Claim for loss relief under s 393A(1)(a)

	£
Schedule D Case I	nil
Schedule D Case V (£12 000 × 100/80)	15 000
	15 000
s 393A(1)(a)	(15 000)
PCTCT	nil

Loss memo	(£)
YE 31/3/03	(30 000)
s 393A(1)(a)	15 000
C/f	(15 000)

2. Claim DTR and carry the loss forward

	£	£
Schedule D Case I		nil
Schedule D Case V		15 000
PCTCT		15 000
CT @ 19% × £15 000		2 850
less DTR lower of:		
(a) UK tax or	2 850	
(b) Foreign tax	3 000	(2 850)
GCT		nil

Loss memo	(£)
YE 31/3/03	(30 000) c/f

This alternative depends on:

- future profits
- cash flow situation
- rates of CT/foreign tax.

3. Claim expense relief under ICTA 1988, s 811

	£
Schedule D Case I	nil
Schedule D Case V	15 000
less s 811 relief	(3 000)
	12 000
less s 393A(1)(*a*)	(12 000)
PCTCT	nil

Loss memo	(£)
YE 31/3/03	30 000
s 393A(1)(*a*)	(12 000)
C/f	(18 000)

By claiming expense relief, the amount of loss available to carry forward is increased by the amount of foreign tax paid, which may be a better alternative where the company has a poor cash flow.

From 17 March 1998, where a claim for DTR proves to be excessive because all or part of the overseas tax has been repaid, then the company must notify the Revenue, in writing, of any adjustment to the foreign tax on which DTR has been claimed. The notification must be made within 12 months of any such adjustment, and failure to comply may result in financial penalties equal to the excess amount of DTR claimed.

Major changes to the system of double taxation relief where announced in the FA 2000, the main changes being as follows:

- underlying tax to be capped at a rate equal to the UK corporation tax rate;
- foreign tax on dividends and profits of overseas branches can be carried forward without time limit, or carried back for one year;
- credit relief cannot be claimed where there is a double tax agreement in force;
- companies can no longer specify from which profits a dividend is paid;
- changes to the way in which relief for underlying tax is calculated;
- relief will be available to non-residents for foreign tax paid on the income of UK branches or agencies;
- provisions to deny relief where there is a special relationship between the payer and recipient of royalties.

Anti-avoidance legislation

Without some sort of control, UK resident companies with subsidiaries established in countries with a low tax jurisdiction could use those companies purely as a means of tax avoidance. The main areas covered by the legislation to control tax avoidance by the use of overseas subsidiaries are as follows:

1. Controlled foreign companies

The overseas subsidiary could be used to accumulate income by withholding dividends that would otherwise be paid to the UK parent company; or by setting up an intermediate holding company overseas to receive dividends from the subsidiary, UK corporation tax could be avoided.

The FA 1984 introduced legislation to combat tax avoidance by the use of overseas subsidiaries under the control of UK resident companies. These provisions are now contained in the ICTA 1988, ss 747–56. A controlled foreign company (CFC) is one that is:

(a) under UK control (from 21 March 2000, control is redefined for this purpose if at least 40 per cent control is exercised by the UK company and at least 40 per cent by a foreign company; prior to this, a company was a CFC where it was more than 50 per cent controlled from the UK);

(b) resident overseas; and

(c) subject to a lower level of taxation, i.e. less than 75 per cent of the tax that would be payable if the company was UK resident in the same period. (Prior to 16 March 1993, the figure was 50 per cent and accounting periods straddling this date are calculated pro rata.)

The provisions of the ICTA 1988, ss 747–56 give the Revenue power to direct that the profits of the CFC are apportioned to UK corporate shareholders controlling at least 25 per cent of the CFC, together with their associates.

The charge is calculated by reference to the profits of the overseas company, and for accounting periods after 23 March 1995, s 133 and Sch 25 of the FA 1995 provides that the overseas currency is used to calculate the profits and then translated on a closing rate basis.

Apportionment can be avoided if any of the following tests can be satisfied:

(a) Acceptable distribution test

For accounting periods after 28 November 1995, the CFC must distribute 90 per cent of its taxable profit, less capital gains and foreign tax, within 18 months after the end of that period in order to avoid apportionment. From 9 March 1999, routing UK dividends through a CFC, so that the acceptable distribution exemption is satisfied without paying the low taxed profits to the UK, will no longer be effective.

From 7 March 2001, where dividends are paid by a CFC to UK banks, insurance companies etc., they will not count towards the acceptable distribution exemption if they are involved in a UK tax avoidance scheme.

(b) Exempt activities test

Apportionment can be avoided where:

- the CFC has a business establishment overseas;
- its business affairs are managed there; and
- its main business does not consist of investment business or dealing in goods for delivery to or from the UK.

For accounting periods beginning on or after 17 March 1998, the legislation relating to the exempt activities test has been redrafted, to make the definitions more specific, e.g.:

- 'intellectual property' will specifically include trademarks and know-how;
- 'banking and similar business' will be made more specific as to what the definition includes, e.g. factoring debts will be specifically included.

From 21 March 2000, holding companies with foreign subsidiaries will only be exempt if at least 90 per cent of their income is in the form of dividends from subsidiaries exempt from the CFC rules. Also, from Budget day, the exempt activities test will not apply to service companies where 50 per cent of the CFC's income is derived from the group.

(c) Motive test

The Revenue will not make a direction where there are *bona fide* commercial reasons for setting up the CFC rather than simply to avoid tax.

(d) Public quotation

The CFC will be excluded from the provisions if at least 35 per cent of the ordinary share capital is held by the public and dealt in on a recognised stock exchange during the accounting period.

(e) Profits less than £50 000

Where the profits of the CFC are less than £50 000 for a 12-month period, no direction to apportion the profits will be made.

Under self assessment, companies must include in the tax return any amounts taxable under the CFC rules.

The CFC legislation will be incorporated into the self assessment regime for accounting periods ending on, or after, 1 July 1999.

Some countries have tax regimes designed to allow companies to circumvent the CFC rules, often referred to as 'designer rate regimes'. In order to clamp down on this abuse, for accounting periods beginning on or after 6 October 1999, companies paying tax under designer rate tax regimes will fall within the definition of a CFC regardless of the level of tax paid.

As a result of the Budget 2002 the Treasury are to be given wide- ranging powers to deny exemption from the CFC legislation to those companies operating in those jurisdictions failing to remove harmful tax practices.

2. Transfer pricing

The overseas subsidiary could be used to generate profits in the country with a lower tax jurisdiction, by manipulating transfer prices, thus avoiding UK CT as a result. The Revenue have the power under the ICTA 1988, s 770 to substitute market value, known as an 'arm's length price', in situations where:

- sales are made by a UK company to an overseas company at an undervalue; or
- purchases are made by a UK company from an overseas company at an overvalue.

Section 772 of the ICTA 1988 gives the Revenue wide powers to enter premises and examine documents to obtain information relating to transfer prices. The legislation applies not only to trading activities but also to:

- sale or purchase of fixed assets
- letting or hiring of property
- loan interest
- patent royalties
- management charges.

Transfer pricing legislation is also to be incorporated into the self assessment regime for accounting periods ending on or after, 1 July 1999. The rules regarding transfer prices are modified, both to facilitate the move to self assessment, and to bring the rules more into line with international principles, i.e.:

- a narrower definition of 'control';
- transitional provisions to exclude existing joint venture arrangements from the new rules for a maximum of three years from 17 March 1998;
- advanced pricing arrangements to be introduced.

3. Transfer of company residence from the UK

Prior to 15 March 1988, it was unlawful for a company to cease to be UK resident and transfer its trade overseas without obtaining Treasury consent. With the change in the law relating to company residence in 1988, the situation is as follows:

1. A company incorporated in the UK cannot migrate unless Treasury consent was given prior to 15 March 1988.

2. A company incorporated overseas, but with its central management and control in the UK, so it is classed as UK resident for tax purposes, can change its residence to overseas provided the following conditions are satisfied:

    (a) the company notifies the Revenue stating the date it intends to become non-resident;

    (b) the company issues the Revenue with a statement of all its tax liabilities up to the date when UK residence ceases; and

    (c) the company makes an arrangement with the Revenue to pay the tax due up to the date of migration.

The company is then subject to an 'exit charge' on the date it ceases to be UK resident, i.e. the company is deemed to dispose of all its assets and immediately reacquire them at their market value on the date of migration from the UK.

The gain on this deemed disposal may be modified in the following circumstances:

(a) where the company concerned retains a UK branch, any assets held by the branch for the purpose of trade can be excluded from the charge; and

(b) where assets are held outside the UK, the gain on these foreign assets can be deferred if immediately after becoming non-resident the company is a 75 per cent subsidiary of a UK resident company, and both companies elect for deferral within two years.

The gain attributable to the foreign assets will crystallise to the UK holding company if any of the following occurs:

(a) the assets are disposed of within six years;

(b) the migrating company ceases to be a 75 per cent subsidiary of the UK resident company; or

(c) the UK company ceases to be resident in the UK.

In the event of the deferred gain crystallising to the UK resident company, any unrelieved capital losses of the migrating company can be set against the gain provided both companies elect in writing within two years.

In order to prevent tax avoidance by migrating companies, ss 765–6, ICTA 1988 provide that control cannot be reduced without consent from the Treasury. A UK resident company with a controlling interest in an overseas subsidiary must obtain Treasury consent before:

● the overseas subsidiary can issue shares or debentures;

● the UK resident company disposes of any of its interest in the overseas subsidiary.

Failure to comply with these provisions can render the UK company liable for severe penalties.

Note: Where the non-resident subsidiary is resident in the EU, Treasury consent is not required.

4. Purchase of foreign tax credits

UK companies can mix low taxed dividends from overseas subsidiaries, with dividends from high taxed foreign subsidiaries in an overseas holding company before the dividends are remitted to the UK in order to preserve DTR for underlying tax.

The FA 1997 amends the ICTA 1988, s 801 by restricting the DTR available for underlying tax where an arrangement exists purely to shelter low tax dividends. The restriction applies to dividends paid on/after 26 November 1996 where there is a scheme to obtain highly taxed income, purely to mix with low taxed income to obtain credit relief for the underlying tax. In this situation the credit relief is calculated as if the highly taxed income had been subject to tax at 33 per cent.

Overseas businesses

The tax treatment of UK resident companies trading overseas depends on whether the overseas business operates through a branch, which is merely an extension of the UK company's business, or as a subsidiary, in which case it is treated as a separate company. There may be many non-tax factors that influence this decision, however, it is necessary to be aware of the taxation effects involved in this choice.

Overseas branch

As UK resident companies are chargeable to CT on their worldwide income gains, they will be charged to CT on the profits arising in the overseas branch, and on assets disposed of overseas. If the branch is controlled from the UK, the profits are assessed under Schedule D Case I, and all the normal rules of computation, capital allowances and loss relief will apply; chargeable disposals will be eligible for roll-over relief.

If the branch is set up and controlled abroad, the profits will be assessed on the UK company under Schedule D Case V. The rules for computing trading income under Schedule D Case V are the same as for Schedule D Case I except that losses under Schedule D Case V may only be carried forward and set off against future Schedule D Case V income.

Overseas subsidiary

Profits arising in the overseas subsidiary will not be chargeable to CT, provided that it is treated as non-UK resident, i.e. it is established that its central management and control are in the foreign country. The reliefs available to companies in a group situation (*see* Chapter 36) do not extend to non-UK resident group members, however, when considering the limits for small companies rate, foreign subsidiaries count as associated companies.

SELF ASSESSMENT QUESTION

37.1 Copperfield Ltd is a UK resident company with no associated companies. The following information relates to its year ending 31 March 2003:

	£
Schedule DI	260 000
Schedule A	30 000
Bank interest received	8 000
Taxed income (gross)	12 000
Chargeable gain	18 000
Overseas dividend received (net of 15% withholding tax)	29 750
Trade charges paid (gross)	6 000
Charitable deed of covenant paid (gross)	2 000

Copperfield Ltd holds 15 per cent of the shares in the overseas company; the dividends were paid out of after-tax profits of £400 000 and foreign tax paid was £90 000.

All charges were paid under the deduction of income tax

REQUIRED

Calculate Copperfield Ltd's corporation tax liability for the year ended 31/3/03.

PRACTICE QUESTIONS

1. Pat Ltd, a company with no associated companies, was incorporated in 1980.

The following information relates to its financial accounting period of 12 months ended on 31 December 2002 :

Income:	£
Schedule D Case I profits as adjusted for taxation	980 000
Bank interest	8 000
Loan interest (gross)	6 000
Capital gains	32 000
(there were also capital losses b/f 1/1/02 – £12 000)	
Rents received	10 000

Dividends from UK companies (gross):	
Received 13 April 2002	12 000
Received 20 August 2002	8 000

Charge paid:	
Trade charges (gross)	10 000
Covenant to cancer research (gross)	2 000

Dividends paid:	
28 March 2002	96 000
13 October 2002	25 600

Additional information:

The bank interest and loan interest were the same as the amounts calculated on an accruals basis for the year.

The company has accumulated ACT brought forward at 1 January 2002 amounting to £24 000.

You are required:

to compute the CT payable for the above chargeable accounting period, showing clearly your treatment of ACT.

(16 marks)

(Source: CIMA, Nov 90)

2. Pro Ltd, a company with no associated companies, which started trading on 1 July 2000, produces the following information in respect of its first three accounting periods:

	12 months to 30/6/01 £	9 months to 31/3/02 £	12 months to 31/3/03 £
Trading profits	24 000	–	8 000
Trading loss	–	30 000	–
Bank interest received	7 000	4 000	2 000
Rents received	2 000	2 000	1 000
FII	4 000	3 000	–
Dividend paid	–	19 200	–
Charitable covenant paid (gross amount)	1 000	1 000	1 000

The bank interest received in the year to 31 March 2003 is the same as the amount calculated on an accruals basis.

You are required to show how the trading loss for the CAP 9 months ended 31 March 2002 would be dealt with on the assumption that all loss claims are made at the earliest opportunity.

(20 marks)

(Source: CIMA, May 91)

3. X Ltd acquired 100 per cent of the voting share capital of Y Ltd on 31 March 2002.

At that date, Y Ltd had accumulated trading losses of £35 000 brought forward under the Income and Corporation Taxes Act 1988, s 393(1) together with unrelieved surplus advance corporation tax (ACT) of £5000. In addition, it had £25 000 of unused capital losses.

The results for each company for the twelve-month accounting period ended 31 March 2003 were:

	X Ltd £(000s)	Y Ltd £(000s)
Income:		
Adjusted Schedule D Case I	160	4
Patent royalties (gross amount)	8	–
Bank interest	6	–
Capital gain on sale of property	20	–
Loan interest (gross amount)	16	3
FII	18	12
Charges paid (gross)	15	2
Dividends paid	76.5	9

The bank interest and loan interest were received on 30 September 2002 and 31 March 2003 respectively.

You are required:

(a) to compute the corporation tax position for each company in respect of the above accounting period, showing clearly your treatment of ACT.

(17 marks)

(b) to advise the directors of X Ltd on the current and future treatment of the brought-forward trading losses and ACT of Y Ltd;

(6 marks)

(c) to discuss if a more tax-efficient method could have been employed for disposing of the property sold by X Ltd.

(3 marks)
(Total: 26 marks)
(Source: CIMA, Nov 93)

4. (a) In the context of the legislation dealing with close companies, explain the terms:
    (i)   control;
    (ii) director;
    (iii) associate.

(9 marks)

(b) Describe the taxation implications for a company deemed to be a close company.

(6 marks)
(Total: 15 marks)
(Source: CIMA, Nov 95)

5. A Ltd is the holding company for a group of five companies. The relationships between the companies in the group are shown in the diagram below:

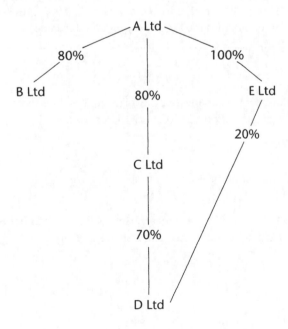

All of the companies are UK resident except for E Ltd, which is resident in a country where the rate of tax is 5 per cent. For the purpose of this question, E Ltd can be regarded as a controlled foreign company.

All of the companies have an accounting year ending 31 March 2002 and their income/(losses) for this year were as follows:

	Adjusted trading profit/(loss) £	Bank interest £
A Ltd	100 000	–
B Ltd	110 000	15 000
C Ltd	(110 000)	12 000
D Ltd	(25 000)	–
E Ltd	15 000	–

The bank interest has been credited on an accruals basis.

(a) From the above diagram, identify
   (i) which companies will be treated as associated companies;
   (ii) which companies form a group (or groups) for relief purposes.

(4 marks)

(b) On the assumption that the most efficient use is made of any trading losses, compute the CT payable by each company.

(9 marks)

(c) You have been advised by the directors that during the year ending 31 March 2003, D Ltd is expected to make a Schedule D Case I trading loss of approximately £100 000, and that E Ltd will have chargeable profits of £30 000. Advise the board of any steps it should take to minimise next year's corporation tax liabilities.

(7 marks)
(Total: 20 marks)
(Source: CIMA, May 93)

6. MN Ltd, a UK resident company, has the following holdings of ordinary voting shares in other companies, which apart from O Ltd are all UK resident:

   65% in B Ltd
   80% in C Ltd
   90% in O Ltd (a foreign resident company)
   80% in D Ltd

D Ltd holds 90 per cent of the ordinary shares of E Ltd, A Ltd holds 12 per cent of the shares in B Ltd and O Ltd holds 5 per cent of the shares in E Ltd.

The trading results for each for company for the year ended 31 March 2002 were as follows:

		£
A Ltd	Loss	60 000
B Ltd	Profit	70 000
MN Ltd	Profit	55 000
C Ltd	Loss	12 000
D Ltd	Profit	265 000
E Ltd	Loss	5 000
O Ltd	Loss	10 000

No company had any other income.

(a) Assuming the above losses are used in the most efficient manner, compute the corporation tax payable by each of the above companies for the CAP 12 months ended 31 March 2002.

(16 marks)

(b) Outline the reliefs which may be available to any of the above companies in respect of inter-company transfer of assets.

(4 marks)
(Total: 20 marks)
(Source: CIMA, May 89)

7. CCD Ltd, a company resident in the United Kingdom with no associated companies, provides the following information in respect of its twelve-month accounting period ended 31 December 2001:

Income	£
Adjusted trading profits (before deduction of loan interest)	980 000
Rents receivable	30 000
Bank interest receivable	42 000
Patent royalties (gross) – received 30 September 2001	60 000
Chargeable capital gain	120 000
Foreign dividends (net of withholding tax of 20%)	20 000
Dividends from UK companies (including tax credit)	100 000

Charges and interest paid (gross)	£
Loan interest – paid 30 June 2001 and 31 December 2001	30 000
One-off payment to charity – paid 1 August 2001	5 000

Dividends paid (actual amounts)	£
25 March 2001	450 000
30 September 2001	57 600

You are required:

(a) to compute the CT payable by CCD Ltd for the above accounting period, showing clearly your treatment of foreign tax.

(20 marks)

(b) to show the effect on your computation in (a) above if the foreign dividends were received from a company in which CCD Ltd has a 15 per cent holding. The dividends were paid out of distributable after tax profits of £300 000 and the foreign tax payable on those profits was £125 000.

(5 marks)
(Total: 25 marks)
(Source: CIMA, May 1995)

PART 5

Introduction to value added tax

Value added tax (VAT) is the common indirect consumer tax adopted by the European Community (EC); art 99 of the Treaty of Rome stated that indirect taxation would be harmonised within the EC in order to promote the free movement of goods and services between member states. After joining the EC in 1972, the UK introduced VAT, to be effective from 1 April 1973, as a first step towards harmonising indirect taxation with the rest of the Community.

Value added tax is a multi-stage, self assessed tax, which is effectively borne by the final consumer. At each stage in the chain the supplier collects output tax on the taxable supplies the business makes, and deducts any input tax suffered, so that essentially VAT registered traders are acting as unpaid tax collectors for HM Customs and Excise (C&E).

Value added tax is levied on both goods and services. In the UK, it replaced both purchase tax, which was an indirect tax on goods, and selective employment tax, a very unpopular tax levied on labour employed in the service industries in the hope that it would encourage increased employment in manufacturing industries at a time when manufacturing industry in the UK was in decline.

Value added tax is a very efficient tax that raises vast amounts of revenue for the government, the main charging provisions being contained in the Value Added Tax Act 1994 (VATA 1994). Section 4(1) of the VATA 1994 states that 'tax shall be charged on any *supply of goods or services*, made in the UK, where it is a *taxable supply*, made by a *taxable person*, in the course or furtherance of any *business* carried on by him'.

All the elements of s 4(1), VATA 1994 need to be present for a transaction to be within the scope of VAT, that is to say:

- there must be a supply of *goods* or *services*;
- the supply must be made in the UK;
- the supply must be a *taxable* supply;

- the supply must be made by a *taxable person*;

- the supply must be made in the course or furtherance of any *business* carried on by the taxable person.

The next two chapters analyse the basic charge to VAT by expanding the elements of s 4(1), VATA 1994 on supplies made within the UK and examines the changes in the rules that were necessary in order to deal with transactions between member states after the introduction of the single market in 1993.

CHAPTER 38

The supply of goods and services

Supplies of goods or services

For VAT purposes, a supply is generally something that is exchanged for a consideration, so that if there is no consideration, there is no supply, unless the legislation specifically provides otherwise. Schedule 4, para 1 of the VATA 1994 states that the transfer of property in goods is a supply for VAT purposes, so that where there is a supply of goods, they do not need to be exchanged for a consideration to be within the scope of VAT. For example, business assets that are the subject of a gift, or taken out of the business for personal use amount to a supply for VAT purposes. However, the following gifts of goods are exempt:

- industrial samples
- gifts costing less than £50 (£15 prior to 8th March 2001).

Generally a supply of services without consideration is outside the scope of VAT. However, from 1 August 1993, if input tax has been reclaimed on services that are supplied and then those services are used for non-business purposes for no consideration, there is a deemed supply. This deemed supply will not apply in the following situations:

- if the input tax on the original supply was not allowed in full; or
- to services used for staff catering or accommodation.

Consideration was defined in the second directive (1967) as 'everything received in return for the supply of goods or the provision of services'. This gives consideration a very wide meaning and includes not only money but also the value of goods received in exchange for goods or services supplied, for example, part exchange deals.

Whether there is consideration or not, the legislation provides that the following are supplies for VAT:

1. Deregistration

Goods held when a person ceases to be VAT registered are deemed to be supplied to that person unless input tax has not been recovered or it is within the *de minimus* limit of £1000 (£250 prior to 1 April 2000).

2. Certain self supplies

For example:

(a) Stationery

Where a business produces stationery for internal use prior to 1/6/02, and its supplies are exempt or partially exempt from VAT, there may be a self supply, unless the amount of tax involved is negligible. From 1/6/02 this measure will be abolished.

(b) Motor cars

Where input tax is deductible on a car, e.g. bought by a garage for resale, and then the car is put to some other use, e.g. a staff car, then a self supply arises.

Some supplies are outside the scope of VAT, i.e. they are categorised as a supply of neither goods nor services in the legislation:

- sale of a business as a going concern, provided certain conditions are met;
- supplies held in a bonded warehouse.

Supplies within the scope of VAT are either a supply of goods or a supply of services. In categorising these supplies the legislation provides that the following are a supply of goods:

(a) transferring the whole ownership in goods either immediately or under a hire purchase agreement;

(b) the processing of another persons goods, e.g. a tailor making clothing using the customer's own materials;

(c) the supply of heat, power, refrigeration or ventilation;

(d) granting or assigning a major interest in land, i.e. a freehold or lease exceeding 21 years; and

(e) business assets that are gifted or taken out of the business for personal use (even without consideration).

A supply exchanged for a consideration which is not a supply of goods is a supply of services. The legislation specifies that the following are supplies of services:

- transferring part of an interest in goods
- transferring the possession, but not the ownership in goods, e.g. rental or loan of an asset.

Supplies made in the UK

Once it is established that there is a supply of goods or services, the place of supply then needs to be considered, as UK VAT is charged on *supplies made in the* UK. Generally, goods are treated as supplied in the UK if they are located in the UK when they become the subject of the particular supply, unless the goods need to be assembled or installed, in which case they are treated as supplied where the assembly or installation takes place: VATA 1994, s 7(3).

The following rules apply to the supply of services.

(a) The basic rule is that services are supplied in the place where the supplier 'belongs', i.e. where the supplier has a business establishment, and if he or she does not have a business establishment, the supplier is treated as 'belonging' where he or she usually resides.

(b) Services connected with land are treated as supplied where the land is located.

(c) Artistic and cultural services are treated as supplied where they are performed.

Exempt supplies

Some supplies are specifically outside the scope of VAT. The VATA 1994, Schedule 9 lists 12 groups containing supplies which are exempt from VAT:

Group 1 – Land

The assignment of any interest in, right over or licence to occupy land is exempt from VAT with the following exceptions:

- hotel and holiday accommodation
- camping facilities
- fishing and hunting rights
- car parking facilities
- mooring and hangar facilities.

These are considered to be a supply of services taxable at the standard rate.

Note: From 1 August 1989, a taxpayer can elect to treat supplies of land as taxable rather than exempt. Once made, the election is irrevocable and applies to all supplies of land made by the elector. However, the FA 1997 denies this option on the sale or lease of property where the purchaser or lessee is not registered for VAT or if they are registered they are not entitled to recover at least 80 per cent of the input tax. The legislation applies to leases granted after 26 November 1996.

Group 2 – Insurance

The exemption covers the supply of services in arranging insurance and handling insurance claims but does not include the services of loss adjusters in assessing claims.

Group 3 – Postal services

Postal services provided by the Post Office are exempt. The sale of unused postage stamps by other traders is exempt provided they are sold at face value. However, all other stamps including first day covers are standard rated.

Group 4 – Betting, gambling, lotteries

Exemption applies to the facilities for placing bets, etc. but does not include admission charges or subscriptions to clubs or supplies of gaming machines which are all standard rated.

Group 5 – Finance

Exemption applies to a wide range of financial services including:

(i)   banking

(ii) credit card services

(iii) making of loans

(iv) dealing with money

(v)   dealing in stocks and shares for money.

Note: Investment advice, however, is standard rated.

The 1999 Budget narrowed the exemption for supplies made from 10 March 1999. Exemption does not include:

- market research
- product design
- advertising
- credit management services.

Group 6 – Education

Education and vocational training provided by schools, universities and other non-profit making bodies are exempt services. Private tuition provided by independent tutors in subjects normally taught in schools or universities, except for recreational subjects and the teaching of English as a foreign language (even if provided by a commercial tutor) are also exempt.

Group 7 – Health

This group exempts supplies made by doctors and other health workers. Related goods are only exempt if they are a minor part of the service or the supply is made in hospital.

Group 8 – Burial and cremation

Services provided in the disposal of the dead, i.e. burial or cremation are exempt, but not headstones, etc.

Group 9 – Trade unions and professional bodies

Supplies made by trade unions, professional bodies and certain trade associations in return for membership subscriptions are exempt, provided that the body concerned is non-profit making.

Group 10 – Sport competitions, sport

Exempts entry fees for sports competitions where the fees are returned as prizes, and services in relation to sport supplied by non-profit making organisations, but only to its members.

From 18 March 1998, this exemption will not be available to clubs if any person with an interest in the club can obtain profits, by making charges for land or facilities etc.; also from 1 January 1999 exemption will be denied unless profits are used to maintain, or improve, the club's sporting facilities.

Group 11 – Works of art

Works of art supplied to public bodies are exempt supplies, i.e. where they are exempt from capital gains tax, and conditionally exempt from inheritance tax.

Group 12 – Fund raising

Goods and services supplied in connection with one-off fund raising events are exempt if made by charities, non-profit making sports bodies and those bodies within group 9. This exemption was extended in the Budget 2000 to include repeat events at the same site and on-line events.

NB: Events where accommodation is provided for more than two nights, however, are specifically excluded.

It is not sufficient, therefore, just to examine the group headings, these only identify potential exemption; to be exempt the supplier must fall within the categories or exempt supplies under the group headings.

If a supply is exempt, it is outside the scope of VAT, and as such the supplier cannot deduct the input tax associated with the exempt supply, although there are special rules for partially exempt businesses.

Taxable supplies

Any supply of goods or services made in the UK which is not an exempt supply is a taxable supply.

Taxable supplies made in the UK by a taxable person in the course of business are charged to VAT at either the standard rate of 17.5 per cent, 5 per cent, or 0 per cent if they fall into the zero rated category of supply. From 1 January 1998, the rate of VAT on insulation and energy saving material supplied under grant funded schemes, was reduced from 17.5 per cent to 5 per cent, in line with domestic fuel.

The FA 2000 extended this 5 per cent rate, which is the lowest rate allowed under EU agreements, to the following, provided that they are funded by government grants:

- installation of energy saving materials, including solar panels, for qualifying pensioners;
- installation of security goods installed at the same time as energy saving materials for qualifying pensioners;
- installation of heating measures in the homes of the less well off, room heaters, boilers, radiators, etc.

From January 2001, a 5 per cent rate will also be applied to women's sanitary products. The FA 2001 extended the 5 per cent rate to include children's car seats and certain property conversions.

If a supply is zero rated rather than exempt, input tax is reclaimable, i.e. the supply is taxable, but taxable at 0 per cent. One of the main reasons for zero rating is to ensure that consumers do not pay tax on items that are considered to be essential.

Schedule 5 of the VATA 1994 lists 16 groups containing supplies that are zero rated. Again, it is not sufficient to examine the group headings alone, they merely indicate that certain items within that category may be subject to zero rating. It is possible for a supply to fall within both a zero rated category and an exempt category, in which case zero rating takes precedence. The groups for zero rating are as follows:

Group 1 – Food

Food for human consumption, animal foodstuffs, livestock of a kind generally used for human consumption, seeds for producing plants for human consumption or animal foodstuffs are all zero rated with the following exceptions:

- food supplied in the course of catering, including hot take away food;
- non-essential food items including ice cream, crisps, peanuts, sweets, alcohol, soft drinks, chocolate biscuits, etc.;
- pet food;
- livestock not considered to be for human consumption.

Group 2 – Water and sewerage services

Supplies of water for non-industrial use and the disposal of sewerage are zero rated but this group does not include distilled water and mineral water which are both considered to be non-essential.

Group 3 – Books

Most books, newspapers, leaflets, music, and maps are zero rated, but as stationery is standard rated, books to be written in, e.g. diaries, are also standard rated with the exception of children's painting books which are zero rated.

Group 4 – Talking books and wireless sets

Talking books, wireless sets, cassette recorders for the disabled or supplied to the disabled by charities are zero rated.

Group 5 – Construction of buildings

New construction or sales of new buildings used for residential or non-business charitable purposes are zero rated.

Group 6 – Protected buildings

Alterations made to listed buildings or the sale of reconstructed listed buildings, provided that they are used for residential or charitable purposes, receive zero rating.

Group 7 – International services

Since 1 January 1993 most items in this category are now contained in the place of supply provisions.

Group 8 – Transport

Passenger transport by road, rail, sea and air if the transport is designed to carry more than 10 persons. From April 2001 includes vehicles adapted for disabled persons.

Note: Transport for pleasure is standard rated.

Group 9 – Caravans and houseboats

Zero rating applies to caravans and houseboats that are used as private residences.

Group 10 – Gold

Gold supplied to a central bank and London gold market when held in the UK is zero rated. From 1 January 2000, investment gold is exempt and producers, refiners and certain other suppliers can elect to tax their sales; however, failure to comply with the special scheme for investment gold may result in a financial penalty of 17.5 per cent of the value of the transaction.

Group 11 – Bank notes

Zero rating applies to the issue of bank notes by banks.

Group 12 – Drugs, medicines, aids for the handicapped

Drugs and medicines supplied on prescription and specialised equipment and modification of buildings supplied to handicapped persons, or to a charity which makes it available to a handicapped person, all receive zero rating.

Group 13 – Imports/exports

This group provides certain zero ratings in relation to international trade.

Group 14 – Tax free shops

Group 14 zero rates limited supplies of tobacco etc. when supplied in a duty free shop.

Group 15 – Charities

This group zero rates a number of supplies to or by charities if certain conditions are met. It does not give a blanket zero rating for matters relating to charities.

However, from 1 April 2000, zero rating is specifically extended to cover the following:

- advertising;
- sales of donated goods to disabled people and those receiving means tested benefits, as well as the general public. This includes the hire of goods but excludes the supply of land;
- extending or adapting bathrooms for disabled people in day centres and other charity premises.

Group 16 – Clothing and footwear

Zero rating is given to the following:

- children's clothing
- protective clothing for industrial use if it conforms to British standards
- cycle helmets, provided that they conform to British standards.

Imports and exports outside the EU

UK VAT is not only charged on taxable supplies made in the UK but also on imports of most goods and some services whether or not the importer is a taxable person. When goods are imported from outside the EU, or removed from a bonded warehouse, VAT is charged as if it were a supply of goods in the UK. This charge arises whether or not the goods enter the UK directly or via another EU country. If the goods are imported in the course of business, the importer can recover the tax due on importation as input tax. Private individuals, however, importing goods from outside the EU cannot reclaim the tax as input tax.

There are no exempt categories for imports from outside the EU, but where imported goods fall into the zero rated categories, there is no liability to tax on importation except that the following imported goods are excluded from zero rating:

(a) gold

(b) building materials

(c) drugs and aids for handicapped persons, unless they are imported by the handicapped person for personal use or by a charity that will make them available to a handicapped person for personal use.

Goods exported from the UK are normally zero rated, provided that the exporter holds proof of export.

From 18 March 1998, non-EU businesses leasing assets to non-business UK customers are required to register for VAT in the UK if the value of their income exceeds the VAT registration limit.

The single European market (1 January 1993)

Transactions between members of the EU are no longer regarded as imports and exports but 'acquisitions of goods in the UK from' and 'supplies of goods from the UK to' other member states:

Supplies of goods from the UK to other member states

Where the supplier and the customer are both VAT registered, the supplier can zero rate the supply provided the following conditions are met:

(a) the goods leave the UK and are acquired by a registered trader elsewhere in the EU;

(b) the suppliers registration number shows the prefix GB on the tax invoice; and

(c) the supplier has documentary evidence that the goods have left the UK.

The customer will have to pay VAT on entry but can recover the tax as input tax. This is known as the destination system, as VAT is paid in the customer's country. Where the customer is not VAT registered, the supplier charges VAT at the UK rate. This is known as the origin system as tax is due in the supplier's country. However, once the value of such supplies reaches the annual threshold, the supplier is liable to register for VAT in the country of destination.

Acquisitions of goods in the UK from other member states

If the supplier and customer are both VAT registered, the UK customer is liable to VAT when the goods enter the UK but the tax can be reclaimed as input tax.

If the UK customer is not VAT registered, tax is imposed in the country of origin; however, a UK customer will be liable to register if the relevant supplies exceed £55 000 (previously £54 000).

CHAPTER 39

Registration

To be within the scope of VAT, the taxable supply must be 'made by a *taxable person*, in the course or furtherance of any *business* carried on by him'.

The terms 'taxable person' and 'business' therefore need to be considered in more detail.

A 'taxable person' is one who makes, or intends to make, taxable supplies and that person is either:

- registered for VAT;
- ought to be registered for VAT; or
- has requested to be voluntarily registered for VAT.

'Person' includes individuals, partnerships, companies, clubs, etc. As it is the 'person' who is registered for VAT rather than the business, if the 'person' carries on more than one business activity, these are aggregated for VAT purposes. For example, if a sole trader also carries on a partnership, the individual and the partnership are separate 'persons' for VAT, but all the activities of the partnership will be aggregated as will all the activities of the sole trader.

For VAT the term 'business' is given the wide meaning of any activity concerned with making supplies for a consideration regardless of the profit motive. Section 94 of the VATA 1994 states that 'business' includes:

(a) trade, profession, vocation;

(b) admission to premises for a consideration; and

(c) benefits provided by a club or association in return for membership fees unless the association is for public purposes, and subscriptions provide no benefit other than to receive annual reports and to participate in its management.

The EC sixth directive (1977) refers to 'economic activities' rather than 'business':

> **'producers, traders, persons supplying services including mining and agricultural activities, and the activities of professions. The exploitation of tangible or intangible property for the purpose of obtaining income therefrom on a continuing basis shall also be considered to be an economic activity'.**

The rest of this chapter is concerned with registration for VAT.

Compulsory registration

The conditions making registration mandatory are related to the trader's taxable turnover, i.e. the volume of taxable supplies and not profit. Any person making or intending to make taxable supplies in the course of business must notify HM Customs and Excise that he should be registered for VAT when either of the following occurs:

(a) At the end of any month the taxable supplies for the 12 months just ended exceed the statutory limit of £55 000 from 25 April 2002 (previously £54 000). Therefore, it is essential for persons making taxable supplies to keep a running total of their taxable turnover for the year just ended at the end of every month.

HM Customs and Excise must be notified within *30 days* of the end of the month in which the threshold was exceeded, of the liability to be registered for VAT, and registration takes effect from the end of the following month, e.g. if the taxable turnover for the 12 months to 31 March is over the limit, registration will take effect from 1 May, or an earlier date if agreed between the taxpayer and C&E.

(b) If at any time the person believes that taxable supplies in the next *30 days* will exceed the statutory limit, HM Customs and Excise must be notified before the end of the 30-day period and registration takes effect from the beginning of that period.

In determining whether or not a person is liable to be registered for VAT, disposals of fixed assets which have been used in the business are ignored, taxable supplies of land, however, which are taxable at the standard rate must be included.

The taxable turnover is the value of all zero and standard rated supplies made by the business (excluding VAT). When calculating the value of taxable turnover, certain services received from overseas are treated as if they were supplies made by the customer and so are added to the taxable turnover in determining whether the statutory limit has been exceeded. This is known as the *reverse charge*; services subject to a reverse charge are listed in the VATA 1994, Schedule 5.

Penalties will be incurred for failure to notify HM Customs and Excise of the liability to be registered. It is possible for a trader to claim exemption from registration where this would not jeopardise the revenue from VAT, e.g. where a trader makes mainly zero rated supplies. *Fong* v *CCE* [1978] VAT TR 75.

Voluntary registration

It is possible for a 'person' to register for VAT voluntarily, even if the taxable turnover is below the statutory threshold, where the 'person' makes, or intends to make taxable supplies. Voluntary registration may be beneficial in the following situation:

(a) the 'person' may not wish to make it known to competitors and customers that the business is not large enough to be compulsory VAT registered;

(b) the 'person' makes mainly or wholly zero rated supplies and wishes to reclaim input tax;

(c) where the customers are mainly VAT registered themselves.

The administrative burden of being VAT registered must, however, be weighed against these potential benefits.

Pre-registration input tax on *goods* can be recovered, provided that:

(a) the goods were supplied to the 'person' who is now registered and they were obtained for the business covered by the VAT registration; and

(b) the goods are still held at the date of registration or they have been used to make other goods which are still held at registration.

Note: VAT incurred on consumables before registration cannot be reclaimed, e.g. fuel.

Pre-registration input tax on *services* can be recovered, provided that:

(a) the services were supplied to the 'person' who is now registered and were obtained for the business covered by the VAT registration;

(b) the services were received not more than six months before registration; and

(c) the services were not related to goods that were disposed of before registration.

Deregistration

A person may request deregistration or HM Customs and Excise may compulsorily deregister the person:

1. Voluntary deregistration

A taxable person may be deregistered if they can satisfy HM Customs and Excise that the value of taxable supplies for the next 12 months, excluding the supplies of capital assets, will not exceed £53 000 from 25 April 2002 (previously £52 000).

The registration will be cancelled from the date of the request, or some other agreed date.

2. Compulsory deregistration

Deregistration may be compulsory where:

(a) HM Customs and Excise are satisfied that the 'person' is no longer making or intending to make taxable supplies; or

(b) there is a change in the legal status of 'person', for example:
   - partnership reverts to a sole trader, or vice versa
   - incorporation of an unincorporated business and vice versa.

Any goods that are held when the person is deregistered are deemed to be supplied to that person unless the input tax has not been reclaimed, it is within the *de minimus* limit of £1000 or the business is sold as a going concern to another taxable person (or by taking over the business the purchaser becomes a taxable person).

Group registration (VATA 1994, s 43; FA 1995, s 25)

Companies can elect to be treated as a group for VAT purposes where one company controls the other(s) or one person controls them all. The election must be made within *90 days* before it is to be effective.

All members of a group need not be included in a group election, for example, if one company in the group makes only zero rated supplies, it may be more advantageous for that company to remain outside the VAT group. Similarly, by including companies making exempt supplies, the amount of input tax that would be reclaimable by the group may be jeopardised. The consequences of group registration are:

(a) goods and services supplied within the VAT group are outside the scope of VAT; and

(b) only one VAT return is submitted by the 'representative member' of the group to account for supplies made and received by all the companies included in the group registration.

From 26 November 1996, the special status of the representative member does not pass to other group members as a result of the group being treated as a single taxable person.

From 29 November 1995, where there are changes to the VAT group or its activities which result in VAT not being charged on the full value of the supply, HM Customs and Excise have the power to direct that:

(a) supplies between the VAT group can be brought within the scope of VAT;

(b) retrospectively (but not before 29 November 1995) a member of the VAT group can be removed from a specific date; and

(c) retrospectively (but not before 29 November 1995) an eligible company can be treated as part of the VAT group from a specified date.

Note: Arrangements made for *bona fide* commercial reasons are outside the scope of these powers.

Other changes introduced by the FA 1997 having effect from 26 November 1996 are as follows:

(a) supplies made to a UK group member from an overseas group member are liable for VAT under the reverse charge provisions; and

(b) companies applying to leave one VAT group and join another can have the change made retrospective by up to 30 days before the application.

As a result of consultations following the 1998 Budget, the rules relating to group registration are to be amended with effect from the FA 1999 as follows:

- the 90-day notice period is to be withdrawn;
- non-UK group members will be restricted to those with UK establishments;
- Customs & Excise will be given the power to degroup companies where they consider it necessary, e.g. the company is no longer eligible, or the revenue is in jeopardy;
- the right of appeal, with respect to group registrations, will be extended.

CHAPTER 40

The VAT system and accounting for VAT

VAT is collected by taxable persons at each stage in the manufacturing and distribution chain, but as the VAT suffered by taxable persons on purchases, expenses and assets is generally reclaimable, the taxable person merely acts as an unpaid tax collector for HM Customs & Excise (C&E), the burden of VAT being borne by the final consumer. This chapter examines the practical workings of the VAT system.

Output tax and input tax

The supplies of taxable goods/services made by a taxable person are called outputs, on which VAT must be charged, this is known as *output tax*. Normally *output tax* is calculated by applying the rate of VAT to the tax exclusive selling price.

EXAMPLE

Standard rated goods supplied for £240 exclusive of VAT.

Output tax = £240 × 17.5% = £42

However, sometimes the output tax has to be calculated from the VAT inclusive selling price using the VAT fraction:

$$\text{VAT fraction} = \frac{\text{Rate of VAT}}{100 + \text{Rate of VAT}}$$

Standard rate VAT fraction (1997/8) = 17.5/117.5 = 7/47

EXAMPLE

Standard rated goods supplied for the VAT inclusive price of £282.

Output tax = £282 × 7/47 = £42

Purchases made by a taxable person are called inputs, on which the VAT can be reclaimed, this is known as *input tax* and includes:

- the VAT on the supply of goods/services;
- the VAT on the supply of goods from other EU member states;
- the VAT on the importation of goods from outside the EU.

The taxable person can deduct the input tax from the output tax and account to C&E for the difference provided that the inputs were used for the purpose of the business.

EXAMPLE

During a VAT period a trader had a taxable turnover of £60 000 and taxable inputs of £28 000.

	£
Output tax:	
£60 000 × 17.5%	10 500
Input tax:	
£28 000 × 17.5%	(4 900)
[Payable to C&E]	5 600

Where the inputs are used only partly for business purposes, the tax is apportioned and only the business portion is reclaimable, or the input tax is reclaimable in full and output tax charged for the private use.

Car maintenance and running costs

Where cars are used partly for business purposes and partly for private use, the following rules apply:

1. Repairs and maintenance

The input tax on the cost of repairs and maintenance is recoverable in full, even if there is some private use.

2. Fuel

Where all the fuel is provided and there is some private use, the input tax on the fuel is reclaimable in full and output tax is charged for the private portion.

Table 40.1 Charges for VAT output tax on a quarterly basis per car

	2001/02		2002/03 from 1/5/02	
	Petrol (£)	*Diesel (£)*	*Petrol (£)*	*Diesel (£)*
Up to 1400 cc	242	225	226	212
1401 cc – 2000 cc	307	225	286	212
Over 2000 cc	453	286	422	268

The VAT output tax due per car is calculated by applying the VAT fraction to the scale charge.

EXAMPLE

The output tax charged for a 1600 cc petrol engine for the VAT quarter ended 31 July 2002:

$£286 \times 7/47 = £42.60$

If the taxable person accounts for VAT on a monthly basis, the scale charges are as follows:

Table 40.2 Charges for VAT output tax on a monthly basis per car

	2001/02		2002/03 from 1/5/02	
	Petrol (£)	Diesel (£)	Petrol (£)	Diesel (£)
Up to 1400 cc	80	75	75	70
1401 cc – 2000 cc	102	75	95	70
Over 2000 cc	151	95	140	89

EXAMPLE

The output tax charged on a 2200 cc petrol car for a monthly VAT period during 2002/03 (from 1/5/02):

$£140 \times 7/47 = £20.85$

There are, however, certain supplies on which the input tax is non-deductible:

1. Business entertaining

If the entertainment is disallowed for Schedule D Case I purposes under the ICTA 1988, s 577, then no input tax is recoverable. Therefore, the input tax incurred on staff entertainment would be reclaimable provided that the cost is reasonable.

2. Provision of domestic accommodation for directors

The input tax on the costs incurred in providing domestic accommodation to company directors is not reclaimable.

3. Motor cars

Generally the input tax on cars is not reclaimable except in the following situations:

(a) cars acquired by dealers for resale, in which case they are purchases of stock and the input tax is reclaimable;

(b) cars acquired for use in the following businesses:
  – taxi firms
  – driving schools
  – self-drive car rental firms;

(c) from 1 August 1995, the input tax on cars purchased for leasing, or wholly for business purposes, is fully recoverable, in which case VAT output tax must be charged if the car is sold. However, if there is any private use of such a car, only 50 per cent of the input tax is recoverable.

Pre-registration input tax

Input tax incurred before registration can be reclaimed, provided that the person has documentary evidence of the input tax suffered and the following conditions apply:

1. Goods

Input tax on goods acquired prior to registration can be reclaimed, provided that the goods are still on hand at the date of registration. From 1 May 1997, legislation introduced a three-year capping of input tax claims; for businesses registered after 1 May 1997, pre-registration input tax on goods can only be claimed, provided that the goods were supplied within three years of the business being registered.

2. Services

The input tax on services can be reclaimed if they were obtained within six months of registration.

In charging the output tax and reclaiming the input tax for a VAT period, it is important to establish the time of supply, known as the *tax point*, so that the tax is accounted for in the correct period, at the rate in force during that period, unless the trader has elected for cash accounting.

Tax point

1. Goods

The basic tax point for the supply of goods is the date on which they are removed, or made available to the customer.

Where goods are supplied on sale or return the basic tax point is the earlier of:

- the date on which the goods are accepted;
- the date on which the time limit to return the goods has expired;
- 12 months after they are issued if no time limit has been set for approval of the goods.

2. Services

The basic tax point for the supply of services is the date on which the service is completed. Where payments are received regularly for services supplied on a continuous basis the tax point is the earlier of:

- the date the payment is received; or
- the date the invoice is issued.

In practice, the basic tax point is substituted for the actual tax point as follows:

(a) Where payment is made or an invoice is issued before the basic tax point, the actual tax point is the earlier of:
   - the date the payment is received; or
   - the date the invoice is issued.
(b) If a tax invoice is issued within 14 days of the basic tax point, the invoice date becomes the actual tax point. This is known as the 14-day rule. However, it is often more convenient for businesses to issue invoices monthly, in which case the taxable person can request that C&E approve an extension to the 14-day rule.

The VAT return and accounting for VAT

The VAT 100 form used for VAT returns, must be submitted to C&E within 30 days of the end of the VAT period. The VAT accounting period is normally three months ending on a date specified by C&E. So that there is a steady flow of VAT returns to C&E. The VAT periods are staggered as follows:

Group 1

Return periods:

31 March	30 June	30 September	31 December

Group 2

Return periods:

30 April	31 July	31 October	31 January

Group 3

Return periods:

31 May	31 August	30 November	28 February

If the trader wishes to have the accounting year end to coincide with the return periods, then C&E should be notified of this when the person first registers for VAT.
Exceptions to quarterly VAT periods are as follows:

1. Monthly return periods

Monthly return periods may be allowed by C&E where the trader normally receives a repayment of VAT, i.e. where the trader makes wholly or mainly zero rated supplies.

Note: Monthly return periods are not allowed where the trader voluntarily registers for VAT.

2. Annual accounting scheme

This is considered in more detail in Chapter 41.

3. Large VAT payers

Large VAT payers, i.e. over £2 million per annum, are allowed to make quarterly returns but must make monthly payments on account. From 1 June 1996, businesses in this scheme have the option of paying the actual monthly VAT liability instead of estimates based on the previous year, in which case electronic payment is compulsory and there is no seven-day period of grace available.

4. Registration/deregistration

The first period after registration and the last period before deregistration may be for a longer or shorter period than the usual three-month period.
At the end of the VAT accounting period, the trader submits the VAT 100 form showing the following:

- the output tax for the period;
- the input tax reclaimed;

- any adjustments of earlier periods;
- the net tax due or refundable;
- value of outputs;
- value of inputs;
- value of supplies made to other EU member states;
- value of acquisitions from other EU member states;
- a declaration signed by, or on behalf of, the taxable person stating that to the best of their knowledge the information contained in the VAT return is true and correct.

The tax invoice is the principal document for VAT as it shows the output tax charged on the supply and is documentary evidence to reclaim the VAT paid by registered traders on their inputs.

Unless the tax invoice has been issued under the 14-day rule, a VAT invoice must be issued within 30 days of the tax point arising. A tax invoice should show:

(a) an identifying number;

(b) the supplier's name, address and VAT registration number;

(c) the time of the supply;

(d) the customer's name and address;

(e) the type of supply, for example:
  - sale
  - hire purchase
  - loan
  - exchange
  - hire/lease/rental
  - process
  - sale or return;

(f) a description and quantity of the goods/services supplied;

(g) the cost of the supply excluding VAT;

(h) the rate of any cash discount offered; and

(i) the total VAT payable (in sterling).

Retailers may supply modified tax invoices where the supply is £100 or less, including the VAT. Modified tax invoices should show the following:

- the supplier's name, address and VAT registration number;
- the time of the supply;
- a description of the goods/services supplied;
- the cost of the supply including VAT;
- the rate of VAT.

Cash discounts

Value added tax is calculated on the amount net of any discount offered, whether or not the customer takes it, thus:

Tax value of supply = value of supply *less* discount

Where there are alternative discounts, the VAT is based on the highest discount available.

EXAMPLE

A trader supplies goods to a customer for £2000 subject to a 5 per cent discount for prompt payment. The VAT is calculated on the amount net of the discount:

£2000 – (5% × £2000) = £1900

The output tax = £1900 × 7/47 = £282.98

Credit/debit notes

From 1996, when a change in price alters the amount of tax due after an invoice has been issued, credit/debit notes must be issued showing the following:

- identifying number;
- the supplier's name, address and VAT registration number;
- the customer's name and address;
- the reason for the credit;
- a description of the goods/services;
- the quantity and amount credited;
- the total amount credited excluding VAT;
- the rate and amount of VAT credited.

If possible, the number and date of the original tax invoice should be shown.

Accounting for VAT

The way in which VAT is treated in the accounts primarily depends on whether or not the trader is registered for VAT:

1. Non-registered traders

Non-registered traders will have to pay VAT on their purchases, expenses and assets, but as they are not registered they cannot reclaim the input tax through the VAT system. In this case it is the VAT inclusive amount that is included in the profit and loss account and capital allowance computations.

2. Registered traders

Registered traders will reclaim the input tax through the VAT system and as such the VAT exclusive amount is included in the profit and loss account and capital allowance computations. The following situations also affect the accounting procedure:

(a) *Non-deductible input tax.* Where the input tax is not deductible through the VAT system, the VAT inclusive amount is included in the profit and loss account and capital allowance computations.

(b) *VAT owing/due for repayment.* Amounts of VAT owing to C&E and repayments due from C&E should be included as part of the creditors and debtors figures.

(c) *Partially exempt traders.* The portion of input tax that cannot be recovered through the VAT system should be added to the cost of those items in the profit and loss account and capital allowance computations. Partial exemption is considered later in this chapter.

Reverse charge supplies

Where certain services, viz. accountancy, legal, intellectual property and supplies of staff, are received from outside the UK, the supply is treated as if it had been made by the customer. This is known as a reverse charge supply. If the customer is a taxable person, the output tax must be accounted for on the supply, and an equal amount treated as input tax, which may be reclaimable depending on whether the supplies are used for business purposes or not.

Note: Reverse charge supplies count towards the turnover limit for registration purposes.

Mixed/composite supplies

For VAT purposes it is important to make the distinction between one supply that consists of several goods/services and a supply of several goods/services in one transaction, as their treatment for VAT purposes is somewhat different.

1. Mixed supplies

One supply involving several goods or services is a mixed supply. Problems arise when the individual components are taxable at different rates, but the whole transaction is charged at a single inclusive price. For example, a correspondence course is a mixed supply; the supply of the course involves the supply of textbooks, which are zero rated, and a supply of tuition, which is standard rated. Where there is a mixed supply, the total price must be apportioned between the component parts on a fair and reasonable basis for VAT purposes.

EXAMPLE

A mixed supply is sold at an inclusive price of £450. The VAT exclusive cost of each component of the supply is as follows:

	£
Zero rated element	140
Standard rated element	112

$$\frac{112}{112 + 140} \times £450 = £200 \text{ [portion of selling price attributable to standard rated element]}$$

VAT on standard rated element = £200 × 7/47 = £29.79

	£
Standard rated element	170.21
VAT on standard rated element	29.79
Zero rated element	250.00
Total VAT inclusive selling price	450.00

2. Composite supplies

Where several goods/services are provided in one single supply at an all-inclusive price, it is known as a composite supply. For VAT purposes, no apportionment is made on a composite supply, i.e. it is treated as a single indivisible supply at one VAT rate, for example, launderette services.

Partial exemption

A person making entirely exempt supplies cannot reclaim input tax through the VAT system as exempt supplies are outside the scope of VAT. Registered persons making both taxable and exempt supplies are known as partially exempt traders.

Partially exempt persons can reclaim the input tax attributable to taxable supplies but not the input tax attributable to exempt supplies. However, some taxable inputs are made in order to support the business generally, e.g. overhead expenses, and the input tax is reclaimable to the extent that it is attributable to taxable supplies using the following standard method:

$$\text{Input tax attributable to taxable and exempt supplies} \times \frac{\text{Taxable outputs (net of VAT)}}{\text{Total outputs (net of VAT)}}$$

EXAMPLE

The following information relates to the VAT quarter ended 31 July 2001 for Jones Ltd, a partially exempt business:

	£
Exempt supplies	170 000
Zero rated supplies	100 000
Standard rated supplies	250 000

Input tax is attributable as follows:

	£
Exempt supplies	15 300
Zero rated supplies	9 500
Standard rated supplies	18 500
Overheads	10 000

Deductible input tax for overheads:

$$£10\,000 \times \frac{100\,000 + 250\,000}{100\,000 + 250\,000 + 170\,000} = £6730$$

VAT due 31/7/01:

	£	£
Output tax:		
£250 000 × 17.5%		43 750
Input tax reclaimable:		
Standard rate	18 500	
Zero rated	9 500	
Overheads	6 730	(34 750)
VAT due		9 020

When applying the formula to calculate deductible input tax, the following items are excluded:

- capital items
- cars
- entertainment expenses
- provision of domestic accommodation for company directors
- self supplies.

The standard method of attributing deductible input tax, must be used unless C&E agree to an alternative method.

From 30 November 1994, a business can deduct all its input tax provided that the exempt input tax falls below the following *de minimus* limits:

(a) £625 per month on average (£7500 pa); and

(b) no more than 50 per cent of the total input tax.

For input tax incurred after 17th April 2002 businesses will be required to override the standard method and make an adjustment at the end of the tax year where the result does not reflect the use of the purchases, and the difference is substantial, i.e.:

- £50 000, or greater; or
- 50% or more of the value of the residual input tax, but not less than £25 000.

Capital goods scheme

The capital goods scheme was introduced to prevent partially exempt traders from claiming the input tax on capital goods by using them for a taxable purpose in the year of acquisition and then switching them to exempt use when the input tax had been recovered.

The capital goods scheme applies to input tax arising on or after 1 April 1990 on the supply or importation of:

(a) computer equipment costing £50 000 or more per item; and

(b) land, buildings, including extensions or alterations if they increase the floor area by 10 per cent or more, in excess of £250 000.

The adjustment periods are:

(a) five years for computer equipment and leases with less than ten years to run; and

(b) ten years for other property.

If there is a change in the extent to which they are used in making taxable supplies in the adjustment period, the input tax is adjusted accordingly.

Premises may have been acquired while making taxable supplies so that all the input tax was reclaimed, however, if in the adjustment period it is used for exempt purposes some of the input tax will have to be repaid.

The FA 1997 further extended the scope of the capital goods scheme by applying the value limit of £250 000 and an adjustment period of ten years from 3 July 1997 to:

(a) the restoration and re-equipping of existing properties; and

(b) civil engineering works.

Anti-avoidance legislation will also be enacted with effect from 10 March 1999 to:

- prevent the spurious reduction in the adjustment period;
- direct the repayment of input tax recovered where goods are disposed of at a loss; and
- include the prepayment of rent by more than 12 months in the value of the capital goods.

SELF ASSESSMENT QUESTION

40.1 RST Ltd had the following transactions for the VAT quarter ended 30/4/02:

Sales:	£
At standard rate (VAT inclusive)	305 500
At zero rate	55 000
Exempt	100 000

Purchases:	
New car (60% business use)	16 000
Overheads (VAT inclusive)	29 375
Purchases (note 1)	223 000

Note (1)
Purchases are VAT inclusive where applicable and are analysed as follows:

	Std-rated £	Zero-rated £	Exempt £
Attributable to std-rated sales	70 970	7 000	19 000
Attributable to zero-rated sales	23 500	3 500	10 000
Attributable to exempt sales	51 230	3 800	34 000
	145 700	14 300	63 000

Note (2)
Overheads are all at standard rate.

REQUIRED

Calculate the VAT payable by RST Ltd for the quarter ended 30/4/02.

CHAPTER 41

The administration of VAT

The administration of VAT is the responsibility of HM Customs and Excise (C&E) and not the Inland Revenue, as is the case with other major UK taxes. Because VAT is a self assessed tax, there is a legal requirement for taxable persons to keep accounts and records relating to all their transactions.

This chapter examines these requirements along with the function and organisation of the commissioners of Customs & Excise in the administration of VAT, and concludes by considering the penalty regime for failure to comply with the VAT requirements.

Sources of VAT law

The sources of law relating to VAT are as follows:

1. Value Added Tax Act 1994 (VATA 1994)

The main charging provisions are contained in the VATA 1994, which consolidates previous legislation to that date, amendments being made by the Finance Act (FA) each year.

2. Customs and Excise Management Act 1979 (CEMA 1979)

As VAT is under the care and management of the commissioners of HM Customs and Excise, the provisions of the CEMA 1979 apply to VAT where reference is made to them in the VAT legislation.

3. Orders, rules and regulations

The VATA 1994 gives the Treasury and Commissioners of HM Customs and Excise wide powers of discretion to make orders, rules and regulations that are imposed by statutory instrument. The power to make orders, which are usually of a policy nature, is vested in the Treasury, whereas regulations concerning the administration of VAT are generally the responsibility of the commissioners. These orders, rules and regulations contain detailed operating provisions for VAT, for example the following changes may be made *via* orders made by statutory instrument:

- the rates of VAT may be altered, within prescribed limits;
- exempt and zero rated categories may be altered;
- determining those goods that are to be treated as self supplies.

However, orders that affect the rate or burden of VAT must be approved by Parliament within 28 days; Parliament also has the power to void orders made under the VATA 1994.

4. HM Customs and Excise publications

The commissioners of HM Customs and Excise issue booklets and leaflets that explain their interpretation of the legislation. These publications are provided mainly for guidance and do not generally have any effect in law; however, leaflets relating to retail and second hand goods schemes, and those regarding records and accounts all appear to have legislative effect.

5. EU Legislation

There is a binding obligation on member states to give the force of law to policy directives issued by the EU in order to encourage the free movement of goods within the union. However, member states can give effect to these directives in a way that they consider to be nationally appropriate, e.g. the rights and duties of a taxable person are given under national law and not by EU directives. Despite this, the European Court of Justice will intervene in those cases where community law confers rights on individuals in member states, therefore a distinction should be made between those provisions that require member states to take legislative action, and those conferring rights to persons in member states. Decisions in the European Court of Justice are binding on the UK courts.

6. The Isle of Man Act 1979

This largely applies to VAT as the Isle of Man and the UK form a single area for VAT purposes.

7. Case law

VAT tribunals issue written decisions, and selected decisions are published by HM Stationery Office in the *Value Added Tax Tribunal Reports*.

The organisation of HM Customs and Excise

The department of C&E is administered by a Board of Commissioners, who get their authority from the Treasury. The departments concerned with VAT are as follows:

1. Internal taxation directorate

Headed by a Commissioner and based in London, this directorate is concerned with the policy aspects of VAT.

2. VAT control directorate

Headed by a Commissioner and based in Southend-on-Sea, this directorate deals with issuing tax returns, collecting tax and making repayments of VAT.

3. Local VAT offices

Headed by an Assistant Collector and divided into eight to ten districts. Each of these districts is headed by a surveyor and deals with the following aspects of VAT:

- enquiries
- registration and deregistration
- keeping traders' records
- collecting outstanding tax
- audits and control visits.

The Commissioners are given wide powers in the management of VAT, including:

(a) issuing court proceedings to recover unpaid VAT in the UK courts that is due to:
   - Isle of Man C&E service; and
   - authorities in other EU member states;

(b) the power to disclose information to:
   - Inland Revenue
   - Business Statistics office
   - authorities in other EU member states
   - Isle of Man C&E service
   - the charity commissioners;

(c) the power to make directions, impose conditions and specify the records to be kept by certain traders, usually by a series of leaflets issued by the VAT Commissioners, some of which have been given legal standing by the courts, e.g. record keeping requirements and used goods schemes.

Accounts and records

Schedule 11, para 6(1) to the VATA 1994 gives C&E the power to require taxable persons to keep any records that they may require in order to verify that the correct amounts of output tax and input tax have been recorded in the VAT 100 form.

The general accounts and records that C&E require are set out in the VAT (Accounting and Records) Regulations 1989 (SI 1989/2248) and include:

- copies of sales invoices
- purchase invoices
- import/export documentation
- intra-EU supplies made and received
- evidence of changes to amounts paid and received, i.e. debit and credit notes
- a VAT account.

There is no set way of keeping the VAT account, but it must be possible for C&E to check the figures in the VAT return from the VAT account and so it must include:

(a) taxable supplies made and received in the course of business:
- standard rated supplies
- zero rated supplies
- any exempt supplies made by the business

(b) summary of input tax and output tax for each VAT period.

If the business records do not allow C&E to verify the input and output tax, then they have the power to direct that any necessary changes are made. Accounts are normally required to be kept for six years, but a shorter time may be allowed, provided that it is agreed in advance with C&E.

Special VAT schemes

The VAT legislation provides special schemes for the payment of VAT in certain situations. Additional records may be required where taxpayers operate any of the following special VAT schemes:

1. Bad debt relief

Generally a taxable person accounts for VAT when the supply is made, regardless of whether payment has been received. If the debt later proves to be irrecoverable, bad debt relief is available on supplies made after 1 April 1989 provided:

(a) the debt is at least six months old (12 months prior to 1 April 1993); and

(b) the debt has been written off in the accounts.

If the above conditions are met, the supplier can recover the original output tax on the supply; if, however, payment is later received, the relief must be repaid to C&E.

In order to be eligible for bad debt relief, the supplier must keep a 'refund for bad debts account' in respect of each claim, showing the following:

- the amount of VAT charged on the original supply;
- the return period in which the VAT was accounted for and paid to C&E;
- information that verifies when, what and to whom the supply was made;
- the amount of the bad debt;
- the amount of the claim; and
- the return period in which the claim is made.

From 26 November 1996, input tax reclaimed by the debtor is claimed back where the supplier subsequently claims bad debt relief. From 17 December 1996, the relief can be claimed up to six months from the due date of payment rather than the time of supply to reflect deferred payment terms.

The FA 1997 also introduced the following amendments to bad debt relief:

(a) title in the goods need not pass before bad debt relief can be claimed;

(b) on the transfer of a business as a going concern the transferor can claim bad debt relief on debts incurred before the transfer; and

(c) taxpayers who account annually for VAT are allowed to claim bad debt relief on the same returns.

The concession dealing with bad debt relief on barter transactions was given legislative effect in the FA 1998.

2. Flat rate schemes

Section 54 of the VATA 1994 provides for a flat rate scheme available to farmers under the provisions of the sixth directive (1977). If a farmer opts for this scheme, he ceases to be registered for VAT, so input tax cannot be recovered. The farmer can then charge a flat rate of 4 per cent on supplies made to taxable persons, which they can recover as input tax, but the farmer is not liable to account to C&E for the flat rate addition. A farmer operating this scheme must issue invoices showing the flat rate addition and keep copies along with his other accounting records.

From 25th April 2002 businesses can opt to join a flat rate scheme if the following conditions are met:

- Tax exclusive annual taxable turnover of up to £100,000; and
- Tax exclusive annual turnover, including the value of exempt, and, or other non taxable income, of up to £125,000.

Different flat rate percentages will apply to different trade sectors.

3. Tour operators

Section 53 of the VATA 1994 provides a marginal scheme where tour operators obtain goods and services which are resupplied without alteration. If the tour operator opts for this scheme, input tax cannot be reclaimed in respect of these services but the value of the supply on which VAT is due is calculated at the margin, i.e. the difference between the amount charged for the service and the amount paid in respect of those services:

	£
Amount charged by tour operator for services	X
less:	
Amount paid by tour operator for service	(X)
Margin on which VAT is due	X

Note: If travel services are supplied from the tour operator's own resources rather than being bought in, the scheme does not apply.

4. Special schemes for small businesses

Two schemes are available to reduce the administrative burden of VAT for small businesses:

(a) Cash accounting]

Businesses with an annual turnover not exceeding £600 000 (VAT exclusive) can account for VAT on a cash basis rather than an accruals basis, provided that:

(a) VAT returns are up to date and paid;

(b) no penalties, surcharges or interest are due;

(c) the taxpayer has not been convicted of a VAT offence within the last three years; and

(d) the taxpayer has not been expelled from the scheme within the last three years.

The conditions in (a) and (b) may be waived if agreement is reached with C&E to pay by instalments.

Under the cash accounting scheme the tax point for input and output tax is the later of:

- the date on the cheque; or
- the date the payment is received/made.

Once in the cash accounting scheme, the taxpayer must stay with it for at least two years unless either:

(a) the value of taxable supplies exceeds £750 000 during any 12-month period (taken at the end of the VAT return period) (SI 1987/1427, reg 6(2)); or

(b) the value of taxable supplies is expected to exceed £600 000 in the next 12 months.

In either case, the taxpayer must leave the scheme. Normal records and accounts must be maintained, the main advantages to cash accounting being that cash flow is improved where customers are slow to pay, and the scheme by its very nature provides automatic bad debt relief.

(b) Annual accounting

Businesses with an annual turnover not exceeding £600 000 can apply to account for VAT annually rather than quarterly, provided that:

(a) the taxpayer has been registered for at least 12 months;

(b) the VAT returns are up to date;

(c) the taxpayer was not a repayment trader in the last year, i.e. supplying mainly zero rated goods; and

(d) the taxpayer has not been expelled from the scheme within the last three years.

Under the annual accounting scheme the taxpayer makes nine monthly payments of VAT on account, taken as 10 per cent of the estimated VAT due for the year, based on the VAT paid in the previous year, with a balancing payment being made at the end of the year when the return is submitted. From 1 June 1996, businesses have the option of paying actual monthly VAT instead of estimates based on the previous year.

Normal accounts and records must be maintained, the main advantage being that it alleviates the administrative burden of submitting quarterly returns for small businesses.

Internet filing of VAT returns: for small VAT registered businesses with turnovers below £600 000, a one-off discount of £50 will be available for one year only, from April 2001, for filing VAT returns on-line and electronically paying the tax due.

From 25th April 2002 the 12 month qualifying period has been removed for businesses with a taxable turnover of up to £100 000.

5. Second hand goods scheme

Because input tax is recoverable by taxable persons, VAT is effectively borne by the final consumer. This does not present a problem for goods that are consumed by the person who purchases them. However, the durability of some goods means that sometimes goods with a second hand value may be sold back to taxable persons and supplied to another individual, so that the same goods could be taxed more than once.

Under the VATA 1994, ss 32, 50A and the FA 1995, s 24, the Treasury has the power to make orders reducing the tax due on the sale of second hand goods to provide a measure of relief against this double taxation. Under the second hand goods scheme, VAT output tax is calculated on the trader's margin rather than the selling price, so that VAT is only due if there is a profit on resale.

$$\text{Output tax} = \text{Gross profit} \times 7/47 \quad (17.5\%/117.5\%)$$

Note: The output tax is calculated on the gross margin, i.e. expenses incurred in putting the goods into a saleable condition are not deductible. The scheme can only be used if the goods being supplied were acquired either from:

- a private individual, i.e. no tax is charged;
- from another dealer in the scheme, i.e. no tax invoice is issued; or
- a self supply;

and when the goods are sold no tax invoice is issued.

In other words, goods cannot be sold under this scheme if a tax invoice is received when purchased or issued when sold.

Section 24 of the FA 1995 gives effect to the sixth directive (1977) to introduce a common scheme for taxing second hand goods. From 1 January 1995 the Commissioners announced the following changes:

(a) existing schemes are extended to include all second hand goods, works of art, antiques and collectors items except precious metals and gemstones; and

(b) a simplified method of accounting, known as global accounting is to be introduced; as a general rule the margin calculation must be made for each item separately, but a global scheme can be used for goods costing £500 or less.

In order to be eligible for the second hand goods scheme, the following additional records must be maintained:

(a) Stock book

This should contain detailed information as follows:

- identification of individual goods
- the person they were bought from
- the person they were sold to
- the cost
- the sale price
- the margin
- the output tax due.

(b) Sales invoice

Special sales invoices and a certificate signed by the retailer and customer.

(c) Purchase invoice

Special purchase invoices and a certificate signed by the retailer and the person from whom the goods were bought.

EXAMPLE

George is a second hand car dealer and bought a car for £1500. He spent £250 including VAT on repairs, and sold the car for £2675.

$$\text{Output tax} = (2675 - 1500) \times 7/47 = \underline{\underline{£175}}$$

The repair costs are ignored, but the VAT on the repairs is available for input tax credit. Goods acquired when a business is transferred as a going concern will not qualify under this scheme unless the goods were eligible before the transfer.

Dealing with HM Customs and Excise

Control visits

The requirement to keep records stems from the fact that VAT is a self assessed tax, and consequently the legislation provides for C&E to carry out periodic audits on taxable persons. The audits, known as 'control visits' enable C&E to verify the accuracy of the VAT returns by examining the business records and, of course, act as a deterrent to tax evasion.

Officers from the local VAT office carry out the visits and in this respect C&E have the power to:

- enter premises
- examine the business records
- obtain a search warrant where fraud is suspected.

All businesses are not visited with the same frequency. How often a 'control visit' is made will be influenced by the following factors:

- the size of the business, i.e. the larger the business the more frequent the audits;
- the trader's track record as regards compliance with the VAT requirements;
- noticeable changes in activity levels when the VAT return is submitted.

Assessments and appeals

Generally the amount of VAT that is due is submitted by the taxable person with the VAT 100 form. However, the commissioners have the power to make an assessment where:

- returns are not submitted;
- the return is incomplete or incorrect;
- records have not been maintained;
- details on the VAT return cannot be verified by the VAT officers;
- a repayment has been made by mistake.

For an assessment to be valid it must comply with the following requirements:

1. The assessment must be correct in law.
2. Section 73, VATA 1994 provides that where the commissioners make an assessment, they must do so to the *best of their judgement*, taking into account all material information to hand.

3. The time limit for making an assessment is the later of:

(a) *two years* from the end of the accounting period; or

(b) *one year* after evidence justifying the assessment was known. However, the assessment must be made within three years (from 18 July 1996), unless fraud is involved, in which case, the time limit is extended to *20 years*, but an assessment may not be made more than three years after a person's death.

4. The taxpayer must be notified correctly. The legislation does not prescribe how this should be achieved, but the courts have held that the notification should state in clear terms:

(a) *who* is being assessed;

(b) the *amount* of the assessment;

(c) the *reasons* for the assessment; and

(d) the period to which the assessment relates.

Failure by C&E in any of these areas, and situations where the taxpayer can produce evidence to show that the assessment is wrong and what the correct amount should be, are all grounds for appeal. Disputed assessments can be settled by negotiation with the local VAT office (LVO), especially in cases where the taxpayer can furnish them with information that he believes has not been taken into account. The taxpayer should apply to the LVO within *30 days* for the decision to be reconsidered, after which the LVO may either:

● revise the original decision; or

● uphold the original decision.

Negotiations at a local level do not preclude the right of appeal to an independent VAT tribunal.

If the taxpayer then wishes to bring the dispute to a tribunal, he must observe the following time limits:

(a) where the LVO issues a *revised* assessment, the taxpayer must lodge an appeal with a VAT tribunal within *30 days* of the revised decision;

(b) where the LVO upholds the original decision, the taxpayer must lodge an appeal with a VAT tribunal within *21 days* of confirmation to uphold the original assessment; or

(c) in the absence of local negotiations, taxpayers wishing to appeal against a decision must apply within *30 days* of the disputed decision to have the case heard by an independent VAT tribunal.

Independent VAT tribunals

There is a VAT tribunal centre for each part of the UK; viz. London, Manchester, Birmingham, Cardiff, Leeds, Exeter, Newcastle, Edinburgh, Belfast and Castletown (IoM). Applications for a dispute to be heard by a tribunal must be made directly to the appropriate tribunal centre, and not the LVO, within the prescribed time limits. Provided that VAT returns and payments are up to date, a tribunal will hear appeals concerning the following matters which are listed in the VATA 1994, s 83:

- registration
- assessments made out of time
- estimated assessments made by C&E
- the amount of output tax chargeable
- the amount of input tax reclaimable
- the proportion of input tax reclaimable by partially exempt persons
- C&E refusal to allow cash accounting
- disputes regarding retail schemes
- bad debt relief claims
- refunds under the DIY house builders scheme
- disputes regarding civil penalties, interest and surcharge
- C&E refusal to pay interest on overpaid tax
- value of goods/services
- C&E requirement that the taxpayer provides security as a condition of making taxable supplies
- claims for repayment of tax on imported goods which the taxpayer does not wholly own
- requirements concerning computer invoicing.

The overall responsibility for the tribunals is vested in the President of VAT tribunals, appointed by the Lord Chancellor; this person must be a barrister, solicitor or advocate of at least ten years' standing. At least one member of a tribunal panel must be a full-time paid chairman, who may sit alone or with other panel members as follows:

(a) a chairman with two other members – in which case the decision is by majority vote;

(b) a chairman with one other member – in which case the chairman has the casting vote; and

(c) a chairman sitting alone.

The detailed rules regarding the procedure to be followed in VAT tribunals are contained in the VAT (Tribunals) Rules 1986 (SI 1986/590). In particular, the tribunal has the power to:

- require the taxpayer to furnish them with any information they need in order to determine the appeal;
- inspect the taxpayer's records;
- summon witnesses who may be asked to give evidence on oath;
- award costs;
- mitigate penalties.

Either party may appeal against the tribunal decision on a *point of law* to the Queen's Bench division of the High Court, the Court of Appeal and finally the House of Lords. Provided that both parties agree, appeals from the tribunal can be heard in the Court of Appeal, thereby by-passing the High Court. Failure to comply with a VAT tribunal direction may render the taxpayer liable to penalties of up to £1000.

The penalty regime

Prior to the Keith Committee report in 1985, the recourse afforded to C&E for non-compliance was under criminal law; where a person is deemed innocent until proven guilty beyond a reasonable doubt, the onus of proof resting with C&E. Following the Keith Committee report, the FA 1985 introduced a number of civil penalties for non-compliance with the VAT requirements. The standard of proof for civil actions is less rigid, being based on a balance of probabilities; under civil law the burden of proof generally rests with the taxpayer. The main penalties afforded by the legislation are as follows:

1. Late registration (VATA 1994, s 67)

Failure to register for VAT at the correct time, or failure to notify a change in the nature of supplies made by an exempt person, renders the taxpayer liable to a financial penalty depending on the lateness of the notification of the liability to be registered for VAT. The penalty is calculated as the greater of:

- £50; or
- a percentage of the tax due from the date the person should have been registered to the date when notification is made or C&E discover the taxpayer's liability to be registered.

The percentage depends on the lateness of the registration as follows:

Up to 9 months late	5 per cent
Between 9–18 months late	10 per cent
Over 18 months late	15 per cent

From 1 January 1996, this penalty applies to the failure to notify a liability to register when a business is transferred as a going concern.

2. Unauthorised issue of VAT invoices (VATA 1994, s 67)

If an unregistered trader issues an invoice, falsely including an amount for VAT, the unregistered trader is liable to a penalty, calculated as the greater of:

- £50; or
- 15 per cent of the VAT included in the invoice.

3. Breaches of VAT requirements (VATA 1994, s 69)

The legislation provides a series of penalties for failure to comply with the VAT requirements. The amount of the penalty depends on the type and frequency of non-compliance. Some breaches of the regulations carry a fixed penalty, others are subject to a fixed daily rate.

In cases where the breach attracts more than one penalty, C&E must decide which penalty to impose, e.g. failure to notify cannot be penalised under the late registration penalty and the breach of regulations penalty, i.e. they are mutually exclusive.

If C&E choose to penalise the taxpayer for breach of regulations, s 76(2) of the VATA 1994 provides that they must have given the person concerned a written warning within two years. Breaches of regulations carry the following penalties:

Table 41.1 Penalty for breach of VAT regulations

Breach	Penalty
Failure to preserve records for six years	Fixed penalty of £500
Failure to submit a return or payment by the due date	Greater of: 1. Fixed daily rate; or 2. Tax geared percentage rate
Any other breach of the regulations	Fixed daily rate

1. *Fixed daily rate* is calculated as:
   (a) basic penalty of £5 per day while the breach continues;
   (b) if the taxpayer has breached the same regulation in the previous two years the penalty is increased to £10 per day;
   (c) if the taxpayer has breached the same regulation more than once in the previous two years the penalty is increased to £15 per day.

2. *Tax geared percentage rate* is calculated as:
   (a) $\frac{1}{6}$ per cent of VAT due whilst breach continues (equivalent to an annual rate of 61 per cent);
   (b) if the taxpayer has breached the same regulation in the previous two years the percentage is increased to $\frac{1}{3}$ per cent of the VAT due (equivalent to 122 per cent pa);
   (c) if the taxpayer has breached the same regulation more than once in the previous two years the percentage is increased to $\frac{1}{2}$ per cent of the VAT due (equivalent to 183 per cent pa).

Penalties imposed under these provisions are subject to:

- minimum penalty of £50; and
- maximum penalty of 100 days.

4. Default surcharge (submission of late returns)

The first time a taxpayer submits a return it does not give rise to a penalty charge but it starts the ball rolling. From 1 October 1993, a *surcharge liability notice* may be issued after the first late return. The surcharge notice stipulates the surcharge liability period which commences when the notice is issued and ends 12 months after the end of the period in which the taxpayer defaulted. If the taxpayer is late during this period penalties will arise as follows:

Table 41.2 Penalty rate in surcharge liability period

Number of defaults in surcharge period	Penalty
First	2%
Second	5%
Third	10%
Fourth and subsequent	15%

These penalties are subject to a minimum penalty of £30. Each time the taxpayer is in default, the surcharge period is extended, therefore, in order to avoid penalties, the taxpayer needs to submit returns on time during the period covered by the surcharge notice. Nil or repayment returns do not attract a financial penalty, but the surcharge liability period will be extended.

EXAMPLE

Quarter ended:

31/12/00	Late
31/3/01	On time
30/6/01	On time
30/9/01	Late
31/12/01	On time

The VAT return due in Southend by 31 January 2001 was late and will result in a surcharge liability notice being issued effective from 14 February 2001–31 December 2001. A late return is submitted for the quarter ended 30 September 2001, which will attract a penalty of 2 per cent of the tax due, and the surcharge period is extended to 30 September 2002.

5. Tax evasion

Depending on the nature and extent of the tax evasion, C&E can commence criminal or civil proceedings against the taxpayer.

(a) Criminal Fraud (VATA 1994, s 72)

The fraudulent evasion of VAT by providing false information or using false documents can render the taxpayer liable to criminal prosecution. The level of penalties for criminal fraud depends on whether a conviction is obtained by the magistrates' court or the Crown Court:

- *Magistrates' court* (summary conviction) – Conviction in the magistrates' court is punishable by imprisonment for up to 12 months and a fine of up to three times the amount of tax evaded.
- *Crown Court* (conviction on indictment) – Conviction in the Crown Court is punishable by imprisonment for up to seven years and an unlimited fine.

(b) Civil fraud (VATA 1994, s 60)

Proceedings for civil fraud may be brought against the taxpayer who has behaved dishonestly in order to evade tax. The maximum penalty for civil fraud is 100 per cent of the tax evaded.

The FA 1994 introduced the offence of misdeclaration to replace serious misdeclaration and persistent misdeclaration. The offences covered by misdeclaration are:

(a) submitting returns that understate the VAT due or falsely claim a repayment of VAT (this offence was previously called serious misdeclaration).

(b) failing to notify C&E within 30 days that an assessment issued by them understates the tax due (previously called serious misdeclaration).

(c) VAT returns understating the liability by the greater of:

- £500 000; or
- 10 per cent of the sum of the output tax and the input tax that should have been shown on the tax return.

The penalty for offences under (a) above, is 15 per cent of the tax that would have been lost had the error above not been discovered subject to a *de minimus* limit of the greater of:

- £1 000 000; or
- 30 per cent of the sum of the output tax and the input tax that should have been shown on the return.

EXAMPLE

VAT return submitted should have shown the following amounts:

	£
Output tax	24 000
Input tax	9 000

The penalty will only be imposed if the error in the return is more than:

30% × (24 000 + 9000) = £9900

The penalty for offences under (b) above, is 15 per cent of the tax that would have been lost had the error not been discovered, subject to a *de minimus* limit of the greater of:

- £1 000 000; or
- 30 per cent of the tax liability shown on the corrected return.

EXAMPLE

Assessment issued by C&E should have shown the following amounts:

	£
Output tax	18 000
Input tax	6 750

The penalty will only be imposed if the amount understated is more than:

30% × (18 000 − 6750) = £3375

Offences under (c) above are known as material inaccuracies and were previously referred to as persistent misdeclaration. These offences carry a penalty of 15 per cent of the tax that would have been lost had the error not been discovered.

6. Mitigation of penalties

Penalties will not be imposed where the taxpayer can show he has a 'reasonable excuse'. The legislation does not define reasonable excuse but provides that the following are *not* to be taken into account:

- insufficient funds;
- errors made by a person whom the taxpayer relied on.

For assessments made after 27 July 1993, the following penalties may be mitigated by up to 100 per cent by C&E or a VAT tribunal:

- civil fraud
- misdeclaration
- late registration
- unauthorised issue of tax invoices.

Note: A VAT tribunal can reduce the mitigation allowed by C&E as well as increase it.

7. Interest on unpaid VAT (VATA 1994, s 74)

These provisions apply to tax which is recovered by assessment or which could have been assessed but is covered by the tax returns. *Note*: It does not apply to the late payment of VAT that is correctly stated in the VAT return, this is covered by the default surcharge provisions.

Interest runs from the date that the VAT should have been paid to the date of payment; for assessments calculated after 16 March 1993, interest will not start from more than three years prior to the assessment date. The rate of interest is fixed by the Treasury and reflects the commercial rate of interest.

8. Repayment supplement

The taxpayer is entitled to a repayment supplement from C&E where they fail to make a repayment of VAT within 30 days of the later of:

- the end of the return period; or
- the date when C&E received the return.

The amount of repayment supplement payable is the greater of:

- 5 per cent of the repayment due; or
- £50.

For returns received on or after 9 March 1999, the basis for calculating the 30-day period will ignore any days before the end of the accounting period to which the returns relate.

PRACTICE QUESTIONS

1. (a) VAT is charged on the supply of goods or services made 'in the course or furtherance' of a business. What general test can be applied to decide whether a business exists?

    (6 marks)

    (b) When a person ceases to be a taxable person for VAT purposes any goods then held by him are treated as disposed of by him in the course of his business immediately before he ceases to be a taxable person. When can this rule be waived?

    (5 marks)
    (Total: 11 marks)
    (Source: ACCA, Dec 87)

2. Mr D advises you that he is about to commence a business on 1 December 2001 as a sole trader.

    He will be engaged in selling motor accessories which are all standard rated for value added tax purposes. His business plan indicates that his turnover will be approximately £4000 for each of the first three months, thereafter rising to £6000 per month.

    In the first few months he will have substantial expenditure on equipment and stock.

    He is new to business and seeks advice on the VAT implications of running this sort of business.

    You are required to draft a report setting out the matters relating to VAT on which Mr D will require guidance.

    (15 marks)
    (Source: CIMA, Nov 93)

3. You have been approached by the finance director of a group of eight UK trading companies. He seeks advice on certain aspects of VAT. The group companies are involved in both the manufacture and the retailing of goods, some of which are standard rated and some zero rated. About one-third of the total sales are exported to both EU and non-EU countries. At present all of the companies are in a single group VAT registration.

    You are required to draft a report to the finance director on the way in which the present arrangements for VAT could be altered in order to improve the cash flow of the group as a whole.

    (15 marks)
    (Source: CIMA, Nov 94)

4. (a) The VAT rules impose a system of penalties for a trader who pays his quarterly VAT late.

    You are required to outline the current state of the law in respect of both:

    (i) financial penalties; and
    (ii) appeals to VAT tribunals.

    (10 marks)

(b) A VAT-registered business had the following transactions for the quarter ended 31 March 2002.

	£
Sales at standard rate	172 500
Sales at zero rate	50 000
Exempt sales	75 000
Purchases at standard rate	115 575
Purchases at zero rate	7 200
Purchased new motor car	10 150
Purchased second-hand motor car	4 500

All the above amounts are inclusive of VAT where this is applicable.

The business allows its employees to use the cars for private motoring.

You are required to calculate the amount of VAT to be accounted for to HM Customs and Excise for the quarter ended 31 March 2002. Ignore the annual adjustment.

(5 marks)
(Total: 15 marks)
(Source: CIMA, Nov 87)

5. **You are required:**

(a) to explain the meaning of the term 'tax point' in relation to value added tax on the sale of goods and to state the exceptions where the basic rule concerning its determination may be amended; and

(8 marks)

(b) to explain why it may be beneficial for an individual who is carrying on a business to register voluntarily even though there is no legal requirement for him to do so.

(4 marks)
(Total: 12 marks)
(Source: ACCA, Dec 84)

6. With regard to value added tax:

(a) Outline the different effects where a person makes supplies which are:
   (i)   zero rate only;
   (ii) exempt only;
   (iii) a mixture of zero rated and exempt.

(10 marks)

(b) A tax invoice is often regarded as one of the most important documents in the operation of VAT. State the items which must be contained in such an invoice where the value of taxable supply exceeds £100.

(10 marks)
(Total: 20 marks)
(Source: ACCA, Dec 83)

PART 6

The administration of direct taxation in the UK

CHAPTER 42

Administration of income tax and capital gains tax

The taxation of income and gains is under the care and management of the Board of the Inland Revenue (IR). The Taxes Management Act 1970 (TMA 1970) sets out the powers and responsibilities of the IR in administering income tax (IT), capital gains tax (CGT) and corporation tax (CT) and substantial changes have been made to the TMA 1970 following the introduction of self assessment.

The Finance Act 1994 (FA 1994) contained legislation for the introduction of self assessment, radically changing the system for the administration and collection of direct taxes in the UK. Under self assessment there is a shift in responsibility for the assessment of direct taxes from the Inland Revenue (IR) to the taxpayer.

One of the main aims of self assessment is to simplify the tax system, however, in reality, while the IR will be streamlined, making direct taxes cheaper to administer, the compliance costs for the taxpayer are likely to increase. Self assessment took effect from the tax year 1996/7 onwards and is the biggest change to the system of direct taxation in the UK since the introduction of the Pay As You Earn (PAYE) scheme in 1944, affecting all those taxpayers who normally receive a tax return.

This chapter examines the administrative machinery for the collection of IT and CGT under the self assessment regime.

The role of the taxpayer

The introduction of self assessment has changed and increased taxpayers' responsibilities and, in particular, they must fulfil the following obligations:

1. Notification of a liability to tax (TMA 1970, s 7 (as amended))

Prior to self assessment, the TMA 1970, s 7 provided that it was the taxpayer's duty to inform the Revenue of a liability to tax within 12 months from the end of the tax year in which the liability arose. Under self assessment, the onus is still on the taxpayer to declare a liability to tax, but the TMA 1970, s 7 is now amended and the time limit is reduced to six months from the end of the tax year in which the liability to tax arose.

Failure to notify the Revenue within the prescribed time limit may result in a financial penalty if the tax remains unpaid by 31 January following the tax year in which the liability was incurred, e.g. a liability to tax for 2000/01 not notified and not paid by 31 January 2002. This means that even if the liability is notified after 5 October 2001 (six months after the end of the 2000/01 tax year), a penalty will not arise if the full amount of the tax due is paid by 31 January 2002.

2. Requirement to submit a return of income and gains (TMA 1970, s 8 (as amended))

Under self assessment, the emphasis is on the tax return, which allows the taxpayer to assess the amount of tax due for a fiscal year, and which must be submitted within the prescribed time limits. The tax return should show the net amounts of any income and gains for the fiscal year concerned.

Pages 1–8 of the tax return requires information concerning the following:

- income from savings and investments;
- claims for allowances and relief;
- casual earnings;
- income from pensions and social security benefits.

Where the taxpayer has other sources of income, (e.g. employment, self-employment, income from land and property, etc.) or chargeable capital gains, the taxpayer must complete the relevant supplementary pages. In pages 1–8 of the return the taxpayer can either calculate the tax due for the fiscal year in question or request that the IR calculate the tax due; in either case, the calculation of the tax liability will be based on the figures supplied in the return, and are, therefore, both treated as a self assessment.

The FA 2000 provided for a number of improvements to be introduced in order to make the system more user friendly, viz.:

(1) clearer statements and forms;
(2) more convenient ways to pay:
    - by debit card online or by telephone,
    - payments on account by direct debit;
(3) reduction in the number of PAYE taxpayers with minor sources of income being required to complete a self assessment tax return.

The *Taxback* Website found at www.inlandrevenue.gov.uk/taxback provides information for non-taxpayers or those paying little tax on how to claim back tax repayments on savings income that has been deducted at source. It also instructs non-taxpayers how to make sure future savings income is paid gross.

Under self assessment, there are strict deadlines for the submission of returns and the payment of the tax due. If the taxpayer opts to calculate the tax due, the return must be submitted by:

(a) 31 January following the fiscal year to which the return relates, e.g. the return of income and gains for 2000/01 will have to be submitted by 31 January 2002; or
(b) three months after the return is issued, where it is issued after the 31 October following the fiscal year to which it relates, e.g. the return of income and gains for 2000/01 issued on 6 December 2001 will have to be returned by 5 March 2002.

Where the taxpayer asks the IR to calculate the tax due, the return must be submitted by:
(a) 30 September following the fiscal year to which the return relates, e.g. the return of income and gains for 2002/03 will have to be submitted by 30 September 2003; or

(b) two months after the return is issued, where it is issued after 31 July following the fiscal year to which the return relates, e.g. return of income and gains for 2002/03 issued on 6 October 2003 will have to be returned by 5 December 2003.

3. Requirement to keep records (TMA 1970, s 12B(1))

From 6 April 1996, taxpayers are obliged to keep the records necessary to enable them to submit a correct return for the fiscal year in question and the TMA 1970, s 12(1) and 12 (2)(b) further provides that these records should be preserved for prescribed periods of time after the return has been filed with the Revenue as follows:

(a) for taxpayers who are in business the records must be preserved for five years after the filing date; and

(b) for other taxpayers the records must be preserved for 12 months after the filing date.

Note: With regard to taxpayers with a business, the five-year time limit applies to all their records and not just the business records.

These time limits may be altered in cases where the return is subject to a formal enquiry. All records that support business transactions, the receipt of income and the disposal of chargeable assets should be maintained, for example:

- purchase and sales invoices
- expenses
- business accounts
- bank statements
- dividend vouchers
- P60
- evidence of taxable benefits
- records relating to chargeable assets and calculations of a gain or loss on disposal.

Photocopies are acceptable if they are full and complete copies. Failure to maintain the correct records to support the return of income and gains may render the taxpayer liable to a financial penalty.

The role of the Inland Revenue

Under the self assessment regime, the role of the IR has changed which has required substantial reorganisation within the Revenue. The FA 1994 and subsequent FAs contain provisions for the amendment of the TMA 1970 to cater for these changes and the old 'Inspectors' and 'collectors' of taxes are now referred to in the legislation as 'officers of the Board'.

Self assessment has brought with it a shift in responsibility from the IR to the taxpayer. The main responsibilities of the officers of the Board under the new regime are as follows:

1. Calculation of the self assessment (TMA 1970, s 9)

Where the taxpayer makes a request and files the return within the prescribed time limits, the Revenue will calculate the tax due. It is still, however, treated as a self assessment because it is based on the figures supplied by the taxpayer in the return, which are not audited at the time when the calculation is performed.

The calculation will also be made by the Revenue where the taxpayer does not calculate the tax due, even if no formal request is made, provided that the return is filed within the prescribed time limits. In either of these cases, the officer of the Board must issue a copy of the calculation before the due date for payment.

Returns submitted without completing the self assessment but outside the prescribed time limit are strictly incomplete. In these cases the Revenue will still perform the calculation but they are under no obligation to inform the taxpayer before the due date for payment with the result that interest may become payable if the tax is paid late.

2. Making a determination of tax due (TMA 1970, s 28C)

The officer of the Board has the power to estimate the tax due where the taxpayer fails to submit a return. The assessment must be made to the officer's best information and belief and the determination, which must state the date of issue, is payable by the taxpayer and enforceable by the Revenue until such time as it is replaced by the actual self assessment.

Determinations made by the Revenue in this way are treated as self assessments. When the taxpayer files an actual self assessment, it replaces the Revenues determination, so that an appeal against the determination is unnecessary. The time limit for making a determination is five years from the original filing date, e.g. the correct filing date for the 2002/03 assessment is 31 January 2004, in which case the Revenue has until 31 January 2009 in which to make a determination.

Interest will often accrue on determinations as the due date for payment is the original due date if the return had been filed on time. Actual self assessments can only replace the determination if they are made:

- within the five year limit; or
- if later, within 12 months of the determination.

3. Power to enquire into returns (TMA 1970, s 9)

Prior to self assessment, the Revenue did not have the authority to make random enquiries into returns but they were obliged only to make assessments on those returns believed to be correct. Where the Inspector believed a tax return to be incorrect, the taxpayer may have been called for questioning in order to verify the accuracy of the return, but there was no statutory procedure to be followed, with the result that the process was time consuming and often caused taxpayer resentment.

Under the self assessment regime, the Revenue adopt a 'process now, check later' approach and only obvious mistakes will be corrected when the returns are initially submitted. The Revenue are given statutory powers under the TMA 1970 to enquire into any tax return at random, to check its accuracy and completeness, without the need to justify the enquiry, within the following prescribed time limits:

(a) Returns filed by the fixed filing date

The officer of the Board must notify the taxpayer in writing that the tax return is the subject of an enquiry within 12 months of the fixed filing date, e.g. the return of income and gains for 2002/03 must be filed by 31 January 2004 in which case the Revenue have until 31 January 2005 in which to issue a notice of enquiry.

(b) Returns filed after the fixed filing date

In this case, written notice must be given by the end of the quarter following the anniversary of the actual filing date, the quarter dates being given as 31 January, 30 April, 31 July and 31 October, e.g. the return of income and gains for 2001/02 was filed on 1 March 2003 in which case the Revenue will have until 30 April 2004 in which to issue a notice of enquiry.

A percentage of returns subjected to an enquiry will be selected at random but many enquiries will continue to be based on information obtained by the Revenue or gleaned from the return in much the same way as before the introduction of self assessment.

Where a taxpayer is subject to an enquiry under the TMA 1970, s 9, the officer of the Board can also issue a notice requesting that the taxpayer provide documentary evidence to support the accuracy and completeness of the return under enquiry, and the taxpayer must be given at least 30 days to produce the documents.

The taxpayer may appeal on the grounds that:

(a) the information is irrelevant in verifying the accuracy and completeness of the return; or

(b) insufficient time has been given to comply with the notice.

Note: There is no right of appeal against the Revenue's statutory right to commence an enquiry.

Once the enquiry is complete, the officer of the Board must notify the taxpayer stating:

(a) the enquiry is completed; and

(b) the corrections to be made to the self assessment.

The taxpayer must then amend the assessment within 30 days of this notice.

Further amendments may be made by the officer of the board within 30 days after the taxpayer's 30-day limit has expired, and the taxpayer has the right to appeal against any such amendments.

The FA 2000 introduced measures to revise the formal enquiry notice to make it less 'threatening' than the one presently in use.

4. Making a discovery assessment (TMA 1970, s 29)

The only assessments to be raised by an officer of the board under the self assessment regime are 'discovery' assessments, i.e. where information comes to light that results in a tax loss to the Revenue. Where a self assessment has become final, the Revenue can only make a discovery assessment where there has been:

(a) incomplete disclosure; or

(b) fraudulent or negligent conduct.

The time limits for making a discovery assessment are as follows:

(a) five years from the 31 January following the year of assessment, e.g. discovery assessments relating to the fiscal year 2000/01 must be made by 31 January 2007; or

(b) the five-year limit is extended to 20 years where fraudulent or negligent conduct is involved, e.g. discovery assessment involving fraud for the fiscal year 2000/01 can be made at any time up until 31 January 2022.

Section 29 of the TMA 1970 prevents the Revenue from making a discovery assessment where a self assessment has become final and all the material facts were presented to an officer of the Board at the time; this codifies in statute the principles established in *Scorer* v *Olin Energy Systems Ltd* [1985] BTC 181.

Correction of errors in the tax return (TMA 1970, s 9)

An officer of the Board can correct any obvious errors in a tax return within nine months of the return being filed, e.g. arithmetical errors, which may reduce or increase the tax liability. Where these corrections result in an underpayment and fraudulent or negligent conduct is involved, the taxpayer may be liable to penalties.

The taxpayer can also correct a self assessment that has been filed, e.g. estimated figures may have been used that have since been ascertained. The time limit in this case is 12 months from the filing date, however, alterations cannot be made while a return is under an enquiry, the taxpayer must wait until the enquiry is complete.

Errors discovered after the time limits above may still be corrected but the method of correction depends on whether the error results in an overpayment or underpayment of tax:

1. Errors resulting in an overpayment of tax

A claim for error and mistake relief can be made under the provisions of the TMA 1970, s 33 within five years of the annual filing date, e.g. return of income and gains for 2002/03 can be subject to an error or mistake claim up until 31 January 2009.

2. Errors resulting in an underpayment of tax

Depending on when the error is uncovered the Revenue may take the following action:

- start an enquiry
- make a discovery assessment.

Note: Taxpayers who knowingly have underpaid tax after the time limit for corrections has expired under the TMA 1970, s 9 are under an obligation to notify the Revenue so that action can be taken to rectify the situation.

Appeals and complaints procedures

1. Appeals procedures

Prior to self assessment, the taxpayer had a right of appeal against any assessment made by the Revenue, provided that a claim was made in writing within 30 days of the issue of the assessment, setting out the grounds for the appeal. Application could also be made to postpone some or all of the tax demanded until the appeal was determined. The process was time consuming and costly and resulted in tax revenue being delayed for long periods of time in many cases.

The introduction of self assessment will reduce the number of appeals, making the system more administratively efficient. Under self assessment, the taxpayer retains a statutory right of appeal against any of the following:

- automatic penalties and surcharges
- tax geared penalties
- requests for documents and accounts
- discovery assessments
- amendments made by an officer of the Board following an enquiry.

Although there is no statutory right of appeal against a Revenue enquiry, the taxpayer may apply to the Commissioners of the Inland Revenue to have the enquiry closed. The commissioners will then make a determination on the request as if it were an appeal.

The appeal procedures under the TMA 1970, s 31 are otherwise unchanged under self assessment. The time limit for lodging an appeal is 30 days from the date of notification of the issue in dispute.

Once an appeal has been made, an officer of the Board will try to reach an agreement with the taxpayer in order that the matter can be settled. Where the appeal cannot be settled in this way, the officer of the Board or the taxpayer can request that the case be heard by the Commissioners of the Inland Revenue (CIR).

The CIR are appointed by the Lord Chancellor and may be general commissioners or special commissioners:

(a) General commissioners

The General CIR are usually local businessmen with no specialised tax knowledge and are unpaid except for expenses. The General CIR usually sit in pairs to hear an appeal and where they believe the case requires specialised knowledge or is likely to take a long time they have the authority to have the appeal passed to the Special CIR.

(b) Special commissioners

The Special CIR are full-time paid civil servants and must be barristers, solicitors or advocates of at least ten years' standing. The Special CIR are tax specialists and usually sit alone on an appeal. The Special CIR can have the case transferred to the General CIR where they believe there is no special reason for the case to be heard by the Special CIR.

There is no further appeal from the CIR on a question of *fact* and their decision is final. The taxpayer or officer of the Board may, however, appeal to the High Court on *a point of law* within 30 days. Appeals from the Special CIR may 'leapfrog' the High Court straight to the Court of Appeal. From the High Court there is a right of appeal to the Court of Appeal and with leave to the House of Lords (*see* Fig 42.1).

Case law is an important part of Revenue law; however, judges do not make new laws, they merely interpret the statutes as they apply to the particular facts of the case. In the judgment of a case it is important to distinguish between the following:

(a) Ratio decidendi (reason for the decision)

These are based on the material facts of the case and so set a precedent for future cases which is binding on lower courts.

(b) Obiter dicta (comments by the way)

These are comments that the judge may make that are not based on the facts of the case and so have no binding effect on future cases, they are merely persuasive.

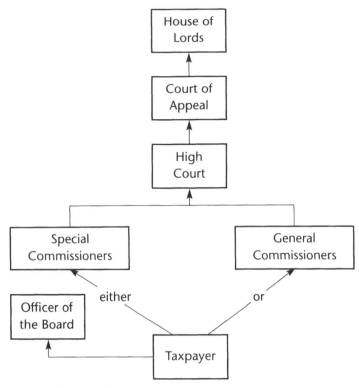

Fig 42.1 Summary of the appeals structure

2. Complaints procedure

Complaints concerning the quality of service supplied by the IR can be made free of charge, to an independent adjudicator where agreement cannot be reached with the local tax office. The adjudicator will consider the matter and attempt to bring about an agreement between the Revenue and the taxpayer. Where such an agreement cannot be reached, the adjudicator will make recommendations to the Revenue on dealing with the complaint and send a copy to the taxpayer, and only in rare circumstances will these recommendations not be followed. Complaints concerning HM Customs and Excise and the Contributions Agency of the DSS are now also dealt with by the adjudicator.

The taxpayer's charter sets out the standard of practice in dealing with the public.

The FA 2001 introduced a number of measures aimed at improving self assessment procedures as follows:

- disputes concerning a point of law can be settled prior to an enquiry being completed;
- simplifying amendments following an enquiry;
- re-write of the rules regarding self-assessment, amendments and enquiries to make the taxpayers rights easier to understand;
- clearer rules regarding the collection of tax;
- where a relief is carried back, giving rise to a repayment of tax from an earlier year, the taxpayer will be entitled to interest on the repayment.

The Taxpayer's Charter

You are entitled to expect the Inland Revenue

To be fair

- By settling your tax affairs impartially
- By expecting you to pay only what is due under the law
- By treating everyone with equal fairness

To help you

- To get your tax affairs right
- To understand your rights and obligations
- By providing clear leaflets and forms
- By giving you information and assistance at our enquiry offices
- By being courteous at all times

To provide an efficient service

- By settling your tax affairs promptly and accurately
- By keeping your private affairs strictly confidential
- By using the information you give us only as allowed by the law
- By keeping to a minimum your costs of complying with the law
- By keeping our costs down

To be accountable for what we do

- By setting standards for ourselves and publishing how well we live up to them

If you are not satisfied

- We will tell you exactly how to complain
- You can ask for your tax affairs to be looked at again
- You can appeal to an independent tribunal
- Your MP can refer your complaint to the ombudsman

In return, we need you

- To be honest
- To give us accurate information
- To pay your tax on time

CHAPTER 43

Due dates, interest and penalties

Before 1996/97 assessments raised by the Revenue were formal demands for tax to be paid by the due date, each source of income having its own particular due date for payment. Under self assessment, all income and gains for the fiscal year in question are entered in the self assessment return and the tax is automatically payable, without demand on set payment dates. The interest and penalty regime has also been amended to take account of these changes. This chapter examines the payment of income tax (IT) and capital gains tax (CGT) and the new rules for interest and penalties.

Payment of income tax and capital gains tax

Under self assessment, taxpayers are required to make two payments on account of their income tax liability, on 31 January during the fiscal year and 31 July following the fiscal year; the balance of any tax payable or repayable will be adjusted on the filing date together with the payment for the CGT liability for a fiscal year.

EXAMPLE

The 2003 tax return of income and gains for the 2002/03 fiscal year will be payable as follows:

31/1/03 – first payment on account of income tax
31/7/03 – second payment on account of income tax
31/1/04 – balance of IT plus any CGT liability

1. Payments on account of income tax (TMA 1970, s 59A)

The payments on account of IT are based on the assessment for the previous year. This is known as the relevant amount and is calculated as:

Relevant amount = Tax liability in previous year *less* Tax deducted at source

EXAMPLE

David, a single man aged 36 years, has the following income for 2002/03:

	£
Schedule D Case I	25 000
Schedule E (gross)	8 000
PAYE deducted	1 750

2002/03	£
Schedule D Case I	25 000
Schedule E	8 000
	33 000
less PA	(4 615)
Taxable income	28 385

	£
£1920 × 10%	192
£26 465 × 22%	5 822
	6 014 Tax liability 2002/03

The payment on account of IT for 2003/04 is calculated as:

£6014 – £1750 = £4264, paid in two equal instalments of £2132 on 31 January 2004 and 31 July 2004.

Payments on account are also necessary in respect of class 4 NICs based on the amount payable in the previous year.

EXAMPLE

The following information relates to Susan for the two years ended 5 April 2002:

	YE 5/4/01 (£)	YE 5/4/02 (£)
Gross tax liability	17 000	20 000
Class 4 NICs	700	880
Tax deducted at source	3 500	4 000

Payments on account for 2001/02:

IT: £
31/1/02   50% (£17 000 – £3500) 6750 + NICs $\frac{1}{2}$ × 700 = £7100 1st payment on A/C
31/7/02   50% (£17 000 – £3500) 6750 + £350 NICs = £7100 2nd payment on A/C

Payments on account for 2002/03:

IT:
31/1/03   50% (£20 000 – £4000) 8000 + NICs £440 = £8440 1st payment on A/C
31/7/03   50% (£20 000 – £4000) 8000 + NICs £440 = £8440 2nd payment on A/C

Payments on account will not be necessary where the relevant amount is less than £500 or more than 80 per cent of the previous year's liability was deducted at source.

Taxpayers can make a claim under the TMA 1970, s 59A(3) and (4) to have payments on account reduced or cancelled where they believe that:

- no tax liability will arise in the current year;
- the tax liability will be covered by any tax deducted at source; or
- the overall tax liability will be less than the payments on account, based on the previous year.

Claims under s 59 must be made by 31 January following the tax year, and the Revenue are bound to accept any such claims, however they will be examined by the Revenue in order to exclude fraudulent or negligent claims being made.

2. Balancing payments (TMA 1970, s 59B)

The final tax liability for a fiscal year is calculated in the self assessment return and any balance of IT is paid/repaid along with the CGT liability on the normal filing date. Where returns are received on time, the normal filing date is 31 January following the year of assessment; if the return is issued late, i.e. after 31 October following the year of assessment, it must be filed within three months of the issue date (*see* Chapter 42).

EXAMPLE 1

The 2003 tax return of income and gains for 2002/03 was received on 1 May 2003. The payment dates are as follows:

31/1/03 – first payment on account of IT for 2002/03
31/7/03 – second payment on account of IT for 2002/03
31/1/04 – balance of IT and CGT liability for 2002/03

EXAMPLE 2

The following information relates to Ahmed, a single man under 65 years old:

	2000/01	2001/02
	(£)	(£)
Schedule D Case I	18 265	20 000
Schedule E (gross)	10 000	12 000
Class 4 NICs	660	780
PAYE deducted	2 219	2 573
CGT liability	3 000	1 000

The payments on account of IT for 2001/02 are calculated with reference to his 2000/01 liability as follows:

2000/01	£
Schedule D Case I	18 265
Schedule E	10 000
	28 265
less PA	(4 385)
Taxable income	23 880

	£	
£1520 × 10%	152	
£22 360 × 22%	4919	
	5071	Income tax liability 2000/01

Class 4 NIC liability 2000/01 = £660

Payments on account of 2001/02 are calculated as: (£5071 + £660) − £2219 = $\dfrac{£3512}{2}$

	(£)
First payment on account	1756
Second payment on account	1756

2001/02	£
Schedule D Case I	20000
Schedule E	12000
	32000
less PA	(4535)
Taxable income	27465

	£	
£1880 × 10%	188	
£25 585 × 22%	5629	
	5817	2001/02 income tax liability

The total income tax and NIC class 4 liability for 2001/02 is:

£5817 + £780 = £6597

The balancing payment due on 31/01/03 is calculated as:

	£	
IT + NIC liability	6597	
less Tax deducted at source	(2573)	
	4024	
less Payments on A/C	(3512)	
Balancing payment	512	due 31/01/03

The CGT liability of £1000 is due on 31/01/03, along with the first payment on account of the 2002/03 IT + NIC liability, calculated as:

50% × £4024 = £2012

Payments on account 2002/03

	(£)
31/1/03	2012
31/7/03	2012

The balancing payment will be made when the 2002/03 tax return is filed along with any CGT liability for 2002/03, and must be made by 31/1/04.

Automatic surcharges and interest (TMA 1970, s 86)

1. Surcharges

A fixed charge is made on the late payment of tax with respect to:

- balancing payments
- amendments
- discovery assessments.

The surcharge imposed depends on the lateness of the payment as follows:

Table 43.1 Surcharge penalty rate for late payments

Date of payment	*Surcharge*
(a) tax paid within 28 days of the due date	nil
(b) tax paid more than 28 days late	5% of unpaid tax
(c) tax paid more than six months late	10% of unpaid tax

Note: Surcharges do not apply to late payments on account of income tax.

EXAMPLE 1

Alice received her 2002 tax return in May 2002. Her final tax liability for 2001/02 was £5000 and payments on account had been made as follows:

31/1/02	£1 750
31/7/02	£1 750

Assume that the balancing payment of £1500 was paid:

(a) 16 February 2003
(b) 31 March 2003
(c) 9 September 2003

As Alice had received her tax return before 31 October 2002, the annual filing date and hence the due date for the balancing payment is 31 January 2003.

(a) As the balancing payment is made within 28 days of 31 January 2003, no surcharge liability arises.

(b) The balancing payment is made 59 days late, therefore, Alice is liable for a surcharge calculated as:

$5\% \times £1500 = £75$

(c) The balancing payment is made 221 days late, therefore, Alice is liable for a surcharge calculated as:

$10\% \times £1500 = £150$

EXAMPLE 2

Mr Green had made the following payments in respect of his 2001/02 income tax liability:

	£
31/1/02 first payment on account	2250
31/7/02 second payment on account	2250
31/1/03 balancing payment	1850

The 2002 return was subject to an amendment which was notified on 16 March 2003 showing additional tax of £600. Assume that this additional tax was paid:

(a) 30 April 2003
(b) 6 June 2003
(c) 6 December 2003

As Mr Green received notification of additional tax due on 16 March 2003, this becomes due and payable on 15 April 2003 (30 days from notification).

(a) As the payment is made within 28 days of 15 April 2003, no surcharge liability arises.

(b) The payment is made 52 days after it became due for payment, therefore, Mr Green is liable to a surcharge calculated as:

$5\% \times £600 = £30$

(c) The payment is made 235 days late, therefore, Mr Green is liable for a surcharge calculated as:

$10\% \times £600 = £60$

Officers of the Board have discretionary powers to mitigate a surcharge, for example, in cases of hardship.

2. Interest on overdue tax (TMA 1970, s 86)

Interest under the TMA 1970, s 86 is automatically charged on any tax paid late as follows:

(a) Payments on account and balancing payments

Interest runs from the due date to the date of the payment.

EXAMPLE

The following information relates to Mrs Pink's income tax payments for 2001/02:

Due date	Amount (£)	Paid
31/1/02 first payment on account	6500	20/3/02
31/7/02 second payment on account	6500	25/9/02
31/1/03 balancing payment	5000	16/2/03

As the balancing payment is made within 28 days of the due date, no surcharge liability will arise. However, interest is charged on the late payments from the due date to the date of payment. Assuming an interest rate of 8.5 per cent, interest is calculated as follows:

Interest under s 86, TMA 1970: £

(a) First payment on account

From 31/1/02 to 20/3/02

$$\frac{48}{366} \times 8.5\% \times £6500 \qquad \underline{72.46}$$

(b) Second payment on account

From 31/7/02 to 25/9/02

$$\frac{56}{366} \times 8.5\% \times £6500 \qquad \underline{84.54}$$

(c) Balancing payment

From 31/1/03 to 16/2/03

$$\frac{16}{365} \times 8.5\% \times £5000 \qquad \underline{18.63}$$

Where a claim to reduce payments on account has been made which later proves to be unfounded, the taxpayer will be liable to interest on the shortfall.

EXAMPLE

George's tax liability for 2000/01 was £8000 so that payments on account of his 2001/02 liability are set as follows:

    31/1/02   £4000
    31/7/02   £4000

A claim was made to reduce the payments to £2000 each and these payments were paid on time. His 2001/02 tax liability proves to be £7000 and George pays the balancing payment of £3000 on 31 January 2003. George will be charged interest on the difference between half of the actual 2001/02 liability and the payments made on account from each payment date.

	Actual liability	Payments made	Difference
31/1/02	($\frac{1}{2}$) £3500	£2000	£1500
31/7/02	($\frac{1}{2}$) £3500	£2000	£1500

Assuming an interest rate of 8.5%:

		£
from 1/2/02 to 31/1/03	£1500 × 8.5%	127.50
from 1/8/02 to 31/1/03	£1500 × 8.5% × $\frac{6}{12}$	63.75
		191.25

Similarly, if payments on account have been excessive, interest will be repaid to the taxpayer. In the above example, if George had made the £4000 payments on account, and the Revenue repaid £1000 to him on 31 January 2003 interest would be credited as follows:

Assuming an interest rate of 4%:

		£
1/2/02 to 31/1/03	£500 × 4%	20
1/8/02 to 31/1/03	£500 × 4% × $\frac{6}{12}$	10
		30

(b) Additional tax

Interest on additional tax due as a result of a discovery assessment or an amendment runs from the annual filing date to the date of payment.

EXAMPLE

The following information relates to Miss Brown's 2001/02 tax liability:

Due date	Amount (£)	Paid
31/1/02 first payment on account	2250	31/1/02
31/7/02 second payment on account	2250	31/7/02
31/1/03 balancing payment	3500	31/1/03

An amendment was notified on 10 March 2003 showing additional tax due of £1800. This was paid on 16 April 2003. The additional tax is due and payable by 9 April 2003, however interest runs from the annual filing date to the date of payment:

	£
From 31/1/03 to 16/4/03	
$\dfrac{75}{365} \times 8.5\% \times £1800$	<u>31.44</u>

3. Interest on overpaid tax (ICTA 1988, s 826)

Where tax has been overpaid interest runs from the later of:

- due date for payment; or
- the date the payment was made to the date it is repaid by the Revenue.

4. Interest on unpaid surcharges

If a surcharge is imposed on the late payment of tax, it is due for payment within 30 days of the surcharge being made. If the surcharge is paid late, the interest runs from the due date to the date the surcharge is paid.

The penalty regime

The taxpayer may be liable to financial penalties for failure to comply with the tax legislation:

1. Failure to file a return

Failure to file a return on time can give rise to the following penalties:

(a) Automatic penalties (TMA 1970, s 93(2) and (4))

There is a fixed penalty of £100 for failure to file a return on time. If the return is still outstanding six months after the filing date, a further £100 may be imposed.

Note: The financial penalty cannot exceed the tax due for the year.

(b) Additional daily penalties (TMA 1970, s 93(3))

Where the fixed penalty of £100 is insignificant compared with the tax involved, an officer of the Board can apply to the CIR to obtain a daily penalty of up to £60 per day while the return remains outstanding. If this is sanctioned within six months of the filing date, the second £100 fixed penalty does not apply.

(c) Tax geared penalties (TMA 1970, s 93(5))

If the return has not been filed 12 months after the filing date, a penalty of 100 per cent of the tax involved may be imposed.

2. Failure to notify a liability to tax (TMA 1970, s 7(8))

A financial penalty of 100 per cent of the tax unpaid by the annual filing date may be imposed.

3. Failure to preserve records (TMA 1970, s 12B(5))

A financial penalty of up to £3000 may be imposed for the failure to maintain records in support of a self assessment return.

4. Fraudulent/negligent conduct (TMA 1970, s 95)

Where an incorrect return is submitted involving fraudulent or negligent conduct, s 95, TMA 1970 provides for a penalty of 100 per cent of the tax underpaid.

Claims for reduced payments on account that involve fraudulent or negligent conduct are liable to a penalty under the TMA 1970, s 59A(6) of an amount equal to the difference between the correct payment on account and the actual payment on account made.

SELF ASSESSMENT QUESTIONS

43.1 Alfred's income tax liability for 2000/01 was £7600, so that his payments on account were set at £3800. As business had taken a downturn, he claimed to have his payments on account of his 2001/02 liability reduced to £1800, the payments being made by the due dates. His 2001/02 liability was finally determined to be £7000. Alfred paid the balancing payment of £3400, in respect of his 2001/02 liability, on 31/1/03.

REQUIRED

Calculate any interest that Alfred will be charged, assuming an interest rate of 8 per cent.

43.2 Hazel has been self-employed for many years. Income tax liabilities for the last three years were as follows:

1999/00	£8 000
2000/01	£10 500
2001/02	£14 000

Payments on account and balancing payments were always paid by the due dates.

REQUIRED

(a) State the amount of payments on account, balancing payments and due dates in respect of the 2000/01 and 2001/02 liabilities.

(b) What would be the effect if the 2000/01 tax return was the subject of a Revenue enquiry which showed additional tax of £2000, with Hazel paying the extra £2000 for 2000/01 on 31/1/03 Assume an interest rate of 8 per cent.

CHAPTER 44

The pay as you earn system

Brief outline of the PAYE system

The majority of income tax payable on Schedule E income is collected under the PAYE system. The system is administered by completing the various Revenue forms relating to the PAYE system. The employer is responsible for collecting the income tax and NICs due for each tax month during the fiscal year, and the amounts collected are due and payable 14 days after the end of the tax month. From 6 April 2000, employers will be required to pay the Working Families Tax Credit (WFTC) and the Disabled Persons Tax Credit (DPTC) through the PAYE system, where the Revenue directs them to do so. Student loans are also to be recovered through the PAYE system. (See Appendix 2 for tax credit rates.)

EXAMPLE

Tax month	Due date
6 April to 5 May	19 May
6 May to 5 June	19 June
6 June to 5 July	19 July

The operation of the PAYE system can prove particularly burdensome for small employers, and to mitigate this an election is available which enables the employer to pay the amounts due on a quarterly basis rather than monthly. This election, first introduced in 1991 and between 6 April 1995 and 5 April 1999, was available to employers, provided that the income tax and NICs due, on average, was £600 per month or less. In the FA 1999 this limit was increased to £1000 per month for periods after 6 April 1999. The FA 2000 again increased the threshold to £1500 per month for periods beginning after 5 April 2000. The payment limit is based on the average net monthly payment due to the IR for PAYE, NICs and student loans recovered (CSL), but after taking into account the tax credits paid to employees and funded from the PAYE, NICs and CSL due to the Revenue, e.g. WFTC and DPTC, payments being required for the quarters ended:

Tax quarter	Due date
6 April to 5 July	19 July
6 July to 5 October	19 October
6 October to 5 January	19 January
6 January to 5 April	19 April

The amount of tax deducted by the employer is calculated using tax tables provided by the Revenue and will depend on the employee's tax code.

Legislation introduced in the FA 1994 required employers to account for PAYE on the provision of 'tradeable assets'. Since that time many artificial schemes have been operated in an attempt to take non-cash forms of remuneration, outside the scope of PAYE and NICs, amounting to a deferral in the tax due until the end of the tax year, and an avoidance of NICs.

In order to counter this avoidance of PAYE obligations, the FA 1998 extended the 1994 legislation by amending the wording of 'tradeable assets' to 'readily convertible assets', making it clear that where employees are paid in assets that can readily be converted into cash, such payments will be within the scope of PAYE and NICs. With effect from 2 July 1997, remuneration in the form of trade debts was specifically brought within the scope of PAYE; for assignments of trade debts made on or after 2 July 1997, employers will have to account for PAYE by 19 April 1998.

Small employers who file the PAYE end of year returns on-line, and electronically pay the tax due will be eligible for a discount of £50. In addition to this, a further £50 discount is available to employers who qualify for the PAYE discount and who pay tax credits to any employee in 2000/01. These discounts are in addition to the discount available for VAT (*see* Chapter 41), making a total discount available of £150.

Tax codes

The tax code is calculated taking into account the individual's personal circumstances, so that the tax deducted at source is reasonably accurate. The final tax code is arrived at by taking one-tenth of all the individual's reliefs and allowances, rounded down to a whole number.

Suffixes are also used in the tax code, essentially to make tax changes more simple to apply in practice. The following are the most common suffixes:

Table 44.1 The meaning of tax code suffixes

Suffix	Meaning
L	Basic personal allowance.
P	Personal age allowance for persons aged 65–74.
V	Personal age allowance and married couples age allowance for persons aged 65–74.
BR	Tax should be deducted at basic rate.
NT	No tax should be deducted.

EXAMPLE

A single person entitled only to a personal allowance will have the following tax code for 2002/03:

Personal allowance = £4615

$\frac{1}{10} \times £4615$

Tax code = 461 L

The most usual suffixes are H and L, and the use of suffixes enables tax changes to be made without issuing new code numbers to all employees. From April 1993, the K prefix was introduced. The K code is effectively a negative code introduced for situations where benefits in kind are in excess of allowances, so that income tax on benefits can be collected via the PAYE system rather than by assessment.

Tax tables

PAYE is generally calculated on a cumulative basis using Revenue tax tables and the tax deduction working sheet.

1. Table A

Two types of table A are available, one for those employees paid weekly and one for those paid monthly. The tables show the cumulative total allowances or 'tax free pay' for each code number. The tax free pay is then deducted from the total pay to give taxable pay.

2. Table B

The taxable pay is given in table B together with the total tax due on the income. From this figure, the tax already paid in the previous period(s) is deducted in order to arrive at the tax liability for the current period.

Tax forms

The following revenue forms are important in the operation of PAYE:

1. Form P2

The form P2 is sent to the employee and shows the notice of coding based on information supplied in the tax return.

2. Form P6

The employee's notice of coding is sent to the employer on form P6.

3. Form P9D

The employer must submit a form P9D for each lower paid employee in receipt of taxable benefits and expenses.

4. Form P11D

The employer must submit a form P11D in respect of each higher paid employee or director in receipt of expense allowances, reimbursed expenses or benefits in kind.

5. Form P11

The PAYE is calculated on a cumulative basis using the tax deduction working sheet form P11.

Note: The employer may only use another form provided the Revenue agree.

6. Forms P14 and P60

This form is in three parts, the first two parts (P14) are sent to the Revenue and the third part (P60) is given to each employee at the end of the fiscal year. The return for each employee must show the following details:

- personal details
- total emoluments
- final pay code
- total tax for year
- total NICs for year.

7. Form P35

At the end of the fiscal year the employer must submit an annual statement using the form P35 showing:

- a summary of tax and NICs deducted for the year;
- a statement of working sheets not used because the employees concerned were below the income tax threshold;
- a questionnaire to ensure compliance;
- a signed declaration and certification that all year end returns have been completed and submitted.

8. Forms P45, P46 and P15

These forms are concerned with employees joining or leaving the company.

(a) Form P45

The P45 is in four parts and shows the following details:

- PAYE reference and National Insurance number;
- employee's name and date of leaving the old employment;
- PAYE code number at the date of leaving the old employment;
- the last entries on the tax deduction working sheet (P11) showing cumulative pay and tax deducted.

The new employer receives parts two and three; part two is retained by the new employer who enters details of the new employment in part three before sending it to the Revenue.

(b) Form P46

If the P45 is not available the employee completes a P46 certifying that:

- it is the employee's first full-time job (certificate A), in which case the code 461L (2002/03) will be applied on a full cumulative basis; or

● in other cases, certificate B is signed and the emergency code 461L (2002/03) will be applied on a non-cumulative basis until the correct code number is issued.

(c) Form P15

Form P15 is completed by the employee at the same time as the P46 and sent to the Revenue in order that the correct tax code can be allocated to the employee.

The end of year returns, i.e. P14, P35, P60, will need to be amended to take account of the tax credits, etc., payable through the PAYE system.

PAYE and the move to self assessment

Self assessment will generally only apply to those employees whose tax affairs are complicated, that is, those employees who normally receive a tax return. In order for employees to complete the self assessment tax return, they will need details of all their emoluments. For emoluments received after 6 April 1996, the employer is required to:

(a) return the P11Ds to the Revenue and provide the employee with a copy by the 6 July following the year of assessment;

(b) disclose the cash equivalent of benefits in kind;

(c) disclose payments and benefits provided by third parties, the third party is then responsible for providing the employee with written details together with the case equivalent of benefits in kind that have been provided. These details must be provided by 6 July following the year of assessment; and

(d) provide the employee with the P60 by the 31 May following the year of assessment.

Support for small and new employers

In the FA 2000, a series of measures were introduced over the following two years, aimed at helping small businesses in operating a payroll, including:

● a telephone support service for new employers;
● offering visits by Business Support Teams to new and small employers to discuss payroll issues;
● offering a one-to-one visit when a new employer appears to be having difficulties;
● offering to check an employer's payroll system to see that it is operating efficiently.

CHAPTER 45

The administration of corporation tax

For accounting periods ending on or after 1 October 1993 and before 1 July 1999, corporation tax was collected under the Pay and File system. Prior to the introduction of Pay and File, a company would receive a tax assessment based on the information contained in the tax return, and in the absence of a return an estimated assessment would be issued, with the company having the right of appeal. Companies could, therefore, use the tactic of failing to submit a return and then appeal against the estimated assessment in order to delay the payment of CT. The Pay and File system was a means of ensuring that payments of CT were made by the normal due date instead of being delayed until the appeal was determined. For accounting periods ending on or after 1 July 1999, companies must make a self assessment of their corporation tax liabilities. This chapter examines the corporation tax system under self assessment and the rules for interest and penalties.

Due date for payment and notification of liability

The normal due date for the payment of mainstream corporation tax (MCT) is nine months after the end of the accounting period; for example, a company whose year end is 31 January must pay the MCT liability by 1 November in the same year. The company's MCT is the gross CT less deductible advance corporation tax (ACT) and income tax repayable.

Section 10(1) of the TMA 1970 provides that a company must notify the Revenue of any CT liability within 12 months of the end of an accounting period if a return has not already been made. Failure to notify a liability renders the company liable to a financial penalty.

From 6 April 1999, ACT was abolished; any surplus ACT that has been accumulated at 6 April 1999 can be recovered through the system of 'shadow ACT' (*see* Chapter 32).

For accounting periods ending after 1 July 1999, large companies will be required to pay quarterly instalments on account of their expected CT liability for the current year, to be phased in over a period of four years. Small and medium-sized companies will not be required to pay instalments on account of their CT liabilities, and companies becoming large in an accounting period will not be required to pay their CT by instalments if:

- taxable profits for that period are £10 million or less; *and*
- they were a small or medium sized company in the previous year.

Note: Small, medium and large companies for this purpose are as defined for small companies rate purposes, i.e.:

Large company – profits in excess of £1 500 000

Medium company – profits between £300 000 and £1 500 000

Small company – profits less than £300 000.

When the quarterly payment system was introduced, it was subject to a *de minimis* limit of £5000. This limit was increased in the FA 2000 so that companies with a tax liability of £10 000 or less for accounting periods ending on or after 1 July 2000 will not be required to pay by instalments. For companies which do not have to make quarterly payments on account, the CT is due nine months after the end of the accounting period.

Payment by instalments will commence for accounting periods ending on, or after, 1 July 1999, i.e. with the introduction of self assessment for companies, with payments starting in month seven of the accounting period.

EXAMPLE

A large company's corporation tax accounting period ends on 31 March 2003, instalments will be due on the following dates:

    14 October 2002 (in the accounting period)
    14 January 2003 (in the accounting period)
    14 April 2003 (in the following accounting period)
    14 July 2003 (in the following accounting period)

If the company's year end was 31 December 2002, the payment dates would be as follows:

    14 July 2002 (in accounting period)
    14 October 2002 (in accounting period)
    14 January 2003 (in following accounting period)
    14 April 2003 (in following accounting period)

During the four-year phasing in period, the company will pay a percentage of the corporation tax liability by instalments, with the balance being due nine months after the company's year end as follows:

Year One: 60% by instalments, balance of 40% nine months after year end
Year Two: 72% by instalments, balance of 28% nine months after year end
Year Three: 88% by instalments, balance 12% nine months after year end
Year Four: 100% of the corporation tax liability by instalments.

Self assessment for companies (CTSA)

Self assessment for companies will come into effect for accounting periods ending on, or after 1 July 99, so the earliest that companies can enter the self assessment regime will be 2 July 98.

In many ways, the introduction of Pay and File was the first step on the road to self assessment for companies as it included many of the characteristics of self assessment, for example, fixed dates for filing returns and paying the CT due, with automatic penalties for failure to comply with the requirements.

There were, therefore, very few changes needed to be made in order to convert the Pay and File system to self assessment:

(a) Under self assessment, the computation of CT submitted with the tax return will constitute the self assessment, bringing companies in line with other taxpayers.

Note: There is no rule requiring the Revenue to calculate the tax if the return is submitted early as there is for individuals.

(b) The rules and time limits applicable to individuals will apply equally to companies, for example:

- revenue enquiries;

- discovery assessments;

- rules regarding when the assessment becomes final;

- as the Revenue will not generally issue assessments, the rules regarding the determination of self assessments apply equally to companies;

- appeal procedures.

(c) The annual filing date for CT self assessment returns remains unchanged from the Pay and File system, i.e. 12 months after the end of the accounting period, or, if later, three months after notice to file the return is made. The self assessment will be regarded as final 12 months after the filing date.

(d) A company must notify its chargeability to CT within 12 months of the end of the accounting period. Failure to notify a chargeability to tax may result in a financial penalty of an amount equal to the tax unpaid at the end of the 12-month period.

(e) A claim for capital allowances must be included in the self assessment return. The time limit for claims, amendments, or withdrawals of a claim must be made by the *later* of:

- 12 months after the filing date;

- 30 days after notice to close an enquiry is given;

- 30 days after notice of amendments following an enquiry is given;

- 30 days after a determination is given following an appeal against a Revenue amendment.

Interest and penalties

1. Interest on overdue tax (TMA 1970, s 87A)

Interest is charged on any CT liability that is not paid by the normal due date. The interest is calculated from the normal due date to the date that payment is made.

EXAMPLE

Dee Ltd prepares accounts to 31 December each year. On 1 October 1999 Dee Ltd paid CT of £37 000 on account of the CT liability for the year ended 31 December 1998. The CT return for the year ended 31 December 1998 was submitted by 31 December 1999 showing further tax due of £15 000, which was paid on 15 January 2000.

The normal due date for the payment of the CT with respect to 31 December 1998 is 1 October 1999. The tax return was filed on time but interest is charged on the underpayment of £15 000 from the normal due date to the date that payment is made, i.e. from 1 October 1999 to 15 January 2000. Assuming an interest rate of 6.25 per cent, the interest charged is calculated as:

$$\frac{107}{365} \times 6.25\% \times £15\,000 = \underline{£275}$$

Where a claim for loss relief or carry back of ACT amends the CT liability, interest will be charged on the original CT liability up to the normal due date for the payment of CT for the accounting period in which the ACT or loss arose.

EXAMPLE

Calder Ltd prepares accounts to 31 December each year. Results for the year ended 31 December 1998 show profits chargeable to CT of £2 000 000, but it is anticipated that the period to 31 December 1999 will show a loss. ACT paid for each period is as follows:

	£	
20 April 1998	100 000	
25 April 1999	96 000	(paid before 1 April 1999)

Consequently, a claim is made to carry back £96 000 ACT to the previous year. The maximum ACT set off for the year ended 31 December 1998:

£2 000 000 × 20% = £400 000

Therefore, all the £96 000 can be carried back:

YE 31 December 1998	£	£
CT @ 31% × £2 000 000		620 000
less ACT paid	100 000	
ACT carried back	96 000	(196 000)
MCT		424 000

The company paid £424 000 CT on 1 October 1999, i.e. by the normal due date. However, Calder Ltd will be charged interest on the £96 000 from 1 October 1999 to 30 September 2000 because the £96 000 was not generated until the year ended 31 December 1999 and the normal due date for that accounting period is 1 October 2000:

£96 000 × 6.25% = £6000

2. Interest on overpaid tax (ICTA 1988, s 826)

Overpayments of CT are repaid with interest calculated at a lower rate than interest on underpaid tax. The interest is paid to the date that the repayment is made from the *later* of:

- the normal due date; *or*
- the date the tax was paid.

EXAMPLE

Ribble Ltd prepares accounts to the 31 March each year. On 15 December 2001 Ribble Ltd paid CT of £70 000 with respect to its year ended 31 March 2001. The CT return for the period ended 31 March 2001 was submitted on 31 March 2002 showing a total CT liability of £60 000 for the period.

The overpayment of £10 000 was repaid by the Revenue on 6 June 2002. Assuming interest at 3.25 per cent the interest due to Ribble Ltd on the repayment is calculated as follows:

Interest is payable from the later of:

(a) 1/1/02, i.e. the normal due date; or
(b) 15/12/01, the date the CT was paid.

Therefore, interest runs from 1/1/02 to 6/6/02:

$$\frac{157}{365} \times 3.25\% \times £10\,000 = \underline{£139.79}$$

Repayments of CT may also arise due to the following:

- ACT carried back
- loss relief carried back
- repayments of income tax.

Repayments of CT as a result of any of these are only eligible for interest from the normal due date for the accounting period in which they were incurred.

EXAMPLE

Shannon Ltd prepares accounts to 31 March each year. Recent results have been as follows:

	£
YE 31/3/01 profit	200 000
YE 31/3/02 loss	(60 000)

YE 31/3/01	£
CT @ 20% × £200 000	40 000

The CT of £40 000 was paid on 1/1/02.

Following the loss for the period to 31 March 2002, a claim was made under s 393A(1)(*b*) of the ICTA 1988 to carry back the loss to the period ended 31 March 2001:

	£
Trading profits	200 000
less s 393A(1)(*b*)	(60 000)
Profit chargeable to corporation tax	140 000

CT @ 20% × £140 000 = £28 000

Therefore, Shannon Ltd is due a repayment of CT for the year ended 31 March 1998: for £12 600.

However, as the loss arose in the accounting period ended 31 March 2001, interest on the repayment will only accrue from 1 January 2002, i.e. the normal due date for the year ended 31 March 2001.

If the repayment of CT was made on 4 April 2002 interest is calculated as:

$$\frac{94}{365} \times 3.25\% \times £12\,000 = \underline{£100.44}$$

The rate of interest applying to underpayments of CT under the quarterly accounting system was reduced in the FA 2000 from 2 per cent above the base rate to 1 per cent above the base rate, to take effect 21 days after the changes are made to the interest rate regulations.

3. The penalty regime

Failure to comply with the tax legislation may result in financial penalties being imposed:

(a) Failure to file a return (TMA 1970, s 94)

Automatic penalties
Fixed penalties are imposed for failure to file a return on time. The amount of the penalty depends on the lateness of the return.

- *Up to three months late* – £100. This amount is increased to £500 if the return is late for three consecutive accounting periods.
- *Over three months late* – £200. This amount is increased to £1000 if the return is late for three consecutive accounting periods.

Additional tax geared penalties
If the return is more than six months late tax geared penalties are applied as follows:

- *6–12 months late* – 10 per cent of the tax due
- *over 12 months late* – 20 per cent of the tax due.

(b) Failure to notify a liability to tax (TMA 1970, s 10(3))

A penalty of up to 100 per cent of the tax unpaid by the annual filing date may be imposed.

(c) Failure to preserve records (TMA 1970, s 12 B(5))

Under the self assessment regime, a financial penalty of up to £3000 may be imposed for failure to maintain records in support of the self assessment.

(d) Fraudulent/negligent conduct (TMA 1970, s 96)

Where an incorrect return is submitted involving fraudulent or negligent conduct, a penalty of 100 per cent of the tax lost may be imposed.

(e) Failure to produce documents (FA 1998, Schedule 18, para. 29)

A penalty of £50 may be imposed for failure to produce documents after formal notice is given during a Revenue amendment or enquiry, and where failure continues, daily penalties may be imposed under the TMA 1970 of £30 per day, increased to £150 per day, if determined by the commissioners.

PRACTICE QUESTIONS

1. The introduction of self assessment from 1996/97 has resulted in changed responsibilities for both the taxpayer and the Inland Revenue. Explain the respective roles of the taxpayer and the Inland Revenue under the new regime.

2. (a) Explain the duties, powers, necessary qualifications, remuneration, method of operation and method of appointment of both General and Special Commissioners.

    (9 marks)

    (b) Explain what further appeal(s) are open to the party who has lost an appeal before either body of Commissioners.

    (2 marks)
    (Total: 11 marks)
    (Source: ACCA, June 1992)

3. Jane received her 2002 tax return in May 2002. The tax liability for 2001/02 was £8000 and payments on account had been made as follows:

	£
31/1/02	1800
31/7/02	1800

    Calculate any interest and surcharge payable if the balancing payment of £4400 was paid on:

    (i)   25 February 2003
    (ii) 5 May 2003
    (iii) 1 September 2003.

    Assume an interest rate of 7%.

4. (a) A change of employment for a person paying tax under the the 'pay as you earn' system is dealt with by the P45 procedure. Explain the working procedure in the case of a person who has no intervening period of unemployment and also state what information has to be entered on the form P45.

    (10 marks)

    (b) Income tax is deducted under the 'pay as you earn' system by means of a code number. **You are required** to state:

    (i)   the reason for the introduction of code numbers;
    (ii) how the code number for an individual is arrived at; and
    (iii) the meaning and reason for the introduction of the following suffixes L and T after the code number.

    (10 marks)
    (Total: 20 marks)
    (Source: ACCA, June 1984)

5. Explain the system of self assessment for companies.

Important case law

Ball (HMIT) v Johnson (1971) 47 TC 155

Problem: Were cash awards for passing examinations taxable emoluments?

Facts: The taxpayer was employed by a bank which gave its employees cash awards for passing the Institute of Banking examinations. The taxpayer passed his examinations and the Revenue assessed the award as emoluments.

Held: The cash awards were made in recognition of the employee's success in passing the examinations, and were not emoluments and so not assessable under Schedule E.

Batey v Wakefield [1981] STC 521

Problem: Did a bungalow built in the grounds of the principal private residence also qualify for relief?

Facts: The taxpayer owned a house and land elected to be his main residence. He did not occupy the house and so had a bungalow built in the grounds for the use of a caretaker to look after the property. When the taxpayer returned to the house, he had no further need of the caretaker and sold the bungalow together with 0.2 acres of land.

Held: The bungalow was occupied by a person providing a service to the owner and so the whole is treated as the principal private residence and so qualified for exemption.

Benson v Yard Arm Club [1979] STC 266

Problem: Did the purchase of a ship and barge and expenditure on modifications to use the vessel as a floating restaurant qualify as expenditure on plant?

Facts: The taxpayer company acquired a ship and a barge and converted them for use as a floating restaurant, removing the engines and altering the hull and permanently mooring the vessel.

Held: The ship and barge did not qualify as expenditure on plant, they were mere setting, i.e. the place where the business was carried on.

Bentley v *Pike (HMIT)* (1981) 53 TC 590

Problem: Should consideration received in a foreign currency be translated into sterling before the gain is calculated?

Facts: The taxpayer's wife inherited property in Germany when her father died in 1967. She was not entered as the owner in Germany until 1972. The property was sold in 1973 and she received the proceeds in Deutschmarks.

Held: The date of acquisition is the date that the beneficiary becomes absolutely entitled, i.e. 1967, and the gain should be calculated by taking the sterling equivalent of the acquisition value and disposal proceeds.

British Insulated and Helsby Cables Ltd v *Atherton* (1925) 10 TC 155

Problem: Was a payment made into a pension fund a revenue expense or a capital expense?

Facts: The taxpayer company set up a pension scheme for its employees. To allow past years' service to rank for a pension, the company paid £31 784 into the fund, claiming that the expense was a revenue item.

Held: The House of Lords held that the payment was a capital expense on the basis that expenditure is capital if it is 'made not only once and for all, but with a view to bringing into existence, an asset or an advantage for the enduring benefit of the trade' (Viscount Cave LC).

Brown v *Bullock (HMIT)* (1961) 40 TC 1

Problem: Was the requirement to join social clubs a duty of the employment, or merely a condition of the employment?

Facts: The taxpayer was a bank manager and was required under the terms of his contract to join clubs in order to promote the business of the bank. Accordingly, he joined two West End clubs, one for luncheons, and the other to play golf, when entertaining clients. The bank reimbursed the costs which were taxable on the bank manager as emoluments. The taxpayer claimed a deduction for the subscriptions under s 198, ICTA 1988.

Held: The subscriptions were not incurred wholly, exclusively and necessarily in the performance of his duties as a bank manager, they were merely imposed on him as a condition of his employment and as such they were not allowable business expenses for Schedule E purposes.

Burmah Steamship Co Ltd v CIR (1930) 16 TC 67

Problem: Was compensation a trading receipt or a capital receipt?

Facts: A shipping company and another company bought a second hand motor boat together and sent it for repairs to be completed by a set date. The repairs took too long and damages were claimed based on the loss of profit due to the delay. The taxpayer company received compensation of £1500 which the Revenue assessed to income tax under Schedule D Case I.

Held: As the compensation was a payment for a loss of profit, it was properly chargeable to income tax under Schedule D Case I as a trading receipt.

Cailbotte v Quinn (1975) 50 TC 222

Problem: Was the expense wholly and exclusively incurred for the purpose of trade?

Facts: The taxpayer was a self-employed joiner who worked from home. The cost of his lunch at home was 10p but if he worked away from home the average cost was 40p. The taxpayer claimed the difference as incurred wholly and exclusively for his business.

Held: The lunch had a duality of purpose, to enable him to work and to keep him alive. Consequently, none of the expenditure was allowable in computing his Schedule D Case I profits.

Campbell Connelly & Co Ltd v Barnett [1994] STC 50

Problem: Can a gain be rolled over if there is some delay in bringing the replacement asset into use?

Facts: The taxpaying company sold its premises and moved into the same premises as its parent company. At a later date premises were acquired and the taxpayer company sought to roll over the gain on the disposal of the first premises. However, the new premises could not be brought into use immediately.

Held: As the premises could not be brought into use for a period of nine months, the company was not eligible for roll-over relief.

Cape Brandy Syndicate v IR Commrs (1921) 12 TC 358

Problem: Did the purchase of South African brandy which was subsequently blended with French brandy before being sold amount to trading?

Facts: Three independent traders joined forces and purchased some South African brandy. When the brandy was shipped to the UK, it was then blended with French brandy and recasked and sold to several purchasers.

Held: The Court of Appeal held that the activity was trading. The act of carrying out work on the product to make it more saleable indicated the intention to trade.

CIR v Barclay Curle & Co Ltd (1969) 45 TC 221

Problem: Was the expenditure incurred on excavation and concrete lining for a dry dock eligible as expenditure on plant?

Facts: The taxpayer company was in the business of building ships. The construction of the dry dock included expenditure on valves and pumps to alter the water level so that ships could be lowered and raised. The company claimed that the whole of the expenditure including excavation, concrete lining and ancillary equipment should be treated as plant.

Held: The whole of the expenditure qualified as plant, as the whole dock performed an active role in the business, it was not merely a passive container for ships.

CIR v Plummer [1979] STC 793

Problem: Could there be an income settlement if the taxpayer received consideration?

Facts: The taxpayer, in an attempt to avoid paying surtax, entered into a covenant with a charity to pay £500 pa for at least five years, for which he received £2470 from the charity.

Held: There was not an income settlement as there was no element of bounty involved.

CIR v Richards' Executives (1971) 46 TC 626

Problem: Can the cost of obtaining probate for an asset be set off when calculating the CGT liability?

Facts: The executors sold certain stocks and shares of the deceased realising a capital gain of £1183. The total costs of obtaining probate was £525 of which £242 related to the stocks and shares. The executors claimed that £242 was an allowable deduction when calculating the gain.

Held: The £242 was an allowable deduction.

CIR v Scottish and Newcastle Breweries Ltd [1982] STC 296

Problem: Could expenditure on decor and lighting be considered to be plant?

Facts: The taxpayer company incurred costs of £104 000 refurbishing its hotels in order to create a certain ambience to attract the right clientele.

Held: The House of Lords held that the expenditure qualified as plant as the items concerned were performing a function in the business in creating the required atmosphere.

Cole Bros v Phillips [1982] STC 308

Problem: Was expenditure on lighting performing a function in the business?

Facts: The taxpayer company incurred expenditure of £945 600 on electrical installations in a new retail store. The Revenue accepted that wiring, heating, ventilation systems, fire alarms, etc. qualified as plant but refused the claim in respect of transformers and specially designed lighting.

Held: The transformers were used for carrying on the business and therefore qualified as plant, however, the main switchboard and special lighting were mere setting and performed no other function other than to light up an area that was otherwise dark and as such these items were not plant.

Cook v Beach Station Caravans Ltd [1974] STC 402

Problem: Was the whole cost of constructing a swimming pool plant or mere setting?

Facts: The company operated a caravan park and installed swimming and paddling pools for holidaymakers. In order to provide safe swimming facilities, the pools were fitted with elaborate filtering, chlorinating and heating systems. The Revenue accepted that these items constituted expenditure on plant but argued that the cost of excavation, pool construction and terracing was not plant but mere setting.

Held: The whole of the expenditure qualified for capital allowances. The water in the pools could not be separated from the structure and as a whole performed an active role in the business.

Copeman v Coleman (1939) 22 TC 594

Problem: Was the arrangement a settlement or a *bona fide* commercial transaction?

Facts: The taxpayer transferred his business to a company in 1935, the shares being owned by the taxpayer and his wife. The share capital was increased in 1937 to £6000 by issuing 25 preference shares of £200 each to his relatives on the basis of £10 payable on allotment and £190 uncalled. The taxpayer's two minor children received one share, and the company declared a preference dividend of £40 per share free of tax and his two children received £40 each. Shortly after, the company called up £40 on each preference share. The taxpayer claimed, on behalf of his children, repayment of tax deducted from their preference dividends.

Held: The arrangement constituted a settlement within the meaning of the ICTA 1988, s 670 and the taxpayer and his wife were the settlors as they had provided the funds, albeit indirectly, and as such income received by the children from the dividends should be treated as income of the settlors within the ICTA 1988, s 663.

De Beers Consolidated Mines Ltd v *Howe* [1906] STC 198

Problem: Could a company incorporated overseas be UK resident for tax purposes?

Facts: The taxpayer company was registered in South Africa where the mines were situated. Its head office was also situated in South Africa and shareholder meetings took place there. The diamonds, however, were sold through a London syndicate. Directors' meetings were held in both South Africa and London but the majority of directors were resident in the UK. The Revenue claimed that the company was UK resident for tax purposes.

Held: The company was UK resident as its central management and control was exercised in the UK.

Dixon v *Fitches Garage Ltd* [1975] STC 480

Problem: Was a metal canopy covering the service area of a self-service petrol station plant or mere setting?

Facts: The taxpayer company constructed a metal canopy to protect the pumps, customers and employees from the elements, and claimed capital allowances on the grounds that it was an integral part of the business for delivering the petrol.

Held: The canopy did not constitute expenditure on plant, it was performing no other function in the business other than to provide shelter and make the delivery of petrol more comfortable for customers and staff.

Fitzpatrick v *IRC* [1994] STC 237

Problem: Were newspapers and periodicals purchased by journalists a legitimate expense of their employment?

Facts: A journalist employed by a national newspaper claimed that the expenses of buying newspapers and periodicals were incurred wholly, exclusively and necessarily in the performance of his duties as a journalist.

Held: The newspapers and periodicals were obtained for reference and were not necessary in order for the taxpayer to perform the duties of his employment.

Glenboig Union Fireclay Co Ltd v *CIR* (1922) 12 TC 427

Problem: Was compensation received by the taxpayer company a revenue receipt or a capital receipt?

Facts: The taxpayer company manufactured fireclay goods and leased fireclay beds which ran underneath the Caledonian Railway lines. The railway owned the land but not the fireclay beds. In 1911 it exercised its power to prevent the taxpayer company from working part of the fireclay and paid the company compensation. The taxpayer company claimed that the compensation was a capital receipt and should not form part of its profits for Schedule D Case I purposes.

Held: The payment was a capital receipt as it was made for the sterilisation of a capital asset.

Gordon and Blair v CIR (1962) 40 TC 358

Problem: Did a new trade exist? If so, the losses of the old trade could not be set off against the profits of the new trade.

Facts: The taxpayer company was in the business of brewing beer and suffered heavy losses. In order to become more profitable, it ceased brewing beer in October 1953 and arranged with another brewing company to be supplied with beer which it then bottled and sold. The company claimed that it was carrying on the same trade and so the brewing losses could be set off against the profits arising from bottling and selling the beer that was supplied to it.

Held: The company's trade of brewing beer ceased in October 1953 from which date it carried on a new business of selling beer, consequently the brewing losses could not be set off against the bottling profits.

Griffiths v Jackson [1983] STC 184

Problem: Was managing the letting of furnished rooms liable to income tax under Schedule D Case I as trading rather than Schedule D Case VI?

Facts: The taxpayer let furnished flats and bed sitting rooms mainly to students, and provided services such as cleaning and laundry etc. The 180 or so rooms were supervised by the taxpayer himself and he claimed that the profits should be assessed under Schedule D Case I as trading income.

Held: The taxpayer was letting furnished accommodation and, therefore, the profit was taxable under Schedule D Case VI.

Note: The FA 1984 introduced legislation to treat the provision of furnished holiday accommodation as if it were a trade, provided that certain conditions are met (ss 503 and 504, ICTA 1988), effectively overturning the above decision.

From 6 April 1995, individuals are liable to income tax under Schedule A on all rented accommodation.

Higgs v Olivier (1952) 33 TC 136

Problem: Was a payment made for preventing the taxpayer from carrying on his vocation an income receipt or a capital receipt?

Facts: Laurence Olivier, a well-known actor, was producer, director and actor in the film *Henry V*. The film did not achieve instant success and the film company paid Olivier £15 000 not to appear in any other film for 18 months. The £15 000 was assessed to income tax under Schedule D Case II.

Held: The taxpayer had received the sum from not carrying on his vocation rather than from exercising his vocation and as such the £15 000 was not an income receipt but a capital receipt.

Hinton v *Madden and Ireland Ltd* (1959) 38 TC 391

Problem: Were assets with an expected life of three years considered to be plant?

Facts: The taxpayer company was in the business of manufacturing shoes and claimed that expenditure on lasts and knives used for cutting the leather was expenditure on plant and eligible for capital allowances.

Held: The knives and lasts were held to be plant indicating that the items need only have a measure of durability.

Hobbs v *Hussey (HMIT)* (1942) 24 TC 152

Problem: Was payment received for the sale of the rights to publish a life story assessable to income tax?

Facts: The taxpayer, a solicitor's clerk, sold the serial rights of his life story to a newspaper for £1500. The Revenue assessed the payment under Schedule D Case VI, and the taxpayer claimed the disposal of the copyright in the articles was a capital receipt and, therefore, not liable to income tax.

Held: The amount received less expenses was taxable under Schedule D Case VI as it represented a supply of services by the taxpayer; the disposal of the copyright was incidental.

Hunt v *Henry Quick Ltd*; King v *Bridisco Ltd* [1992] STC 633

Problem: Was expenditure on mezzanine flooring and ancillary lighting qualifying expenditure on plant?

Facts: The taxpayer companies were wholesale merchants. Expenditure on mezzanine platforms was incurred in order to increase storage space.

Held: The mezzanine platforms constituted plant as they were performing a function in the business, ancillary lighting, however, performed no function other than to provide light and did not qualify.

IRC v Aken [1990] STC 497

Problem: Could a trade exist even where the trade is unlawful?

Facts: The taxpayer had operated for many years as a prostitute under the name of Lindi St Clair. In 1980 she appeared on television about her 'business'. The programme was seen by the tax inspector and estimated assessments were issued. The taxpayer defended the claim on the basis that the prostitution was unlawful and could, therefore, not be chargeable to tax.

Held: The courts held that profits from prostitution were taxable under Schedule D Case I as her services were provided for reward which amounted to trading.

Jarrold v John Good & Sons (1962) 40 TC 681

Problem: Did moveable partitioning qualify as plant or was it just mere setting?

Facts: The taxpayer company's workload as a shipping agent fluctuated widely and to provide flexible office accommodation they acquired moveable partitioning and claimed that it was expenditure on plant qualifying for capital allowances.

Held: The courts rejected the Revenue's argument that the partitioning was mere setting and the expenditure qualified for capital allowances.

Kelsall Parsons & Co v CIR (1938) 21 TC 608

Problem: Was compensation for the cancellation of a contract a revenue receipt or a capital receipt?

Facts: The taxpayer was agent for manufacturers, being charged tax under Schedule D Case I on the commission received. A three-year agency contract was cancelled at the end of the second year and £1500 paid in compensation, and the taxpayer claimed it was a capital receipt.

Held: The court held that the compensation was revenue as the cancellation of the contract with only one year to run did not affect the whole profit-making apparatus of the company; it was a payment for a loss of profit and properly chargeable to income tax under Schedule D Case I.

Kirkby v Hughes [1993] STC 76

Problem: Was trading more likely to be present if the transaction is related to the trade which the taxpayer normally carries on?

Facts: The taxpayer was a builder who bought houses and then sold them after they had been renovated. In 1978 he had bought a property, carried out improvements and sold the property having lived in it for a while, although not as his main residence.

In 1981 he bought a building plot, built a house on the site and sold it in February 1984. In March 1984 he bought a barn, converted it to a house but did not live there permanently. The taxpayer was assessed to income tax under Schedule D Case I in respect of the first property and he contended that it was his principal private residence.

Held: The courts found in favour of the Revenue that the property had been held as a trading asset. As he was a builder by trade, he was unable to prove that he had bought the property with the intention of living in it as his main residence.

Law Shipping Co Ltd v CIR (1923) 12 TC 621

Problem: Was the repair expenditure capital or revenue?

Facts: The taxpayer company bought a ship that was already loaded with cargo and about to set sail. After the first voyage under this new ownership, repairs amounting to £51 558 were necessary. The company claimed that the repairs were revenue expenditure.

Held: Generally, if something is acquired in a dilapidated state, this is reflected in the sale price, and repairs necessary to bring the item up to standard would be treated as capital expenditure.

However, it was held that £12 000 of the expenditure related to repairs necessary after acquisition and, therefore, were allowed as a revenue item, the balance was treated as capital expenditure.

Lewis v Rook [1992] STC 171

Problem: Was a cottage in the grounds of the main residence eligible for principal private residence exemption?

Facts: Lady Rook's estate comprised a large house, an adjacent coach house and two cottages. In 1974 her gardener moved into one of the cottages until 1978 when he moved to the converted coach house. The cottage was sold 18 months later.

Held: The cottage did not qualify for the exemption as it was insignificant to the main house.

Lyon v Pettigrew [1985] STC 107

Problem: What is the date of disposal when the asset is disposed of under a hire purchase agreement?

Facts: The taxpayer agreed to sell six taxis and the licences for £6 000 each payable in instalments over three years. Assessments were raised for 1979/80 in the year the agreement was made. The taxpayer claimed that the contract could only take effect when it was completed.

Held: The contract for the disposal was made in 1979/80 and was unconditional therefore the CGT liability arose in 1979/80.

Lysaght v CIR (1928) 13 TC 511

Problem: Was the taxpayer resident and ordinarily resident in the UK for 1922/23 and 1923/24?

Facts: The taxpayer was the managing director of a UK company until 1919 when he retired from the company but retained an advisory post. In 1920 he and his family moved to Ireland. In 1922/23 and 1923/24 he visited the UK for about 100 days in his advisory capacity, staying mainly in hotels.

Held: The House of Lords held that the taxpayer was both resident and ordinarily resident in the UK for the two years concerned regardless of the fact that his return to England was for business purposes and that he stayed mainly in hotels.

McGregor v Adcock [1977] STC 206

Problem: Did the disposal of part of the taxpayer's farmland qualify for retirement relief?

Facts: The taxpayer owned 35 acres of land which he had farmed for over ten years. He sold five acres of the land together with planning permission and realised a gain of £64 481. The taxpayer was 68 years old but continued to farm the remaining 30 acres after the disposal. The taxpayer claimed that he was entitled to retirement relief on the sale of part of his business.

Held: The sale of the five acres was the sale of a business asset and retirement relief can only be claimed on the sale of a business asset if the asset is capable of being managed as an independent business. As the business continued unchanged after the disposal it was held that the land did not form part of the farming business and retirement relief was not available.

Makins v Elson [1977] STC 46

Problem: Was a caravan eligible for principal private residence exemption?

Facts: The taxpayer acquired some land on which he intended to build his principal private residence. During the building he moved onto the site with his family and lived there in a touring caravan jacked up on bricks. The caravan was supplied with electricity, water and a telephone. Three years later the taxpayer sold the caravan and site at a profit and claimed principal private residence exemption.

Held: The gain qualified for relief as the caravan constituted a dwelling house within the meaning of the TCGA 1992, s 222.

Mallalieu v Drummond (1983) 57 TC 330

Problem: Was expenditure on clothing wholly and exclusively for the purpose of business?

Facts: The taxpayer was a lady barrister who claimed that she only wore black clothes because her profession required her to do so, and as such she claimed the cost of the purchase and maintenance of the clothes as incurred wholly and exclusively in carrying on her profession.

Held: The expenditure was not allowable because there was a duality of purpose; the clothes not only allowed her to practise her profession but also kept her warm and properly clothed.

Markey v Sanders [1987] STC 256

Problem: Did a bungalow form part of the main residence and so qualify for exemption?

Facts: The taxpayer owned a 12-acre estate which included the main house, outbuildings and a bungalow occupied by domestic employees. The whole estate was rated as a single property, and sold in one lot.

Held: The bungalow was held not to be part of the main residence, it was not closely adjacent to the main house.

Marson v Morton (1986) 59 TC 381

Problem: Was the sale of land, initially bought as an investment, to be construed as trading when it was eventually sold?

Facts: The taxpayer and his brother were potato merchants and in 1977 they purchased some land for £65 000 for which they borrowed £30 000. They had not invested in land previously and had no intention of using it or developing it. It was their intention to hold it merely as an investment for a few years. In September 1977 they sold the land for £100 000 and the Inspector raised an assessment under Schedule D Case I in respect of dealing in land.

Held: The court held in favour of the taxpayer that no trade was being carried on.

Martin v Lowry (HMIT) (1927) 11 TC 297

Problem: Did the purchase and resale of government surplus stocks of aircraft linen amount to trading?

Facts: The taxpayer who was in the business of selling agricultural machinery, bought 44 million yards of surplus stocks of aircraft linen. He was unable to dispose of the linen in one sale and so set up an organisation to sell the linen in smaller lots, and the linen was sold within a year.

Held: The taxpayer was carrying on a trade and the profits were liable to income tax under Schedule D Case I.

Massey v Crown Life Assurance Co [1978] 1 WLR 676

Problem: The employment/self-employment distinction.

Facts: The taxpayer was employed as branch manager of an insurance company under two contracts. Under one contract he was a freelance agent and paid on commission, and under the other he was a Schedule E employee. In 1973 he renegotiated his position and was re-engaged as manager on a self-employed basis. The Revenue accepted that he was self-employed for tax purposes. When the taxpayer was dismissed in 1975 he claimed unfair dismissal.

Held: As the plaintiff was not employed by the company, he could not bring a case for unfair dismissal.

Moore v Griffiths (1972) 48 TC 475

Problem: Were bonus payments made on winning the 1966 World Cup emoluments for Schedule E purposes?

Facts: The taxpayer was the English football captain. He received two payments, one was his share of a bonus paid by the Football Association, the other was a prize paid by a company for the best player.

Held: As the amounts paid to the taxpayer were not a reward for services, they were not emoluments for Schedule E purposes.

Moore v Thompson [1986] STC 170

Problem: Was a caravan that had no mains services and used only occasionally a dwelling house under the TCGA 1992, s 222?

Facts: The taxpayer and her husband bought a farm, which included an old farmhouse, which was to be their main home. A wheeled caravan was purchased for use by the couple until the farmhouse was renovated, but no services were connected to the caravan. Three years later the couple separated before the farmhouse was complete and the taxpayer sold the caravan and entire farm for a substantial profit.

Held: The gain was not exempt from CGT as the caravan was not found to be a dwelling house within the TCGA 1992, s 222.

Odeon Theatres Ltd v Jones (1971) 48 TC 257

Problem: Was repair expenditure revenue or capital?

Facts: The taxpayer company purchased several cinemas at the end of the Second World War. Because of restrictions on building work during the war time years the cinemas were in a poor state of repair. The repairs were carried out over a ten-year period from 1945 during which time they were operated commercially and the condition of the cinemas had not affected the purchase price. The Revenue claimed that the repairs were of a capital nature on the principle laid down in the *Law Shipping* case.

Held: The repairs were a revenue expense as the cinemas operated on a commercial basis both before and after they were acquired by the taxpaying company, i.e. the disrepair had not affected the ability to earn profits, and as such were properly chargeable to revenue.

Oram (HMIT) v Johnson [1980] 1 WLR 558

Problem: Was the taxpayer's time and labour qualifying expenditure for CGT?

Facts: The taxpayer bought a dilapidated cottage in 1968 for £2250. After extensive improvements the cottage was sold for £11 500 in 1975. The taxpayer claimed his labour as a legitimate expense of the improvements (charged at £1 per hour).

Held: The taxpayer's labour was not qualifying expenditure within the TCGA 1992, s 38(1).

Owen v Pook [1970] AC 244

Problem: Were travelling expenses incurred by a doctor allowable expenses under the ICTA 1988, s 198?

Facts: The taxpayer was a doctor who besides having a private practice also worked for a hospital. The hospital appointment was assessable under Schedule E and the hospital contacted him at home when it required his services.

Held: Since the doctor commenced his duties when the hospital telephoned him, the travelling expenses were incurred wholly, exclusively and necessarily in the performance of those duties and as such they were an allowable expense.

Pepper (HMIT) v Hart [1992] STC 898

Problem: What is the cost to an employer of supplying 'in-house' benefits?

Facts: The taxpayer was a teacher at a private school and his son received an education from the school at a special rate of 20 per cent of the normal fees payable. The Revenue claimed that the difference was a benefit in kind assessable on the taxpayer.

Held: The cost of providing the benefit was not the total cost to the employer but should be based on the marginal cost of providing the benefit.

Pickford v Quirke (HMIT) (1927) 13 TC 251

Problem: The purchase of a mill which is then asset stripped would normally be considered to be a capital transaction. Where this process is undertaken frequently, is a trade being carried on?

Facts: The taxpayer bought a mill and stripped it of its assets. This was repeated four times in all.

Held: Although the transaction would generally be considered to be of a capital nature, the fact that it was repeated frequently indicated a trade was being carried on, and as such the profits were liable to income tax under Schedule D Case I.

Proctor and Gamble Ltd v *Taylerson* [1990] BTC 462

Problem: The time limit of two years to claim a carry back of ACT can be a problem if the surplus ACT is generated as a result of a loss claim.

Facts: In December 1979 a claim was made for surplus ACT arising in the accounting period ending 30 April 1979 to be carried back. The accounts were settled in 1981 and the surplus ACT arising in 1979 was carried back to the previous year. Subsequently, the company incurred a loss in 1982 and as some of the loss was due to FYA's on plant and machinery part of the loss was carried back to 1979 with the result that surplus ACT was again generated for that period. As a claim had already been made for that year, the company claimed the ACT could be carried back.

Held: The claim in 1979 was settled in 1981 when the ACT was agreed, thereby settling the 1979 claim. The 1984 claim was a new claim and outside the two-year limit for the surplus ACT generated in 1979 as a result of the loss in 1982 being carried back. The additional surplus ACT arising in 1979 was out of time and, therefore, could not be carried back.

R v *IRC ex p Fulford-Dobson* [1987] STC 344

Problem: Was the taxpayer protected by ESC D2?

Facts: In 1977 the taxpayer's wife inherited a farm. By 1980 the farm had substantially increased in value and consideration was given to selling the property. In order to avoid CGT, the wife transferred the farm to her husband who was about to become non-UK resident when he took up employment in Germany. The farm was then disposed of a few days after he left the UK.

Held: The taxpayer was not protected by ESC D2 and the gain was chargeable to CGT as the concession had been used for tax avoidance.

Ricketts v *Colquhourn* (1926) 10 TC 118

Problem: Were travelling and subsistence expenses incurred while travelling between two occupations allowable expenses?

Facts: The taxpayer, who was a barrister, was also employed as a Recorder. His law practice was in London, where he lived, and the occupation of Recorder took place in Portsmouth. He claimed travel expenses between London and Portsmouth and hotel accommodation against his Schedule E emoluments.

Held: The expenses were disallowed as they were not incurred in the performance of his duties as a Recorder.

Rutledge v *CIR* (1929) 14 TC 490

Problem: Was a single isolated transaction trading and liable to income tax under Schedule D Case I?

Facts: The taxpayer purchased one million toilet rolls cheaply while in Germany. On his return to the UK, he sold them to one purchaser for a substantial profit. The Revenue assessed him to income tax on the basis that it was an adventure in the nature of trade.

Held: The toilet rolls had not been purchased for personal use, and the nature of the items made it unlikely that they had been bought as an investment, making the resale at a profit an adventure in the nature of trade.

Schofield v *R&H Hall Ltd* [1975] STC 353

Problem: Did a concrete silo constitute plant?

Facts: The taxpayer company built a concrete silo together with a supporting framework, conveyors and chutes and claimed the expenditure as plant.

Held: The expenditure qualified as plant, the silo was not just a storage container for grain but also provided a means by which the grain could be conveniently loaded for transportation.

Scorer v *Olin Energy Systems Ltd* [1985] BTC 181

Problem: Could an assessment be reopened where an error is discovered after agreement between the taxpayer and the Inspector had been reached under the TMA 1970, s 54 ?

Facts: The taxpayer company operated a manufacturing trade and between 1961 and 1967 also engaged in a second trade involving chartering a ship. Interest on a loan to purchase a ship exceeded the shipping profits and when the shipping trade ceased in 1967 excess interest from the shipping trade was set off as a loss against profits of the manufacturing trade. The computations were agreed, with minor amendments, under the TMA 1970, s 54 and the loss relief given. Four years later another Inspector realised that the loss relief had been given erroneously and sought to raise an additional assessment to correct the mistake.

Held: The House of Lords held that where agreement had been reached under s 54 and all material facts had been presented at the time, the taxpayer is protected by the original agreement and no additional assessment could be made.

Sharkey v Wernher (1955) 36 TC 275

Problem: What value should be placed on goods taken from a business other than a sale at arm's length?

Facts: The taxpayer's wife had a stud farm business and also trained and raced horses as a hobby, the hobby not being liable to taxation. She transferred several horses to the racing stables from the stud farm at cost. The Revenue contended that they should be transferred from trading stock at market value.

Held: Appropriations of trading stock must be shown at market value rather than cost for tax purposes.

Shilton v Wilmshurst (HMIT) [1991] STC 88

Problem: Was an inducement payment taxable under Schedule E?

Facts: The taxpayer, a professional footballer, was transferred to Southampton from Nottingham Forest, who paid him £75 000. The Revenue claimed that the payment was an inducement to move to Southampton, the taxpayer claimed it was a termination payment from Nottingham Forest.

Held: The payment was an inducement to move to Southampton and taxable as an emolument arising from the new employment even though it was paid by Nottingham Forest. Section 19 of the ICTA 1988 provides that Schedule E covers the emoluments from the employment and not just emoluments from the employer.

Smith (HMIT) v Schofield [1993] BTC 147

Problem: Should indexation be applied before or after time apportionment for assets acquired before 1965, i.e. does the unindexed gain mean the chargeable gain after time apportionment?

Facts: The taxpayer had bought a Chinese cabinet and a French mirror for £250 in 1952, and sold them for £15 800 in 1987.

Held: Section 53(2), TCGA 1992 provides that the unindexed gain is the whole of the gain between acquisition and disposal and as such the House of Lords took the view that the indexation should be set against the whole of the gain before time apportionment is made.

Strong & Co of Ramsey Ltd v Woodifield [1906] STC 215

Problem: Was the expenditure incurred wholly and exclusively for the purpose of trading?

Facts: The taxpayer company was in the trade of brewing and innkeeping. During a storm a chimney of a public house fell in injuring a guest who subsequently successfully claimed compensation for personal injury. The company paid the damages but claimed that the amount was deductible as a revenue expense.

Held: The expenditure on damages was too remote from the trade, i.e. the expense had been incurred in a non-trading capacity and as such was disallowed in computing the Schedule D Case I profits.

Taylor v Good (1974) 49 TC 277

Problem: Was there an adventure in the nature of trade if it had not been the taxpayer's intention when acquiring the property that it would be resold at a substantial profit?

Facts: The taxpayer bought a country house at auction for £5100 in 1959 with the intention of living in the house. His wife, however, refused to live in the house and he applied for planning permission to build 90 houses on the land. The property was subsequently sold to a property developer in 1963 for £54500.

Held: The Court of Appeal held that as the property was not acquired initially with a view to resale at a profit the remaining transactions to enable him to sell the land were not sufficient to establish trading.

Tucker v Granada Motorway Services Ltd (1979) 53 TC 92

Problem: Was a payment to alter the terms of a lease revenue or capital expenditure?

Facts: The taxpayer company leased a motorway service area from the Minister of Transport for a term of 50 years. Rent payable under the lease comprised a fixed rent plus a percentage of the previous year's gross takings. The company paid the landlord a sum of £122200 to vary the terms of the lease so that tobacco duty was excluded from the gross takings for the remaining 40 years of the lease. The company claimed the payment was a revenue expense.

Held: The payment was a once-and-for-all expense on a capital asset, the lease, to make it more favourable, and as such the expense was a capital expense.

Van der Berghs Ltd v Clark (1935) 19 TC 390

Problem: Was compensation received for the cancellation of a contract a capital receipt or a revenue receipt?

Facts: In 1908 the taxpayer company made an agreement with a competing Dutch company to regulate their activities and share profits and losses. The agreement was intended to remain in force until 1940. However, the Dutch company terminated the agreement during the 1914–18 war and paid compensation of £450000.

Held: The receipt was a capital receipt as it affected the whole profit-making structure of the company, it was not a payment for a loss of profit.

Varty v Lynnes [1976] STC 508

Problem: Was the sale of part of the garden after the disposal of the main residence eligible for relief?

Facts: The taxpayer bought his principal private residence in 1968 together with less than one acre of garden for £6920. He sold the house and part of the garden for £10000 in 1971 which was eligible for principal private residence relief. He obtained planning permission for the rest of the land and sold this for £10000 in 1972.

Held: The sale of the remainder of the garden did not qualify for relief. Principal private residence relief is only available where at the time of the disposal it is the taxpayer's principal private residence.

Whitehead v Tubbs (Elastic) Ltd (1984) 57 TC 472

Problem: Was a payment made to release the company from a restrictive loan agreement a revenue or capital expense?

Facts: In 1975 the taxpayer company made a loan agreement to borrow £80000 for a period of nine years secured by a fixed and floating charge over the company's assets. In addition, the agreement stated that the taxpayer could only borrow a maximum of £35000 on an overdraft facility from banks. As the company's business was expanding, it paid the finance company £20000 to release the company from this restricted borrowing and the floating charge.

Held: The payment was a capital payment as release from the restriction and floating charge enhanced the company's identifiable assets.

Williams v Evans (HMIT) [1982] STC 498

Problem: Does the word 'fixed' in the phrase 'fixed plant and machinery' within s 155, TCGA 1992 apply to both plant and machinery?

Facts: The taxpayers were in the business of civil engineering and plant hirers. They sold earth moving equipment at a profit and bought new earth moving equipment. The taxpayers claimed roll-over relief under the TCGA 1992, s 155 on the basis that 'fixed' applied only to plant and not to machinery.

Held: The word 'fixed' applies to both plant and machinery and as such the taxpayers did not qualify for roll-over relief.

Wimpy International Ltd v Warland [1989] STC 273

Problem: Was expenditure on fixed items installed in restaurants to create ambience and attract the right clientele considered to be expenditure on plant?

Facts: The taxpayer company operated a chain of fast-food restaurants which were refurbished with fixed items such as raised floor areas, tiling, etc. and removable items such as carpets, pictures, etc.

Held: The fixed items of expenditure represented mere setting and did not qualify for capital allowances. On the other hand, the removable items qualified as plant and were eligible for capital allowances.

Wisdom v *Chamberlain (HMIT)* (1968) 45 TC 92

Problem: Was the purchase and resale of silver bullion an adventure in the nature of trade?

Facts: The entertainer Norman Wisdom bought silver bullion in 1961 and 1962 as a 'hedge against inflation' when there were prospects of the pound being devalued. In October 1962 and January 1963 the taxpayer sold the silver bullion at a profit.

Held: Although the nature of the silver bullion was such that it could have been considered to be an investment, the short time between acquisition and disposal indicated an adventure in the nature of trade and as such liable to income tax under Schedule D Case I.

APPENDIX 2

Summary of rates and allowances

Income tax

1. Allowances	2002/03	2001/02
	£	£
Personal allowances	4615	4535
Age allowance (65–74 yrs)	6100	5990
Age allowance (over 75 yrs)	6370	6260
Income limit for age allowance	17900	17600
Blind person's allowance	1480	1450

2. Tax reducers (relief given at 10%)	2002/03	2001/02
	£	£
Married couples' age allowance (65–74 yrs)*	5465	5365
Married couples' age allowance (over 75 yrs)	5535	5435
Income limit for age allowance	17900	17600
Children's tax credit	5290	5200
Children's tax credit – baby rate	10490	N/A

3. Rates and bands	2002/03	2001/02
Lower rate	10%	10%
Basic rate	22%	22%
Higher rate	40%	40%
	(£)	(£)
Lower rate band	0–1920	0–1880
Basic rate band	1921–29900	1881–29400
Higher rate band	over 29900	over 29400

4. Rent a room relief	2002/03	2001/02
	£	£
	4250	4250

* The married couples' age allowance is only available where either spouse is over the age of 65 years at 5 April 2000, and the minimum amount for 2002/03 is £2110.

From 6 April 2000, maintenance relief is withdrawn, except where one of the parties to the agreement is over the age of 65 years, in which case relief is available at 10 per cent on a maximum amount of £2110 (2002/03), the relief being given as a tax reducer.

5. Fuel scale rates

	2002/03		2001/02	
	Petrol	*Diesel*	*Petrol*	*Diesel*
Cylinder capacity	£	£	£	£
Up to 1400 cc	2 240	2 850	1 930	2 460
1401–2000 cc	2 850	2 850	2 460	2 460
Over 2000 cc	4 200	4 200	3 620	3 620

Car benefit charges for cars with an approved CO_2 emissions figure

CO_2 emissions in grams Per kilometre 2002/03	Percentage of cars price to be taxed	
165	15*	The basic car benefit will be
170	16*	price x percentage charge
175	17*	subject to :
180	18*	(1) diesel supplement, or
185	19*	(2) discount for cars using
190	20*	alternative fuels.
195	21*	
200	22*	
205	23*	* Add 3% if car runs on diesel
210	24*	
215	25*	** Add 2% if car runs on diesel
220	26*	
225	27*	***Add 1% if car runs on diesel
230	28*	
235	29*	**** Maximum charge so no
240	30*	diesel supplement
245	31*	
250	32*	
255	33**	
260	34***	
265	35****	

6. Pension contribution limits

Age at beginning of tax year	*Personal pension schemes* %
Under 35	17½
36–45	20
46–50	25
51–55	30
56–60	35
Over 61	40

Personal pensions earnings cap 2002/03: £97 200 (£95 400 for 2001/02).

Notes

i) Personal representatives pay income tax at basic rate.

ii) Discretionary trusts are liable to income tax at 34%, other trusts are only liable to income tax at basic rate.

iii) Savings income is taxed at 10%, 20% or 40%, i.e. it is not liable to income tax at basic rate.

WFTC and DPTC (£ per week)

	2002/03 (from 9th April 02) £	2001/02 (from April) £	2001/02 (from June) £
Basic WFTC	60.00	54.00	59.00
DPTC			
– Single	62.10	56.05	61.05
– Lone parent/couple	92.80	86.25	91.25
30 hours' tax credit (WFTC & DPTC)	11.65	11.45	11.45

Child tax credits (£ per week)

	2002/03 £	2001/02 from April £	2001/02 from June £
WFTC & DPTC			
Under 16*	26.45	26.00	26.00
16–18*	27.20	26.75	26.75
Disabled child tax credit			
– WFTC	35.50	30.00	30.00
– DPTC	35.50	30.00	30.00
WFTC threshold	94.50	92.90	92.90
DPTC threshold			
– Single	73.50	72.25	72.25
– Lone parent/couple	94.50	92.90	92.90

* The child tax credits apply from 1 September following the 16th birthday.

National Insurance contributions

Class 1

1. Employee contributions (Primary)

Limits	2002/03 £	2001/02 £
Lower earnings limit:		
weekly	75	72
annually (directors)	3900	3744

Upper earnings limit:

weekly	585	575
annually (directors)	30420	29900

Primary threshold per week:	89	87

Rates 2002/03

	Non-contracted out	*Contracted out of SERPS*
Weekly		
First £89	0%	0%
£90–£585	10%	8.4%
Annually (directors)		
First £3900	0%	0%
£3901–30420	10%	8.4%

2. Employer contributions (Secondary)

There is no ceiling for secondary contributions. Prior to April 1999, employers paid secondary contributions in respect of their employees according to:

- the level of income in the earnings period;
- whether the employee was contracted in or out of SERPS;
- whether the contracted out scheme was a salary related or money purchase scheme.

From April 1999, a lower earnings threshold for secondary contributions has been introduced. The secondary threshold for 2002/03 is £89 per week. Employers will not pay secondary contributions unless the employee's earnings exceed the threshold for a contribution period. Earnings in excess of this limit are liable to secondary contributions at a single rate of 11.8% where the employee is not contracted out of SERPS; where the employee is contracted out of SERPS, the rate depends on the type of scheme. (*See* Chapter 14)

Class 2

	2002/03	*2001/02*
Weekly rate	£2.00	£2.00
Small earnings limit	£4025	£3955

Class 3

	2002/03	*2001/02*
Weekly rate	£6.85	£6.75

Class 4

	2002/03	*2001/02*
Upper limit	£30420	£29900
Lower limit	£4615	£4535
Rate	7%	7%

Rates of corporation tax

	Financial years					
	1997	*1998*	*1999*	*2000*	*2001*	*2002*
Full rate	31%	31%	30%	30%	30%	30%
Small companies rate	21%	21%	20%	20%	20%	19%
Marginal relief fraction	$\frac{1}{40}$	$\frac{1}{40}$	$\frac{1}{40}$	$\frac{1}{40}$	$\frac{1}{40}$	$\frac{11}{400}$
Upper limit	1 500 000	1 500 000	1 500 000	1 500 000	1 500 000	1 500 000
Lower limit	300 000	300 000	300 000	50 000	50 000– 300 000	50 000– 300 000
ACT rate	20%	20%	nil	nil	nil	nil
Limit for starting rate	–	–	–	0–10 000	0–10 000	0–10 000
Starting rate	–	–	–	10%	10%	0%
Starting rate marginal relief fraction	–	–	–	$\frac{1}{40}$	$\frac{1}{40}$	$\frac{19}{400}$

Marginal relief formula

$$\text{Fraction} \times (\text{upper limit} - \text{'profits'}) \times \frac{\text{'income'}}{\text{'profits'}}$$

'Income' = PCTCT

'Profits' = PCTCT + FII

Marginal relief:
(1) 10 001–50 000 (fraction $\frac{19}{400}$ FY 2002
(2) 300 001–1 500 000 (fraction $\frac{11}{400}$ FY 2002

Rates of value added tax

	From 25/4/02	*From 1/4/01*
Standard rate	$17\frac{1}{2}$%	$17\frac{1}{2}$%
VAT fraction	$\frac{7}{47}$	$\frac{7}{47}$
	(£)	(£)
Registration limit	55 000	54 000
Deregistration limit	53 000	52 000

Capital gains tax – retail price index

	1982	1983	1984	1985	1986	1987	1988	1989	1990	1991	1992	1993	1994	1995	1996	1997	1998	1999	2000	2001	2002
Jan.	–	82.6	86.8	91.2	96.2	100.0	103.3	111.0	119.5	130.2	135.6	137.9	141.3	146.0	150.2	154.4	159.5	163.4	166.6	171.1	173.3
Feb.	–	83.0	87.2	91.9	96.6	100.4	103.7	111.8	120.2	130.9	136.3	138.8	142.1	146.9	150.9	155.0	160.3	163.7	167.5	172.0	173.8
Mar.	79.4	83.1	87.5	92.8	96.7	100.6	104.1	112.3	121.4	131.4	136.7	139.3	142.5	147.5	151.5	155.4	160.8	164.1	168.4	172.2	174.5
Apr.	81.0	84.3	88.6	94.8	97.7	101.8	105.8	114.3	125.1	133.1	138.8	140.6	144.2	149.0	152.6	156.3	162.6	165.2	170.1	173.1	174.8*
May	81.6	84.6	89.0	95.2	97.8	101.9	106.2	115.0	126.2	133.5	139.3	141.1	144.7	149.6	152.9	156.9	163.5	165.6	170.7	174.2	175.2*
June	81.9	84.8	89.2	95.4	97.8	101.9	106.6	115.4	126.7	134.1	139.3	141.0	144.7	149.8	153.0	157.5	163.4	165.6	171.1	174.4	175.5*
July	81.9	85.3	89.1	95.2	97.5	101.8	106.7	115.5	126.8	133.8	138.3	140.7	144.0	149.1	152.4	157.5	163.0	165.1	170.5	173.3	175.9*
Aug.	81.9	85.7	89.9	95.5	97.8	102.1	107.9	115.8	128.1	134.1	138.9	141.3	144.7	149.9	153.1	158.5	163.7	165.5	170.5	174.0	176.3*
Sept.	81.9	86.1	90.1	95.4	98.3	102.4	108.4	116.6	129.3	134.6	139.4	141.9	145.0	150.6	153.8	159.3	164.4	166.2	171.7	174.6	176.7*
Oct.	82.3	86.4	90.7	95.6	98.5	102.9	109.5	117.5	130.3	135.1	139.9	141.8	145.2	149.8	153.8	159.5	164.5	166.5	171.6	174.3	177.2*
Nov.	82.7	86.7	91.0	95.9	99.3	103.4	110.0	118.5	130.0	135.6	139.7	141.6	145.3	149.8	153.9	159.6	164.4	166.7	172.1	173.6	177.6*
Dec.	82.5	86.9	90.9	96.0	99.6	103.3	110.3	118.8	129.9	135.7	139.2	141.9	146.0	150.7	154.4	160.0	164.4	167.3	172.2	173.4	178.1*

*Estimated figures

	2001/02	2002/03
	(£)	(£)
Annual exemption	7500	7700
Chattel exemption	6000	6000

Answers to self assessment questions

Chapter 10

10.1(a)

	£	£
Net profit as per a/cs		12 990
Add back:		
– motor expenses (40%)	1 476	
– drawings	12 000	
– depreciation	1 800	
– health club	650	
– legal fees re new lease	550	
– lease written off	5 000	21 476
		34 466
Deduct:		
– rental income	6 000	
– building society interest	1 200	
– capital allowances	1 302	
– lease premium relief (W1)	2 460	(10 962)
Adjusted Schedule DI		23 504

W1	£
Premium	30 000
less:	
2% (10 – 1) × £30 000	(5 400)
Assessable to Schedule A on grantor	24 600

Premium relief for Charlotte:
$$\frac{24\,600}{10} = £2460 \text{ pa for 10 years}$$

10.1(b)

2000/01	*Assessments*
1/1/01 – 5/4/01	**(£)**
$\frac{3}{16} \times £23\,504$	<u>4407</u>

2001/02
No a/cs in current year so:
6/4/01 – 5/4/02
$\frac{12}{16} \times £23\,504$ <u>17628</u>

2002/03
12 months to 30/4/02
$\frac{12}{16} \times £23\,504$ <u>17628</u>

Overlap profits $= \frac{11}{16} \times £23\,504 = $ <u>£16 159</u>

10.2

	(£)	*Assessments*
		(£)
1996/97		
1/7/96 – 5/4/97		
1/7/96 – 31/12/96	13135	
1/1/97 – 5/4/97: $\frac{3}{12} \times £25\,300$	<u>6325</u>	<u>19460</u>
1997/98		
YE 31/12/97		<u>25300</u>
1998/99		
YE 31/12/98		<u>30000</u>
1999/00		
YE 31/12/99		<u>28000</u>
2000/01		
YE 31/12/00		<u>26600</u>
2001/02 (year of cessation)		
1/1/01 – 30/9/01	10000	
less Overlap profits	(6325)	<u>3675</u>

Chapter 11

11.1

(£)	Pool (£)	Car (1) (£)	Car (2) (£)	Allowances
1/1/97 – 30/6/98 (18 months)				
Additions:				
1/1/97 plant	7000			
1/1/97 car		10000		
12/6/97 lorry	10000			
	17000	10000		
WDA: $25\% \times \frac{18}{12}$	(6375)			6375
WDA: $25\% \times \frac{18}{12}$		(3750) × 60%		2250
C/f	10625	6250	nil	
				8625
1/7/98 – 30/6/99 (12 months)				
Additions:				
20/5/99 car			15000	
Disposals: 31/10/98	(7000)			
20/5/99		(5000)		
	3625	1250	15000	
WDA: 25%	(906)			906
WDA: 25% (restricted)			(3000) × 60%	1800
Balancing allowance		(1250) × 60%		750
Additions qualifying FYA:				
1/9/98 plant 8000				
10/11/98 equip 4000				
15/5/99 m/c 12000				
24000				
FYA (40%)	(9600) 14400			9600
C/f	17119	nil	12000	13056
1/7/99 – 30/6/00				
Disposal: 30/9/99	(6599)			
	10520	nil	12000	
	(2630)			2630
WDA: 25%			(3000) × 60%	1800
Additions qualifying FYA:				
30/9/99 lorry 20000				
FYA 40%	(8000) 12000			8000
C/f	19890	nil	9000	12430

11.2(a)

As the building is used for manufacturing purposes, the canteen is allowable. The office will be allowable if the cost is not more than 25 per cent of the total cost:

	£
Architect's fees	8 000
Preparation of land	10 000
Cost construction	230 000
Total cost	248 000

$\dfrac{50\,000}{248\,000} = 20.16\%$ Therefore, offices are allowable.

	Factory (£)	Allowances (£)
YE 31/12/96		
Cost	248 000	
WDA (4%)	(9 920)	9 920
C/f	238 080	
YE 31/12/97		
WDA (4%)	(9 920)	9 920
C/f	228 160	
YE 31/12/98		
WDA (4%)	(9 920)	9 920
C/f	218 240	
YE 31/12/99		
WDA (4%)	(9 920)	9 920
C/f	208 320	
YE 31/12/00		
WDA (4%)	(9 920)	9 920
C/f	198 400	

YE 31/12/01

Building sold during this period, therefore, no WDA available.

Tax written down value	£198 400
Total allowances given	£ 49 600

11.2(b)

As building is sold for more than cost, a balancing charge arises, lower of:

(i) £300 000 – £198 400 = £101 600

or (ii) £49 600

Therefore, BC = £49 600

11.2(c)

The building has 20 years remaining of tax life.

Allowances available to Keats Ltd:

$$\frac{\text{Tax written down value} + \text{BC}}{\text{Remaining tax life}}$$

$$\frac{198\,400 + 49\,600}{20}$$

$$= \text{£}12\,400 \text{ pa}$$

Chapter 12

12.1

(a) *2001/02 priority claim*

	Assessment (£)	Loss memo (£)
2001/02		
Schedule DI	15 000	(20 000) YE 30/6/01
Investment income	7 000	
	22 000	
s 380 relief	(20 000)	20 000
	2 000	
less PA (restricted)	(2 000)	
2002/03		
Schedule DI	nil	
Investment income	7 000	
	7 000	
less PA	(4 385)	
Taxable income	2 615	

12.1

(b) *2002/03 priority claim*	Assessment (£)	Loss memo (£)
2002/03		
Schedule DI	nil	(20 000) YE 30/6/01
Investment income	7 000	
s 380 relief	(7 000)	7 000
		(13 000)
2001/02		
Schedule DI	15 000	
s 380 relief	(13 000)	13 000
	2 000	
Investment income	7 000	
	9 000	
less PA	(4 335)	
Taxable income	4 665	

So as not to waste the personal allowance, the s 380 claim should give priority to 2001/02.

12.2 (a) *Assessments*

	(£)
1998/99	
1/1/99 – 5/4/99	
$\frac{3}{15} \times £5\,000$	1 000
1999/00	
12 months to 31/3/00	
$\frac{12}{15} \times £5\,000$	4 000
2000/01	
YE 31/3/01	nil
2001/02	
YE 31/3/2002	18 000

	1997/98 (£)	*1998/99* (£)	*1999/00* (£)	*2000/01* (year of loss) (£)
(b)				
Schedule E	13 000	10 000	nil	nil
Schedule DI	nil	1 000	4 000	nil
Investment income	1 200	1 200	1 200	1 200
	14 200	12 200	5 200	1 200
s 381	(14 200)	(12 200)	(5 200)	
	nil	nil	nil	1 200

Loss memo
YE 31/3/01	(36 000)	
s 381 97/98	14 200	
s 381 98/99	12 200	
s 381 99/00	5 200	
Unrelieved loss	4 400	c/f s 385

(c) *2000/01*
STI	1 200
less PA (restricted)	(1 200)
Taxable income	nil

2001/02	£		*Loss memo*	£
Schedule DI	18 000		b/f	(4 400)
s 385	(4 400)			4 400
	13 600			
Investment income	1 200			
	14 800			
less PA	(4 535)			
Taxable income	10 625			

Chapter 13

		£		£
13.1	*Car*			
	£18 000 × 20%	3 600		
	Fuel scale charge	2 850		6 450
	Suits			
	£600 × 20%			120
	BUPA			500
	House			
	GAV	3 600		
	Additional charges			
	(120 000 − 75 000) × 7%	3 150		6 750
			Total benefits	13 820
			Salary	28 000
			Schedule E emoluments	41 820

13.2

	£
Cost property	75 000
Improvement October 2001	12 000
	87 000

2002/03	£
GAV	2 000
Additional charges	
$(87\,000 - 75\,000) \times 7\%$	840
Taxable benefit	2 840

13.3(a) *Car*

	£	£
£15 000 × 21%		3 150
Accommodation		
Basic charge	3 000	
Additional charge:		
$(130\,000 - 75\,000) \times 7\%$	3 850	6 850
Ancillary benefits		
Electricity	600	
Council tax	900	
Gardener	1 560	3 060
	Total benefits	13 060
	Salary	30 000
	Total emoluments	43 060

13.3(b)

Net emoluments:	£
Salary	30 000
Car benefit	3 150
	33 150
less Pension	(2 000)
Net emoluments	31 150

Therefore, maximum ancillary benefit
$10\% \times £31\,150 = £3\,115$

Accommodation job-related:	£
Basic charge	nil
Additional charge	nil
Ancillary benefits	3 060
	3 060

Chapter 14

14.1   £

Primary

52 [(400 − 89) × 10%]   1617.20

Secondary

52 [(400 − 89) × 11.8%]   1908.30

14.2

Class 1 paid

52 (585 − 89) × 10%   2579.20

Class 2 paid

52 × £2.00   104.00

                                   2683.20

less Maximum class 1 and 2:

53 (585 − 89) × 10%   (2628.80)

Repayable   54.40

Chapter 15

15.1

Year	NRE	% Relief	Max. relief	Used	Unused	C/f
1996/97	13000	17.5	2275	2200	75	75
1997/98	17000	17.5	2975	2200	775	850
1998/99	18000	17.5	3150	2200	950	1800
1999/00	25000	20	5000	2200	2800	4600
2000/01	20000	20	4000	2200	1800	6400
2001/02	16000	20	3200	4200	nil	5400

Robin has £1000 excess contributions for 2001/02 and can be relieved from earlier years on a LIFO basis. Robin could contribute an extra £5400 in 2001/02 and obtain relief.

Chapter 16

16.1

2002/03	£	£
Rents receivable (£300 × 10)	3000	
less Expenses	(480)	2520
Premium	4000	
less 2% (5 − 1) × £4 000	(320)	3680
	Schedule A	6200

16.2 2002/03 £

	£
Premium	10 000
less: 2% (12 – 1) × £10 000	(2 200)
	7 800
less Sub-letting relief	
$\frac{12}{25}$ × £18 200 (W1)	(8 736)
Premium assessable	nil
Unrelieved premium	936
Rent received ($\frac{9}{12}$ × £6 000)	4 500
Rent paid	(4 000)
	500
Relief: $\dfrac{936}{12} \times \frac{9}{12}$	(59)

Schedule A   441

W1   £

	£	
Premium	35 000	
less: 2% (25 – 1) × £35 000	(16 800)	
	18 200	Premium assessable on head lease

Chapter 17

17.1	*Non-savings* (£)	*Savings* (£)	*Dividends* (£)	*Tax* (£)
Schedule E	27 000			6 100
Schedule DI	6 500			–
Schedule A	5 200			–
BSI		1 500		300
Bank int.		75		15
NSB (180 – 70)		110		–
Dividends			3 200	320
	38 700	1 685	3 200	6 735
less Charges	(500)	–	–	
	38 200	1 685	3 200	
less PA	(4 615)	–	–	
Taxable income	33 585	1 685	3 200	

Non-savings:	£
1 920 × 10%	192
27 980 × 22%	6 156
3 685 × 40%	1 474
Savings	
1 685 × 40%	674
Dividends	
3 200 × 32.5%	1 040
	9 536
add Tax on charge	110
	9 646

9 646   Income tax liability 2002/03

17.2

	Non-savings (£)	Savings (£)	Dividends (£)	Tax (£)
Salary	27 865			
Dividends ($3600 \times \frac{100}{90}$)			6 000	600
BSI ($1020 \times \frac{100}{80}$)		1 275		255
NSB		250		
	27 865	1 525	6 000	855
less PA	(4 615)			
Taxable income	23 250	1 525	6 000	

Non-savings	£
$1920 \times 10\%$	192
$21 330 \times 22\%$	4 693

Savings	
$1525 \times 20\%$	305

Dividends	
$5125 \times 10\%$	512
$875 \times 32.5\%$	284
	5 986 Tax liability 2002/03

17.3

	Non-savings (£)	Savings (£)	Dividends (£)	Tax (£)
Schedule E: Salary	7 000			
Pensions	8 500			
Dividends			2 100	210
Bank interest		1 225		245
STI	15 500	1 225	2 100	455
PA	6 100			
less:				
$\frac{1}{2}$ (18 825 – 17 900) (463)	(5 637)			
Taxable income	9 863	1 225	2 100	

Non-savings	£
$1920 \times 10\%$	192
$7943 \times 22\%$	1 747

Savings	
$1225 \times 20\%$	245

Dividends	
$2100 \times 10\%$	210
	2 394 Tax liability

Chapter 19

19.1

2001/02	Non-savings (£)	Dividends (£)	Tax (£)
Schedule E: Salary ($\frac{6}{12}$)	19 000		4 900
Director's remuneration:			
6 × £2 000	12 000		
Dividends			
(5000 × 16p) $\frac{100}{90}$		889	89
	31 000	889	4 989
PA	(4 535)		
	26 465	889	

Non-savings	£
1880 × 10%	188
24 585 × 22%	5 409

Dividends	
889 × 10%	89
	5 686

less Tax paid	(4 989)	
	697	Income tax payable by PRs

Chapter 20

20.1(a)

	£
BSI (net)	2 320
less Trust expenses	(500)
Net savings income available for Mary	1 820

	£
Schedule A	7 650
less Tax @ 22%	(1 683)
Schedule A income available for Mary	5 967

	Net	Tax	Gross
Savings income	1 820	455	2 275
Schedule A income	5 967	1 683	7 650
	7 787	2 138	9 925

20.1(b) £

Tax on savings income used for expenses:

$(500 \times \frac{100}{80}) \times 20\%$ 125

Tax on rest of savings income:

$(1820 \times \frac{100}{80}) \times 20\%$ 455

Tax on Schedule A income $\underline{1683}$

Total tax liability for trustees $\underline{\underline{2263}}$

20.2(a)

As Amy is over 18 years old, she is entitled to an interest in possession of $\frac{1}{3}$ of the trust income:

	Savings		Other income	
	£	£	£	£
Taxed income:				
$(3465 \times \frac{100}{78}) \times \frac{1}{3}$			1481	326
Building society interest:				
$[(4600 - 400) \frac{100}{80}] \times \frac{1}{3}$	1750	350		
	$\underline{1750}$	$\underline{350}$	$\underline{1481}$	$\underline{326}$

20.2(b) £ £ Tax

Taxed income:

$(3465 \times \frac{100}{78}) \times \frac{2}{3}$ 2961 651

BSI:

$[(4600 - 400) \frac{100}{80}] \times \frac{2}{3}$ $\underline{3500}$ $\underline{700}$

  $\underline{\underline{6461}}$ $\underline{\underline{1351}}$

  £

Tax @ 34% × £6461 2197

less Tax credits (1351)

Trustees' s 686 liability $\underline{846}$

Chapter 22

22.1		£	£	£ Gain
(a) Proceeds			50 000	

less Cost:

$$45\,000 \times \frac{50\,000}{50\,000 + 70\,000}$$

			(18 750)	
			31 250	

less Indexation to April 1998

$$\frac{162.6 - 97.7}{97.7} = 0.664 \times £18\,750$$

			(12 450)	18 800

less Taper 15%				(2 820)
				15 980

	Cost	*MV*		
(b) Proceeds	66 000	66 000		
less Cost/mv	(20 000)	(40 000)		
	46 000	26 000		

less Indexation to April 1998:

$$\frac{162.6 - 79.4}{79.4} = 1.048 \times £40\,000$$

	(41 920)	(26 000)		
	4 080	nil	nil	

(c) Proceeds			25 000	
Cost			(10 000)	
			15 000	

less Indexation to April 1998:

$$\frac{162.6 - 126.7}{126.7} = 0.283 \times £10\,000$$

			(2 830)	
Gain eligible taper relief			12 170	
Taper relief 75%			(9 128)	3 042

Total chargeable gains	19 022
less AE	(7 700)
Taxable gains 2002/03	11 322

22.2	Cost (£)	MV (£)
Proceeds	400 000	400 000
less Cost / mv	(100 000)	(130 000)
	300 000	270 000
less Improvements (1990)	(50 000)	(50 000)
	250 000	220 000

less Indexation:

(1) $\dfrac{162.6 - 79.4}{79.4} = 1.048 \times £130\,000$

	(136 240)	(136 240)
	113 760	83 760

(2) $\dfrac{162.6 - 126.7}{126.7} = 0.283 \times £50\,000$

	(14 150)	(14 150)
Indexed gain	99 610	69 610
Taper relief 15%		(10 442)
		59 168

Chargeable gain = £59 168

Chapter 23

23.1	£	£	£ Gain
(a) Exempt			nil
(b) Proceeds		15 000	
less Cost of sale		(1 500)	
Net proceeds		13 500	
less Cost		(5 000)	
		8 500	

less Indexation to April 1998:

$\dfrac{162.6 - 129.3}{129.3} = 0.258 \times £5\,000$

		(1 290)	
less		7 210	
Taper 15%		(1 082)	6 128
(c) Proceeds		7 000	
less Cost		(2 000)	
		5 000	

less Indexation to April 1998:

$\dfrac{162.6 - 144.0}{144.0} = 0.129 \times £2000$

		(258)	
		4 472	

Restricted to: 5/3 (7000 − 6000) = £1 667

less Taper 15%	(250)		
			1 417
Total chargeable gains			7 545

23.2	£	£	£ *Gain*
(a) Proceeds		8000	
less Cost		(5000)	
		3000	

less Indexation to April 1998:

$$\frac{162.6 - 139.2}{139.2} = 0.168 \times £5000$$

		(840)	2160
less Taper 15%			(324)
			1836

	Cost	*MV*	
(b) Proceeds	80000	80000	
less Cost /MV	(20000)	(25000)	
	60000	55000	

less Indexation to April 1998:

$$\frac{162.6 - 79.4}{79.4} = 1.048 \times £25000$$

	(26200)	(26200)	
	33800	28800	
Taper relief 75%	(25350)	(21600)	
	8450	7200	7200
		Chargeable gains 2002/03	9036

Chapter 24

24.1	£	£
Disposal 1994/95		
Proceeds		5000

less Cost: $20000 \times \dfrac{5000}{5000 + 16000}$

		(4762)
		238

less Indexation:

$$\frac{147.5 - 126.8}{126.8} = 0.163 \times £4762 \text{ (restricted)}$$

		(238)
Deemed part disposal 1994/95		nil

Disposal 2002/03		
Proceeds		30000
less Cost: (20000 – 4762)		(15238)
		14762

less Indexation to April 1998:

$$\frac{162.6 - 126.8}{126.8} = 0.282 \times £15238$$

		(4297)
Untapered gain		10465

24.2

	£	£
Proceeds		20 000
less Cost		(8 000)
		12 000

less Indexation to April 1998:

$$\frac{162.6 - 111}{111} = 0.465 \times £8000$$

	£	£
		(3 720)
Indexed gain		8 280
less Roll-over relief: indexed gain	8 280	
less Proceeds not used	(2 000)	(6 280)
Untapered gain		2 000

Base cost of replacement asset:	£
Cost	18 000
less Rolled over gain	(6 280)
Base cost	11 720

Chapter 25

25.1

	£
Proceeds	150 000
less Allowable cost: $80\,000 \times \dfrac{82.496}{87.330}$	(75 572)
	74 428

Gain eligible taper relief.

25.2

Schedule A

(1) *On head lease*

	£
Premium	50 000
less 2% (40–1) × £50 000	(39 000)
Schedule A	11 000

(2) *On sub-lease*

	£
Premium	80 000
less 2% (20–1) × £80 000	(30 400)
	49 600
less Sub-letting relief:	
$\frac{20}{40}$ × £11 000	(5 500)
Schedule A	44 100

	£
Premium on sub-lease	80 000
less Allowable cost – 50 000 × $\dfrac{(88.371 - 50.038)}{95.457}$	(20 079)
	59 921
less Indexation to April 1998:	
$\dfrac{162.6 - 140.6}{140.6} = 0.156 \times £20\,079$	(3 133)
	56 788
less Schedule A assessment	(44 100)
Gain eligible taper relief	12 688

Chapter 26

26.1

	No. of shares	Unindexed (£)	Indexed (£)
June 1986	4000	18000	18000
August 1989			
$\dfrac{115.8 - 97.8}{97.8} \times £18000$			3313
Rights: 1 for 4 @ £4	1000	4000	4000
	5000	22000	25313
March 1990			
$\dfrac{121.4 - 115.8}{115.8} \times £25313$			1225
Acquisition	3000	15000	15000
	8000	37000	41538
January 1998			
$\dfrac{159.5 - 121.4}{121.4} \times £41538$			13037
Acquisition	4000	20000	20000
	12000	57000	74575
August 2002			
$\dfrac{162.6 - 159.5}{159.5} \times £74575$			1450
	12000	57000	76025
Disposal	(10000)	(47500)	(63355)
Balance	2000	9500	12670

	£
Proceeds	80000
less Cost	(47500)
	32500
less Indexation (63355 – 47500)	(15855)
Untapered gain	16645

26.2

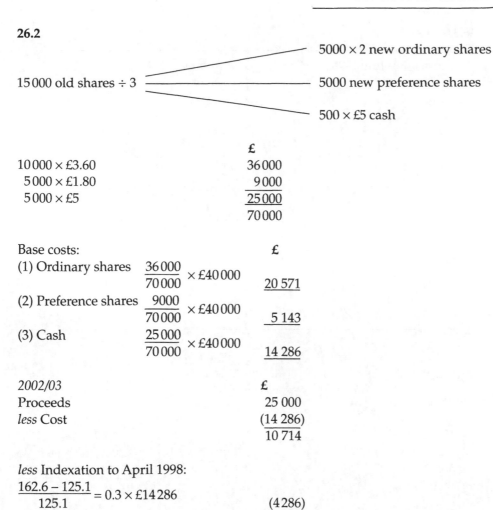

15 000 old shares ÷ 3 ——————— 5000 × 2 new ordinary shares

—————— 5000 new preference shares

—————— 500 × £5 cash

	£
10 000 × £3.60	36 000
5 000 × £1.80	9 000
5 000 × £5	25 000
	70 000

Base costs: £

(1) Ordinary shares $\dfrac{36\,000}{70\,000} \times £40\,000$ 20 571

(2) Preference shares $\dfrac{9000}{70\,000} \times £40\,000$ 5 143

(3) Cash $\dfrac{25\,000}{70\,000} \times £40\,000$ 14 286

2002/03	£
Proceeds	25 000
less Cost	(14 286)
	10 714

less Indexation to April 1998:

$\dfrac{162.6 - 125.1}{125.1} = 0.3 \times £14\,286$

	(4 286)
Untapered gain	6 428

26.3

The shares will be matched as follows:

(1) acquisition July 1998	1500 shares
(2) FA 1985 pool	500 shares
Disposal	2000 shares

1985 pool	*No. of shares*	*Unindexed* (£)	*Indexed* (£)
March 1984	1000	2600	2600
$\dfrac{94.8 - 87.5}{87.5} = 0.083 \times £2600$			216
Balance 6/4/85	1000	2600	2816
June 1993			
$\dfrac{141 - 94.8}{94.8} \times £2816$			1373
Acquisition	500	1600	1600
	1500	4200	5789
September 1995			
$\dfrac{150.6 - 141}{141} \times £5789$			395
Acquisition	1000	3600	3600
	2500	7800	9784
September 2002			
$\dfrac{162.6 - 150.6}{150.6} \times £9784$			780
	2500	7800	10564
Disposal	(500)	(1560)	(2113)
Balance	2000	6240	8451

		£	£
(1)	*Acquisition July 1998*		
	Proceeds $\frac{1500}{2000} \times £17200$	12900	
	less Cost	(4500)	8400
			Untapered gain
(2)	*FA 1985 Pool*		
	Proceeds $\frac{500}{2000} \times £17200$	4300	
	less Cost	(1560)	
	less Indexation (2113 – 1560)	(553)	2187
			Untapered gain

Chapter 27

27.1		*Cost*	*MV*
		(£)	(£)
Proceeds		480 000	480 000
less Cost / MV		(60 000)	(80 000)
		420 000	400 000

less Indexation to April 1998:

$$\frac{162.6 - 79.4}{79.4} = 1.048 \times £80\,000$$

		(83 840)	(83 840)
		336 160	316 160

Gain eligible for relief:	£	
Land and buildings	250 000	
Goodwill	85 000	$£316\,160 \times \dfrac{415}{465}$
Plant and machinery	80 000	
Chargeable business assets	415 000	
Investment property	50 000	$= £282\,165$
Total chargeable assets	465 000	

Maximum retirement relief	£
(lower limit)	50 000
Plus ½ (200 000 – 50 000)	75 000
Maximum retirement relief	125 000

	Business assets	*Non-business assets*	*Total*
	(£)	(£)	(£)
Gain	282 165	33 995	316 160
less R/R	(125 000)	nil	(125 000)
	157 165	33 995	191 160
less Taper relief 75%	(117 874)	(25 497)	(143 371)
Chargeable gain	39 291	8 498	47 789
Total chargeable gain	£47 789		

27.2

June 1988	*Cost*	*MV*
	(£)	(£)
Proceeds	70000	70000
less Cost / MV	(30000)	(40000)
	40000	30000

less Indexation:

$$\frac{106.6 - 79.4}{79.4} = 0.343 \times £40\,000$$

	(13720)	(13720)
	26280	16280
less Roll-over relief		(16280)
Chargeable gain		nil

October 2002		
Proceeds		150000
less Cost	70000	
	(16280)	(53720)
		96280

less Indexation to April 1998:

$$\frac{162.6 - 106.6}{106.6} = 0.525 \times £53\,720$$

		(28203)
Untapered gain		68077

Chapter 31

31.1(a)	£	£
Net profit as per a/cs		1414000
Add back:		
– repairs	20000	
– depreciation	60000	
– entertaining	6000	86000
		1500000
Deduct:		
– bank interest received	18000	
– dividends received	160000	
– debenture interest received	35000	
– building society interest received	9000	
– debenture interest paid (gross)	20000	
– capital allowances	38750	(280750)
Schedule D profit		1219250

31.1(b)

	£
Proceeds	250 000
less Cost	(90 000)
	160 000

less Indexation:

$$\frac{175.5 - 105.8}{105.8} = 0.659 \times £90\,000$$

	(59 310)
Chargeable gain	100 690

	No. of shares	Unindexed (£)	Indexed (£)
March 1984	2000	5600	5600
$\frac{94.8 - 87.5}{87.5} = 0.083 \times £5600$			465
Balance 1/4/85	2000	5600	6065
June 1990			
$\frac{126.7 - 94.8}{94.8} = \times £6065$			2041
Acquisition	3000	18600	18600
	5000	24200	26706
November 2002			
$\frac{177.6 - 126.7}{126.7} = \times £26\,706$			10729
	5000	24200	37435
Disposal	(5000)	(24200)	(37435)

	£
Proceeds	85 000
less Cost	(24 200)
	60 800

less Indexation:

(37 435 − 24 200)	(13 235)
Chargeable gain	47 565

Total chargeable gains	£
Investment property	100 690
Shares	47 565
Total gains	148 255

31.1(c)

	£
Schedule DI	1 219 250
Schedule DIII (18 000 + 9000)	27 000
Debenture interest received	35 000
Chargeable gains	148 255
	1 429 505
less Charges paid	(14 000)
PCTCT	1 415 505
add FII: $160 000 \times \frac{100}{90}$	177 778
'Profit'	1 593 283

Therefore, Wellbetter Ltd is a large company.

	£
GCT @ 30% × £1 415 505	424 652

31.2

	£	£
Trading income	360 000	
less Debenture interest paid:		
	(25 000)	
Schedule DI		335 000
Schedule DII		7 000
Schedule A		10 000
Taxed income		12 000
Chargeable gains		20 000
		384 000
less Charges paid:		
Trade charge	8 000	
Covenant	2 000	(10 000)
PCTCT		374 000
add FII $(18 000 \times \frac{100}{90})$		20 000
'Profits'		394 000

Profits fall into two financial years, FY 2001 and FY 2002. The main rate of CT was the same but the fraction for marginal relief changed.

MR 2001 : ($\frac{3}{12}$ of profit falls in FY 2001)

$\frac{1}{40}(375 000 - 98 500)\,\dfrac{93 500}{98 500} = £6 562$

MR 2002 : ($\frac{9}{12}$ of profit falls in Fy 2002)

$\frac{11}{400}(1 125 000 - 295 500)\,\dfrac{280 500}{295 500} = £21 654$

Total MR YE 31/12/02 = £28 216

	£
CT @ 30% × 374 000	112 200
less Taper relief	
	(28 216)
Corporation tax liability	83 984

Chapter 32

32.1

	£	£
Trading income	490 000	
less Debenture interest paid $(8\,000 \times \frac{100}{80})$	(10 000)	
Schedule DI		480 000
Schedule DIII		20 000
Schedule A		10 000
Taxed income $(20\,000 \times \frac{100}{80})$		25 000
Chargeable gains		80 000
		615 000
less Charges paid:		
Patent royalties $(4\,680 \times \frac{100}{78})$	6 000	
Deed convenant $(2\,340 \times \frac{100}{78})$	3 000	(9 000)
PCTCT		606 000
add FII: $(11250 \times \frac{100}{90})$		12 500
'Profits'		618 500

Limits: $\frac{150000}{2} = £750\,000$; $\frac{300000}{2}$ £150 000

Therefore, Swallow Ltd is a marginal relief company.

	£
CT @ 30% × £606 000	181 800
less: $\frac{11}{400}$ (750 000 – 618 500) $\times \dfrac{606\,000}{618\,500}$	(3 543)
	178 257
less Income tax suffered (W1)	(1 020)
Corporation tax liability	177 237

W1		£	£
Tax on income: £25 000 × 20%			5 000
less Tax on payments:			
– royalties	£6000 × 22%	1 320	
– covenant	£3000 × 22%	660	
– debenture interest	£10 000 × 20%	2 000	(3 980)
Income tax suffered			1 020

32.2

Workings

(1) *Limits*

$\frac{150000}{3} = £500\,000; \frac{300000}{3} = £100\,000$

Therefore, Sparrow Ltd is a large company.

	£
'Profits'	550 000
less PCTCT	(480 000)
F11	70 000

$\therefore 90\% \times £70\,000 = $ Net dividend

(2) *Shadow ACT*

Dividend paid	180 000
less Dividend received	(63 000)
	117 000 $\times \frac{1}{4} = £29\,250$

(3) *Maximum ACT*

£480 000 × 20% = £96 000

	£	£
CT @ 30% × £480 000		144 000
less:		
Maximum ACT set-off	96 000	
less 'Shadow ACT'	(29 250)	(66 750)
Corporation tax liability YE 31/3/03		77 250

	£
Surplus ACT b/f 1/4/02	110 000
less Used YE 31/3/03	(66 750)
Accumulated ACT c/f	43 250

Chapter 33

33.1

	2000	31 December 2001	2002
	(£)	(£)	(£)
Schedule DI	60 000	nil	100 000
s 393(1)	(5 000)	–	(10 000)
	55 000	nil	90 000
Schedule A	15 000	15 000	15 000
Schedule DIII	7 000	8 000	10 000
Chargeable gains	nil	6 000	8 000
	77 000	29 000	123 000
s 393A(1)(a)	–	(29 000)	–
	77 000	nil	123 000
Trade charges	(8 000)	–	(8 000)
	69 000	nil	115 000
s 393A(1)(b)	(69 000)	–	–
	nil	nil	115 000
Non-trade charges	–	–	(1 000)
PCTCT	nil	nil	114 000
CT @ 20%			22 800

Loss memo		*Capital gains/losses*	
b/f 1/1/00	(5 000)	YE 00 gain	18 000
YE 31/12/00	5 000	YE 00 loss	(20 000)
YE 31/12/01	(100 000)	c/f	(2 000)
s 393A(1)(a)	29 000	YE 01 gain	10 000
	(71 000)	YE 01 loss	(2 000)
s 393A(1)(b)	69 000	YE 01	6 000
c/f s 393(1)	(2 000)	YE 02 gain	15 000
YE 31/12/02	2 000	YE 02 loss	(7 000)
Trade charges YE 01	(8 000)	YE 02	8 000
s 393(1) YE 02	8 000		

33.2

	31st March		
	2001	*2002*	*2003*
	(£)	*(£)*	*(£)*
Schedule DI	10 000	35 000	nil
Taxed income	8 000	8 000	8 000
Taxed income	12 000	12 000	12 000
Chargeable gains	10 000	nil	5 000
	40 000	55 000	25 000
s 393A(1)(*a*)	–	–	(25 000)
	40 000	55 000	nil
Trade charges	(5 000)	(5 000)	–
	35 000	50 000	nil
s 393A(1)(*b*)	–	(35 000)	–
	35 000	15 000	nil
Non-trade charges	(2 000)	(2 000)	–
PCTCT	33 000	13 000	nil

Loss memo

YE 31/3/2000	(60 000)
s 393A(1)(*a*)	25 000
	(35 000)
s 393A(1)(*b*)	35 000

Trade charges YE 2001   (5 000) c/f

	2001	*2002*	*2003*
PCTCT	33 000	13 000	nil
CT @ 20%	6 600	2 600	nil
Less:			
(1) 1/40 (50 000–33 000)	(425)		
(2) 1/40 (50 000–13 000)		(925)	
CT liability	6 175	1 675	nil

Chapter 36

36.1(a)

H Ltd, A Ltd, B Ltd and C Ltd are all associated for SCR purposes:

Upper limit: $\frac{1500000}{4}$ = £375 000 starting rate: $\frac{10000}{4}$ = £2 500

Lower limit: $\frac{300000}{4}$ = £75 000 $\frac{50000}{4}$ = £12 500

H Ltd, A Ltd and B Ltd are a group for group relief purposes.

	Year ended 31 March 2003			
	H Ltd	*A Ltd*	*B Ltd*	*C Ltd*
	(£)	*(£)*	*(£)*	*(£)*
Schedule DI	170 000	nil	90 000	nil
Schedule A	10 000	20 000	nil	2 000
Taxed income	12 000	8 000	nil	5 000
	192 000	28 000	90 000	7 000
s 393A(1)(*a*)	–	–	–	(7 000)
	192 000	28 000	90 000	nil
Trade charges	(8 000)	nil	(2 000)	–
	184 000	28 000	88 000	
s 402	(47 000)	–	(13 000)	–
PCTCT	137 000	28 000	75 000	nil

Loss memo A Ltd		*Loss memo C Ltd*	
YE 31/3/2003	(60 000)	YE 31/3/2003	(10 000)
s 402 B Ltd	13 000	s 393A(1)(*a*)	7 000
	(47 000)		(3 000)
s 402 H Ltd	47 000	Unrelieved charges	(1 000)
		c/f s 393 (1)	(4 000)

	H Ltd	*A Ltd*	*B Ltd*	*C Ltd*
	(£)	*(£)*	*(£)*	*(£)*
PCTCT	137 000	28 000	75 000	nil
CT @ 19%		5 320	14 250	nil
CT @ 30%	41 100			
less: $\frac{11}{400}$ (375000 – 137000)	(6 545)			
CT liability	34 555	5 320	14 250	nil

36.1(b) C Ltd c/f £ (4000) s 393(1)

36.2

The transfer in 1998 is on a no gain/no loss basis:

	£
Cost (August 1986)	100 000
Indexation:	
(from August 1986 to November 1998)	
$\dfrac{164.4 - 97.8}{97.8} = 0.681 \times £100\,000$	68 100
Deemed cost to Nelson Ltd	168 100

As Nelson leaves the group within six years of the transfer, the gain becomes chargeable in the year Nelson leaves the group, i.e. YE 31/3/03.

	£
YE 31/3/03	
Deemed proceeds (MV November 1998)	200 000
less Deemed cost	(168 100)
Chargeable gain	31 900

Chapter 37

37.1

	£
Schedule DI	260 000
Schedule A	30 000
Schedule DIII	8 000
Schedule DV (W1)	42 875
Taxed income	12 000
Chargeable gain	18 000
	370 875
less Charges paid (6000 + 2000)	(8 000)
PCTCT	362 875

	£
CT @ 30% × £362 875	108 863
less: $\frac{11}{400}$ (1 500 000 − 362 875)	(31 271)
GCT	77 592
less DTR (W2)	(9 504)
Corporation tax liability YE 31/3/03	68 088

W1

	£
Net dividend	29 750

WT ($29750 \times 100/85$)

	£
	5 250
	35 000

Underlying tax:

$90000 \times \dfrac{35000}{400000}$

	£
	7 875
	42 875 Sch DV

W2

DTR: Lower of:

(1)   O/S tax: £5250 + 7875 = £13 125

or

(2)   UK tax: $80434 \times \dfrac{42875}{362875} = £9\,504$

DTR = £9 504

Chapter 40

40.1

VAT payable for quarter ended 30/4/02

	£	£
Output tax: £305 500 × $\frac{7}{47}$		45 500
Input tax:		
(1) Standard rated purchases:		
70 970 × $\frac{7}{47}$	10 570	
(2) Zero rated purchases:		
23 500 × $\frac{7}{47}$	3 500	
(3) Overheads (see note 3 below)	3 320	(17 390)
	VAT due	28 110

Notes:
(1) Input tax on motor car is non-deductible.
(2) Input tax attributable to exempt supplies is non-deductible.
(3) As the *de minimus* limits are exceeded RST Ltd is a partially exempt business, and the input tax on overheads is apportioned:

Input tax on overheads = £29 375 × $\frac{7}{47}$ =   <u>£4 375</u>

$$\frac{\text{Value of taxable supplies (VAT excl)}}{\text{Value of total supplies (VAT excl)}} \quad \times \quad 4375$$

$$\frac{260\,000 + 55\,000}{260\,000 + 55\,000 + 100\,000} \quad \times \quad 4375$$

Deductible input tax on overheads   =   <u>£3 320</u>

Chapter 43

43.1	*Actual liability*	*Payments made*	*Difference*
	(£)	(£)	(£)
31/1/01	3500	1800	1700
31/7/01	3500	1800	1700

Interest:	£
1/2/01 – 31/1/02 £1700 × 8%	136
1/8/01 – 31/1/02 £1700 × 8% × $\frac{6}{12}$	68
Interest due	<u>204</u>

43.2(a)   £

2000/01

31/1/01 1st payment on a/c	4000
31/7/01 2nd payment on a/c	4000
31/1/02 balancing payment	2500

2001/02

31/1/02 1st payment on a/c	5250
31/7/02 2nd payment on a/c	5250
31/1/03 balancing payment	3500

43.2(b)

Interest is due on the £2000 from the due date to the date of payment:

$1/2/02 - 31/1/03 : £2000 \times 8\% = £160$

The additional tax due will also have a knock-on effect in respect of the 2001/02 payments on a/c:

	Payments due (£)	Payments made (£)	Difference (£)
31/1/02	6250	5250	1000
31/7/02	6250	5250	1000

Interest:	£
$1/2/02 - 31/1/03 \; £1000 \times 8\%$	80
$1/8/02 - 31/1/03 \; £1000 \times 8\% \times \frac{6}{12}$	40
	120

INDEX